The Attalids of Pergamon and Anatolia

Historians have long wondered at the improbable rise of the Attalids of Pergamon after 188 BCE. The Roman-brokered Settlement of Apameia offered a new map – a brittle framework for sovereignty in Anatolia and the eastern Aegean. What allowed the Attalids to make this map a reality and leave their indelible Pergamene imprint on our Classical imagination? In this uniquely comprehensive study of the political economy of the kingdom, Noah Kaye rethinks the impact of Attalid imperialism on the Greek polis and the multicultural character of the dynasty's notorious propaganda. By synthesizing new findings in epigraphy, archaeology, and numismatics, he shows the kingdom for the first time from the inside. The Pergamene way of ruling was a distinctively noncoercive and efficient means of taxing and winning loyalty. Royal tax collectors collaborated with city and village officials on budgets and minting, while the kings utterly transformed the civic space of the gymnasium. This title is also available as Open Access on Cambridge Core.

NOAH KAYE is Assistant Professor in the Department of History at Michigan State University. He is an ancient historian who has worked extensively throughout the eastern Mediterranean, in Greece, where he was the Heinrich Schliemann Fellow at the American School of Classical Studies at Athens; in Israel, where he was a Fulbright Postdoctoral Fellow at the University of Haifa; and in Turkey, where he was a Senior Fellow at the Koç University Research Center for Anatolian Civilizations. He has conducted and published archaeological fieldwork in Greece (Molyvoti Thrace Archaeological Project) and Turkey (Boğsak Archaeological Survey, Cilicia). He is also an epigrapher and a numismatist, and has contributed to the multilingual corpus of inscriptions *Corpus Inscriptionum Iudaeae/Palestinae*.

The Attalids of Pergamon and Anatolia

Money, Culture, and State Power

NOAH KAYE
Michigan State University

University Printing House, Cambridge CB2 8BS, United Kingdom

One Liberty Plaza, 20th Floor, New York, NY 10006, USA

477 Williamstown Road, Port Melbourne, VIC 3207, Australia

314–321, 3rd Floor, Plot 3, Splendor Forum, Jasola District Centre, New Delhi – 110025, India

103 Penang Road, #05-06/07, Visioncrest Commercial, Singapore 238467

Cambridge University Press is part of the Cambridge University Press & Assessment

It furthers the University's mission by disseminating knowledge in the pursuit of education, learning, and research at the highest international levels of excellence.

www.cambridge.org
Information on this title: www.cambridge.org/9781009279574
DOI: 10.1017/9781009279567

© Noah Kaye 2023
Reissued as Open Access, 2023

This work is in copyright. It is subject to statutory exceptions and to the provisions of relevant licensing agreements; with the exception of the Creative Commons version the link for which is provided below, no reproduction of any part of this work may take place without the written permission of Cambridge University Press & Assessment.

An online version of this work is published at doi.org/10.1017/9781009279567 under a Creative Commons Open Access license CC-BY-NC-ND 4.0 which permits re-use, distribution and reproduction in any medium for non-commercial purposes providing appropriate credit to the original work is given. You may not distribute derivative works without permission. To view a copy of this license, visit https://creativecommons.org/licenses/by-nc-nd/4.0

All versions of this work may contain content reproduced under license from third parties. Permission to reproduce this third-party content must be obtained from these third-parties directly.

When citing this work, please include a reference to the DOI 10.1017/9781009279567

First published 2023

A catalogue record for this publication is available from the British Library.

Library of Congress Cataloging-in-Publication Data
Names: Kaye, Noah, 1981- author.
Title: The Attalids of Pergamon and Anatolia : money, culture, and state power / by Noah Kaye.
Description: New York : Cambridge University Press, 2021. | Includes bibliographical references and index.
Identifiers: LCCN 2021041821 (print) | LCCN 2021041822 (ebook) | ISBN 9781316510599 (hardback) |
  ISBN 9781009017626 (paperback) | ISBN 9781009038935 (epub)
Subjects: LCSH: Attalid dynasty, 282 B.C.-133 B.C. | Pergamum (Extinct city) | Bergama (Turkey)–History. |
  Bergama (Turkey)–Politics and government. | Money–Turkey–Bergama. | BISAC: HISTORY / Ancient / General
Classification: LCC DS156.P4 K39 2021 (print) | LCC DS156.P4 (ebook) | DDC 939/.26–dc23
LC record available at https://lccn.loc.gov/2021041821
LC ebook record available at https://lccn.loc.gov/2021041822

ISBN 978-1-009-27957-4 Paperback

Cambridge University Press & Assessment has no responsibility for the persistence or accuracy of URLs for external or third-party internet websites referred to in this publication and does not guarantee that any content on such websites is, or will remain, accurate or appropriate.

Sevgili oğlum Yunus'a

Contents

List of Figures   [*page* viii]
List of Graphs   [x]
List of Maps   [xi]
Acknowledgments   [xii]
List of Abbreviations   [xv]

Introduction   [1]

1 Eating with the Tax Collectors   [34]

2 The Skeleton of the State   [74]

3 The King's Money   [129]

4 Cities and Other Civic Organisms   [188]

5 Hastening to the Gymnasium   [234]

6 Pergamene Panhellenism   [283]

Conclusion   [354]

Appendix of Epigraphical Documents   [364]
Bibliography   [370]
Index Locorum   [425]
Subject Index   [433]

Figures

1.1 Ilgın Plain, vicinity of ancient Toriaion   [*page* 63]
2.1 The Roman Via Sebaste, retracing an earlier Attalid route, emerges from the Klimax Pass (Döşeme Boğazı) into the plain of Pamphylia   [122]
3.1 Silver tetradrachm of Eumenes II minted in the name of Philetairos   [132]
3.2 Silver tetradrachm of Side minted ca. 210–190 BCE, bearing countermark of bow-in-case + ΠΕΡ   [133]
3.3 Cistophoric silver tetradrachm of Pergamon, ca. 160–150 BCE   [134]
3.4 Cistophoric silver didrachm of Tralles, ca. 145–140 BCE   [135]
3.5 Cistophoric silver drachm, ca. 134–128 BCE   [135]
3.6 Standing serpent on reverse of large module (hemiobol?) bronze coin in the name of Philetairos, ca. 270s–200 BCE   [138]
3.7 Fragmentary bedroom scene from the Telephos Frieze with standing serpent warning hero and Auge   [139]
3.8 Silver tetradrachm of Eumenes II, ca. 166–162 BCE   [143]
3.9 Silver tetradrachm in the name of Athena Nikephoros, reign of Eumenes II, ca. 180–165 BCE   [143]
3.10 Silver drachm of Ephesus with legend "of the Ephesians," ca. 150 BCE   [144]
3.11 "Wreathed" silver tetradrachm of Myrina, ca. 160–135 BCE   [146]
3.12 Cistophoric silver tetradrachm of Ephesus, ca. 150–140 BCE   [152]
3.13 Proconsular cistophoric silver tetradrachm, signed by C. Pulcher and Aristokles, 55–53 BCE   [155]
4.1 Hellenistic grave stele of Doidalses from Mustafakemalpaşa   [208]
4.2 The Çan Sarcophagus from the Granikos Valley, early fourth century BCE   [217]
4.3 Late Hellenistic bronze coin of the Mysoi Abbaeitai   [220]
5.1 Plan of the gymnasium of Pergamon in relation to adjacent monuments and current reconstruction of street grid   [239]
5.2 Gymnasium of Pergamon, looking east across the palaistra of the upper terrace   [239]

5.3 Hellenistic Sikyon, view east/southeast from the terraces of the city's gymnasium toward the adjacent agora [273]
6.1 Yığma Tepe [298]
6.2 View to the southwest of the Kaikos Valley from the acropolis of Pergamon [307]
6.3 Model of ancient Athens [308]
6.4 Model of Hellenistic Pergamon [309]
6.5 Archaic terrace walls of Sardis, reconstruction drawing by Philip Stinson [311]
6.6 Late Hellenistic terraces at Arykanda [312]
6.7 Late Hellenistic Pergamene market building of the unidentified city at Melli in Pisidia [341]
6.8 Late Hellenistic frieze of Gigantomachy in the agora of the unidentified city at Melli in Pisidia [343]
6.9 Left: reverse of silver tetradrachm of Demetrios II depicting Athena Magarsia, ca. 145–142 BCE; right: reverse of silver tetradrachm in the name of Athena Nikephoros, reign of Eumenes II, ca. 180–165 BCE [348]

Graphs

1.1 Philanthropic foundations of the Hellenistic world   [*page* 37]
1.2 Royal gifts of money   [38]
1.3 Royal gifts of grain   [38]
5.1 Royal gifts to gymnasia   [237]

Maps

I.1 Anatolia, ca. 200 BCE [*page* 3]
I.2 Pergamon and its environs [16]
I.3 The core of the Attalid kingdom and the Rhodian *peraia* after 188 BCE [23]
2.1 The Kayster Valley [99]
2.2 Pisidia and the Milyas [120]
3.1 The Maeander Valley and Rhodian Caria [156]
4.1 Eastern Lydia and Mysia Abbaitis [194]
6.1 Tumuli recorded in salvage excavations (*Müze Çalışmaları ve Kurtarma Kazıları Sempozyumu Yayınları*, 1990–2016) and ancient settlements in the Pleiades data set (pleiades.stoa.org) [303]
6.2 Central Anatolia [324]

Acknowledgments

This book represents the culmination of over a decade's worth of research and writing, and I am grateful for the training, support, and indeed nurturing, which made it all possible. It began as a Berkeley PhD dissertation that took root as I studied Bradford Welles' *Royal Correspondence in the Hellenistic Period* and the *Bulletin épigraphique* in the Art History/Classics room of the Doe Library. I am grateful to my supervisors, Emily Mackil, Erich Gruen, and Andrew Stewart, for giving me the courage to take on the topic of the entire political economy and ideological program of a major Hellenistic kingdom, and to my classmates, especially Ryan Boehm, Lisa Eberle, Joel Rygorsky, and Randall Souza, for their input. At the time, I was also receiving crucial training and support in epigraphy and numismatics from my dear teachers, Nikolaos Papazarkadas, Peter Van Alfen, Andrew Meadows, and Alain Bresson. I received institutional support in the form of a dissertation completion fellowship from the Sarah B. Aleshire Center for the Study of Greek Epigraphy in Berkeley, and I completed summer programs at the American Numismatic Society in New York and on Delos with the École française d'Athènes. I also found myself poking around the Stoa of Attalos in the Athenian Agora and the Epigraphical Museum of Athens with support from the American School of Classical Studies at Athens. Thanks go also to Jaime Curbera at *Inscriptiones Graecae* in Berlin for a fun day with squeezes. During this early period, utterly indispensable support for my project arrived by email from two scholars in Oxford, themselves working on the Attalids, John Ma and Peter Thonemann, who assured me that I was in fact on to something.

During a post-doc supported by the Binational US-Israel Fulbright Commission and the University of Haifa, I was able to refine many of the ideas in the dissertation. Seeing Asia Minor from the Levant was enormously beneficial, and I thank my sponsor in the Fulbright program, Ory Amitay, for the opportunity and intellectual comradery, as well as Jonathan Price, for inviting me to present Chapter 5 at Tel Aviv University in the Department of Classics, and Uri Yiftach, for invitations to present parts of Chapter 2 to the Legal Documents in Ancient Societies colloquia. Thanks to Aurélie Carrara, I was able to workshop parts of the book at the

Université de Bordeaux with Veronique Chankowski in 2013. Veronique provided me with so much inspiration all along the way. I also received important feedback on the ideas that are contained in Chapter 4 from Stephen White at the University of Texas-Austin. I traveled extensively in Attalid lands in the summer of 2013, and I was generously hosted by Nicholas Cahill at Sardis.

When for several years, the manuscript languished while I taught Classics and archaeology at the University of Oregon and Indiana University, I received unstinting support from my PhD advisors, while mentors such as Nicholas Purcell and Andrew Monson, to name two, continued to show me, each in their own way, how to make a contribution to scholarship. Arthur Eckstein's feedback on Chapter 4 was a real boost and encouraged completion of the book. The Classicists at Indiana University, especially Adam Gitner and the Homerist Jon Ready, left their mark on Chapters 4 and 6, and Matt Christ helped me jump-start the project again by sending me to New York to join the discussion and festivities around the Met's 2016 exhibition *Pergamon and the Hellenistic Kingdoms of the Ancient World*. Thanks in particular to Susan Rotroff for her encouragement and exchange at the exhibition colloquium. During this period, I was also given an apprenticeship in archaeology by Nathan Arrington and Tom Tartaron, under whom I worked on the Attalid frontier in Aegean Thrace, as well as Nicholas Rauh and Günder Varinlioğlu, with whom I investigated the ramifications of the Settlement of Apameia on the ground in coastal Rough Cilicia. It was of great importance that I finish the book by looking at the Attalids from an Anatolian perspective, and I was fortunate to receive a fellowship at Research Center for Anatolian Civilizations (ANAMED) at Koç University in Istanbul for 2017–18. Special thanks are due to Koray Konuk for his support in this endeavor, and I had many interesting conversations with the director, Christopher Roosevelt, who taught me a lot. While in Turkey, I benefited from presenting the project at Boğaziçi University, thanks to Julia Shear. I am so very grateful for the warm reception, aid, and intellectual exchange I received from members of the Pergamon Excavation Project of the German Archaeological Institute, namely, director Felix Pirson, Ute Kelp, Ulrich Mania, Sarah Japp, Güler Ateş, Bernhard Ludwig, and Kıvanç Başak, and to Turgut Saner of Istanbul Technical University for discussions about his work at Larisa-on-the-Hermos. Finally, I signal here my warmest appreciation for my traveling companion in Turkey, Evin Taş: I hope one beautiful morning at the

Klimax Pass (Döşemealtı) compensated for a dreadful evening in the Milyas (Korkuteli).

In its final stages, the book has benefited from the patient support of Michael Sharp at Cambridge University Press and from the anonymous reviewers, who greatly improved the manuscript. In 2019, I was able to present a draft of Chapter 6 to Classics crowds at the University of Massachusetts–Amherst, by invitation of Simon Oswald, and at Harvard, by invitation of Paul Kosmin. I warmly thank my Harvard hosts, Supratik Baralay and Felipe Soza, for their hospitality and feedback. The History Department of Michigan State University supported a year in Turkey, which Walter Hawthorne helped arrange with funding from the Lab for Education and Advancement in Digital Research. My faculty mentor, Liam Brockey, has been a model and a bulwark. Amanda Tickner of the MSU Library patiently guided the cartography. Illustrations were funded by the Humanities and Arts Research Program Production grant that Kayla Van Dyke truly made happen. The illustrations elicit many expressions of gratitude: to Elena Stolyarik at the American Numismatic Society, Amelia Dowler at the British Museum, Karsten Dahmen at the Staatliche Museen zu Berlin, Frédérique Duyrat and Julien Olivier of Bibliothèque nationale de France, Brian Rose of the Troy Excavation Project, Elmar Schwertheim of Westfälische Wilhelms-Universität Münster, Sylvie Dumont and Craig Mauzy of the Athenian Agora Excavations, Veli Köse and Lutgarde Vandeput of the Pisida Survey Project, both Baha Yıldırım and, again, the ever supportive Nicholas Cahill of the Archaeological Exploration of Sardis.

In the end – in the beginning, actually – I was just curious about the way the Attalids used language and money to shift shape, about the vestiges of the Kingdom of Pergamon, which led me to a hunt in the library – and for that curiosity, for a love of books and of libraries, I have only my dear parents to thank, Dianne Vidmar and Michael Kaye.

List of Abbreviations

AA	*Archäologischer Anzeiger*
ANS	American Numismatic Society
Arthur S. Dewing	L. Mildenberg, *The Arthur S. Dewing Collection of Greek Coins* (New York, 1985)
BCH	*Bulletin de correspondance hellénique*
BE	*Bulletin épigraphique*
BMC	*Catalogue of the Greek Coins in the British Museum*
BNJ	*Brill's New Jacoby*
CAH	*The Cambridge Ancient History*
CH	*Coin Hoards*
CID	*Corpus des inscriptions de Delphes*, 4 vols. (Paris, 1977–)
CIG	*Corpus inscriptionum graecarum*, 4 vols. (Berlin, 1828–77)
CLA	Customs Law of Asia
Claros I	L. Robert and J. Robert, *Claros I: Décrets hellénistiques* (Paris, 1989)
FD	*Fouilles de Delphes III: Épigraphie* (Paris, 1929–)
FGrHist	F. Jacoby, *Fragmente der griechischen Historiker* (1923–)
HN	B. V. Head, *Historia Numorum: A Manual of Greek Numismatics*, 2nd ed. (Oxford, 1911)
Hunterian	*Catalogue of Greek coins in the Hunterian Collection, University of Glasgow* (Glasgow, 1899–1905)
I.Adramytteion I	J. V. Stauber, *Die Bucht von Adramytteion, Teil I: Topographie Lokalisierung antiker Orte/Fundstellen von Altertümern* (Bonn, 1996)
I.Adramytteion II	J. V. Stauber, *Die Bucht von Adramytteion, Teil II: Inschriften – Literarische Testimonia – Münzen* (Bonn, 1996)
I.Delos	*Inscriptions de Délos*, 7 vols. (Paris, 1926–72)
I.Didyma	A. Rehm, *Didyma, II: Die Inschriften* (Berlin, 1958)
I.Ephesos	*Die Inschriften von Ephesos*, 8 vols. (Bonn, 1979–)
I.Erythrai	*Die Inschriften von Erythrai und Klazomenai*, 2 vols. (Bonn 1972–73)
IG	*Inscriptiones Graecae*
IGCH	C. M. Kraay, M. Thompson, and O. Mørkholm, *An Inventory of Greek Coin Hoards* (New York, 1973)

IGR	*Inscriptiones Graecae ad Res Romanas Pertinentes*, 3 vols. (Paris, 1911–27)
I.Histriae	D. M. Pippidi, *Inscriptiones Scythiae Minoris Graecae et Latinae I: Inscriptiones Histriae et Viciniae* (Bucharest, 1983)
I.Iasos	W. Blümel, *Die Inschriften von Iasos*, 2 vols. (Bonn, 1985)
I.Ilion	P. Frisch, *Die Inschriften von Ilion* (Bonn, 1975)
I.Iznik	S. Şahin, *Katalog der antiken Inschriften des Museums von Iznik (Nikaia)*, 2 vols. (Bonn 1979, 1981–82)
I.Kyzikos II	E. Schwertheim, *Die Inschriften von Kyzikos und Umgebung, Teil II: Miletupolis, Inschriften und Denkmäler* (Bonn, 1983)
I.Kyme	H. Engelmann, *Die Inschriften von Kyme* (Bonn, 1976)
I.Magnesia	O. Kern, *Die Inschriften von Magnesia am Maeander* (Berlin, 1900)
I.Metropolis	B. Dreyer and H. Engelmann, *Die Inschriften von Metropolis I* (Bonn, 2003)
I.Milet	*Inschriften von Milet*, 3 vols. (Berlin, 1997–2006)
I.Mysia (und Troas)	M. Barth and J. Stauber, *Inschriften Mysia & Troas* (Packard Humanities Institute CD #7)
I.Oropos	V. Ch. Petrakos, Οι επιγραφές του Ωρωπού (Athens, 1997)
I.Pergamon	M. Fränkel, *Die Inschriften von Pergamon*, 2 vols. (Berlin 1890–95)
I.Pessinous	J. Strubbe, *The Inscriptions of Pessinous* (Bonn, 2005)
I.Priene	F. Hiller von Gaertringen, *Inschriften von Priene* (Berlin, 1906)
I.Prusa	T. Corsten, *Die Inschriften von Prusa ad Olympum*, 2 vols. (Bonn, 1991–93)
I.Sardis	W. H. Buckler and D. M. Robinson, *Sardis VII: Greek and Latin Inscriptions, Part I* (Leiden, 1932)
Iscr.Cos	M. Segre, *Iscrizioni di Cos*, 2 vols. (Rome, 1993)
ISE	L. Moretti and F. Canali de Rossi, *Iscrizioni storiche ellenistiche*, 3 vols. (Florence, 1967–2008)
I.Sestos	J. Krauss, *Die Inschriften von Sestos und der thrakischen Chersones* (Bonn, 1980)
I.Smyrna	G. Petzl, *Die Inschriften von Smyrna*, 2 vols. (Bonn, 1982–90)
I.Sultan Dağı	L. Jonnes, *The Inscriptions of the Sultan Dağı I* (Bonn, 2002)
I.Thespiai	P. Roesch, *Les inscriptions de Thespies* (Lyon 2007–9)
I.Tralleis	F. B. Poljakov, *Die Inschriften von Tralleis und Nysa, Teil I: Die Inschriften von Tralleis* (Bonn, 1989)
Jameson	*Collection R. Jameson*, 4 vols. (Paris, 1913–32)

Keil and Premerstein, *Bericht über eine Reise*	J. Keil and A. von Premerstein, *Bericht über eine Reise in Lydien und der südlichen Aiolis* (Vienna, 1908)
LSCG	F. Sokolowski, *Lois sacrées des cités grecques* (Paris, 1969)
MAMA IV	W. H. Buckler, W. M. Calder, and W. K. C. Guthrie, *Monumenta Asiae Minoris Antiqua, Vol. 4: Monuments and Documents from Eastern Asia and Western Galatia* (Manchester, 1933)
MAMA VI	W. H. Buckler and W. M. Calder, *Monumenta Asiae Minoris Antiqua, Vol. 6: Monuments and Documents from Phrygia and Caria* (Manchester, 1939)
MDAI(A)	*Mitteilungen des deutschen archäologischen Instituts (Athenische Abteilung)*
Michel, *Recueil*	*Recueil d'inscriptions grecques*, 2 suppl. (Brussels, 1900–27)
Milet I 3	G. Kawerau and A. Rehm, *Das Delphinion in Milet* (Berlin, 1914)
ML	R. Meiggs and D. M. Lewis, *A Selection of Greek Historical Inscriptions to the End of the Fifth Century BC*, 2nd ed. (Oxford, 1988)
New Pauly	*Brill's New Pauly: Encyclopaedia of the Ancient World* (Leiden, 1996–2011)
OGIS	W. Dittenberger, *Orientis Graeci Inscriptiones Selectae*, 2 vols. (Leipzig, 1903–5)
P.Cair.Zen	C. C. Edgar, *Zenon Papyri, Catalogue général des antiquités égyptiennes du Musée du Caire* (Cairo, 1925–40)
P.Rev.	B. P. Grenfell, *Revenue Laws of Ptolemy Philadelphus* (Oxford, 1896)
PSI	*Papiri greci e latini*
P.Tebt.	*The Tebtunis Papyri* (London, 1902–)
RC	C. B. Welles, *Royal Correspondence in the Hellenistic Period* (New Haven, CT, 1934)
RE	A. Pauly, G. Wissowa, W. Kroll, et al., *Paulys Real-Encyclopädie der classischen Altertumswissenschaft, Neue Bearbeitung* (Stuttgart, 1893–1997)
RO	P. J. Rhodes and R. Osborne, *Greek Historical Inscriptions 404–323 BC* (Oxford, 2003)
Robert, *Carie* II	L. Robert and J. Robert, *La Carie: Histoire et géographie historique, avec le recueil des inscriptions antiques. Tome II, Le plateau de Tabai et ses environs* (Paris, 1954)

Robert, *OMS*	L. Robert, *Opera Minora Selecta*, 7 vols. (Amsterdam, 1969–90)
RPC	*Roman Provincial Coinage* (London, 1992–)
SEG	*Supplementum Epigraphicum Graecum*
SGDI II	H. Collitz, F. Bechtel, and J. Baunack, *Sammlung der griechischen Dialekt-Inschriften II: Epirus, Akarnanien, Aetolien, Aenanien Phthiotis, Lokris, Phokis, Dodona, Achaia und seine Kolonien, Delphi* (Göttingen, 1885–99)
SH	H. Lloyd-Jones et al., *Supplementum Hellenisticum* (Berlin, 1983)
SNG Copenhagen	*Sylloge Nummorum Graecorum: Danish National Museum* (Copenhagen, 1942–)
SNG Leipzig	*Sylloge Nummorum Graecorum, Deutschland: Sammlung der Universitätsbibliothek Leipzig, 1. Band, Autonome Griechische Münzen* (Munich, 1993)
SNG München	*Sylloge Nummorum Graecorum, Deutschland: Staatliche Münzsammlung München* (Munich, 1968–)
SNG Paris	*Sylloge Nummorum Graecorum, France: Bibliothèque nationale, Cabinet des médailles* (Paris, 1983–)
SNG von Aulock	*Sylloge Nummorum Graecorum, Deutschland: Sammlung von Aulock*, 8 vols. (1957–63)
Staatsverträge	H. Bengston and H. H. Schmitt, *Die Staatsverträge des Altertums*, 3 vols. (Munich, 1969–75)
Swoboda, *Denkmäler*	H. Swoboda, J. Keil, and F. Knoll, *Denkmäler aus Lykaonien, Pamphylien, und Isaurien* (Vienna, 1935)
*Syll.*³	W. Dittenberger, *Sylloge Inscriptionum Graecarum*, 3rd ed., 4 vols. (Leipzig 1915–24)
TAM III	R. Heberdey, *Tituli Asiae Minoris III: Tituli Pisidiae* (Vienna, 1941)
TAM V	P. Herrmann, *Tituli Asiae Minoris V: Tituli Lydiae*, 3 vols. (Vienna, 1981–2007)
Waddington	*Inventaire Sommaire de la Collection Waddington acquise par l'état en 1897 pour le Départment des Médailles et Antiques de la Bibliothèque Nationale* (Paris, 1898)
Wilhelm, *Neue Beiträge*	A. Wilhelm, *Neue Beiträge zur griechischen Inschriftenkunde*, 6 vols. (Vienna, 1911–32)

This title is part of the Cambridge University Press *Flip it Open* Open Access Books program and has been "flipped" from a traditional book to an Open Access book through the program.

Flip it Open sells books through regular channels, treating them at the outset in the same way as any other book; they are part of our library collections for Cambridge Core, and sell as hardbacks and ebooks. The one crucial difference is that we make an upfront commitment that when each of these books meets a set revenue threshold we make them available to everyone Open Access via Cambridge Core.

This paperback edition has been released as part of our Open Access commitment and we would like to use this as an opportunity to thank the libraries and other buyers who have helped us flip this and the other titles in the program to Open Access.

To see the full list of libraries that we know have contributed to *Flip it Open*, as well as the other titles in the program please visit http://www.cambridge.org/fio-acknowledgements

Introduction

From Berlin to Bergama

In the sunny, austere central hall of the Pergamon Museum in Berlin, wrapping around the room's walls like a serpent, then rising halfway to the ceiling on marble steps, stands a strident, if also fragmentary statement of empire. It is an unfinished wedding cake of a building. Tourists recline languidly on its ascent, like guests with nowhere to sit. The room is just too small; it is overtaken by the object on display: the Great Altar of Pergamon. The Altar, with its two sculptural friezes, the outer depicting the Battle of Gods and Giants, the inner, the tale of Telephos, son of Herakles and heroic ancestor of the Attalid dynasty, was discovered in 1871, the year in which the Second German Empire was born. The engineer Karl Humann stumbled upon the marble fragments while building infrastructure for Ottoman Turkey, making the Altar as we know it a pure product of German, French, and British competition for influence in the Middle East. Today, Turkey has regained confidence, and officials from the Prussian Cultural Heritage Foundation expect Ankara to ask for it back.

These sinuous marbles seem to speak to ascendant world powers. The Great Altar exudes confidence. Below the surface, however, does it also betoken demise? King Eumenes II and his brother Attalos II, their faces conspicuously absent among the Altar's myriad sculpted figures, were responsible for the construction of this colossal monument in the mid-second century BCE. The Attalids were the last of the great dynasties to emerge in Eurasia in the wake of the conquests of Alexander the Great, and the Altar is the loudest expression of their arrival. "We belong," it seems to say. Consider the themes of its two friezes. On the outside, savage Giants, half-man and half-beast, challenge Olympus for supremacy in the world. Zeus, Athena, and the other Olympian gods are shown battling down the threat of chaos. The barbarians are beaten back from the gates, a Classical example of classic fear mongering. And the message is simple: In an insecure world, the Attalids belong at the helm. On the inside, the Greek exiles from Arkadia, the retinue of princess Auge and her foundling son Telephos, arrive in non-Greek Mysia. Local king Teuthras and his indigenous Mysians receive and absorb them. Together, they even fend off an attack of Greeks on their way to Troy. In short, the Attalids belong in Anatolia.

Yet also ringing out from the marble, from its distended and seething bodies, is the death knell of a Hellenism without Rome. Within a generation, the Attalids were gone, their finery transported to Rome, their kingdom converted into a province, their library and collection of art picked over by Roman looters, their customs houses occupied and their cities picked over by Roman tax collectors. During an 1882 viewing, Jacob Burckhardt, one of the Altar's first sympathetic critics, was thrilled with its rippling dynamism.[1] What he saw as a terrifying creativity breaking free of the straitjacket of convention could also be interpreted as the equally mortifying last gasp of the Hellenistic World. In the end, royal Pergamon disappeared as suddenly as it had emerged onto the stage of history.

The Subject of the Inquiry

The Attalids' was an overnight empire. The story in a nutshell is that in 188 BCE, Rome defeated the Seleukid army of Antiochos III "the Great" and promptly parceled off to allies the winnings of Aegean-based Asia Minor and inland Anatolia (**Map I.1**). Those allies were the Attalid kingdom and the island republic of Rhodes. While the Rhodians failed to secure their share of the spoils, the Attalids succeeded, chiefly, by using a set of flexible and noncoercive tools of empire building. These tools were both fiscal and ideological in nature. The Attalids exploited the potent mechanisms of public finance in ancient Greece to bind an urbanized Aegean zone to rural Anatolia in a way that assured both populations of cultural autonomy. It was taxation – not predation – that afforded the Attalids their legacy as patrons of arts and culture in the polis and as prestige brokers in parts of the Anatolian countryside where an Iron Age way of life persisted well into the Roman period. In fact, for fifty years, the Attalids raised such a bountiful harvest of taxes that the Pergamene cartouche is still visible in nearly all of the most prestigious venues of Old Greece. Today, the Stoa of Attalos in the ancient marketplace of Athens stands for Pergamon's inclusion in Greece and – ever since John D. Rockefeller reconstructed it and

---

[1] On the discovery of the Altar in its historical context, as well as the reactions of intellectuals such as Burckhardt and Friedrich Nietzsche, see Gossman 2006. For its rapid reception across Germany, see Bohne 2012, 399–400.

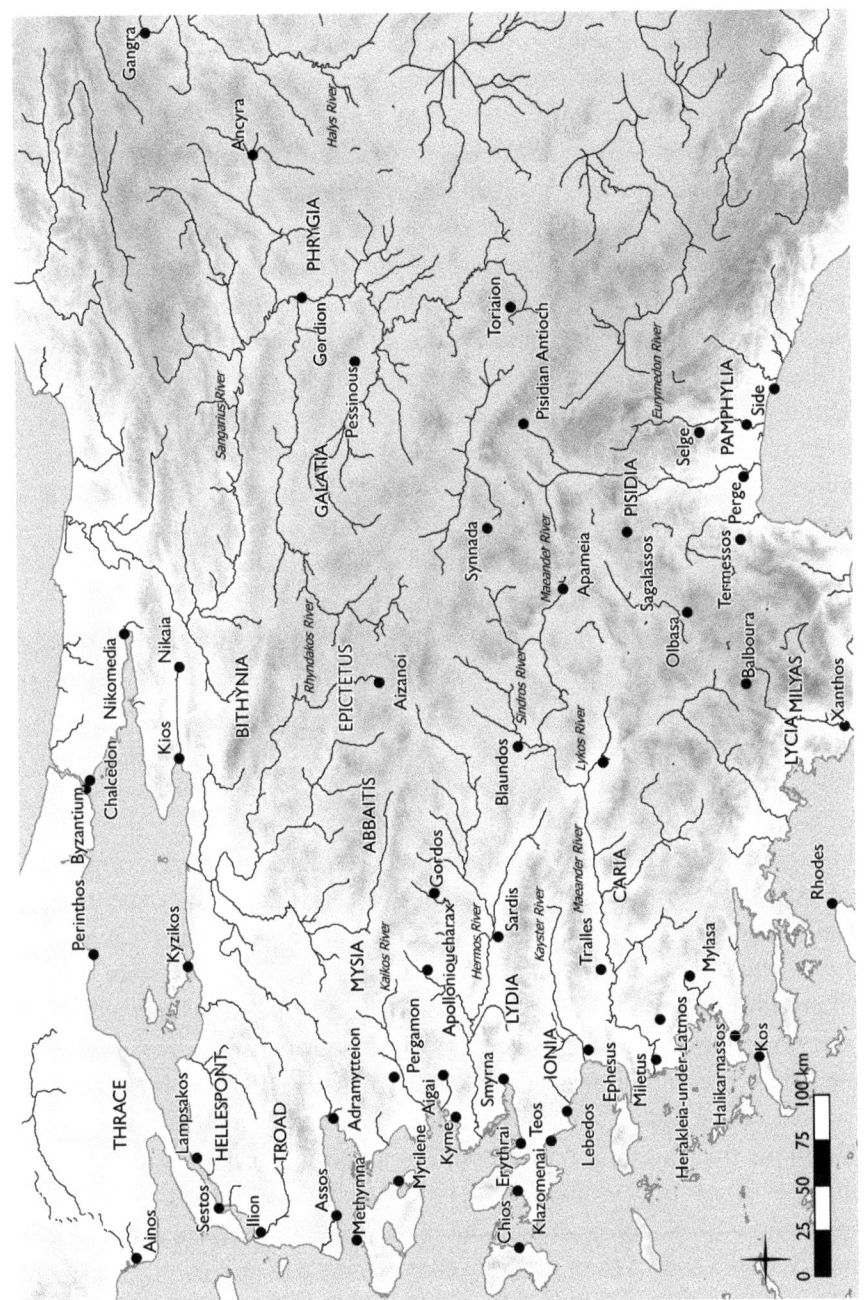

Map I.1 Anatolia, ca. 200 BCE.

Dwight D. Eisenhower rededicated it in 1956 – Greece's belonging to the West. Overwhelmed by the aesthetic blitz of the Altar, or perhaps with the benefit of hindsight, seeing the hubris of a soon-to-be defunct dynasty in its monuments, we have yet to explain how this young and lightweight empire so effectively raised the money.

The explanation is that the Attalids made culture depend on taxation. It is important to remember that for the average Greek of 188 BCE, only death was certain, not taxes. Surely, the new imperial overlord would demand tribute, an outflow of resources – but that amounts to confiscation, not taxation. A fiscal system that works sustains the fiction of reciprocity. With the tax return that Pergamon sent back, a bundle of money and fiscal privileges, the taxpayers funded the reproduction of their own culture. Naturally, lent such dignity, they agreed to pay up. It was all rather like the gambit that C. P. Cavafy imagined in his poem "In a Large Greek Colony, 200 B.C." (lines 18–20). An outsider appears, a "political reformer," who meddles with the local economy, making radical changes under cover of carefully chosen words. Just so the Attalids seem to have coaxed their subjects, by arguing, in Cavafy's telling, "Give up this revenue and that other similar one, and this third, *as a natural consequence*" (emphasis added).

It is a remarkable fact that the Attalids extracted resources from vast new territories without militarizing them or succumbing to a revolt. Rather, the great revolt, the War of Aristonikos, broke out under the shadow of the extinction of their line. Instead of imposing bureaucrats and garrisons, the Attalids ruled through an extraordinarily wide range of local actors, from the elite of the old Greek cities of the Aegean coast to the tribal leaders of the interior of Anatolia. Instead of abolishing local institutions and identities, they harnessed them. The cities' budgets were written into the royal tax code. The king inscribed the cities' emblems on coins, not his own portrait. In the cities, the Attalids profited from ancient civic institutions, a well-oiled administrative machine. In the countryside, a civic awakening was afoot, and Pergamon nimbly helped generate new institutions that instantly meshed with their own. They ruled under the banner of a new universalism, which drew on Panhellenism's traditional appeal to the Greek polis, but built out their own cosmopolis to encompass zones of backwoods Anatolia as yet unknown to state power.

As a subject of inquiry, the rise and fall of an empire is as old as the writing of history itself. In the fifth century BCE, Herodotus described the formation of imperial Persia, while Thucydides analyzed the origins of the Athenian Empire. In Hellenistic times, the Greek historian Polybius, a contemporary and an admirer of Pergamon's most famous kings, the brothers Eumenes II and Attalos II, explained to Greece how Rome had risen to Mediterranean-wide power. Philosophically, Polybius' view was that every great empire must eventually fall, though he left that theme to the likes of eighteenth-century English historian Edward Gibbon, whose *Decline and Fall of the Roman Empire* very much speaks to the concerns of our own age.[2] Indeed, with American power on the wane, Europe's cohesion evaporating, and the postcolonial order in the Middle East crumbling, understanding imperial and civilizational collapse is once again on the agenda. Yet between these two poles of birth and demise stands another issue, one now of pressing concern to sovereigns of young empires like China's or to those who rule over pieces of failed states, namely, the question of how a "successful" empire actually functions. If we define "success" in terms of the capacity of the few to dominate the many, to extract or control the resources of extensive territories, to integrate populations ideologically, and to substitute cooption for coercion, then the Attalid Empire, short-lived as it was, ranks among the most successful of Classical Antiquity.

The subject of the inquiry here, then, is not how an empire came into being or disappeared. The Attalids gained their empire by shrewdly allying themselves with the Romans, who simply created it by fiat to fill a power vacuum and avoid the burden of direct rule. In turn, Attalos III bequeathed his kingdom to Rome, ultimately preserving its unity in the form of Rome's new Province of Asia, contributing a major building block to the kind of "composite monarchy" that we later find in early modern Europe.[3] For such perspicacity and timeliness, the Attalids have been rewarded with little attention from historians.[4] Yet what most sorely awaits investigation, the subject of the inquiry here, is how the Attalids' empire came to be so entrenched, so quickly. Consequently, what follows is micro-history on an imperial scale. It is the story of how an empire embedded itself in society, how an empire came to be a state. While both terms, "empire" and "state," are notoriously difficult to define, and even vexing when we import to the ancient past the categories of European colonialism or the nation-state, it is important to mind the distinction. Empire implies the effective sovereignty of one polity, the dominant metropole, over another, the subordinated

---

[2] See recently, e.g., Morris 2010; Ober 2015.
[3] On "composite monarchy," see, e.g., Koenigsberger 1989.
[4] The last synthesis of Attalid history was Hansen 1971 (first ed. 1947). Allen 1983 is a more specialized treatment. For renewed interest, see the papers collected in Thonemann 2013a.

periphery.⁵ That domination, of course, rests on the recognition of sharp differences in identity. A state, by contrast, in Max Weber's famous definition, is a continuous and compulsory political organization, which upholds its monopoly on the legitimate use of physical force in the enforcement of its order on a specific territory.⁶ Here, local elites cooperate and common identities predominate. Rome handed Pergamon an empire, but it was the Attalids who pursued the path of the state. The task is to narrate and explain the rapid and relatively bloodless conversion of an imperial periphery into a coherent state. Along the way, a further objective is to illustrate the texture of Attalid state power in order to provide a fuller account of the historical development of Hellenistic monarchy and enrich our knowledge of its many regional inflections.

If we step back and survey the grand history of ancient empires, we see a great variety of solutions to the problem of governance. On one extreme, certain empires integrate conquered territories with only the credible threat of violence. The Neo-Assyrian Empire of the early Iron Age operated on this basis. The vanquished faced either integration or annihilation, a choice vividly illustrated on the stone reliefs that show cities toppled, bodies impaled, and all that is sacred profaned. However, that form of integration was administrative and fiscal, but never ideological. On the other extreme, we find empires that can take a step beyond merely attracting the loyalties of local elites on the periphery; they open up new identities for broad segments of the conquered population. The Roman Empire, which turned its provincial Gauls, Africans, and Syrians all into card-carrying Romans, lasted centuries because it penetrated society to an unprecedented depth. This is the fundamental question in the comparative study of empire: To what extent do empires convert their peripheries into parts of their original state?⁷

It is a question that remains unanswered for the Hellenistic kingdoms of western Eurasia, which form the chronological and geographical bridge between the Ancient Near East and Rome. In his magisterial *The Sources of Social Power*, Michael Mann calls them "loose, Persian-style states," with Greeks holding sway.⁸ With a wealth of evidence unearthed in recent decades, we can now see the Pergamene iteration of Hellenistic empire in a different light. This late-breaking version, strapped for charisma if not for cash and administrative acumen, evinces a clear break with the old Achaemenid tradition of minimal interference in local affairs. As Peter

---

⁵ Doyle 1986, 19–48. ⁶ The paraphrase of Weber is drawn from Monson and Scheidel 2015, 6.
⁷ Goldstone and Haldon 2009, 16. ⁸ Mann 2012, 247.

Thonemann argues, the Attalids now came "creeping into their subjects' lives in a new and intrusive way," leaning on the Greek polis and other, non-Greek civic organisms to generate ever more of what Mann calls *infrastructural power*.[9]

Classics

If the Renaissance rediscovered Classics, the original discovery took place in Antiquity itself. Those ancient tastemakers whom we have labeled since the nineteenth century the so-called Hellenistic Greeks are often credited in romantic narratives with spreading Hellenism across the Middle East. Johann Droysen, the Prussian monarchist who coined the term "Hellenistic," celebrated the scientific and philosophical achievements of their age and exalted their mixing of cultures. Hellenism and Judaism were combined to produce Christianity, on his account.[10] We have inherited Droysen's fascination with cultural mélange, if the fracturing of academic disciplines has also meant a turn away from his mode of synthesis. Yet we can understand the mix only as well as we know the ingredients. Hellenism may have been generalized in the wake of Alexander the Great, but it was also classicized. Drawing on their inheritance, scholars in the Ptolemies' Library of Alexandria and the Attalids' Library of Pergamon selected and refined, catalogued, preserved, and transmitted the corpus of literary and artistic output that we call Classics. Not just the shape, then, but also the prestige attached to Classics in its primeval form derives from a specific historical context, in which the new Hellenistic kings gambled on a new conception of culture.

While Alexandria's earlier role in this process is well recognized, we tend to look past Pergamon, Hellenistic latecomers, toward Rome, though ironically, the Romans themselves believed wholeheartedly that the Attalids were the agents of cultural transfer.[11] Pergamon commands a crucial, if relatively unexamined position in the mediation of the Classical Tradition. Gregory Nagy describes the Library of Pergamon as both rival and alternative to the centers of Alexandria and Athens. It operated according to a different notion of comprehensiveness, verging on

---

[9] Thonemann 2013b, 46–47.
[10] For the origins of this grand hypothesis, which Droysen himself never put to the test, see Momigliano 1970.
[11] Kuttner 1995.

encyclopedism. This is no triviality if it meant that a much larger corpus of Aristotle and more poetry attributed to Homer and Hesiod survived.[12] The Attalids were omnivorous and voracious collectors across media. Theirs was a truly bibliophilic city; an ancient etymology for the word "parchment" links it to Pergamon. They collected Athenian intellectuals and refashioned the legacy of Pericles, erecting a replica of Pheidias' statue of Athena from the Parthenon inside their library. They purchased the island of Aegina and then plundered it for statues, including a portrait of the poet Sappho. They participated in the Sack of Corinth and picked out the paintings of old masters from the rubble. They were no more or less opportunistic than their peers in this regard, only more successful at making their mark with the detritus of Greece's heyday. Yet inevitably, each king and court with the requisite institutions shaped Classics for the ideological use best suited to the needs of the moment. By focusing on the historical moment of urgent state formation in the decades after the Treaty of Apameia of 188 BCE, and by providing a full account of the ideological challenges and proclivities of the Attalids, who decorated Delphi, Delos, and Athens and built a capital with a royal library and the largest gymnasium on record in the Hellenistic world, we can supply the missing context for a key stage in the development of the Classical Tradition.

Taxation

We live in the most financialized economy in the history of the world. Money is more ubiquitous, fungible, and powerful than ever before; it permeates every aspect of life and of death too. It flies around the globe with ferocious velocity and underwrites American dominance. The differences are striking, if we juxtapose to ours the world into which Philetairos, founder of the Attalid dynasty, was born. Imagine an agrarian society, in which many people rarely laid eyes on a coin, in which there was so much that money could *not* buy. Kings ruled only as long as they proved themselves worthy on the battlefield; their lands were "spear-won," and therefore also their right to consume the fruits conspicuously.[13] And yet money is a central theme of the story of the improbable rise of Philetairos and the Attalids. Generations ago, when money was newer and perhaps viewed with more suspicion, this oddity was frequently noted. Theodor

---

[12] Nagy 2011.
[13] For "spear-won" land, the essential sources are collected by Austin 2006, 84 n. 4.

Mommsen, for example, cast the Attalids as the Medici of Antiquity, while a historian of the 1920s bemoaned the "money power of Pergamon."[14] An Anatolian archaeologist of the 1950s and 1960s, as if charging stray ruins to their account, opined, "Pergamenes always preferred gold and diplomacy to force of arms."[15] In fact, an ancient critique of the Attalids relates to their moneyed origins: Philetairos was a eunuch and a treasurer (*gazophylax*), not a king. Indeed, they did descend from this rogue official, a Hellenized Paphlagonian who managed to embezzle 9,000 talents of royal silver stored in a citadel of Lysimachus.[16] This was a large amount of silver, if we compare it with the estimated cost of the construction of the Parthenon, around 500 talents, or take these 9,000 talents as roughly equivalent to Herodotus' guess for the annual tribute of Achaemenid Persia. If minted, Philetairos' silver would have equaled almost eight years of the copious coinage issued in the name of Alexander the Great (ca. 332–290 BCE).[17] On the other hand, hypothetical revenues for the Seleukid kingdom in this period reach 14,000–19,000 talents; the cash income of Ptolemy II Philadelphus of Egypt has been registered at 14,800. In short, the Attalid dynasty was born into money, but not much more than a middling-to-large Hellenistic kingdom collected in a year.[18]

Yet money came to define the Attalids because of how they deployed it – as a means of girding subjects to express their own communal identities and granting those expressions increased prestige. With characteristic subtlety, they delivered cultural autonomy, status, and risk buffering to many a polis and village, but also, the bonds of dependence. For a Hellenistic king, conspicuous consumption was a given, as was pandering to the cultural prejudices of those he ruled. So why, centuries later, was the Christian moralist Tertullian still railing against "Attalid riches" (*attalicae divitiae*)?[19] Clearly, money was the basis of their power. However, the mechanisms and ideological maneuvers through which Pergamon obtained money and used it to gain an empire have long been opaque. Any investigation into the roots of the Attalid imperial project must shed light on systems of public finance.

The Attalids were heirs to a long line of thinking about taxation that stretches from Xenophon's reflections on a specifically economic Athenian

---

[14] Ure 1922, 285. [15] Winter 1966, 129. [16] Strabo 13.4.1.
[17] Hdt. 3.89–95. For the Parthenon, see Stanier 1953. For an estimate of just 10% minted, see Marcellesi 2012, 80.
[18] Callataÿ 2011, 20; Manning 2007, 454; Aperghis 2004, 251. On the historical insignificance of these 9,000 talents, see already Rostovtzeff 1923, 360.
[19] Tertullian, *De ieiunio adversus psychicos* 294.

Empire through the political economy of Pseudo-Aristotle's *Oikonomika*, written at the dawn of the Hellenistic period. What makes the Attalids unique is that their question was not just how to raise more taxes, but how to involve the populace more deeply in its own taxation. Pergamon maintained a modest army and fell back behind sturdy walls when attacked.[20] The Attalids' subjects did not revere them as pharaohs, nor as the successors of the Great Kings of Persia and Babylonia, nor as the representatives of a Macedonian kinship group. If only for survival, cunning choices about taxation were essential; though just as important were decisions about redistribution, which is why the term "taxation" and not "tribute" is maintained in what follows. The case of Pergamon may even disprove the dictum now attributed to the Austrian economist Joseph Schumpeter: "The budget is the skeleton of the state stripped of all misleading ideologies."[21] On the contrary, everything we know about fiscal practice in the Attalids' empire shows that culture and ideology were inscribed in their tax code.

Taxation provokes debate. Behind arguments about what the state must purchase and how to distribute the costs are debates about the very nature, essential fairness, and even definition of taxation. In the United States, where the Constitutional Convention of 1787 failed to agree on an unambiguous definition of "direct taxes," taxation is a divisive issue and consensus elusive.[22] As recently as 2011, the Supreme Court disagreed over whether to qualify as a tax the individual mandate provision of Obamacare.[23] Different taxes have received the public's approbation and its scorn, cast as natural, habitual obligations and sacrifices, or foreign and un-American confiscations. Slavery and its legacy, the impact of industrialization and now globalization, the American way of life, are all debated in the fiscal arena. What we talk about when we talk about taxation is citizenship and democracy, but also the vaunted and loathed exceptional character of American culture.

It turns out that the ancient Greeks were just as divided over taxation. They had budgets.[24] They also had fiscal preferences and prejudices. From the assembly of Classical Athens to the battlefield of Alexander's Babylon, public spending debates were surprisingly sophisticated.[25] The average citizen knew how much was in the treasury and how to investigate the

---

[20] Ma 2013a, 59–62. [21] Schumpeter 1991, 100, quoting Rudolph Goldscheid.
[22] Einhorn 2006; Huret 2014; Hutchins 2016.
[23] *National Federation of Independent Business* v. *Sebelius.* [24] Rhodes 2013, 217–18.
[25] Perikles on eve of Peloponnesian War: Thuc. 2.13.3. Alexander at Opis: Arr. *Anab.* 7.9.6.

costs of added benefits in new taxes or public borrowing.[26] Then too, definitions were contested. Greeks had a bewildering number of different names for these taxes. Vocabulary depended on imperial ideology, on one's vantage point in the economy, or simply on belief.[27] Was the tax just? Was it *Greek*? What end did it serve? As Demosthenes once complained, merchants failed to see that the taxes they called "gifts," in fact, paid for the security of their ships at sea.[28] In their own way, the Attalids of Pergamon won the perennial debate on taxation. They taxed to build the Great Altar and the Stoa of Attalos in the Athenian Agora, to purchase art and buy Aegean islands, and to fight the wars and fund the festivals, which proffered them a place at the table of high politics. They picked their words carefully, but they also shed the specter of taxation without representation, a plague on the Athenian Empire and the rest of its Hellenistic successors. Throughout the kingdom, the Attalids broadcast on stone the goals of taxation, and they advertised on coins the taxpayers' role in a credible and profitable fiscal system.

A focus on taxation takes advantage of a generation's output of empirical studies, but it also builds on a more recent wave of work on ancient Greek political economy that highlights a fiscal system's power to integrate.[29] It is no exaggeration to claim that for many ancient Greeks, taxes determined identity. When, where, and how they paid turned a discursive reality into a hard, cold one. Their world was both ecologically and politically fragmented, filled with more than a thousand small city-states, between which they often traveled in search of necessities or profit. In the harbors and at the gates, discriminatory tax collectors checked identities, demanding an answer: Who *are* you? Are you an Athenian or a Pergamene? In coastal Iasos, for example, the question was more complicated: Are you Iasian? Or are you *like* an Iasian, that is, a foreigner granted "tax equality"?[30] Here, taxes effectively assimilated the noncitizen to the citizen. Hellenistic kingdoms contained much larger and more diverse populations. Revenue-hungry rulers relied on fiscal systems that integrated individual subjects and entire subject communities. In Ptolemaic Egypt, this meant a shift from a traditional emphasis on controlling labor to raising revenues in cash. The attendant institutional changes – tax farming, banking, receipts, coinage, and the census – all constrained relationships

---

[26] Public spending debates: Pritchard 2015, 16–24. Public borrowing: Migeotte 1984.
[27] Vocabulary: Chankowski 2007, esp. 313.   [28] Dem. *On the Chersonese* 25.
[29] Public finance in the cities of ancient Greece: Migeotte 2014.
[30] *SEG* XXXVI 982A; Bresson 2016, 289–90.

with the new state.³¹ For the cities of Seleukid Anatolia and Antigonid Macedonia, we can now recognize a process of integration alongside the subterfuge and resistance. Paradoxically, what in the Macedonian cities were known as "city dues" were actually services rendered to the central administration of the kingdom.³² Old Greek cities gradually found themselves sharing accounts with Seleukid kings, as the royal treasury became a fixture of their fiscal landscape.³³

The Attalid case is of particular value, then, as a relatively well-documented Hellenistic fiscal system, in which taxes and transfers reinforced local identities and created imperial ones. The last scholar to fully assess the political economy of Pergamon was the White Russian émigré Mikhail Rostovtzeff in 1930. In fact, Rostovtzeff identified the crux of the Attalids' success, musing, "It is, however, curious that while taxing heavily the population of the subject cities with one hand, the kings paid with the other hand both to the cities and to the temples, and to the associations of the young men (probably to the Gymnasia) certain subsides in specie and kind."³⁴ For Rostovtzeff, what made this behavior so curious was an anachronistic idea that the Attalids were half-baked liberals. In our own neoliberal age, it continues to haunt the scholarship.³⁵ It helps that the Attalids purposively hid their faces, muted their dynastic cult, eschewed the pageantry through which Hellenistic royalty typically circulated images of its power, and sought in every medium and venue merely to blend in. It also helps that Polybius praised one Attalid as a singular champion of "Greek cities."³⁶ Yet Rostovtzeff's facts have only multiplied, showing even greater interleaving of royal and civic systems of public finance in the Attalid kingdom. By Hellenistic standards, this was big government. Yet, fascinatingly, it was combined with radical decentralization.

Interest in the economic history of ancient Greece and Rome has grown tremendously in the past several decades. Outside academia, the prestige of economics as a mode of analysis only grows in a period of heightened economic insecurity. Inside academia, humanists fatigued with a history of representations have drawn inspiration from historicizing trends within economics and economic sociology, which question the genesis and performance of institutions. Whereas mainstream economics treats

---

[31] Manning 2009, 128.   [32] Hatzopoulos 1996, 1:438–39.
[33] Capdetrey 2004; 2007, 425–28, contrasting the Achaemenid system.
[34] Rostovtzeff 1930, 605.
[35] Kertész 1992. On the historiographical trope of Attalid liberalism, see Savalli-Lestrade 2001, 78–80.
[36] Polyb. 32.8.5.

institutions, the human constraints of formal and informal rules for interaction, as an aberrance, the so-called New Institutional Economics (NIE), associated with the names Coase, North, and Williamson, treats them as a determinant. Ronald Coase is credited with introducing transaction costs as a factor in economic analysis. They are the price we pay to interact at an acceptable level of uncertainty, the price of having institutions that mitigate risk. As Alain Bresson writes, "NIE substitutes a science of contract in lieu of a science of choice."[37] As the new orthodoxy, it has achieved remarkable popularity in ancient history because it broke an impasse and made economic theory relevant again to Classics. The old quarrel between "primitivist" and "modernist" approaches to ancient economic life is absurd if contemporary capitalism is no longer the ultimate reference point.[38] Under the banner of NIE, much recent scholarship is devoted to demonstrating the extent of markets and the existence of economic rationality in Antiquity.[39] Ever more, the "glory that was Greece" is chalked up to growth-oriented economic policy.

This book owes an intellectual debt to those who have insisted on the importance of institutions for understanding coordination. The goal is to explain Pergamon's successful capture of an empire and rapid state formation. The explanation, it is argued, lies in the choice of specific fiscal institutions that gave taxpayers a say and a stake in taxation. The case I am making is therefore primarily qualitative, though as in the case of the dynasty's 9,000 talents of start-up funds, I try wherever possible to provide the reader with a sense of the quantitative scale by which the distinctiveness of the Pergamene way is also registered. Undoubtedly, the Attalids, just like the other Hellenistic kings, strove to "maximize revenue" within ecological and institutional constraints.[40] They needed to maximize in order to combat the Galatians, Seleukids, Rhodians, Bithynians, Pontos, and other rivals in the anarchic ancient Mediterranean. The more interesting problem relates to how their fiscal system ensured high returns *and* its own survival. Did the Attalids spread markets? Political unification seems to have strengthened interregional exchange in Anatolia. Did they produce growth? We lack the data to answer such a question, though the city-states that have been credited of late with driving growth in ancient Greece loom

---

[37] Bresson 2016, 19.   [38] Bresson 2016, 25; Ober 2015, 2–3.
[39] On the trend toward chronicling the extent of markets, specialization, and economic rationality in ancient Greece, see, e.g., Harris, Lewis, and Woolmer 2016.
[40] So-called revenue maximizing: Aperghis 2004, 297–303; for critiques, see Ma 2007b; Capdetrey 2007, 426. Hellenistic empire triumphing over ecological and institutional constraints: Manning 2009, 120–30.

large in this story. In the Mediterranean of the second century BCE, the polis, the privileged partner of Pergamon, with its centuries of experience, was by far the most efficient tax authority around. Yet it was also the Greeks' primary site of cultural reproduction. By taxing through the polis, but also through civic organisms on its margins, the Attalids, to an unprecedented extent, tied their own economic reproduction to the cultural reproduction of their subjects. Attalid taxes were indeed, to paraphrase Oliver Wendell Holmes, the price of civilization.[41]

History

In order to clear the ground for the analysis of the specific character of Attalid state power that forms the heart of the book, it may be helpful to lay out a narrative of political history in advance. A wide-lens perspective can enrich our understanding of many of the documents presented later in their local context. Narratives of the history of the fortunes of the Attalid dynasty and the development of the city of Pergamon already abound in scholarship.[42] The basic facts of battles and indeed regnal dates are still debated, even which Attalos, on which visit to Athens, made such an indelible mark on its acropolis, not to mention the question of which monarch was responsible for the Great Altar. This fuzziness is in part due to holes in the literary sources – the text of Polybius is fragmentary for the entire period 188–133 BCE; the only complete account of Attalid history per se is Strabo's neat summary in two paragraphs.[43] It is also due to our heavy reliance on epigraphical evidence. For example, the over two decades-long reign of Eumenes I is known from just a handful of inscriptions. Fortunately, new inscriptions turn up all the time, while new readings of old inscriptions help us fine-tune the chronology of events. However, I have not made the traditional timeline, from Philetairos to Attalos III, or a series of Roman interventions in the East, the structuring principle of this book, because my objective is to explain Pergamon's impact on Anatolia by way of teasing out the distinctive features of Attalid imperialism.

---

[41] *Compania de Tabacos* v. *Collector*.
[42] For dynastic history, see Gehrke 2014; Marek 2016, 207–10. For the city of Pergamon, see Pirson 2019a; and in long-term perspective, Evans 2012.
[43] Strabo 13.4.1–2.

Appropriately, the story begins with the problem of trust and its relation to money. In ca. 302 BCE, Lysimachus, one of Alexander's Successors, put an official named Philetairos son of Attalos in charge of the citadel and treasury of Pergamon. Belittled in Antiquity as a eunuch, an unheroic "keeper of the treasury" (*gazophylax*), Philetairos had arrived from Tieion, a mixed city on the southern coast of the Black Sea where Greeks lived alongside Paphlagonians. Indeed, we know that his mother Boa was an Anatolian. However, contrary to an oft-repeated assertion, we cannot be certain that his unknown father was a Macedonian. Certain cognates of the name Attalos are in fact Phrygian, and the dynasty's later claims of Arkadian and Heraklid descent echo the foundation stories of the people of Tieion, recalling too those of Mausolus of Caria.[44] The family was evidently powerful in Paphlagonia itself, as Lysimachus placed a brother of Philetairos named Eumenes over his new mega-city of Amastris. Ultimately, both brothers were alienated from Lysimachus by ca. 283, the date from which court chronographers later counted the reign of Philetairos. Sensing danger, Eumenes turned Amastris over to Ariobarzanes of Pontos and fled to Pergamon.[45] For his part, Philetairos switched his allegiance to Seleukos I Nikator shortly before his defeat of Lysimachus at Koroupedion in Lydia in 281. When Ptolemy Keraunos subsequently murdered Nikator in Europe, Philetairos was quick to ransom the body, cremate it in Pergamon, and dispatch the remains to Antioch, thereby securing his position as a trusted Seleukid vassal on the western periphery.

As lord of Pergamon, Philetairos occupied a stronghold in the Kaikos Valley that had been host to the Gongylids (**Map I.2**), Greek exiles in the employ of the Achaemenid Persia, during the fifth and early fourth centuries. From the time of the Peace of Antalcidas of 387/6, the site seems to have functioned as a kind of sub-satrapal capital and to have grown into a minor polis. After 362, the ambitious Bactrian satrap Orontes resided there, governing a satrapy of Mysia that seems to have encompassed much of western Anatolia. The strategic value of the place was also recognized in the age of Alexander. The conqueror's son and potential heir, known as Herakles, along with his mother Barsine, the daughter of a Persian aristocrat, lived in Pergamon from ca. 325 until their murder in 309. A consensus now holds that either Lysimachus or Barsine built the Temple of Athena on the acropolis, which bore a Lydian-Greek inscription on one of the

---

[44] Kuttner 2005, 158.   [45] *FGrHist* 434 F9; Marek 1989, 376.

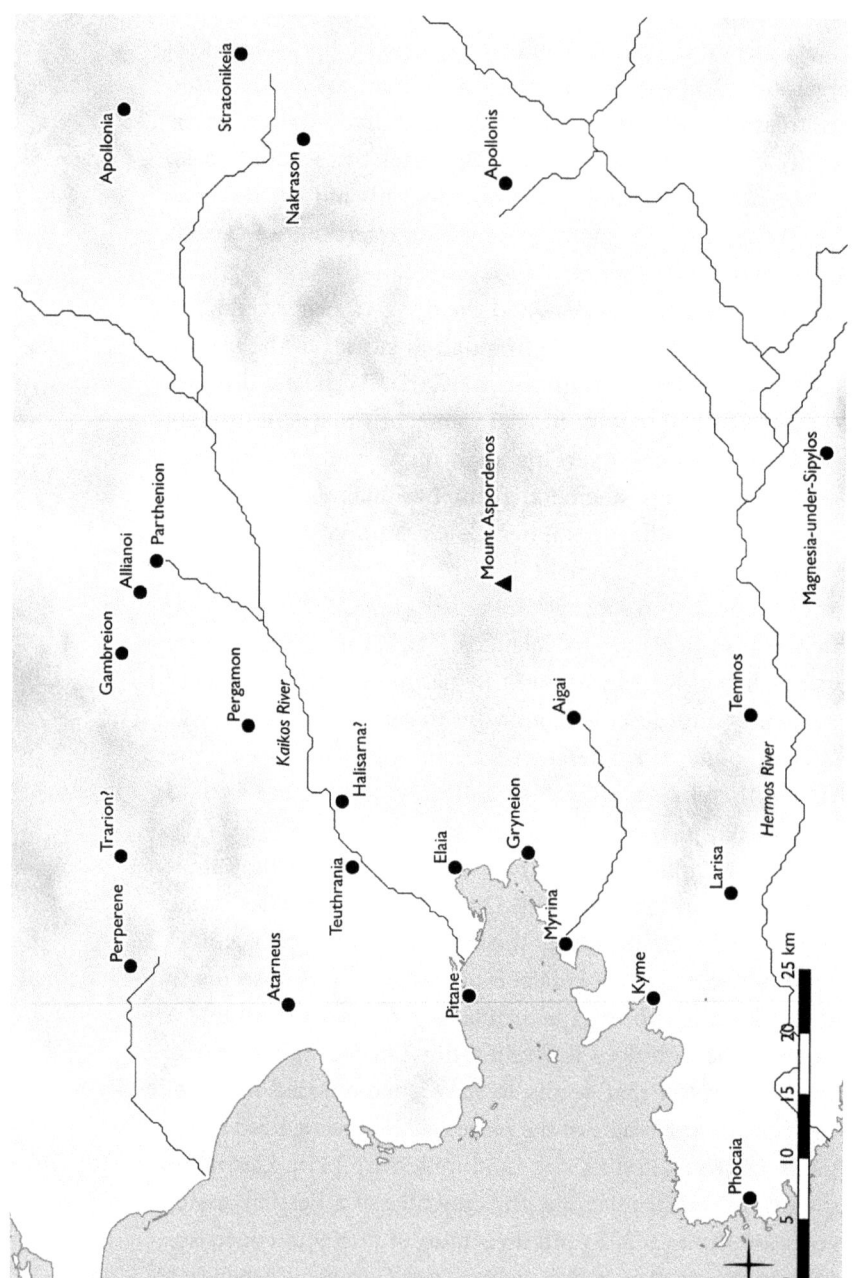

Map I.2 Pergamon and its environs.

columns of its pronaos. This act and the inauguration of a Panathenaia festival effectively substituted the goddess for Apollo at the top of the civic pantheon.[46] Yet this means that next to no evidence exists for any particular orientation toward Athens on the part of Philetairos.[47] He inherited a fortress with strong defenses, to which he added an arsenal. A late Classical or early Hellenistic wall, the so-called Philetairan Wall, which reinforced an earlier line of possibly prehistoric fortifications, is now considered an achievement of the pre-royal polis.[48] Philetairos, therefore, was not a city founder, but he may have developed the street plan; he certainly embellished what was in his time an extramural sanctuary of Demeter and Kore and projected influence into the surrounding countryside.[49] Just 30 km away on Mount Aspordenos, Philetairos monumentalized a Phrygian sanctuary of Mater with a Doric temple in trachyte. His benefactions are recorded for many of the cities of the region of Aeolis, such as Aigai, Pitane, Temnos, and Cyme. A series of gifts over several years to the Propontic city of Cyzicus established an important and lasting relationship by proffering aid during, among other conflicts, the crisis that attended the migration of the Galatians into Asia in the 270s. Finally, Philetairos also made a name for himself on the Greek mainland by spending money with tasteful discrimination. He followed in a grand tradition of Anatolian rulers as a benefactor of Delphi, where he gained proxeny for himself and his family. Less conventional were his dedications at the sanctuary of the Heliconian Muses at Thespiai in Boeotia, associated with the archaic poet Hesiod, which included oil for a gymnasium. From the beginning, with targeted giving, the Attalids were attaching themselves to high culture as much as to local culture.[50]

Childless, the dynasty's founder had at some point adopted his nephew Eumenes (son of his brother Eumenes), who succeed him in 263. Eumenes

---

[46] See Ohlemutz 1968, 16–21, for a date ca. 283 for the arrival of Athena Polias in Pergamon under Philetairos, taken as the beginning of a policy of emulation of Athens. New, high date for the temple of ca. 330–325: Schalles 1985, 20; Pirson 2019a, 76.

[47] Despite contact via philosophers under Eumenes I, sustained relations between the two cities emerged only under Attalos I. See Habicht 1990, 562.

[48] Radt (2014, 191) describes the Philetairan wall as late Classical/early Hellenistic, built along the line of a rudimentary fortification of the second millennium. Cf. Radt 1994 for an early third-century wall on top of an archaic one. A revised stratigraphy with an initial phase of the Middle Bronze Age will be published by Peter Pavúk; see already Bielfeldt 2019, 167 n. 7.

[49] Pirson (2019a, 78) argues that Philetairos did not expand, perhaps did not even significantly develop the urban plan of Pergamon. Cf. Orth 2008, 485: "Zu seiner Zeit kam es zu durchgreifender urbaner Neugestaltung: das städtische Areal wurde durch die Oberstadt Philetaireia ganz erheblich vergrößert."

[50] For sources for the donations of Philetairos, see conveniently Orth 2008, 486.

I gives us our first glimpse of the relationship of the Attalids to the city of Pergamon, by now a full-fledged polis with civic institutions at least as old as the first half of the fourth century. He pushed the city's assembly to honor the powerful board of officials known as *stratêgoi* for resolving a fiscal crisis born of malfeasance.[51] He is also the first on record to honor Athena as Polias at Pergamon.[52] One of the only other facts known about his reign of 22 years is that he defeated Antiochos I in a battle at Sardis in 262. A momentous victory on its face, it is not actually clear what effect if any the battle had on the shape or character of Eumenes' fiefdom (now a *dynasteia*, in Strabo's account).[53] The temptation to tell Attalid history as a number of steps toward emancipation from Seleukid control should be resisted. Client rulers on the margins of the Seleukid space were constantly winning and surrendering sovereignty.[54] At any rate, Philetairos had already minted coins in his own name and – seemingly, at the end of his life – coins bearing his own image. Further, while the Pergamene mint issued coins under Philetairos in the name of Seleukos I, it never minted in the name of his son and successor Antiochos I.[55] Eumenes may have enjoyed a greater freedom of action while Antiochos II was busy fighting Ptolemy II during the Second Syrian War (260–253), which affected coastal Asia Minor. Thanks to the preservation of an oath sworn between the king and mercenaries who had recently been in revolt, we know that Eumenes I possessed the military settlements of Attaleia in the upper Lykos valley near Thyateira and Philetairea on Mount Ida.[56] Both were attempts to exploit rural resources, but it is also possible that the forests of the Troad provided the timber that now allowed the Attalids to further engage the urbanized Aegean. The same mercenary oath alludes to ships, and an archaeological investigation of Elaia has concluded that the port came

---

[51] *OGIS* 267. It was once thought that the Attalids directly appointed *stratêgoi* in Pergamon and in subject cities as well, in order to control city administration. For a summary of views, see Allen 1983, 165–68. This view has fallen out of favor. See Müller 2012, 255–56.

[52] *I.Pergamon* 15.

[53] Many have seen *OGIS* 335, the arbitration of a dispute between Pitane and Mytilene that involved Eumenes I, as evidence of an expansion of Pergamene territory in this context. Against this view, see the nuanced critique of Savalli-Lestrade 1992, 226–28.

[54] Chrubasik 2013.

[55] This is Westermark Group II, dated by Georges Le Rider to 270–263. See Meadows 2013, 157. Historical works tend to take no account of this finding in narrating the reign of Eumenes I. See Allen 1983, 24; Shipley 2000, 312; Gehrke 2014, 124.

[56] *OGIS* 266. Chrubasik (2013, 90) and Couvenhes 2020 both view these settlements as foundations of Philetairos.

under Attalid control shortly after the mid-third century and saw its harbors militarized and city plan transformed.[57]

The 44-year reign of Eumenes' adopted son Attalos I (241–197) witnessed the birth of the kingdom as such. Livy tells us that Attalos was the "first of the inhabitants of Asia (*primus Asiam incolentium*)" to refuse the Galatians tribute (38.16.14). War ensued, with what Attalid memory cast as the decisive defeat of the barbarians taking place "around the source of the river Kaikos" or, according to Pausanias, "in Mysia."[58] In his eulogy for Attalos, Polybius relates that by vanquishing the Galatians, the king "established his rule and first showed himself to be a king (ταύτην ἀρχὴν ἐποιήσατο καὶ τότε πρῶτον αὑτὸν ἔδειξε βασιλέα)" (18.41.7–8). Despite uncertainty about whether Polybius was in fact referring to the battle at the Kaikos, his testimony has often been used to date the event to the first years of the reign and, by extension, give us a date for the assumption of the royal title (*basileus*), the donning of the diadem, and the appellation Sotêr (savior).[59] The father of Attalos was the son of another nephew of Philetairos, but his mother was a Seleukid, Antiochis daughter of Achaios the Elder. Ultimately, he won his kingdom by taking advantage of internecine conflicts within his mother's family. In 239, the younger Antiochos Hierax defeated his brother Seleukos II at Ankyra and established himself as the independent ruler of cis-Tauric Asia. By ca. 228, Attalos had in turn defeated Hierax and his Galatian allies in Lydia, inland Caria, and on the Hellespont, and presumably claimed a certain portion of this territory. In Pergamon, these victories were memorialized on monuments set up in the sanctuary of Athena Polias, which indeed spotlighted the Galatian victory at the Kaikos on the spectacular Round Monument, but also trumpeted the defeat of Seleukos III (r. 225–222) and his general Lysias, probably of the rival Anatolian dynasty of the Philomelids from Phrygia Paroreios.[60] Some of the new territories were soon lost to Achaios, a Seleukid pretender who in 220 broke with Antiochos III Megas and claimed the cis-Tauric kingdom vacated by Hierax. To suppress the usurper, Antiochos was compelled to

---

[57] Work on the northern, closed harbor seems to have begun earlier, roughly the fourth and third centuries, according to pollen studies. See Pirson 2014a, 354. On the militarization of the waterfront, clearly a process that stretched into the reign of Eumenes II, see Pirson 2015, 38–41.

[58] *I.Pergamon* 24 = *OGIS* 276; Paus. 1.25.2.

[59] Well summarized by Allen 1983, 195–99, dating the battle to 238 or 237. Note that one can find dates for the Kaikos battle as high as ca. 240 (Mitchell 2003, 284) and as low as 234/3 (Müller 2012, Kat. 5.29 on *I.Pergamon* 20 = *OGIS* 269).

[60] *OGIS* 269, 273–79, with Austin 2006, 405 n. 7 on Lysias as a Philomelid. For the victory monument – a colossal bronze Athena Promachos in the style of Pheidias? – see Stewart 2004, 197; Kästner 2012, 185–88.

contract an alliance with Attalos, and the subordinate's sovereignty seems to have been formally recognized by 212.[61] In 218, with the army of Achaios busy fighting Pisidians, Attalos for a time secured his two key domestic constituencies, the Aeolian cities and the villages of rural Mysia Abbaitis, in the process settling his own Galatian clients deep inside the boundaries of his own kingdom.[62]

To a far greater extent than his ancestors or contemporary Anatolian rivals, Attalos I pursued reputational and territorial aggrandizement in Greece and the Aegean. He was the first Attalid active at the Panhellenic sanctuary of Apollo on Delos, where he publicized both his Galatian victories and his family's Mysian origins. At Delphi, he built a stoa dressed with historical paintings that is the sole monument to break the line of the sanctuary's framing *peribolos* wall. He also placed his own portrait statue on a column that occupied prime real estate directly in front of the Temple of Apollo.[63] These construction projects surely required the acquiescence of the Aetolians, who then held sway at Delphi and had gained Attalos as an ally against Philip V in the First Macedonian War (214–205). Pergamene forces entered the fray, consisting now of ever fewer mercenaries and more call-ups from places such as Cyzicus, hometown of queen Apollonis. Still, Attalos used cash to purchase the storied island of Aegina from the Aetolians, with all its artistic heirlooms, ca. 210. At around the same time, the crucial relationship with Rome began with an alliance that hardly required Attalos to fight to the end, despite his appearance as a signatory on the Roman side of the Peace of Phoinike at the war's conclusion. With his own kingdom under attack by Philip's kinsman Prousias I of Bithynia,[64] Attalos crossed back into Asia already in 209. The war with Prousias lasted four years, at the end of which, Attalos seems to have conquered the Aezanitis in Phrygia Epictetus and the Galatian borderlands around Pessinous with its sanctuary of Mater/Cybele.[65] From Pessinous, Attalos was able to transfer to the Romans, who were seeking a divine intervention against Hannibal, the aniconic cult stone of the Magna Mater, transported up the Tiber in 205.

When Ptolemy IV of Egypt died the following year, leaving a child of five in power, Philip and Antiochos formed a pact to divide up his kingdom.[66] The collapse of the century-old state system in the Mediterranean was a grave danger to middling powers such as Pergamon and Rhodes, which now found common cause. By 200, their ambassadors

---

[61] Shipley 2000, 314 with references.   [62] Polyb. 5.77–78.
[63] On the building activities of Attalos I in Delos and Delphi, see Schalles 1985, 60–68, 104–27.
[64] Gruen 1984, 530.   [65] Mileta 2010.   [66] Eckstein 2012, 121–80.

were in Rome for the first time, begging the Senate to launch what we call the Second Macedonian War. Meanwhile, Antiochos III had returned from a seven-year campaign of eastern reconquest to seize parts of Caria from Rhodes in 204 and 203. Philip had taken his own Carian positions and had invaded the Propontic area in 202. Rhodes and Pergamon joined forces with a coalition of smaller maritime states to confront Philip, leading to a destructive sea battle near Chios in 201. Attalos narrowly escaped his wrecked ship, leaving gobs of royal paraphernalia on deck, shiny loot to divert the Macedonian seamen, as he hurried back to a capital that Philip had severely damaged. Polybius tells us that Philip destroyed the Nikephorion at Pergamon, our first indication that Athena Polias had taken on the additional epithet "victory-bearer" (16.1.5–6).[67] In the end, Attalos had a hand in persuading not only the Romans to join the war but the Athenians and the Achaean *koinon* (league) as well. In addition to military leadership, Attalos offered the Greeks financial support and received immediate recompense in the form of honors in places such as Sikyon. The Athenians, deprived of their rural sanctuaries by Philip, welcomed Attalos in 200, showering him with honors.[68] In turn, he seems to have deposited the so-called Little Barbarians sculptural program on the Acropolis at this time, which inserted the Attalid Galatian victory into a cycle of civilizational triumphs.[69] The war allowed Attalos to strengthen his foothold in the Aegean, gaining the Cycladic island of Andros in 199 after making a play for Euboea. He died in 197, exhorting the Boeotians to join a war that was concluded the same year at Kynoskephalai.

Eumenes II, devoted son of Attalos I and Apollonis, Polybius tells us, inherited a small, diminished kingdom (32.8.3). The Seleukid alliance notwithstanding, already by 209, Antiochos III had taken back core Mysian territories bordering the upper Kaikos.[70] From 198 to 193, Antiochos reconquered much of western Asia Minor, and we find Eumenes pushing for another Roman intervention. Cagily, in 192 Antiochos offered the Pergamene king a final chance to return to vassalage by marrying one of

---

[67] On the location of the Nikephorion, conventionally understood to be an undiscovered extramural sanctuary, see Kohl 2002. On Athena's acquisition of the epithet Nikephoros in Pergamon, Attalos I is usually given credit for establishing his Nikephoria festival in the late 220s (Polyb. 4.49.3). See Ohlemutz 1968, 29; Jones 1974; Agelidis 2014, 383. Cf. Allen (1983 pp. 121–26), who places the event ca. 197 under Eumenes II.

[68] On Philip's destruction of Attica, see Livy 31.26.9–13 with Gawlinski 2015, 66, for archaeological evidence.

[69] Stewart 2004, 218–36; cf. Papini 2016, 43, not ruling out Attalos II as the dedicant of the Little Barbarians.

[70] Such is the evidence of a stele from Pamukçu near Balıkesir, SEG XXXVII 1010.

his daughters. Rebuffed, Antiochos crossed to Europe the same year to join his Aetolian allies, then lost his first engagement with the Romans in a battle at Thermopylae. The Seleukid then retreated to Asia, where in 190/89 he was vanquished again by the Romans at Magnesia-under-Sipylos, this time certainly with an Attalid army present. The greatest opportunist in a dynasty full of them, as R. E. Allen puts it, Eumenes II sprang into action to take full advantage of a power vacuum.[71] He set off to Rome to plead his case for Antiochos' cis-Tauric territories, which the Rhodians wanted to see set free from kings. Meanwhile the future Attalos II, the brother of Eumenes, joined the new consul Manlius Vulso on a punitive expedition against the Galatians, some of whom had fought with Antiochos. Tellingly, Livy tells us that the consul regretted Eumenes' absence, since the king possessed thorough knowledge of the people and places of Galatia (38.12.6; *gnarus locorum hominumque*). The Attalids had clearly long been active in inner Anatolia, but now had a chance to extend their power. The expedition of Vulso took a path that left from Ephesus and reached Apameia at the headwaters of the Maeander, then turned south into Pisidia, the Milyas, and the Cibyratis, and only then headed for Galatia proper. Much of the journey traversed lands that became – in theory – Pergamene once Roman legates had drawn up a new map at Apameia in 188. In addition to European territories, principally the Thracian Chersonese, the Attalids received all of cis-Tauric Asia north of the Maeander, the Carian outpost of the Hydrela region and the Lycian port of Telmessos, while the Rhodians were awarded most of Caria and Lycia (**Map I.3**).[72]

---

[71] Allen 1983, 76.

[72] The crucial territorial clause describing cis-Tauric Asia is missing from the text of Polyb. 21.43.5–6. Possible corruption of the corresponding text of Livy 38.38.4–5 has led to multiple understandings of the so-called Taurus line, which was confusingly defined by a mountain range, a valley, and a river (the "Tanais" according to the manuscripts, or the river Halys, according to many emendators, most recently Gehrke 2014, 132). For a summary, see Magie 1950, 757–58, who follows Holleaux 1957, 208–43, in accepting a boundary on the "middle Halys." In an important study, Giovannini (1982, 229) retains Tanais (Don), which makes a Seleukid evacuation of cis-Tauric Asia the true crux of the treaty. At stake was also the definition of an eastern border for the expanded Attalid kingdom. Notably, Mommsen (1879, 527–32) and McDonald 1967 reject the emendation of Tanais to Halys. Their readings of the geography would have limited the Seleukids to Cilicia in 188. However, for a critique of McDonald's view that the Tanais is the Calycadnus River (and further bibliography), see Gruen 1984, 641 n. 145. In sum, if Livy is not emended in a phonologically perverse way – and the Tanais *is* the Don – then Antiochos was excluded from both sides of the Halys. The Treaty of Apameia, then, did not prevent the Attalids from conquering or absorbing central Anatolia, the heart of the earlier Hittite and Phrygian empires.

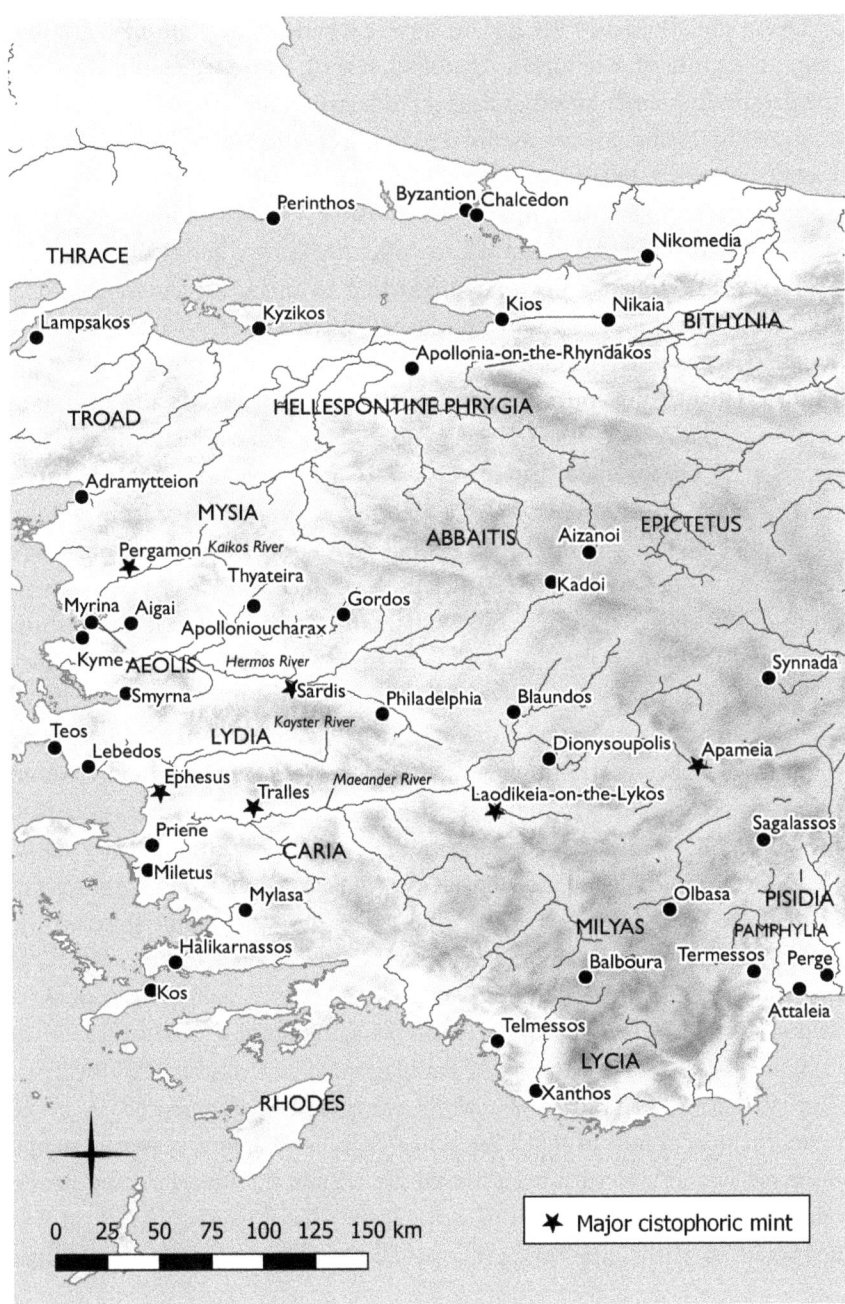

Map I.3 The core of the Attalid kingdom and the Rhodian *peraia* after 188 BCE.

Overnight, Eumenes seemed to have exchanged the diminished kingdom of his inheritance for an Anatolian empire. However, more wars and the patient implementation of the techniques of domination described and analyzed in this book were required to vindicate the settlement. An alliance was struck with Ariarathes IV of Cappadocia, who now betrothed his daughter Stratonike to Eumenes in penance for his earlier support of Antiochos. However, the first decade after 188 saw a series of challenges from rival Anatolian kings that threatened to block the emergence of a cis-Tauric kingdom. First, Prousias I of Bithynia, having allied with the Galatian leader Ortiagon, marched and sailed against Eumenes in 184/3. Hannibal was at the court of Prousias and famously advised the stratagem of hurling pots of snakes at Pergamene ships in a naval battle that is still occasionally glimpsed on the Great Altar's Gigantomachy.[73] Eager to finish off Hannibal, the Romans offered diplomatic support. Yet from a local perspective, the last stand of the Carthaginian was a sideshow at most. We learn from a decree of Telmessos that the conflict was viewed by contemporaries as a crucible for "all of the inhabitants of Asia," with Eumenes now playing the role of Sotêr.[74] It is not clear how much Bithynian territory accrued to the Attalid victors, though for a time, Philetairos' old city of Tieion became a Pergamene outlet on the Black Sea. The treaty that settled the war also brought Bithynia into alliance, but Eumenes now found himself at odds with Pharnakes I of Pontos. In 183, Pharnakes occupied the entrepot of Sinope, panicking both the Attalids and the mercantile Rhodians. Roman diplomacy did not prevent war, but rather a protracted conflict (183–179) broke out, drawing in nearly every major state on the Anatolian peninsula.[75] Eumenes traveled deep into Galatia, as far as the Halys, the riverine counterpart to the eastern Taurus line of Asia Minor. There, he rendezvoused with his father-in-law Ariarathes IV of Cappadocia, as well as Morzius of Paphlagonia and Prousias II of Bithynia. The various tribal polities of Galatia were further fragmented. A peace treaty included a host of Black Sea states, both Greater and Lesser Armenia. Eumenes was able to turn his attention to helping the Rhodians suppress a rebellion in Lycia. It was in this context that the Nikephoria festival was upgraded to truly international, so-called iso-Olympic and iso-Pythian

---

[73] An idea that originated in an 1880 article of W. H. Roscher. See Hansen 1971, 99 n. 90.
[74] Allen 1983 no. 7 line 7. Cf. Shipley 2000, 316: "Victory over the Gauls led the Greeks of Asia Minor to call Eumenes 'Nikephoros.'" Savalli-Lestrade 2018 places the Toriaion Dossier (**D8**) in the context of this conflict.
[75] On the scale of this war, see Eckstein 2012, 379, a war "which roiled all of Asia Minor 179–182 BC, and which several embassies of mediation sent by the Senate failed to stop."

status in 182/1. Pergamene sacred embassies were sent out in all directions to request recognition, from Delphi, from the old Greek cities of the Aegean, and from new cities of the Anatolian interior.

Polybius also tells us that Eumenes enjoyed an unparalleled reputation for benevolence among Greek cities and private citizens (32.8.5). He squandered some of that goodwill, earned in a popular war against the Spartan king Nabis (195) and in the Antiochene War, by coaxing the Romans into a decisive clash with Perseus, son of Philip V and ruler of Antigonid Macedon since 179. Whether with policy or with charisma, Perseus simply bested Eumenes in the court of public opinion and isolated him by making marriage alliances with both Prousias II and Seleukos IV, whose daughter Laodike the Rhodians conveyed to Pella in 178. In response, Eumenes helped his own man Antiochos IV grasp the diadem after a minister murdered Seleukos in 175. With Eumenes outwitting him at Rome, Perseus turned to violence. In 172, assassins hurled a boulder at the Pergamene king in a narrow pass below Delphi. Eumenes was feared dead, but the Attalid state did not crumble. In an act of loyalty that was quickly canonized in official memory, the future Attalos II Philadelphos ("the brotherly") took power and even temporarily married Stratonike, later abdicating and renouncing the marriage when his brother Eumenes recovered.[76] The Third Macedonian War (172–168) ended with the defeat of Perseus at Pydna and the Roman dismemberment of the Antigonid kingdom. The strongest of the Attalids' rivals had been eliminated or neutralized, but the Romans promptly withdrew their support over suspicions of double-dealing with Perseus. While the Rhodians received the same cold treatment and consequently lost control of Caria, Lycia, and their position in maritime commerce, the Attalids seem to have consolidated their post-Apameian kingdom at precisely this time. First, they took on a Galatian war (168–165) that touched their own Lydian and Phrygian territories but also secured them. The people of Sardis were so relieved to have survived the war that they instituted sacrifices and a joint festival in honor of Athena and Eumenes, which commemorated the removal of the "great danger."[77] The Ionian League proclaimed him the "common benefactor of the Greeks."[78] Diodorus tells us that Eumenes now subjugated the whole of the Galatian *ethnos* (tribal state), no doubt an exaggeration, but

---

[76] The name "Philadelphos" was applied to Attalos already in Eumenes' lifetime (*OGIS* 308; Hopp 1977, 59 n. 2). For the image of brotherly solidarity in dynastic self-representation, see, e.g., Polyb. 22.20.1–8. On Attalid "family values," see Thonemann 2013b, 38–44.
[77] *OGIS* 305 lines 11–12. [78] *RC* 52 lines 7–8.

evidence of territorial ambitions on the plateau.[79] Further, it appears that at this time the Attalids launched a new monetary system of their own in order to integrate the urban and rural, Aegean and Anatolian components of their kingdom.

Eumenes II was responsible for a major expansion of the city of Pergamon that extended its walls to the foot of the great hill, increasing the fortified area from 21 to 91 ha with a circuit of 4 km.[80] Under his rule, at least according to the Roman antiquarian Pliny, the cultural rivalry with Ptolemaic Alexandria finally burned hot (*HN* 13.70). Ptolemy V is said to have imprisoned Aristophanes of Byzantium rather than see him decamp for the Library of Pergamon, but Eumenes did nab an intellectual superstar in the Stoic philosopher Crates of Mallos. Ptolemy's ban on the export of papyrus is said to have compelled the Pergamenes to invent parchment.[81] We know that Eumenes dramatically increased the grandeur of the royal capital.[82] He was certainly responsible for at least the beginning of construction of the Great Altar.[83] Archaeological soundings show that he devised an entirely new grid plan for the city, with possibly the largest gymnasium of the time as its anchor point and architectural centerpiece. Remarkably, the development of a prestigious imperial metropole did not destroy the partnership of the sons of Apollonis. Roman attempts to woo Attalos away in 167 by offering him an independent kingdom in Aegean Thrace failed. Rather, by 160, he was co-regent. Twin inscriptions from Delphi show that both brothers financed educational foundations in 159, a final collaborative act for Eumenes, who died that year or the next.[84]

Finally succeeding his brother at the age of sixty-two, Attalos II successfully protected the achievement of his brother, replicated many of his accomplishments, and safeguarded the inheritance of the future Attalos III. The landscape of Athens provides an illustration. Whereas Eumenes had built a stoa adjacent to the Theater of Dionysus, Attalos built his own

---

[79] Diod. Sic. 31.14; Allen 1983, 142.

[80] Pirson 2019a, 80. For the proposal that Attalos I was responsible for the new fortification wall, see Lorentzen 2014.

[81] *Suda* s.v. Ἀριστοφάνης (A3933), Ἀριστώνυμος (A3936), Κράτης (K2342).

[82] Strabo (13.4.2) gives the credit to Eumenes. For the archaeological evidence, see Pirson 2014c, 217–24; Pirson 2019a, 80–84.

[83] Pollitt 1986, 97: begun ca. 180. For low dating, see Ridgeway 2000, 21–22: inception just before Eumenes' death in 159, lack of completion because of turmoil surrounding death of Attalos III in 133. See also Kästner 2014a, 458, for stratigraphy and stylistic indicators in favor of construction 170–150.

[84] *Syll.*³ 671 and 672. For 158/7 as final regnal year of Eumenes II, see Petzl 1978, 263–67; Mulliez 1998; Marek 2016, 565.

in the agora early on in his reign. In addition, both brothers seem to have left chariot monuments in Athens.[85] Alliances with the cities of Crete, which had been essential to the victory of Eumenes over Pharnakes, were maintained.[86] In Anatolia, Attalos further extended Pergamene dominance. Already in 165, Prousias II had brought to the Senate's attention the complaints of certain Galatians and of the citizens of Selge, perhaps the most developed and belligerent city in Pisidia. We know that Attalos had personally campaigned in Pisidia in 160, and we find him in the nearby region of the Milyas in 138/7.[87] It seems probable that the Pergamene impact on Pisidia that is so evident in the region's distinctive form of urbanism owes something to the king's active presence. We know that he dedicated a stoa on the agora of Termessos.[88] He also seems to have attempted to improve the kingdom's harbors, both at Ephesus and with the foundation (?) of a Mediterranean port in Pamphylia, christened Attaleia (Antalya). Mastery over upland Pisidia facilitated passage from Antalya overland to the river systems that finally terminate in the Aegean in places such as Ephesus.

Strife with Prousias II resulted in yet another war in which the Pergamenes abandoned arms and watched from behind their walls as the enemy wreaked havoc on the plain below and in several other cities of the Aeolian core (156–154). While the Romans imposed another set of unfavorable terms on Prousias, this time a cash indemnity, by 149, Attalos II had fully eliminated his Bithynian rival by cleverly using a patricidal civil war to install the more pliant Nikomedes II. Subsequently, he seems to have punished Thracian allies of Prousias with a European raid in 145.[89] In a family feud over Cappadocia, he was just as wildly successful in protecting Attalid interests with a mix of soft power and threats. Ariarathes V, his brother-in-law and former schoolmate in Athens, had lost his kingdom to Orophernes II in 158. While the parties argued it out at Rome, Orophernes managed to deposit 400 talents in a banking institution located in Attalid territory, the temple of Athena Polias in Priene. When Ariarathes regained sole power, despite the Senate's recommendation of power sharing, he claimed the 400 talents for the Cappadocian monarchy.

---

[85] Korres 2000.
[86] Eumenes: *Syll.*³ 671. Attalos: *OGIS* 270. Relations with Crete and its stock of mercenaries actually extend back to the reign of Attalos I. See the inscription from Malla, Allen 1983, no. 3.
[87] *RC* 54. For the date of 138/7 (not 159) for the decree of Olbasa (*SEG* XLIV 1108), see Savalli-Lestrade 2001, 87.
[88] Bringmann et al. 1995, no. 303.
[89] Date from the Gelembe inscription (*OGIS* 330). On this campaign, see Hopp 1977, 96–98.

The people of Priene refused to release what they considered a private deposit. Ariarathes attacked Priene, with the connivance and encouragement of Attalos, says Polybius (33.6.6), though the city dispatched embassies to Rhodes and Rome. In the end, the money was returned to Orophernes.[90] Ultimately, Attalos was not willing to destroy confidence in private property rights or civic institutions of public finance.

Attalos II has often been accused of obeisance to Rome in foreign policy. This conclusion is largely based on his letter of 156 to Attis the priest of Cybele in Pessinous, regarding a military action in Galatia. The letter purports to describe internal deliberations at court, the final decision to consult the Romans, since "to go ahead without consulting them seemed to involve considerable danger."[91] However, this is not quite the admission of powerlessness that the textbooks relate. Rather, it is the Attalid regime's own representation of the relationship with Rome, produced for its own advantage.[92] In any case, as has long been pointed out, the king was able to intervene in the affairs of his neighbors without Roman interference.[93] Like Eumenes, he helped raise up his own contender for the Seleukid throne. This was Alexander Balas, a youth from Pergamene Smyrna, who with Ptolemaic and Cappadocian help ousted Demetrios I in 150. Attalos thereby settled a score with Demetrios for his support of Orophernes. Admittedly, the Senate had recognized Balas, and as an ally, Attalos was never far behind when the Romans campaigned in Greece. Yet it is not difficult to find domestic concerns behind Attalid support for the war of Metellus against the pseudo-Philip (Andriskos) in 148. The Antigonid pretender was born in Adramyttion, recruited supporters in Miletus and in Thrace, and perhaps even meddled in the marriage of the Pergamene prince Athenaios. In other words, he was also a domestic problem.[94] In the Achaean War, an Attalid army participated in the destruction of Corinth (146), but also in the appropriation of its legacy. Pausanias describes works

---

[90] On this episode, see *OGIS* 351 with Polyb. 33.6; Habicht 1989, 360–61.

[91] Trans. Austin 2006, no. 244 = *RC* 61. For the traditional view, see Shipley 2000, 318–19 (citing Habicht 1989); Hansen 1971, 141: "Attalus II had advanced the vassalage of Pergamon by acquiescing in Roman interference in Galatia."

[92] Gruen 1984, 591. Compare Eumenes' invocation of the Romans in the Toriaion Dossier (**D8** lines 17–23).

[93] Hopp 1977, 68; Gruen 1984, 591: "The Pergamene ruler now had protégés on the thrones of Syria, Cappadocia, and Bithynia. His stature as preeminent power in Anatolia went unchallenged." Cf. Eckstein 2012, 379, on the considerable amount of choice in foreign relations for Greek states down to 168.

[94] Diod. Sic. 32.15 with Daubner 2011, 53. On Andriskos, Kallipa the ex-concubine of Perseus, and "Athenaios of Pergamon," see discussion of Hopp 1977, 93–94.

of art looted in the sack still visible in his day at Pergamon (7.16.8). Perhaps, a divergence of interest among the victors is part of the point of the libelous story about the Roman general, which depicts Attalos inadvertently alerting Mummius to the value of the painting his legionaries were using as a dice board.[95]

Whether or not he was in fact the biological son of Eumenes II, Attalos II chose to describe the future Attalos III that way in a letter sent to Ephesus concerning the boy's tutor.[96] Also, co-regent or not, already as an adolescent in the late 150s, young Attalos was associated with his guardian in acts of royal administration.[97] Thus, when the octogenarian Attalos II died in 138, Attalos III Philometer (Mother-lover) Euergetes (Benefactor) succeeded him according to plan.[98] However, the nearly preternatural solidarity of the dynasty was finally breaking down. The literary sources agree that Attalos began his five-year reign by executing many of his own kin, the entire upper echelon of courtiers and administrators. While it is a sensational claim and hardly would have been practicable, the portrait of Attalos III as an eccentric, paranoid, and violent man, who butchered the courtiers whom he suspected of killing his mother and wife, probably derives from the polemics and dustups of this first – and remarkably late – succession crisis in Attalid history. In other respects, the accounts of Diodorus and Justin are just too contradictory to salvage. Justin describes a recluse, the pharmacological gardener known also from Galen, who essentially abandons his kingdom; but according to Diodorus, Attalos III ran his kingdom into the ground.[99] What we know from the documentary evidence is that he did rule actively and largely in a traditional manner, even insofar as his innovations in the domain of public religion were not necessarily unusual. For example, after an epiphany he promoted to co-equal status with Athena Nikephoros the syncretized Zeus Sabazios, reputedly his mother's import from Cappadocia but increasingly popular

---

[95] Paintings as dice board: Polyb. 32.9.2. The high bid of Attalos: Plin. *HN* 35.24. On the true interests of Mummius, see Gruen 1992, 123–29; Yarrow 2006, 62. Further on Attalid collecting, see Kuttner 2015.
[96] Austin 2006 no. 246 = *I.Ephesos* 202.
[97] *RC* 65. On the chronological problems with making Attalos III the biological son of Eumenes II, see summary of problem by Allen 1983, 189–94, with co-regency ruled out despite Plut. *De frat. amor.* 489f.
[98] On the chronology of the transition between the reigns of Attalos II and Attalos III, see Petzl 1978, 275–76. Year 21 for Attalos II and year 1 for Attalos III may have coincided in 138/7.
[99] Diod. Sic. 34.3; Just. *Epit.* 36.4.1–5; references from Galen collected by Hansen 1971, 145.

all across Anatolia.¹⁰⁰ Nevertheless, a long decree of the city of Pergamon, which was issued to celebrate an undated military victory, granted Attalos III a string of unprecedented lifetime cultic honors.¹⁰¹ With a ruler cult of the sitting king now performed daily in civic space and those rituals enshrined in the sacred laws of Pergamon, Attalos may have hoped to insulate himself from looming challenges. His perception of a threat from an illegitimate son of Eumenes II named Aristonikos may have prompted him to make the Roman people his testamentary heir, copying the ploy of Ptolemy Euergetes in 155.¹⁰² With even a potential Eumenes III waiting in the wings, the Attalids were in a sense finally normal. They now began suffering from the typical infighting of Hellenistic courts. Attalos is said to have sent gifts to Publius Africanus in distant Numantia (Spain).¹⁰³ That Attalos leveraged his relationship with Rome to secure his position does not mean that the annexation of his kingdom was inevitable. The end of the Attalids was not what Mommsen called "merely a further recognition of the practical supremacy of Rome."¹⁰⁴ It took the Romans a decade to finish deliberating and then to fully convert the kingdom into a province. The contingent fact is that in 133, after a century and a half of carefully planned and executed power transitions, a Pergamene ruler less than 40 years of age died unexpectedly without a consensus successor. This set off what amounted to a brutal war of succession, the War of Aristonikos (133–129), which drew in not only the Romans, but all the other Anatolian kings, vying for supremacy over Pergamon's former partners, scavenging for pieces of the Attalid state. A grand coalition fragmented, but many structures held up and reappeared later as fundaments of the Roman province of Asia.

Road Map

Money and culture were both key to the success of the Attalids. These two themes structure the book. The first part of the book, Chapters 1–3, treat taxation and coinage. Chapter 1 presents the practice of earmarking as a prominent and distinctive feature of a fiscal system that forced cities across the empire to participate in their own taxation, but did so in a way that sustained civic identity. Through bilateral negotiations with taxpayers, the

---

¹⁰⁰ *RC* 67; Melloni 2018, 205.   ¹⁰¹ *OGIS* 332.   ¹⁰² *SEG* IX 7.   ¹⁰³ Cic. *Deiot.* 19.
¹⁰⁴ Mommsen 1881, 53 (English trans. Hansen 1971, 149). Cf. Gruen 1984, 594, with n. 94, compiling scholarly speculations on motives of Attalos III.

kings honed the tool of earmarking – tagging, case-by-case, specific revenues for specific public goods. For the cities, public life and with it collective identity came to depend on cooperation with the kings. This habit of earmarking entailed risks for the Attalids, as the king often ventured into the realm of private property. However, the opportunity it afforded to demonstrate a providential interest in removing risk from subjects' lives was priceless.

Zooming out from budgets to capture a snapshot of the full fiscal system, Chapter 2 presents the first comprehensive analysis of Pergamene taxes. It presents what comparative economic historians have termed a "fiscal constitution," the tax morphology of the Attalid state, that is, the scope, incidence, and modalities of taxation. It argues that the distribution of risk in the system was carefully managed, local customs were faithfully maintained, tax rates were negotiable, and tax collectors were local men who answered to their communities. By premodern standards, the system was supple and light on coercion. Certainly, the Attalids were hungry for revenue. In fact, their deep fiscal reach is refracted in a legend about the fate of Aristotle's library. The heritors of the books were Pergamene subjects, who buried them to hide their wealth from the kings' inspectors. Indeed, revenue seeking took the form of a deepening of the incidence of taxation, rather than the creation of new fiscal categories, which states under pressure, such as the Ancien Régime, are want to invent. Principally, the Attalids targeted mobility, the movement of goods and people, by investing in an infrastructure of surveillance.

Coinage, the subject of Chapter 3, allowed Pergamon to further reorder economic life by introducing a startlingly innovative currency. No one had ever seen anything like it. They erased the king's face, the convention for royal coinage since Philip and Alexander, and replaced it with ecumenical religious iconography and the badges of cities. A lightweight coin known as the "cistophorus" was issued at a value above its weight in silver. This helped close off the currency system, which in turn helped Attalid Anatolia cohere into a solid whole without cutting it off from exchange with the Aegean, the Black Sea, and the Levant. The participation of old Greek cities like Ionian Ephesus and new ones like Phrygian Toriaion guaranteed the experiment's success. The profits that accrued were shared all around, as the new money reproduced the local symbolic repertoire on a visual plain devised at the imperial level.

In the second part of the book, the ramifications of Attalid rule for the patterning of culture take center stage. Chapter 4 assesses the urbanization of inner Anatolia under the Attalids. The surprising conclusion is that the

Attalids achieved fiscal and ideological integration without the heavy-duty city building that we have come to associate with Hellenistic kings and Roman emperors. In the countryside, the Attalids drew towns and villages into their orbit without forcing people to move or change their way of life. They also capitalized on an upsurge in civic consciousness among Anatolian peasants. They stoked the fire of ethnogenesis for the tribesmen of Mysia, who came to see themselves as heroes of the Attalid army, immortalized in myth on the inner frieze of the Great Altar. For the rural and indigenous population, joining up with the Attalids did not mean being pushed into a city, relinquishing a territory or the prerogatives of a body politic. On the contrary, that these civic organisms held on to their own fiscal territories and maintained their own memberships is what enabled resource extraction and interaction with the state.

Chapter 5 offers a twist on the history of the gymnasium of the Greek polis, which aims to explain why and with what effect the Attalids pumped so much money into that cultural institution. Why did the gymnasium – of all the institutions of the polis – attract the interest of kings and courtiers? Answering this question requires rethinking the gymnasium. Against the standard view of a "city writ small," an incubator for citizens, I marshal the evidence for sharp distinctions between the gymnasium and everyone else. This kind of philanthropy allowed Pergamon to play the part of civic benefactor without getting dirty with city politics, while city elites gained their own line out to power. That the gymnasium eventually became the ancient city's new center for politics and self-representation was part of the legacy of the Attalid fiscal system.

Finally, having drawn our attention to this monarchy's ability to disappear into the background, I attempt in Chapter 6 to specify Pergamon's own cultural politics. An old-fashioned view describes the Attalids as inauthentic Greeks, deploying an aggressive Panhellenism aimed to erase a cultural deficit. Yet their particular brand of cultural universalism can be historicized and explored through figures from the Library of Pergamon. In the works of the periegetic writer Polemon of Ilion, we find an emphasis on topographical authenticity and the parity of Asia Minor with Old Greece. Another intellectual often associated with the Library, Demetrios of Skepsis, is seen to have strengthened the dynasty's claim to the mantle of Troy. Fundamentally, the Attalids claimed the kingship of Asia, and we need to take that claim seriously. I argue that the deficit they faced was one of prestige, rather than Hellenicity, and I try to uncover their true cultural background. The picked-over Classical sources record a trail of Asian money, the cash behind Horace's *Attalicae condiciones* – "Attalid offers," slightly foreign but just too good to turn down (*Carm.* 1.1).[105] Largely unrecognized, however, is the Greco-Anatolian background of the Attalids that was a crucial ingredient of their success. Within their kingdom, they posed as the successors of Mausolos, Midas, Gyges, Croesus, and indeed Priam, whose very territory they occupied. Their ability to do so authentically is glimpsed in the urban landscape of the capital and in the tumuli in which they were buried. Further, rather than simply coopt or Hellenize the great Anatolian sanctuaries in Galatia and Phrygia Epictetus, it appears that the creative and culturally hybrid Pergamene rulers transformed these cult sites into august, so-called temple estates, which extended their reach into the countryside. The imaginary Galatian barbarian, who blocked Pergamene supremacy in Asia, required expulsion, but the real-life one needed blandishment. The cultural impact of the Attalids both on Galatia and on rapidly urbanizing Pisidia was profound.

---

[105] On echoes of Midas and Gyges in Horace's ode, see West 1976.

1 | Eating with the Tax Collectors

Resolved by the Council and the People; Menemachos son of Archelaos moved: since Korragos son of Aristomachos, the Macedonian, when he was appointed general (*strategos*) of the regions (*topoi*) about the Hellespont, continuously applied all his enthusiasm and goodwill to the improvement of the People's condition and made himself serviceable both publicly and in private to all the citizens who had dealings with him, and when he took over the city he requested from the king the restoration of our laws, the ancestral constitution, the sacred precincts, the funds for cult expenses and the administration of the city, the oil for the young men (*neoi*) and everything else which originally belonged to the People, and as the citizens were destitute because of the war, he supplied at his own expense, cattle and other victims for the public sacrifices and after mentioning the matter to the king he secured the provision of corn for sowing and for food, and he enthusiastically assisted [the king] in preserving the private property of each of the citizens and in providing those who had none with some from the royal treasury, and as exemption (*ateleia*) from all taxes (*prosodoi*) had been granted by the king for three years, he secured a further exemption for two years, wishing to restore the citizens to a state of prosperity and increase, acting in conformity with the king's policy; so that the people may be seen to be rendering adequate thanks to its benefactors, be it resolved by the People [to praise] Korragos the general and [to crown him] with a gold [crown...].[1]

---

[1] **D1** = *I.Prusa* 1001. Trans. Austin 2006, no. 235. ἔδοξεν τῆι βουλῆι καὶ τῶι δήμωι· Μενέμαχος Ἀρχελάου εἶπεν· ἐπεὶ Κόρραγος Ἀριστομάχου Μακεδών, τεταγμένος στρατηγὸς τῶν καθ' Ἑλλήσποντον τόπων, διατελεῖ τὴμ πᾶσαν σπουδὴν καὶ εὔνοιαν προσφερόμενος εἰς τὸ συναύξεσθαι τὸν δῆμον, καὶ κοινῇ καὶ ἰδίᾳ τοῖς ἐντυγχάνουσιν τῶν πολιτῶν εὔχρηστον αὐτὸ[ν] παρασκευάζει, ὑπό τε τὴν παράληψιν τῆς πόλεως ἠξίωσεν τὸν βασιλέα ἀποδοθῆναι τούς τε ν[ό]μους καὶ τὴν πάτριον πολιτείαν καὶ τὰ ἱερὰ τεμένη καὶ τὸ εἰς τὰ ἱερὰ καὶ πόλεως διοίκησιν ἀργύριον καὶ τὸ τοῖς νέοις ἔλαιον καὶ τὰ ἄλλα ἅπερ ἐξ ἀρχῆς ὑπῆ[ρ]χεν τῶι δήμωι, ἐνδεῶς τε ἀπαλλασσόντων τῶν πολιτῶν διὰ τὸν πόλεμον παρ[ά] τε αὐτοῦ ἐχαρίσατο εἰς τὰς δημοτελεῖς θυσίας βοῦς καὶ ἱερεῖα, καὶ τῷ βασιλε[ῖ] μνησθεὶς ἐξεπορίσατο σῖτον εἰς σπέρμ[α] καὶ διατροφήν, καὶ τὰς ἰδίας ἑκάστῳ τῶν πολιτῶν κτήσεις συνέσπευσεν διαμεῖ[ναι] τοῖς τε μὴ ἔχουσιν δοθῆναι ἐκ τοῦ βασιλικοῦ, καὶ ἀτελείας ἐπικεχωρημένης πασῶν τῶν προσόδων ὑπὸ τοῦ βασιλέως ἐτῶν τριῶν ἔσπευσεν καὶ ἄλλα δύο ἔτη ἐπιδοθῆναι, βουλόμενος εἰς εὐδαιμονίαν καὶ ἐπίδοσιν καταστῆσαι τοὺς πολίτας, ἀκόλουθα πράσσων

The decree for Korragos the Macedonian, the Attalid governor of Pergamon's new Hellespontine province, recalls catastrophic conditions in an anonymous city, ca. 188 BCE. It describes a postwar landscape of both material want and profound social disorder. Still suffering from the effects of the War of Antiochos, the city could not so much as feed itself, let alone plant crops. Naturally, public sacrifices, rituals, and politics – the institutions that had preserved collective identity over generations – had all gone into abeyance. The very basis of ancient social structure, the distribution of landed property, felt insecure. It was as if everything had broken down all at once. This was the breach into which the Attalids and their administrators stepped after the Treaty of Apameia. In cities such as this, the first task of postwar governance was simply to reconstitute the community. In the case of Korragos on the Hellespont, a royal official personally provided the animals for the initial public sacrifices and feasting. He was also the catalyst for the king's own benefactions, prevailing upon Eumenes II to distribute seed and, in the meanwhile, sustenance. Ultimately, the Attalids even paid to preserve the city's social order, assuring those with property of their rights and granting land to the landless.[2] For these kings, the initial steps of assembling an empire required getting their hands dirty. Building up this city entailed deep familiarity with its social fabric and institutions.

Remarkably, the citizens of this devastated city, who were the recipients of so much strings-attached aid, seem to have negotiated rather ably. Weakened as they were by the recent war, they still managed to drive a hard bargain with Eumenes. In the near term, what had been envisioned as a three-year tax holiday was extended for two more years. In the long term, Eumenes acceded to their request for a return to certain privileged conditions of the past. In the felicitous shorthand of civic memory, those privileges are described as "everything else which originally belonged to the People" (ἅπερ ἐξ ἀρχῆς ὑπῆ[ρ]|χεν τῷ δήμῳ)."[3] That term "originally" was chronographically ambiguous by design. Demands for privileges

---

τ[ῇ] τοῦ βασιλέως προαιρέσει· ἵνα δὲ καὶ ὁ δῆμος φα[ί]νητα<ι> ἀποδιδοὺς χάριτας ἀξίας τοῖς αὐτὸν εὐεργετοῦσιν, δεδόχθαι τῶι δήμῳ· [ἐπαινέσαι τε] Κόρραγον τὸν στρατηγὸν κα[ὶ στεφανῶσαι αὐτὸν] χρυσῶι στεφ[άνῳ — — — — —

[2] The unnamed city is commonly identified as Apollonia-on-the-Rhyndakos. On its relationship with the Attalids, see Aybek and Dreyer 2016, 12–14. For the identification of Korragos with Livy's Corragus Macedo (38.13.3, cf. 42.67.4), see, *I.Prusa* 1001 ad loc.

[3] D1, lines 12–13.

backdated to the hoary past were more likely to succeed.⁴ Equally vague and malleable was the notion of an "ancestral constitution (*patrios politeia*)," which Eumenes also promptly returned to them without modification. Yet we know that one trumpeted privilege was almost certainly of very recent vintage: "[royal] funds for cult expenses and the administration of the city" (τὸ εἰς τὰ ἱερὰ καὶ πόλεως διοίκησιν ἀργύριον)."⁵

This practice of earmarking, of injecting royal money directly into the organs of civic finance, has long been considered, if not an exclusively Pergamene habit, a trademark of the Attalids.⁶ By nature, the injection was not a one-time gift, but like the "oil for the *neoi*" mentioned in the same breath, a routine, regularized, usually annual disbursement of money.⁷ Earmarks also allowed donors to give targeted gifts, which in this case were subsidies that sustained a local culture under threat of extinction. While they did not invent the practice, the Attalids were the most prolific issuers of what is usefully labeled the "earmark": the designation of specific future revenues for specific public goods.⁸ These are promised gifts; the money is anticipated. These are also gifts with a purpose. Pergamon, for example, dominates our records for foundations, the endowments, the pots (sometimes literally) of money, which priests and other magistrates of Greek cities and sanctuaries managed in order to fund public life. As **Graph 1.1** shows, no other dynasty matched the Attalids for giving on this score.⁹

---

⁴ Holleaux (1924, 29) already recognized the rhetoric. On similar *per sempre* arguments, see Boffo 2013, 230. Cf. in *CID* 4 104, line 7, the tendentious claim of the city of Delphi to rights "comparable to what they have always had (καθὼς πάτριον αὐτοῖς ἐξ ἀρχῆς [ἦν])," with commentary of Lefèvre, ad loc. Further on ἐξ ἀρχῆς, see Chaniotis 2004, 192–93, esp. n. 35; Ager 1996, nos. 37, 74, 126, and 129A.

⁵ D1, line 11.

⁶ Holleaux 1924, 25. Holleaux's axiom that the practice always signifies an Attalid presence is no longer valid. It is twice attested under Antiochos III: *SEG* XXXIX 1285, from Sardis (213 BCE), and *SEG* XXXVII 849, from Herakleia-under-Latmos (196–193). Cf. also in this regard a case from Ptolemaic Halikarnassos, *P.Cair.Zen.* 59036. Three thousand drachmas in the royal bank, owed to Alexandria for the tax of the *stephanos* (crown), are applied provisionally to the city's trierarchy.

⁷ Holleaux 1924, 25: "subvention réguliere."

⁸ See Black, Hashimzade, and Myles 2012, s.v. "earmarking": "A linkage between a particular tax and a particular type of state expenditure. In the UK, for example, television license revenue goes to support the British Broadcasting Corporation."

⁹ Source for data: Bringmann et al. 1995. For high counts of the Attalids, see already Laum 1964, 14. The strength of the epigraphical habit in Asia Minor may have favored documentation of Attalid gifts, but not enough to invalidate the global pattern. The Seleukids had held the same inscription-rich territory for over a century, while the Ptolemies and the Antigonids both turn up enough in civic epigraphy to make the absence of their earmarks meaningful.

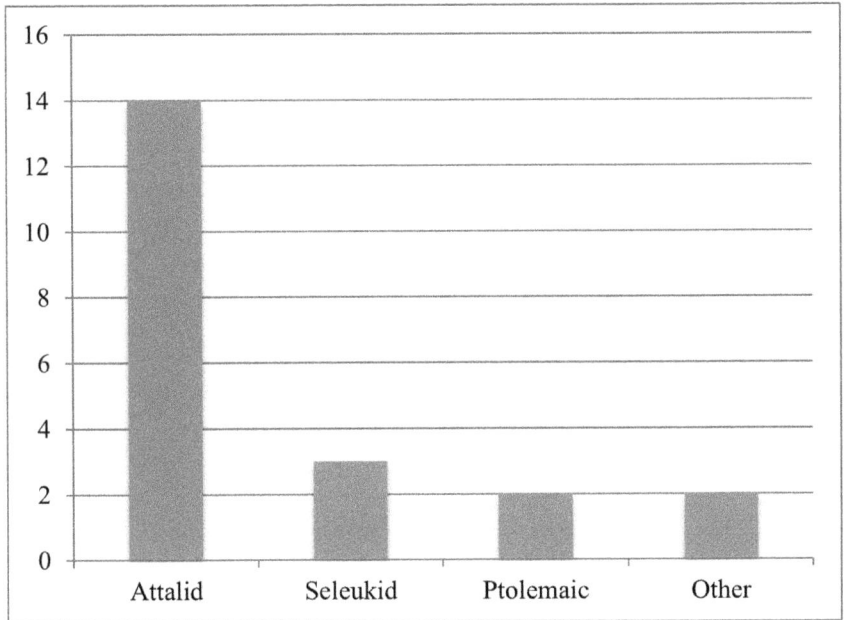

Graph 1.1 Philanthropic foundations of the Hellenistic world (data from Bringmann et al. 1995).

Earmarks reflect the Attalids' exceptional facility with moving money. Around Anatolia and throughout the Aegean, they shifted cash between accounts and polities more often than any of their peers (**Graph 1.2**), and they moved grain, the most money-like commodity of their day and the most easily converted into cash, at a rate rivaling the Ptolemies with their Nilotic cornucopia (**Graph 1.3**). Fascinatingly, while Attalid gifts of money are so numerous, they tended to be very small. Numbers are scarce, but Attalid donations make up a mere 9% of the total (recorded) amount of money comprised by the gifts of Hellenistic kings. Moreover, while the median gift size for a king was 45 talents, the Attalids' was just 10. Many Attalid subventions were even smaller. Perhaps, as has been suspected, Polybius was aiming a barb their way when he complained of miserly kings who gave four or five talents and expected the highest honors in return. By the standards of Hellenistic royalty, these were small gifts, but by contemporary standards of public finance, these were sophisticated gifts.[10]

---

[10] Source for data: Bringmann et al. 1995. For the notion of Attalid miserliness in Polybius' account of the reaction to the Rhodian earthquake, see Holleaux 1923. Holleaux suggests that Polybius has in mind the gifts of Eumenes II and Attalos to Delphi (*Syll.*³ 671 and 672).

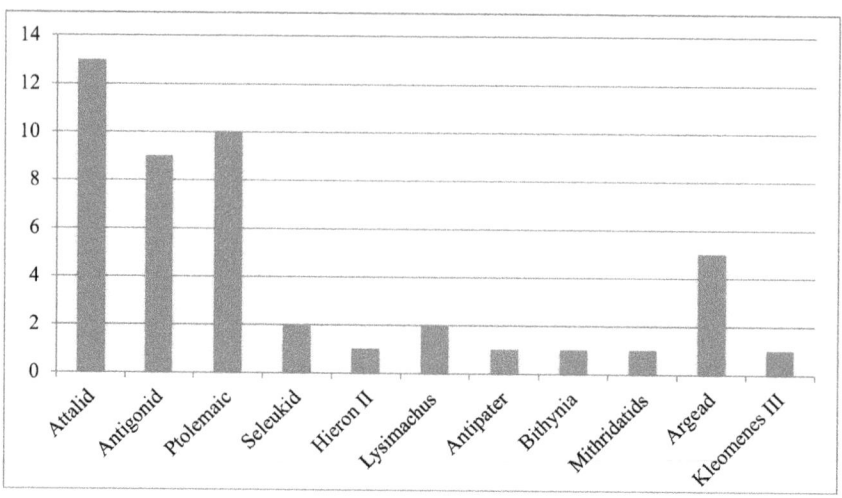

Graph 1.2 Royal gifts of money (data from Bringmann et al. 1995).

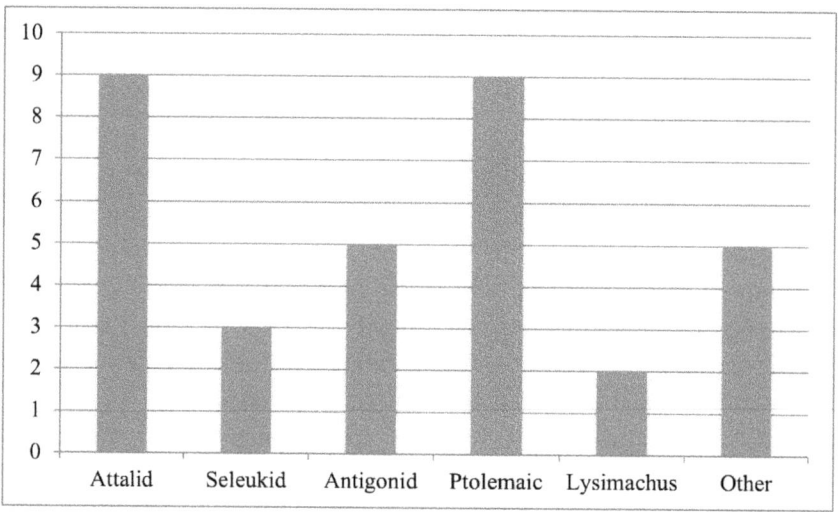

Graph 1.3 Royal gifts of grain (data from Bringmann et al. 1995).

The so-called Korragos Decree from modern Bursa, Turkey, highlights the modesty, frequency, and indeed the rationality of an Attalid earmark. This was not a one-off transaction. Nor was it a windfall bonus of mysterious origins. Admittedly, the Korragos Decree is silent about the source of the money promised in perpetuity. However, those texts which do speak to the issue invariably specify a local source of revenue. In other words, the money is not assumed to issue forth from a distant, centralized treasury. Either some portion of those royal taxes collected locally is rerouted into the city's coffers or another source of revenue is provided. This could be a piece of property or the taxes of an entire village. According to Greek fiscal categories, it did not make much difference. Rather, to a Greek, these revenues were all *prosodoi* of one kind or another, the taxes and endowment income of the modern fiscal lexicon.[11] We may not always hear about the source of the earmark, or one text may refer to the public good while another designates the revenue source, but we can be sure that royal bureaucrats and Attalid subjects both knew the details well. This is because they were the ones who had hammered them out. Earmarking was a social process.

By the time that Korragos and the Attalids appeared on the Hellespont, ancient political communities had been earmarking money for a very long time. The practice of reserving future revenues for specific public goods such as security had been a feature of the Classical polis.[12] What was new and distinctive about the Attalids was the extent to which they employed earmarking as a tool of empire. How to explain this? A review of the evidence will not support an explanation that relies exclusively on either top-down, royal, or local, civic initiative. Both parties clearly reaped benefits from these arrangements. So were the Attalids simply sweetening the bitter pill of imperialism?[13] While earmarking contributed to the ideological accommodation of Attalid subjects, it also circumscribed the king's freedom of action and exposed the limits of his power. This chapter explores the dynamics of earmarking as a social process, arguing that the static earmarking arrangements of our sources were negotiated into existence. The dynamics of earmarking will be seen to include frequent royal forays into the sphere of private property, the devolution of agency, and an interleaving of civic and royal institutions that implies deep familiarity. Finally, a set of culturally specific meanings emerges for earmarking, which rendered it a privileged solution to the problems of risk and governance in the expanded Attalid kingdom.

---

[11] On *prosodoi*, see Gauthier 1976, 7–19.
[12] See, e.g., the Athenian Grain-Tax Law of 374/3, which earmarks revenue for the *stratiotika* fund (Stroud 1998, lines 53–55). Stroud (1998, 78) writes: "Thus the 8 1/3% tax on the grain from the islands and the *pentekoste* eventually produced in Athens revenue that was earmarked in advance for this specific purpose."
[13] Just so, Rostovtzeff 1930, 605–6; Jones 1971, 55.

Earmarking as a Social Process

Before delving into the dynamics and meanings of earmarking in the Attalid kingdom, it is worth considering how insights from economic sociology can help us reanimate a practice that has become fossilized in our inscriptions. Earmarking is one way of relating to money by means of differentiating it, and if we step back from any particular artifact, from ingots to coins, cowry shells to bricks of tea, paper to plastic, we can see that money has always taken many different forms. Theoretically, as an economic instrument, money is homogeneous. And so the tautology goes, a dollar is a dollar; any dollar *works* like any other. The conventional, fourfold definition of money as a means of exchange, a means of payment, a store of value, and a unit of account takes money to be perfectly fungible.[14] Historically, the homogeneity of money is what has given it economic significance. Money lowers transaction costs because different goods and services are priced according to a standard unit. As Aristotle remarked in his imagined history of coinage, the convenience of money for partners to an exchange is irresistible (*Pol.* 1.3.1257a31–42). Because in such a world money is perfectly fungible, the existence of money by itself promotes an increase in the volume of exchanges, as all money finds acceptance in all transactions. However, such a world does not exist; not today, nor in Antiquity.[15]

Certainly, money is an economic instrument of enormous significance. Exchange looks very different without money. Yet as social scientists have demonstrated, human beings steadfastly refuse to treat all money as equal. In a monetary regime that contains multiple forms of money, different monies may be appropriate for different transactions, sometimes exclusively so. One pays a dowry in, say, bronze ingots, but the services of a seer can only be had for token money – seashells, for example, even if these must be bought with bronze. These are the "special-purpose monies" of the work of Karl Polanyi.[16] Moreover, money is still differentiated and restricted in its fungibility in a monetary regime in which a single form of money predominates or even achieves monopoly status.[17] We

---

[14] Carruthers 2005, 356 (paraphrasing a textbook definition of Joseph Stiglitz); Von Reden 2010, 1–6.
[15] Earlier scholarship focused on the ways in which premodern or primitive societies mark money, supposedly in contradistinction to modern societies. For the modern world, see Zelizer 1997.
[16] Polanyi 1957, 246–66.
[17] Monopoly status was rare if not inconceivable in ancient monetary systems. Indeed, as Chapter 3 emphasizes, contrary to what is often claimed, the Attalids did not achieve it with the

differentiate money in a great number of ways. To take just two examples, we make distinctions between "clean" and "dirty" money, or between "windfall" money and regular income. The crucial factor here that dictates the ways in which the money can be employed is the *source* of the money. A purely utilitarian or functionalist account of money misses the link between the variable meaning of money and its uses. Money is both an economic and a symbolic instrument.[18] When the two modalities collide, a friction is produced that we can observe.

Research in the social sciences has heightened our awareness of the diverse properties and possibilities of money. Among economic sociologists, Viviana Zelizer has led the charge in exposing the limits of money's fungibility and highlighting the socially and culturally constructed nature of its meaning.[19] She places special emphasis on the practice of earmarking money, both according to its source and according to its use.[20] Earmarking is a prime example of the way in which notionally homogeneous money becomes differentiated. Fundamentally, earmarking is the differentiation of money, whether by source, by use, or as in the Attalid practice, by both: money from a particular source is designated for a particular use. Anthropologist Mary Douglas studied how so-called primitive societies mark off monies into separate spheres of sacred and profane, fungible and nonfungible, as well as the way money moves in and out of those categories.[21] Zelizer's contribution was to show that modern economic life is also full of earmarking, and not as the result of the survival of a primitive, precapitalist practice. In fact, she argues, in American history we see a proliferation of earmarking and more broadly of the social differentiation of money precisely when the federal government imposes with its full weight a single, uniform, and generalized form of money, a process that began with the National Banking Act of 1863. In Zelizer's late nineteenth- and early twentieth-century households, the money is not kept under the mattress in one lump sum. It is divided between a set of tin cans: one for mortgage payments, another for the children's education, and another for

---

introduction of the cistophoric system. Even in the United States, it did not obtain for much of the nineteenth century.

[18] Carruthers 2005, 358.

[19] Zelizer 1989 and 1997. For a review of scholarship on the social meaning of money and its relevance for ancient economic history, see Boldizzoni 2011, 160–61.

[20] Zelizer 1997, 21–25.

[21] Douglas 1967. Indeed, tracking the movement of funds was a particular preoccupation of public finance in the Greek polis. See Fröhlich 2004a, 439; and on sacred finance in particular, see Von Reden 2010, 156–85.

emergencies. "Pin money" is set aside for the wife's consumption. Earmarking, however, is by no means the exclusive strategy of nonstate actors. The modern state itself engages in earmarking in its budgets, routing cigarette taxes into college scholarships and gas taxes into roads. The state might even encourage households to adopt the practice of budgetary earmarking in an ideological struggle over the shape of home economics.[22]

Earmarking and Greek Epigraphy

An earmark is often the end result of a long process of negotiation. Even then, the process can continue as earmarks are met with counter-earmarks. Relations of domination and subordination are articulated and rearticulated. "The earmarking of money is thus a social process: money is attached to a variety of social relations rather than to individuals."[23] A large number of Greek epigraphic documents bear witness to this very process. To choose from countless examples, we may consider a debate that took place in the context of an Athenian cultic association of the third century.[24] In a decree, the association published new rules for the source and use of its patron goddess' money: rents from sacred land were thenceforth earmarked exclusively for sacrifices. In the background, we can glimpse a dispute, which had concerned the differentiation of money. The question had been, "Was income from sacred land 'clean' or 'dirty'?" It had also been unclear whether members (*orgeones*) were entitled to borrow money from the goddess for worldly ends.[25] Methodologically, we must be aware that such an inscription records the outcome of the dispute, while the process by which it was resolved tends to be obscured. Another difficulty is discovering a social process when earmarking appears in the context of imperial domination. The *orgeones* of an Athenian cultic association met on egalitarian terms. Was earmarking any less of a process in Hellenistic Asia Minor, with its vast disparities of power between kings and cities? The case of Antigonos and the cities of Teos and Lebedos suggests it was not. The ill-fated attempt of the Macedonian to execute the synoicism of Teos and Lebedos involved a negotiation over the constitution of a public grain fund.

---

[22] Walker and Carnegie 2007 (on Australia of 1850–1920).   [23] Zelizer 1997, 25.
[24] On this type of association and its administration, see Aneziri 2012, 72–73.
[25] *IG* II² 1289. See *SEG* LII 132 (resuming Sosin 2002) for the conclusion that the *orgeones* did not prohibit the renting of the land as such, but only a certain kind of leasehold. For a new edition of the complete text and similar conclusions, see Papazarkadas 2004–9, 91–95.

Lebedos had earlier requested of Antigonos that 1,400 gold staters "be set aside from the revenues (ἐξαιρεῖσθαι ἀπὸ τῶν προσόδων)" for a complicated grain scheme. In other words, certain revenues were to be reserved for the provision of the new city's grain supply. Antigonos did not act on the initial request of Lebedos, but when Teos later petitioned for an even larger amount, he rejected the idea. Any exigent import of grain, Antigonos argued, ought to come from his own "tribute-bearing (*phorologoumenê*)" land, effectively claiming a royal monopoly. Yet in the end, the cities prevailed over the king: Antigonos agreed to earmark the 1,400 gold staters, per the original request of Lebedos.[26]

The Dynamics of Earmarking in the Attalid Kingdom

Our sources are fragmentary, but together they capture many different stages of the earmarking process. The Korragos Decree, which shows Eumenes II resuscitating one community after the War of Antiochos, demonstrates the power of earmarks to bind subjects and rulers together. Though rich with information, the document is also lacunose. It only alludes to the process of negotiation lurking behind Eumenes' decision to extend the city's tax holiday. The Korragos Decree tells us little about the institutional arrangements put in place. We only hear that royal funds are earmarked for the religious life of the city and for its administration. The tap is turned on, the money set to flow in regularly, but how regularly? Annually or in installments? According to which calendar, the city's or the king's? Eumenes also promises a provision of oil for the *neoi* (young men of the gymnasium), presumably disbursed in like manner, but the language of the inscription is even cloudier on this point.[27] So much is left out or left ambiguous. Should we imagine two separate funds, one for sacrifices and another for "the administration of the city" (*dioikesis*) – or is it a joint fund?[28] How much money will be earmarked for each purpose? And finally, where exactly will the money come from?

---

[26] *RC* 3, lines 72–94, esp. 73. For interpretation, see Gabrielsen 2011, 238–45. Gabrielsen (2011, 241) argues that the 1,400 gold staters were "excluded from the total revenue of the city," i.e., from what Antigonos could tax. On the agency of these cities, see further Boehm 2018, 20–21, 102.

[27] τὸ τοῖς νέοις ἔλαιον (line 12). The finances of the civic gymnasium are treated in Chapter 5.

[28] Thomas Corsten (*I.Prusa* 1001) understands a single fund ("Kasse") linked to two different public goods, sacred and profane. Cf. the decree of Colophon for Polemaios, *SEG* XXXIX 1243 Column V lines 51–53, in which it is equally difficult to distinguish grammatically a joint

Private Property and Sale

In 2007, an extraordinarily rich document for the Attalid earmarking process was published, a double-sided inscription from the modern village of Taşkuyucak, west of Lydian Daldis (**D2**). The inscription was discovered in the Keçi Dağ mountain range, north of Lake Koloe/Gygaia, near a pass that connects the plain of Sardis to the road to Thyateira and the upper Kaikos Valley. After 188, this was a vital link between the old Attalid core and what had been the primary Seleukid administrative center in cis-Tauric Asia Minor. The site of the town (*katoikia*) and fortress of Apollonioucharax must have been nearby since the inscription shows the town's ambassadors appealing to Eumenes II in the wake of the destructive conflict with the Galatians (168–166). Soldiers as well as civilians lived in this town. The soldiers, largely Mysian, were not necessarily professional, as evidenced by a partial conscription alluded to in the text. This inscription shares many similarities with the Korragos Decree, from its script to its postwar setting.[29] Once again, Eumenes II aimed to ameliorate the devastation of war with a variety of fiscal privileges and outright gifts. Side B appears to be a petition of Apollonioucharax. Side A appears to be the response of Eumenes II to the requests. The text reads in Peter Thonemann's translation and edition (my modifications in underlined italics):[30]

Side B:

> ... of these ... registered ... (we request that) these privileges should persist, and (we request that you) annul the [punishments?] of those reported as having deserted from the army in Year 32 (166/5 BCE), and that they should have the same (privileges) as the others. (We request

---

fund from a single-purpose one: ἀπὸ τῆς φυλακῆς καὶ τῆς διοικήσεως. For P. J. Rhodes (2007, 356) the term *dioikesis* does not refer to a "fund" at all, if by fund we mean treasury (*contra* Schuler 2005). It is the remainder of a subvention after earmarked funds have been taken out.

[29] Similarity of script: Herrmann and Malay 2007, 53.

[30] The ordering of B before A was first suggested by Wörrle 2009, 427 n. 76; developed by Thonemann 2011a. This solves certain major problems of interpretation, but it opens up others. In general, the corporate identity of Apollonioucharax is curiously absent from the entire text. One place to look for it might be in the expression ἐπεὶ δημόται ἐσμέν, which Thonemann translates unsatisfactorily as "because we are poor" (Side B lines 10–11). Also left somewhat incomplete is his interpretation of the final lines of Side B, which clearly do not represent the voice of Apollonioucharax. He makes no mention of the stray letters below the text on Side B, engraved and then deleted, which Herrmann and Malay read tentatively as [α]ὐτὸς ἔκοψα Ἱέρων ("Hieron engraved it himself"). Finally, on this interpretation Apollonioucharax seems to reprimand Eumenes for failing to return certain dependent villages to the *katoikia*. The tone of the reproach is striking and deserves further consideration.

that) there should be inviolability for Zeus Stratios, and instead of the seven stadia previously granted, it should extend to ten stadia. In order that the priest Bacchios might make a golden wreath, (we request that) our registered debts, both in silver and grain, should be remitted until the third year, unless anyone has already exacted and sequestered them. Concerning the houses in the suburb (of Apollonioucharax) which were burned and pulled down, (we request that you) take care that, because we are *co-citizens*, some grant be given for their reconstruction. *(We request that) the village of Sibloe, which was earlier ours – about which it is written that "it will be restored to us when we have settled up a price with Meleager, who bought the village, (vacat), 448 drachmas and 1.5 obols" – that it should now be conveyed to us without a price, so that the revenues of the village shall provide for the sacrifices for Zeus Stratios and for those on your behalf. (We also request that) the village should remain for us sacred and tax-free, and that the money for it should be given to Meleager from the royal treasury.* (We request that) villages should be granted to meet the shortfall of *kleroi* and associated buildings. Since those (villages) which were previously taken from us have not been restored in the way in which you promised, (we request that you) mark out for this purpose Thileudos and Plazeira as hunters' settlements, and move the inhabitants of these villages to whatever settlements Lykinos the land-distributor may decide. (Royal official) – For we have ordered him to look into the matter and mark them out.[31]

Side A:

... Kournoubeudos ... [made] demonstrations [sc. of their loyalty] in the war; [I was intending] to move the Mysians living in this place to Kastollos, since fresh land certainly exists there in an uncultivated

---

[31] [- - 10 - -]PE[- - 12 - - το]ύτων δὲ τῶν ΑΝ[- - 12 - -][.]δριαι ἐπιγέγραπ[ται . . 3-4 . . ὑ]πάρχειν τὰ φιλάνθρωπ[α - - 8 - -] νας τῶν συναναφερομένων λιποστρατῆσαι ἐν τῶ β′ καὶ λ′ ἔτει περιελεῖν, ὑπάρχειν δὲ ταῦτα τοῖς ἄλλοις· τὴν ἀσυλίαν τοῦ Διὸς τοῦ Στρατίου ὑπάρχειν, ἀντὶ τῶν προσυνκεχωρημένων σταδίων ἑπτὰ ἔσται ἐπὶ στάδια δέκα· καὶ ἵνα Βάκχιος ὁ ἱερεὺς ποῇ στέφανον χρυσοῦν, τὰ ἀναφερόμενα ὀφειλήματα τὰ ἐν ἡμῖν ἀργυρικὰ ἢ σιτικὰ ἕως τοῦ τρίτου ἔτους ἀπολῦσαι, εἰ μή τινες πράξαντές τινα αὐτοὶ κατεισχήκασι· περὶ τῶν ἐνπεπυρισμένων καὶ καθειλκυσμένων οἰκίων ἐν τῶι προαστίῳ προνοηθῆναι, ἵν', ἐπεὶ δημόται ἐσμέν, μεταδοθῆ τι εἰς τὴν κατασκευὴν αὐτῶν· Σιβλοην κώμην τὴν πρότερον οὖσαν ἡμετέραν, περὶ ἧς γέγραπται, ἵνα διορθωσαμένων ἡμῶν τὴν τιμὴν Μελεάγρῳ τῷ ἠγορακότι αὐτὴν δραχμῶν vac. ΥΜΗ – C ἀποδοθῇ, κομίσασθαι νῦν ἄνευ τιμῆς, ὅπως ὑπάρχωσιν αἱ ἐξ αὐτῆς πρόσοδοι εἴς τε τὰς τοῦ Διὸς τοῦ Στρατίου καὶ τὰς ὑπὲρ ὑμῶν συντελουμένας θυσίας καὶ διαμένῃ ἡμῖν ἱερὰ καὶ ἀτελής· τὸ δὲ ἀργύριον δοθῆναι ὑπὲρ αὐτῆς ἐκ τοῦ βασιλικοῦ τῶι Μελεάγρωι· εἰς τὰ ἐλλείποντα τοῖς κλήροις καὶ προσδομ(ήμ)ασιν δοθῆναι κώμας· ἐπ(ε)ὶ αἱ πρότερον ἀφαιρεθεῖσαι ἡμῶν οὐκ ἀποκατεστάθησαν ὃν τρόπον συνεκεχωρήκεις, παραδεῖξαι Θίλευδον καὶ Πλάζειρα κατοικίας κυνηγῶν, τοὺς δ' ἐν τούτοις μετάγειν εἰς ἃς ἂν κρίνῃ κατοικίας Λυκῖνος ὁ γεωδότης. – συντετάχαμεν γὰρ τούτῳ ἐπιβλέψαντι παραδεῖξαι.

condition. But [ambassadors] from Apollonioucharax came to meet me, and said that they were grateful for the . . . of their territory; they also said that, since the Mysian settlers at Kournoubeudos [were . . .] and had become well-acquainted/friendly with them, they wished to . . ., in whatever way they might decide among themselves. And so, in recognition of their good sense and moderation, I have granted this just as they have requested. I have also ordered Lykinos the land-distributor to [take thought] whence we might be able to add a further stretch of land to their territory. Since they deserve great consideration, having been destroyed last year by the enemy, I grant another five years' exemption from customs-dues in addition to the five years granted previously, just as I have done for the Mysians at Kadooi. Registration for compulsory military service will fall only on one man in three, for I know that if some emergency occurs, they will provide more soldiers of their own accord because of their eagerness and goodwill. They shall all be exempted from the collection of the tithe on produce for the current year, and those on whom the *eisphora*-taxes are levied are also exempted for the current year. Since they are making a start on the rebuilding of the settlement, I have also agreed to provide masons for them.[32]

Here, a document speaks to the crucial issue of the source of an earmark. The earmark's source was property purchased by the king. By purchase and redemption of private property from third parties, the Attalids funded the public goods that earned them loyalty at home and accolades abroad. It bears emphasizing that this was an unusual pattern of kingly behavior, but one detectable in the dynasty already with Philetairos, who acquired real estate in Thespiai in the 270s. Lands which the dynast purchased and designated as sacred fed the cult of the Muses, provided for the festival of

---

[32] [- - - ca.15 - - -]ΤΙ[- - - ca.8 - - - ἀπο]δείξεις ἐν [τῷ πο]λέμῳ Κουρνουβευδος· τοὺς δ' ἐν τούτῳ τῷ τόπῳ κατοικοῦντας Μυσοὺς [ἐπενόου]ν εἰς Καστωλλὸμ μετάγειν, ἐπεὶ και[νὴ γῆ (?) παν]τελῶς [ὑ]πάρχει ἐκεῖ περισσή· ἐντυχόντων δ' ἐ[μοὶ e.g. τῶν ἀπὸ] τοῦ Ἀπ[ολ]λωνιουχάρακος καὶ φασ[κόντων ἐπὶ (?) - ca.4 -]δ[- ca.4 -] τῆς χ[ώ]ρας εὐχαριστεῖν, ἐπεὶ δὲ ο[ἱ κατοικ]οῦντες ἐν τῶι Κ[ουρ]νουβευδει Μυσοὶ κατ[- - - ca.9 - - -]καὶ γεγόνασιν α[ὐ]τοῖς συνήθεις, βούλεσθ[αι - - - ca.10 - - -]αι ὅπως ἄ[ν] δι' ἑαυτοὺς δοκῶσιν· ἐγὼ? καὶ [- - - ca.12 - - -]ν ἀπ[ο]δεξάμενος τὴν εὐγνωμοσύ[νην καὶ με[τρι]ότ[η]τα α[ὐ]τῶν, τοῦτο μὲν συνεχώρησα ὡς ἠξίουσαν, Λυκίνωι δ[ὲ] τῶι γεωδότῃ συνετάξαμεν [φροντί]ζειν ὅθεν δ[υ]ναίμεθα χώραμ προσορίσαι αὐτοῖς· ἐπεὶ δὲ κατεφθ[ι]μένοι πέρυσι ὑπὸ τῶμ πολεμίωμ πολλῆς προμη[θεί]ας ἄξιοί εἰσιν, συγχωρῶ πρὸς οἷς ἐπεχωρήσαμεν πένθ' ἔτεσιν ἀτελείαν αὐτοῖς καὶ ἄλλων πέντε, καθὰ καὶ τοῖς ἐγ Καδοοις Μυσοῖς συν[ε]χωρήσαμεγ, καὶ ἀπὸ τριῶν τὴν καταγραφὴν γ[ί]γνεσθαι· ὅταν γὰρ ἀναγκαιοτέρα χρεία γίνητα[ι], αὐτοὶ διὰ τὴμ προθυμίαν καὶ εὔνοιαν οἶδ' ὅτι δώσ[ου]σιν πλείονας σ(τ)ρατιώτας· καὶ τῆς ἐφ' ἔτους δεκ[α]τείας παρεθήτωσαμ πάντες, ὁμοίως δὲ καὶ οἷς τὰ εἴσφορα ἐπιγέγραπται· ἐπεὶ περὶ τὴν τοῦ χωρίου οἰκοδομίαν γίνονται, καὶ ἡμεῖς λατύπου[ς] ὡμολογήκαμεν αὐτοῖς χορηγήσειν. vac. Γ vac.

the Philetaireia, and maintained the supply of oil for a local gymnasium.[33] Another episode involves the visit of Attalos I to Sikyon in 198. The city had lost control of land sacred to Apollo, evidently being held as private property. Attalos purchased it – for a steep price, notes Polybius – and restored to the Sikyonians their sacred lands.[34] That the Attalids built their redistributive system by routinely transacting with private partners is now further underscored by the inscription from Taşkuyucak.

In postwar Apollonioucharax, the breakdown of order was again complete. With some soldiers homeless and others deserting, both social stability and state control were in doubt. Again, Eumenes' goal was to reconstitute a community, this one rural and in certain ways non-Greek. For his generosity, the king demanded an easy conscription in yet tougher times. Eumenes provided the settlers with land allotments, building materials, and masons. He instructed his official to find and survey the land, transfer out other populations, distribute construction materials, and bring in know-how. He also provided support for the ancient Anatolian cult of Zeus Stratios ("the army leader"), first, by expanding an unparalleled grant of territorial immunity (*asylia*) to a sanctuary outside the control of a Greek polis.[35] Second, he employed a pair of earmarks: taxes in arrears, both cash and kind, were remitted for a period of three years so that the priest Bacchios might furnish a golden wreath.[36] To fund the worship of Zeus and sacrifices on his own behalf, the king earmarked revenues that he redeemed from the nearby village of Sibloe, perhaps the place once attached to an indigenous sanctuary known from a fourth-century Aramaic inscription from Kenger (Side B lines 11–19).[37]

Financially, Apollonioucharax was in over its head. Apparently, the town had sold the usufruct of the village of Sibloe to an individual named Meleager for cash. The town retained the right of redemption, but could not come up with the money. The ambassadors seem to have asked the king to unwind this old transaction. It is helpful to think of the new transaction of Eumenes with Meleager as the unwinding of the old one because it allows us to make sense of the odd number on the stone: 448 drachmas and 1.5 obols. Thonemann finds the price too low for an

---

[33] *I.Thespiai* 58–61.
[34] Polyb. 18.16.1–2. The sale/redemption seems to be the resolution of the transaction known in Greek as *prasis epi lusei*. To raise money for the First Macedonian War, the Sikyonians appear to have mortgaged property to outsiders, before defaulting. See Walbank 1957–79, ad loc.
[35] Zeus "the army leader": Henrichs, *New Pauly* sv. "Zeus." On the Anatolian origin of the cult, see Parker 2017, 103. On the supposed inexistence of *asylia* outside of the polis: Rigsby 1996, 20.
[36] Chaniotis 2010, no. 266; cf. Ricl 2011, 144 n. 3.   [37] Lemaire 2002, 183.

entire village's revenues and so postulates a missing numeral in the *vacat*.³⁸ However, this assumes that the price recorded in the inscription was the original price paid by Meleager. Peter Herrmann and Hasan Malay, working from the stone itself, note, "It looks as if the amount had been added later in a space left blank."³⁹ This does not fit well with the model of interpretation put forward by Thonemann, which sees here a contract quoted verbatim ("about which it is written" περὶ ἧς γέγρα|πται). Perhaps, we should consider the lowball price as the result of Eumenes' "settling up" with Meleager. In fact, settling is exactly what the act of *diorthôsis* ("setting to right") implies – the "sticker price" was not necessarily the final price.⁴⁰

Quoted in the moral register of setting to right, the 448 drachmas and 1.5 obols may have sounded like a just price, given the circumstances. An implicit contrast is then drawn with Eumenes' own conveyance of Sibloe back into the patrimony of Zeus Stratios. Trenchantly, that transaction is described as "without price (ἄνευ τιμῆς)." For the king who forgoes a sale, earmarking becomes an arena for the display of a particularly economic royal virtue. That we are told that the final transfer of the village to the cult was a specifically priceless conveyance is an indication of what is at stake when it comes to earmarking. One must describe these transactions, and description is a gambit of ideological risks and rewards. Without a price, Eumenes and Apollonioucharax meet at a point, as it were, above and beyond the market.⁴¹ In the end, neither party assumes the dreaded role of buyer. Yet what of Meleager, the original buyer? We can only guess at how he really fared in all this. If he had not as yet collected the usufruct of the village and marketed it, the whole business would have at best approximated an interest-free loan to Apollonioucharax for whatever period of time had elapsed since the original sale. If he had collected anything at all, this was profit, maybe even a windfall, if on account of the tumult of war the revenues of Sibloe were unlikely to equal 448 drachmas and 1.5 obols any time soon. We should note that the inscription makes clear that some

---

³⁸ Thonemann 2011a, 8–9.   ³⁹ Herrmann and Malay 2007, 51.
⁴⁰ For διορθοῦσθαι, see discussion of Gauthier 1989, 20: "payer ou *régler* une somme due" (emphasis added). Cf. Thonemann's translation of Side B lines 13–14: "it will be restored (ἀποδοθῇ) when we repay (διορθωσαμένων) to Meleagros the price (τὴν τιμήν) at which he bought it (ἠγορακότι)."
⁴¹ Angelos Chaniotis (2004, 203–4) treats the legitimacy of interstate sales of territory with regard to transactions between different kings and between kings and cities or *koina* (e.g., Attalos I and the Aetolians over Aegina in 210), but he does not discuss any between private individuals and kings.

partial collection of taxes has already taken place: the remission of arrears explicitly excludes those taxes that are already in the hands of tax farmers (Side B Lines 7–9).

It is impossible to know what became of Meleager. However, to focus on one of the key relationships in earmarking – the king and his private business partner – it is necessary to speculate. One can compare the Lycian dynast Ptolemaios, who transferred land to another *katoikia* town, the Kardakon Kome near Telmessos, but did not receive the money promised from the community in return. In a letter of 181, Eumenes II freed the Kardakoi from their debt, even if, he added, they happened to have the money on hand (*SEG* XIX 867; **D3**, lines 7–10). Just as in the case of Meleager and Apollonioucharax, the fate of the Lycian creditor Ptolemaios or his heirs is effaced. Presumably, Eumenes settled up with them, too. In both cases, we can infer that private third parties transacted with the king over the fate of subject communities. The inscription from Taşkuyucak shows the Attalid king purchasing private property in order to provide a source of revenue for an earmark. Indeed, it is one more piece of evidence to belie the old scholarly notion that only two forms of land tenure existed in Hellenistic Asia Minor: royal/nonprivate land and the territory (*chora*) of the polis, on which private property existed alongside public.[42] In fact, private property has a distinctly high profile in earmarking.

However, the full significance of Eumenes' purchase becomes clear only when we can see it as part of a reciprocal exchange with the community of Apollonioucharax. With the *diorthôsis*, the king brought to an ethical conclusion a transaction that had not gone according to the original participants' plan. We should note that Eumenes does nothing to perpetuate the relationship with Meleager. He does not ask the land-distributor Lykinos to find a different village for Meleager. It seems that Meleager just walks away with the money that he receives from the royal treasury. By contrast, the earmarking arrangement construes the relationship between king and community as fixed and everlasting. The earmarking of revenues for sacrifice takes the form of a purpose clause that contains the almost atemporal verb ὑπάρχειν in the subjunctive.[43] The agreement is open-ended and eternal. One does not dare imagine a time when the revenue stream will *not* provide for sacrifices.[44] Eumenes promises that the village

---

[42] Mileta 2008, 8–19.   [43] See Hedrick 1999, 421.
[44] In her study of Greek foundations, the legal historian Anneliese Mannzmann (1962, 147–51) identifies this tendency toward unlimited temporal horizons as "Verewigungstendenz."

of Sibloe will remain perpetually earmarked. And while Apollonioucharax and its priest may avoid negotiating any further with Meleager, they are involved in an exchange with Eumenes. They are now responsible for the cost of revenue collection in the village. In turn, they will perform sacrifices to Zeus Stratios on the king's behalf.

The inscription from Taşkuyucak may also illuminate the transactions echoed in a very fragmentary text found in Pergamon itself, long known but poorly understood (*RC* 48; **D4**). A lamentable four discrete fragments of it survive. It is a letter of Eumenes II to the Aeolian polis of Temnos, a city of the old kingdom. The Attalids likely had an especially good knowledge of local institutions in Temnos. The city had even exchanged political rights (*isopoliteia*) with Pergamon in predynastic days, which makes it all the more intriguing to find in Temnos those same dynamics of earmarking that proliferated in the new territories.[45] Bradford Welles could not interpret any further what he termed "certain subsidies" of Eumenes II for Temnos, but he saw in this inscription the same "financial policy" as that instantiated in the Korragos Decree.[46] In other words, the Temnos letter was another important building block in the early twentieth-century theory of Attalid penetration into civic finance.

The crucial passages are in Fragment D. Welles' text here, however, must be used with caution, as he himself admitted. Though the script is "fine and even," the right margin of Fragment D, the measure by which he determined line length elsewhere, is irregular. Francis Piejko, who has published several major restorations of Fragment D, provides slightly different line numbers.[47] According to the text of Welles, the opening lines of Fragment D tell us: (1) land had been purchased (πε]πραμένης χ[ώρας); (2) a 1/10 tax (*dekate*) on agricultural produce was at issue (μ]έρη τῆς δεκ[άτης); and (3) funds are being earmarked for the city's administration (εἰς τὴν διο]ίκησιν τῆ[ς π]όλεως καὶ [. . .). Welles asks an important question: "Does this mean that crown land had been sold to the city, from which a part of the revenue would be available for the city's running expenses?"[48]

The model of Apollonioucharax and Sibloe, Eumenes II and Meleager, suggests a different interpretation. In the case of Temnos too, a third party – a private property owner – is likely lurking. Again, earmarking entails

---

[45] *OGIS* 265. For the designation of Temnos as "tributary" in this period, see Allen 1983, 111; Allen's sovereignty rubric, however, is based solely on the dubious criterion of "independent coinage."

[46] *RC*, 195–96, invoking Holleaux, Louis Robert, and Rostovtzeff for the Pergamene "financial policy."

[47] Piejko 1987, 724; Piejko 1989, 401. [48] *RC*, 197.

recourse to the purchase of private property. The reasoning behind this supposition is both methodological and philological. First, Welles takes as his starting point the old conception of land tenure in Hellenistic Asia Minor as a two-tiered system consisting of royal land and polis territory, with no place for private property of any form beyond the *chora* of the poleis. This view is now untenable. Eumenes is the buyer, not the seller. We can note that the king divides up his purchase into "parts" (μέρος [D 14]; μέρη [D3]).[49] Further, the postulated earmark will feed Temnos "every year" (κατ' ἐνια[υτὸν [D15 and 16]). While Piejko's bold restorations are unsustainable, they suggest a general framework for interpretation. He has restored, first, the remission of two parts of the *dekate* and, second, an earmark for the purpose of "sacred things" (*hiera*) and "the administration of the city (*dioikesis tes poleos*)," the source of which will be the revenues from a stoa that the king undertakes to build.[50] Yet this restoration does not solve the problem posed by Welles of the purchased land. In the remainder of Fragment D, nothing is said of a stoa, but in fact everything concerns the fiscal status of land. Mention of a place called the Bomitis, of an official land survey (*katametresis*), and of the notification of an official named Pyrrhos regarding the act of "taking over" (*paralêpsis*) land follows a series of illegible fiscal prescriptions.[51] The land at issue may have once been part of a gift estate granted in early Hellenistic times, or it may have fallen more recently into private hands through public borrowing and default. The point is that Eumenes must purchase this land in the process of constructing an earmark for Temnos. Once set in motion, the mechanics of earmarking trigger a sale.

Brokering the Earmark

Though earmarks at times required the Attalids to take on the risks of transacting with private third parties, the community's input was also crucial. Other documents depict the civic elites who served as ambassadors to the court and its regional outposts brokering earmarks. Local leaders used their embassies to negotiate the terms of earmarks and therefore the impact of Attalid power on their cities. By nature, earmarks are ad hoc solutions to local problems. With information scarce, local people

---

[49] Noted by Fränkel, *I.Pergamon* 157.
[50] For a harsh critique of Piejko's method, see Gauthier 1989, 171–78. For the finance of Attalid stoa building, see Kaye 2016.
[51] For a discussion of *paralepsis*, see the remarks of Corsten, *I.Prusa* 1001.

represented their own problems to the Attalid state, and in the end, local people gained even more agency by helping execute the earmark. As coauthors of these line items, the Pergamene chancery and local elites, quite simply, needed each other.

The role of a man named Apollonios in the creation of an earmark for Ionian Metropolis is on display in an inscription that records his city's appreciation for his deeds (*I.Metropolis* 1; **D5**). Metropolis was a minor city of the Kayster Valley, easily overshadowed by Ephesus. Little of its Hellenistic remains have come to light, but strong ties to imperial Pergamon are evidenced by an altar of Attalos II, a dedication to Queen Apollonis, a private association's use of the regnal year in a dating formula, and the local onomasticon – Apollonios' father was named Attalos.[52] A decree for Apollonios on one side of the stone dates itself to 144/3, the fifteenth year of the reign of Attalos II. Metropolis praises Apollonios for a life full of service, listing his good deeds, while all along emphasizing that his stature outstripped humble Metropolis. Insofar as Apollonios spent time in other cities, the fair reputation he earned abroad redounded to the benefit of Metropolis. Back home, citizens could count on him in a pinch to travel away again on embassies "to kings and others" (Side B lines 12–13). Owing to his characteristic perseverance and sacrifice of private advantage to public, the embassies accomplished the city's aims.

What follows then are three positive outcomes of embassies. These are presented in a narrative passage that is closed by one final sentence before the formal expression of motivation: "(and) in all other respects he consistently engages in politics (πολιτευόμενος διατελεῖ) incorruptibly and eagerly" (Side B line 27). The three positive outcomes are as follows. First, in land disputes with neighbors, likely with Colophon, Smyrna, or Ephesus, or with some combination of such adversaries, Apollonios saw to it that the city suffered no loss. Here, editors Boris Dreyer and Helmut Engelmann, as well as Christopher Jones, who has challenged many of their interpretations, hypothesize an embassy not to the king but to the Attalid governor in Ephesus.[53] We do know that such an official (*strategos*) was responsible for the Kaystrian plain.[54] Next, a dispute with a mysterious group of tax farmers drew Apollonios into a formal arbitration (*diakrisis*) (Side B line 23). Who presided? We are not told, though we know that the

---

[52] *I.Ephesos* 3407 and 3408. On archaeology, see Meriç 2004. Regnal date: *SEG* LX 1257. Onomasticon: Aybek and Dreyer 2012, 212.
[53] *I.Metropolis*, 50–7; Jones 2004, 476. [54] *SEG* XXVI 1238.

Attalids settled a fiscal dispute between Parion and Priapos.⁵⁵ The tax farmers had in some way altered the fiscal status of Metropolis with respect to the "Kaystrian harbor (*limen Kaïstrianos*)" (Side B line 20).

The result of the embassy seems to have been a return to the status quo: Metropolis received its tax privilege back. Yet perhaps the city gained even more in the bargain. It is curious that the third and final good deed of Apollonios is not set off like the other two with an introductory clause. For the story about the land dispute: κατά τε τὰς γινομένας πρὸς τοὺς παρακειμένους ὑπὲρ χώρας ἀμφιζβητήσεις ("concerning the disputes that had risen with the other parties over land"; Side B line 14). For the story about the harbor taxes: ὑπὲρ τῶν ἐφευρισκομένων ἡμεῖν τελῶν ("over the taxes that had been invented for us"; Side B line 19). However, for the third case, we have only a pair of conjunctive particles: δὲ καὶ (Side B line 24). Here, Apollonios obtained (ἐξεπορίσατο in Side B lines 23–24) from the Attalid king an earmark of 500 drachmas for oil for the youth of the gymnasium (*neoi*) and 500 drachmas for lessons for freeborn youth each year (καθ' ἕκαστον ἐνιαυτὸν) (Side B line 25). In other words, Apollonios facilitated Attalid participation in the year-by-year financial planning of Metropolis. When did he secure the earmark? Jones does not treat the issue directly, but he counts at least two embassies. "Since the text praises Apollonios just above for his embassies to 'the kings and to the others' (12), both issues, that of the land and that of the tax-farmers, must have required recourse either to one of the kings or to an official."⁵⁶ And what of that other issue, who will pay for oil for the gymnasium and for the education of the freeborn youth? The text holds out the possibility that Apollonios used the same embassy to obtain both the old fiscal regime for the Kaystrian harbor *and* the two annual pledges of 500 drachmas. This is why we lack a new introductory clause after the story of the tax-farming dispute concludes. The process of repealing the harbor taxes may have resulted in a new earmark.⁵⁷ Certainly, Apollonios used an identical channel of communication in each case.

The Metropolis inscription points to the active participation of local notables like Apollonios in the process of cobbling together earmarks.

---

⁵⁵ Strabo 13.1.14. It is difficult to discern from Strabo's report of Parion's sycophancy (*therapeia*) whether the Attalid arbitration might have been in any sense formal. With kings, Sheila Ager (2007, 50) argues, "The line between arbitral and arbitrary is quite fuzzy." On the other hand, for Dreyer and Engelmann, as well as Jones, the tax farmers are royal, which necessarily implies an Attalid role in the dispute's resolution.

⁵⁶ Jones 2004, 476.

⁵⁷ This interpretation is also consistent with the translation of Virgilio 2004, 264.

Thus, alternative reconstructions, in which minimal interaction precedes an earmark, are to be rejected.[58] On that model, cities simply petition for benefactions, and kings reply. Or kings seem to parachute into local contexts, rearrange cities' budgets, and leave. Earmarks, however, require intermediation and, therefore, the devolution of agency. In the Attalid kingdom, earmarking required subjects to participate in their own governance. The interactive character of earmarking was also showcased in an incident that took place in Apameia in the mid-160s, a city which then once again found itself at the center of a conflict, the aforementioned war with the Galatians. Kephisodoros son of Ariston was a leading citizen of Apameia and perhaps also a courtier.[59] For Apameia, he clearly played an important role in public finance. One of his descendants may have served as the city's financial administrator in the first half of the first century BCE.[60] For Pergamon, Kephisodoros was a key supporter stationed in one of the kingdom's lynchpin cities. A decree of Apameia honors him for erecting statues of the royal family during his tenure as gymnasiarch, while also maneuvering to set conditions on an earmark (**D6** lines 1–16):

> Decreed by the Council. Since Kephisodoros son of Ariston is a good and noble man, whose deeds are worthy both of the reputation of his ancestors and of his own love of goodness; both earlier when he made demonstrations ever fitting his character and benefited the People, he met with appropriate honors, which have been set down in decrees inscribed about him; and from that time up until now he has not let off excelling in all earnestness for the commons and showing a love of honor, and always doing whatever was advantageous for the People, serving as gymnasiarch [splendidly with his own funds?], and when he was honored by *neoi*, he dedicated statues of Eumenes and Attalos the brother of the king; and now, with the King having granted 3,000 drachmas, to [our?] People who provided grain to the soldiers in the war and in many other needs of war [?] furnishing fine demonstrations of our goodwill towards the king's affairs, he [Kephisodoros] has made on behalf of the King a

---

[58] Scholarship has advanced two different versions of this model of royal-civic relations that posits minimal interaction. The earlier model presented strong kings, unconcerned with the local affairs of cities. See, e.g., Rostovtzeff 1941. More recently, scholars have tended to see a vibrant Hellenistic city, which can act unilaterally or in concert with other cities, setting its own priorities without royal approval or participation. Here see, e.g., A. Chankowski 2009.

[59] Courtier: Jean and Louis Robert *BE* (1939) no. 400; Kephisodoros does not meet the formal criteria for inclusion in the catalogue of courtiers of Savalli-Lestrade 1998.

[60] *BMC* 47. W. H. Buckler (*MAMA* 6, 173) suggests that the moneyer was the son of Kephisodoros, but the downdating of this second series of Apameian bronze to the late 90s–50s BCE by Ashton 2016 excludes the possibility. Also, if a kinsmen, he was not a homonymous one, since the *BMC* reading of ΑΡΙΣΤΑ/ΚΗΦΙΣ has proven correct (Ashton 2016, 423 n. 61).

dedication of [X many] drachmas on condition that every year there shall be an assembly [in the gymnasium] of the ephebes and the boys of the gymnasium (*paides*) when they celebrate the Hermaia and Heraklea ...

The document shows the Attalid king magnanimously rewarding a city's loyalty with a cash subsidy, but also relinquishing a certain amount of control over the shape of an earmark. It highlights the degree to which earmarking devolves agency. Initially, Eumenes II had promised Apameia 3,000 drachmas as a reward for providing grain and other assistance to Attalid troops operating nearby during the recent war.[61] Kephisodoros, however, then modified the king's gift in two different ways. First, he added more money to the original grant, a top-up dedication vowed on behalf of the king. Second, surprisingly, he attached conditions to the gift: Apameia would receive the money provided that a gathering of ephebes and other youths of the gymnasium took place each year at the festival of the Hermaia and the Heraklea. This event may also have been the legally prescribed occasion for the public proclamation of his own honors.[62] We can safely assume that the money promised, the start-up capital for a foundation, was earmarked to pay for these festivals. Yet the grammar of a provisory clause is unusual for an earmarking arrangement. The typical construction is: *apo* + genitive (source); then *eis* + accusative (purpose). On the other hand, ἐφ' ᾧ ἔσται ("on the condition that ...") may be proper to the language of dedications. One can compare a late second-century Delphic manumission that vows a slave to Apollo, according to the convention, "on the condition that the slave be free (ἐφ' ὧιτε ἐλεύθερον εἶμεν)" (*SGDI* II 2086 line 7). While its grammar may be unusual, by introducing the contingency of the young men's synod, the decree of Apameia for Kephisodoros exposes what may have been a commonplace: a local agent succeeded in altering the terms of an Attalid earmark. For the king, the dedication of his money to a divinity always provided a measure of security against repurposing. However, it was invariably the local councils and assemblies that enshrined foundations in law and encased subventions in the procedures and rituals of civic finance. For Attalid subjects, earmarking provided numerous opportunities to exercise their own agency.

---

[61] The nature of that benefaction was obscured so long as the beginning of line 12 was read: [καὶ τοῦ δήμου, ἀργ]υρίου, and so on; and line 13 was read: [τῶι ταμίαι (?) τῶι ἐν τ]ῶι πολέμωι, and so on. The king belongs in line 12 and the *demos* belongs in line 13, for which see Jean and Louis Robert *BE* (1939) no. 400. Robert (1960, 124) gives a date of 168–166, which rests on the identification of the war mentioned in one of the crucial lines as the Galatian War. For confirmation of the date on the basis of royal titulature, see also Thonemann 2003, 104–5.
[62] Savalli-Lestrade 2010, 73.

The anecdote raises a series of important if ultimately unanswerable questions. Do the citizens receive the king's 3,000 drachmas with strings attached? In other words, did Kephisodoros, who tacked on his own contribution to the king's gift, change the earmarking arrangement? In short, who is the author of the earmark? As the local gymnasiarch, Kephisodoros had converted his own honors into honors for the royal family in the form of a statue group (lines 10–11). So he plainly conducted his local affairs against the backdrop of the kingdom at large. His interests were certainly not at odds with those of the Attalids nor, however, were the two identical. By making an annual assembly of the gymnasium a condition, he may have guaranteed himself perennial public honors that were not available at all in any other forum. This means that Eumenes was not solely responsible for the Apameia earmark, manipulating Kephisodoros and using his stature in his community to legitimate an intrusive intervention in civic affairs. Rather, Kephisodoros' piggy-backing of his contribution on top of the king's gift speaks to the frequent division of agency in earmarking.

This last-minute rider to a royal writ reminds us how much local agency is unleashed in the earmarking process. On the one hand, the implementation is left to those on the ground, which entails tasks of coercion and the monitoring of the arrangement. As we have noted, the settlers of Apollonioucharax and the priests of Zeus Stratios received from the Attalids not just the right but also the responsibility to collect revenue from the village of Sibloe. In the very complaint of those settlers that other dependent villages had not been returned to them in the manner Eumenes II authorized, we may have an admission of failure in the implementation of an earlier earmark (**D2**, Side B lines 20–21). On the other hand, the creation of earmarking arrangements implicates multiple agencies from the start because earmarks are tailored to highly local circumstances. Infamously, this is what is called "pork-barrel spending" in the United States. There is no one-size-fits-all earmark. Kephisodoros occupied a privileged niche in the social hierarchy of the kingdom. He was therefore in a position to frame the needs of his city before the king, to be part of the conversation that ends with an earmark.

Certain documents give the impression that the king's *only* role was to provide money. The royal treasury (*to basilikon*) dispensed the capital for a foundation of the city's choosing, or made annual payments to a slush fund bearing the opaque name "for the administration (*dioikesis*) of the city" (**D1** line 11). Left unexpressed, the source of the money can appear inconsequential. How the money is invested and differentiated between the various organs of civic finance and their attendant ideological categories, even the particular type of money, which currency, is on this account the city's prerogative alone. The Attalids do not actively participate in the social process of earmarking, or so it appears. A notable example is a decree of Teos that describes the establishment of a foundation for the support of an actors' guild, the koinon of Dionysian *technitai*, the powerful, inter-city association that would eventually spar with Teos over festival revenues, prompting an Attalid mediation (*SEG* II 580; **D7**).[63] Its date is placed variously after 188 or at the end of the third century, late in the reign of Attalos I.[64] This text is most often cited as surefire evidence for Attalid intervention in city finance in the form of a fund, "for the administration (*dioikesis*) of the city" (lines 17–18).[65] Attalid money, which is earmarked for the general administration of the city, grants Teos financial flexibility and security. To create the actors' foundation, citizens combined 3,000 drachmas of royal *dioikesis* funds with 3,000 drachmas of city money. Interestingly, this latter amount was twice re-earmarked: it is filched from the grain fund, which was formerly known as the fortification fund! The combination of Attalid and civic monies is facilitated by the merging of the civic and royal financial calendars: on taking up their office, the city's treasurers receive 3,000 drachmas as the first installment of the year's royal *dioikesis* funds. The royal role here seems to begin and end with disbursement. The process by which the city arranges to provide for purchase of property to support the actors is complex, laid out in detail, and, as far as we can see, free of royal participation. The king, it seems, grants a certain number of subventions per year, and the citizens of Teos do with the money what they will.

J. D. Sosin argues that the Attalid kings played a similarly passive role in the establishment of four endowments at Delphi in 159/8.[66] Delphi lay far outside the Attalid kingdom but promised the Pergamenes a Panhellenic stage and the opportunity to politick with the Aetolians. Moreover, the city of Delphi was also a polis, with the requisite institutions to make the most of Attalid gifts so modest that Polybios may have singled them out for condemnation. The polis of Delphi stretched Attalid money into years of

---

[63] For the Attalid mediation, see *RC* 53.
[64] However, for a date ca. 210, see Le Guen 2001, 202–10.
[65] P. J. Rhodes (2007, 360–61) seems to cast the intervention as extraordinary, while as Stefano Fanucchi (DOI: 10.25429/sns.it/lettere/GEI0041) notes, the future participle δοθησομένων reveals that these contributions were regular.
[66] Sosin 2004. See also Domingo Gygax 2009, 176, arguing for a Delphic initiative designed to obtain benefactions from the king by proleptically offering excessive honors.

pageantry, cult, and public education. To summarize events, in a period of months, the city sent four embassies to Pergamon, which resulted in two gifts containing a total of four endowments. First, the co-regent Attalos II gave 21,000 attic-weight drachmas, labeled "Alexanders," three talents of which were earmarked for teachers' salaries, the education of Delphi's citizen youth, and the remaining half talent for the celebration of a new festival in honor of the king and dynasty called the Attaleia.[67] One inscription describes the stringent terms on which the funds would be managed, splashing local rules about sacred and public money, guarantors and defaulters, across the base of an equestrian statue for Attalos II on which the text was inscribed ($Syll.^3$ 672). A few months later, the dying Eumenes II endowed a grain fund (three and a half talents) and another new festival, the Eumeneia (one talent). A second inscription records that Eumenes II also paid in those "Alexander" drachmas ($Syll.^3$ 671).

Together, the two gifts amounted to an injection of eight talents of "Alexanders" into a monetary system dominated by other, regional currencies. The so-called Alexanders, by contrast, were an international currency. These tetradrachms, whether or not they bore the face of the Macedonian conqueror, had been minted on the old Attic standard, meaning they now commanded a premium in long-distance trade.[68] For Sosin, this fact unlocks the dynamic that produced these earmarking arrangements. Because the Delphic elite planned to borrow the Alexanders at a lower cost than the price of that premium currency on the open market, they stood to gain the most from the arrangement, and on his account, would have plowed the coins back into international transactions. Sosin astutely demonstrates what certain Delphic citizens stood to gain. However, while this dogged pursuit of *cui bono* demystifies the claims of the ὅπως clause of the decree for Attalos II, which construes the whole affair as a royal plot to earmark interest "for all time" for the maintenance of sacrifices, the king's own honors, and the teachers' salaries, it papers over much of the complexity of the transaction.

Sosin describes the Delphic elite as "crony capitalists," casting the Attalids as partners to a simple "gift exchange," cash for honors. He writes, "Though these texts are inevitably studied as specimens of royal gifts, there is no reason to think that the idea to establish the endowments or the

---

[67] For the date of the co-regency, based on these documents, see Hansen 1971, 127. For the Attalid endowments at Delphi, see now Jacquemin et al. 2012, nos. 165–68.

[68] For "Alexanders," see Knoepfler 1997. On the reduction of the Attic standard and the monetary situation in the Aegean in this period, see Chapter 3.

restrictions under which they were to operate came from Attalos or Eumenes. Both pairs of endowments were established only after Delphi sent embassies to the kings in support of the idea. Kings provided money. Rich Delphians provided initiative and ingenuity."[69] The question of origin and invention here seems misplaced. Again, Attalid earmarks matched local wants and needs with the floating resources of a redistributive system. It took four embassies to produce the four earmarks contained within these two diplomatic acts. The rhetoric of Delphi's decree was, in short: the city asked, and it received (*Syll.*³ 672 lines 6–7). Beneath the rhetoric, however, the back-and-forth of the emissaries reflects painstaking negotiations. If not those details of the final arrangement subject to strictly local politics, then the basic shape of the earmark was bargained out. Cash or kind? We know that the Attalids skillfully deployed grain from surplus tribute in this economy of gifts. If cash, which currency? The Attalids traversed many different monetary systems and concocted their own. We can also consider the gifts' amounts and delivery schedules; for royal honors, if a statue, its location; if a festival, its place on the religious calendar. All this and more was up for negotiation.

Institutions and Earmarking

The image of Delphi's rules and regulations scrawled like a caption beneath the statue of Attalos II on horseback is jarring. High and low politics are combined. The king seems to get mired in the city's red tape. One lesson to be drawn from the juxtaposition is that earmarking afforded the two parties an opportunity to gain familiarity with each other's financial institutions. The more Attalid officials and civic elites shared information, the greater the prospects for fiscal and indeed ideological integration. Yet with power so unevenly distributed inside the kingdom, it must be demonstrated, not assumed, that subjects of the nascent Attalid empire offered kings a candid look at their finances and, conversely, that kings cultivated an interest in local institutions. Inscriptions brought to light in recent years provide two key pieces of evidence in this regard. The first is a dossier from Kyme in Aeolis, like Temnos, a city long in the Pergamene orbit (*SEG* L 1195).[70] The dossier emerges from an episode in the reign of Philetairos (either 280–278

---

[69] Sosin 2004, 195–96.
[70] Ed. pr.: Manganaro 2000; see also Fröhlich 2004b on the administration of the gift. See Hamon 2008 on Kyme's political history and institutions, vicissitudes between Seleukid and Attalid influence and control.

or ca. 270), but it gives us a striking impression of an aspect of Attalid political culture that endured into the second century.[71] It consists of three documents: the decision of the beleaguered city of Kyme to send ambassadors to Philetairos urgently requesting military equipment, the dynast's positive response, and a decree of Kyme on the administration and safeguarding of Philetairos' gift, which also outlines his honors. Initially, the city had sent an embassy to Philetairos to negotiate the provision of a large number of shields for the protection (*phylake*) and security (*asphaleia*) of its citizens.[72] Philetairos obliged, confessing that while the competent Pergamene workshops had closed, he happened to have the shields on hand and would provide them as a gift.[73] We know that Hellenistic Kyme was particularly exercised by monarchical and oligarchical threats to its democracy.[74] Remarkably, we learn that the dynast who armed the citizens of Kyme also became a citizen of the Aeolian polis (line 30). Even further, the name of this super-citizen was etched into each of 600 shields alongside the name of one of the twelve tribes of Kyme. In separate musters, the *phylarch* (tribal leader) would have distributed shields bearing his particular tribal insignia – and the name of Philetairos.[75] The city's proposal of an earmark, the circuit that connects centers of arms production at Pergamon and the customs houses of Kyme, appears in the first document:

συγχωρήσαντα τὰγ γινομέναν πέλταν ἐπιχάλκ[ω]ν παρ' ἑαυτῷ
κατιστα|μένω ἀναλώματος δόμεναι ὅπλα ἑξακόσια ἵνα εἰς ἑκάσταν φυλὰν
κα[τ]αταχθέωσι πεντήκον|τα, εἰς δὲ τὸ ἀνάλωμα τὸ ἐσσόμενον πόρον
ὑπάρχην τὰμ πρόσοδον τὰν [ἀ]πὸ τῶ διαγωγίμω σίτω|ἐπεί κε
ἀποδοθέωισι τοῖς τε ἰρέ[ε]σσι καὶ τοῖς ἀρχόντεσσι καὶ [τ]οῖς ἄλλοισι τὰ
προεψαφισμένα ἐπὶ|πρυτάνιος Λυσανία, τοῖς δὲ ἄρχοντας δόμεναι τούτων
γραφὰ[ν] τοῖς πρεσβέεσσι.

---

[71] Dates: *SEG* LIV 1230; Claude Brixhe *BE* (2001) no. 373.
[72] See Hamon 2008, 86, 104. These key terms marked the decree with solemnity. Decrees deemed "for defense and security" formed a distinct class of public documents of importance at Kyme. It is conjectured that the historical context is a major incursion of Galatians in the second quarter of the third century.
[73] On the Attalids and their workshops, see Robert 1984, 496–99.
[74] The key documents are *I.Kyme* 12 and *SEG* LIV 1229. Epigraphists have dated both variously, with Hamon (2008, 102–5) arguing most recently for roughly the same third-century context as the Philetairos dossier *SEG* LIV 1230. See also Claude Brixhe and Philippe Gauthier *BE* (2005) no. 396.
[75] For tribal organization in the military context at Kyme, see Kunnert 2012, 301; for archaeological evidence for the convention of the king's name alone as an emblem on Macedonian shields, see Sekunda 2012, 18.

(We ask that) Philetairos allow 600 of the bronze shields available to him to be given for the customary cost, so that 50 may be distributed to each tribe. As for the future cost of the shields, (we ask that) the means come in the form of the revenue from the tax on grain in transit – after the monies earmarked in the decree of the prytany of Lysanias have been apportioned between the priests, the archons, and the others. The archons are to give the ambassadors a written account of all this. (lines 7–11)

While Philetairos chose not to execute an earmark designed to match his manufacturing resources with Kyme's coastal ones, the encounter provides a model of interaction. Rather, in the end, Philetairos chose to trade shields for honors – not money. Yet the original proposal of Kyme forecasts a transfer of information. Kyme was prepared to buy the shields, but hoped to negotiate a good price by pleading for the "customary cost" (κατισταμένω ἀναλώματος; lines 7–8).[76] The city could not offer payment upon delivery, but promised future payment by earmarking taxes on grain in transit. To reassure Philetairos of creditworthiness, Kyme disclosed a great deal of information about its finances: still yet to be collected, the tax on grain in transit was already earmarked for a number of other purposes, but Philetairos, too, would get his money. In order to lay out the plan, the city's ambassadors delivered to Philetairos a document called a *grapha*, a written account of Kyme's fiscal outlook, perhaps including the master document known as "the decree passed in the prytany of Lysanias." Philetairos, then, received a detailed map of Kyme's finances. In exchange for the shields, the city had laid bare its institutions, the present state of its finances, and its projected revenues. The earmarking process continually fed the Attalids valuable information, which inevitably informed rational taxation and redistribution.[77]

Kyme and Pergamon were old friends and once peers. Kyme even counted the dynast Philetairos among its own citizens. In such a city, the Attalids could hardly hope to revamp institutions to better fit their fiscal system or cultural preferences.[78] On the other hand, in the rural eastern

---

[76] Cf. Bresson 2000, 183–206, on the "recommended price (*kathestekuia time*)."
[77] Andrzej Chankowski (2010, 321 n. 10) adduces the inscription as evidence for a robust civic army in the Hellenistic polis. A. Chankowski 2009, moreover, insists on the independence of polis armies in Hellenistic Asia Minor. The dossier from Kyme would seem to nuance those claims, as soldiers don a uniform that bears the dynast's name, and military preparedness is predicated on fiscal coordination with the Attalid state.
[78] In fact, the case of Kyme's *strategeia* shows just how diverse civic institutions were in cities under Pergamene control. The Attalids, contrary to an old scholarly hypothesis, did not impose the *strategeia* on city governments. See Hamon 2008, 64–69.

territories awarded at Apameia, opportunities arose to tailor civic institutions. This was especially true at the moment when a new polis was born, when an Anatolian town was refounded with Greek institutions. Another new epigraphical dossier, this one from Toriaion in Phrygia Paroreios, depicts the Attalids gathering data on civic institutions, engineering them to complement their own, and founding public life on earmarking (*SEG* XLVII 1745; **D8**; **Fig. 1.1**). Under the Seleukid regime, Toriaion had been a *katoikia*, another multiethnic military town, the kind which occupied a rung just below the polis in the settlement hierarchy of the kingdom. Probably in the 180s, Eumenes II granted Toriaion the status and institutions of a polis in a process documented in the dossier of three royal letters. In the first epistle, the king addresses himself to settlers (*katoikountes*), in the second and third, he speaks to the freshly minted council (*boule*) and people (*demos*) of Toriaion. While it is nearly impossible to judge the pace of acculturation, the political transformation was decisive and momentous.[79] Desperate to solidify their sovereignty in the vast new territory, the Attalids turned Toriaion into an administrative hub.[80] They also ceded to it the ultimate ideological defense weapon, the title of polis, but not before predicating polis identity on paying taxes.

In the inscription, Eumenes gives the Toriaeitai permission to organize themselves, along with τοῖς μεθ' ὑμῶν συνοικοῦσιν ἐγχωρίοις ("those of the indigenous cohabiting with them"), into a single polity (*politeuma*), and to use their own laws (*idioi nomoi*) (line 28).[81] On the shelves of city archives around the Hellenistic world, royal orders (*prostagmata* and *diagrammata*) shared space with city laws. It seems to have been a common practice, even a standard practice in the Attalid kingdom, to send city laws up to the king for validation.[82] However, Eumenes presents Toriaion with an interesting choice. He demands that if Toriaion wishes to use its own laws, the city

---

[79] Scholarship has tended to focus on the issue of the integration of non-Hellenes, the *enchorioi* of line 27 (cf. in line 27 of ed. pr.'s text and translation ἐγ χωρίοις "in the fortified places," corrected by Schuler 1999, 128–29). Cf. Virgilio 2008, on a mostly indigenous population. At issue is whether Toriaion provides a paradigm for the assimilation of non-Hellenes into Hellenistic urban foundations or refoundations on the polis model. For Kennell 2005, it is the paradigm.

[80] If Thonemann (2008, 51–52) is correct in assigning a so-called cistophoric countermarking authority to Toriaion, the site became for several decades a major administrative center.

[81] The grant of *idioi nomoi* has – rightly or wrongly – prompted many commentators to compare the situation of the population of Toriaion to that of the Jewish settlers moved to Phrygia and Lydia by Antiochos III (Joseph. *AJ* 12.151). Gruen (2002, 17) has argued for the authenticity of the grant of Antiochos III.

[82] On royal documents in polis archives, see Boffo 2013, esp. 205–7. While Gauthier (1993, 48) considers royal validation of the laws and decrees of the polis unremarkable, several key examples are Attalid. These include the documents referred to in *OGIS* 329, honors for Cleon,

Figure 1.1 View of the Ilgın Plain, vicinity of ancient Toriaion, with Nodalar Höyük in the middle ground (© Yalburt Yaylası Archaeological Landscape Research Project).

submit them for review, lest any of them conflict with "their" interests – or "his" interests, depending on whether one accepts the restoration of ‹ἡ›μῖν for ὑμῖν in line 30.[83] On the other hand, if the city wishes, Eumenes offers to coordinate even more. He promises to send the budding polis the full package: ready-made laws, a council, magistracies, civic tribes, and an oil fund for the *neoi* of the gymnasium.[84] This was no empty gesture. The Attalids vied for more than the elimination of legal contradictions smoldering in city archives. They urged the adoption of democratic institutions that were compatible with their own monarchical political economy, framing the choice for Toriaion. They set bounds around the field of legal production. The goal was to achieve the level of institutional homogeneity and interoperability necessary to implement an earmark.

---

the Pergamene governor of Aegina. From Olbasa in the Milyas, the decree in honor of the governor Sotas was also sent to Attalos II for review (SEG XLIV 1108).

[83] Philippe Gauthier BE (1999) no. 509. Gauthier points out that the photo of the ed. pr. is illegible. According to Herrmann and Malay (2007, 58 n. 76) the inscription from Taşkuyucak (**D2**) exhibits the same mistake (or phonological ambiguity?) on Side B lines 16–17.

[84] Here, one has to decide whether ἐπιτηδείους is a substantive, i.e., a commission of men "ready" to craft laws, divide up tribes, etc.; or rather an adjective referring to the *nomoi* (line 31). The most recent editor, Bencivenni (2003, 124–25) understands *nomoi* as the referent.

In fact, an earmark did emerge from these negotiations along with Toriaion's new institutions. Eumenes and the delegation led by a man with the Celtic name Brennos agreed to designate certain taxes collected in Toriaion for the purchase of oil for the new city's ephebic class. In the second letter, the gymnasium of the polis of Toriaion gained royal support for its provision of oil.[85] For the time being (κατὰ τὸ παρὸν) – and here the political horizon is hazy – the revenue from the *agoranomia*, a certain market tax or fee, was earmarked for the oil. Eumenes ordered a financial official called the *hemiolios* to use his discretion in substituting a different set of revenues. While the nature of these revenues is imperfectly understood, they are clearly taxes on land, as the use of the term *dekate* (tithe; lines 41–47) implies. Of the third and final letter we have only the first few lines, but they mention another embassy. It would seem that the contingent and provisional terms of the earmarking arrangement laid out in the second letter had generated this second embassy and a third royal letter. As the new citizens of the new polis of Toriaion bargained out the shape of their institutions, they were also arguing with Eumenes over earmarks. The king traded benefaction for tax collection. The Attalids were not intervening in polis affairs so much as embedding their authority inside local institutions from their very inception.

Each of these anecdotes describes a recursive relationship between the process of arranging an earmark and the process of crafting institutions for the polis or the *katoikia*. Ambassadors met with kings to negotiate fiscal privileges, and when they returned home, they reshaped local institutions of public finance in ways that reflected new realities of domination. Or civic leaders aimed to shape local institutions in ways that maximized the likelihood of securing fiscal privileges from new rulers. The exchange of information and personnel between imperial centers and peripheries probably picked up in western Asia Minor during the stormy 180s, as both new hegemons, Pergamon and Rhodes, struggled to find a footing. Not only was sovereignty still shaky, but the Romans had left behind a quagmire of fiscal quarrels and territorial disputes.[86] Polybius writes:

> Ὅτι κατὰ τὴν Ἀπάμειαν οἵ τε δέκα καὶ Γνάιος ὁ στρατηγὸς τῶν Ῥωμαίων, διακούσαντες πάντων τῶν ἀπηντηκότων, τοῖς μὲν περὶ χώρας ἢ χρημάτων ἤ τινος ἑτέρου διαφερομένοις πόλεις ἀπέδωκαν ὁμολογουμένας ἀμφοτέροις, ἐν αἷς διακριθήσονται περὶ τῶν ἀμφισβητουμένων.

---

[85] There is debate over whether the gymnasium predates the foundation of the polis of Toriaion. See Philippe Gauthier *BE* (1999) no. 509; Savalli-Lestrade 2005, 14–15; Kennell 2005, 14.

[86] For example, at Aphrodisias, see Chaniotis 2010, 461.

> After listening to the claimants, Manlius Vulso and the ten legates assigned to those cities that were disputing land, money, or something else, different cities that had been agreed upon to act as arbitrators. (21.45.1)

Indeed, the Romans ruled on such issues in only a limited number of cases. For example, the cities of Chios, Smyrna, and Erythrai were all successful in petitions for pieces of taxable territory (21.45.6). Once the Romans left, Rhodes and Pergamon must have decided the lion's share of cases. Unfortunately, we lack a well-documented case from north of the Maeander. Strabo merely alludes to a dispute between Parion and Priapus, settled by the Attalids (13.1.4). However, we can look to the Rhodian sphere to fill in the picture. The career of Pamphilos of Apollonia Salbake in Caria shows us how bargaining over taxes with the new regimes went hand-in-hand with the development and adaptation of local institutions of public finance. The decree in his honor reads (lines 1–27):[87]

> [When the ten legates from] Rome (were) settling (affairs) with Gnaeus (Manlius Vulso), the proconsul at Apameia, (Pamphilos) met them and conducted himself beautifully and fully in the interest of his fatherland. At that critical time, he neither looked away from the danger before his very eyes, nor did he dodge the distress, but he settled each matter with all his energy and love of honor. Later, when sent to Rhodes, with colleagues he debated our enemies among the *enchorioi*, and in the most advantageous way possible, he concluded an agreement with the Rhodians. Having completed many other embassies in the public interest, and on all of them, comported himself appropriately and managed affairs correctly, he was responsible for many of the city's blessings. When the city's finances were being administered messily, and there were regular discrepancies of account, he drafted and submitted to the Council and People a decree, which had the effect of saving the city's finances. The men elected each year governed according to his decree with the result that there were no more shortfalls. In general, saying, writing, and doing what was best for the People in each situation, he continued to show his brilliant energy in everything which he did on behalf of the city.

The formulaic nature of the language of praise notwithstanding, it is clear that Pamphilos had an extraordinary impact on his city. With everything at stake, he had represented Apollonia's interests before Manlius Vulso and the Romans conferencing at Apameia in the summer of 188. When his city

---

[87] Robert, *Carie* II, 303–12 no. 167.

was assigned to Rhodes, he hastened to the island to defend its interests. Among these, Jean and Louis Robert suspected, were the revenues of certain sacred villages in the vicinity of Caria's Mount Salbake, a plausible conjecture, but one that depends on taking the ambassadors' antagonists as indigenous Carians (*enchorioi*).[88] Christof Schuler, by contrast, has argued that the *enchorioi* are in fact "native" Rhodians hostile to the interests of Apollonia.[89] At present, it does not seem that Pamphilos played the culture card in order to secure his goal. What is important for our purposes is that at some point the energetic ambassador returned home to find the city's revenues (*demosiai prosodoi*) in disarray and public monies gone missing. His technocratic solution, delivered in a lexicon more papyrological than epigraphical, was to overhaul public finance at Apollonia with a new founding document.[90] His decree (*psephisma*) appears to have functioned like a budget, preventing future shortfalls, in part, one assumes, by taking account of the recently formalized fiscal relationship with Rhodes.[91]

Interaction with one of Asia Minor's new hegemons may have spurred Pamphilos to reform. New institutions arrived in Hellenistic cities through different means. In this political ecosystem, cities constantly looked around at each other, which meant institutional change could occur through outright imitation.[92] When Teos and Lebedos needed a new set of laws for their synoikism, though, it was a king who urged them to take over the law code of a peer-polity, Kos (*RC* 3 lines 57–61). Sometimes, fear of nonconformity sparked a change. When the citizens of second-century Beroia noticed that "in the cities that have gymnasia and have established an oil fund," there were also gymnasiarchal laws, they considered it only fitting (καλῶς ἔχει) that they pass those laws too (*SEG* XLIII 381 lines 6–8). Human mobility also played a role: when people moved about, they took institutions with them. Therefore, the many embassies of Pamphilos no

---

[88] Robert, *Carie* II, 307. [89] Schuler 1999, 129 n. 21.

[90] Papyrological lexicon: Robert, *Carie* II, 310–11, e.g., διάπτωμα (shortfall), which appears just three times in *Syll.*³, but is a very common term in accounts on papyrus, e.g., *P.Tebt.* 3.2 894 Fr5, r, 2 line 8.

[91] Pamphilos brokered a formal agreement with Rhodes: *synthekai* (lines 12–13). For Rhodian taxation of Apollonia Salbake, see Robert, *Carie* II, 306–9. Compare Erythrai, which passed a *psephisma* for *dioikesis* in the first half of the second century (*I.Erythrai* 112 line 114). According to Schuler (2005, 397), this template for the apportionment of public money best approximates what we would call a budget, and Pamphilos employed it at Apollonia.

[92] Cf. the argument of the citizens of Sardis before Antiochos III (*SEG* XXXIX 1285 lines 8–10). The Sardians seem to know what taxes "other cities (*allai poleis*)" pay on workshops. Cf. also the suggestions of Schuler (2004a, 185–87) that civic elites modeled gymnasia at home on what they observed abroad.

doubt influenced his reform, for we find widespread centralization of public finance in precisely this period.[93] Perhaps his experience negotiating fiscal arrangements abroad had even conditioned what he considered "messily kept (μὴ ὀρθῶς)" books at home (line 19). If we accept that these sorts of interactions could affect a city's choice of institutions, it is not difficult to conceptualize earmarking as an arrangement between ruler and subject that is the outcome of a social bargain struck in the name of a subject community by men such as Apollonios of Metropolis, Kephisodoros of Apameia, Brennos of Toriaion, and Pamphilos of Apollonia Salbake. In other words, part of brokering the arrangements was matching royal resources – not only cash, but the means of coercion – with civic resources – not only manpower, but institutions like public banks and the sacred repositories of temples.

On the Attalid side of the Maeander, the kings continued to deepen their familiarity with local civic institutions in order to use them as conduits and safeguards for their money, as well as tools for investment. Earmarking could not work otherwise. Beneath the bombast of self-advertisement lie humdrum details of institutional coordination. For example, in the winter of 167/6, the Ionian koinon, with the Milesians taking the lead, passed a decree that conferred a series of honors on Eumenes, including a gold statue, proclaiming him the common benefactor of the Greeks (*euergetes ton hellenon*). Ionian ambassadors, including Eirenias of Miletus, intercepted the king on Delos and presented him with the decree. While that decree does not survive, two other documents may contain portions of its contents. One is the king's letter of reply to the Ionians (*RC* 52); the other is a fragmentary decree of Miletus found at Didyma (*I.Didyma* 488). In his letter, Eumenes writes:

> ὅπως δὲ καὶ εἰς τὸ λοιπὸν ἐν τῇ πανηγύρει|τῶν Πανιωνίων ἡμέραν ἐπώνυμον ἄγοντες|ἡμῖν ἐπιφανέστερον τὴν ὅλην ἑορτὴν συν|τελῆτε, προσόδους ὑμῖν τὰς ἱκανὰς ἀνα|[θήσ]ω ἀφ' ὧν ἕξετε τὴν καθήκουσαν ἡμῖν|[ἀνατιθ]έναι μνήμην. τὸν δὲ χρυσοῦν ἀνδρι|[άντα ποιή]σω μὲν ἐγὼ προαιρούμενος ἀδά|[πανον πάν]τως [τὴν] χάριν εἶ|ναι τῷ κο[ινῷ].

> In order that forever after, celebrating a day in our name during the Panionia, you should make the whole festival more illustrious, I shall dedicate for you sufficient revenues, from which you shall be able to make an appropriate dedication to our memory. I shall make the gold statue myself, preferring that this be a cost-free gift for the koinon. (*RC* 52 lines 51–58)

---

[93] See Migeotte 2006 on *planification* of public spending.

At first glance, this looks like paternalism: the Ionians play no role in earmarking revenues for their own festival. The king magnanimously assumes the cost of one of several days' festivities during the Panionia, and his subjects agree to rename the day in his honor, rendering him cult.[94] They propose a gift of a gilded statue, but he commutes their gold into *charis* – the intangible currency of gift exchange – and then orders them to erect his portrait in his sacred precinct in Miletus. It would appear that the king alone decides the source of this earmark and, moreover, that he determines without input from the Ionians just how much revenue will be appropriate. "This project," writes Welles, "as far as the evidence of the letter goes, originated with Eumenes. It was not proposed in the [original] decree."[95] As usual, we can only guess at the origin of the earmark. Yet our question is not one of first impetus. Rather, we want to discover the dynamic that produces the earmarking arrangement in its final form.

Welles points us in the right direction by suggesting that the earmarking arrangement anticipated in *RC* 52 may very well have resembled the one we know from a fragmentary Milesian decree from sanctuary of Apollo at Didyma (*I.Didyma* 488). In fact, the first editor of both documents, Theodor Wiegand, believed that the two inscriptions reflect the same portfolio of honors.[96] What remains of the fragmentary decree from Didyma is concerned with the financing of activities associated with the celebration of Eumenes' birthday, rather than the king's name day during the Panionia. Yet the institutional underpinnings of both royal galas were likely comparable. *I.Didyma* 488 mentions two foundations, one at the beginning of the fragment, the "revenues from the gift funds" ἀπὸ [τῶν πρ]οσό[δων|τῶν ἐκ τῶν δεδωρ]ημένων χρημάτων (lines 2–3), and, later, the "revenues from the maritime loans" ἀπὸ τῶν ὀφειλομένων ἐμπορικῶν|δ]ανείων (lines 24–25). The revenues of the first are earmarked for the festivities of the king's birthday: sacrifices and feasting, a parade of ephebes in full armor, "and everything else according to the *stephanephorikos nomos* (wreath-wearing law) and the *diagraphe* (ordinance) of the priesthood" (lines 13–15). The revenues of the second fund, which are 30 talents of retiring maritime loans, are linked to a grain fund. That fund is to provide for a public grain distribution on Eumenes' birthday. Each Milesian receives six *hemiekteia* of grain in an event that packages together citizenship, commensality, and fealty to Pergamon.

For Welles and Wiegand, the first foundation is certainly royal, while the second is also likely to be so, as it is under the control of two officials

---

[94] For this form of name-day cult (ἡμέρα ἐπώνυμος), see Habicht 1970, 156. [95] *RC*, 217.
[96] Wiegand 1911, 27.

"appointed for the construction of the gymnasium"), one of whom is the same person – Eirenias of *RC* 52 with his Attalid connections. *I.Didyma* 488 may not be conclusive evidence for direct Attalid involvement with the Milesian grain fund, but it illuminates precisely what the statement of Eumenes in *RC* 52 occludes. An earmarking arrangement of enormous ideological import for the king, aiming as it does to implant the king's name in civic memory, rests squarely on Milesian institutions. Eumenes' gift of "sufficient revenues" presupposes Milesian cooperation. The king provides the seed money, while the city grows its own subsidy. This earmarking arrangement needs the public bank of Miletus and its personnel (lines 26, 31); local grain commissioners, who manage the fund in such a way that sufficient grain is produced (lines 17–18); and the legal guardrails provided by the *stephanephorikos nomos* and the *diagraphe* of the priesthood. Also aiding its chances of success are the procedural sanctions that Miletus institutes to protect against its dissolution or the repurposing of the funds (lines 46–49) – and even the facility of the Didymaion, which as the repository of the decree, lends it an aura of the permanent and sacred. Earmarking allowed the Attalids to profit handsomely from the elaborate organizational resources of the Hellenistic polis.

The Meanings of Earmarking in the Attalid Kingdom

If earmarking is a social process that produces meaning by differentiating money, which kinds of meanings did the Attalids manufacture with it? What made it such an attractive and successful solution to the problems of risk, governance, and ideological accommodation for a second-tier Hellenistic power on the rise? In the first instance, earmarking was a familiar fixture from the sphere of religion, which lent it legitimacy. At the most basic level, the practice of pre-designating portions of a sacrificial victim for the consumption of certain priests or particular members of the cultic community must go back far beyond our records in the Aegean. In the Hellenistic period, we know that priests divided up their revenues according to source and slated expenditure. On Kos, an extraordinarily rich picture has now emerged of revenues from the sales of priesthoods earmarked for cultic silverware and furniture, a theater, and other public buildings.[97] We can also look to Delos, where priests took up management of the treasury of the city of Delos for the first time in the year 192, neatly

---

[97] Meier 2012.

using jars to divide funds earmarked by civic decrees for specific public goods, their own working capital, and a reserve (*I.Delos* 399).[98]

Moreover, earmarking specific revenues for cultic activity had long been a way of protecting them from misappropriation by the body politic, future magistrates, or other worshippers with their own ideas about the use of sacred wealth. For example, when the Athenians, in the time of Lykourgos, acquired a windfall, the new and soon-to-be controversial source of revenue known as the Nea, they earmarked it for the cost of the Little Panathenaia (*RO* 81). For Hellenistic and Roman Asia Minor, Beate Dignas has argued for the independence of cultic authorities, their sense of corporate identity, and the autonomy of the sphere of sacred finance in a study of temple administration.[99] Unsurprisingly, earmarking is at issue in one standoff at the heart of her study, the conflict between the priests of Zeus at Labraunda and the Carian city of Mylasa. That earmarking does not seem to have prevented Mylasa from claiming revenues that once belonged to Zeus Labraundeus is telling. Earmarking is one of the means by which priests and city magistrates in Dignas' account articulate their different corporate identities. An earmarking arrangement may for a time place restrictions on public money, or create obstacles to its free employment, but these arrangements can almost always be dissolved. Accordingly, procedures were put in place for safeguarding earmarking arrangements that directed revenues into sacred coffers. The danger was ever present: we can see cities re-earmarking funds time and again through procedures like *metaphora* (reappropriation). The citizens of Delphi may have designated the cash gift of Attalos II as *hiera chremata* (sacred funds) to ensure that a charge of *hierosylia* (shrine robbing) would stick against anyone who diverted them from their original purpose, but they also took the extra step of decreeing fines for anyone who would so much as attempt *metaphora*, "by a vote or otherwise" (*Syll.*³ 672 lines 15–18). An even wider repertoire of procedural safeguards is on full display in the charter of the foundation of Eudemos of Miletus (*Syll.*³ 577 lines 64–66). Finally, in Pergamon itself, aspects of ruler cult in the reign of Attalos III depended on funds of Asklepios designated with the peculiar technical term ἀμέτοιστοι πρόσοδοι – nontransferable revenues (*I.Pergamon* 246 line 19). The Attalids could rely on the sanction of polis religion to endow their earmarks with lasting awe.

---

[98] On earmarking and sanctuaries, see V. Chankowski 2011, 144–59. See also Pafford 2013, for priests' intensive differentiation of monies deposited as cult fees in *thesauros* boxes.
[99] Dignas 2002.

In Hellenistic cities, this administrative routine became a distinctive way to exchange gifts for honors. Of the many ways that Greeks bore gifts, earmarking puts the most emphasis on the creation of long-term bonds. In earmarking, the relationship of the donor to the recipient is conceptualized as everlasting, just as it is continually reenacted with each fiscal cycle. Earmarking puts the future at stake, while also securing it. The Attalids were demonstrating the virtue of providential care precisely when the future lurched into the epigraphic record. For many second-century philanthropists, both royal and civic, a gift's worth was reckoned in terms of providence (*pronoia*). For example, a major philanthropist from Teos named Polythrous took forethought for his city (προνοήσας) when he established a fund for the education of the freeborn youth (*Syll.*³ 57 line 3). Cities honored these benefactors for their providence, not for anticipating a rainy day so much as for troubling themselves with accomplishing the long-term goals of the community, in particular, the creation of continuity by means of regularizing revenue streams.[100] A few fixed points in the city's fiscal landscape could go a long way in reducing anxiety about risk. The acceptance of Attalid earmarks was predicated on this culturally specific approach to risk. Yet the kings still needed to make their case, which is why the language of *pronoia* is so common in Attalid documents.[101] In an exhaustive study of the expression πρόνοιαν ποιεῖσθαι (to take forethought), J.-L. Mourgues even suggests that the formula was in origin a creation of the Attalid chancery, a diplomatic convention transmitted to the Greek-speaking administrators of the Roman province of Asia.[102]

Yet *pronoia* was by no means the preserve of the Attalids in this period. We also find it in the civic epigraphy of Asia Minor: in the 180s in the Maeander Valley (*Milet* I 3 149 line 16) and ca. 140 in Cilicia Pedias (*SEG* XII 511 line 5).[103] One could see here larger-than-life civic benefactors of the later Hellenistic period imitating kings. A priest in Metropolis was praised for his *pronoia*, while the association that honored him dated its documents by the Attalid regnal year.[104] When the settlers of Apollonioucharax ask that "thought be taken for their needs (προνοηθῆναι)," we could see the Attalids snared by their own ideology

---

[100] Byzantine Greek may provide a wider semantic field for administrative *pronoia*, as the word comes to mean "maintenance" or "pension." See Bartusis 2012, 14–31; further on *pronoia* as a Byzantine fiscal concept, see Kazhdan 1995.
[101] E.g., *RC* 53 Fragment II A line 2; *SEG* IV 632 line 4. [102] Mourgues 1995, 432.
[103] On *SEG* XII 511, see also *SEG* LIV 1473. See also, e.g., *SEG* LXII 1489 line 16, from Rhodiapolis.
[104] *SEG* LX 1257 line 7.

(**D2** Side B line 10). However, we now have an example of a different royal chancery boasting of "having taken the greatest *pronoia* (πλείστην πρόνοιαν ποιούμενοι)" in a letter of Seleukos IV, the so-called Heliodoros Stele of the year 178, a text published long after Mourges' study (*CIIP* IV 2 no. 3511 line 14). In fact, the *pronoia* language of the Heliodoros Stele is echoed in several inscriptions from the city of Pergamon.[105] Clearly, the Attalids did not invent the virtue of *pronoia*. Rather, they embraced it, and they chose to emphasize earmarking because the practice instantiated this political ideal of capacious significance. *Pronoia* not only points to the future; it also projects an inclusive vision of the past. When a benefactor boasts of having taken forethought for his beneficiaries, he shares with them the deliberative process behind the gift.[106] By the same token, part of the meaning of earmarking was conveyed through a startlingly transparent vision of the kingdom's fiscal structure: suddenly the subject caught sight of the logic behind royal patrimony. The thin membrane separating the city's patrimony dissolved. In the end, earmarking arrangements bore the traces of social process.

The primary goal of this chapter has been to reveal the dynamics of earmarking in the Attalid kingdom. For Pergamon, the choice of earmarking presupposed knowledge of civic institutions, a drive to get to know them, even a desire to transform them. It also opened up a range of transactions with private individuals, all of which were conducted in the public eye. This encounter with private property owners, as much as the confrontation of city and ruler (*Stadt und Herrscher*), presented its own ideological risks and rewards. Throughout this chapter, the process, negotiation, and contingency behind the earmark have been emphasized in order to highlight the agency of subject communities. Was the Attalid state, then, especially weak? If measured by its capacity to penetrate society, it was in fact remarkably strong. Even the first leviathan-states of the nineteenth century, such as France of the Third Republic, built up their prodigious fiscal capacity by strategically dividing central authority.[107]

Earmarking was neither simple apportionment nor the confiscation of revenues. Nor was it a matter of two states, one hegemonic, dividing up a

---

[105] The language of *pronoia* alone may not give away the Attalid authorship of documents, but I do think it can be used to support dating royal documents to the second century. To give an Attalid example, *Syll.*³ 270 is a letter of a certain King Attalos to the Cretan city of Aptera. The phrase πρόνοιαν ποῆται ("demonstrates providence"; line 3) suggests Attalos II or III. Inscriptions from the city of Pergamon: *I.Pergamon* 167 line 9; *MDAI(A)* 33 (1908) 375,1 lines 13–14.

[106] Cf. Savalli-Lestrade 2003 on the elaboration of royal decisions.   [107] Sawyer 2016.

single revenue base. We can contrast a case from Hellenistic Crete, where the polis of Praisos, having vanquished neighboring Stalai, took for itself half of Stalai's customs dues, but left the rest, as well as "(the revenues of) the land, the city, and the islands that the citizens of Stalai now hold" (*Syll.*³ 524 lines 3–8). In Attalid Asia Minor, earmarking created new sources of revenue, even as it obscured a community's loss of autonomy or the transfer of its surplus to the imperial center. At once parasitic and redistributive, earmarking never involved the complete destruction of a city's tax base or any of its means of cultural reproduction. On the contrary, as both the Korragos Decree and the Toriaion Dossier show, the Attalids preferred to employ earmarking in order to reconstitute or reorganize cities, or in the case of Apollonioucharax, a *katoikia*. Chiefly by rationalizing the impact of royal power on civic finance, this age-old administrative practice contributed to the success of the Attalid imperial project.

2 | The Skeleton of the State

> And when he had gathered the Greeks and all the other peoples who inhabited that part of Asia around Pergamon, as well as those who were present on embassies seeking a treaty, and still others who had been summoned, Antony addressed them as follows: "Your King Attalos, O' Greeks, left you to us in his will, and straightaway we proved better to you than Attalos had been, since we released you from those taxes which you had paid to Attalos, until popular agitators also among us made these taxes necessary. But when they became necessary, we did not impose them upon you according to a fixed valuation so that we could collect revenue without risk, but we required a portion of your yearly harvest, in order that we should share with you the vicissitudes of the seasons. When wronging you the publicans asked for much more, Julius Caesar remitted to you one-third of what you had paid to them and put an end to their outrages: for he turned over to you the collection of the taxes from the cultivators of the soil." (Appian, *B Civ.* 5.1.4) (trans. after Loeb)[1]

This speech of Mark Antony, which the Roman historian Appian places in the triumvir's mouth, was purportedly delivered in 42 BCE at Ephesus.[2] While the aim of the speech was to promote the benefits of Roman rule, it transmits important information about the redistributive political economy undergirding Hellenistic Pergamon's characteristic earmarks. Antony tells us the basics: that the direct taxation of the land and its produce was paramount; that each community was taxed according to a fixed assessment, meaning that the annual rate of taxation will have varied, according

---

[1] τοὺς δὲ Ἕλληνας καὶ ὅσα ἄλλα ἔθνη τὴν ἀμφὶ τὸ Πέργαμον Ἀσίαν νέμονται, κατά τε πρεσβείας παρόντας ἐπὶ συνθέσει καὶ μετακεκλημένους συναγαγὼν ἔλεξεν ὧδε· "ὑμᾶς ἡμῖν, ὦ ἄνδρες Ἕλληνες, Ἄτταλος ὁ βασιλεὺς ὑμῶν ἐν διαθήκαις ἀπέλιπε, καὶ εὐθὺς ἀμείνονες ὑμῖν ἦμεν Ἀττάλου· οὓς γὰρ ἐτελεῖτε φόρους Ἀττάλῳ, μεθήκαμεν ὑμῖν, μέχρι δημοκόπων ἀνδρῶν καὶ παρ' ἡμῖν γενομένων ἐδέησε φόρων. ἐπεὶ δὲ ἐδέησεν, οὐ πρὸς τὰ τιμήματα ὑμῖν ἐπεθήκαμεν, ὡς ἂν ἡμεῖς ἀκίνδυνον φόρον ἐκλέγοιμεν, ἀλλὰ μέρη φέρειν τῶν ἑκάστοτε καρπῶν ἐπετάξαμεν, ἵνα καὶ τῶν ἐναντίων κοινωνῶμεν ὑμῖν. τῶν δὲ ταῦτα παρὰ τῆς βουλῆς μισθουμένων ἐνυβριζόντων ὑμῖν καὶ πολὺ πλείονα αἰτούντων, Γάιος Καῖσαρ τῶν μὲν χρημάτων τὰ τρίτα ὑμῖν ἀνῆκεν ὧν ἐκείνοις ἐφέρετε, τὰς δ' ὕβρεις ἔπαυσεν· ὑμῖν γὰρ τοὺς φόρους ἐπέτρεψεν ἀγείρειν παρὰ τῶν γεωργούντων."

[2] For Antony's "specious plea," see Magie 1950, 165. Further on the perilous practice of using Appian's evidence here, see Pelling 1996, 4, 9–13.

to the quality of the harvest; and he seems to imply that the Attalids did not employ outsiders as tax farmers. Clearly, Antony's rhetorical aim was not to accurately represent administrative details but to persuade *his* new subjects of the superiority of Roman – as opposed to Attalid – imperialism. He outlines two different "tax morphologies" for two different states, with the Attalids functioning as a foil. Nevertheless, the statement of Antony is at least a reminder that fiscal regimes could change suddenly even in the conservative climate of Antiquity. More importantly, it is clear evidence of the contention that had come to surround public choices about taxation, that is, of the existence of a healthy public discourse on taxation. The triumvir had stepped into the late Attalid world. Here, the ruler justified taxation to the ruled, to his subjects whom he flattered from the start by addressing each and every one as a *Hellēn*. Here, he would need to assert the justness of the particular forms of taxation he selected. Here, the Roman would need to tax the inhabitants of Asia like Greeks.

We can safely assume that whatever morsels of veracity are contained within Antony's description of Attalid taxation, the Attalids themselves would have represented their fiscal practices differently. Just so, earmarking, which a modern historian like Rostovtzeff could cast as a bait-and-switch, was a form of beneficent providence in the Attalids' own account of themselves.[3] We have seen that earmarking redistributed the risks of taxation and of provisioning culturally privileged public goods. Yet Antony casts the Attalids as after "revenue without risk (*akindynos phoros*)," shifting risk, in other words, onto the taxpayers, whereas, the Romans, he claims, share the risk. He characterizes the Attalid fiscal assessment (*timema*) as arbitrary and rigid, the Roman state as responsive. With this rhetorical maneuver, Antony focalizes for us what was at stake in the public discourse on taxation: the perception of the distribution of risk between ruler and ruled in a world of endemic shortage. The success of the Attalid imperial project hinged on this perception. Pergamon gave taxpayers a vested interest in the collection of taxes. About earmarks the Attalids would have argued precisely as Antony did about his flat tax: they spread risk.

Yet beyond earmarking lay a range of fiscal practices unmoored from specific public goods and the rest of the fiscal apparatus on which so much depended – the maintenance of king and court, military expenditure, Pergamon's ability to have a seat at the table of high politics. This chapter

---

[3] Rostovtzeff 1930, 605.

analyzes that broader Attalid fiscal system. I argue that what slight evidence we have for its design and for how it worked in practice suggests that Antony's picture is a distortion. Like the process of cobbling together an earmark, the process of assessment was a social one. War, famine, bad harvests – what Antony calls *ta enantia* (adversities) – these were cause for a renegotiation of levels of taxation. In general, royal fiscal modalities were predetermined by civic fiscal institutions, and a patrimonial logic militated against the destruction of the traditional revenue base of the polis. To meet ballooning needs, the incidence of taxation broadened after 188, but it also deepened. Yet where they pursued fiscal intensification, the Attalids succeeded because they prudently relied on revenue from indirect taxes and the exploitation of extra-urban domains long claimed by kings.

Framing the Fiscal Constitution of the Attalids

Premodern fiscal systems as a rule lack the internal consistency of their modern successors.[4] Yet practitioners of the "New Fiscal History" have been able to delineate in broad outline the so-called fiscal constitutions of a wide range of medieval and early modern European states by aiming for "the particular form that a prevailing type of fiscal system takes in a specific country at a given moment in its history."[5] Our evidence simply does not permit such precision for the Attalid kingdom at its acme. We can only guess at the relative importance of different forms of revenue to the system as a whole; our identification of key modalities of taxation must remain provisory. Granted, in a period of 55 years dramatic change, even "fiscal revolution" was possible, as the first century of Roman rule in Asia Minor would show all too clearly. Yet ever more, one tends to see the Attalids adopting the Seleukid system almost wholesale, which means that the study of late Attalid taxation is properly subsumed under the study of fiscality in Hellenistic Asia Minor.[6] The fiscal constitution of the Attalid kingdom is best approached by posing three questions: Which taxes were collected? Who collected them? How much was collected?

To organize our presentation of the Attalid fiscal system, it will be helpful to distinguish between "direct" and "indirect" taxes, a distinction

---

[4] Consider here the nineteenth-century Ottomans' attempt to impose consistency on the fiscal system of Anatolia, as analyzed by İslamoğlu 2004.
[5] Bonney 1999, 5; see also Bonney 1995; Ormrod et al. 1999; Monson and Scheidel 2015.
[6] Schuler 2004b.

that will prove salient for assessing the grand strategy of the Pergamene kings. Véronique Chankowski has argued persuasively that these were not the foundational categories for the ancient Greeks themselves.[7] However, they do allow us to identify patterns and, ultimately, to place the Attalids in a comparative historical perspective. By direct taxes, we mean taxes on income, property, and persons, which are generally tailored to the taxpayer. By indirect taxes, we mean taxes on consumption, exchange, and mobility, which often allow "shifting," whereby one taxpayer can shift the tax burden onto another by raising prices, or shift away altogether by avoiding certain economic activities.[8] The use of the term *tax* to the exclusion of *tribute* also requires a word of explanation. To oversimplify, taxes imply reciprocity and redistribution, to which the epigraphy and architecture of Attalid Asia Minor well attest. Tribute, by contrast, is a mark of subjection, a one-way transfer from periphery to center. The difference between the two forms of extraction, it should be noted, was often in the eye of the beholder. It is a distinction that is articulated on two planes: both in discourse and in economic or institutional reality. The success of the Attalid imperial project depended on the kings' ability to persuade their subjects that it was taxes, not tribute, which they were after.[9]

Direct Taxation

Of direct taxes, the two most important will have been those that struck at the productive capacity of the land.[10] These were of two kinds: taxes levied on whole communities, reckoned in silver money, and taxes on certain categories of land, reckoned as a percentage of output or property value. For the first, we have only a single notice, the letter of the future Attalos II

---

[7] V. Chankowski 2007, 305. Her lexical study both assails the anachronism of the terms "direct" and "indirect" taxation and seems to admit their utility by confirming the widely held view that Greeks preferred what we call indirect taxation.

[8] For "shifting," see Einhorn 2006. Einhorn also underscores how fraught the debate on what constitutes direct taxation has been in US history, a constitutional inheritance from the thought of early modern Europe; for a discussion of the history of the direct-indirect problem in which the individual characteristics of the taxpayer makes the difference, see Atkinson 1977.

[9] For tax, tribute, and redistribution, see Briant 1989; for V. Chankowski (2007, 306–7), certain "prélèvements" are more "tributaires" than others, which seems to mean, for her, a greater mark of subjection. She points in particular to the ubiquitous *phoros*. The *phoros*, however, was at times redistributed, as when Antigonos Monophthalmos offered Teos and Lebedos grain from *phorologoumene chora* (RC 3 line 83).

[10] As Ps.-Aristotle writes of the six species of (satrapal) revenue: αὐτῶν δὲ τούτων πρώτη μὲν καὶ κρατίστη ἡ ἀπὸ τῆς γῆς ("Of these the first and most significant is revenue from land") (Arist. [*Oec.*] 2.4).

to the Pisidian city of Amlada, ca. 160 (*RC* 54; **D12**). There, Attalos first speaks of an annual tax payment of 2 talents (τῶν δύο ταλάντων ἃ τελεῖτε κατ' ἐνιαυτόν) (line 7). He later seems to characterize the same payment as φόρος καὶ τέλεσμα (lines 13–14). That collocation, *phoros kai telesma*, calls to mind the similarly enigmatic phrasing of the first decree of Teos for Antiochos III and Laodike III, probably of 203, which praises the king for designating the city as *aphorologos* and releasing the citizens from the *syntaxeis* of Attalos I (*SEG* XLI 1003). While the citizens speak of ὧν ἐφέρομεν συντάξεων ("those *syntaxeis* we used to pay"; line 19), Antiochos speaks of ὧν συνετάξαμεν φόρων ("those *phoroi* we have assessed"; lines 33–34). The task of distinguishing *phoros* from other levies called *syntaxis*, *telos*, *telesma*, and so on, has proven exceedingly difficult, especially in light of a comment of Polybius on the Treaty of Apameia:

> ὅσαι μὲν τῶν αὐτονόμων πόλεων πρότερον ὑπετέλουν Ἀντιόχῳ φόρον, τότε δὲ διεφύλαξαν τὴν πρὸς Ῥωμαίους πίστιν, ταύτας μὲν ἀπέλυσαν τῶν φόρων· ὅσαι δ' Ἀττάλῳ σύνταξιν ἐτέλουν, ταύταις ἐπέταξαν τὸν αὐτὸν Εὐμένει διδόναι φόρον.

> Whichever of the autonomous cities had earlier paid *phoros* to Antiochos, and had then kept faith with the Romans, the Romans released them from *phoroi*. Those cities which had paid *syntaxis* to Attalos I, the Romans ordered them to give the same *phoros* to Eumenes II. (21.46.2–3)

For the ancients, we know, each term carried different connotations. Classical Athens provides a case in point. During a second go-round of empire, known as the Second Athenian League, Athens' leaders substituted the term *syntaxis* in deliberate contradistinction to the earlier Delian League's *phoros*.[11] Put simply, contribution sounds better than tribute. The scholarly debate is over just how fungible the fiscal lexicon was in practice. Most scholars have given up on trying to recover a distinctive institutional reality behind each term.[12] Yet the connotations are elusive, too. The payment of *phoros* was clearly a mark of subjection, but as Polybius suggests, political *autonomia* was not incompatible with this way of taxing – or talking about taxation. Still, it may be possible to draw

---

[11] *RO* 22 line 23; Plut. *Sol.* 15.2; Theopompos of Chios, *FGrHist* 115 F 98 with discussion of V. Chankowski 2007, 324–25.

[12] E.g., on the problem of defining *eisphora*, Gauthier writes, "La plupart du temps … les modalités d'assiette de ces contributions nous restent inconnues" (Gauthier 1991, 67, with n. 93); Capdetrey 2004, 107–11, represents the view that *phoros*, *syntaxis*, and *telê* can refer to the same institutional reality, while V. Chankowski (2007, 324–28) argues for a differentiated institutional reality and semantic limits; see further Schuler 2007.

a few concrete conclusions about the nature of the *phoros* in the Amlada letter. First, in terms of incidence, this tax falls on the community as a whole. Ultimate responsibility for payment may fall on elites like Oprasates, an ambassador of the Amladeis who happened to enjoy the Attalids' favor (line 12).[13] However, the *phoros* of the Amlada letter is exacted from the community, and it also seems to have been assessed on that basis. The polis as collective forms the basic taxable unit. Second, in terms of punctuality, far more than any of these other terms, *phoros* implies regularity and indeed perpetuity, hence κατ' ἐνιαυτόν (annual) payment.[14] The annual payment of 2 talents, while not explicitly named *phoros* in Attalos' paraphrase of the Amladeis' request, is likely just that. What is less clear is whether the remission of a half-talent ἀπὸ τοῦ φόρου κα[ὶ] τε[λέ]σ[ματ]ος ("from the *phoros* and *telesma*") will be subtracted in its entirety from the *phoros* sum.[15] Unless the pairing is simply hendiadys, the introduction of the term *telesma* raises the specter of a broad range of indirect taxes and irregular contributions. Attalos may have had something very specific in mind by *telesma*: corvée labor, quartering, or grain. Yet the promise to subtract the 2 talents ἀπὸ τοῦ φόρου κα[ὶ] τε[λέ]σ[ματ]ος introduces an element of ambiguity. It will have allowed the Amladeis room to maneuver. They may have been able to shift the burden, or at least spread the benefit of the half-talent remission around their local economy.

That direct taxation of the polis invariably took the form of a collective obligation in cash, on the model of Amlada, has come in for debate in light of the puzzling final lines of the second letter of Eumenes II to Toriaion (**D8** lines 43–47). Eumenes, we recall, had set in place an earmarking arrangement, which "for the present" routes revenue from the *agoranomia* into an oil fund for the gymnasium. The arrangement is envisioned as temporary: ἕως ἂν|ἐπισκεψάμενος Ἡρωίδης ὁ ἡμιόλιος ἀποτάξη ἑτέραν,|ἐάν τε ἀπό τινος κτήματος ἢ χώρας, ἐάν τ' ἀφ' ἑτέρου ε[ὐ]|δοκιμάζηι, καὶ τῶν πάντων γενημάτων φέρειν [τὴν]|δεκάτην.[16] The central problem is the

---

[13] In the case of the Tobiads of the tale told by Flavius Josephus, Joseph the Tobiad put to death the nobility of Ascalon in order to force the community to pay the Ptolemies arrears (*AJ* 12.181).

[14] Typically, scholars juxtapose the irregularity of the *syntaxis* to the regularity of the *phoros*, but the ambiguity of *SEG* XLI 1003 in this regard is cause for caution; for κατ' ἐνιαυτόν, cf. *SEG* XXIX 1516; on the other hand, the *syntaxis* of **D3** line 10, the so-called Attalid poll-tax, is clearly annual.

[15] This is the general assumption of scholars, e.g., Virgilio 2008, 217.

[16] Austin 2006 no. 236: "until such time as Herodes 'one and a half' investigates the matter and determines other sources of income, / whether from some property or piece of land or any other

relationship of the last clause to what precedes, and as of yet, no one has clarified the grammar. φέρειν is clearly an imperatival infinitive, but the conjunction καί seems redundant. Only Schuler has argued for breaking the connection with the instructions for an official, the *hemiolios* Herodes. Provocatively, he proposes that the land in question, subject to a tax of one-tenth on all of its produce, has nothing to do with the land (*chora* or *ktema*) designated by Herodes to replace with its revenues the *agoranomia* as the source of the royal earmark.[17]

On this interpretation, the one-tenth "of all agricultural products" is the general tax rate on all land in the new polis of Toriaion and its territory. Were Schuler right, this would imply that the individual landholders of Toriaion all paid a *dekate* directly to the royal fisc, though perhaps payments were pooled into a single sum. However, as Helmut Müller points out, the conjunction ἐάν ensures a relationship between the two clauses: whether Herodes chooses this *ktema* or that *chora* – whichever piece of property he ultimately chooses – it will pay the one-tenth on all of its produce. As we shall soon see, the convention of royal administration was rather to tax the different products of the land at different rates. Thus the mention of the *dekate* is a further articulation of the revenue demanded of the land that one day will be set aside for the oil fund. Eumenes either was prescribing an unusual tax rate for that land or was emphasizing that it remained subject to the *dekate* over and above its contribution to the gymnasium. Either way, this text does not prove the existence of an alternative to the method of direct taxation of the polis known from Amlada. The Toriaion letter does not support the claim that the Attalids took 10% of all agricultural production in a polis, even a nascent "subject" polis, since the land in question will have been royal property or a royal dependency – the details are left up to Herodes to decide – which lay outside, but necessarily in the vicinity of, Toriaion's territory. Exactly as Antony boasted of the Romans in Appian's account, the Attalids left to the communities themselves the right of taxing agriculture on their territories.[18]

---

he might choose, on which a tenth of all the produce would be levied." Note that this translation takes no account of καί. Similarly, Bencivenni 2003, 336: "in modo che (da qui) si raccolga la decima di tutti i prodotti."

[17] For interpretations, see *SEG* XLVII 1745; Philippe Gauthier *BE* (1999) no. 509; Jones and Ricl 1997 (ed. pr.), 26–27; Schuler 2004b, 535 n. 194. Müller (2005, 356–58) declares the problem an *aporia*. For this tenth as instead a civic tax, see Reger 2007, 464 n. 16.

[18] Jonnes and Ricl 1997, 27: "In Tyriaion [*sic*], even after its promotion to the status of a Greek city, the tax of ten per cent of the harvest seems to have remained in force, and this can be

Direct taxes were also levied on plots of land (*kleroi*) assigned to military settlers (cleruchs). We have already had occasion to discuss the *katoikia*-type towns in which they lived. Under the Attalids, such towns came increasingly to resemble poleis, with respect to both territoriality and institutions. From the case of the *katoikia* of Apollonioucharax and its various dependent villages (**D2**), we can see that these communities raised revenues of their own.[19] Individual cleruchs seem to have paid the king tax on their allotments. The key text here is *RC* 51 (**D13**), a letter to cleruchs holding plots in the hinterland of Pergamon, dated by Welles to the second century. Each *kleros* included arable and vine-land. The produce of that land was taxed variously. A proportion of the harvest was demanded, a twentieth from the vines (*eikoste*), and a tenth (*dekate*) of the grain and "the other fruits" (τούτων εἰ[κοστήν, ἐκ δὲ το]ῦ τε σίτου καὶ τῶν λοιπῶν καρπῶν δεκά|την; lines 16–17). We also know that the settlers at Apollonioucharax paid an annual tithe of 10%, the *dekateia*, from which they were *all* released (for one year?) by Attalos II (καὶ τῆς ἐφ' ἔτους δεκ[α]||τείας παρεθήτωσαμ πάντες) (**D2** Side A lines 22–23).[20] In contrast to the citizen of a polis, the cleruch paid an individuated tax on the produce of the land. In the end, it was land that he had received from the king.

There is reason to suspect that the tax liability of a *kleros* was in fact greater than the annual tithes of 5, 10, or 12% reported in the sources, if we can extrapolate from the details of the valuation of the estate of Mnesimachos, from third-century Seleukid Sardis (*I.Sardis* 1). In an influential treatment of that inscription, Raymond Descat has argued that the gift-estate (*dorea*) allotted to Mnesimachos was subject to both an annual tithe of a notional 10% and a *phoros* reckoned as one-twelfth of the cash value of the estate.[21] Thonemann has modified Descat's conclusions

---

interpreted as another favour from the king eager to increase the prosperity of the new city by prescribing a more equitable taxation of its soil." I can see no reason why this *chora* or *ktema* should be in polis territory, which is the basis for using the text to generalize about how the Attalids taxed poleis. Yet why should Toriaion then be privy to the information in lines 43–47? On the one hand, this is a side effect of an epistolary habit: a kind of internal memorandum is embedded within the royal letter. On the other hand, the information may have been publicized because Herodes' ultimate decision will have affected local claims on royal land. One thinks here of the distinct possibility of reappropriation of a gift-estate envisioned in the case of Mnesimachos (*I.Sardis* 1). The power brokers of Toriaion, perhaps even the ambassadors named in the dossier, were being given notice.

[19] On civic finance in rural Asia Minor as a historiographical blind spot, see Walser 2015, 413–17.
[20] ἐφ' ἔτους is translated "this year" in Thonemann's text (Thonemann 2011a), but cf. the ed. pr. of Herrmann and Malay (2007, 52) for the alternative translation "annual," as in the "annual 1/10 tithe."
[21] Descat 1985.

slightly, casting the *phoros* as one-twelfth of the cash value of the produce of the *nonarable* part of Mnesimachos' estate.[22] It is of course conjectural whether the system of "mixed *phoroi*," an Achaemenid inheritance, which Thonemann sees as standard for early Hellenistic gift-estates, can simply be assumed for late Attalid cleruchic land. Yet the language of lines 16–17 of **D13**, concerning land just outside Pergamon, suggests that the mixed-*phoros* regime was indeed retained under the Attalids.

On the one hand, we have tax rates for two specific crops, grapes and grain, corresponding to the two different forms of land granted, *gê psilê* and *gê ampelon*. On the other hand, we have one tax rate for "the other crops (τῶν λοιπῶν καρπῶν δεκά|την)." This "tenth" on the non-vine and nonarable parts of the allotments may not be a tithe at all, but a fixed sum of cash, the *argyrikos phoros*, paid annually in addition to one-tenth of the land's grain and one-twentieth of the produce of its vines. On this account, each year, instead of delivering to the royal fisc one-tenth of his figs, fruits, and nuts, all the sundry perishables of his allotment, the cleruch makes a single cash payment. This is in essence an arbitrary figure, but it is understood as one-tenth of the cash value of those "other crops." To carry one step further the analogy with Mnesimachos and also with the estate of Krateuas of Gambreion, if the cleruch alienates the land, a possibility that our text envisions (**D13** lines 25–27), he transfers this bundle of fiscal liabilities too.[23] Thus in doling out fertile plots to cleruchs, the Attalids chose a traditional – and administratively efficient – land tenure regime, not dissimilar to the one employed by their predecessors on their gift-estates. And like the owners of those earlier gift-estates, the cleruchs were tethered to the monetary system of their kingdom via the mixed-*phoros* regime. If, as we shall argue, the cistophori appeared simultaneously with the buildup of a belt of *katoikia*-type towns in the 160s, then these new communities, sited remotely at the heads of river valleys and the edge of the Anatolian steppe, were from the beginning linked to the kingdom's urban centers, the cities which issued the coinage in which the settlers perforce paid an important part of their taxes.

Beyond its poleis and *katoikia*-type towns, Anatolia contained vast stretches of territory worked by populations bound by different relationships to the Attalid state. Some of these were organized on a regional basis,

---

[22] Thonemann 2009, 385–89.
[23] Krateuas' estate is the subject of Thonemann 2009, which adduces it to explicate Mnesimachos'; we also possess a lamentably fragmentary land conveyance document from Pergamon, which speaks of *gê psilê*, *I.Pergamon* 230. It may also have spelled out fiscal liabilities.

and identified themselves as a *demos* or an *ethnos*; others were organized as villages, either attached to gift-estates and sanctuaries or even, one now admits, independent.[24] Presumably, all of this land might have been taxed, although we have next to no evidence from the period of Attalid control.[25] It may have been that the different populations related to royal fiscal authority through different channels, depending on the status of the land they farmed. For example, in a dossier of the future Attalos II from 185 concerning the settlers (*katoikoi*) of Apollo Tarsenos in the upper Kaikos Valley, the cult's high priest seems to play a significant role in securing a grant of tax privileges (*RC* 47; **D14**).[26] Were such priests also collecting tax on sacred land and transmitting a portion to the crown?

This would make sense, given the implied dependence of the *katoikoi* of Apollo Tarsenos on the sanctuary and the close connection of local priests to Attalid officials tasked with sacred affairs. The fiscal system of the Attalids certainly preserved the power of the old priesthoods, but it also seems to have monitored the priests' finances ever more closely. This is best observed north of Sardis in the sanctuary of Apollo Pleurenos, where two inscriptions reflect the Attalids' interaction with a community of initiates (*mystai*), arrayed under the local priests. One local priest goes so far as to obtain permission to put up a stele inscribed with the initiates' names, submitting his request to a royal official called *archiereus* (high priest) (*SEG* XLVI 1519). The post seems to have been taken over from the Seleukids, but the nature of the request signals an intensification of control. Another priest honors a local man, ὁ ἐπὶ τῶν ἱερῶν προσόδων (overseer of sacred revenues), which may suggest that the Attalids refined the Seleukid system,

---

[24] In an important contribution, Schuler 1998, 160–80, contests the century-old dogma that these communities were all subject either to a polis or directly to the king. That dogma is a correlate of the view that private property did not exist outside the polis and its territory, only the royal domain of *chora basilike*, the meaning of which is itself a subject of dispute (see Mileta 2008, 8–19). Schuler replaces this dichotomous picture with a highly differentiated one. Yet all of the communities he describes are understood to have paid *phoros* to the crown: "φόροι leisteten nicht nur die λαοὶ βασιλικοί, sondern Dorfgemeinden, δῆμοι und ἔθνη verschiedenster Couleur, und die χώρα βασιλική war deshalb nur ein Teil der χώρα φορολογουμένη" (p. 171).

[25] Schuler 1998, 162, though often in Schuler's work the reconstructed Seleukid system is assumed to have obtained under the Attalids, and Attalid evidence is used conversely to shed light on the earlier period; for the panoply of taxes and liturgies to which these non-polis communities were subjected, our best example is the royal document discovered just outside Aigai, Malay 1983 (*SEG* XXXIII 1034). However, the identity of the king and the precise nature of the community are both uncertain. See Chandezon 2003, no. 52; cf. Descat 2003, 160–65.

[26] A similar context is suggested by Schuler (1998, 193–94) for *RC* 69, a very fragmentary letter of Attalos III to the *katoikountes* of Hiera Kome near Tralles, granting, so it seems, a form of *ateleia* (tax immunity).

adding a layer to the hierarchy in order to increase access to sacred wealth (*SEG* XXXII 1237).[27] Yet as Robert suggested, the source of that wealth is likely to have been the fecund Lake Koloe/Gygaia, not land.[28] In sum, direct evidence for the taxation of the majority of cultivable land in the Attalid kingdom is unavailable.

We know that the Attalids levied a tax on persons, now commonly termed a poll tax or a head tax. This is what Ps.-Aristotle calls the *epikephaleion* or *cheironaxion*, while the epigraphy of Greek cities generally speaks of taxes on the body or person (*soma*), as in the expression ἀτέλεια τοῦ σώματος (immunity from personal tax).[29] Our only direct indication of an Attalid poll tax is the letter of Eumenes II of 181 concerning the fiscal status of the inhabitants of a village called the Kome Kardakon, in western Lycia, adjacent to the polis of Telmessos (**D3**).[30] The Kardakes were required to pay an annual tax in cash, referred to euphemistically as a *syntaxis* (contribution), on "each adult person (ἑκάσ|του σώματος ἐνηλίκου)" (lines 10–11).

Two other inscriptions suggest the practice was not out of the ordinary. In Apollonioucharax, the Attalids raised an annual (?) *eisphora* (**D2** Side A line 24). That this *eisphora* was not a collective obligation but a poll tax is implied by the fact that it fell not on the entire adult population but only on certain registered settlers.[31] The other comparandum also comes from western Lycia, but its author and addressee are both a matter of dispute.

---

[27] As suggested by Dignas 2002, 53; for *SEG* XXXII 1237, cf. *SEG* LV 1300; also, in connection with these two documents, see *SEG* IV 632, honors for Timarchos, the former Attalid *riskophylax*, a high financial official at court, appointed *neokoros* of Artemis at Sardis under Eumenes II.

[28] Robert 1982, 366. One could very easily imagine a similar situation surrounding the dedication of the inhabitants of the Attalid *katoikia* of Daphnous, where a shrine of Apollo Daphnousios was located. (Tanrıver and Kütük 1993). Schuler (1998, 191), in an exhaustive study of these terms, assimilates these people to "Tempeldörfer." In other words, the settlement is based around the shrine. This is all taking place on the southern shore of Lake Apolloniatis, perhaps not "in the territory of Apollonia ad Rhyndacum," as Tanrıver and Kütük allege. In fact, the decree may represent honors for (Attalid?) officers, a *doryphoros* and a *strategos* for precisely the service of excluding Daphnous and its resources in the lake from the fiscal territory of Apollonia; cf. Habicht 1956 on "Attalos" and sacred land of Aizanoi.

[29] Arist. [*Oec.*] 2.4: these are revenue "from the people (ἀπὸ τῶν ἀνθρώπων)," the sixth form of revenue in the satrapal *oikonomia*; for the 10 cases of civic taxes τοῦ σώματος, see Gauthier 1991.

[30] For Maier (1959–61, vol. 1, p. 258), the Kome Kardakon fell within the territory of Telmessos. Cf. Schuler 1998, 192: the village was near Telmessos, but itself situated in *chora basilike*.

[31] For *eisphora* as poll tax, see Gauthier 1991, 67 n. 93. Thonemann (2011a, 6) conjectures that, as on the Athenian model, these may have been the wealthier inhabitants of Apollonioucharax. Is the *eisphora* annual or is the remission "for this year?" The question turns on the interpretation of **D2** Side A line 22: ἐφ' ἔτους.

This is the royal document first published by Michael Wörrle as a fragment of a letter of Eumenes II or Antiochos III to the city of Telmessos (*SEG* XXIX 1516).[32] Certain members of an unnamed community, artisans who seem to be "recently arrived," are released from the *cheironaxion* on condition that they take up a public service called *(h)orophylakia* (τοῦ χειρωναξίου παρεθήσονται οἱ μεταπορευ|[όμε]νοι τεχνῖται τὴν ὀροφυλακίαν αἱρόμε[νοι]; lines 7–8). Again, we know from Ps.-Aristotle that the *cheironaxion* was a tax on persons, applied discriminatorily, as we can see from this document, on certain craftspeople.[33] The question here is the status of the taxpayers and the tax authority. Wörrle hypothesized that the artisans in question were metics, which would make the *cheironaxion* a civic tax of Telmessos, albeit one that the king summarily abolishes.[34] Others have countered that the text is rather an analog to that very letter of Eumenes II concerning the Kardakes and their poll tax (**D3**), which makes the addressee a royal official and the community at issue a *katoikia* or *kome* (village), but certainly not a polis.[35]

In sum, the evidence permits us to posit an Attalid poll tax for certain populations discernible within non-polis communities. Ideologically, taxation of these persons was risk-free. Administratively, however, all Hellenistic bureaucracies faced a shortage of knowledge about such people, relying on the dragnets of temples, craft guilds, and military institutions to identify them and collect their poll tax. So it is hazardous in the extreme to assume the direct taxation of persons was universal, or even consistently applied outside the polis. As Philippe Gauthier writes of one of the scarcely attested civic poll taxes, "Though the Greeks were hardly consistent, one is tempted to believe that here too the *épiképhalion* was related to war, or was at least episodic."[36] The royal poll tax may not have been any more regular, and one can supply a multiyear crisis of Galatian troubles or other wars as the historical context for each of the confirmed Attalid cases.[37] Yet in quest of quantitative models of royal economy in Asia Minor, one has been

---

[32] Wörrle 1979.
[33] In other words, it is not a tax on practicing a craft as such, or on craft output, as the name might suggest. Thus for V. Chankowski (2007, 308), it is a form of "capitation."
[34] Wörrle 1979, 94.
[35] Jean and Louis Robert *BE* (1980) no. 484. They translate μεταπορευ|[όμε]νοι as "recently arrived."
[36] Gauthier 1991, 62.
[37] A parallel from the civic context would be the "Galatian fund," τὰ Γαλατικά. It was regular enough, at least in the case of Antiochos II and Erythrai, to have been accounted for in a portfolio of fiscal exemptions, but it is juxtaposed with all the ordinary royal taxes collected in the polis. See comment of Welles at *RC* 15 line 28. For this tax, see also *SEG* XXXVII 923 line 41.

tempted to make the leap, even though we know how variegated the political landscape of inner Anatolia must have been.[38] It is preferable to understand these direct taxes on persons as part of a greater fiscal burden that included inheritance taxes on cleruchic land and various corvée labor obligations, from which only the name and ideology of the polis provided ultimate defense.[39] Meanwhile, even for non-polis communities, the typically ad hoc character of these exactions made the poll tax a subject of negotiation with the king, as the case of Apollonioucharax demonstrates.

Indirect Taxation

For taxation of the exchange and movement of goods we are better informed. Yet both of our key texts from the context of sale require commentary. In the case of Toriaion, the revenue (*prosodos*) earmarked for the oil fund is termed, ambiguously, "from the *agoranomia*" (**D8** line 43). That institution, however, is usually translated "the office of *agoranomos*."[40] Accordingly, *SEG* translates in line 43, "the revenue accruing from the office of *agoranomos*." Naturally, the office governed exchange in the market, but did the *agoranomos* raise a tax on sale? Does the Toriaion dossier in fact demonstrate that the Attalids taxed sale? Much of the evidence for the function of such magistrates relates not to sale but instead to the maintenance of social order in the market, price regulation, the enforcement of standards of quality and measurement, and the adjudication of disputes.[41] For example, an *agoranomos* from Hellenistic Tralles is honored

---

[38] For example, see Aperghis 2004, 164–66, on Seleukid head taxes. Crowns offered up by poleis to kings were in his view head taxes. He then notes our sole evidence from the Seleukid kingdom for tax "on the *kephalē*," the problematic testimony of Joseph. *AJ* 13.49, asserting finally, "Therefore a royal head tax (ἐπικεφάλαιον) on a city's citizens and slaves is quite possible, although not attested." For the Attalids, Mileta (2008, 208–18) models on the assumption that the entire population outside the cities was taxed in the same manner as the Kardakes.

[39] For inheritance taxes levied on cleruchs, see **D13** lines 25–26; for corvée labor, note that the Kardakes are themselves responsible for the repair of fortifications, and Eumenes II only promises to send a foreman (*technitēs*) (**D3** lines 17–20); clearer indications of corvée obligations come from Seleukid documents, e.g., the *phoros letourgikos* of the Mnesimachos inscription (*I.Sardis* 1 Column I line 12); see also the *ergazomenoi* (laborers) of the Aigai royal document (Malay 1983 = Chandezon 2003, no. 52 = *SEG* XXXIII 1034 Side B lines 2–3).

[40] This sensible translation is based on, e.g., *I.Magnesia* 269, *I.Iznik* 1260, or, perhaps most germane, *I.Pergamon* 183. See Jonnes and Ricl 1997, 5; Dmitriev 2005, 24.

[41] Citing Arist. [*Ath. Pol.*] 51.3–4, but also a wider body of evidence, Bresson (2007–8, 22) summarizes the duties of the *agoranomos* in the following way: "de veiller à la régularité des transactions effectuées sur le marché." From Athens, there is no clear testimony that the *agoranomos* collected sales taxes. See Rhodes 1993, 575–76; cf. Aperghis 2004, 285, suggesting sales tax at Toriaion. This is an unsettled debate with roots in the nineteenth century.

exclusively for jurisprudence (*I.Tralleis* 32). A third- or second-century *agoranomos* from Metropolis dedicated a measuring table.[42] It is then likely that a portion of the *agoranomia* revenue of Toriaion came from fines.[43] On the other hand, it is explicit neither in the text nor in any of the comparanda adduced in the *editio princeps* that the rest of the revenue came from sales taxes, from the farming out of those taxes, or from what are commonly called "market dues."[44] Sales taxes are well known from Greek public finance.[45] Yet to associate them with the office of *agoranomos* is to ignore a large body of evidence, particularly rich from Hellenistic Delos, that points to the enforcement of market rules, some of which were no doubt fiscal, as the primary duty of the magistrate.[46]

Our best evidence for an Attalid tax on sale is the aforementioned dossier concerning the high priest and *katoikoi* of Apollo Tarsenos (**D14**). It is important to note both the nature of the community, cult dependents, seemingly without a polis as overlord, as well as the specific occasion. This has been shown by Adolph Wilhelm and Piejko (against Welles) to be a festival, the *panegyris* restored in lines 4 and 12 of Text A.[47] The inscription merely records that Attalos awards the cult community *ateleia probatôn*, a tax remission on livestock (Text A lines 5–6 and Text B line 4). This could mean freedom from a head tax on livestock or their progeny, from customs levied on the movement of livestock across political boundaries, or from sales tax. Rostovtzeff read here a head tax, and indeed Christophe Chandezon's analysis of Greek civic taxes on pastoralism shows

---

[42] Aybek and Dreyer 2012, 208–9.   [43] As emphasized by Dmitriev 2005, 34.
[44] Jonnes and Ricl 1997, 24: "the revenues collected through the office of *agoranomoi*, the bulk of which came from taxes on sales (τὰ ἀγοραῖα τέλη, ἐπώνιον, ἀνδραποδικόν), taxes on the registration of documents, as well as revenues produced by tax farming and fines." However, they do not provide the evidence to support this conclusion. For τὰ ἀγοραῖα τέλη, they cite a proxeny decree from Zeleia that provides immunity from these market taxes. The phrase has been restored by Matthias Barth and Josef Stauber in *I.Mysia (und Troas)* 1137 and 1138, in place of H. G. Lolling's ἔγγαια τέλη in *MDAI(A)* 9 (1884) 59–60. Nowhere does that text speak of *agoranomia* or an *agoranomos*. More to the point, they cite *I.Erythrai* 503, a third-century decree that sets out rules for the maintenance of the statue of the tyrant-slayer Philitos, which is to be set up in the agora. There, the charge of the *agoranomos* is to keep the statue clean and to attend to the production of honorific crowns. The officials (restored) in lines 27–28 are to sell the contract (*ônê*) for the production of the crowns in the course of the year.
[45] Andreades 1933, 144–46; on sales tax and royal administration, see Kaye 2015.
[46] For Delos, see Vial 1984, 232–35; and further, Bresson 2006. From late Hellenistic Athens, the agoranomic inscription from the Piraeus illustrates nicely the twin concerns of price regulation and measurement. See Bresson 2000, 151–82, and cf. the measuring table dated with an inscription by two *agoranomoi* to 143/2 from Marisa (Idumaea), Finkielsztejn 2010.
[47] Piejko 1989.

direct taxation predominates, either on pastures or on the animals themselves.[48] On the other hand, Chandezon's evidence for *royal* taxes on pastoralism points toward indirect taxation as the norm, and the festival surely provoked the movement of large numbers of animals toward the shrine of Apollo and precipitated their sale. Accordingly, with the festival more firmly established in the restoration of the text, scholarly opinion has settled on an interpretation of sales tax.[49]

As for customs duties, we can surmise that the Attalids, like most in the premodern Mediterranean, relied heavily on what amounted to taxes on mobility and interdependence.[50] We catch sight of the customs regime already ca. 280–275, when Cyzicus honors Philetairos for a grant of tax immunity on the movement of livestock and other wealth into his territory, as well as on the export of purchased animals (*OGIS* 748 lines 8–12). In order to make sense of the fact that the territories of Cyzicus and Philetairos were not contiguous, but in fact separated from each other by Seleukid territory, Christophe Chandezon suggests transport by sea, making the tax an *ellimenion* of some kind collected in the Pergamene port and satellite city Elaia.[51] Yet the fiefdom of Philetairos need not have shared a border with Cyzicus for the dynast to have claimed customs on the flocks that the Cyzicenes shepherded into his territory in time of war. We know from contemporary interstate agreements from Crete that pastoralists en route from one polis territory to another routinely crossed the territory of a third city.[52] Moreover, Hellenistic Asia Minor was a patchwork of different fiscal authorities, the kind of place that is not easily represented on a textbook map. In the end, it matters little whether we place the customs house of Philetairos in Elaia or on his northern frontier. The point is that the fiscal territoriality of the Attalid state had already taken shape at this early stage.

After 188, the Attalids extended their customs regime over much of the territory allotted to them at Apameia. This is evident in the long inscription from Ephesus known as the Customs Law of Asia (*CLA*), which is a

---

[48] Chandezon 2003, 309–30; Rostovtzeff 1941, 1440.

[49] Chandezon 2003, 196, though cf. 315, allowing for the possibility that it is a head tax; Piejko 1989, 400; Schuler 1998, 193: "Verkaufsteuer auf Schafe, von der Festmarkt befreit werden sollte."

[50] Purcell 2005.

[51] Chandezon 2003, 186; see V. Chankowski 2007, 313–19, for the vocabulary of the *ellimenion* harbor tax.

[52] Making it of course desirable to obtain fiscal privileges from the third city as well. See Chaniotis 1999, 196–204.

Neronian compilation of regulations on the collection of customs in the Roman province of Asia.[53] The first version of this accretive and palimpsestic document may date all the way back to the years 129–126 BCE, during which the Romans first organized the province. If so, it captures an image of the kingdom of Attalos III at the very moment when the proconsul Manius Aquilius received and began to reshape it. That the *CLA* transmits information about the late Attalid kingdom is not in doubt. However, one has not completely disentangled the Attalid bits from the rest.[54] Stephen Mitchell has shown that the scope of the first version of the law, which includes the Bosphorus and Pamphylia, both regions that did not belong to province of Asia in Nero's time, gives away an Attalid template.[55] After all, long before Pompey organized the province of Pontus and Bithynia, much of the Bosphoran territory covered in the *CLA* had belonged to Pergamon. As for Pamphylia, the Attalid hold on this region has been questioned, but not their claim.[56] Nevertheless, the Attalid template has its unresolved problems. For example, in a section on import and export by sea, the *CLA* lists coastal cities with customs stations, moving in geographical order south and southeast from the Bosphorus to Pamphylia, but passing through Caria along the way (lines 23–26). It seems unthinkable that these coastal Carian cities in the heart of the Rhodian mainland territory (*peraia*) ever belonged to the Attalid kingdom. In other words, regrettably, we cannot discern an Attalid core to the *CLA*.[57]

---

[53] Ed. pr.: Engelmann and Knibbe 1989; for authoritative edition and commentary, see Cottier et al. 2008.

[54] Cottier et al. 2008, 4 n. 4: "M. H. Crawford notes that the order of the clauses in ll. 9–69 excludes the possibility that we have to do *simply* with an Attalid nucleus and a Republican supplement."

[55] Mitchell 2008, 167–69.

[56] It is common to adduce Livy 44.14.3-4 as proof that Pamphylia was free of Pergamene control by or at least after 169 when certain ambassadors (*legati Pamphylii*) approached the Roman Senate "to renew the alliance (*amicitiam renovare*)" – e.g., Meadows (2013, 186–87), who argues that Attalos II conquered Pamphylia in the 150s. For in-depth treatment, see McNicoll and Milner 1997, 118–19; Gruen (1984, 90) also takes these for the Pamphylians of southwest Asia Minor. It is possible that Livy's *Pamphylii*, who follow a delegation of Gauls, and whose ethnic is reported variously in the manuscript tradition as Pampyli and Pamphyli (see Briscoe's Teubner), are tribesmen not of Asia Minor but of Transalpine Europe. There may be a numismatic clue to their identity in Livy's description of their gift: a crown of *philippi*. On the entire Pamphylian question, see conveniently Hopp 1977, 104–6.

[57] Cf. Mitchell (2008, 192), who dates the list of harbors in lines 23–26 to the 120s, given the inclusion of Pamphylian cities, which belonged to the original Roman province of Asia. However, the inclusion of cities of Caria in the *CLA* remains problematic because Caria seems to have entered the Roman province of Asia decades later, in 84 BCE after the First Mithridatic War. See Marek 2016, 277.

That disclaimer notwithstanding, the *CLA* is crucial for our reconstruction of the Attalid customs regime. The first of two key passages, lines 26–27, follows immediately after the list of maritime customs stations:

ὁ κατὰ γῆν εἰσάγων ἐν τούτοις τοῖς τόποις προσφω|[νείτω καὶ ἀπογραφέσθω ἐν οἷς ἂν τελώνιον τοῖς ὅροις τῆς χώρα]ς πρὸ τῶν βασιλείας ἢ ἐλευθέρων πόλεων ἢ ἐθνῶν ἢ δήμων ὑπάρχῃ, ἐπὶ τοῦ τελώνου ἢ ἐπι- vacat

The person importing by land [is to] declare [and register], in those places [in which] there is [a customs station on the boundaries of the land] formerly of <the> monarchy or of free cities (*poleis*) or of peoples (*ethnê*) or of communities (*demoi*). (trans. M. H. Crawford in Cottier et al. 2008)

The extent to which Hellenistic customs regimes targeted the transport and smuggling of goods by land has been underappreciated.[58] This passage depicts the interior of Asia Minor as a patchwork of fiscal zones, each of which contained its exaction points. Navigating them all may have cost traders more than a simple import and export through coastal harbors. There is no consensus on how to understand these four categories of land, introduced from the end of the lacuna. It is especially difficult to see what makes these cities "free," but they are obviously not free of a customs regime imposed from above.[59] The origin of all four, however, seems to lie in the Attalid kingdom, which treated separately with poleis, *ethnê*, and *demoi* in the interior, all the while directly governing certain rural lands, termed here, as restored, *chora basileias* ("land of the monarchy"). In fact, the tripartite collocation of poleis, *ethnê*, and *demoi*, to which the Romans here add former royal land, seems to anticipate the membership of the Koinon of Asia. It suggested to the document's first editors that an inheritance from the Attalids lay behind the Koinon.[60]

Clearly, the Attalid kingdom contained within its political boundaries a patchwork of fiscal zones. No single, contiguous customs barrier surrounded Attalid territory. On the political frontiers, not only in the busy Aegean harbors, but also in the mountainous Mysian borderlands opposite Bithynia, or in the Maeander corridor running through Tralles, the Attalids surely exacted customs. The *CLA* pulls the curtain back on the interior, which proves to be riven with enclaves of royal fiscal authority, in addition to royal land, a variety of polities that stood in various relationships of

---

[58] See Chandezon 2003, 312, with n. 20, *contra* Andreades 1933, 148; Francotte 1909, 11–12.
[59] See the discussion of Mitchell 2008, 184–87.   [60] Engelmann and Knibbe 1989, 73–74.

dependence to the kings. In fact, the Attalid state had no interest in rendering all of this territory fiscally homogeneous. The taxation of goods moving between the many different zones of the interior was sufficiently profitable to justify investment in physical infrastructure. As a matter of shared sovereignty, the best point of comparison is the federative koinon. For example, the Lycian customs law from Andriake, also emanating from Nero's reform, shows that while the Lycian Koinon collected one set of customs in the various harbors, a part of which were sent on to Rome, the constituent poleis also raised their own dues.[61]

A second passage from the *CLA*, lines 67–70, which mentions Attalos III by name, shines a light on the infrastructure of taxation:

> ἐποίκια|[καὶ σταθμοὺς βασ]ιλικοὺς οὓς βασιλεὺς Ἄτταλος Εὐμένους υἱὸς τελωνίας χάριν ἔσχ[εν] ὁ [δ]ημο[σιώνης] οὕ[τως] καρπευέσθω. ταῦτά τε ὁποῖα ἂν παραλάβῃ||[τῷ ἐσομένῳ δημ]οσιώνῃ ἢ ἀνδρὸς ἀγαθοῦ ἐπικρίσει παραδιδότω{ι}. vacat αἵτινες πόλεις ἔθνη ὑπὸ βασιλεῖ Ἀττάλ[ῳ] Εὐμένους υἱῷ οὐκ ἐγένοντο, ἐν οἷς τόποις ἢ|[μερίσι (?) τῆς Ἀσία]ς τελῶναι κατὰ τὸν τῆς μισθώσεως νόμον ἀπογράψασθαι προσφωνῆσαι δεήσει, τούτων ἐν ἑκάστῃ πόλει πρὸς θαλάσσῃ, εἰς τὸ προσ- vacat

> With respect to the buildings and royal [staging posts] which king Attalus the son of Eumenes had for the purpose of exaction of *telos*, [the *publicanus*] is to use (them) [as he (the king) did]; and he is to hand over *viri boni arbitratu* to [the incoming] *publicanus* whatever of these he may take over. Whatever cities and peoples were not under King Attalus the son of Eumenes, in whatever places or [regions (?) of Asia] it is necessary to register with or declare to a collector according to the *lex* of the *locatio*, in each city by the sea there. (trans. Crawford in Cottier et al. 2008)

Unfortunately, even here, the evidence for the Attalid system may not be unadulterated. Mitchell takes the passage as the very end of the first version of the law, drafted perhaps between 129 and 126, while Helmut Engelmann and Dieter Knibbe give a *terminus ante quem* of 75.[62] Crawford holds out the possibility that these lines are a post-Sullan supplement to the original

---

[61] See Takmer 2007 for a detailed summary of the unpublished text, esp. p. 176 for lines 41–45 (on the taxation of saffron) as a reproduction of fiscal conditions in the Hellenistic period. For the Seleukid kingdom, it has long been recognized that multiple customs regimes were operative within the political boundaries of the *basileia*. See comments of Dreyer and Engelmann, *I.Metropolis*, 51–52. See further on the customs law of Andriake – and on federal sovereignty over taxation in a koinon that includes both coastal and landlocked member poleis – Mackil 2015, 495–96.

[62] Mitchell 2008, 200; Engelmann and Knibbe 1989, 89.

document, pointing out that the lacuna at the beginning of line 70 makes it particularly difficult to generalize about the Attalid kingdom, since we may have lost a reference to parts of the province of Asia that had not belonged to Pergamon.[63] Still, we receive precious information about the built environment of royal customs collection. The Attalid infrastructure appears substantial: two different sets of structures, the *epoikia* and a plural masculine supplement for βασ]ιλικούς, for now, the vague *stathmoi* (barracks, stables, or the like).[64] From the instructions to register and declare in each city by the sea in their absence, we can recognize these as maritime customs houses, either in poleis or in the coastal territory of *ethnê*. From the perspective of the *CLA* (and no doubt for the inhabitants of Attalid Asia Minor, too), the presence of these structures was a mark of subjection. Yet the text does not permit us to place those poleis and *ethnê* without royal customs infrastructure outside the kingdom – or even beyond the reach of its fiscal authority. As these very lines from the *CLA* remind us, the same state can collect the same tax with or without its own infrastructure; Roman tax farmers were required to make use of old Attalid customs stations *if available*. The Attalids, by contrast, seem to have created a new infrastructure for tax collection, increasing surveillance and revenues. A measure of transparency was also gained, an encouragement to the very quasi-voluntary compliance that Nero was pursuing. Yet to be clear, the Attalid customs houses did not delineate the political or economic boundaries of the Attalid state.[65]

Saltpans, Lakes, and Lagoons

Our evidence for Attalid taxation includes two references to coastal lagoons and lakes containing saltpans – and presumably much else of value

---

[63] Cottier et al. 2008, 126.
[64] Ed pr.: δούλους, as preferred restoration, meaning that Rome also took over slaves who served as royal customs agents. Subsequent commentators have rejected the suggestion; the replacement of ed. pr.'s ἐσ[τήσατο] with ἔσχ[εν] precludes certainty that the Attalids built this infrastructure, though it seems likely.
[65] Cf. Engelmann and Knibbe, who depict (1989, 90) a single customs barrier encircling the kingdom, which therefore operated as a closed market ("ein geschlossener Binnenmarkt") and a closed currency zone. This is more than an unjustified extrapolation from this particular text. As Chapter 3 argues, no closed currency zone existed in Attalid Asia Minor, while this broader concept of closed "national" markets in ancient Greece, here protected by a customs barrier, has played a long and even insidious role in scholarship. See Laum 1933, which conscripts the ancient Greeks to demonstrate the virtue of not just autarky but closed markets.

besides.⁶⁶ This is a special case both because indirect and direct taxation were combined in the exploitation of this domain, and because it represents one of our best opportunities to register fiscal intensification, as well as outright confiscation, topics to which we shall return. The first episode involves the city of Priene, which at the beginning of the first century BCE disputed with certain Roman tax farmers called *halonai* over revenues from saltpans (*haleai*) in a coastal lagoon in the Maeander Delta called the Gaisonis.⁶⁷ For our purposes, the following is the significant passage of the honorific decree for Krates (*ISE* 182 = *I.Priene* 111 Column XVI lines 112–17):

> [...... c.16 ...... ἃ π]ρότερο[ν] εἰργάζετο βασιλεὺς Ἄτταλος, οὔτε διακατέχει ὁ δῆμος ἡμῶν οὔτε|[ἡ σύγκλητος ἐξουσίαν οὐ]δεμίαν εἰς τοὺς δημοσιώνας πεποίηται· τὰς δὲ κατασκευασθείσας ὑφ' ἑαυ|[τοῦ ἁλέας τὰς ἀνακειμέ]νας ἐκ πλείονος χρόνου τῆ Ἀθηνᾶ τῆ Πολιάδι, ἃς κατέχει καὶ καρπίζεται|[ὁ δῆμος, ἀνέσωσεν, π]αρακαλῶν τὸν ἀνθύπατον τοῖς μὲν ὑπὸ τῶν ἁλωνῶν λεγομένοις μὴ προσ|[έχειν, ἀκέραια δὲ ἐᾶσ]αι τῶι δήμωι τὰ πράγματα, μέχρι ἂν ἐπιγνῶμεν τὸ κριθησόμενον ὑπὲρ| [αὐτῶν ὑπὸ τῆς συγκ]λήτου

> .... which earlier King Attalos worked, and which neither our People possesses nor has the Senate granted to tax farmers as a concession. About the saltpans that he [Krates] had fitted out himself, which had long ago been reserved for Athena Polias, which the People currently possesses and exploits, he asked the proconsul not to listen to the things said by the *halênai*, but to preserve untaxed (ἀκέραια) (the saltpans) for the People until we know the Senate's decision on the matter.

To divine the Attalid role here we are required to imagine what it was King Attalos (II or III) had exploited earlier, since the object of εἰργάζετο is lost in the opening lacuna. In her study of salt in the Greek world, Cristina Carusi lends little credence to a restoration of saltpans. She notes the text's juxtaposition between, on the one hand, the saltpans that Priene claims it possesses and exploits and, on the other, whatever King Attalos was working.⁶⁸ Yet, as Thonemann argues, what is contrasted here is rather two different historical property claims on two different saltpans. In one

---

⁶⁶ On the "underestimation of Mediterranean wetlands," see Horden and Purcell 2000, 186–90; Marzano 2013.
⁶⁷ Von Gärtringen's text was significantly amended by Holleaux 1907, 387. De Rossi's *ISE* text is the most recent and reproduced here. There is some dispute over the identification of the contested saltpans as the Gaisonis, on which see Carusi 2008, 83; with Van Rookhuijzen 2018, 279, on the location.
⁶⁸ Carusi 2008, 237.

case, the Attalids staked a claim, perhaps rooted in a confiscation of Alexander, rather than in a confiscation of their own. The Attalid claim gave the Roman tax farmers legal ground to stand on. In the case of the Gaisonis it had – by contrast, so the argument goes – always belonged to Priene, always been exploited by its citizens, and always been reserved for Athena Polias. Thus Thonemann, invoking those same lines 67–68 of the *CLA* just discussed, restores the lacuna: [τὰς μὲν ἁλέας τὰς βασιλικὰς, ἃς π]ρότερον εἰργάζετο βασιλεὺς Ἄτταλος. "the royal saltpans, which earlier King Attalus had worked."[69]

The second episode occurred in Ephesus, which, Strabo tells us, won its own dispute with tax farmers over the "great revenues (*megalai prosodoi*)" of a seaside lake called Selinousia, as well as a second, contiguous lake:[70]

> Μετὰ δὲ τὴν ἐκβολὴν τοῦ Καΰστρου λίμνη ἐστὶν ἐκ τοῦ πελάγους ἀναχεομένη (καλεῖται δὲ Σελινουσία) καὶ ἐφεξῆς ἄλλη σύρρους αὐτῇ μεγάλας ἔχουσαι προσόδους, ἃς οἱ βασιλεῖς μὲν ἱερὰς οὔσας ἀφείλοντο τὴν θεόν, Ῥωμαῖοι δ' ἀπέδοσαν· πάλιν δ' οἱ δημοσιῶναι βιασάμενοι περιέστησαν εἰς ἑαυτοὺς τὰ τέλη, πρεσβεύσας δὲ ὁ Ἀρτεμίδωρος, ὥς φησι, τάς τε λίμνας ἀπέλαβε τῇ θεῷ.

> After the outlet of the Kayster there is a lake next to the sea. It is called Selinousia, and just after, confluent with it, is another lake. They provide great revenues, which though they were sacred, the kings confiscated from the goddess. But the Romans gave them back. And then the tax farmers took the taxes for themselves by force. Artemidoros went on an embassy, so he says, and got the lakes back for the goddess. (14.1.26)

Consensus holds that "the kings" who confiscated the sacred lakes were the Attalids.[71] We know that already in the archaic period, the temple of Artemis Ephesia raised revenues on salt (*I.Ephesos* 1). If those same revenues belonged to Pergamon after 188, this would represent a major reconfiguration of power in the Kayster Delta. The particular products that provided these revenues have been the subject of debate. Yet it is more than unhelpful to quibble over whether the revenues came from salt, fish, or

---

[69] Thonemann 2011b, 329, with n. 85 for restoration; 327–32 for the historical context, as well as observations on the intensive exploitation of the rich saltpans in the Maeander Delta in Ottoman times.

[70] Strabo seems to locate the lakes north of the Kayster estuary. See Davies 2011, 180, for the lakes and the patrimony of Artemis Ephesia.

[71] See Radt 2002–11, ad loc.; Debord 1982, 148. Moreover, Strabo has just referred to Attalos II at 14.1.24. Proof that Strabo could refer to the Attalids as "the kings" comes at 14.1.39, the distich of Daphitas the grammarian. He was crucified for poking fun at "the kings" for descent from a treasurer of Lysimachus, i.e., Philetairos.

other sources.⁷² It obscures the multifaceted character of the ecological niche exploited by the Attalids in the hinterland of both Priene and Ephesus. A useful point of comparison is the so-called Little Sea (*mikrê thalassa*) near coastal Iasos, which was far more than a large fishing ground, but also a source of salt and seasonal pasturage on a regional scale.⁷³ Moreover, human mobility across these coastal lagoons produced revenues. A fine example from our period was then known as the *Iônopolitikos Kolpos*, but today as the inland Lake Bafa due to coastline change, poised between Miletus and Herakleia-under-Latmos. In the late 180s, those two cities jointly farmed a τέλος τῆς πορθμίδος (ferry tax) on the marshy gulf (*Syll.*³ 633 lines 100–104).⁷⁴ One quickly understands why Roman tax farmers resorted to violence: only with arms could they wrest these places away from owners as powerful as the goddesses Athena Polias and Artemis Ephesia. These were lucrative monopolies, though we should not extrapolate from the evidence of Priene and Ephesus a universal Attalid monopoly on salt, compulsory purchase of salt, or a salt tax as head tax.⁷⁵ Fundamentally, these were taxes on the usage of distinctive natural resources (*enkyklia telê*). Under the Attalids, the revenues of certain coastal lagoons, the mainstays of local economies, were absorbed into the royal patrimony.⁷⁶

The Personnel of Tax Collection

One of the lessons of Mark Antony's tendentious gloss on the tax history of Asia Minor is the significance of the state's choice of collection agents.

---

⁷² Thonemann (2011b, 331) tentatively suggests fish rather than salt here, though he, as is the norm, pairs this text with the aforementioned *I.Priene* 111 in his interpretation; Carusi (2008, 85) cautiously reads salt among the revenues of the lakes described by Strabo, but rightly, as one part of a portfolio of resources; Debord 1982, 148: fisheries.

⁷³ Vacante 2011, 333.

⁷⁴ It is tempting to interpret similarly the dispute mentioned in *I.Priene* 111 line 129, τὸ κατὰ τὸν εἴσπλουν, which traditionally has been understood as maritime passage into the Gaisonis past the Mykale Peninsula. However, Carusi (2008, 82–83) disassociates this dispute from the quarrel over the saltpans in lines 112–17.

⁷⁵ Precisely what Aperghis (2004, 154–56) suggests for the Seleukid kingdom; cf. review of evidence in Carusi 2008, 202–35.

⁷⁶ We might also consider the taxation of these coastal lagoons in terms of what V. Chankowski (2007, 310–13) calls "taxes d'usage," in her view, those described in the sources as *enkyklia telê*. Finally, a minor miscellany of other taxes has been deemed Attalid. In particular, Crawford (1985, 160) suggests that two Roman-period taxes were originally Pergamene, but having examined both the "door tax" of Caesar *BCiv.* 2.32.2 and the "nail tax" from Aphrodisias (see Reynolds 1982, no. 15), I cannot determine what makes them Attalid.

This was not simply a matter of choosing the most efficient agents, but of engineering compliance. As with rates and economic incidence, personnel choices affect the perception of fairness in taxation. As the Greeks knew incredibly well, tax farming had its advantages, chiefly, the off-loading of risk, but also the outsourcing of assessment and surveillance.[77] Tax farming was ubiquitous in the public finance of the cities and non-polis communities of Hellenistic Asia Minor, so much so that it would be otiose to enumerate examples. As is well known, the problem with tax farmers is that they are hard to control; their abuses can lead to diminishing returns, as taxpayers lose their appetite for compliance. This is of course precisely what happened in Asia Minor of the Late Republic. Indeed, Antony admits that the Italian tax farmers acted outrageously. Yet had the Romans not acted outrageously – in the first place – by farming out agricultural taxes to outsiders? This put basic sustenance in the hand of men "unknown and unaccountable."[78] Perhaps, and hence the corrective: Julius Caesar turned over to the communities of Asia Minor the responsibility for the collection of those taxes. This prompts the question of whether these communities had known an imperial power to tax them through its own tax farmers, rather than demand lump sums and fixed percentages of revenues, which the communities themselves collected through their own, internal tax farming or by other means; that is to say, whether the institution of *royal* tax farming ever existed on any significant scale in Hellenistic Asia Minor.[79]

---

[77] "Incredibly well," because we see in Ptolemaic Egypt the sophisticated innovation of using tax farmers to guarantee returns and supervise the system, without actually using tax farmers to collect the taxes themselves. This system may have also existed in Ptolemaic Cyprus, Cyrenaica, and the Levant. See Bagnall 1976, 6, 240.

[78] Consider an incident from early American history, in which Rhode Island resisted paying a federal impost in 1783. Rhode Island's legislature found the collection of the tax by agents "unknown and unaccountable" to be in violation of the state's constitution. See Einhorn 2006, 139.

[79] "On any significant scale," because we know of tax farming in Ptolemaic enclaves such as Lycia. According to Bagnall (1976, 227), it was the norm there. For the specific taxes and documentation, see Domingo Gygax 2001, 174, on *OGIS* 55. His discussion of the process at work in third-century Telmessos, which was a Ptolemaic *dôrea* ruled by semi-autonomous dynasts, provides several useful points of comparison (pp. 167–82). There, we know of tax farmers called *dekatônai*, who presumably collect a *dekatê* (*OGIS* 55 line 19). And we know that the Ptolemies farmed out in Alexandria the tax collection for their possessions in Lycia (*P.Tebt.* 8). Yet we have reason to believe that many of the tax farmers were local Lycians. In the case of one tax, the πορφυρική, the Ptolemies specify in *P. Tebt.* 8 that the tax farmer is a Lycian. Domingo Gygax also suggests that the *dekatônai* of *OGIS* 55 may be local subcontractors or that the tax was sold locally in the first place (p. 175). In other words, as Rostovtzeff (1941, 338) once

Since the Attalids took over so many Seleukid administrative practices after 188, it makes sense to ask the question first of the earlier period. Little has changed since John Ma admitted, "It is still not clear whether Seleukid indirect taxation was farmed out."[80] Yet G. G. Aperghis can write, "There is no specific mention in the sources of the use of Seleukid tax-contractors, other than the high priests of Judaea, but one cannot discount the possibility, certainly for the revenue of cities."[81] In the case of the Attalids, the evidentiary basis has in fact changed of late, as the honorary decree for Apollonios from Metropolis (ca. 144) has been published and pored over (*I.Metropolis* 1 Side B; **D5**). One of Apollonios' services to his community concerns a tax dispute (Side B lines 18–23):

ὑ|πὲρ τῶν ἐφευρισκομένων ἡμεῖν τελῶν ὑπὸ τῶν ὠνησαμένων τὰ διαγώγι|α τοῦ Καϊστριανοῦ λιμένος, εἰς ἀγωνίαν καὶ ταραχὴν παραγενομένων|ἡμῶν τὴν μεγίστην, ὑπολαβὼν ἴδιον εἶναι τὸ συμβεβηκὸς ἐλάσσωμα τῆι πό|λει, πάντα παριδὼν τὰ καθ' ἑαυτόν, ὑπέστη παρακληθεὶς καὶ τὴν πρὸς τούτους|διάκρισιν, δι᾽ ἧς ἐτήρησεν τὴν ὑποκειμένην ἐν τοῖς τέλεσιν φιλανθρωπίαν.

(And) with reference to the taxes devised for us by those who had bought (the right to levy) the tolls of the Kaystrian harbor [*sic*], when we had fallen into the greatest anxiety and perturbation, (Apollonios), considering the loss that had befallen the city to be his own, neglecting all his own concerns, when called upon underwent judgment against these too, through which he preserved the established concession in the matter of the taxes. (trans. C. P. Jones 2004)

Here is a dispute between anonymous tax farmers and the polis of Metropolis, submitted to royal judgment (*diakrisis*). Presumably, a representative of the king heard the case, perhaps the *strategos* in Ephesus, whose title as invoked elsewhere in a dedicatory inscription portends involvement: "the *strategos* appointed over Ephesus and the places around Ephesus and the plain of the Kayster (ὁ στρατηγὸς ἐπί τε Ἐφέσου καὶ τῶν κατ᾽ Ἔφεσον τόπων καὶ Καΰστρου πεδίον)" (*SEG* XXVI 1238 = *I.Ephesos* 201).[82] The nature of these taxes and the fiscal privileges of Metropolis

---

argued, the model put forth in the "Tale of the Tobiads" (Joseph. *AJ* 12.4.1–11), of royal tax farming administered through local elites, may actually also fit Ptolemaic Asia Minor.

[80] Ma 1999, 139 n. 120.
[81] Aperghis 2004, 283. Note further that Aperghis' characterization of the priests of Judaea as tax contractors/farmers under the Seleukids (as opposed to tax *collectors*) is highly debatable. See Honigman 2014, 352–61.
[82] That this official may have heard the case is suggested in both the ed. pr. and Jones 2004, 476.

underlying the conflict require scrutiny. It is generally agreed that τῶν ἐφευρισκομένων ἡμεῖν τελῶν in line 18 means new taxes that had been contrived *for* the Metropolitans. Boris Dreyer and Engelmann argue in the ed. pr. that these taxes were produced *for the benefit* of the Metropolitans; and, so their argument goes, the tax farmers violated the right of the polis to the new revenue by not transmitting it. C. P. Jones, who marshals all the evidence for grants of portfolio of tax immunities (ἀτέλεια τῶν πασῶν προσόδων, κτλ.), often tailored to specific local economic conditions, sensibly reinterprets the "invented taxes" as a violation of a particular fiscal immunity.

To a certain extent, this helps us to make sense of the tax, τὰ διαγώγια τοῦ Καϊστριανοῦ λιμένος ("the *diagôgia* of the Kaystrian harbor") – the cancellation of which was absolutely vital for the citizens of Metropolis. They argued that the *diagôgia* – whatever it was – did not apply to them.[83] As the name implies, this is a tax on passage, a tax on mobility of some kind. Is it a tax akin to that on *diagôgimos sitos* in Kyme, the taxable grain in-transit (*SEG* L 1195 line 9)? It is difficult to be more precise, as the term is an epigraphical hapax.[84] Yet the confidence of Jones that this is "a toll on goods conveyed through the 'Caystrian harbor'" is perhaps not unwarranted. Jones places that harbor in the territory of Ephesus, which is to say, at the mouth of the Kayster. Since tiny Metropolis lay upriver, the city relied on a major coastal harbor under the control of a regional rival for its basic needs (**Map 2.1**). In fact, the *limên Kaïstrianos* must be a harbor in

---

[83] *Contra I.Metropolis*, 54. The editors see in this *diagôgia* a toll ("Maut"), which Metropolis has the privilege of charging. On their interpretation, as a "subject city," Metropolis does not raise its own customs dues ("Gebühren"), a point to which we shall have occasion to return. Instead, it has the privilege of exacting this toll on passage through its harbor, on river traffic and land traffic – since they make much of the fact that the Kayster is not perennially navigable.

[84] "Hapax," because restoration [διαγ]ώγιον in *I.Milet* 54 line 15 is tentative; for *diagôgê*, we have, e.g., of people: τῶν ἀνδρῶν διαγωγὴν in *BCH* 13 (1889) 334,4 line 36; and *diagôgê* of goods, as is fairly well attested in proxeny decrees, e.g., *I.Magnesia* 91 line 19. Neither the English word "toll" nor "customs" captures the standard interpretation of Ps.-Aristotle's (ἡ πρόσοδος) ἡ ἀπὸ τῶν ἐμπορίων καὶ διαγωγῶν (Arist. [*Oec.*] 2.1.5). This can be found in Velissaropoulos 1980, 214–15, under "péages." Velissaropoulos sees in *diagôgai*, "droits de passage levés sure les marchandises en transit." This tax is supplementary to the usual customs dues, *pentakostê*, etc. As for *diagôgion*, it does occur in Polybius in the context of the Byzantine episode ca. 220 (4.52.5). Polybius first describes a Byzantine *paragôgizein* (4.47.1), but later describes their extraordinary tax as a *diagôgion* on those sailing to the Pontus (4.52.5). Strabo (4.3.2) writes of quarrels between communities in Gaul over τὰ διαγωγικὰ τέλη, which Velissaropoulos is agnostic about. The gloss of Jones 2004, 477, "tolls on goods conveyed through the 'Caystrian harbor," captures well the philological difficulty.

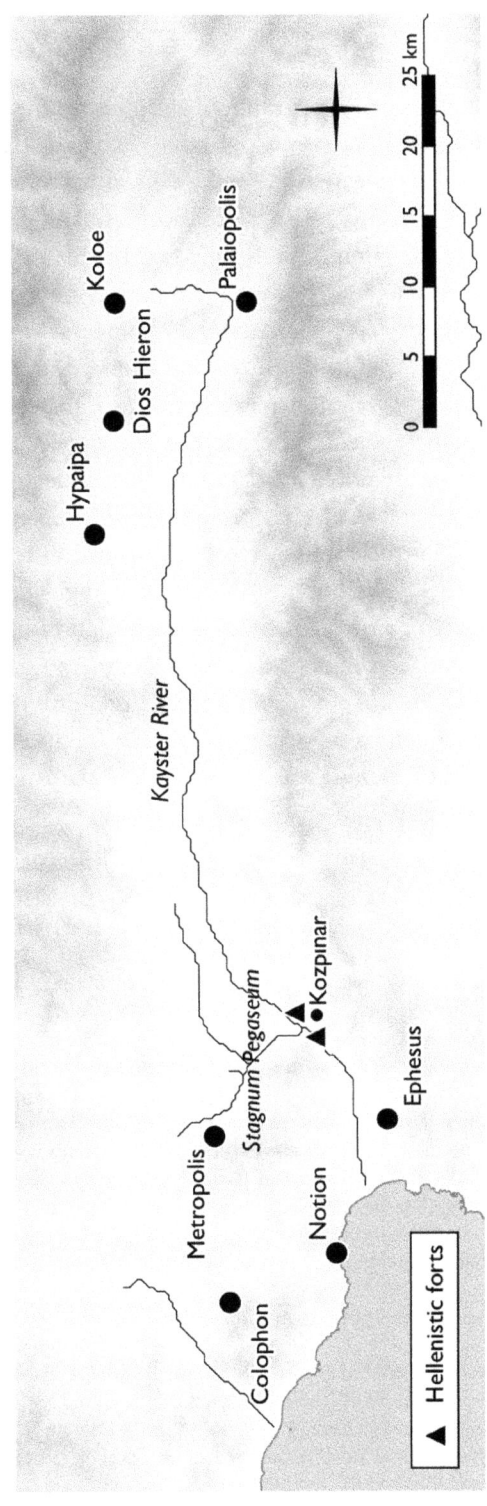

Map 2.1 The Kayster Valley. (After Roelens-Flouneau 2019, fig. 36)

99

the Kayster Delta. For to the Metropolitans, their local harbor would have been simply ὁ λιμήν.[85]

The extra designation, Καϊστριανοῦ, may help identity the anonymous tax farmers. Both Jones and the text's first editors suggest that these are royal tax farmers.[86] To be clear, by "royal tax farmers," we mean tax collectors who answer directly to royal authorities, and who are not necessarily members of the communities they tax. In this case, such men would have been stationed in the Kayster Delta, having purchased the *diagôgima* tax farm directly from the Attalids. The decree for Apollonios would then be the first, unique, positive indication that the Attalids employed royal tax farmers.[87] Yet it is unlikely to be so. Instead, we should see here tax farmers of the polis of Ephesus, who likely collected both civic and royal taxes, even if we are not in a position to determine how to classify the *diagôgima*. In general, the same civic personnel routinely collected both royal and civic taxes.[88] Furthermore, Metropolis' choice to leave Ephesus and its territory out of its description of the tax is telling. Their language, τὰ διαγώγια τοῦ Καϊστριανοῦ λιμένος, recalls the titulature of the Attalid official who may have judged the case: ὁ στρατηγὸς ἐπί τε Ἐφέσου καὶ τῶν κατ' Ἔφεσον τόπων καὶ Καύστρου πεδίον. In the titulature, the Kaystrian plain is conceptually distinct from the city of Ephesus and its environs. The so-called Kaystrian harbor as much as the Kaystrian plain represents the

---

[85] The epigraphical evidence is overwhelming: poleis rarely qualify their harbors with toponyms. Athens is one obvious exception, which speaks of λιμένος τοῦ ἐν Ζέᾳ (e.g., *IG* II² 835 and 1035); or we have a named harbor precisely in the context of a dispute, as in the Megarid, where Aigosthenai and Pagai both claimed Panormos (λιμένος τοῦ Πανόρμου) (*SEG* XIII 327). Note that Roelens-Flouneau (2019, 101–2) places the "Kaystrian harbor" of the decree at inland Kozpınar, with its two Hellenistic forts, from which the Ephesians would have surveilled the confluence of the Kayster with a tributary that may have been navigable in winter as far as Metropolis itself. Therefore, the harbor of Metropolis would have been the Stagnum Pegaseum (Celat Gölü).

[86] *I.Metropolis*, 55: "Die Erhebung der Maut war augenscheinlich (vom König oder in dessen Auftrag) verpachtet an Unternehmer, die jenseits der festen Pachtsumme, die an den König oder abzuführen war, mit der Zielsetzung einer möglichst hohen eigenen Gewinnspanne arbeiteten"; for Jones (2004, 477), the tax collectors are "probably royal"; cf. Chandezon 2004, 141–42, which does not treat *I.Metropolis* 1, but suggests that royal *telônai* did not exist in Hellenistic Asia Minor, offering the same interpretation of Antony's speech on this score as that advanced here.

[87] It may be objected that tax farmers appear at Apollonioucharax (**D2** Side B lines 8–9): "Those who may have already sequestered funds (τινες πράξαντές τινα αὐτοὶ κατεισχήκασι)." As the conditional clause implies, the Attalid state does not have full knowledge of their operations or perhaps not even full control over them. These are *local* tax farmers.

[88] For royal and civic taxes collected together, e.g., *SEG* XXXVII 859 Column III lines 2–4, the earmark of oil for the gymnasium of Herakleia-under-Latmos, which comes from the farmed-out harbor tax. See discussion of Wörrle 1988, 460–63.

supra-poliad perspective of the monarchy.[89] For the Ephesians, this may have been just another *limên*. Therefore, the citizens of Metropolis assumed the royal perspective as a way of enlisting Attalid power on their side, as embodied by the *strategos*. Part of this official's brief was keeping the peace in an ecology on which several communities had claims, namely, what the Attalids called the Kaystrian plain.[90] In an analogous fashion, citizens of the poleis of Metropolis, Colophon, and Ephesus, among others, would have all sought passage through the Kayster Delta. The task of the *strategos* of the Attalid state, in the final analysis, was to minimize the resultant strife – especially since royal revenues were at stake.[91]

The king himself did not dispatch tax farmers to collect these revenues from communities, but he did employ royal officials in a fiscal apparatus. Hovering above, and seemingly apart, was the *strategos*. We have noted the possibility that a *strategos* judged the dispute between Metropolis and the unnamed tax farmers. We are on firmer ground in two other cases. It was Korragos, στρατηγὸς τῶν καθ' Ἑλλήσποντον τόπων, who requested fiscal privileges of Eumenes II for the unnamed community of **D1**. Moreover, while it has long escaped notice, another clue as to the role of the *strategos* in fiscal politics may be found in the fragmentary dedicatory inscriptions from the epistyles of two stoas on the steep Theater Terrace at Pergamon (*I.Pergamon* 152–55).[92] The fragments of *I.Pergamon* 152A + B clearly read προσόδων ("revenues"), which is echoed, albeit in smaller letters, on 154B. As a restoration of the title of the dedicant for 154A, Max Fränkel suggested [στρατηγ]ὸς τῆς κ[ατά] κτλ., on the model of στρατηγὸς τῆς Χερρονήσου καὶ τῶν κατὰ τὴν Θράκην τόπων (*I.Sestos* 1; paralleled in *OGIS* 330). Since Fränkel's time, new comparanda for this titulature have come to light, the aforementioned dedication from Ephesus (*SEG* XXVI 1238)

---

[89] Chaniotis (2010, 458–60) suggests that the term *topos* already places us outside polis territory.

[90] Note that while Strabo (13.3.2) conceives of the Kaystrian plain as part of the Ephesia, the Attalid imperial geography of *SEG* XXVI 1238 distinguishes it from the *topoi kat'Epheson*. The plain has an interesting role to play in Attalid imperial geography. Note that in the upper Kaikos Valley, it may even have been possible to form an ethnic from a plain, the Apias Pedion, part of the modern Balıkesir Plain. See the ephebic list form Pergamon, *MDAI(A)* 35 (1910) 425,12 Column II line 5: Ἀνδρικὸς Ἀσκληπίδου τῶν ἐξ Ἀπιασίωνος ἀγροῦ.

[91] On fierce inter-polis ecological competition in the region, see Robert and Robert 1976. Cf. *SEG* XLVIII 1404, which documents charges of abuse leveled against tax farmers from Colophon who purchase tax contracts "from elsewhere" – likely from nearby poleis. As for the royal (Ptolemaic or Seleukid?) role, it is not fully understood: the *dikai telônikai* (tax arbitrations) refered to in lines 22–24 are conducted according to a royal protocol (τὸ διάγραμμα τοῦ βασιλέως). As Étienne and Migeotte emphasize (1998, 155), the institutions of tax farming at work are steadfastly civic, even if some of the taxes so farmed are royal.

[92] On these buildings, see Seaman 2016, 412.

and the ostotheke from Tralles (*SEG* XLVI 1434). Aperghis has argued that the Seleukids deprived the *strategos*/satrap of a direct role in financial administration.[93] This may have been the case for the Attalids as well, but these two texts suggest that the *strategos* could in certain circumstances bring his weight to bear on fiscal matters.

Tellingly, the *strategos* is absent from a list of Attalid administrative titles ritually invoked by a cultic association in the hinterland of Pergamon, near Apollonia in the Kaikos Valley (*SEG* LII 1197 Side A lines 9–12; dated ca. 168–164).[94] Many of these officials would appear to be part of the Attalid fiscal apparatus: *archiereus, hêmiolios, ho epi tês poleôs, dioikêtês, archeklogistês, oikonomos, eklogistês*. They are listed, according to Müller and Wörrle, in roughly descending order of seniority, though each office came with a different mandate.[95] For example, the *hêmiolios*, familiar from the figure of Herodes in the Toriaion dossier (**D8**), will have been responsible for revenues from royal patrimony.[96] In other cases, it is more difficult to determine which part of an official's brief might have been fiscal, as in the case of *ho epi tês poleôs*, a strictly civil official at any rate. Overall, this document adds validity to the axiom that the Attalids took over much of the Seleukid system, especially since it excludes the *strategos* from the fiscal apparatus.[97] As positive evidence, it gives us a confirmed Attalid tax collector in the *eklogistês*, the one who "collects (ἐκλέγειν)," but once again, no indication whatsoever that Pergamon auctioned off its taxes to the highest bidder.[98] Finally, a model begins to emerge. Pergamon's tax collectors were local tax farmers, operating within civic institutions – and, therefore, socially embedded in their communities. Crucially, they were known and accountable to taxpayers. For their part, royal officials such as those named in the inscription from Apollonia provided a different service: coordination between communities, cultic associations, tax farmers, and the central administration. Finally, the *strategos* will have interfered only in extraordinary circumstances.

---

[93] Aperghis 2004, 295; endorsed by Ma in his review, Ma 2007b.
[94] Müller and Wörrle 2002, 194.   [95] Müller and Wörrle 2002, 220–33.
[96] See Müller 2005, a full study of this official. We should perhaps think of two different fiscal apparatuses: one connecting the court and the royal patrimony, to which the *hêmiolios* would belong, but also the *riskophylax*, known from Sardis (*SEG* IV 632); and a second, which raised revenues from the kingdom at large.
[97] Müller and Wörrle 2002, 228. For the Seleukid system, see Aperghis 2004, 263–96. It should be noted, many of the presumed antecedents also stand in need of clarification.
[98] See Müller and Wörrle 2002, 229 n. 184; cf. Aperghis 2004, 282, on *eklogistês*, "responsible for tax assessment and, probably, collection."

It must be admitted that we have no evidence for how the Attalids conducted tax assessment. For the Seleukids, at least, we have slim evidence for a cadaster system.[99] However, there is scattered evidence for Attalid land survey and surveyors: καταμέτρησις [δὲ τῆς] χώρας (measuring out of land) in Temnos (**D4** Fragment D line 18); Lykinos, the γεοδώτης, active in the vicinity of Apollonioucharax (**D2** Side B lines 23–24) and possibly also among the Mysians of Emmodi (*SEG* XL 1062). The techniques employed in land distribution probably facilitated tax assessment as well. Finally, for the levels of taxation, the record is again poor, but intriguing. We have already discussed attempts to quantify revenues on the basis of the few numbers that have survived. These are, principally, the head tax of the Kardakes, "one Rhodian drachma and an obol," and the *phoros kai telesma* of Amlada of 1.5 talents (**D3** and **D12**). Each case has its idiosyncrasies, which makes generalization hazardous. In each case, negotiation has reduced an original level of taxation to our final number. One other tax rate is available from the anonymous city T-, possibly Temnos (*I.Sardis* 2). A royal rescript, either Attalid or Seleukid (difficult to determine which, as the stone perished in a modern war), fixes that city's annual rate at a mere one-third of a talent. To put these numbers in perspective, Aperghis has estimated revenues of 1–2 talents per 1,000 people in the Seleukid empire.[100] The small, nascent Pisidian polis of Amlada seems to fit well within those parameters. These numbers contrast markedly with those reported by Polybius for the Rhodian zone: Kaunos and Stratonikeia, the Rhodians claimed, produced 120 talents per year, surely a mix of direct and indirect taxation (30.31.7). Given the sovereignty challenges that the Attalids faced and their penchant for solving their problems with money, these are surprisingly low rates. They suggest a lighter, though perhaps broader burden than the one that Rhodes imposed on its *peraia*, and indeed the Rhodians' subjects did complain to Rome of their overlords' "heaviness (*barytês*)."[101] Pergamon's need for revenue must have been met

---

[99] For the Seleukids, the key evidence is again from Herakleia-under-Latmos (*SEG* XXXVII 859 Column III line 6). The cadastral unit there seems to be the *zeugos*. See discussion of Wörrle 1988, 464–65; see also Chandezon 2004, 142–44, which also treats the question of whether the cadaster system in Asia Minor goes back to Achaemenid times, on the evidence of Hdt. 6.42, (Artaphernes' activities in 493/2); Thonemann 2009, 381–84, makes a strong case that land was assessed according to its productive potential in both Achaemenid and Hellenistic Asia Minor. There, in early Hellenistic Gambreion, the issue is evaluation of land in terms of *kyproi*, a unit of measurement of seed; but he also adduces Magnesia (*I.Magnesia* 8). In that case, allotments of land of equal surface area are sold for a range of prices, implying both a cadaster and a system of valuation according to productivity.

[100] Aperghis 2004, 251.   [101] Polyb. 25.4.4.

by broadening the tax base to include large parts of Anatolia that had been loosely integrated if at all into the Achaemenid or Seleukid political economy. The typically light tax rates of the Aegean coastal poleis may have become even lighter, while new cities, towns, and other civic organisms in inner Anatolia traded arbitrary, unpredictable, and harsh exactions for the regularized and lenient coastal rate.

To summarize the conclusions of this survey of the evidence: Pergamon's direct taxes fell on communities, not landholders – unless those landholders were cleruchs, in which case they paid the traditional mixed-*phoros*: a tithe on grain and often vines, a cash sum for "the other fruits." Villagers who were dependents of temples and sacred estates might also pay taxes on the land that they farmed, but they paid those taxes to their local priest, who became ever more accountable to the royal bureaucracy. For indirect taxes, cautious interpretation of key documents was urged. Poll taxes, which fell on non-polis communities as a rule, were nevertheless both irregular and ad hoc. The Attalids collected sales tax, but not in the form of Toriaion's *agoranomia*, the source of one of their earmarks. Customs dues were likely the most important form of indirect taxation, as evidenced by the *CLA*. The Attalids built up an infrastructure of surveillance in order to capture revenue from the flow of goods between the sea and the highlands – and between a multitude of fiscal zones within Anatolia. Taxes on the usage of parts of the royal patrimony such as saltpans and lagoons will also have been significant. These resources may long have been claimed by outside powers, but the interests of the surrounding poleis and priesthoods were at stake in a battle over natural resources. Finally, the personnel of tax collection did not include royal tax farmers. This was the most significant of the many respects in which the Attalid system of personnel mirrored its Seleukid forbearer.

The Rules of the Game

1. Negotiation Is Routine

Certain generalizations now present themselves. In accusing the Attalids of raising a "riskless revenue (*akindynos phoros*)," Antony aimed his criticism at their system of assessments (*timemata*), implying that a community's *timema* was fixed, arbitrary, and immutable. Yet the cases of Amlada and the Kardakon Kome belie this characterization. The Kardakes achieved a 72% reduction of their head tax, while the Amladeis knocked 25% off their annual collective payment. There is no way to determine the representativeness of these figures. By contrast, can we assume that the amount of negotiation that went into each assessment was typical? Just how appropriate was this kind of bargaining in the fiscal arena? On the one hand, we have already tried to demystify the process of earmarking by bringing the attendant negotiations out into the light. It makes sense to check for negotiation elsewhere in the fiscal system. On the other hand, we have to contend with both the admittedly tendentious evidence of Antony's speech that makes of the *timema* a fixed sum, as well as the idiosyncrasies of Pisidia ca. 160 and western Lycia in 181.

With their origins still in dispute, we cannot describe the *katoikountes* of the Kardakon Kome simply as military settlers, although the Attalids clearly had a strategic interest in reconstituting the community in 181.[102] In 184, Eumenes II had repulsed what was, according to Attalid propaganda, a major incursion into the region by Prusias I and the Galatians under Ortiagon.[103] This war may have been behind the failure of the Kardakes to pay their taxes. Yet this is not explicit in the letter of Eumenes II to his official Artemidoros, which resumes the community's request for a lightening of their tax burden (**D3**). Artemidoros had transmitted the request to Eumenes and checked into (ἐξετάζων) the claims of poverty. Not only had bad harvests befallen the village; the villagers had actually started to flee the land. Artemidoros' investigation implies that claims of poverty may have been commonplace, a hint that negotiation was widespread. The position of Eumenes was in its own way rather weak, as the king needed to incentivize the Kardakes with tax privileges and the aid of a skilled mason in order to repopulate and refortify the village.

Unlike the Kardakes, the Amladeis could communicate directly with the king, even if he could answer them only as "polis and *gerousia*," not the normative "*boulê kai demos*" (**D12**).[104] In this case, a large embassy delivered the community's request to Attalos II. Again, the conditions seem catastrophic. Pisidian Amlada had proven disloyal in the recent *Galatikos polemos*, so much so that they had been compelled to surrender hostages and now owed the Attalids reparations for "repairs (ἐπισκευ[ῆς ἕνε]|κ]ε) (?)" (lines 6–7). It is difficult to know whether these hostilities were

---

[102] See *SEG* LIII 1706.   [103] We know of the war from a single inscription, Segre 1932.
[104] Welles (*RC*, 239) sees this as evidence that Amlada had only recently become a Greek-style polis and was as yet partially Hellenized. Was it actually the case that in communicating with the king through the *gerousia* Amlada was at a disadvantage vis-à-vis other, more "advanced" poleis?

a continuation of the Great Revolt of the Galatians or a separate series of local wars that eventually involved Prousias II in the revolt of Selge in 156.[105] Like the Kardakes, the Amladeis represented themselves as impoverished: "since you are now weak from many financial burdens (ἐπεὶ θλιβέντες ἐμ πλείοσιν ἀσθενῶς [νῦν ἔ]|χετε" (lines 8–9).[106] We would not expect self-abasement from Attalos, but was his position so much more secure? The sources provide a mixed picture of the Attalid hold on this part of southwestern Anatolia.[107] Nearby Olbasa evidently felt the need to send its honorific decree for two Attalid officials to the king for confirmation.[108] However, we know the region to have been restive. For example, Selge's battle with kings for parts of the plain of Pamphylia was worthy of Strabo's retelling (12.7.3).

The historical contexts for the negotiations between the Attalids and the Kardakon Kome and Amlada may have been extraordinary, but not the tenor of those negotiations, nor the rules of the game. If these two small, semi-Hellenized communities on the periphery of the kingdom could engage the Attalids over tax assessments, it is likely that a polis of the core could too. Amlada's ambassador Oprasates enjoyed royal favor, but other cities launched their own native sons into senior positions at court and in the administrative hierarchy. We can consider Adramyttion as the model. In the 160s, it issued a decree honoring its citizen Pamphilos (*SEG* XXXVII no. 1006). He was no ordinary citizen, but in his trustworthiness and moderation was deemed worthy of appointment to a position in the Attalid court (συστα]θεὶς τῶι βασιλεῖ Εὐμένει) and taken into the confidence of Queen Stratonike (lines 3, 9). The decree records in typically vague and heavy-handed language that Pamphilos continued to serve his polis and its citizens with honor (lines 13–18). Unfortunately, we are not given a narrative in the motivation clause to describe what is likely taken for granted, namely, that many of these services of representation before the monarchy were fiscal in nature.[109]

Rather more is spelled out in a long honorary decree of the city of Pergamon for a royal courtier (*I.Pergamon* 224 + *I.Pergamon* II p. 509;

---

[105] See Kearsley 1994, 52–53; for Attalid "local wars," see Ma 2013a, 52–56.

[106] Thonemann (2011a, 7) interprets similarly the claim of the *katoikountes* of Apolloniocharax to be *dēmotai* (**D2** Side B line 11). Giovanni Marginesu has made the interesting suggestion to me that *dēmotēs* there is rather a term of political status imbued with local meaning.

[107] Kosmetatou 1997, 24–35.   [108] *SEG* XLIV 1108.

[109] For Pamphilos, see Savalli-Lestrade 1996, 168–71, esp. 170: the lasting bond with the city of origin is common.

OGIS 323).¹¹⁰ Most discussion of the text concerns the identity of the courtier, given here the title of *syntrophos* (royal age-mate), and usually identified as the powerful Andronikos, who was a representative of the Attalids at Rome in their quarrels with the Bithynians and ultimately a key figure in the coup of Nikomedes II against his father Prousias II.¹¹¹ By contrast, recent treatments of the *Stadt und Herrscher* relationship have not made much use of this important statement, perhaps because Pergamon was no ordinary polis under the Attalids.¹¹² In honoring a courtier for his administrative virtue, the Pergamene *demos* provides an ideal framework for negotiation between kings and cities:

> τήν τε πατρίδα σπε[ύ]|δων, ὅσον ἐφ' ἑαυτῷ, διαφέρειν παρὰ τὰς ἄλλας πόλεις ἐν ταῖς κατὰ τὴ[ν]|πολιτείαν οἰκονομίαις, τὰ μὲν παραλελειμμένα εἰσηγησάμενος ἐπὶ τῶ[ι]|συνφέροντι διώρθωσεν, τὰ δὲ λοιπὰ ἀκολούθως τοῖς νόμοις συνεπείσ|[χ]υσεν
>
> ... aiming as much as he could to distinguish his fatherland [i.e., the city of Pergamon] among other cities in matters of administration according to *politeia*, [meaning that] on matters neglected, having proposed something useful, he straightened them out. As for the rest, he saw to it that the laws were closely followed ... (lines 11–14)¹¹³

Admittedly, while we may suspect that a range of governmental affairs lie under the rubric of "matters of administration (*oikonomiai*)" – the language of "straightening out (*diôrthosis*)" is redolent of public finance. Generically, the honorific decree represents an ideal, which those "other cities" surely trotted out in negotiations with the monarchy: we have a distinctive constitution (*politeia*) and certain laws (*nomoi*) that preclude some forms of taxation and guard us from arbitrarily high rates. If this argument carried weight in Pergamon, which was under tight royal control,

---

¹¹⁰ Date: Fränkel in *I.Pergamon* proposed the Bithynian war of succession 149/8, perhaps signified in line 21, as a *terminus post quem*, while Dittenberger in *OGIS* proposed 156/5 or shortly thereafter, on the basis of the embassy. It dates to the reign of Attalos II, in any case; Allen 1983, 132 n. 203, reports the *phi* of σύντροφος is visible on a squeeze.

¹¹¹ For the sources for Andronikos, see the entry in Savalli-Lestrade 1998, 143–44, as well as her discussion in Savalli-Lestrade 1996, 158–68. It may have been the brother (or son?) of Andronikos, Philopoimen, who was the Attalid commander under Mummius in the Achaean War in 146. See further Hopp 1977, 98.

¹¹² For the citizens of the polis of Pergamon under the Attalids, see Bielfeldt 2010, with a legible photo of this inscription on p. 143.

¹¹³ On the verbs εἰσηγοῦμαι and συνεπισχύω, see Savalli-Lestrade 1998, 164–65. She and many others have been interested in this inscription as evidence for the *strategeia* of the polis of Pergamon, since the introduction of legislation alluded to here would make of Andronikos a *strategos*.

it is all the more likely to have resonated farther afield. Interestingly, it is a tactic of negotiation known from the peer–polity context, too. In 205, for instance, the city of Xanthos replied to the request of the city of Kytenion for financial aid, pleading that "no extraordinary levy on (our) citizens is possible because we have decreed a nine-year *oikonomia* (ἐπιβαλεῖν τε τοῖς πολίταις | οὐδεμίαν ἔξεστιν ἐπιβολὴν διὰ τὴν γεγενημένην οἰκονομίαν μετὰ ψηφίσματος εἰς ἔτη ἐννέα)" (*SEG* XXXVIII 1476 lines 53–55).[114] In the end, Xanthos gave Kytenion 500 drachmas, but the institution of the nine-year *oikonomia*, ratified unilaterally, had set limits on the negotiation. *I.Pergamon* 224 shows that the city of Pergamon, in its agonistic competition with other poleis, strove to place an analogous set of limits on royal power.[115]

2. Royal Fiscality Is a Calque

We have been using Antony's polemic as a guide through the tax morphology of the Attalid state, but it is not primary evidence for the indignation of the taxpayer. For that, we must pay attention to the outrage in Metropolis where new taxes had been "invented (ἐφευρισκομένων)" (**D5** Side B line 19). As we have argued, the Attalids had not invented these taxes for the Metropolitans, though in the end, they succeeded in cancelling them. Yet the episode could have been a cautionary tale for royal power: the creation of new domains of fiscality remained taboo. The best way to reduce compliance was to invent new taxes – or to be perceived as doing so. As for inventions, nothing had changed with the advent of the Attalids. It was an old imperial habit in Asia Minor to assimilate the cities' own fiscal

---

[114] Ma (2003b, 12) is probably incorrect in translating *oikonomia* as "budget." On "budgets," see Schuler 2005; Migeotte 2006; Rhodes 2007. For *oikonomia*, cf. from the Archippe dossier from Kyme, *SEG* XXXIII 1039 line 43, which Picard 2006 translates "la gestion administrative"; cf. *SEG* XXXII 1109, on the *sympoliteia* of Euromos (?) and Chalketor, with translation of Jean and Louis Robert *BE* 1983 no. 401: "règlement d'administration."

[115] Obviously, the city of Pergamon is a special case. However, scholarship is still working out the nature of its distinctiveness. See Müller 2012, 255–58. Most glaringly, the kings are often thought to have had a hand in the appointment of the civic *strategoi*, whom we know to have had powerful pro-bouleutic powers. The key text is *OGIS* 267, in which Eumenes I honors an outgoing board of *strategoi* for their competence. Again, Andronikos (?) has been suspected of taking the actions described in lines 11–14 of *I.Pergamon* 224 in his capacity as civic *strategos*. Yet clearly, the horizon here is a larger cadre of poleis beyond Pergamon: "to distinguish among other cities" (διαφέρειν παρὰ τὰς ἄλλας πόλεις).

categories.[116] Conceptually, if not always economically, royal taxation was epiphenomenal.[117]

Our best example of this effect comes from Toriaion, where Eumenes II earmarked for the oil fund "for the present, the revenue from the *agoranomia* (κατὰ τὸ παρὸν τὴν ἀπὸ τῆς ἀγορανομ[ί]ας πρόσοδον)" (**D8** line 43). It is unclear which institutions Toriaion possessed prior to its upgrade to polis status. And as we have explained above, the nature of the revenue from the office of *agoranomos* is also obscure. Yet the implication of the directive *for the present* is that the revenue stream for the oil fund already exists. It at least takes logical precedence over the procedure of earmarking. In other words, Eumenes did not trample into new social and economic fields in order to pay for his new expenditure. In the history of Asia Minor, the observation may appear banal, but not in the history of monarchy. For example, France of the *ancien régime*, at least in its last hundred years, worked very differently.[118] The principal direct tax in France since the fifteenth century had been the *taille*, but from 1695 to 1789 the monarchy introduced a series of new direct taxes, the *capitation* and the *dixième*, later renamed the *vingtième*, in order to fund increasing expenditures. These new taxes have been termed "universal" in that they were designed to penetrate the barriers of status and privilege that had previously shielded many French royal subjects from taxation. In search of revenues, the French monarchy created new fiscal categories, a radical innovation on the road to the Revolution.[119]

That Attalid fiscal policy was less creative does not mean it was more benign. In fact, if we can rely on earlier evidence from Asia Minor, the calque of royal fiscality could just as easily be used to wound the polis. The classic case comes from Sardis under Antiochos III. In order to punish the city for siding with Achaios, the king added a royal *eikostê* (twentieth) tax to a preexisting civic (*politikê*) one.[120] To what extent this form of "double taxation" was practiced is a matter of debate, but the calque need not have always been a perfect copy: the royal share of a given revenue source may have been more or less than one-half. It is clear from the letter of Zeuxis to Herakleia-under-Latmos that the same local tax farmer was collecting royal taxes and civic taxes in the harbor, even if a fixed amount of the royal

---

[116] Chandezon 2004, 131–33.
[117] *Contra* Rostovtzeff 1930, 605: "The difference was that the kings introduced some new taxes." There is no evidence to support this claim, and Rostovtzeff did not attempt to provide any.
[118] Bresson 2000, 297–304. [119] Kwass 1999.
[120] *SEG* XXXIX 1283 lines 5–6, with explication of Gauthier 1989, 33–36.

receipts remained in Herakleia, earmarked for the oil fund.¹²¹ Thus cooperation, or at least coexistence, was possible, which is why recent scholarship has highlighted not only the competition between the two fiscalities, but, to borrow the French, "connivance" and "cohabitation."¹²² If the latter were a matter of dividing up a single revenue stream, the former was a fight over which revenue streams – in a more or less timeless fiscal portfolio – each side would claim. In essence, what was up for negotiation was sovereignty (*kyrieia*) over the different revenue streams (*prosodoi*), not their number and location in the civic economy. This is why royal grants of tax immunity (*ateleia*) so often speak of "the taxes over which the city is sovereign (ὧν ἡ πόλις κυρία ἐστίν)."¹²³

Just which taxes those might be was subject to change, a possibility that Iasos tried to foreclose by binding an official of Ptolemy I with this oath:

> τὰς δὲ προσόδους ἐάσω Ἰασε[ῖ]ς|λαμβάνειν τὰς τῆς πόλεως πάσας καὶ τοὺς λιμένας, σύνταξιν δὲ φέρειν αὐτοὺς|ἣν ἂν ὁ βασιλεὺς συντάξῃ.
>
> ... that I [Aristoboulos] should allow the Iaseians to collect all civic revenues and (taxes from) harbors, and themselves to raise whatever extraordinary contribution the king might call for. (*I.Iasos* 3, lines 13–15)

The Ptolemaic state threatened the sovereignty of Iasos over one or another of its *prosodoi*. Hence the gist of the oath was: let all revenues be civic (*politikai*). The atmosphere was of course competitive, but again, the two fiscalities could just as easily cooperate. The point is that the city defined the categories of fiscality to which both parties wholeheartedly subscribed.

We have a beautiful illustration of this dynamic in a text that may very well be Attalid and post-188. It is a royal rescript (?) discovered in Sardis, but addressed to another polis, which W. H. Buckler and David Robinson suggested may have been Temnos, on account of the T in line 7 (*I.Sardis* 2).¹²⁴ Judging from the script, they dated the inscription to 225–175. The historical context is the familiar and generic one of postwar devastation and royal euergetism, so it is very difficult to choose between a Seleukid author like Antiochos III and Eumenes II, acting on the model found in the Korragos Decree (**D1**). In response to a petition, a royal

---

[121] *SEG* XXXVII 859 Column III lines 2–4. V. Chankowski (2007, 323–28) argues for "double taxation" in several domains in the case of Herakleia. For the debate on "double taxation" with reference to Sardis, see Martinez-Sève 2004, 95.
[122] Connivance: Capdetrey 2004. Cohabitation: Chandezon 2004.   [123] Chandezon 2004, 133.
[124] Unfortunately, the stone seems to have perished in the Smyrna/İzmir fire of 1922. If the letter were addressed to Temnos, part of the old Aeolian core of the Attalid kingdom, it would very likely be a Pergamene document.

official grants the unnamed city of *I.Sardis* 2 a seven-year tax holiday, and the following permanent arrangement starting in the eighth year: "they should pay in three installments out of all the revenues produced, twenty minae in total per year, and should be taxed in no other way (διδόναι τρε[ῖς ἀναφοράς]|[ἐκ] πασῶν τῶν γινομένων προσόδων πα[ρ' ἕκαστον]|ἐνιαυτὸν ἀργυ[ρ]ίου μνᾶς εἴκοσι καὶ ἄλλ[ως μὴ ἐν]οχλεῖσθαι)" (lines 16–19). In other words, royal fiscality has a role in designing the punctuality of taxation (three installments) and in calculating the tax burden (20 minas), but it does not take part in defining *any* of the revenue sources (πασῶν τῶν γινομένων προσόδων). Those were left to the city's discretion. The calque of royal fiscality meant that the battle for sovereignty was effectively circumscribed. The result was that the much larger sovereignty claims of the Attalids – the absolute claims of the Treaty of Apameia – were camouflaged.

3. The Survival of Civic Fiscality Is Guaranteed

The historical problem of the relationship of royal fiscality to civic fiscality presupposes the survival of a civic fiscal apparatus and the preservation of much of the traditional tax base of the polis within the Attalid kingdom. This is well recognized in Francophone scholarship on civic institutions in the tradition of Louis Robert and in the formulation of the problem by Frédérique Duyrat and Véronique Chankowski in their 2004 volume *Le roi et l'économie*. Moreover, the most recent German scholarship on the identity and institutions of the city of Pergamon under the kings makes the point expressly.[125] However, in the technical literature on certain key sources, one reads that the Attalids, in the first instance, claimed *all* revenues. Only then did the kings remit to the cities whichever portions suited them. This notion may continue to warp interpretations, which justifies a brief consideration of its merits. The idea goes back to the grand syntheses of Rostovtzeff and later A. H. M. Jones, but has leaked into numismatic and epigraphical studies.[126] Fred Kleiner's standard treatment of the cistophoric coinage and Robert Bauslaugh's of the so-called cistophoric countermarks both quote the judgment of Jones in summing up

---

[125] Most recently, see Bielfeldt 2010; for the *politikai prosodoi* of Pergamon, see, e.g., *I.Pergamon* 246 lines 40–41.
[126] Rostovtzeff (1930, 605–6) postulates civic taxes alongside royal taxes, but his view was that the royal tax burden was so heavy as to destroy the city's ability to pay for its own needs. For Rostovtzeff, this explained the practice of earmarking and royal patronage of the gymnasium!

their views on the historical import of the coins: "The policy of the kings seems to have been to appropriate nearly all the taxes, and then to make grants from the royal treasury to the cities 'for the administration of the city.'"[127]

Another version of this argument transposes the ideal type of the "subject city," which is a convention of modern historiography, onto the ancient reality. Subject cities, then, were a class of poleis, which by virtue of that status surrendered not just some vague sense of *autonomia* and freedom of action, but specific domains of fiscality. Thus Lloyd Jonnes and Marijana Ricl write, "In the case of Tyriaion [sic], the king presently relinquishes revenues collected by *agoranomoi*, which in case of a subject city went εἰς τὸ βασιλικόν," citing the Korragos Decree (**D1**).[128] The interpretation of Dreyer and Engelmann of the *diagôgion* of *I.Metropolis* 1 (**D5**) is based on an analogous and equally unjustified assumption. Since they take Metropolis to be a "*sujette ville*," the city was, as it were, "constitutionally" barred from raising its own customs dues. The *diagôgion* must then be a toll (*Maut*) and not customs dues (*Gebühren*).[129] Rather, the rule of thumb should be formulated thus: each domain of fiscality was potentially an arena for negotiation, the domains themselves remaining fixed. So if we were to learn that Metropolis raised its own customs dues, it would not be any more surprising than the recent discovery that member poleis of the Lycian Koinon exercised that right.[130]

And for the Attalids, efficiency was gained by leaving the civic fiscal apparatus in place.

Finally, from this perspective, the sundry evidence for civic fiscality requires cautious interpretation. For example, an inscription reading ὅροι Περγαμηνῶν ("boundary of the Pergamenes"), albeit in a Roman-period script, was found in the vicinity of modern Aliağa, *in situ* but over 40 km from Pergamon (*I.Kyme* 27). The stone appears to mark an exclave of the polis of Pergamon, a source of revenue, which was perhaps already available to the city in days of the monarchy.[131] Nearby in the mountain country northwest of Manisa, two more boundary stones were found, reading: ὅροι Αἰγαέων ("boundary of the people of Aigai").[132] While the

---

[127] Jones 1971, 55, *apud* Bauslaugh 1990, 59 n. 54; Kleiner and Noe 1977, 125 n. 19.
[128] Jonnes and Ricl 1997, 26.   [129] *I.Metropolis*, 51–54.   [130] Takmer 2007, 176.
[131] Sommerey 2008, 149; Heinle 2015, 137 n. 962. Cf. Hansen 1971, 23: "in characters of the early period of the dynasty." Earlier scholarship used the inscription to establish the borders of the realm of Eumenes I.
[132] Keil and Premerstein, *Bericht über eine Reise* nos. 204 and 205; the stones also bear dates, δ' and π', respectively, which may hold the key to their eventual interpretation. Admittedly,

upland Aeolian city thrived under the Attalids, the conclusions that we can draw from this evidence are rather modest. Aigai claimed this rocky terrain as part of its fiscal base, and perhaps the productive ecological niche in which the stones were erected was a matter of dispute, with another city or with the sanctuary of Apollo Chresterios. However, we cannot use this evidence to assign Aigai a political status ("autonomous" or "subject" city) in the Attalid kingdom or, by circular reasoning, to date these texts according to a status that we presume Aigai received at Apameia or after the War with Achaios. In the same vein, we should not exclude the Pisidian poleis of Adada and Termessos from the Attalid kingdom because they swore an oath to guard against the dissolution (*kataluein*) of each other's laws and revenues (*prosodoi*).[133] Such an oath is an index not of Attalid control in Pisidia, but rather of the lengths to which cities might go to protect their revenues.[134]

Digging around for Revenues

Surveillance

> Θεόφραστος δὲ Νηλεῖ παρέδωκεν: ὁ δ' εἰς Σκῆψιν κομίσας τοῖς μετ' αὐτὸν παρέδωκεν, ἰδιώταις ἀνθρώποις, οἳ κατάκλειστα εἶχον τὰ βιβλία οὐδ' ἐπιμελῶς κείμενα: ἐπειδὴ δὲ ᾔσθοντο τὴν σπουδὴν τῶν Ἀτταλικῶν βασιλέων ὑφ' οἷς ἦν ἡ πόλις, ζητούντων βιβλία εἰς τὴν κατασκευὴν τῆς ἐν Περγάμῳ βιβλιοθήκης, κατὰ γῆς ἔκρυψαν ἐν διώρυγί τινι. ὑπὸ δὲ νοτίας καὶ σητῶν κακωθέντα ὀψέ ποτε ἀπέδοντο οἱ ἀπὸ τοῦ γένους Ἀπελλικῶντι τῷ Τηίῳ πολλῶν ἀργυρίων τά τε Ἀριστοτέλους καὶ τὰ τοῦ Θεοφράστου βιβλία.

Theophrastus bequeathed (his library) to Neleus, who having taken it to Skepsis, bequeathed it to his relations – lay people – who kept it locked up and in disarray. But when they learned of the zeal of the Attalid kings for pursuing books in order to found a library in Pergamon, Skepsis being

---

I have no reason to believe that these were inscribed under the Attalids rather than the Seleukids. The methodological lesson remains the same.

[133] *TAM* III 1 2 lines 13–15; Rudolf Heberdey's date for this text was 200–102. We know that the Attalids were active in Termessos. See Kosmatatou 1997, 32–33. While there is no way to securely date the treaty, the fact that the two cities possess their own revenues is of course no criterion for making 133 the *terminus post quem*.

[134] Cf. *Syll.*³ 633 lines 40–41, for an almost identical clause from the *isopoliteia* agreement of Miletus and Herakleia-under-Latmos, ca. 180; see further on these clauses V. Chankowski 2007, 301.

subject to the Attalids, they hid it in a kind of pit in the ground. But much later, when the books had been damaged by moisture and moths, their descendants sold them to Apellicon of Teos for a large sum of money, both the books of Aristotle and those of Theophrastus. (Strabo 13.1.54; trans. after Loeb)

A nightmarish anxiety about the long reach of the state pervades Strabo's story, which contrasts a king's curated rapaciousness with the absurdity of his subject's method of escaping detection. Truly, the descendants of Neleus were not scholars, but they knew how to hide their wealth. The historicity of its details aside, the story reminds us that the ancient world perceived the Attalids as fiercely hungry for cultural capital and money.[135] Elevated by Rome to a notional position of great power in an unstable, anarchic Mediterranean system still reeling from the collapse of its hegemons, Pergamon's budget ballooned overnight. Yet in their pursuit of revenue, the Attalids, as we have seen, adhered to certain rules. These traditions and norms limited the scope of tax collection. By contrast, the kings could change the scale of taxation – but only by sharpening surveillance. It was not sufficient to loosely integrate new territories into a tributary system, especially when cities like Adada and Termessos were oath-bound to march out to war over revenues. Rather, it was necessary to deepen the incidence of taxation *and* maximize compliance. As Strabo's story about the heirs of Theophrastus suggests, the Attalids surely met resistance from taxpayers. Therefore, critical to Pergamon's success was the implementation of fiscal arrangements that encouraged what sociologist Margaret Levi calls quasi-voluntary compliance.[136] In the section on saltpans and coastal lagoons, we discussed one form of outright confiscation. There may have been more.[137] However, arbitrary confiscation is inimical to any sense of tax fairness. The only sustainable approach was to deepen the incidence of taxation. We do not hear of a major reassessment of tax rates, such as, for example, the Athenians implemented in 425/4 (*ML* 69). Instead, just as the Athenians did in eventually focusing their energies on

---

[135] Historicity: Hendrickson 2014, 396.   [136] Levi 1988, 48–70.
[137] The most telling indication is the property mentioned in *I.Pergamon* 249 line 25, as "having become royal (τῶν οὐσιῶν τῶν γεγενημένων βασιλικῶν)." Cf. *SEG* XLVIII 1532 line 10, from Olbasa, a hint of confiscated property passed on to another new (?) polis: [— — — —]Σ οὐσίας κατατάξητε. While the issue of confiscation needs further exploration, the evidence seems to point to a focus on the kind of extra-urban resources that Alexander and his immediate successors claimed as an inheritance from the Achaemenids: forests, saltpans, lakes, mines, quarries, perhaps beehives and brickworks. The notion of Mileta (2008, 49–52) of the "Königliches Gebiet" beyond royal land is helpful here.

collection of an empire-wide harbor tax (the *eikostê*), the Attalids taxed what they could see best. Catering to the cultural preference of their subjects, they became masters of indirect taxation.[138]

The richly documented history of imperial Venice reminds us that this preference for indirect taxation is a consistent feature across Mediterranean empires.[139] It is to be expected that the Attalids structured their fiscal system in such a way as to progressively deepen the incidence of indirect taxation in an effort to touch more transactions, groups, and individuals. In fact, the evidence points to a focus on capturing revenues from movement and exchange. Recall that in documents like the *CLA*, Anatolia appears as a patchwork of different fiscal regimes. This patchwork effect represented an impediment to trans-Anatolian movements of goods and people, and, naturally, it engendered on-the-ground adaptations. For example, Laodikeia-on-the-Lykos and Stratonikeia in Caria may have granted each other tax immunities late in the second century in order to reduce – by at least one – the number of fiscal boundaries a trader crossed in participating in a regional economy around the Maeander Valley.[140] On the other hand, from the king's perspective, the patchwork effect will have been a boon. The more that traders passed in and out of enclaves of Attalid control, the more taxes on mobility accrued.[141] Yet the king could only profit from as much of this mobility as he could observe. While Purcell has emphasized the role of customs houses in ports, assembling a model of the "Mediterranean of *ellimenia*," we must also picture toll stations lining a network of inland roads.[142] Unfortunately, archaeologically, these structures are indistinguishable from fortifications and rural towers of other function. Texts, however, demonstrate that beyond the harbor lay a range of checkpoints and surveillance mechanisms, revenue officers checking

---

[138] For *eikostê*: Thuc. 7.28.4. Migeotte 2003 collects all the neglected evidence for direct taxation in ancient Greece, but still concludes that indirect taxation was predominate and universal and, in the cadre of the polis, the preferred form of taxation (p. 313).

[139] See Hocquet (1999, 387) for Venetian resistance to direct taxation on income, movable and immovable assets, and property.

[140] Ritti et al. 2008, no. 3. Francesco Guizzi's restoration of the *Stratonikeis* (lines 24–25) as the counter-party to the agreement remains a hypothesis – see Saba 2020, 124–25 – but a plausible guess on grounds of economic geography.

[141] Relevant here is the hypothesis that the Attalids rebuilt the road from Ephesus to Sardis, proposed on the basis of the milestone *I.Ephesos* 3601. However, several scholars now date the inscription to 306 BCE and attribute it to Antigonos Monophthalmos. See Roelens-Flouneau 2019, 58–59; cf. Thonemann 2003, 95–96.

[142] Purcell 2005, 204.

bags at gates and fortified customs houses set in narrow passes.¹⁴³ So it is no surprise that the *CLA* is concerned with preventing smuggling by land (lines 26–28). In addition to customs houses (*telôneia*), the law refers to other guard posts called *paraphylakai* (e.g., lines 31–33, 37–39).¹⁴⁴ The Romans and the Attalids were both after what Ps.-Aristotle calls the revenue of *telê kata gên*, taxes levied along land routes ([*Oec.*] 2.4).

A central plank of the strategy for increasing revenues without provoking revolt, then, was the construction of a new and more sophisticated infrastructure for surveillance. In addition, the Attalids must have also dispatched units of armed men to occupy it. In the sources, these groups of guards appear as *orophylakes* and *paraphylakitai*. Already from the late fourth century on, Greek cities had organized troops of *orophylakes*, literally, "boundary guards."¹⁴⁵ Following Louis Robert, Cédric Brélaz has produced the spelling ὀροφύλακες, that is, "mountain guards," which reflects the difficulty of deciding in any particular case whether a mountain or a border is under surveillance.¹⁴⁶ Often in Asia Minor, the mountain *is* a border. Thus the *orophylakes* of Miletus and Herakleia-under-Latmos are responsible for capturing and ransoming the slaves that escape from one city's territory into the other via the mountainous divide (*Syll.*³ 633, lines 88–99). Andrzej Chankowski, however, has argued on linguistic grounds against the notion of mountain guards. Moreover, he adduces a wide range of evidence, from a fifth-century inscription from Chios to the Zenon Papyri, which places boundaries, public and private, under the guard of such men.¹⁴⁷ Significantly, several royal documents that seem to emanate from the late Attalid kingdom also make mention of these terms. The first is a fragmentary royal document found in Telmessos, introduced earlier in the section on direct taxation. To recapitulate, traced to the chancery of Eumenes II, the document records the king's offer of a tax privilege to craftsmen in exchange for the service of *orophylakia* (*SEG* XXIX 1516).

As the Roberts argued, the *orophylakes* of *SEG* XXIX 1516 would have actually patrolled the mountainous borderlands high above the coastal plain of western Lycia.¹⁴⁸ Descriptions of these patrols as simply policing

---

¹⁴³ For revenue officers checking bags, see Aen. Tact. 29.5, where the context is arms smuggling. Interestingly, although the officers are posted at the city gates, they are called *ellimenistai*. Cf. the taxes taken at the city gates of Jerusalem (Joseph. *AJ* 12.138–44).

¹⁴⁴ For the debate on the precise meaning of *paraphylakê*, Brélaz (2005, 123) concludes, "[L]e substantif ἡ παραφυλακή désigne la garde, la garnison et, dans un sens figuré, la protection, la surveillance, la circonspection."

¹⁴⁵ A. Chankowski 2010, 347.   ¹⁴⁶ Brélaz 2005, 157–58.   ¹⁴⁷ A. Chankowski 2010, 347–59.

¹⁴⁸ Jean and Louis Robert *BE* (1980) no. 484.

marginal land, the wilds that the Greeks called *eschatiai*, miss the mark. Indeed for Brélaz too, the service of *orophylakeia* is one of "securité publique" on such terrain, and he carefully notes the lack of direct evidence for the involvement of *orophylakes* in tax collection in Hellenistic or Roman Asia Minor.[149] However, working from a wider body of evidence, Angelos Chaniotis describes such groups as "not simply policing the countryside but primarily safeguarding the revenues expected from the countryside."[150] What were these revenues? Chaniotis' examples tend to show cities taxing land in liminal and vulnerable locations. Therefore, they send armed men out for surveillance, to protect the crops and guard those bringing it in. The mountainous terrain of Asia Minor bore a different kind of fruit, which is probably why the *oreinê chora* (mountainous territory) is disputed in the aforementioned *Syll.*³ 633 (line 78). In certain seasons, this terrain surely bloomed, but the harvest that the *orophylakes* were responsible for was perennial. Since people and goods were always moving across the fiscal patchwork of Asia Minor, manning the interstices was always profitable. It seems reasonable to propose that the boundaries of *horophylakeia* could at times be fiscal. At least some of the revenue collection ensured by the Attalid *orophylakes* of Lycia was customs on goods transported in and out of the Pergamene exclave of Telmessos. Otherwise, the concern of Eumenes II (?) for the "public security" of the mountains of western Lycia is left curiously unmotivated.[151]

The Attalids' funding of these patrols is of a piece with their placement of groups of guards called *paraphylakitai* in permanent, fortified installations outside urban centers. In each case, the goal will have been to capture revenues from territorial surveillance. Our evidence from civic contexts is slightly more verbose on the subject. In late Hellenistic Pisidian Antioch, where the Attalids were active, a *paraphylax* was attached to the plain known as the Killanion Pedion (*SEG* XXXI 1201).[152] On this plain (Şarkikaraağaç), a mixed population of Phrygians and Pisidians worked grand estates. It also contained the city of Neapolis, an Attalid

---

[149] Brélaz 2005, 157–71.   [150] Chaniotis 2008, 141.
[151] On internal customs boundaries within a Hellenistic kingdom, evidence is available from the Seleukid Levant (Joseph. *AJ* 12.142 and 1 Macc 10:34). It is also worth considering *PSI* 4 406, from the Zenon Papyri. It records the existence of a *horophylax* in Pegai/Antipatris, in Ptolemaic Koile-Syria. For discussion, see Chankowski 2010, 350–52. It seems entirely plausible that a guard at Antipatris (Rosh-ha-Ayin), at the conjuncture of the Sharon Plain with the foothills of Samaria, monitored a customs boundary. In Rabbinic sources (e.g., m. Gittin 7:7), Antipatris is the proverbial northern frontier of Judaea.
[152] Attalids and Pisidian Antioch: Mitchell and Waelkens 1998, 68.

stronghold on the future Via Sebaste.¹⁵³ Or consider that Termessos built (or rebuilt?) a *paraphylakeion* on a so-called royal road (*basilikê hodos*) (ca. 135 CE; *TAM* III 1 14 line 14). For cities, the point of these watches was to observe activity where revenues were at stake. It seems reasonable then to infer that, for their part, royal *paraphylakitai* were also guarding revenues linked to the topography of the kingdom. As in the case of the *orophylakes*, we should try to pin down which revenues they were guarding. The suspected Attalid *paraphylakitai* can be found in two places: the hinterland of Pergamon, and the Milyas. We have had occasion to mention the letter of Attalos II to Olbasa in the Milyas (*SEG* XLIV 1108). A second letter to an unnamed community was found nearby (*SEG* XLVIII 1532). It mentions *basilikoi topoi* (royal estates) and *paraphylakitai* (lines 5, 16). In part on grounds of epistolary style, Nicholas Milner suggests an Attalid author and so a date after 188, yet there is also a danger here of circular reasoning, as *paraphylakitai* come to stand in for the Attalids.¹⁵⁴ From Alassos, also in the Milyas, another dedication of *paraphylakitai* has surfaced (*SEG* XLVII 1601).¹⁵⁵ Finally, the city of Pergamon includes precisely such guards among those granted citizenship after 133 (*I.Pergamon* 249 lines 17–18).¹⁵⁶

Unless a new source comes to light that describes the territorial charge of a group of Attalid *paraphylakitai* in the genitive case, à la the officer of Pisidian Antioch who watched over the Killanion Plain (Κιλλανί[ο]υ Πεδίου), we cannot pinpoint assignments. However, even if we knew in every case the name of the territory to which they were assigned, we would still need to explain the nature of the revenues that territorial control was meant to guarantee. The current scholarly bias leans toward landed wealth. For example, Brélaz suggests that the *paraphylakitai* of *SEG* XLVIII 1532 guarded royal estates, namely, the *basilikoi topoi* mentioned in the text.¹⁵⁷ Yet in that inscription, it is not possible to make out what if any relation these *topoi* have to the guards in question.

A consideration of the economic geography of the regions in which these inscriptions have come to light suggests that the Attalids used *paraphylakitai* to monitor taxable movement in the countryside. To start with the hinterland of Pergamon, which produced *I.Pergamon* 249: it was certainly linked in this period to a form of specialized pastoralism that

---

[153] Strabo 13.4.13; Talloen 2013, 17; Bru 2017, 49–61. [154] Milner 1998, 65–66 (no. 145).
[155] Schuler (1999, 124 n. 2) suggests on palaeographic grounds an earlier, Seleukid date.
[156] For discussion of this famous inscription, see Brélaz 2005, 125–26, with bibliography.
[157] Brélaz 2005, 127.

fed the fabled textile production of the city.[158] In fact, this is a pattern that we can also trace in the other large urban centers of western Asia Minor like Ephesus, Miletus, and Teos. Specialized pastoralism implies distinctive fiscal modalities, which is to say, it requires a great deal of moving first flocks and then semi-processed and finished textiles.[159] This is why in a fourth-century synoikism document of Teos, a fiscal distinction is made between cloaks of Milesian wool that are imported to be sold and those that are brought into the city to be worked.[160] The density of connections formed by specialized pastoralism in western Asia Minor made surveillance of the pathways between cities, countryside, and markets a constant preoccupation. There was a palpable desire to be able to move animals and products, but also to observe others doing so – and to charge them for it. Thus it was useful for the Colophonian garrison commander who guarded the contested pass between Colophon and Lebedos ("*Ta Stena*") to keep a pack of dogs.[161] The worry was not a surprise frontal assault. It was undetected movement through the pass. The *paraphylakitai* of the Pergamene citizenship grant are more likely to have monitored movement related to specialized pastoralism than agriculture on royal estates in the Kaikos Valley.

The other testimonia come from the Milyas, specifically from around Olbasa, in the Lysis Valley (**Map 2.2**). The mountainous Milyas region, in its geography and history very similar to Pisidia (to its east), separates the upper Maeander, that is, Laodikeia-on-the-Lykos and Apameia, from the coastal plain of Pamphylia. The Attalids were neither the first nor the last imperial power to sink resources into the region. Alexander had fought the Pisidians of Termessos for the narrows (*stena*) connecting the Milyas to Pamphylia.[162] Augustus would later found a colony on the site of Olbasa.[163] The two regions that the Milyas could tie together, if so compelled by outside imperial powers, were in fact oriented in opposite directions: the Maeander Valley toward the Aegean and Pamphylia toward

---

[158] See Rostovtzeff 1923, 379–82, esp. 380–81, for treatment of the treaty between Aigai and the Olympenoi (Chandezon 2003, no. 51).
[159] Chaniotis 1999, 211–12. [160] *MDAI(A)* 16 (1891) 292–93,17 lines 13–16.
[161] Robert and Robert 1976, esp. 206–9. Cf. *SEG* XXIV 154 + XL 135, the Athenian decree of Epichares for the defense of Rhamnous. Epichares employed both dogs and lookouts (the mysterious *kryptoi*) to defend isolated crops around the time of the Chremonidean War.
[162] Strabo 14.3.9.
[163] For the significance of the Hellenistic road from Laodikeia-on-the-Lykos to Pamphylia, see Mitchell 1994, 132, 136; Mitchell 1999, 17–21. This road was the first to receive the attention of Manius Aquilius, 129–126. Parts of this road were included in the Via Sebaste, constructed in 6 BCE in order to link Pamphylia to central Anatolia.

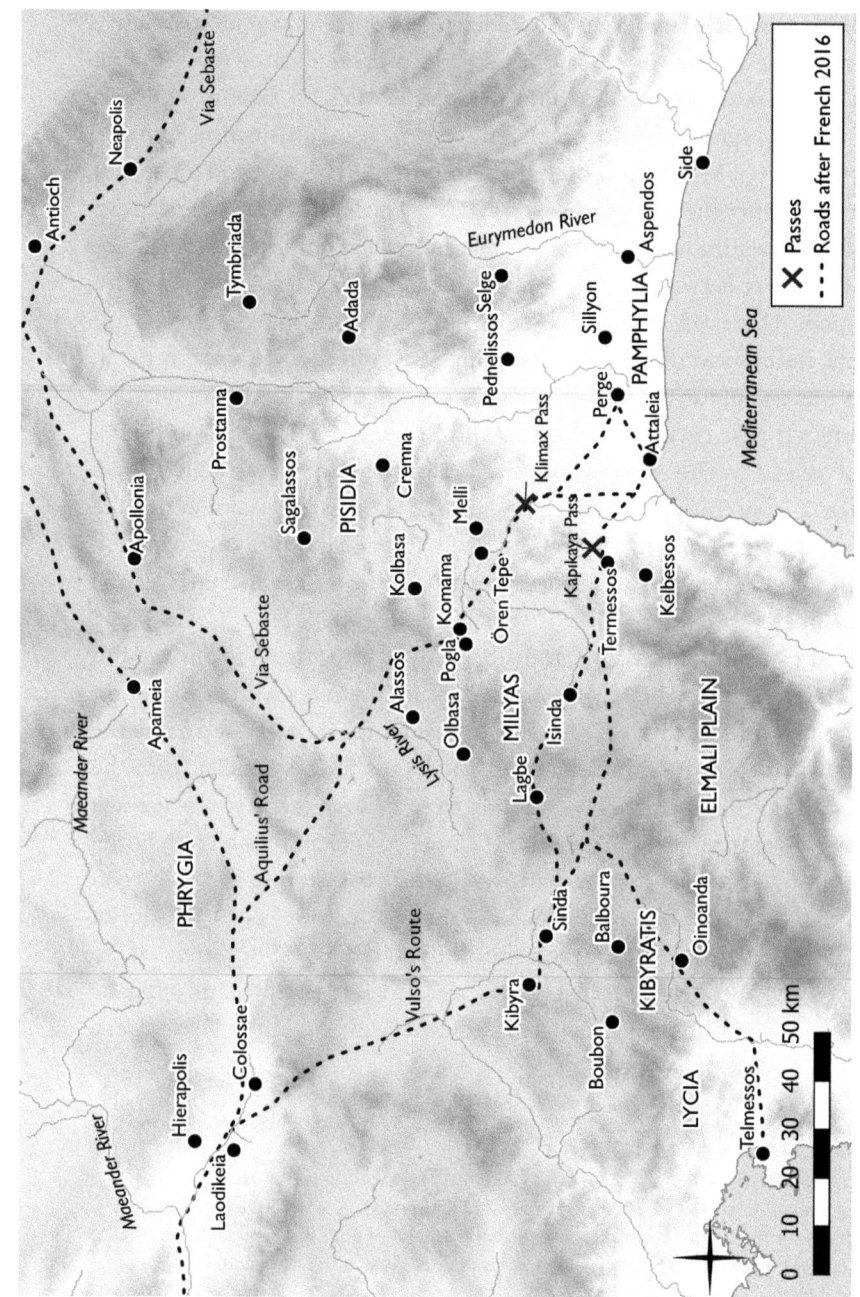

Map 2.2 Pisidia and the Milyas.

the Levant. In terms of the "natural" economic geography of Anatolia, the Milyas is not a vital link. Rather, the Attalids were interested in configuring it into one for profit. The resources of the fertile Lysis Valley notwithstanding, the strategic value of the region was enormous. Yet this was not simply a matter of being able to move armies through. Commerce between Pamphylia and the Attalids' Aegean core was funneled through a series of rocky passes. The Attalid *paraphylakitai* of this region were not watching over out-of-the-way royal estates. The place was no longer out of the way, as was indicated by establishment of a cistophoric mint at Kormasa, on the eastern side of the Lysis, which Vulso had seized in 189 on his way from Termessos to Apameia.[164] Here, guards were tasked with monitoring an increasing volume of movement between these two great zones of exchange.

Indeed, along the passes that lead into and out of the western fringe of the Pamphylian Plain, archaeology has revealed a concerted buildup of fortifications, which seems to coincide with the arrival of the Attalids. Military historian F. E. Winter drew attention to the long wall at Kapıkaya, at the foot of the Güllük Dağı, a "Pamphylian Dema" as he called it, after the dragnet barrier in rural Attica.[165] Plausibly attributed to the Attalids, the wall would have controlled access between the Pamphylian Plain and the mountainous interior. For Eumenes II, the Kapıkaya wall could have secured a vital overland link between Lycian Telmessos and Pamphylia, crucial before the foundation of the seaport of Attaleia. As Winter emphasized, this was a wall designed to curtail movement, rather than heavy artillery, and, tellingly, he identified an adjoining structure still extant as a fortified Roman toll house. Stephen Mitchell has identified two further installations in the vicinity that may have served similar purposes. At Döşeme Boğazı (Klimax Pass), where a major Hellenistic artery and later the Via Sebaste passed in dramatic fashion into and out of the plain of Pamphylia, a fortress of Hellenistic date was discovered dominating the upper part of the site (**Fig. 2.1**).[166] Further north, in a narrow plain below the Iron Age stronghold of Panemoteichos, Mitchell has also documented the impressive fortress on Ören Tepe, which he attributes to an aggressive Attalid intervention in the landscape.[167] The Sagalassos Survey has also

---

[164] Hall 1986, 141–42; Thonemann 2008, 53–58.
[165] Winter 1966; Winter 1971; McNicoll and Milner 1997, 119–20; Waelkens 2004, 445. Talloen (2013, 31 n. 129) contests Pergamene control, but understands the wall as a customs barrier.
[166] Mitchell 1998b, 173; Roelens-Flouneau 2019, 74 n. 446. Klimax Pass as control on the main route connecting Pamphylian possessions to Pergamon: Talloen 2013, 32.
[167] Aydal et al. 1997, 163–70.

Figure 2.1 The Roman Via Sebaste, retracing an earlier Attalid route, emerges from the Klimax Pass (Döşeme Boğazı) into the plain of Pamphylia. The adjacent building is Late Antique (author's photo).

studied several rural fortifications that may have functioned similarly, especially sites at Insuyu and one near Yarıköy.[168] Finally, one should note the fortification, in this period, of the site of Kelbessos, a so-called *peripolion* outpost also guarding access to the Pamphylia.[169] Granted territory on Anatolia's southern shore, with its lucrative Levantine connections, the Attalids consolidated their winnings with infrastructure designed to monitor mobility.

Centralizing Exchange

A focus on the indirect taxation of economic mobility dulled or obscured the imperial threat to civic identity. However, to meet its pressing need for revenue, the monarchy was still required to shine a light on a far greater number of taxable transactions. Preferring surgical interventions to coercion-heavy city building, the Attalids therefore directed the flow of mobility and concentrated exchange by shoring up old commercial centers and cultivating new ones. Apameia, in southwest Phrygia, is a signal case. As Kelainai, it had been a satrapal capital – an administrative center – but under the Attalids, it grew into what Strabo would call the greatest *emporion* of Asia after Ephesus, though Phrygia remained, as always, thinly

---

[168] Waelkens 2004, 446–47; Talloen 2013, 32 n. 131.   [169] Çevik and Pimouguet-Pedarros 2004.

urbanized (12.8.15). A recent analysis based on coin finds from the site helps us to see Apameia as a trans-Anatolian interchange in a highly integrated economy that linked Pergamon to Pisidia and to Pamphylia.[170] Another Phrygian example is the sanctuary of Pessinous, which Strabo tells us had by his time grown into a booming *emporion* (12.5.3). To a far greater degree than Apameia (modern Dinar), Pessinous has proven accessible to archaeologists, and it is now possible to date the emergence of the *emporion* to the second century BCE.[171] In other words, the Attalid age witnessed the birth of two enormous regional markets on the rural inland fringe of the kingdom. While strong royal connections are in evidence for both, the concentration of commercial exchange in Apameia and Pessinous surely had multiple causes. Across the entire rural southwest Taurus, we find many indications of a rupture in economic life at precisely this time – damaged agro-pastoralist relations and violent competition for resources fueled by and in turn contributing to migration, internal colonization, ethnogenesis, and the formation of a chain of rivalrous peer-polities.[172] Yet the Attalids, as imperial outsiders, figured to profit as the overlords of the newly commercialized regional economy's two great centers.

By contrast, on the Aegean and Mediterranean coasts, older entrepots were reorganized or received enhancements designed to funnel exchange into Pergamene harbors. Strabo tells us that Attalos II founded Attaleia in Pamphylia (14.4.1). There, the archaeological record for the Hellenistic period is just now emerging, but the site – previously occupied – soon became the principal port of the southern coast of Anatolia, the modern Antalya.[173] A long-standing topographical problem relates to Strabo's following comment that, nearby, Attalos also settled Korykos, "another *katoikia*, a fortress that shared its borders, and he cast a greater wall around (them both?)" (πολίχνιον ὅμορον, ἄλλην κατοικίαν καὶ μείζω περίβολον περιθέντος). One solution is to posit another Attalid foundation, but in Lycia, chalking it up to Strabo's confusion. A second solution is to think of Korykos as a satellite military settlement of the entrepot of Attaleia, perhaps on the model of Telmessos and the Kardakon Kome.[174] Both of those solutions fit with behavior patterned elsewhere. What is in any case

---

[170] Bresson 2019, 292.   [171] Verlinde 2015; Coşkun 2018, 218.   [172] Robinson 2007, 126.
[173] Bean 1968, 41; Akman and Tosun 2012, 60.
[174] See Cohen 1995, 337–38. On the corruption of the text, see Radt 2002–11, ad loc. Cf. Roller 2014, 629: "Then there is the city of Attaleia, named after its founder [Attalos II] Philadelphos, who also settled Korykos, a small neighboring town, surrounding the settlement with a larger circuit wall."

clear is that Attalid building activity in harbors always paired military with commercial considerations, though in practice they must have been closely intertwined. For example, Aeolian Elaia was a pre-dynastic maritime polis that under royal rule gave Pergamon access to the sea. Strabo's description of the city as both a "naval station (*naustathmon*) of the Attalid kings" and a commercial harbor (*limên*) is reflected neatly in recent archaeological investigations that depict a seafront split by an extant partition wall (13.3.5).[175] On a much larger scale, Attalid Ephesus was redesigned to serve the Pergamene navy, but when royal engineers dredged its harbors, Strabo tells us, it was also so that large merchant vessels (*megalai holkades*) could enter (14.1.24).[176] The geographer thus confirms that one nonmilitary objective of the ambitious royal civil works project was to increase the volume of exchange focused in Ephesus.

The same interest in economic surveillance may also elucidate the poorly understood Attalid adventure in southeastern Thrace, especially along the route from the the Hellespont to the Hebros River – and also along the Propontic littoral to Byzantium. Where Europe met Asia, heavily trafficked land and sea routes promised a surefire source of revenue to any power that could wrangle a network of settlements and customs houses around them. Scholars have long argued over whether the polis of Bisanthe, known from the Athenian Tribute Lists, and the polis of Panion, not known from any contemporary documents, but thought to be a late Attalid foundation, were one and the same.[177] The crux of the problem is that at the modern village of Barbaros an inscription was found that records a dedication: "On behalf of King Eumenes, savior, benefactor, and founder of the city (ὑπὲρ βασιλέως|Εὐμένου σωτῆρος|καὶ εὐεργέτου καὶ|κτίστου τῆς πό|λεως)" (*OGIS* 301).[178] Barbaros lies just 10 km south of Tekirdağ, the presumed site of ancient Bisanthe, on the Propontic littoral. Since the dedication for Eumenes does not record the name of the city in question, those who contend that Barbaros is the site of Panion use this inscription to make the case that it was an Attalid foundation. Alternatively, Barbaros may indeed be the site of Classical Bisanthe, but Eumenes simply refounded the city and changed its name. Indeed, there exist garbled shreds of evidence for the refoundation and renaming of

---

[175] Pirson et al. 2015, 29–30.
[176] The archaeological sequencing of the harbor of Ephesus is debated. Against the Austrian consensus (e.g., Kraft et al. 2007), Lytle (2012, 222–24) argues that the enormous, silted-up Roman harbor was the creation of Attalid engineers.
[177] Resumed by Cohen 1995, 87.   [178] See *SEG* XLIX 875; Sayar 1999, no. 1.

Bisanthe, but as a different city, the unlocated Hellenopolis. That name rings of Pergamene Panhellenism, and histories of the Attalids typically make mention of the unresolved topographical problem, related to a confusion in the testimonia.[179] We learn from the Apollodoros of Athens, active in the Library of Pergamon:

> Ἄτταλὸς ἐκ τῶν Ἑλληνίδων πόλεων οἰκήτορας συναγαγών, ἔκτισε πόλιν, καὶ ὠνόμασεν αὐτὴν Ἑλληνόπολιν (FGrHist 244 F 77).
>
> Attalos, leading settlers from the Greek cities, founded the city, and named it Hellenopolis.

Topographers have looked for Hellenopolis in Asia Minor, specifically in Bithynia, which is to say, the Bithynia of Hellenistic geography, because of this gloss of Stephanos of Byzantium:

> Ἑλληνόπολις, πόλις Βιθυνίας. μετὰ τὸν ἀνοικισμὸν Βισάλθης. τὸ ἐθνικὸν Ἑλληνοπολίτης. (Steph. Byz. ε 63 Billerbeck, s.v. Ἑλληνόπολις).
>
> Hellenopolis: a city in Bithynia. After the rebuilding of Bisalthe. The ethnic is Hellenopolitan.

The meaning of "Bithynia" has not been sufficiently explored, nor the origin of Hellenopolis as a rebuilding (*anoikismos*) of "Bisalthe." The linguistic phenomenon observed in the change from Bisanthe to Bisalthe is unremarkable.[180] What we need is an historical context for the description of Hellenopolis as πόλις Βιθυνίας. This may come from tracing Stephanos' sources. The Pergamene librarian Apollodoros did not describe the city in these terms, but rather Aelius Herodianus, an Antonine grammarian. Parts of Propontic Thrace belonged to the Roman province of Pontus and Bithynia from 74 BCE until the reign of Septimius Severus, and it is worth noting that Trajan assigned Byzantium to Bithynia. Still, it is difficult to understand how a place southwest of Perinthos, the capital of the Roman province of Thrace from 46 CE, could be described as Bithynian.[181] We are nevertheless left with the impression that an Attalid king refounded or reorganized settlement around Bisanthe. That the *anoikismos* of Hellenopolis also took place along the European shores of the Propontis seems likely given what we know of Attalid expansion across the Hellespont, ca. 148–133 BCE. Thanks to the work of David French on the early Roman roads of Asia Minor and Louisa Loukopoulou on the eastern

---

[179] Hopp (1977, 102 n. 236), rightly criticizes Hansen (1971, 178) for locating the city in Hellenistic Bithynia.
[180] Buck 1955, 64.   [181] Lozanov 2015, 176; Russell 2017, 110.

boundaries of the Roman province of Macedonia, we can take the measure of late Pergamon's European territories.[182] In addition to royal estates on the Thracian Chersonese (Gallipoli Peninsula), later known as the *agri Attalici*, there were also various territories under the authority of the "governor for the Chersonese and the places in Thrace" (στρατηγός τῆς Χερρονήσου καὶ τῶν κατὰ τὴν Θράικην τόπων)" (*I.Sestos* 1 line 13).[183] These included all of the lowlands north and east of the Melas River (Kavak Deresi), up to the Kurudağ range, and would have included at different moments part of the territory of the Thracian Caeni around today's Keşin. Toward the west, it extended along the Aegean coast to the territory of Ainos, and northeastward, it stretched along the Propontic littoral.

On the European side of the Hellespont, then, we must reckon with an indeterminate number of Pergamene projects, some of which seem to have fallen into oblivion with a major expansion of Thracian power seaward in the latter parts of the second century. However, this body of evidence still serves to elaborate the picture of Attalid activity in Propontic Thrace that we receive from reports of skirmishes with Prousias II and his allies the Caeni.[184] This was not simply a matter of burnishing warrior credentials or protecting royal estates in the Chersonese. Rather, it was a concerted effort to build up the royal presence around the heavily commercialized Hellespont and Propontis, and as an inscription from Bizye in the Thracian plain may suggest, to expand the empire (*archê*) in the direction of continental Europe.[185] For the most part, existing poleis seem to have been incorporated into the royal fiscal system, and we might see Attalos II in 167 at Rome requesting revenues from the port cities of Ainos and Maroneia – not political control.[186] As Loukopoulou points out, the

---

[182] Loukopoulou 1987, 67–81; French 2012, 12–18, both *contra* Walbank's view (1983, 145) of a Caenic Chersonese south of the Kurudağ, blocking the Attalids from acquiring a contiguous territory and road system between the Hebros and the Hellespont.

[183] For the *agri Attalici in Chersoneso* (Cic. *Leg. Agr.* 2.50), see Magie 1950, 1044, 1047. The governor's very title implies a broader territory beyond estates on the peninsula, paralleled in the Mysian soldiers' dedication from Gelembe, dated 146/5 BCE (*OGIS* 330). In fact, Loukopoulou (1987, 70) suggests that ca. 146/5 Attalos II first created the province of the Chersonese and the Thracian *topoi*. On the significance of Attalid military manpower in the region, see Daubner 2006, 72–73.

[184] For sources for the conflict with the Caeni, see conveniently Habicht 1989, 375 n. 188.

[185] This is a suggested restoration of Robert for the dedication of courtiers (?) from the Thracian citadel (and later royal capital) of Bizye. See Robert, *OMS* I, 120–23. Line 3 reads: [α]ὔξουσιν τὴ [ν - - - -].

[186] Polyb. 30.1–3; Livy 45.20. Cf. Dmitriev 2010, who sees a request for territorial gifts.

European bridgehead was also significantly expanded into resource-rich rural areas with populations afflicted by war and in need of resettlement.[187] The fiscal exploitation of the Propontis was always contingent on the maintenance of a network of customs stations, which is evinced in the *CLA*'s special treatment of the region.[188] All of the major poleis of the region possessed these outposts and indeed fought over them. Since Bisanthe/Panion – and perhaps also Hellenopolis – overlooked a commercial track that would later form the final extension of the Via Egnatia, we ought to consider the possibility that the Attalids sought their own network of positions in the region. This will have been an experiment in fiscal intensification that never quite got off the ground, leaving an incoherent mark on the historical record.

This chapter has offered a partial reconstruction of the Attalid fiscal system. The paucity of the evidence prevents us from providing the kind of snapshot of the forms, personnel, and levels of taxation for the Attalid kingdom that practitioners of the New Fiscal History have provided for many other premodern states. Yet those three questions guided the inquiry: Which taxes were collected? Who collected them? How much was collected? Direct taxes on the land, paid as the collective obligations of cities, *katoikia*-type towns, and smaller, dependent villages, were the bedrock of the system. It is instructive that these were in fact the only taxes mentioned in Antony's caricature of the Attalid system. However, we have presented evidence for a variety of other levies. Direct taxes also fell on persons, though we cautioned against assuming, for the sake of a quantitative model, that the poll tax fell on everyone who was not a citizen of a polis. As for indirect taxes, the success of an imperial project turned on their collection, on the extent to which Pergamene tax men could blend into the background of economic life. For example, a sales tax must have existed, but it was not the *agoranomia* showcased in the Toriaion earmark. The Attalids demonstrated a preference for taxes on usage, collected in the saltpans and coastal lagoons of Priene and Ephesus, and for taxes on mobility, collected all across the fiscal patchwork of Anatolia. We also tried to demonstrate the speciousness of Antony's claim of innocence in the offense of the Italian tax farmers. For a region that had not known Attalid tax farmers, the very insertion of an outsider into this traditional, socially embedded role was already an offense.

---

[187] Loukopoulou 1987, 71. [188] See Mitchell 2008, 178–83; Russell 2017, 104–13.

A model was also presented for the interaction between the royal fiscal authority and its subjects, a sketch of the rules of the game. Negotiation seems to have been appropriate – indeed, routine – around the collective tax assessment (*timêma*), precisely the place in the system where Antony alleged that the Attalids were unfairly transferring risk to the taxpayer. Just as in our examination of earmarking arrangements, we found much more room for negotiation than at first might meet the eye. In stark contrast, negotiation was out of the question when it came to delineating the categories of fiscality. These came from below, from the conceptual field of the polis, and, thereby, reinforced civic identity. Instinctively cautious and conservative in respecting categories of taxation, the Attalids hewed close to Seleukid precedent. The proposition may seem somewhat counter-intuitive, as fiscality appears in the sources as a primary arena for the negotiation of sovereignty. Yet as Apollonios and Metropolis remind us with their complaint about the tax farmers, a ruler in this world was loath to be accused of inventing new taxes. However oppressive, royal fiscality remained a calque on civic, which ensured the survival of the latter. Therefore, pressed for revenues, the Attalids did not invent new fiscal categories to broaden the scope of taxation. They focused their energies instead on capturing more of those taxes that everyone already agreed were legitimate. As they always were in the premodern Mediterranean, these were chiefly indirect taxes on mobility and exchange. So the Attalids mustered the bodies and facilities necessary for surveillance, and they refounded or refurbished a network of entrepots to centralize exchange.

3 | The King's Money

Up until now, our analysis of the Attalid political economy has traced patterns of interaction between royal and civic actors that help explain the success of the Pergamene imperial project. Whether taxing or gifting, the characteristic Attalid finesse was always on display. Genuine negotiation produced the proliferation of earmarking arrangements. As we shall see in Chapter 5, it also had the effect of channeling royal benefaction into the civic gymnasia. As techniques of domination and accommodation, none of this was new. On the contrary, these were time-honored, culturally privileged solutions to the problems of governance. What was new was the intensity with which the Attalids pursued administrative and ideological cohesion, producing new collectivities as fiscal structures aligned interests. However, we have yet to consider what is usually regarded as the most strikingly new, distinctive, and still mysterious feature of their rule, namely, the coinage and, specifically, the cistophori (plural for cistophorus).

These are curious coins. They were minted on a peculiar weight standard. They also lack the royal portraits that genre prescribed. Their very strangeness has provoked radically divergent interpretations. For Fred Kleiner, whose *Early Cistophoric Coinage* is the standard reference work on the subject, the cistophori were "the king's money," a straightforwardly royal coinage.[1] That position, it must be understood, is polemical. There is a long tradition, stretching back to Alexandre Panel and Joseph Eckhel in the eighteenth century, with Henri Seyrig and Wolfgang Szaivert as its most recent exponents, which regards the cistophori as the federative coinage of cities.[2] In an authoritative study, George Le Rider writes of the "cistophoric coinage of the Attalids," but tentatively puts forward a more nuanced vision, suggesting that the kings negotiated the cistophori into existence, and then shared with the cities of Asia Minor the attendant

---

[1] Kleiner and Noe 1977, 120–25.
[2] Kleiner and Noe 1977, 10; Szaivert 2008; Seyrig 1963. To compare two divergent characterizations in recent scholarship, Daubner (2006, 74) emphasizes the initiative and profits of the cities ("nicht von oben oktroyiert"), while Thonemann (2013b, 33) writes of "projection of this 'pseudo-federal' ideology."

responsibilities and rewards.[3] This chapter argues that the cities' cooperation was key not only to the birth of the cistophori but to the maintenance of the entire Attalid monetary system. As an arena of negotiation between city and king, the coinage elicits our attention.

Neither purely royal nor civic, the cistophori defy labels and epitomize the eclecticism of the Attalid state. On closer inspection, we will find other confounding forms of Attalid money, such as the Wreathed Coinages and the so-called "cistophoric" countermarks. From ca. 170 BCE, we enter a transformative period in the history of Greek coinage. The relationship between sovereignty and coinage becomes ever more difficult to untangle. As Olivier Picard has pointed out, to make sense of large new coinages such as the Athenian New Style or Macedonian Meris coinage, we need to lose old labels such as "imitation" or "pseudo-Roman."[4] Indeed, this chapter will propose one new schema: coordinated coinage. Achaemenid antecedents aside, the monetary system of the Attalid kingdom at its acme involved civic institutions and promoted civic identities to an unprecedented and ultimately unmatched degree. Paradoxically, this had the effect of extending the kings' reach over much new territory. In other words, coinage had a role to play in fostering the integration of the various microregions of the Attalid state. It is interesting to contrast the testimony of Polybius, for whom coinage was merely an index of state formation and integration (*symphronêsis*) (2.37.8–11). For the Megalopolitan, the federal coinage of the Achaean Koinon is just one measure of the remarkable transformation of the Peloponnese into, in his formulation, a single polis but for the walls. It is an expression, not a tool of integration. We can go further, attributing to a Hellenistic coinage the power to bind the smaller polities of a royal state to each other and to the crown.

The narrow question of what to call the cistophori – the binary choice of royal or civic coinage – is a fruitless question of *cui bono*. The cistophoric system generated profits, through the procurement and transfer of bullion, and through the exchange and reminting of old coin. Yet given the present state of our evidence, we cannot so much as guess at the size of these profits and the extent to which the Attalids shared them with the cities. We can, however, observe in the cistophoric system features of both centralized and

---

[3] Le Rider 1989, 189.

[4] Picard 2010, 189–90. Meadows 2018 illustrates the transformation in Greek coin design, ca. 170 to ca. 140, which upended categories of Hellenic and epichoric, royal and civic. See esp. p. 310 on cross-pollination between new civic coinage and unusual royal issues of Antiochos IV and Ptolemy V.

decentralized control. This hybridity permits us to state with confidence that the inherent profits were shared. Decentralization is emphasized in the explanation of the cistophori set out in what follows mainly because previous scholarship seems to overstate the case for centralization. To emphasize cooperation is not to lose sight of the Attalids as the prime movers behind this coinage, nor to discount their role as the indispensable coordinating force behind the system – to ignore the obvious asymmetries of power. It is instead a means, first, of situating the cistophori in the broader context of Attalid money and, second, of highlighting the distinctiveness of Attalid monetary practice. The chapter first lays out a new understanding of the cistophori: neither royal nor civic, but what we term a coordinated coinage. Second, it proposes an explanation of the various changes in the coinage of the Attalid kingdom, 188–133, set against the wider backdrop of the eastern Mediterranean. But before we can explain them, we need to introduce the coins.

Overview of the Coinages of the Attalid Kingdom, 188–133 BCE

The most current numismatic research on the mint of Pergamon undercuts the notion of a decisive change in 188.[5] The Attalids had always minted an Attic-weight, which is to say, international silver coinage, and they continued to do so after the Treaty of Apameia (Marcellesi nos. 26 and 42; **Fig. 3.1**).[6] The Philetairoi, Attic tetradrachms bearing the face of the founder, have been divided into seven groups by Ulla Westermark.[7] With minor modifications, Westermark's groups have been retained, but their absolute dates are not fixed. Andrew Meadows has recently posited a gap in the production of Philetairoi from ca. 190 to ca. 180–175.[8] Yet the Attalids were minting an Attic-weight silver coinage in the 180s, if indeed their posthumous Alexanders continue from the late third century into this

---

[5] Cf. Harl 1991, 281: "The defeat of Antiochus III on the plains of Magnesia wrought major political and monetary consequences for the eastern Mediterranean." On the mint of Pergamon specifically, see Chameroy 2012, 154: no change in the bronze coinage of Pergamon can be linked to the events of 188.

[6] Identifying numbers for Pergamene coin types are given from Marcellesi 2012.

[7] Westermark 1960.

[8] Meadows (2013, 164) posits a gap from the end of Westermark Group VI B2 to the beginning of Group VII; cf. Marcellesi 2012, 122–23, assuming continuous production of Philetairoi. On her chronology, Group VII was launched with the cistophori, just before 190.

Figure 3.1 Silver tetradrachm of Eumenes II minted in the name of Philetairos, Westermark Group VII (16.35 g, ANS 1944.100.43195; courtesy of the American Numismatic Society).

period (Marcellesi no. 32). Meadows has placed a subset of Attalid Alexanders (Price nos. 1491–95) in the 180s, arguing that "Alexander coinage is likely to have been the principal coinage produced by the Pergamene kings during the period of their conflict with Antiochos III, and in the subsequent decade of reorganization of the Pergamene kingdom."[9] In other words, the Attalids seem to have preferred to make payments in Alexanders during the crucial start-up years of the enlarged kingdom. Pergamon now joined Miletus and a host of other cities in the region already minting Alexanders. With an eye to making their coinage acceptable and their royalty inconspicuous, the Attalids paused production of the Philetairoi in favor of generic Alexanders.[10]

At some point in the 180s, a new wave of Attic-weight silver entered the enlarged Attalid kingdom in the form of countermarked tetradrachms of four Pamphylian cities: Phaselis, Perge, Aspendos, and Side.[11] The Sidetan

---

[9] Meadows 2013, 163.
[10] Cf. Marcellesi 2012, 180–83, arguing for continuous production of the Philetairoi, with Group VII minted from the 190s to the 160s. Contemporary Alexanders from Miletus: Marcellesi 2004, 137–39.
[11] For the hoard evidence that points to 188–183, see Bauslaugh 1990, 53–55. Cf. Meadows 2013, 170–73: a date range of 188–180; similarly, Callataÿ 2013, 225. For the Pamphylian host coinage, see Mørkholm 1978; Meadows 2009.

Figure 3.2 Silver tetradrachm of Side minted ca. 210–190 BCE, bearing countermark of bow-in-case + ΠΕΡ (15.91 g, ANS 2015.20.1206; courtesy of the American Numismatic Society).

issues, which predominate, bore that city's own types; the rest, like many other civic coinages of this period, were Alexanders. A second minting authority placed a countermark on the obverse of the host coin, consisting of a bow-in-case alongside an abbreviated city name or ethnic (**Fig. 3.2**). These have been named "cistophoric countermarks" on account of the bow-in-case symbol, shared with the cistophori proper, which would seem to refer to the Heraklid origins of the House of Telephos. The cities evoked by the marks were also all in post-Apameian Pergamene territory: Ephesus, Tralles, Sardis, Synnada, Apameia, Laodikeia-on-the-Lykos, Stratonikeia-on-the-Kaikos, Adramyttium, Toriaion, the long unidentified ΕΛΗΣ, ΕΛ/ΛΗ, ΕΛΛΗ, and Pergamon itself.[12] However, these countermarks and the cistophoric coinage itself were not contemporaneous. The so-called cistophoric countermarking seems to end in the early 170s, just before the cistophori, on the "low chronology," begin.[13] Indeed, seven of the twelve known cities referred to by the countermarks correspond to cistophoric cities. While Sardis appears on the countermarks the most, Ephesus barely registers. This is significant because Sardis plays a minor role and Ephesus

---

[12] For Toriaion and Sala in Lydia, see Thonemann 2008. In a forthcoming contribution to the festschrift for Richard Ashton, Thonemann eliminates Sala from consideration and proposes the *strategeia* of the Hellespont for ΕΛΗΣ, ΕΛ/ΛΗ, ΕΛΛΗ.

[13] Cf. Marcellesi 2012, 136–39: the years ca. 190–ca. 170 witnessed the production of the cistophoric countermarks, in her view, contemporary with the minting of the first cistophori.

Figure 3.3 Cistophoric silver tetradrachm of Pergamon, ca. 160–150 BCE (12.58 g, ANS 1951.5.13; courtesy of the American Numismatic Society).

a major one in the production of cistophori, implying shifting priorities or purpose.[14]

The cistophori are one of the great numismatic puzzles of Classical Antiquity. The term *cistophorus* is an ancient one, usually used by Moderns to refer to the tetradrachms of a system that included didrachms and eventually drachms.[15] It is the tetradrachm alone, however, which, bears on its obverse the wicker chest or ritual basket, the so-called *cista mystica*, with its lid ajar and a serpent emerging (Marcellesi no. 45; **Fig. 3.3**). An ivy wreath wraps around the field. On the reverse, the tetradrachm displays two snakes on either side of a bow in its case (*gorytos*). The reverse also bears various symbols and the name of a city – or an ethnic – usually in abbreviated form, for example, ΕΦΕ or, less often, as a monogram.[16] The didrachms (Marcellesi no. 46; **Fig. 3.4**) and post-Attalid drachms (Marcellesi no. 49; **Fig. 3.5**) share types: on the obverse, a

---

[14] Bauslaugh 1990, 50.

[15] The ancients were more precise. A Delian account specifically refers to the large-module coin as a tetradrachm: κιστοφόρον τετράχμον (*I.Delos* 1443 A1 line 149). For a review of literary references to cistophori, see Szaivert 2005.

[16] I will discuss below the important question of whether we treat these legends as an abbreviation of a city's name or as a proper ethnic. Le Rider 1990, esp. 685, and Drew-Bear and Le Rider 1991, e.g., treat them as an ethnic.

Figure 3.4 Cistophoric silver didrachm of Tralles, ca. 145–140 BCE (5.91 g, ANS 1944.100.37564; courtesy of the American Numismatic Society).

Figure 3.5 Cistophoric silver drachm, ca. 134–128 BCE (2.58 g, ANS 1984.5.35; courtesy of the American Numismatic Society).

club draped with a lion skin, wrapped in a wreath; on the reverse, a bunch of grapes on a vine leaf, and again, various marks and the shortened version of a city's name/ethnic. The tetradrachm, which will be referred to here as the cistophorus, per the convention, is the dominant denomination; the didrachms and the later drachms, which will be referred to as the fractions, are rare by comparison. (By "cistophori," we mean all three denominations.) The cistophoric tetradrachm was minted at a theoretical weight of ca. 12.6 g, the didrachm at 6.15 g, and the drachm at 3.05 g.[17] This weight standard is singular, if also relatable to its contemporaries, with a cistophorus weighing roughly the same as three Attic-weight drachms or Roman denarii, and the drachm a negligible 0.05 g heavier than the Rhodian plinthophoros.[18]

The iconography of the mythological repertoire glimpsed on the cistophori is bewilderingly complex.[19] Perhaps it was meant to be so, and therefore it managed to appeal to a broad range of users, Greek and Anatolian, while remaining politically and culturally anodyne. Alternatively, the peculiar combination of myths depicted eludes conclusive interpretation because it is not preserved in any other media. Commentators since Warwick Wroth in the nineteenth century have emphasized different divine attributes, the snake of Asklepios, ivy and grapes of Dionysos, arms and lion skin cloak of Herakles, without offering a comprehensive interpretation of the visual program.[20] One tends now to describe cistophoric iconography as a mixed bag. For example, asserting that the Attalids "considered Pergamon as a sort of Athens of the east," Elizabeth Kosmetatou argues that the *cista* and snake of the obverse represent the myth of Erichthonius and Athena, while also allowing that the visual frame of the ivy wreath may refer to the dynasty's favored cult of Dionysus Kathegemon.[21] For Marie-Christine Marcellesi, the coins are a savvy mix of Bacchic and Heraklid imagery. The *cista*, then, would be part of the paraphernalia of the mystery cult of Dionysos Kathegemon, while the citizens of Pergamon, as the descendants of Telephos, would be vindicated by the symbols of Herakles.[22] In fact, any number of these

---

[17] Kleiner and Noe 1977, 15.
[18] For the relationship to the denarius, circulating in Greece from ca. 150 BCE, see Harl 1996, 68–69. While the ratio of 3:1 must have facilitated accounts during episodic joint military operations, it does little to illuminate the logic of the cistophoric system, as the denarius arrived in Asia Minor only in the second half of the first century BCE.
[19] The most systematic exposition is Szaivert 2008.   [20] Wroth 1882.
[21] Kosmetatou 1998, 17.
[22] Marcellesi 2012, 146. On the citizens of Pergamon as the Telephidai, see also Heres 1996, 83.

conclusions is open to debate. For example, in an exhaustive study of the cults of Pergamon, Erwin Ohlemutz finds no sign of the mystery cult of Dionysos Kathegemon on the coins.[23] Rather, an ancient viewer may have seen the cult of Demeter and Persephone in the image of a snake-in-a-box.[24] We tend to focus on the *cista*, at least in part, because we happen to have it in a Greek and later Latin term for the coin. Yet the most dominant motif overall is the snake – with one on the obverse and two on the reverse. To a different ancient viewer, these could have been the "snake-bearing coins (*ophiophoroi*)."

It is worth bearing in mind that some or all of these snakes may belong to a class of benevolent serpents (*drakônes*).[25] This distinguishes the cistophori from famous coin types such as the silver of classical Chalchis, which exhibits a predatory eagle holding a serpent in its beak and claws, and the hunch can lead us in several interesting directions.[26] The heraldic pair of standing snakes on the reverse of the cistophorus almost seems to guard the *gorytos* of Herakles. Are these snakes in fact friendly to the house of Telephos? Apparently, some serpents were friendly to the Pergamene hero. In a possibly Sophoclean version of the myth, a snake stood up to prevent the hero from consummating his marriage with his mother Auge, the very scene depicted on Panel 21 of the Great Altar's inner frieze.[27] Moreover, an important precedent among the coin types of Pergamon should be brought into the discussion. A large number of bronzes were minted in the name of Philetairos from the 270s until the early second

---

[23] Ohlemutz 1968, 118–19. On Dionysos and the Attalids, see conveniently Dignas 2012, 134–35. However, the snake-in-*cista* motif does exist in the iconography of the cult of Dionysos (and Asklepios). See Ogden 2013, 363.

[24] Picard 2010, 19. See also the bronze coin of Perinthos in nearby Propontic Thrace (ca. 138–192 CE) that features a veiled Demeter/snake emerging from *cista*: Schönert-Geiß, *Die Münzprägung von Perinthos* no. 173.2, p. 117, pl. 7, pic. 173/2 (Perinthos CN_2164, in Corpus Nummorum: www.corpus-nummorum.eu/CN_2164 [accessed June 29, 2020]). Further, the snake-in-the-box motif also appears in the Talmud (t. Yoma 22b) in connection with the worship of Persephone in Roman Palestine. See Meshorer 1981. See further the important study of Krengel 2016, which argues that both the Palestinian and the Pergamene coins refer to an Orphic theogony. On the cistophoros, therefore, we should see Zeus-Sabazios in the form of a snake on both sides of the coin, begetting Dionysus on the obverse, and on the reverse, mating with Demeter to produce Persephone.

[25] Cf. Szaivert 2008, 29–30, interpreting the snakes of the reverse as those strangled by young Herakles. Generally on benevolent snakes in Greek myth and religion, see Ogden 2013, 271–382.

[26] Chalchis: *BMC Central Greece* nos. 38–40. For the eagle-destroys-serpent motif on grave stelai of late Hellenistic Bithynia, see Akyürek Şahin and Uzunoğlu 2019, 267–68.

[27] The same scene appears on a late Hellenistic votive relief from just outside the Asklepieion. See Bauchhenss-Thüriedl 1971, 69–70.

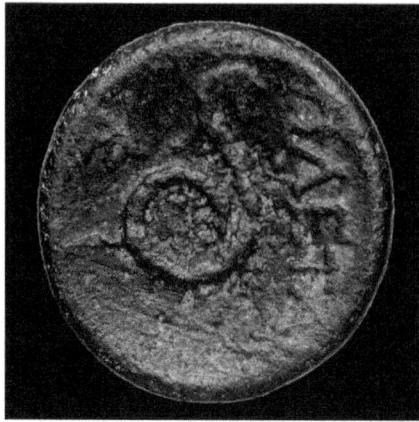

Figure 3.6 Standing serpent on reverse of large module (hemiobol?) bronze coin in the name of Philetairos, ca. 270s–200 BCE (4.27 g, BNF Fonds général 1486; courtesy of Bibliothèque nationale de France).

century that bear a standing snake on the reverse (Marcellesi no. 18; **Fig. 3.6**). A reference to the popular, pre-Attalid cult of Asklepios is certainly plausible given echoes on the god's own bronze and that of Hygieia (Marcellesi nos. 59–60, 62), but the snake on the Philetairos bronze, lacking omphalos or staff, also bears a striking resemblance to the one saving Telephos from Oedipal sin on the Great Altar (**Fig. 3.7**). Indeed, if we cast a wider net, we find plenty of contemporary myths of foundation that involve friendly snakes, most relevant among them, the *argolai*, which are said to have aided Alexander in Alexandria.[28] The Alexander Romance suggests that household snakes as friendly spirits (*agathoi daimones*) had well-known associations with Hellenistic royalty.[29] Meanwhile, Iron Age Anatolia seems to have contained its own tales of founder-snakes and serpentine progenitors. Strabo tells us of the snake-men as heroes of the tribes of the conspicuously pro-Attalid city of Parion, and a recurrent motif on the coinage of Pisidian Etenna shows that non-Greek myth mixed easily with Greek when it came to friendly snakes.[30]

From an administrative standpoint, the cistophori are slightly less mysterious. We can be reasonably certain of the identity of most of the pre-133 cistophoric mints – at least the major ones (**Map I.3**). There are two tiers in

---

[28] Suda s.v. ἀργόλαι (A3781).   [29] Djurslev and Ogden 2018.
[30] Strabo 13.1.14; Nollé 1992, 92–96; Krengel 2016, 18. On the serpentine dragons of Anatolian myth in popular memory of the Roman period, see Rojas 2019, 80–82, 127–37.

Figure 3.7 Fragmentary bedroom scene from the Telephos Frieze with standing serpent warning hero and Auge (T.I. 37, © Antikensammlung, Staatliche Museen zu Berlin – Preussischer Kulturbesitz; Photo: Johannes Laurentius).

terms of volume of production: the large, regular mints, which are Pergamon, Ephesus, Tralles, Apameia, and, to a lesser extent, Sardis (Synnada in Phrygia was once thought to be Sardis-Synnada);[31] and the small, irregular ones: Laodikeia-on-the-Lykos; Adramyttion, which is attested by a single pre-133 coin, though it became a major mint from the time of the Revolt of Aristonikos;[32] and, finally, a smattering of small mints whose identity is contested, but at least four seem to be south Phrygian: Blaundos, Dionysoupolis, Dioskome, and Lysias (or Synnada?). The mystery mint KOP may be Kormasa in the Milyas.[33] Quantitatively speaking, an overall volume of roughly 50 obverse die equivalents per year points to Attalid initiative and bullion resources behind coins that deliberately obscure – and indeed efface – the kings' role. Meanwhile, the

---

[31] Kleiner and Noe 1977, 78–85.
[32] Bauslaugh (1990, 48) announces the discovery of a pre-133 cistophoros of Adramyttion and planned publication. That coin, which is Paris 2600 ex Slg. Garriri, Smyrna, 1853, was later published by Josef Stauber as I.Adramytteion II, 208, no. 94. For a catalogue of cistophoric countermarks of Adramytteion and the city's large production of late cistophori, see I.Adramytteion II, 206–11.
[33] Thonemann 2008, 53–58. For other suggestions, see Marcellesi 2012, 118–20.

cistophori represent Attalid minting on an unprecedented scale. François de Callataÿ has estimated the value of the cistophori at 6.5 times that of the annual average of pre-170 Philetairoi.[34]

Dating the Cistophori

The terms of the debate on the vexed question of the date of the introduction of the cistophoric system have narrowed in recent years.[35] For the high chronology, Karl Harl and Marcellesi rely on the testimony of Livy, who records the display of cistophori in four Roman triumphs between 190 and 187. Marcellesi sees the Attalids minting the new coins at Pergamon in the run-up to the war with Antiochos III. After the victory, the system was expanded to include the other mints in the new territories.[36] Many other numismatists dismiss Livy's testimonia as anachronism, and have instead concentrated on the period between 188, when the political geography of Asia Minor was redrawn, and ca. 166–ca. 150, when the coins start to turn up in the Delian accounts. The debate turns on the dating of a portion of Westermark Group VII Philetairoi, reclassified as Nicolet-Pierre issues 19–25.[37] These Philetairoi share control marks with what are understood to be early cistophori. Leaving aside for a moment the important point that the Attalids struck the cistophori and this Attic-weight regal coinage simultaneously, one needs to decide on dates for this group of the latest Philetairoi. Their presence in the Maaret-en-Nouman hoard (northwest Syria) provides a *terminus ante quem* of 162.[38] But it is difficult to determine how much earlier they began, and how long they took to travel from Pergamon to Syria and into the ground. For the overlap of Philetairoi and cistophori, Meadows argues for the lowest chronology yet, ca. 165–ca. 160,

---

[34] Callataÿ 2013, 239. For the methodology for calculating the original number of dies, see Carter 1983. For the much more controversial calculation of the original size of the coinage from that number, see Callataÿ 2011b. By number of "obverse die equivalents," I mean, according to the widely accepted method of Carter, how many obverse dies were used to strike the coinage, converted into a standard unit of an Attic drachm obverse die. The numbers presented in this chapter make no assumption about average die productivity (20,000 strikes per die?) other than that it was roughly constant.

[35] See Kleiner-Noe 1977, 10–16; Meadows 2013, 175–83, favoring a date of 167. Callataÿ 2013, 218–31, more cautious about the relationship between the Maaret hoard and the inception of the cistophori, offers a loose date in the 170s; Marcellesi 2012, 132–44, with a date just before 190.

[36] Livy: 37.46.3–4, 37.58.3–5, 37.59.3–6, 39.7.1–2, 5. See further Harl 1991 and Marcellesi 2012, 140–44.

[37] Nicolet-Pierre 1989, 208–15.   [38] Mattingly 1993.

and points to a coin of Alabanda minted in 167/6 on the cistophoric standard as supplementary evidence of their existence.[39]

Many scholars posit 181 as a further *terminus ante quem* for the launch of the cistophori on the basis of Richard Ashton's interpretation of a letter of Eumenes II to Artemidoros, the Attalid governor of the Lycian outpost of Telmessos (**D3**).[40] The letter concerns benefactions for the inhabitants of the Kome Kardakon, who had fallen on hard times.[41] The key passage reads: "Since it is necessary for them to pay arrears on the poll-tax, each of them four Rhodian drachmas and one obol, but since, in light of their suffering, this is not within their means, let this amount be remitted this year, and from next year, let them pay one Rhodian drachma and one obol (καὶ ἐπεὶ τῆς συντάξεως δεῖ διορθοῦσθαι αὐτοὺς ἑκάστου σώματος ἐνηλίκου Ῥοδίας δραχμὰς τέσσαρας ὀβολόν, ἀσθενοῦντες δὲ τοῖς ἰδίοις βαρύνονται, τά τε παραγραφόμενα αὐτοῖς ἐκ τοῦ ἑκκαιδεκάτου ἔτους ἐκ τούτων ἀφεῖναι, ἀπὸ δὲ τοῦ ἑπτακαιδεκάτου ἔτους Ῥοδίαν δραχμὴν καὶ ὀβολόν)" (lines 10–14). Ashton calls attention to the significance of what he deems the curiously unrounded number of the tax. He takes it as given that the poll-tax was normally paid at a rate of four "Rhodian" drachms and one obol, which, if the Rhodian coins are indeed Rhodian plinthophori, is equivalent to a total of ca. 12.6 g of silver, the weight of the cistophorus. This would mean that in Telmessos, in the vicinity of the Rhodian zone of control, the Attalids had decided to collect a tax collected elsewhere in the kingdom as a cistophorus in an equivalent amount of Rhodian coined silver. Therefore, the curiously unrounded number of the tax levied at Telmessos tells us that the cistophorus already existed in the kingdom at large. It is an ingenious conjecture, but should not be mistaken for an unimpeachable fact. The decree only states that the Attalids had been unable to collect the 12.6 g of Rhodian silver coins from the Kardakoi. Significantly, they then

---

[39] The 1968 Larissa (Sitochoro) hoard (*IGCH* 237) has always been a problem for advocates of a late date for the cistophoric reform. For the hoard's publication, see Price 1989, who adjusts the *IGCH* listing date of 168/7 to ca. 165. It contained a single cistophorus of Apameia (no. 241, Pl. LV). The existence of the coin had been reported in the Greek newspaper *Estia* in 1968, but the coin itself appeared in the British Museum only in 1979, with the accompanying story that it came from the hoard of 1968. According to Price (1989, 240), it has the same "patchy black patina" as the hoard's Perseus tetradrachms, but scholars on both sides of the debate now favor a prudent exclusion of the Sitochoro cistophorus from discussion: Meadows 2013, 181 n. 77; Marcellesi 2012, 134–35.

[40] Ashton 1994; adopted by, e.g., Thonemann 2011b, 170; Kosmetatou 2003, 164; also Bresson 1996, 71 – though he no longer accepts Ashton's arguments (personal comm.).

[41] Part of the context for those hard times might have been the war with Prousias I and the Galatians referred to in the decree of Telmessos of 184/3, Segre 1932 (Allen 1983, no. 7).

permanently lowered the tax rate to a figure, one Rhodian drachm and one obol (3.5–6 g), which bears little relation to the weight of the cistophoric drachm (3.05 g).[42] Was the attempt to integrate the Lycian outpost into the new monetary system so quickly abandoned? Rather, the Telmessos text only demonstrates that in 181 the Attalids were employing a unit of account that would later be expressed in the cistophorus. The origin of the unit of 12.6 g may lie in fiscal experimentation, but 181 cannot be posited as a *terminus ante quem* for the cistophoric system, which was introduced some time after ca. 175.[43]

Attic-Weight Coinage

Whether we date the cistophoric reform to the 170s or 160s, it is becoming increasingly clear that the introduction of the cistophorus did not spell the end of production of Attic-weight coinage in the kingdom.[44] In fact, we are only just coming to recognize the impressive scale of Attic-weight, "international" coinages minted in the final decades of Attalid rule. Of those that are patently royal, to the aforementioned Group VII Philetairoi we must add an extremely rare issue of tetradrachms bearing a portrait of Eumenes II, dated by Hélène Nicolet-Pierre to 166–159 (**Fig. 3.8**).[45] Two other silver coinages known from a very small number of specimens seem to be related to officially sanctioned cultic activity: the tetradrachms of Athena Nikephoros, usually placed in the mid-160s (**Fig. 3.9**), and a tetradrachm from Teos, but issued in the name of a group with deep ties to the Attalid court, the Association of the Artists of Dionysus, dated by Catherine Lorber and Oliver Hoover to the 150s. Meadows has added a further coinage to the mix from the mid- to late 140s. These are tetradrachms that show Demeter on the obverse and the Kabeiroi encircled by a wreath on the reverse, in much the same fashion as the reverse of the Eumenes II portrait coins.

---

[42] As Marcellesi (2012, 134) points out, the reduced figure does not fit roundly into cistophori. Tietz (2003, 312–13) recognizes the problem, but does not challenge Ashton's theory. He sees in the letter of Eumenes II to Artemidoros a failed attempt to integrate Telmessos into the Pergamene monetary orbit. On the contrary, one could see flexibility and fiscal integration across monetary boundaries. Tietz' conclusion that Telmessos fell squarely in the Rhodian zone is based on counts from the collection of the museum of Fethiye (Telmessos): ca. 600 of ca. 2,500 Hellenistic coins are Rhodian.

[43] For ca. 175 as, in his view, the date of the introduction of the cistophorus, see Bresson 2018, 134.

[44] Marcellesi 2012, 122–27, 149–54; Meadows 2013, 163–75.

[45] On the portrait coins of Eumenes II, see Queyrel 2003, 144–46, boldly arguing that portrait style can confirm the date.

Figure 3.8 Silver tetradrachm of Eumenes II, ca. 166–162 BCE (15.24 g, BM 1849,0717.10 © The Trustees of the British Museum).

Figure 3.9 Silver tetradrachm in the name of Athena Nikephoros, reign of Eumenes II, ca. 180–165 BCE (16.06 g, BM 1975,0208.1 © The Trustees of the British Museum).

Their legend, however, reads not ΒΑΣΙΛΕΩΣ ΕΥΜΕΝΟΥ ("of King Eumenes"), but ΘΕΩΝ ΚΑΒΕΙΡΩΝ ΣΥΡΙΩΝ ("of the Syrioi Kabeiroi"). If Meadows is correct in attributing this coinage to the Attalids, it would be of more than antiquarian interest. By the looks of the die counts, this was a

Figure 3.10 Silver drachm of Ephesus with legend "of the Ephesians," ca. 150 BCE (4.02 g, BNF Fonds général 511 = Kinns 1999 obverse 70; courtesy of Bibliothèque nationale de France).

very large coinage, on the same scale as the cistophori in the same period of production.[46]

Several cities within the Attalid kingdom also minted Attic-weight coinage after the introduction of the cistophorus. For example, the gold drachms of Tralles, minted on the Attic standard, share control marks with the cistophori Kleiner-Noe series 9 and 41.[47] Signaling the city's autonomy, it seems that Tralles minted the two gold issues at two distinct periods of its history. Of much greater importance to the regional money supply were the many Ephesian silver drachms with bee on obverse, stag on reverse (**Fig. 3.10**). Philip Kinns has established an early phase for this coinage that ends ca. 170, as well as a later phase for which he gives only the *terminus ante quem* of ca. 150.[48] It is indeed likely that Ephesus was producing Attic drachms and cistophori in parallel. The cases of Ephesus and Tralles, cities awarded to the Attalids at Apameia as gifts (*dôreai*;

---

[46] Meadows 2013, 184–86. Cf. Queyrel 2003, 146: the posture of the Dioscuri of Eumenes' portrait coin interpreted as symbols of big-brotherly rule, with the figure to the right (Eumenes) leaning on the one to the left (Attalos), who meekly crosses his chest with an arm. On the other hand, the Kabeiroi, who are sometimes identified with the Dioscuri, are positioned identically on the ΘΕΩΝ ΚΑΒΕΙΡΩΝ ΣΥΡΙΩΝ coins. Despite the large differential in volume, Thonemann (2015a, 86) sees both as festival coinages.

[47] Jenkins 1980, 186; Le Rider 1989, 173; Meadows 2013, 189.   [48] Kinns 1999.

Polyb. 21.46.10), point up the difficulty of using coinage to determine the political or fiscal status of a community after 188.[49] The same can be said of Temnos, which, while under tight Attalid control, continued to mint its Alexanders in the 150s and 140s.[50] Monetary production is just one arena for the negotiation of sovereignty. As Thomas Martin has shown, the ancient Greeks possessed little loyalty to an abstract connection between sovereignty and the right to mint.[51] For the cities of the Attalid kingdom, it is not possible to extrapolate monetary behavior from the political status assigned at Apameia.[52]

Finally, the most significant Attic-weight coinages produced in the Attalid kingdom in these years are the so-called Wreathed Coinages.[53] These are silver tetradrachms bearing the civic types and ethnics of coastal cities, the obverse framed by the wreath that gives them their name (**Fig. 3.11**). The cities in question are Aigai, Kyme, Myrina, and Smyrna in the Aeolian core; Lebedos; Magnesia-on-the-Maeander; and Herakleia-under-Latmos. With good hoard evidence and die studies available, Callataÿ has been able to date the Wreathed Coinages ca. 154–135, although the mints operated on different schedules.[54] Still, even on the lowest chronology, the cistophori and the Wreathed Coinages are contemporary developments. It should be noted that several other coinages of the middle two quarters of the second century share the wreath design, for example, coins of Macedonia under Philip V, of Eretria and Cyzicus, and the Athenian New Style tetradrachms. This is evidence not of a monetary union, as some have hypothesized, but of a popular fashion in coin design that may have served to enhance the coins' acceptability.[55]

The Wreathed Coinages circulated similarly to other Attic-weight coinages of Asia Minor. They do not appear in the thin hoard record for mid-second-century Asia Minor, but they do turn up in Levantine hoards of the 150s and 140s.[56] We do not need ad hoc political or military

---

[49] Cf. Allen 1983, 110–11, who uses coinage to determine the tributary status of each city that minted 188–133.

[50] Meadows 2013, 189–90: Temnos' mint as an "active civic apparatus." For Attalid control of Temnos, see *RC* 48 (**D4**). Temnos may also have been the recipient of the inscribed letter *I.Sardis* 2. In addition to these Alexanders of the 150s or 140s, Temnos, according to Seyrig (1973, 70), countermarked Alexanders of Alabanda of the mid-second century. The attribution of these grapes countermarks, however, has been questioned: for the coins and comment, see Meadows 2008, 73.

[51] Martin 1985.   [52] Cf. Psoma 2013, 271 n. 20.

[53] For bibliography, see Callataÿ 2013, 233 Table 6.10.   [54] Callataÿ 2013, 232–36.

[55] For the debate on the meaning of the wreath, see Picard 2010, 175 n. 48, with earlier bibliography.

[56] E.g., Kırıkhan (*CH* 1.87; 2.90), Aleppo (*IGCH* 1562), and Akkar (*IGCH* 1559).

Figure 3.11 "Wreathed" silver tetradrachm of Myrina, ca. 160–135 BCE (14.51 g, ANS 1944.100.44235; courtesy of the American Numismatic Society).

explanations to explain why silver moved from the Aegean to the Near East, where the higher value of silver relative to gold had since Achaemenid times attracted Greek coinage to the Levant.[57] Indeed, the Wreathed Coinages participated in an old circulation pattern that intensified in this period. What needs to be explained is the size of these coinages, which share common designs and originate in cities firmly under Attalid control. Callataÿ estimates a total of 76.8 Attic-drachm equivalent obverses per year for the Wreathed Coinages – compared with just 51.9 for the pre-133 cistophori!derived[58] Tipped off by the size of the issues, scholars since Rostovtzeff have suspected Attalid involvement.[59] The notion of a "proxy coinage" may seem less conspiratorial after the discussion below. Leaving open for now the question of the precise nature of Attalid involvement with the Wreathed Coinages, it is difficult to understand how these cities minted in such quantities without injections of bullion from the outside.

---

[57] Marcellesi 2012, 150.
[58] Callataÿ 2013, 232–36. Compare also the individual Wreathed mints' output (Kyme = 27.9, Herakleia = 22.5, Myrina = 26.2) with that of Pergamon, the largest cistophoric mint (20.3).
[59] Rostovtzeff 1941, vol. 2, 658: "We can hardly suppose that the minting cities – important or unimportant – owned silver mines. It is more than likely that the metal was supplied to them by the kings, who, in all probability were the owners of the mines." See also Rostovtzeff 1939. On Kyme, e.g., Kinns (1986, 169) emphasizes a transfer of bullion from Prousias II in the form of an indemnity.

Explaining the Cistophori

Scholars have struggled to define the character of the cistophoric coinage, vacillating between civic, royal, and federal models of minting. The inherited paradigms fail us, in part, because the coins look so strange. However, their visual strangeness need not be explained away in our analysis. Attalid silver and indeed bronze had always born the portrait of Philetairos, nearly always with the legend ΦΙΛΕΤΑΙΡΟΥ, "of Philetairos." That combination of image and text was standard practice across the Hellenistic world. In their design, the cistophori mark a radical break with the past – and with convention, in a medium that is famously conservative.[60] Not only do these coins renounce the claims of the typical Hellenistic coin legend; they also replace the dynastic portrait with imagery sufficiently generic or enigmatic, it seems, to evoke a wide range of associations. They leave us asking, "Whose money is it?" On the other hand, the coins bear symbols, control marks, which without question derive from the iconographic repertoire of the various cities involved. This is best observed in Ephesus, where the bee and stag (along with the quiver of Artemis), appear on the cistophori; meanwhile, Ephesus had for centuries placed that same imagery on its own coinage, and in fact continued to do so, even after the introduction of the cistophori, on its common Attic-weight drachms.[61] In the markets adjacent to its new harbor, the one built by the engineers of Attalos II, traders handled both coinages in tandem. Or consider the case of Tralles. It provides another clear instance of identifiably civic badges on the cistophori: the humped bull, the meander pattern, and, perhaps, Zeus Larasius. The bull we find on the aforementioned gold coinage of Tralles, and the meander pattern, so important to the civic and regional identity of the city, appears already on pre-188 bronze.[62] Kleiner sought to limit the phenomenon to Tralles and Ephesus, but his own catalogue shows its breadth. Some Apameian cistophori bear flutes (of Marsyas), and Laodikeian ones display the punning wolf (*lykos*) for the Lykos River.[63] To match image with text, then, we are justified in following Le Rider, who

---

[60] Szaivert (2008, 34–37) compares cistophoric imagery to earlier Attalid coin iconography.
[61] See, e.g., Kraay 1976, 356–57, nos. 600 and 601.
[62] For the coin, see *SNG München* Lydien no. 695. For discussion, see Thonemann 2011b, 40–41, with n. 100 on bronze minted in name of Zeus Larasius (e.g., *SNG München* Lydien nos. 702–6). On its date, see Gökyıldırım 2016, nos. 842–46, assigning it to third to second century BCE.
[63] Mørkholm (1979, 53–58) challenges the identification of Apameia as an early cistophoric mint. His view has not carried the day, but it is worth noting that he observes changes in the icon of the flute and argues that it does not belong to Marsyas.

restores cistophoric legends as ethnics, not mintmarks, as, for example, ΕΦΕ[ΣΙΩΝ], "(coin) of the Ephesian (citizens)."[64] The coins represented the citizens – of their respective poleis – just as much as the kingdom.

To cast the cistophori as either strictly royal or civic in nature is to explain away their visual strangeness. Either one argues that the combination of civic iconography and muted reference to the crown signals the withdrawal of the Attalids from the domain of coinage, a restatement of the laissez-faire, constitutional vision of Attalid imperialism, or the coins dissemble and mask the kings' interventions. In that sense, as Kleiner puts it: "The cistophoric coinage is not what it appears to be."[65] Yet a coin in this world was always, in some sense, what it appeared to be. According to the classic formulation of an inscription from Sestos honoring the late Attalid courtier Menas, the benefits of introducing any new epichoric coinage were of two kinds (*I.Sestos* 1 lines 44–45).[66] First, the community was able to place its own *charaktêr* on its coins. Second, the coinage would become a source of revenue (*prosodos*) for the community through mandatory exchange, reminting fees, and so on. Unfortunately, on the present state of the evidence, we cannot say anything about who laid claim to the surely considerable profits of the cistophoric system, or in what proportions. Tellingly, Kleiner relates the fiscal structure of the cistophoric system to the practice of earmarking. In his view, they were both forms of bait-and-switch fiscality, tribute disguised as taxation and redistribution.[67] On the other hand, we must admit that the Attalids ceded away a certain part of the *charaktêr* of this coinage, and the text from Sestos provides explicit confirmation of the significance of that aspect of coinage for late Hellenistic cities. Meadows has gone so far as to suggest that the political significance of minting with epichoric types was changing and in fact intensifying in precisely this period.[68] Therefore, it seems prudent to take the cistophori at "face value," even if this means ruling out conventional models of royal or civic coinage. The strange appearance of the coins hints at the same Attalid sensitivity to civic identity and the same reliance on civic institutions that undergirded the practice of earmarking. Yet any new characterization of

---

[64] Le Rider 1990, 685. Thonemann 2015a, 79: "city ethnics." Cf. Marcellesi 2012, 145: "nom de différentes cités"; Bresson 2019, 294: "names of a series of cities."
[65] Kleiner and Noe 1977, 125.
[66] In the case of Menas and Sestos, the new epichoric coinage was of course bronze.
[67] Kleiner and Noe 1977, 125, with n. 19.
[68] Meadows 2001, esp. 61–62; Meadows 2018, 298–301. Cf. Andrew Burnett et al. in *RPC* I, 1: coinage is a royal prerogative until the breakdown of kingdoms.

the cistophori must rest on the evidence of the coins themselves for the administration of the system.

The Devil in the Administrative Details: The Evidence for Centralization

To underline the point, the coins do not give us a balance of accounts, how much city and king – or indeed third parties, like merchants – each invested in the system, and how much each took out. And this problem is not unique to Attalid Asia Minor. In a programmatic essay on late Hellenistic coinage, Picard has sized up our aporia with the question, "Where does the metal come from?"[69] No metallurgical analysis is available to trace the origin of the various stocks of silver bullion used to mint early cistophori.[70] On the other hand, we can at least try to determine where the minting took place, and how the shape of the money supply and the rhythm of monetary production were managed. To begin with the organization of the cistophoric mints, Kleiner's *Early Cistophoric Coinage* (*ECC*) appears to have overstated the case for centralized production. Le Rider and Otto Mørkholm have offered criticisms of *ECC* on this score, but given the status of Kleiner's book as the standard of reference for the coinage, its arguments deserve further scrutiny, since for Kleiner, what he calls "intercity linkage" would "necessitate a complete reconsideration of the nature of the cistophoric coinage."[71]

ECC does not postulate two tiers of mints, large and small, as we have above. The system of *ECC* contains just three central mints that produce all the coins, whichever their *charaktēr*: Ephesus, Tralles, but, most importantly, Pergamon itself, the administrative hub, minting for a number of smaller pseudo-mints. Central to Kleiner's argument is a notion of intercity linkage that includes not only die links, but also shared symbols, monograms, and, crucially, the stylistic links that Kleiner observes throughout the coinage. Numismatic method privileges the evidence of die links over stylistic links, but the number of die links in the *ECC* corpus is

---

[69] Picard 2010, 187.
[70] Cf. on Roman cistophori, Butcher and Ponting 2014, 465–90, esp. 466. Although hindered by a lack of samples for metallurgical analysis, they note results that highlight the exceptionally high standard of fineness of cistophori of the second century BCE (96–98%).
[71] Kleiner and Noe 1977, 120. For criticism, see Le Rider 1989, 186–88; Mørkholm 1979, 50–53. However, for support, see Bresson 2019, 294–95.

surprisingly low.⁷² In fact, there are only two instances of verifiable die-sharing between mints, both involving Pergamon.⁷³ The first is the link between Kleiner's P24 of Pergamon and S10 (series 6) from "Sardis-Synnada."⁷⁴ Noting that "Sardis-Synnada" series 6 is itself die-linked to the then as yet un-deciphered BA ΣY AP cistophori, Kleiner argued for the unlikelihood of a single die traveling between the royal capital, Lydia, and Phrygia. Since then, Le Rider has suggested that "Sardis-Synnada" is actually two mints, Sardis and Lysias in south Phrygia; that the monogram on the reverse of the obverse die-linked coin at issue should be read "Dionysoupolis"; and that the BA ΣY AP coins come from Blaundos, both Dionysoupolis and Blaundos themselves also lying in south Phrygia.⁷⁵ All this still leaves us with the circulation of at least one die between two or perhaps three regions. Its possible mintmark notwithstanding, Blaundos, for example, does not seem to have been urbanized under the Attalids.⁷⁶ So the need for greater centralization in rural south Phrygia makes sense. We cannot rule out a traveling mint that accompanied the retinue of Eumenes II, who might have faced the Galatians at both Sardis and Synnada.⁷⁷ Edward Robinson demonstrated a roving mint for Aristonikos.⁷⁸ Whatever the arrangement here, it was short-lived, irregular, and confined to an early stage, perhaps under the peculiar conditions of the Galatian War.

Much more suggestive of centralization is the second case of die sharing, known from an impressive five links between Pergamon and Apameia: Kleiner's A17/P38, A24/P46, A28/P54, A38/P75, and A40/P79. Moreover, Kleiner's observation that the pace of production at both mints was increasing simultaneously is intriguing. It at least implies that both mints faced a sharp increase in demand for coinage at the same time and coordinated a response. But were these actually two distinct mints? If one assigns to Pergamon the 16% of production currently credited to Apameia, a more centralized system emerges with just three mints functioning. However, many of the die linkages have been challenged.⁷⁹ It was also

---

⁷² Cf. Callataÿ 2013, 228: "The amount of die sharing between mints strongly points to a single minting place for issues allegedly coming from different mints." Similarly, see Kinns 1986, 164.
⁷³ Kleiner (1980, 50–51) suggests a third.   ⁷⁴ Kleiner and Noe 1977, 80–81.
⁷⁵ Le Rider 1990, 697–99. Cf. Mitchell 1999, 25 n. 30, which places the south Phrygian cistophori in the wake of Sulla.
⁷⁶ For the archaeological discussion, see Filges 2003, esp. 42.
⁷⁷ For sources for Galatians at Sardis and Synnada, see Thonemann 2011b, 170–77.
⁷⁸ Robinson 1954.
⁷⁹ The pi-alpha monogram was once read as Parion (Mørkholm 1979, 56–58), or as Apollonia-on-the-Rhyndakos (Kleiner 1980, 48–51). But the *communis opinio* now reads it as Apameia – see here Le Rider 1990, 687–89; and Le Rider's comments in Drew-Bear and Le Rider 1991, 366–69,

quite common for dies and die-cutters to pass between mints.[80] The detailed study of Christophe Flament on the mechanics of minting in Classical Greece highlights the pitfalls of using hand studies to demonstrate centralized production.[81] Yet Kleiner's observations of hands is what sustains much of his model of centralization, from Apameia to the mystery mint KOP to his claim that Tralles struck for Laodikeia.[82] There are clear signs of coordination by a central authority, but we also find hints of local participation and information sharing. Apameia seems to have minted its first civic bronze coinage about now, which shares the symbol of the *pilos* with early cistophori.[83] For the late cistophori, the civic mint was certainly involved, as the magistrate KOKOY appears on both the silver cistophori and the civic bronze coinage.[84] In sum, it still seems probable that Apameia possessed a mint under the Attalids.

It must be admitted that the cistophori display remarkable uniformity of type. The imagery is consistent, as is the placement of the ethnic and the symbols (**Figs. 3.3** and **3.12**). The weight of the coin and the size of the flan do not change much either.[85] Most importantly, the repetition of symbols on the coins of different mints implies a coherent administrative system. On the other hand, we find striking anomalies, such as the letters on a limited number of series from Ephesus (33–35) and Apameia (27–28), usually taken to be regnal years. Whether the letters on either of these coinages actually represent regnal dates, and why these cities alone and not Pergamon itself would have marked time in this way are both open questions.[86] The salient point is that different administrative systems were at work in different places. This implies that local actors and institutions influenced the production of the cistophori. We get a sense of just how important local officials might have been under the Attalids from the behavior of their mints immediately after 133. While the Ephesians were

---

also for challenges to some of Kleiner's attributions of certain obverses in the above sequence to Pergamon. Cf. Bresson 2019, 296, opting for Kleiner's theory of a central mint at Pergamon serving Apameia, as well as less significant Sardis and Synnada.

[80] See, e.g., Robert 1967, 87–105. Mackil and Van Alfen 2006 argue incisively (p. 227 n. 78) that die sharing implies centralization, but does not correspond to a particular state form.
[81] Flament 2010, 31–73.
[82] Kleiner and Noe 1977, 88–89, 101, and 98 for the prediction that – *one day* – die links may substantiate the claim about Tralles and Laodikeia.
[83] Ashton and Kinns 2003, 46–47; Ashton 2016, 379, not ruling out a third-century date.
[84] Carbone 2020, 1 n. 4.
[85] See the weight tables of Kleiner and Noe 1977, 128–29; for flans, 121.
[86] Kleiner and Noe 1977, 52, 94. Kleiner 1972, 23: changing of guard from the reign of Attalos II to that of Attalos III is responsible for the anomaly. For regnal dates on the cistophori of Aristonikos/Eumenes III, see Robinson 1954.

Figure 3.12 Cistophoric silver tetradrachm of Ephesus, ca. 150–140 BCE (12.58 g, ANS 1944.100.37502; courtesy of the American Numismatic Society).

quick to place their city's civic era on the coins, the citizens of Pergamon minted cistophori bearing the names of their *prytaneis*.[87] Had those magistrates shared the responsibility for minting with royal officials all along?

The Peculiar Role of Tralles

> ... that they think it just the same, whether they arrive in Tralles or in Formia ...
>
> (Cicero, *Q.Fr.* 1.1.17)[88]

Die sharing is just one of the twin pillars of the case for centralization. The other is the specialization of the mint of Tralles in the production of small denominations. These are the didrachms and drachms that survive in much smaller numbers than the cistophoric tetradrachms (**Figs. 3.4** and **3.5**). This unmistakable peculiarity of Tralles in this respect fulfilled the needs of local users on the border between two large regional monetary systems. Thus, *ECC* lists 16 obverse drachm dies and 18 obverse didrachm dies

---

[87] Ephesus: Rigsby 1979. Pergamon: Kleiner 1978, 79.
[88] ... *neve interesse quidquam putent, utrum Tralles an Formias venerint* ...

for Tralles.[89] No other mint comes close.[90] However, the traditional view is that the Attalids arbitrarily assigned small change to Tralles. "It is unlikely that the silver currency needs of Tralles differed substantially from those of the other large Attalid cities," writes Kleiner.[91] On this interpretation, royal needs motivated Tralles' designation, which represents the ultimate instantiation of the "royal design" behind the cistophoric system. Even those who model decentralized production assume centralized control of the shape of the supply of coin. For example, Callataÿ: "The fact that the mint of Tralles was in charge of nearly all the fractions points too in the direction of a general policy established at a higher level."[92] It is also commonly assumed that the Attalids decided unilaterally to focus the production of fractional coinage in Tralles. As Thonemann writes, "The cistophori were produced at a number of decentralized mints. Their production, however, was closely directed from the centre.... [Tralles' specialization] strongly suggests that the distribution and scale of the mints did not necessarily reflect the coinage's circulation."[93]

In fact, the special role of Tralles was neither arbitrary nor the outcome of a unilateral royal decision. Further, the case of Tralles may even shed light on circulation patterns. Consider first that the city continued to specialize in fractions – and even intensified its production of small denominations after the fall of the Attalid dynasty. In his study of the very large coinage known as the "late cistophori," minted from ca. 133 to ca. 67, Kleiner found that Tralles retained its traditional role.[94] The only hoard of late cistophori that contains fractions is *IGCH* 1460 (unknown provenance in Asia Minor). It contains 2 drachms and 7 didrachms, all of them, except for a single drachm of Ephesus, from Tralles. Kleiner did not make a companion die study of the late cistophori, but he does note that the late fractions of Tralles are overwhelmingly dominant in both public and

---

[89] Callataÿ (2013, 228) lists under "Tralles Half-Cistophori" 20 obverse and 30 coins, *ECC* lists 20 didrachm obverses and 25 coins. Note further the recent appearance of a cistophoric drachm of Tralles in the collection of Lydian Coins in the Istanbul Archaeological Museum, Gökyıldırım 2016, no. 722.

[90] For the rare cistophoric hemidrachm in the form of fractional silver minted at Pergamon in the name of Athena Nikephoros, see Marcellesi 2012, 121–22.

[91] Kleiner and Noe 1977, 122.   [92] Callataÿ 2013, 228.

[93] Thonemann 2011b, 170–71. Cf. Marcellesi (2012, 120), suggesting limited local initiative in the choice of denomination. On circulation, however, cf. *CH* IX 535 (Ahmetbeyli), from the territory of ancient Colophon, buried ca. 120. Of its 25 cistophoric tetradrachms, 15 come from nearby Ephesus – see Travaglini 1997, 137–42. Similarly, *IGCH* 1415 (Afyonkarahisar), buried ca. 133: of 120+ cistophori, the 10+ described came from nearby Apameia.

[94] Kleiner 1978. The drachms may have only begun ca. 125. See Marcellesi 2012, 184.

private collections.[95] In trying to understand the persistence of the pattern, it is important to remember that early Roman administrators were cautious and practical. We could see here simply the rote reproduction of an administrative procedure and the inertia of bureaucracy.

However, a meaningful pattern emerges when we consider a yet later stage in the long history of the cistophori. When production of the late cistophori ended ca. 68/7 in the context of Pompey's operations in the East, a 10-year hiatus ensued.[96] Around 58, the cistophori appeared again, this time bearing the names of cities, but also two personal names, one Greek and one Latin. These are the so-called proconsular cistophori, which carry the names of Roman proconsuls and local Greek magistrates. The coinage ends ca. 49 BCE with the issue of the propraetor L. Aemilius Lepidus Paullus. Gerd Stumpf's corpus of proconsular cistophori does not record any fractions.[97] Yet this is because the one fraction that can be associated with the proconsular cistophori does not bear the typical two names, but just the Greek one. The coin is a didrachm minted by a certain ΑΡΙΣΤΟΚΛ[ΗΣ] (*BMC* Lydia 335, no. 55).[98] The same Aristokles of Tralles, we presume, is known to have minted proconsular cistophori (tetradrachms, bearing the city's ethnic) for both C. Claudius Pulcher (**Fig. 3.13**) and C. Fannius (Stumpf nos. 55, 63, and 65). It is unclear whether Aristokles' name appears alone on the didrachm due to considerations of space in the visual field or whether this is an expression of a different institutional arrangement. Either way, it appears that Tralles – and perhaps only Tralles – was minting fractions after a decade-long hiatus.

After all the intervening disruption, why was it Tralles, yet again, which specialized in fractions? We need not imagine that its citizens held a monopoly on the technological know-how. Rather, we need to take seriously the possibility that the monetary needs of this city had been distinctive all along. In other words, we need to examine the economic and historical geography of the Maeander Valley. Thonemann's study of the long-term history of the Maeander region illustrates how it can either connect or separate different stretches of Anatolia. He views Apameia both as a limit point for the Attalid imperial space and as an interchange between the steppe of inner Anatolia and the coastal lowlands.[99]

---

[95] Kleiner 1978, 90.   [96] Crawford 1985, 206–9.   [97] Stumpf 1991.
[98] Another example has turned up in commerce, reported in Valverde 2007, 34 n. 68.
[99] Thonemann 2011b, 99–129.

Figure 3.13 Proconsular cistophoric silver tetradrachm, signed by C. Pulcher and Aristokles, 55–53 BCE (11.95 g, ANS 1959.48.6; courtesy of the American Numismatic Society).

The Maeander after 188 was very much a political frontier, chosen to mark the boundary between Rhodes' domain on the mainland (*peraia*) and the expanded Attalid kingdom. In economic terms, perhaps this frontier was more permeable. Thonemann's study does not offer us any idea of what an interchange would look like that connected the Rhodian zone of southwestern Asia Minor to the Attalid Maeander and beyond. Tralles fits the bill perfectly.

Positioned at the junction of several important trans-Anatolian routes, Tralles also joined Attalid Lydia to Rhodian Caria (**Map 3.1**). Branching off from the primary route between the coastal delta and the upper Maeander, the major route south into Caria took off from Tralles. In Pergamene terms, it connected Tralles to Alabanda, and, ultimately, Telmessos. But another branch connected Alabanda to Lagina, Stratonikeia, and, finally, Physkos (Marmaris), on the mainland opposite Rhodes.[100] The road from Alabanda to Tralles connected Caria to the Attalid's southern highway, a stretch of the road that was to become one of the main arteries of the

---

[100] French 2016b, 83; French 2016a, 52 for maps. This is what French calls the Tralles-Alabanda-Telmessos route.

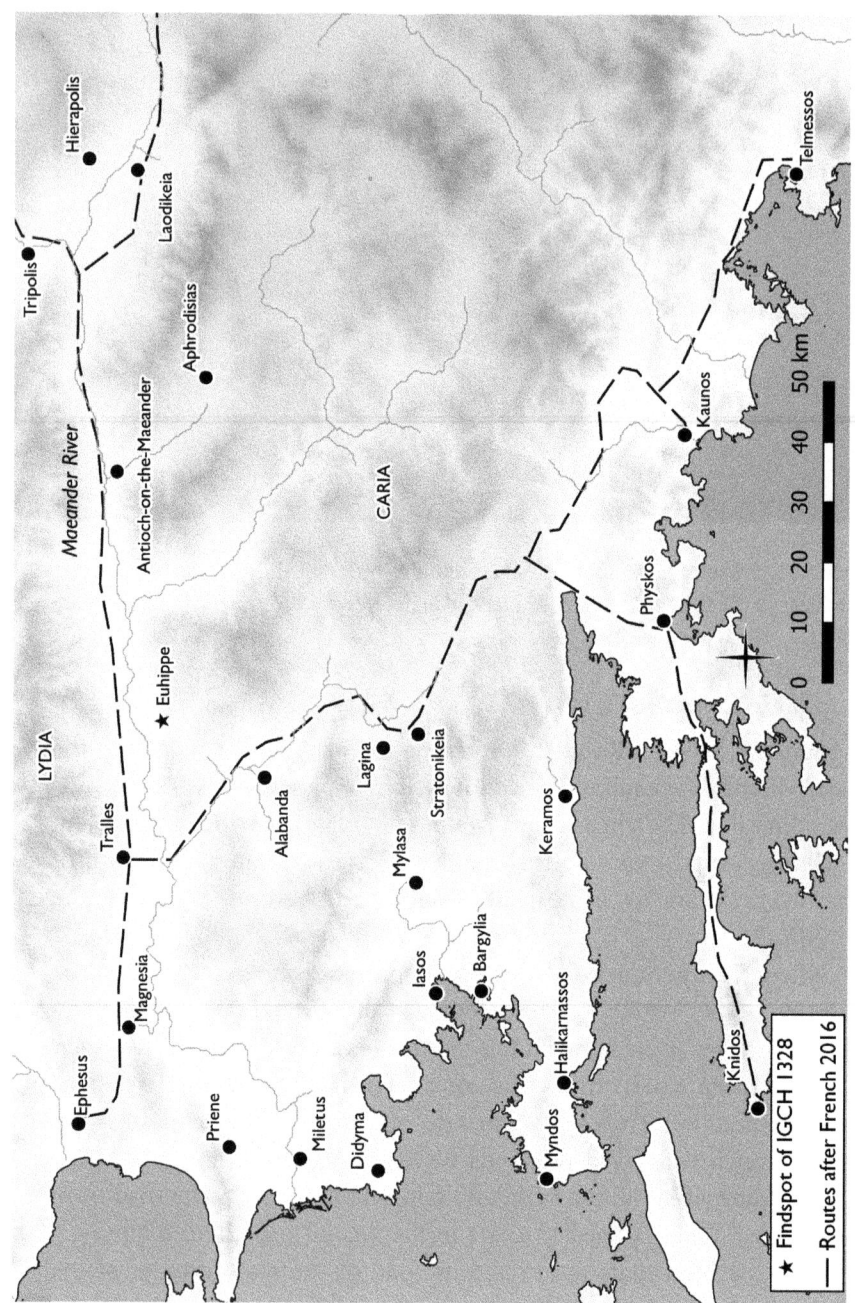

Map 3.1 The Maeander Valley and Rhodian Caria.

Roman province of Asia.[101] Strabo's source Artemidoros of Ephesus (fl. 104–101 BCE) traveled it. In his testimony, Artemidoros is explicit about how he conceptualizes the road. For him, the road was part of a route from Physkos to Ephesus. Thus, Strabo: "Artemidoros says that the journey from Physkos, on the coast opposite Rhodes, towards Ephesus, as far as Lagina is 850 stadia; thence to Alabanda 250 stadia; to Tralles 160. About halfway, on the road to Tralles, the Maeander is crossed, and here are the boundaries of Caria. The whole number of stadia from Physkos to the Maeander, along the road to Ephesus, is 1180 stadia" (14.2.29).[102] For Artemidoros, note, Tralles was the middle point on this route, in terms of both distance and conceptual geography. Tralles was the end of Caria.[103]

By location, therefore, Tralles was a monetary interchange between, on the one hand, the Rhodian zone to the south, where Rhodian and pseudo-Rhodian coinages on epichoric standards dominated for centuries, and, on the other, the young cistophoric zone. After 188, but seemingly before the advent of the cistophorus, the Rhodians reformed their own coinage, minting the plinthophoros.[104] The Rhodians may have designed the plinthophoros to be even more epichoric than other Rhodian and pseudo-Rhodian coinages in circulation.[105] In any case, the plinthophori, like other coinages on the various "Rhodian" standards, circulated throughout the Rhodian *peraia* and rarely left the zone. For their part, the cistophori almost never left the Attalid kingdom. The Maeander Valley, then, formed the border between two large, relatively impermeable regional monetary systems.[106] Passage between the two would have necessitated an exchange of currencies. And if the volume of those exchanges were higher

---

[101] French 2012, 10 and milestone no. 6 for Tralles as station on the road of Aquilius with Ephesus as *caput viae* and Side as terminus.

[102] Trans. Loeb. Φησὶ δὲ Ἀρτεμίδωρος ἀπὸ Φύσκου τῆς Ῥοδίων περαίας ἰοῦσιν εἰς Ἔφεσον μέχρι μὲν Λαγίνων ὀκτακοσίους εἶναι καὶ πεντήκοντα σταδίους, ἐντεῦθεν δ' εἰς Ἀλάβανδα πεντήκοντα ἄλλους καὶ διακοσίους, εἰς δὲ Τράλλεις ἑκατὸν ἑξήκοντα· ἀλλ' ἡ εἰς Τράλλεις ἐστὶ διαβάντι τὸν Μαίανδρον κατὰ μέσην που τὴν ὁδὸν ὅπου τῆς Καρίας οἱ ὅροι· γίνονται δ' οἱ πάντες ἀπὸ Φύσκου ἐπὶ τὸν Μαίανδρον κατὰ τὴν εἰς Ἔφεσον ὁδὸν χίλιοι ἑκατὸν ὀγδοήκοντα.

[103] For the problem of these puzzling measurements, see Radt 2002–11, ad loc. An interesting prosopographical link suggests itself in the figure of Apatourios of Alabanda, who Vitruvius (*De arch.* 7.5.5) tells us built the *ekklêsiasterion* at Tralles. Further, numismatic evidence from Aphrodisias tells a similar story. According to MacDonald (1992, 15), the circulation pattern of coins of Aphrodisias in the *longue durée* follows this route, from Caria to Lydia and Ionia along the roads of Maeander Valley. Only in late Roman times does Aphrodisian coinage flow east.

[104] For the debated date of the introduction of the plinthophoros, see most recently Ashton 2005b.

[105] Bresson 1993; Bresson 1996.

[106] For Bresson 1993, the Rhodian zone is closed; *pace* Ashton 2001, 95–96, with personal observation from storerooms in Rhodes. For the regional pattern, cf. also *IGCH* 1330 (Priene), which contained both a Rhodian silver coin and a cistophorus of nearby Tralles. Unfortunately,

than elsewhere, the demand for small denominations would also have been elevated. Indeed, if we accept that Tralles linked the Rhodian zone to the cistophoric zone, then as an interchange between two major epichoric systems, Tralles was sui generis as an Attalid mint.[107]

To test the hypothesis of high-volume currency exchange in and around Tralles, we may look to the thin but suggestive hoard record. As noted, fractions of Tralles dominate the only known hoard of late cistophoric fractions, which is the unprovenanced *IGCH* 1460. For the cistophori of the Attalids, we are luckier. We still have just one hoard containing fractions, but it has a provenance. *IGCH* 1328 (Şahnalı) contains 18 pieces of cistophoric silver, 10 of them fractions. Again, among the fractional mints, Tralles predominates, with four didrachms. But the other mints are represented too: one didrachm apiece from Pergamon, Ephesus, Apameia, and "Synnada."[108] While the Şahnalı hoard provides further confirmation of Tralles' special role, it also sheds light on circulation patterns in the system. In other words, it is important to notice that the hoard contains coins from all the major mints, both cistophoric tetradrachms and fractions. It could be what numismatics call, with all due caution, a "circulation hoard," the proverbial snapshot of what was in circulation at a given place and point in time.[109] The hoard was found near the site of ancient Euhippe, which lies just opposite Tralles, south across the plain of the Maeander, not far to the east from where the route of Artemidoros entered and exited the Valley, on the way from Tralles to Alabanda in Caria.[110] We simply do not have the hoard evidence to test the representativeness of the Şahnalı hoard in terms of circulation, though it is unquestionably representative in terms of content; that is, the common fractions of Tralles predominate. This is an isolated piece of evidence, but it suggests a pattern of circulation that

---

the coin of Tralles cannot be located in Berlin and the denomination was not recorded (Karsten Dahmen, personal comm.). For disposition, see http://coinhoards.org/id/igch1330.

[107] The persistence of the specialization of Tralles in fractions in Roman times can be explained by the persistence of the plinthophoric system in Caria, which was both outside the Roman province of Asia until after 84 BCE and full of autonomous civic mints. Eventually, the post-plinthophoric drachm on the so-called light Rhodian standard created a neat equivalence with the drachm of the cistophoric system, as documented in an inscription of the first century CE. See Carbone 2014, 28, with inscription from Kibyra *IGR* 4.915, a, lines 12–14.

[108] Kleiner and Noe 1977, 118–19, suggesting it is *not* a circulation hoard but a product of gradual accumulation. Important supplements in Onat 1959 (http://coinhoards.org/id/igch1328): one didrachm of Ephesus and two uncertain didrachms.

[109] For hoard methodology and circulation, see, Howgego 1995, 88–94.

[110] For the movement of Roman soldiers on this road, see *SEG* XXXVII 1186 from Euhippe.

concentrates fractions from all over the Attalid kingdom in the vicinity of Tralles, on the very edge of the cistophoric zone.

The hypothesis of heavy traffic between the Rhodian and cistophoric zones, channeled through Tralles, which produced a high volume of currency exchange, motivating the special role of Tralles in the cistophoric system, finds support in the behavior of mints south of the Maeander after the introduction of the cistophorus. In reaction to the creation of the cistophoric zone, these cities minted a portfolio of coinages on different standards, which allowed them to maintain their economic ties to the Maeander and profit from their own position of connectivity. After 167, the Rhodian political hegemony in Caria and Lycia began to collapse, but southwest Asia Minor was still very much part of the Rhodian monetary *koinê*.[111] In Caria, Alabanda in the 160s minted not only Attic-weight Alexanders, but also a coinage on the cistophoric standard.[112] With this coinage, Alabanda was not pledging fealty to Pergamon. It remained outside the Attalid kingdom, even if Eumenes II was inching into the power vacuum.[113] The Alabandan "cistophori" imply significant traffic back and forth along the first stretch of the Tralles-Physkos corridor, and represent one state's attempt to integrate the two regional systems to its advantage. Similarly, Carian Stratonikeia, which lay further south along the same route, minted a curious denomination in this period, an Attic tridrachm alongside an Attic drachm in a system otherwise dominated by plinthophoric drachms and hemidrachms.[114] Meadows has pointed out that the weight standard of Stratonikeia's Attic-weight tridrachm, ca. 12–12.5 g, made it interchangeable with a cistophorus. In northern Lycia, Oinoanda may have pursued a similar strategy, minting silver didrachms

---

[111] For Carian and Lycian revolts of 168, see Polyb. 30.5.11–16. In 167, the Senate ordered Rhodes to remove garrisons from Caunus and Stratonikeia, and then formally granted freedom to Caria and Lycia (Polyb. 30.21, 24). However, Rhodian influence on the mainland was not extinguished (see, e.g., Strabo 14.2.3; Cicero, *Q.Fr.* 1.1.33). For Caunus restored to Rhodes by Sulla, the Rhodian capture of Calynda in 163 with Roman confirmation (Polyb. 31.5.5), see, generally, Habicht 2006, 174–242. For the coins of independent Lycia before the First Mithridatic War, which remained on the Rhodian standard, see Troxell 1982 with Ashton and Meadows 2008.

[112] See, e.g., *CH* X 302, a hoard of 7+ Alabandan cistophori buried in 150 (from western Asia Minor?).

[113] Errington 2010, 129. See also the letter of Eumenes II to the Tabênoi (Guizzi 2006; *SEG* LVII 1109). If the city is in fact Carian Tabai, the document is evidence of Attalid influence in the former Rhodian domain ca. 165. See Patrice Hamon *BE* (2009) no. 440. According to Livy (37.56.2), the Attalids had been granted the Carian district of Hydrela in 188, between the Maeander and the Lykos. See Magie 1950, 762.

[114] Meadows 2002, 99.

that equated nicely with the cistophorus at the ratio 3:2.[115] Another north Lycian city, late Hellenistic Kibyra followed Alabanda and minted its own cistophoric tetradrachms and drachms (*BMC* Phrygia, pp. 131–32, nos. 1–5). The north Lycian cases are without firm dates, floating between the mid-second and early first centuries BCE. For our purposes, it need not matter. Clearly, the spread of the cistophorus into southwestern Asia Minor was a slow, intermittent, century-long process, still being completed in the early first century BCE.[116] Along the way, it was useful for those cities situated on major routes in and out of the Maeander Valley to mint an appropriately flexible coinage.

Another measure of the extent to which Tralles straddled two monetary zones is the poor survival rate of its coins. Low survival rates may provide indirect evidence that cistophoric fractions were leaking out of the cistophoric zone faster than the cistophori themselves. The loss of small denominations is a case of the notorious "problem of small change" studied by economic historians Thomas Sargent and François Velde.[117] The drachms of Tralles are known from 18 specimens (n) and 16 dies (D), a ratio of nearly 1:1; the didrachms are 30 (n) and 20 (D), exactly 3:2.[118] Numismatists, with theoretical backing from statisticians, typically seek a sample of n/D = 3:1 before undertaking a die study.[119] Using a lower ratio is dangerous because it is not possible to estimate the original number of dies with any degree of certainty. In other words, we must admit that we do not have any idea of the scale of Tralles' production of cistophoric fractions. However, we do know that Tralleian fractions survive very poorly. The average n/D for the entire cistophoric coinage (166–123 BCE) is 2.75 (1,142/416).[120] So, while the sample size is small, the fractions of Tralles are significantly below the average at 1.5 for the didrachms and 1.125 for the drachms. But how do those rates compare with other small silver of second-century Asia Minor? Kinns' study of the copious silver drachms

---

[115] Ashton 2005a, 73. Cf. Callataÿ 2007, for whom this is a Roman proxy coinage from the First Mithridatic War.

[116] The evidence of Aphrodisias is key here. See MacDonald 1992, 17. Unfortunately, the weight standard of much of its first-century BCE silver (ca. 3.5 g = drachm) is unclear. Crawford (1985, 160) mentions a small late-Hellenistic hoard of Aphrodisias. It contained coins of Tralles. Crawford also provides the following information: *SNG von Aulock* 7463, Pergamon, from before 134/3, worn; *SNG Copenhagen* 657, Tralles, ca. 100, fresh, two specimens.

[117] Sargent and Velde 2002.

[118] Kleiner's numbers in *ECC* are 25 (n) and 20 (D), whereas the above numbers, 30 (n) and 20 (D), are taken from Callataÿ 2013, 228.

[119] For methodology, see Carter 1983.

[120] Except for the figure for drachms, all figures from Callataÿ 2013, 228.

of Ephesus (ca. 202–150 BCE), produced an n/D of 8.43 (590/7).[121] On the other hand, the Rhodian plinthophori (ca. 185–84 BCE) survive at a much more comparable rate of 1.91 (1,583/829), as do the Stratonikeian hemidrachms (130–90 BCE) (4.92 = 305/62) and the pseudo-Rhodian drachms of Mylasa (165–30 BCE) (5.79 = 619/107). Hoarding practice may account for the problem. It could be that small silver in a multidenominational system was hoarded differently – that is, less – and so survives less often. An apposite comparison is available from Bithynia of the reign of Prousias II (189–149 BCE). His silver drachms are extremely rare by comparison to his tetradrachms.[122] We may also consider the possibility that the high volume of currency exchange on either side of the "cistophoric frontier" just south of Tralles contributed to a distinctive circulation pattern for the fractions, and so a lower rate of survival. The plinthophoric drachm weighed about as much as the cistophoric drachm (3.05 g), but we can hardly suppose that money changers were willing to make the exchange for free.[123] Did those who went south take the fractions of Tralles with them, exchanging these coins inside the plinthophoric zone, where they eventually met the melting pot?

The weight of the evidence shows that local needs and preferences determined the choice of Tralles as the chief fractional mint in the cistophoric system. Or to put it another way, regionalism inflected the shape of the money supply in the Attalid kingdom. Consider again the regional situation along the Maeander, but now against the backdrop of the wider Hellenistic world. As Picard has illustrated, the typical late Hellenistic monetary system was built around large silver and fiduciary bronze, with little coinage at the intermediary values.[124] Few regional systems reserved an important role for small silver. The exceptions to this rule were two: the symmachic Peloponnese and the Rhodian zone that intersected with the

---

[121] Kosmetatou's unpublished study of the same coinage produced 4.47 (456/102) – see Callataÿ 2013, 236 n. 102.

[122] Kaye 2013 collected 187 silver tetradrachms of Prousias II, but turned up just a handful of silver drachms. Similarly, the drachms are absent from Turkish museum collections, including those of the Bithynian heartland, surveyed by Güney 2015.

[123] For weights, see Ashton 1994, 59. Bresson is the chief advocate of the view that the "interoperability" of denominational systems does not imply that the ancients waved the exchange fee (agio). Rather, he adduces cases like that of Timon of Syracuse to show that one might – as a benefaction – wave it. See Bresson 1996 and 2001; but *contra*, see the arguments on mid-second-century Rhodian coinage of Apostolou 1995. Kleiner's point (1972, 31) that compatibility was not acceptability is helpful. He notes a cistophorus of Tralles now in Berlin, which was overstruck on a pre-plinthophoric didrachm of equal weight.

[124] Picard 2006; Picard 2009.

cistophoric zone at Tralles. In the late third or early second century, Rhodes even raised a tax (or a public subscription?) called the *didrachmia* (*SEG* XLI 649).[125] Moreover, the imitative cistophoric production of Kibyra in northern Lycia seems also markedly biased toward the fraction. No comprehensive study exists, but a survey of major collections reveals a nearly 3:1 advantage for Kibyra's cistophoric drachms over its tetradrachms (30:9).[126] The Tralleian cistophoric fractions are representative of the affinity of southwest Asia Minor for small silver. In the end, there were good reasons for Tralles to specialize; the choice was not arbitrary.

In sum, the case of Tralles is a far cry from proof that the Attalids held fiat power when it came to the shape of the money supply. Naturally, the people of Tralles possessed some notion of how to shape it themselves. Recall that they minted Attic-weight gold staters in two issues ca. 167–133. They may very well have minted civic bronzes in this period too.[127] It also remains possible that civic authorities in Tralles applied a countermark of their own, the bull protome, to certain Attic-weight silver tetradrachms from outside the kingdom.[128] Therefore, one can conceivably find local inflection up and down the complete range of value. Yet for poleis, just as important as the shape of the money supply was the rhythm of monetary production. As noted, the cistophoric system contains several administrative anomalies. From Tralles, we have intriguing signs that the rhythm of minting was not set on high. These are the unusual combinations of letters and monograms on Kleiner-Noe series 33–35, tetradrachms, didrachms, and drachms, which Ashton has read as Macedonian months.[129] Again, the

---

[125] Migeotte and Kontorini 1995.

[126] Collections surveyed: *SNG Copenhagen*, American Numismatic Society, *BMC*, Arthur S. Dewing, *SNG Leipzig*, Jameson, Hunterian, and Waddington.

[127] Discussion in Thonemann 2011b, 40 n. 100; see also Robert, *OMS* III, 290–91, for the possibility that bronze coins from Tralles signed Διὸς Εὐμενοῦ date from post-Apameian Attalid times. See also Marcellesi 2010, 199, who does not discuss this case in particular but argues for the appearance of numerous civic bronzes in the expanded Attalid kingdom *after* the cistophoric reform, even in places which had not coined before, e.g., Apameia, for which see Arslan and Devecioğlu 2011. Note the loose date for several series of bronze of Tralles (second to first century BCE) offered by Gökyıldırım 2016, nos. 847–69.

[128] Two examples of this countermark are known; the first is a tetradrachm of the New Athenian Style (ANS 1944.100.85073), for which see Bellinger 1949, no. 5; Noe 1954, 85; Thompson 1961 no. 184b. Until recently, an ethnic of Tralles was read: ΤΡΑΛΛΙ[ΕΩΝ]. Now, a second coin, a silver tetradrachm of Side, has surfaced on the market bearing the same countermark, as well as a cistophoric countermark of Sardis (Classical Numismatic Group, 364, Lot: 297, https://cngcoins.com/Coin.aspx?CoinID=299730). The second example makes clear that the still undeciphered legend cannot be read as an ethnic of Tralles.

[129] Ashton and Kinns 2003, 41–45. It is interesting to note here that the city of Pergamon under the Attalids employed a modified Aeolian calendar, while the royal chancery used the

sample size is small, and the die links imply a perhaps short-lived experiment. None of this disproves the existence of a central authority in the cistophoric system. It merely alerts us to the existence of countervailing forces of decentralization. When it came to money, Tralles wanted what every Greek state wanted in order to combat the "anarchy" of the ancient monetary world: some measure of control over the rhythm of the production of coinage – and with it, the shape of the money supply; some room for supple reactions to changing conditions.[130]

Closure and Closed Currency Systems: The Ptolemaic Model

So much about Tralles was royal. It had fallen to the Attalids as a "gift" city at Apameia, and it seems to have displaced Sardis as the chief administrative center of the region. In Tralles, the Attalids constructed a palace and may have received extraordinary cultic honors.[131] However, the city's minting reminds us of the complexity of the relationship between sovereignty and coinage in ancient Greece.[132] Yet, prima facie, Tralles seems unlikely to have exercised influence over the design of the scaffolding of the cistophoric system. Just outside the city's gates was an open-air royal military encampment.[133] If the introduction of the cistophorus necessitated negotiation, Tralles was not in a position of strength. Yet the character of the cistophoric coinage was not "royal," if by royal we mean that the

---

Macedonian calendar. See *I.Pergamon* 247 line 14 and 251 line 1, with Daubner 2008. For a discussion of calendrical diversity in Hellenistic federalism, see Graninger 2011, 87–114; cf. Savalli-Lestrade 2010.

[130] The notion of an ancient Greek monetary anarchy dates to the nineteenth century. But see too Rostovtzeff 1941, 655, for a classic example. Regarding monetary *supplicité*, the vision here owes much to Francophone scholarship. See, e.g., Bresson 2005; Delrieux 2007. It is becoming increasingly clear that many cities of the Attalid kingdom, as a matter of course, minted bronze and silver coins. Marcellesi 2010 provides a wealth of evidence of local minting at the lower range of value. Of particular interest here is the small silver (ca. 3 g) of Adramyttion and in the name of Athena Nikephoros (ca. 1.5 g).

[131] For the worship of Zeus Eumenes at Tralles as a possible form of ruler cult, see Robert, *OMS* II, 287–91; however, for the suggestion that the cult, at least as it relates to the month Eumenaios in the Pergamene calendar, has nothing to do with the Attalids, see Daubner 2008. Further on the Attalids and Tralles, see Savalli-Lestrade 2001, 82–86.

[132] Martin 1985 provides a classic account of the relationship between sovereignty and coinage in ancient Greece, but his main focus is Thessaly under Philip II. The more recent study of Ziesmann 2005, largely confirming Martin's conclusions, is also focused on the fourth century. Numismatists have begun to suggest that the second century BCE witnessed a transformation of the traditional, looser relationship between sovereignty and coinage, as outlined by Martin and Ziesmann. See Meadows 2001, 61–62, and the prolegomenon to *RPC*.

[133] *SEG* XLVI 1434.

coinage expresses raw domination. We must reckon with the iconoclastic appearance of the coins, while the role of royal authority in the system also cannot be denied. This is because the cistophoric zone was a closed monetary system. The only state around capable of launching and maintaining an epichoric coinage on this scale and territory was Pergamon, even if nothing was possible without the cooperation of the cities.

Confronted with a closed currency system within a Hellenistic kingdom, scholarship has always turned to well-documented Ptolemaic Egypt as both the historical and interpretive model for the cistophori. From Rostovtzeff to Mørkholm, the Attalids were seen to have taken direct inspiration from the Ptolemies.[134] For Le Rider and Callataÿ, the Attalids imitated the Ptolemies, but the model belonged to no one; closed currency systems were simply the norm in both classical and Hellenistic Greece.[135] Lost in all this is the distinctiveness of the Attalid case. In other words, even more than the term "royal," the notion of *closure* lacks nuance in most accounts and potentially leads us astray. Unchallenged, the inapt Ptolemaic comparison impedes our understanding.[136]

Leaving aside the question of its origins and motivations, how did the Ptolemaic system work in practice?[137] We know surprisingly little, but it is clear from the hoards that foreign coinage, both Attic-weight and foreign

---

[134] Mørkholm 1982, 301: "There can hardly be any doubt that the inspiration came from Egypt"; Marcellesi 2000, 330–31; cf. Rostovtzeff 1941, 1293–94: "The monetary policy of the Attalids was in many respects similar [to the Seleukids']. Their own coinage was sound and abundant. Like the Seleucids they insisted on their monetary prerogative. But Eumenes II, in order to increase the issue of coined silver and thus to promote commerce, did not hesitate to grant several cities of his kingdom the right of minting under his control special uniform coins, the so-called *cistophori*, which soon became a Pan-Anatolian currency and circulated in large quantities both in Asia Minor and abroad. Nor did the Attalids differ from the Seleucids in their policy of allowing the local minting of small change." See further Faraguna 2006, 132–36, comparing "open" and "closed" Hellenistic royal economies.

[135] Le Rider and Callataÿ 2006, 113. Cf. Duyrat 2014, 117–18, for the reverse argument: open systems as the norm and the Attalid zone as closed.

[136] It must be noted that Marcellesi 2010 changed the contours of the debate, and my argument is largely in sympathy with hers. Marcellesi 2008, 250: "un système monétaire fermé. Les monnaies d'argent cistophorique sont désormais les seules qui aient cours à l'intérieur de l'État attalide ... mais celui-ci n'atteint pas la rigidité du système lagide." Fuller exposition of limits of closure in the Attalid system: Marcellesi 2012, 149–61. Rejection of Ptolemaic model: Meadows 2013, 196. Note, however, a harder closure – on a Rhodian model – proposed by Bresson 2018, 108–9, a major study too recent for adequate incorporation here.

[137] Von Reden (2007, 43–45) has provocatively questioned the assumption of a deliberate design behind the Ptolemaic system. For her, the Ptolemies arrived almost haphazardly at their solution, which was a solution to the problem of monetizing rapidly huge volumes of metal. She characterizes the Ptolemaic system as a classic demonstration of the validity of Gresham's law.

epichoric, ceased to circulate in Egypt ca. 310–ca. 300.[138] Over this period, the weight of the Ptolemaic silver coinage descended progressively from the Attic standard of ca. 17.25 g to its own epichoric standard of ca. 14.25. Around the same time, Ptolemy I also introduced reduced-weight gold and bronze coinages.[139] According to Gresham's law, the reduced-weight coinages in precious metals would have forced the full-weight (i.e., Attic-weight) coinage, much of it foreign, out of circulation; and market forces alone would have kept Ptolemaic gold and silver coins from leaving Egypt, since their local value so exceeded their international one.[140] Yet it appears that the Ptolemaic state had a more active role to play in creating the homogeneity of the hoards. Relying on the indirect evidence of *P.Cair.Zen.* I 59021 of the year 258, one generally sees an official prohibition on the use of foreign coinage in the form of a *prostagma* issued ca. 300. Unfortunately, we do not possess the text of a law, just that famous letter of the mint official Demetrios to the royal *dioikêtês* Apollonios. It depicts a frustrated foreign merchant class waiting to change foreign (*epichorion*) gold coins and old Ptolemaic *trichrysa* into new Ptolemaic *mnaieia* after the reform of Ptolemy II. Their money is lying idle. The lesson is that, in Egypt, there were no options. The Ptolemaic state created a system in which the exclusive legal tender was whatever local coinage the king ruled valid. Buying and selling, all payments public and private, were to be conducted in the local coinage sanctioned by the Ptolemaic state.[141]

Therefore, part of the standard reconstruction of economic life in Ptolemaic Egypt is the following scenario. A foreign trader arrives at port. To buy an export cargo, he will have to obtain Ptolemaic coinage. To buy Ptolemaic coinage, he must bring his foreign coinage into the country. It is possible that the import of coinage was taxed.[142] Having paid customs, the

---

[138] The exceptions are gathered in Cadell and Le Rider 1997, 10 n. 11. Only three out of 35 hoards from Ptolemaic Egypt deposited after ca. 300 contain foreign coins.

[139] For an account of Ptolemy I's minting, see Cadell and Le Rider 1997, 9–11.

[140] For precious metal Ptolemaic coinage from hoards outside Egypt, see the table (of Meadows) in Appendix 1 of Von Reden 2007.

[141] For the genre of royal order envisioned here, *prostagma*, see *P.Cair.Zen.* I 59021 line 14. For Ptolemy I's general prohibition of the use of foreign coinage ca. 300, see Cadell and Le Rider 1997, 10. For the comprehensiveness of the ban, see the Olbia Coinage Decree, *Syll.*³ 218 lines 13–16: "to buy and sell everything with the city's coins, both the bronze and the silver of Olbia (πωλεῖν δὲ καὶ ὠν[ε]||[ῖσθαι] πάντα πρὸς τὸ νόμισμα τὸ τῆς [πόλ]εως, πρὸς τὸν χαλκὸν καὶ τὸ ἀργύριο[ν] [τὸ] Ὀλβιοπολιτικόν)."

[142] See *CLA* line 61, which prohibits taxation on import and export of coinage. Does the prohibition imply its existence elsewhere? Just how strictly customs agents controlled monetary flow is difficult to gauge. Bresson 2007 likens the intensity of surveillance in ancient Mediterranean customs regimes to medieval European standards of enforcement. It may be

trader goes to a bank, where he changes foreign coinage into Ptolemaic coinage at officially prescribed rates of exchange – taking a 17% (?) loss on silver, perhaps even more on gold.[143] Of course he keeps some amount of foreign coinage on hand in anticipation of his final departure from Egypt. He wants to avoid repurchasing foreign coinage from the bank, coinage that he will need when he arrives at his next port of call. Foreign coinage was not contraband in Ptolemaic Egypt, but unacceptable as legal tender. This is why it is so rarely found in hoards post-ca. 300, but, occasionally, it does turn up.

To compare the situation in second-century Asia Minor, when the Attalids introduced the cistophorus at a weight 25% below the Attic standard, they ensured that the coins would not travel far. Royal authority clearly granted them a premium above their international value as silver bullion. This explains why we essentially never find a cistophoric coin in a hoard outside the Attalid kingdom – and indeed the singular example of one such coin in the Larissa hoard is usually considered an intrusion (*IGCH* 237; buried ca. 165). The cistophoric zone was closed in the sense that the cistophori did not slip out too easily. As Meadows points out, these silver coins behave just like any epichoric bronze: with all their fiduciary value, they are meant to stay put.[144] Yet the Ptolemaic – or Olbian – notion of closure was something else.[145] There, exchange as such was closed to foreign coinage, whether gold, silver, or bronze. In other words, whatever its real value in Egypt as precious metal, or its fiduciary value elsewhere as coin, non-Ptolemaic coinage could not serve as a means of payment in the Ptolemaic state. Contrary to popular belief, there is no firm basis for the

---

helpful to note a striking example from the Cairo Genizah. Between Old Cairo and the port of Alexandria, a trader was forced to stop and make 45 different payments (Goitein 1967–93, vol. 1, p. 342). If we make this our model for Antiquity, it is not implausible to imagine customs agents of the second century BCE going so far as to search people for coins.

[143] I recognize that the banking system changed over the course of the third century. By the end of the century, currency exchange was no longer the preserve of state-farmed monopoly banks, but for the earlier period, see the evidence of *P.Rev.* lines 73–78: only royal banks and state-farmed monopoly banks collected agio (*allagê*) on currency exchange (Bogaert 1998, 169). For an officially prescribed exchange fee, which varies in the papyri, hence my "about 10%," see Bogaert 1984, 181–82. However, for the exchange rate (*kollybos*, at least in the papyri), we do not know if it was set officially, particularly since parts of the *diagramma trapezôn* of the *P.Rev.* are so fragmentary (Bogaert 1984, 184). For the vocabulary of exchange fees as opposed to exchange rates in ancient Greek banking, see Bogaert 1968, 48–50; Bresson 2014.

[144] Meadows 2013, 202–3.

[145] See also the decree of Gortyn on bronze coinage, ca. 250–200 (*Syll.*³ 525 = Austin 2006, no. 123). Gortyn voted to demonetize its silver obols and mandate the use of its bronze coinage. Again, this is a different, much stronger form of closure than the one we find in the Attalid kingdom.

view that the Attalids similarly banned the use of non-cistophoric coinage within the territory of their kingdom or even within some "cistophoric core," the existence of which is scarcely visible in the hoard record and is in fact contradicted by the epigraphic record.[146] Ultimately, the cistophoric system outlived the Attalids and all their edicts. Yet to argue for a "hard" notion of closure, one often points to the hoard record for pre-133 cistophori, which, again, is poor in the extreme.[147] Almost all of the hoards contain only cistophori. However, the earliest hoard to include cistophori is mixed, the 1962 "Asia Minor" hoard *IGCH* 1453, containing 71+ silver coins, 42 of them cistophori, the rest, various Attic-weight coins, including five Pergamene. Meadows dates the deposit of this hoard to ca. 150 but is agnostic about its findspot.[148] To preserve the picture of a Ptolemaic-style closed system, Christof Boehringer, in publishing the hoard, placed it on the frontier between the cistophoric zone and the neighboring Attic-weight zone within the boundaries of the kingdom of Bithynia.[149] Yet consider also the fact that an unmixed hoard of 37 cistophori was found at Türktaciri on the Upper Sangarius, in the hinterland of Pessinous (*CH* VIII 446). That hoard, known as the Polatlı hoard, does not make the Galatian frontier part of the cistophoric core. Rather, it reminds us that the borders of the monetary zone as much as the kingdom were permeable and mutable. Among its 37 coins is a range of some of the earliest and latest series, right down to autonomous cistophoric issues of Ephesus securely dated 131/0.[150] In addition, all five of the largest mints are represented, in regular proportion to their size, making trade, as much as warfare, a plausible explanation for it on the Sangarius. Either trade or warfare could also explain the Ahmetbeyli hoard from the opposite, Aegean fringe (*CH* IX 535). Further, a large hoard of 120+ cistophoroi was found in the nineteenth century in Afyonkarahisar (*IGCH* 1415). Does it derive from a single military campaign or from healthy trade at the great emporion of Apameia?[151] We must admit our ignorance. In the end, what the evidence

---

[146] Epigraphic record: Marcellesi 2012, 152–54.   [147] Callataÿ 2013, 241–44.
[148] Meadows 2013, 182; cf. Kleiner and Noe, 1977, 108, with date ca. 145–140.
[149] Boehringer 1972, 183: "Sollte die Vermutung der Herkunft des Hortes aus dem pergamenischen Grenzgebiet zutreffen, so ist man versucht, ihn mit den kriegerischen Ereignissen von 150–149 zu verbinden, in denen Attalos II. Kräftig mitmischte"; cf. Kleiner and Noe 1977, 110: "As a rule, the cistophori did not leave Attalid territory, and it is almost certain that this hoard was buried in an area under Pergamene control."
[150] *CH* VIII gives a burial date of ca. 150–140 BCE, reproduced by Callataÿ 2013, 243: "near Ankara." Türktaciri is about 100 km as the crow flies from Ankara. For a burial date not long after ca. 130, see Göktürk 1991.
[151] On both Polatlı and Afyonkarahisar as related to campaigning, see Callataÿ 2013, 230.

of hoards tells us is that the ancient user generally kept separate stores of cistophoric and non-cistophoric coinage, not that the Attalids proscribed the use of foreign coin. Hoarding practice does not necessarily reflect what was used or in circulation.[152]

The logic of such a hoarding practice is that the monetary system is ramified. Different payments require different currencies. For the Attalid kingdom, then, we can reconstruct the following scenario. A foreign trader arrives at an Attalid port or at an inland interchange like Tralles, and he first pays customs. To what extent does he then change his foreign coinage, Attic-weight or epichoric, into cistophori, assuming he does not possess a reserve of them like the merchants of the Antikythera shipwreck?[153] The answer is that it depends on what kinds of payments he will make – and this is the crucial difference between the Ptolemaic and Attalid situations. For in the Attalid system, cistophoric coinage must have been required only for a certain a set of payments. Chief among these payments would have been official payments: taxes, fees, rents, and others, and so our hypothetical foreign trader could certainly not have avoided purchasing some cistophori. Of the official status of the money changer that he went to, we can say nothing. Yet in light of the comparative evidence, we can be fairly certain that the Attalid state fixed either the exchange rate or the exchange fee (agio), or perhaps both. In the fifth century, the Athenians set an official agio for the exchange of foreign coinage into owls in the so-called Coinage Decree (*ML* 45 line 5).[154] The citizens of Pontic Olbia set an official rate of exchange for their coinage against Cyzicene electrum staters (*Syll.*³ 218 lines 24–26). In the end, this is part of the logic of any epichoric

---

[152] The hoard record for Asia Minor of the mid- to late second century BCE is rather poor, which makes it difficult to generalize about hoarding practice. On the other hand, mixed hoards of any kind are very uncommon in *IGCH* for all of Asia Minor of the second century. A hoarding practice that separates epichoric from international coinages may be in evidence in a hoard of 25 cistophori from the territory of Colophon, buried ca. 120 (*CH* IX 535, Ahmetbeyli = Travaglini 1997, 137–42). Colophon was of course participating in a wider zone of circulation in this period, even if this hoard does not reflect it. Consider also the Muğla hoard (*IGCH* 1357; closed 84 BCE), republished in Meadows 2002 (*CH* X 324). Of all its 350+ silver coins of Rhodes and Stratonikeia in the Rhodian peraia, none belongs to Meadows' "Group 1" of Stratonikeian coins, the subset of the city's coinage that was minted on a standard that was compatible with both the Attic and cistophoric standards. According to Carbone 2020 (p. 33), as a rule, cistophori circulated (and were hoarded) unmixed from 133 until the 40s BCE. An exception is the aforementioned *IGCH* 1330 (Priene, ca. 125), which contained a single cistophoros among its 331 coins.

[153] Antikythera: *CH* VIII 521, ca. 75–50 BCE, the only hoard of cistophori (late or early) to be found outside Asia Minor and, significantly, from a shipwreck.

[154] There, the word "to exchange" is restored: κατ]αλλάτειν.

coinage: the state, whether it be a polis like Sestos or the Ptolemaic kingdom, gained revenue by forcing people into currency exchanges, and then profiting from its position of monopoly power over some aspect of those exchanges.[155]

For a host of other payments inside the Attalid kingdom, one might have preferred or been compelled to make payments in Attic-weight silver or gold; or in a different epichoric coinage, the Rhodian, in places with strong economic ties to Rhodes, its *peraia*, and the Cyclades; or for small transactions, in the local epichoric bronze that cities minted without Attalid participation and without reference to the cistophoric standard.[156] It may have been that the deeper one went inland, the greater the number of payments requiring cistophori. But it need not have been so. Wherever you went, people were making payments in multiple coinages.

The Attalid Model

If we adopt a ramified vision of coinage in the Attalid kingdom, we can resolve several outstanding problems. The first is the troublesome matter of the extraordinarily high cost of exchanging non-cistophoric coinage for cistophoric. Assuming one exchanged an Attic-weight silver tetradrachm for a cistophorus, the commission was 25%, plus whatever agio was charged. The conventional agio in ancient Greece seems to have been ca. 5–7%, so the total premium of the cistophorus would have been near 30%.[157] Again, the Ptolemies are seen to have set a precedent with the high rate of exchange of 17%, their agio being around 10%, for a similarly

---

[155] For *Sestos*: *I.Sestos* 1 lines 44–46 with Bresson 2016, 275–76. Was the official exchange rate set only against Attic-weight coinage? Bogaert (1984, 184) adduces the paradigm of the Olbia decree in discussing the possibilities for Ptolemaic Egypt. Olbia mandates an official exchange rate of one Olbian hemistater to one Cyzicene stater, making all other exchanges a matter of "persuasion."

[156] Marcellesi (2010, 198–200) raises the issue of the large number of civic bronze coinages the post-Apameian Attalid territory, though as she admits, it is not always possible for numismatists to agree on dates for these coins. The city of Apameia itself is a particularly interesting case, with some scholars dating at least one series to the period of Attalid control (obverse with Serapis, reverse of two *piloi*, a symbol shared with early cistophori in the name of the same city). See Ashton and Kinns 2003, 46–47; Bresson 2019, 300.

[157] The total premium postulated could be even higher if customs dues on imported coinage are added. For the conventional agio in ancient Greece, see Bogaert 1968, 109, 115, for a norm of around 5%, slightly higher in the Delphic evidence (7–9.5%). See further on all three cases treated here, Le Rider and Callataÿ 2006, 112–14. Their view of the cistophoric system is the traditional one, which likens it to the Ptolemaic system and the experiment of Byzantium and Chalcedon, ca. 235–220. The Attalids are said to have taken a "tax au change" of 25%. For conventional rates of agio, as well as the standard assumption of a 25% premium for the

high total premium of around 30%. Yet how can we compare the alluring resources of Ptolemaic Egypt with those of Attalid Asia Minor? To buy Egyptian grain, the premium was evidently palatable, and the Ptolemies in the Nile Valley enjoyed the perfect ecological niche for enforcing monopoly. In an analogous fashion, and perhaps with Ptolemaic support, the cities of Byzantium and Chalcedon profited from their peculiar ecology on the Bosphorus, but overreached ca. 235–220 when they tried to force an exchange rate of ca. 19% on users.[158] This is a limiting case: it seems that Rhodes went to war over the issue, and the closed currency system failed. Byzantium and Chalcedon lacked the resources to sustain the enterprise. For their part, the Attalids enjoyed neither a preciously unique ecological niche nor a productive base that could have justified a demanded premium of 25+%. There are no echoes in the sources of resistance to such measures, which surely would have represented a painful restructuring of economic life, nor signs of the kind of coercive enforcement necessary to sustain a truly closed currency system on this territory. It is impossible to explain how the Attalids managed to impose and maintain the kind of closed system that succeeded in Egypt but ultimately failed in the Propontis. However, this is a *question mal posée*. Those are inappropriate points of comparison.

We can now also make sense of the large amount of Attic-weight silver minted in Attalid Asia Minor *after* the cistophoric reform, with both royal (Marcellesi nos. 42–44) and civic types. First, we can dispense with the idea that these were "export coinages." By sheer volume, they must have been an important part of the money supply of Asia Minor. Consider, for example, that Myrina produced a total of 445 Attic drachm obverse equivalents in Wreathed Coinage, while Ephesus coined a total of 486 in Attalid-era cistophori.[159] Of course, as international coinage, these coins were particularly useful for exchange with outsiders. Yet we need not doubt that they passed between insiders too, if we can accept that there existed a series of nonofficial payments for which these coins *were* legal tender. Selene Psoma restricts these transactions to the fairs of religious festivals, where in her view, locals were required to use Attic-weight coinage to make purchases.[160] These were largely big-ticket items like slaves and livestock,

---

cistophori, see Mørkholm 1982, 296, 301. See too an exchange fee of 25% on epichoric bronze for symmachic silver at mid-second century Thebes: *SEG* XLV 447.

[158] This is the interpretation of Seyrig 1968 of the episode recorded in Polyb. 4.46–52. See further Russell 2017, 119–32.

[159] Callataÿ 2013, 234.   [160] Psoma 2013, 272–75.

and the vendors were outsiders. She adduces the tetradrachm of the *technitai* of Dionysus (of Ionia and the Hellespont), and the Attic silver called for in the Archippe dossier from Kyme, prescribed for the purchase of a victim. Indeed, one could explain the rare gold staters of Tralles similarly. Like Kyme, the city needed to buy a bull for a festival sacrifice. Yet why should the city be required to purchase the bull (1) from an outsider and (2) under the special conditions of festival commerce? The associations of the *technitai*, after all, were regional; in Asia Minor, they were intimates of the Attalid court – these were not outsiders. Psoma's point is salutary, but she has isolated only one of the contexts for which Attic-weight coinage would have been usable and useful.

It is difficult to shine a light directly on those other contexts for Attic-weight coinage in the Attalid kingdom, but we possess tantalizing clues such as the Athenian New Style tetradrachm with the countermark of bull protome (Thompson no. 184b). Margaret Thompson dated the issue of the coin, in Athens, to 175/4, but the whole series has long been downdated. On David Lewis' influential chronology, the Athenians issued the coin some 33 years later.[161] Picard's downward shift is only 20 years, but he also questions the assumption of uninterrupted minting.[162] On any of these chronologies, a coin minted at least one or two decades before 133 can plausibly be imagined to have entered circulation in the Attalid kingdom. The same is true of a related coin, the Sidetan tetradrachm that recently surfaced at auction bearing *both* the bull protome countermark *and* a cistophoric countermark – this Attic-weight coin obviously circulated in the late Attalid kingdom.

The problem is a familiar one of how to interpret the countermark. Rather than see it as remonetizing a coin that is no longer money once it travels inside the cistophoric zone, we can see it as expanding the range of transactions for which the coin is acceptable. Whoever conveyed this tetradrachm considered it money. The countermark only extended its acceptability, and perhaps cleared up some ambiguity about its value. For example, was the slightly lightweight New Style tetradrachm really worth four Attic drachms? The countermark did not remonetize the coin, but may have allowed it to enter the transactional sphere of local taxes. It is a

---

[161] See Lewis 1962; Mattingly 1971, 34–46, largely endorsing the low chronology of Lewis. See further, Mattingly 1990, and for a summary of the debate, Bresson 2016, 425 n. 43.
[162] Picard 2010, 173. Thonemann 2015a, 126: dating of Thompson no. 184b to 144/3.

stark reminder that civic fiscality had its own relationship with coinage to maintain.[163]

Dispensing with the Ptolemaic model also allows us to clarify the role of bronze coinage in the Attalid monetary system after the cistophoric reform. In Egypt, closure meant the application of standard ratios of value between Ptolemaic gold, silver, and bronze. Thus, when the Ptolemies altered the weights and denominational structure of their bronze, the papryi reflect the consistent application of the new ratio. Around 260, Philadelphos was even able to impose a heavy bronze coin at value equal to his silver drachma.[164] Granted, the Attalid state will have had a hand in fixing the rates at which moneychangers in the kingdom sold their cistophori, rates that were reckoned in gold, bronze, or other silver. The state had to safeguard its profit with a fixed exchange rate – precisely what the Athenians do in the Coinage Decree, or what we see the Roman emperor Hadrian attending to in an Imperial-period decree from Pergamon (*OGIS* 484). Yet the Attalids minted no gold and, at the beginning of the second century, appear to have stopped minting bronze in the name of Philetairos.[165] New bronze issues appear in the era of the cistophori, a civic bronze in the name of the citizens of Pergamon (Marcellesi nos. 63–67) and coins in the name of deities such as Athena Nikephoros and Asklepios Soter (Marcellesi nos. 53–62). Crucially, their denominational structure and, therefore presumably, the values affixed to bronze coinages changed little from the third to the second century. Larger denominations (obols and diobols) are added in the second century.[166] Yet we see no reform of the bronze to match the cistophoric reform in silver, such as is visible in the case of the Rhodian plinthophori.[167] Effectively, the Attalids had at most an indirect influence over the value of bronze coins trading in an entire sea of transactions.[168]

The value of bronze coins was not determined solely by the asking price for cistophori, but far more directly by the issuing authorities. And those

---

[163] Cf. Thonemann (2015a, 126), "suggesting that Athenian coins had to be 'validated' in order to be used" in western Asia Minor. Yet the coin was in any case usable. The situation in the Attalid kingdom was not fundamentally different from Delphi of the Amphyctionic decree (Austin 2006, no. 125) – in both places the value of the coin was potentially ambiguous.

[164] Cadell and Le Rider 1997, 18–19.   [165] Marcellesi 2012, 127.

[166] Marcellesi 2012, 157–58.   [167] Chameroy 2012, 145.

[168] Cf. Evans 2018, 129, introducing the notion of "Attalid 4-unit" and "Attalid 2-unit" bronze coins for two issues of Sardis (nos. 58 and 59; cf. figs. 2.12 and 2.13, the latter terming them Attalid), said to date from 188–133. However, there is no evidence for a specifically Attalid standard in bronze. On the contrary, the denominations of Attalid bronze, various fractions of the obol, conform to the pattern set by the regional civic mints, including Pergamon's. See Marcellesi 2012, 75–77, 157–58.

authorities were the cities of the Attalid kingdom, which granted a fiduciary value to their own bronze coins. This has often escaped notice because it has long been conventional to use 133 as a *terminus post quem* for many late Hellenistic bronzes of Asia Minor, to assume, unjustifiably, an Attalid prohibition of civic bronze.[169] Long-running excavations in the imperial metropole have turned up a restricted range of other cities' bronze.[170] The picture that emerges is of each city attending to its own needs for bronze, choosing the value and acceptability of coin for this tier of the monetary system. We are very far indeed from Ptolemaic Egypt.

The Cistophori: A Coordinated Coinage

Part of the justification for examining in detail the incongruence of the Ptolemaic and Attalid systems is that we can now distinguish the banal from the exceptional. A ramified monetary system, which coupled closure, in the form of a silver coinage removed from the international standard of its day, with an openness absent from Egypt (and Rhodes?) was in fact commonplace. The impermeable Ptolemaic system and the open system of the Seleukids were, in fact, the outliers of the Hellenistic world. The norm for most Greek states was a mixed regime: epichoric coinage was required for one set of transactions, while the rest, to paraphrase the decree of Olbia, was a matter of persuasion.[171] This is just what we have envisioned for the Attalid kingdom. It is instructive here to recall that in the late 180s, the Attalids had twice asked the Kardakes for a certain tax to be paid in Rhodian coin. It should then be no stretch of the imagination to propose that after ca. 167, the Pergamene state was prescribing a specific coinage – the cistophori – for a certain set of official payments. This exposes what is

---

[169] See, e.g., the conclusion of Johannes Krauss in his edition of *I.Sestos* 1. He dates the civic minting episode of lines 44–46 to post-133, applying this rule of thumb. The same rule is applied throughout corpora such as *BMC*. However, cf. MacDonald (1992, 1) calling certain bronzes of Aphrodisias "pseudo-royal petty coinages." More recent scholarship moves toward generic second-century dates. See, e.g., Gökyıldırım 2016, nos. 847–69 (Tralles); Aybek and Dreyer 2016, 12 (Apollonia-on-the-Rhyndakos); Ingvaldsen 2010, 178, on bronze of Metropolis, allowing for possibility that his Type 1 Ares/Thyrsos is pre-133. Evans (2018, 24; 2019, 113) argues for continuous minting of bronze at the civic mint of Sardis across the Seleukid-Attalid transition.

[170] Chameroy and Savalli-Lestrade 2016, 259–84.

[171] Marcellesi 2000, 356. Of course, in Olbia, certain exchange rates were what was a matter of persuasion – and only Olbian coins were legal tender. Regarding the role of persuasion in currency exchange, see the case of the League of Islanders and the banker Timon of Syracuse (*IG* XII 5 817), as interpreted by Bresson 2001; Bresson 2014.

truly strange about the cistophoric system: its size. Instead of imitating the Ptolemies, the Attalids acted rather like a polis with an exceptionally large *chora*.[172]

However, as we have shown, the Attalids did not act alone. They decentralized minting, and they seemed to have ceded to local actors some measure of control over the shape of the money supply and the rhythm of its production. Indeed, the cistophoric experiment succeeded only with the help of the cities. Just consider once more how currency exchange would have worked, our lack of epigraphical or literary sources notwithstanding. Either the exchange rate or the agio (or both) would have been fixed and standard across the kingdom. This is what all our comparative evidence tells us – this is the logic of an epichoric coinage. We have no way of knowing which kinds of banks performed the exchange, but we can be sure that many were in the agoras of cities, not confined to royal customs stations on a kind of cistophoric frontier encircling the kingdom.[173] We know from the subscription of Colophon in 310 and the audit of Teos in the third century that, in western Asia Minor, people were used to holding portfolios of different currencies.[174] By the mid-second century, could things have changed so much? In these conditions, it was difficult to prevent people from making private deals that allowed them to avoid paying the state its due premium. The challenge had motivated earlier Greek cities to appoint official enforcers and impose heavy penalties for noncompliance.[175] The problem was endemic to the ancient Mediterranean, and it still plagued the city of Pergamon in the time of Hadrian. There, the *agoranomoi* failed to suppress an active black market in the city's bronze coins.[176] The problem of compliance was formidable enough in the marketplace or territory of a single polis, but the Attalids needed surveillance, policing, and communication across the wide expanse of their newly expanded kingdom. They needed, in a word, cooperation.[177]

---

[172] Meadows 2013, 202–3.   [173] For a cistophoric frontier, see Psoma 2013, 272.
[174] Colophon: Meritt 1935, 358–72, no. 1, with commentary of Migeotte 1992, 219. Teos: *SEG* XLIV 949 Column III lines 71–102.
[175] Thus in Olbia the penalty for noncompliance was the confiscation of goods; in Gortyn, armed youths called *neotai* enforced a coinage reform (*Syll.*³ 525).
[176] *OGIS* 484. Cf. the incident of clandestine currency exchange in Mylasa, 209/10 CE (*OGIS* 515). Mylasa gained important revenues from its monopoly on exchange. Private, illegal exchange threatened the city's fiscal stability. See the discussion of Bogaert 1968, 266–68.
[177] Cf. Kleiner 1972, 32 n. 30: "The Attalid silver must have had a higher value within Pergamene territory than outside it." That postulate requires another – the postulate of the cities' cooperation, which was absolutely necessary to enforce the overvaluation of the cistophori.

In their prolegomenon to the study of what they call "cooperative coinages," Emily Mackil and Peter van Alfen have drawn attention to a broad category of inter- and intrastate minting arrangements that remain poorly understood. Emphasizing the costs and complexities of the enterprise, Mackil and van Alfen seek explanations for why distinct polities submitted to mint together. Reacting against a tradition that read these coins as a straightforward expression of political union or domination, they propose a variety of economic explanations: "If, however, in each case it is possible to provide an economic explanation for the (functional) cooperation of multiple cities in minting coinage, then we need to ask whether any hegemonic factor is really significant."[178] The point is particularly trenchant for our understanding of a multiscalar polity like the koinon. In the case of the early Boiotian Koinon, for example, cooperative minting preceded political federation. In most other cases, it appears at about the same time as other formal institutions at the regional level. In other words, cooperative minting is not an expression of a new political hegemony, but rather a way to institutionalize preexistent economic interdependence. In fact, instead of a hegemon, an ecological imperative can compel cities to cooperate.[179]

By contrast, the cistophoric coinage entailed a coordinated form of cooperation. Mackil and van Alfen seem to cast kingdom (*basileia*) as another multiscalar polity, but it is left out of their discussion.[180] Yet here, there can be no doubt: political hegemony precedes the cooperative arrangement of minting and using these coins. Here, the significance of the hegemonic factor can be explained. It was the singular role of the Attalid state to coordinate between the different polities. Revenues may very well have been shared, but the fiscal benefits of the system were still distinctly advantageous for Pergamon. Across the kingdom, it became cheaper for the king to collect taxes and make gifts. Also, Attalid Asia Minor was an artificial conglomeration of regional economies, unlike the fragile but coherent economies of Achaia or Boiotia or, to compare an *ethnos*-based kingdom, Antigonid Macedonia with its economically complementary regional divisions (*merides*), purposively shattered by the Romans. For their part, the Attalids imposed a political hegemony on a group of regional economies oriented variously and only loosely interconnected. On Pamphylia, the Propontis, the Troad, and the Maeander Valley,

---

[178] Mackil and van Alfen 2006, 204.
[179] Mackil and van Alfen 2006, 220; Mackil 2013, 264–84.
[180] Mackil and van Alfen 2006, 204. Cf. Mackil 2013, 264, on Antigonid Macedonia.

they had to *impose* economic as well as political integration.[181] The cistophori differ from many other cooperative coinages in that the accent is on the production of new economic behaviors, patterns, and links, rather than on the regularization and maintenance of old ones.

The cistophori, then, represent a special class of cooperative coinage, which is usefully termed "coordinated coinage." We retain the economic raison d'être, but we also take account of the role of the political hegemon, the coordinator. Because a coordinated coinage presupposes the cooperation of civic institutions, it is again important to keep in mind the developmental trajectory of those institutions in the second century. In creating the cistophoric system, the Attalids drew on a reservoir of civic institutional know-how long in the making. They were also able to rely on a network of civic elites, who, increasingly rich and powerful, were asserting ever more control over local institutions.[182] These were men such as Menas of Sestos, who was both an Attalid official and a civic moneyer, someone who cared for the affairs of the king but also for the pride of his city (*I.Sestos* 1, lines 12, 46). As we have seen, the system rewarded cooperation. Cooperation, however, is not the same as coordination. This is one of the conclusions of Levi in her fiscal sociology of revenue collection.[183] She argues that successful fiscal regimes promote "quasi-voluntary compliance," through either institutional or ideological means. Compliance is higher where fiscal institutions are more cooperative. Yet people also cooperate with the tax-collecting state because they believe it is in their interest. The state gives them something in return. Ultimately, the cistophoric system engendered a level of economic integration in Asia Minor that buffered risk for all, and the revenues, along with the responsibilities, were likely shared. The Attalids offered their subjects the service of coordination, itself a public good and a reward worthy of their cooperation.

---

[181] One can see the different economic orientations of these regions in the history of their coinages. Pamphylia, oriented toward the Levant, is obviously an outlier in the Attalid kingdom. The Propontis displays distinctive features, such as the typically Pontic use of electrum and frequent use of countermarking. For the Maeander Valley, consider again *IGCH* 1330, from a house in Priene, buried ca. 125. It includes 329 bronze coins of Priene, epichoric bronze for local needs, but also one silver coin of Rhodes, and one cistophorus of Tralles, an important Maeander city. The hoard is a witness to the region's coherence, vaunted in Thonemann 2011b, as well as to its contiguity to the Rhodian zone.

[182] On local elites in Asia Minor and Hellenistic kings, see Dreyer and Weber 2011. For the enrichment of the great civic benefactors of second-century Asia Minor, see Thonemann 2011b, 249–51; and further on the leading families of Priene, Kyme, and Miletus, see Grandinetti 2010.

[183] Levi 1988, esp. 48–70.

Monetary Change after Apameia

Explaining the Countermarks

In the cistophori, we have explained just one aspect of the monetary change ushered in with the Treaty of Apameia. Yet we have also developed a framework for analyzing two other numismatic puzzles of this period, the so-called cistophoric countermarks, which preceded the cistophori, and the Wreathed Coinages, which were an integral part of the money supply after the cistophoric reform. Again, we need to consider the broader context of Hellenistic coinage, since no one minted into a void. In Asia Minor of the 180s and 170s, the silver coinage of one state countermarked by another would not have been an uncommon sight. While the Seleukid anchor and Helios countermarks seem to begin slightly later than the cistophoric ones, nearby in the Propontis, the practice was time-honored.[184] From precisely this period, the Propontis hoard (*IGCH* 888) contains a tetradrachm of Phaselis bearing a cistophoric countermark of Pergamon.[185] Earlier, Byzantium and Chalcedon had countermarked large quantities of Ptolemaic coinage for much of the third century.[186] Moreover, the Propontis hoard shows that civic countermarks of Cyzicus, the letters KY ZI within a wreath, were contemporaneous with the cistophoric countermarks, stamped on the very same Attic-weight silver tetradrachms from Pamphylia. For Thonemann, the KY ZI countermarks are numismatic evidence that Cyzicus was not part of the expanded

---

[184] For the vexed problem of dating these two Seleukid countermarks of the second or third quarter of the second century, see Le Rider 1999, 229–33. Le Rider cautiously dates them to the years following 175, while for Bauslaugh (1990, 55–56), the hoard evidence points to ca. 170. Bauslaugh also presents the evidence of overstrikes (anchor countermarks struck over cistophoric countermarks), our only evidence for a slightly later date for the Seleukid countermarks. For the two countermarking systems in relation, see also the recently published hoard of silver tetradrachms from Uşak (*CH* X 293), which contained ca. 19 coins with cistophoric countermarks, but just one bearing the anchor.

[185] Waggoner 1979 no. 79 = Bauslaugh 1990, 41, pl. 4 no. 1. For discussion of date of Propontis hoard, which has floated between ca. 180 and ca. 160, see Harl 1991, 277–78.

[186] Marinescu 2000, 334–35: "The countermarking of Attic coins which Seyrig placed at ca. 235 BC can now be shown to be part of a long standing tradition at Byzantium, which began by countermarking Ptolemaic tetradrachms. . . . Therefore the countermarking of Attic weight coins must have commenced around 235 BC and seems to be a direct continuation of the same policy which first used Ptolemaic coinage." Note also a different set of countermarks from Byzantium and Chalcedon that seem to be later than Seyrig's "Phoenician episode." Marinescu (2000, 335) places one countermark from Byzantium in the last decade of the third century. Moreover, the Propontis hoard (*IGCH* 888) contained two countermarks of Byzantium and one of Chalcedon. Seyrig himself dated the Byzantine ones 220–190. See discussion of Waggoner 1979, 23–24.

Attalid kingdom.[187] We should be more cautious. Like the countermark of bull protome, or the Tyche countermarks of Smyrna (?) and the grape cluster of Temnos (?), the Cyzicene one proves only that a city took action to control its local money supply.[188] The cistophori and the Wreathed Coinages both imply that the Attalids regularly afforded cities that latitude.

Therefore, in countermarking, the Attalids adopted a practice seemingly widespread in the nearby Propontis, which a number of other states took up at roughly the same time. Yet why they chose to countermark is not always clear. The standard explanation of the function of the countermark, as embodied by Seyrig's telling of the "Phoenician episode" on the Bosphorus and in an influential essay of Le Rider, has clouded the discussion.[189] For a period of about 15 years (ca. 235–ca. 220), Byzantium and Chalcedon jointly minted silver on a reduced, so-called Phoenician standard, very close to the Ptolemaic standard of 14 or 13.5 g to the tetradrachm. Simultaneously, the two cities seem to have countermarked all Attic-weight silver, mostly foreign, but also their own Lysimachi.[190] Also, since at least the early 260s, Byzantium's countermarks had been placed on Ptolemaic tetradrachms minted at Alexandria. Further, we now know that Byzantium and Chalcedon minted Lysmachi unceasingly into the second century. A number of different monetary experiments, then, seem to have taken place on the Bosphorus between the 260s and the 220s. So while for Seyrig, the "Phoenician" silver created a closed currency system in order to raise revenue during the acute crisis reported by Polybius (4.37.8–10, 4.45.1–53.1), Thomas Russell's treatment of the new evidence concludes that under financial pressure from the Galatians, Byzantium and Chalcedon had already closed the system with Ptolemaic support several decades prior.[191]

The unique ecological niche of the Bosphorus and the aggregate coercive power of Byzantium, Chalcedon, and the Ptolemies may have, for spurts of time, made it possible to close off the region's currency system completely. We should not, however, use the case both as a general template for understanding countermarking and, specifically, to explain the cistophoric

---

[187] Thonemann 2008, 59.

[188] This entire phenomenon of civic countermarks on Attic-weight coinage – of, e.g., Kyme and Alabanda – is poorly understood, though obviously crucial for any understanding of the monetary system of the Attalid kingdom. Noe 1954 was the first to flag the issue. See also Seyrig 1973, 70, on the Tyche and grape cluster countermarks of the Tell Kotchek hoard (*IGCH* 1773). Meadows 2008 dates these countermarks to the 140s.

[189] Seyrig 1968; Le Rider 1975.   [190] See the Büyükçekmece hoard (*IGCH* 867).

[191] Russell 2017, 124; see also p. 131, on the comparability of the cistophoric system.

countermarks. The idea is that it only makes sense to countermark a (foreign) silver coin in order to either remonetize it or retariff it. The theory of remonetization has nothing to commend it. It was plausible when the cistophoric countermarks were seen to accompany the cistophori themselves, or if the cistophoric zone is seen to be hermetically sealed. Yet it is doubtful whether any ancient Greek state, other than Ptolemaic Egypt, could in fact demonetize good silver coinage, especially international *nomisma hellenikon*. The theory of retariffing is more suggestive, if by retariffing a coin, we mean increasing its local value relative to its value elsewhere. With the countermark, the state told the user that the coin was now acceptable for certain local payments. Was its new value reckoned in epichoric coinage, or was it assimilated to an epichoric coin? It is impossible to know, and the situation would have varied. If we want an axiom, it is that countermarking a precious metal coin increased its likelihood of remaining in the local money supply.

From this perspective, the logic of Attalid countermarking becomes clear. We can divorce our discussion of the cistophoric countermarks from speculation about the source of the host coins and the means by which they entered circulation. One tends not to challenge Bauslaugh's suggestion that the Pamphylian host coins represent a part of the Seleukid indemnity paid to the Attalids according to the Treaty of Apameia.[192] With most having given up on the idea of using the indemnity to interpret the monetary behavior of the Seleukids themselves in this period, it makes little sense to place so much weight on it in the Attalid context.[193] Even more problematic is Bauslaugh's reconstruction of the administrative procedure behind the countermarks, for it is based on an untenable notion of "earmarking."[194] In his view, the cities of the Attalid kingdom possessed no revenues of their own, but only received "earmarked" revenues from the royal treasury. In similar fashion, Eumenes II would have received the indemnity directly from Antioch, and then disbursed various portions to twelve cities. Those cities would then have countermarked the coins with

---

[192] The sources for the indemnity are Polyb. 21.43.20–21 and Livy 38.38.14. Bauslaugh 1990, 63, and in substantial agreement, Meadows 2013, 172; also tempted to make the connection is Callataÿ 2013, 225, recalling the suggestion of Meadows 2009 that these Attic-weight Pamphylian coins were already a Seleukid "proxy coinage." However, *contra* the indemnity hypothesis, see Bresson 2018, 74–75.

[193] No one doubts that the indemnity was burdensome, which is the thrust of the literary sources, but see the caution of Le Rider 1993. Further on indemnities, see Meissner 2008; Ungern-Sternberg 2009.

[194] Bauslaugh 1990, 64.

the common symbol of the bow in case and their individual ethnics, releasing the coins into circulation.

Lost in all this is what motivated the costly administrative procedure in the first place. These coins are good Attic-weight silver – if traceable to the indemnity, the "best" (*to argyrion attikon ariston*) (Polyb. 21.43.19). Why go to the trouble? Because the imperative was to keep the silver from leaking out of the local money supply, which the metal was wont to do in a world where its global price was steadily increasing, attracting silver coin to where its buying power was greatest.[195] The countermark reversed the imbalance, making the coin more valuable at home than abroad. Further, in the cistophoric countermarks, we see twelve cities, many of them newly Attalid, previously belonging to diverse monetary systems, suddenly cooperating to meet this challenge on an impressive scale. For presumably, the cistophoric countermark of one city was an expression of the acceptability of the coin in any of the other countermarking cities. The mental map of those who used these coins started to look ever more like the physical one drawn up at Apameia. Functionally, the countermarking system was an initial step in the process of political and economic integration that came to fruition after 167 in the form of the cistophori and Wreathed Coinages.

The Mineralogical Background

Before we turn to that changed landscape of the Greek East after Pydna, we must pause to consider the question of the ostensible scarcity of the silver in the Attalid kingdom, in the geology of western Anatolia. It has often been erroneously assumed that, no less than Egypt, the region lacked deep veins of silver. First, it is important to mind the difference between the general dearth of silver in the eastern Mediterranean of the late Hellenistic period and any local irregularities in its availability.[196] The distinction is crucial for interpreting any monetary behavior that economizes on silver – either the countermarking, as we have conceived of it, or minting on a reduced standard. Granted, Rome withdrew large amounts of precious metal from the money supply of the eastern Mediterranean in the form

---

[195] The flow of Attic-weight silver from western Asia Minor to northern Syria is well documented in the hoards. For its relation to the long-term, incremental increase in the price of silver, see Bresson 2005, 58–63; Bresson 2016, 263–64. For countermarking as way to economize on silver, see already Le Rider 1975, 44; Szaivert 1983, 37. However, neither model gives the coordinating role of the Attalids its due.

[196] Bresson 2005, 62–63.

of spoils and indemnities, and as Pliny the Elder noticed, the Romans preferred to be paid in silver (*HN* 33.15.51).[197] Roman exaction was a major factor, but just one among several behind the gradually increasing scarcity of silver in this period.[198] The consequences of this slow, steady drain of silver were twofold. First, because the demand for silver coinage was basically constant, a silver coin was now worth more relative to its weight in bullion. In other words, the buying power of silver coin was on the rise. This means that the value added to silver bullion by measuring and minting it, by stamping it with the state's imprimatur, was also greater than before. There was plenty of silver bullion around; states just had a greater incentive to monetize it, to mint it on a reduced standard, and to add more fiduciary value. This is most evident in the silver coinage of Antiochos IV, which descended toward a standard 2% below the true Attic.[199]

The second, related consequence was that epichoric standards began to proliferate. Just like the countermarks, epichoric weight ensured that the coin remained nearby, and thus was protection against local irregularities in the supply of silver. But these standards also capitalized on the general uptick in the value of silver. It had become easier for states to add fiduciary value to the coins' real value as a piece of bullion. In fact, the cistophori belong to an entire class of large epichoric coinages, including symmachic (reduced Aiginetan) and Rhodian coinages on various standards, which came to dominate certain regions in this period.[200]

In an ironic twist to the standard explanation of acute shortage, the cistophori point to considerable Attalid reserves in silver. The introduction of a new epichoric coinage – on such a scale and at such a high degree of fineness – presupposes a vast accumulation of metal.[201] For a reform of this

---

[197] Callataÿ 2006, 39. Callataÿ et al. (1993, 92) estimate that one-third of the volume of silver coinage in circulation in the Hellenistic world at the beginning of the third century was in Rome by the end of the second century. To judge the effect of this withdrawal on the supply of silver (coin or bullion), it is necessary to have an idea of the amount of bullion in the system. Callataÿ 2006 concludes that only a paltry amount of bullion was coined. A typical Hellenistic king would have had an estimated 70% of his store of precious metal in bullion, 55% in silver bullion. Cf. Panagopoulou 2007, 335, on the "proliferation of silver during the Hellenistic period."

[198] Consider that the Seleukids' *gradual* reduction of the Attic standard in the second century was accompanied by an increase in the number of coins produced. See Duyrat 2014, 118–19.

[199] Le Rider 1999, 225–26. This 2% descent had already occurred elsewhere when Antiochos IV began to reduce. Before the end of his reign, it is observed only at the mint of Antioch; cf. the full 10% descent for the silver coinage of Perseus, noted by Dahmen 2010, 54.

[200] Thonemann 2015a, 127. See further Grandjean 2007, esp. 21, on the spectacular size of the symmachic coinage in the Peloponnese in this period and the question of silver scarcity.

[201] Fineness of 96–98% silver: Butcher and Ponting 2014, 466.

nature was designed to appear not in fits and starts, but as a deluge, which transforms a supra-regional monetary system. Indeed, the die counts tell us that the cistophori were in fact minted in much greater numbers in the initial two decades than after ca. 150.[202] While the tax receipts of the years 188–ca. 167 may have contained much of the needed silver, according to current archaeometallurgy, it is almost certain that sources of silver were in fact available to the Attalids within their own kingdom.[203] Interestingly, Strabo (14.5.28) tells us of a mining settlement between Atarneus and Pergamon (modern Ovacık?), which by his time had been worked to exhaustion, and also of the evocatively named Argyria on the Aisepos, the so-called birthplace of silver (13.1.45).[204] While the Troad was famed for its metals in Antiquity, it is difficult to match remains to the reports of Homer or Strabo, or to the testimony of early travelers and modern ethnographers about lead and silver mining near classical Neandria.[205] On the other hand, the western plain of the Kaikos contains a gold and silver mine at Ovacık still active today.[206] In the Attalids' own backyard of Mysia, evidence of ancient mining and slag have been found at the well-known deposit of lead-silver at Balya Maaden (Balıkesir province), famous for cannonball manufacturing during Ottoman times, and one of the largest silver mines in the Middle East, exploited during a period of rapid

---

[202] For the pace of cistophoric production, the evidence is based around *IGCH* 1453. See Meadows 2013, 182–83.

[203] Cf. Meadows 2013, 152: "Like the Ptolemaic kings, or the cities of Byzantium and Chalcedon, the Attalids possessed no natural source of silver within their realm." Thonemann (2015a, 80) sees the shuttering of Macedonian silver mines in 167 and "external supplies of silver drying up" as an impetus for launch of cistophori. Already, Will (1962, 99 n. 48) writes of a supposed lack of silver deposits in the Attalid kingdom and modern Turkey (!). Importantly, Bresson (2005, 60) points out that the cistophori have no bearing on whether the Attalids lacked silver. Note also that the Rhodian plinthophoros was heavier than earlier Rhodian and pseudo-Rhodian coins, hence the expression *argyrion rhodion lepton* (lightweight Rhodian silver coins) in the Mylasa leases, for which see Descat and Pernin 2008.

[204] Strabo's source is Kallisthenes (*BNJ* 124 F 54). For skepticism, see Sommerey 2008, 139.

[205] Troad: Panagopoulou 2007, 318 n. 10; also, on the Troad and provenance analysis for ancient silver, see Pernicka 2014, 154–59. For the *pseudargyros* of Andeira: Strabo 13.56.1, though the location of Andeira is debated – see *I.Adramytteion* I, 71–74. For early travelers, see Cook 1973, 298–318: in 1740, Pockocke noted silver, lead, copper, and alum mined near the present-day village of Üsküfçü, in the Skamandros Valley, northwest of the Çığrı Dağ. This is the site of classical Neandria. Winter 1985, studying the fortifications, suggests that some reoccupation followed the late fourth-century abandonment of the site. The study of Schulz 2000 of the walls indeed identifies a second phase with associated habitation. By contrast, Maischatz 2003 concludes decisively that both phases belong to the fourth century. However, ancient mines need not have been associated with settlements. Mines may even have discouraged permanent occupation.

[206] Bayburtoğlu and Yıldırım 2008.

industrialization between 1880 and 1939. Indeed, it is now active again because the entire Biga Peninsula, to which Balya belongs geologically, has been deemed one of the most active metallogenic regions in the world.[207] Further, the ancient route from Pergamon to Cyzicus passes by Balya, and it was on this road that Galen tells us a silver-mining settlement called Ergastêria was located (*De Simp. Med.* XII 229 line 16 to 230 line 5). On the site of Balya, an archaeometallurgical survey catalogued a tremendous number of ancient cuttings, but also clear evidence of Hellenistic occupation.[208] If in Rostovtzeff's time it was simply assumed that the Attalids exploited Balya Maaden, today the archaeological case is much stronger. In 2017, Balıkesir University archaeometallurgist Ahmet Baştürk presented a history of lead-zinc exploitation in the region that takes 500 BCE as its starting point.[209] We have no reason to postulate a lack of silver in the Attalid kingdom.

Explaining the Wreathed Coinages

The Antigonid collapse in the Third Macedonian War permanently altered the political complexion of the Mediterranean. For contemporaries, Polybius tells us, the conflict was a final and decisive battle for absolute hegemony: "viewing the final decision and the subjection of the whole world by one power (ὁρώντων κρινόμενα τὰ ὅλα καὶ τὴν τῆς οἰκουμένης ἐξουσίαν ὑπὸ μίαν ἀρχὴν πίπτουσαν)" (30.6.6). In his speech *Oratio pro Rhodiensibus*, Cato the Elder shows us Greek onlookers reluctant to support Rome for fear of living in a monopolar world: "It was with an eye to their own freedom that they held that opinion, in order not to be under our sole dominion and enslaved to us (*ne sub solo imperio nostro in servitute nostra essent, libertatis suae causa in ea sententia fuisse arbitror*)" (fr. 95b).

---

[207] Pirajno et al. 2019, 164.
[208] Pernicka et al. 1984, 540. For Wiegand (1904, 264–71), the remains at Balya represented the site of Pericharaxis. The identification of Balya as Pericharaxis is often repeated in the literature, e.g., Gentner et al. 1980, 180, and Panagopoulou 2007, 318. However, see *RE*, s.v. Pericharaxis. See also Pernicka et al. 1984, 548, for Kastel Kadıkalesi, 5 km north of Balya, a site Wiegand himself explored, as Pericharaxis.
[209] Rostovtzeff 1923, 367; Magie 1950, 804–5; cf. Cary 1932, 141 n. 4, who presumes that "Bulgar-Maden" was active ca. 246 BCE, seemingly confusing a place in Cappadocia with one in Mysia. Kovenko 1940 lists Balya as one of the largest lead deposits in the world before 1914. See Oy 2017, 13. In an October 2017 conference paper entitled, "Mining History of Balya Pb-Zn Deposit" (https://docplayer.biz.tr/155385604-Oztunali-2017-and-metallurgy-symposium-abstract-book.html), Ahmet Baştürk and Selman Aydoğan assert that mining activity began at Balya in the Classical period and was active in the Roman period.

The destruction of Corinth was yet to come, as well as the creation of the provinces of Macedonia and Achaea, but it was already clear to both Rhodes and Pergamon that the rules of the game had changed.[210] This was the new geopolitical environment in which the cistophori as well as the Wreathed Coinages appeared. The production of both coinages entailed the cooperation of royal and civic institutions. Yet Attalid involvement with the Wreathed Coinages is not self-evident. No less an authority than Le Rider has seen them as purely civic in nature.[211] Taking the Attalid role seriously requires us to briefly consider the phenomenon of proxy coinage in the Hellenistic world. A proxy coinage is a coinage minted in the name of one polity at least in part out of bullion and institutional resources provided by another, larger polity – a cooperative, if not always coordinated minting arrangement.

The practice of coining by proxy was commonplace for Hellenistic kings and early Roman provincial administrators in Greece and Asia Minor. Specific cases may be open to question, but the phenomenon as such is well known. Some of these coinages openly declare the involvement of outsiders. For example, Erythrai, ca. 306–304, minted bronze coins bearing the portrait of Demetrios Poliorketes on the obverse, and the mark EPY along with the name of a local magistrate on the reverse. The citizens of Smyrna under Lysimachus minted bronzes that seem to depict the king's daughter Eurydike, accompanied by their new ethnic ΕΥΡΥΔΙΚΕΙΩΝ ("of the Eurydikeians"). Similarly, the Ephesians, as the Arsinoeis, put the face of Arsinoe II on their bronze, accompanied by distinctly civic control marks.[212] Such marks allow us to understand some drachms of Corinth under Ptolemaic rule as a proxy coinage.[213] Certain proxy coinages are easy to spot, such as the silver didrachms minted in Corcyra, bearing the face of

---

[210] See Kallet-Marx 1995, 11–41; Eckstein 2012, 371. [211] Le Rider 2001.

[212] On all of these examples from Asia Minor, see Delrieux 2007. The case of Kyme (*BMC* Troas 109, no. 58) is especially interesting. Under Antiochos I or II, Kyme minted tetradrachms with royal portrait/Herakles that share control marks with a more straightforwardly civic series, one which seems to bear the face of the Amazon of Kyme and certainly the identifying mint mark KY. We even possess a story of royal proxy minting in the lore of Kyme recorded in the *excerpta politiarum* of Heraklides Lembos (37): "They say that Hermodike, wife of Midas king of the Phrygians, was exceptionally beautiful, but also wise and skilled. They say that she was the first to mint coins for the people of Kyme" (Ἑρμοδίκην δὲ γυναῖκα τοῦ Φρυγῶν βασιλέως Μίδα φασὶ κάλλει διαφέρειν, ἀλλὰ καὶ σοφὴν εἶναι καὶ τεχνικὴν καὶ πρώτην νόμισμα κόψαι Κυμαίοις).

[213] The Chiliomodi hoard (*IGCH* 85) included 14 drachms of Corinth and 12 of Ptolemy I, all fresh and sharing the mintmark ΔΟ. See Martin 1985, 179–84. Consider also the possible civic origin of so-called Peloponnesian Alexanders (Troxell 1971).

Antiochos III on the obverse and the legend ΑΙΤΩΛΩΝ on the reverse.[214] For others, as Hans-Christoph Noeske has shown in attempting to track Ptolemaic gifts in the numismatic record of mainland Greece, we have to look beneath the surface.[215] This is usually a matter of evaluating the appropriate scale of a coinage, using the synthetic scale established for Hellenistic coinages by Callataÿ to measure appropriateness.[216] Interestingly, from ca. 170, suspiciously large coinages in the names of small- or medium-sized polities proliferate: the tetrobols of Histiaea, pseudo-Rhodian drachms from central and northern Greece, the Macedonian Meris coinage – even the Athenian New Style tetradrachms – have come in for interrogation. For the Histiaean and pseudo-Rhodian issues, some postulate Perseus as the source, but in most cases, Rome is the prime candidate, for the triumph of the denarius was yet a long way off in the second century.[217] Meadows has provided a helpful point of comparison for the Wreathed Coinages in the large silver issues of Pamphylian cities associated with Seleucid campaigns of the late third and early second century.[218]

The size of the Wreathed Coinages, in total roughly equal to that of contemporary cistophori, has long seemed suspicious, but our analysis of the monetary habits of the Attalids now allows us to make sense of it. It is important to remember that each city minted on a different schedule, over the course of a generation and beyond.[219] The rhythm of production could reflect an Attalid payment schedule or a local need for coin, but it was most likely some combination of the two. We know that the Attalids ceded more than bullion here, as the iconography of the coins, often the cult image of a patron deity of the city, is expressly civic. The Wreathed Coinages lack the visual nod to the higher order polity that is common to many cooperative coinages of multiscalar states. If this minting arrangement relied on civic institutions and afforded civic actors some measure of control over the shape of their local money supply, it was not unlike the cistophoric system. In fact, these were two complementary and, to a degree, coordinated parts of the money supply of the Attalid kingdom. Yet the full scope of that complementarity is apparent only when we accept that the locally

---

[214] *SNG Copenhagen* 4; *BMC* Thessaly to Aetolia 195, nos. 9–11; Noeske 2000, pl. 30, no. 6.
[215] Noeske 2000 makes a laudable if perhaps quixotic attempt to use metallurgical analysis to unveil royal proxy coinage.
[216] Callataÿ 2011b. Whatever reservations one may have about the absolute figures that Callataÿ has produced, his scale is a major contribution to scholarship and a powerful tool of analysis.
[217] On the late cistophori as "hidden power" of Rome, see Carbone 2020, 14–34.
[218] Meadows 2009. [219] See Meadows and Houghton 2010, esp. 185 (chart).

produced Attic-weight coinage was also exchanged between locals.[220] The monetary needs of the outwardly oriented coastal cities differed from those of communities of inner Anatolia. Yet as the Ahmetbeyli hoard from the territory of Colophon reminds us, cistophori also circulated on the coastal fringe. Ultimately, the nature of the transaction determined the choice of currency, not the geographic zone.[221]

At root, neither the practice of minting a proxy coinage nor even a coordinated coinage sets the Attalids apart. In precisely this period, we see other minting experiments that meet our definition of coordinated coinage. One example is the so-called municipal bronzes of Levantine and Cilician cities under Antiochos IV, featuring royal portraits, civic ethnics, and an array of weight standards.[222] Another example are Macedonian coinages, minted in bronze and silver, in the name of the different *merides*. On the basis of Livy, it was long thought that these administrative regions were Roman inventions, but the numismatic record shows that Philip V and Perseus delegated the power of the mint to these regions.[223] Such coinages are an expression of civic and regional identities that received a new hearing after the humbling of the Antigonids and Seleukids in the early second century. Properly harnessed, the administrative infrastructure by which these identities were being expressed was, ironically, a tool of resistance wielded against the new hegemon, Rome. The coinage, then, from the countermarks to the Wreathed Coinages and cistophori, is simply a

---

[220] Note the two silver tetradrachms and two silver drachms of Myrina recently published from the Arikantürk collection (*SNG Turkey* 9), Tekin and Erol-Özdizbay 2017, nos. 503–6. All coins are said to have been purchased in Burhaniye, ancient Adramyttion.

[221] Ahmetbeyli: *CH* IX 535. Cf. Marcellesi 2010, 200: "Quoi qu'il en soit, les tétradrachmes à la couronne ne font pas véritablement partie de la histoire monétaire du royaume attalide." See also Jones 1979, for whom the Wreathed Coinages are a *response* to the cistophori. On the Wreathed Coinages as a coinage solely for export, see Psoma 2013, 277.

[222] Meadows 2001, 59–60; Mørkholm 1965; Ecker et al. 2017, 194, emphasizing the active role of civic mints in the short-lived experiment.

[223] Thonemann 2015a, 171–72. Livy 45.18: *in quattuor regiones discribi Macedoniam*. Yet *discribere* should mean "distribute/divide into parts," and need not imply the original creation of the parts, for which see, e.g., Livy 31.14.2. Suspicion of Livy's testimony began with the study of the Larissa hoard (*IGCH* 237), deposited in or soon after 168/7. It contained six tetradrachms of the First Meris, while the Romans are thought to have closed the gold and silver mines of Macedonia until 158. Ultimately, we have been forced to recognize that the Roman *merides* were based on much older administrative divisions. (corroborative epigraphic evidence in Hatzopoulos 1996, vol. 1, pp. 231–60). Recently, ever more Meris coinage has been updated to the late Antigonid period. See esp. Kremydi-Sicilianou 2007; Prokopov 2012; and for a summary of recent scholarship, Dahmen 2010, 55. A further point of comparison for the phenomenon of coordinated coinage is the Mithridatic bronze coinage minted in large quantities in the name of Pontic cities. See Callataÿ 2011a.

measure of how much farther the Attalids were willing to go to make use of these forces.

Our interpretations of each of these monetary practices, including our new understanding of the cistophori, do not rely for their validity on the firm dates that numismatics can seldom provide. Rather, they draw on a wide body of comparative material in order to explain the nature of Attalid imperialism, which in this domain, no less than taxation or benefaction, promoted civic identities and instrumentalized civic institutions. Still, if we place the start of the cistophori in ca. 167, with the Wreathed Coinages taking off over the following decade, the historical implications are significant. In terms of the political dynamics of the Mediterranean, we have emphasized the transformative impact of the Antigonid defeat in the Third Macedonian War. For the Attalids, the crisis did not end at Pydna, since the revolt of the Galatians had broken out in 168 and would continue until 165.[224] The notorious Attalid penchant for bolstering their power with the threat, real or perceived, of the Galatian menace, best known from officially commissioned works of art, should not obscure the gravity of the conflict. The anecdote of Polyaenus, which relates how a weakened Eumenes II sat in an open-air throne above a pass to deceive his Galatian pursuers, reminds us of the seriousness of the conflict from the Attalid perspective: this war required the personal attention of the king, who stationed himself on the front lines at Apameia.[225] Indeed, in this context, the short-lived cistophoric production of south Phrygia becomes much more comprehensible. In fact, the entire post-Apameian kingdom appeared to be coming apart at the seams, and the Attalids looked for a way to reconstitute and reinforce an imperial space. Their solution was this puzzling new monetary system, which confounds our categories, those rooted in an antiquarian and artificial distinction between royal and civic. Ptolemaic Egypt was not the model. Rather, this was an unprecedented and daring experiment in the devolution of the power of the mint – successful because it relied on both the pride and know-how of cities and also the silver stock of Anatolia.

---

[224] For the sources for this war, see Mitchell 1993, vol. 1, p. 26; Ma 2013a, 77–82.

[225] Polyaenus, *Strat.* 4.8.1, with no firm date for the incident. For Eumenes at Apameia, see the inscription announced by Drew-Bear 1975, 357.

4 | Cities and Other Civic Organisms

From the start, the Attalids were city people. Philetairos was born in Tieion, a proud Greek city, staked out at the mouth of the river Billaios on the southern coast of the Black Sea. Pinched between semi-barbarous Bithynia and non-Greek Paphlagonia, the people of Tieion boasted of descent from Ionian Greeks of the city of Miletus. The mother of Philetairos was named Boa, an indigenous Paphlagonian name, but the city of his birth counted itself a Greek polis. When it successfully evaded absorption into Lysimachus' new mega-city of Amastris, Tieion minted coins bearing the Greek for FREEDOM and joined Herakleia, Byzantium, Chalcedon, and Kios in the so-called Northern League, a formidable alliance of powerful Black Sea poleis.[1] One can imagine that a young Philetairos carried with him the urbane pretensions of the Hellenic outpost of Tieion, the city that he would have called his fatherland (*patris*), when he first arrived on the hilltop of Pergamon, as the treasurer charged with safekeeping 9,000 talents of silver for the king Lysimachus.

The Pergamon that Philetairos first encountered was as much an old fortress as a young polis. As a city, it lacked a storied past. In the Achaemenid period, it had not been a city at all, but rather the manorial citadel of the Gongylid barons, whom Xenophon in his *Anabasis* depicts lording it over the Kaikos Valley.[2] Indeed, Pergamon is absent from Herodotus' list of the twelve Aeolian cities of mainland Asia Minor.[3] Yet it was precisely those cities, near at hand, which Philetairos soon began to cultivate from the perch of his fortress.[4] Within a few generations, Attalos I would refer to them all as the "cities under" him, the urban core of the early kingdom.[5] Though it was the second-century monarchs who made

---

[1] ΕΛΕΥΘΕΡΙΑ: *HN*² 518. On Philetairos as a Paphlagonian, see *I.Pergamon* 613 B 5.
[2] Xen. *An.* 7.8–24.   [3] Hdt. 1.151.1.
[4] Strabo 13.4.1: ἐγγὺς παρόντα ("near at hand"). Notably, Strabo terms Pergamon a fortress (*phrourion*). On Philetairos' gifts to the Temple of Apollo Chresterios at Aigai and nearby Pitane, see Hansen 1971, 18. For relations with Kyme, see *SEG* L 1195. On Philetairos and Temnos, with which he may have concluded a political union (*isopoliteia*), see *I.Pergamon* 245; Allen 1983, 18–19, on the extent of early Attalid control over the Aeolis.
[5] *RC* 34 lines 12–13.

the city of Pergamon, in Strabo's words, "what it now is," the third-century Attalids took momentous steps to surround the citadel with the trappings of an estimable polis.[6] By origin, the Attalids' was a city-state empire, sustained by taxes collected by other city-states, nourished on their cooperation, and glorified by their prestige. Once assigned their cis-Tauric, continental empire, Eumenes II and his brother must have drawn on these experiences in absorbing major urban centers such as Ephesus and Sardis. Yet cities were only one class of features on the map drawn up at Apameia. The Attalids were also assigned regions called "Lydia" and "Lykaonia," two kinds of "Phrygia" ("Hellespontine" and the ominously named "Greater Phrygia"), a region known as the "Milyas," and contested parts of "Mysia." How were these thinly urbanized territories integrated into the Attalid state? How were these lands and populations rendered legible for Attalid administrators and tax men?[7]

Contrary to expectation, it was not by urbanization that the Attalids achieved the deeper integration of Anatolia, which the Achaemenids and the Seleukids had not.[8] The importance of the cities of the great coastal river valleys is uncontestable. New rulers perforce engaged with them. However, the Attalids were also active at the uppermost reaches of those river valleys, at the headwaters of the Hermos (Gediz), for example, in the town of Kadoi, which gives its name to the modern river. There, in the second century, a visitor found a landscape bereft of cities. Understandably, the cities have shaped our view of the kingdom, for it is primarily through their decrees and coins, the stoas of the urban marketplaces and the statues of the poliad sanctuaries, that the story of Pergamon has been told. Indeed, Polybius lauds Eumenes II as his generation's greatest benefactor of "Greek cities."[9] Yet the city was only one settlement type among several, the polis only one of the different forms of political community with which the

---

[6] Strabo 13.4.2.

[7] Polyb. 21.45.10; Livy 38.39.15–16. Mysia is a moving target. Certain parts of Mysia were contested territory on the Bithynian frontier. On the vexed problem of their location, see Habicht 1956, 92–96; Schwertheim 1988; Avram 2004, 974–75; Dmitriev 2007, 135 n. 14. For an older survey of rural settlement in the Attalid kingdom, see Hansen 1971, 173–87.

[8] Cf. Gehrke (2014, 138) on the Attalids: "Generally tribes tended to aspire to the status of a Greek *polis*. And kings tended to oblige, active as they were in founding cities, knowing that it facilitated the organization of their rule at grass-roots level, and probably aware equally of the importance of such urbanization process for forging cultural identity in their heterogeneous territories." Similarly, see Marek (2016, 292) on Pompey's urbanization of northern Anatolia: "Nothing like it had been seen on such a scale since the Attalids." Bielfeldt 2019, 187: numerous new cities in Lydia and Phrygia under the Attalids. Much closer to the truth is Levick 2007, 107: "Geography and history were against the *polis* in Phrygia."

[9] Polyb. 32.8.5: πόλεις Ἑλληνίδες.

Attalids needed to interact. In some cases, from these towns, villages, and decentralized tribal confederations a new polis was born; more often, the Attalids managed to build places into their political economy without building a city. The Attalids did found cities; Antalya (Attaleia), the greatest port of Anatolia's southern seaboard, still echoes their name. However, in contrast with the earlier Hellenistic kings of the age of Alexander and his Successors, who spent their Persian plunder so freely, the Attalids did not pay to herd large numbers of smaller settlements into imperial mega-cities. They also eschewed the costly and coercive tactics of rivals Philip V and Prousias I, who leveled and rebuilt, in their own image, the Propontic cities of Kios and Myrleia.[10] Instead, with typical agility and economy of effort, the Attalids drew people into their orbit without forcing them to move or change their way of life. Tellingly, recent excavations of a large cemetery in Antalya demonstrate continuity in occupation and burial practice from the third century to the second.[11]

This chapter surveys the settlement landscape of inner Anatolia under the Attalids. Unsurprisingly, a hierarchy does emerge, with the polis planted firmly at the top.[12] What is surprising, however, is not just the range of polities to be reckoned with in the interior of the kingdom, but also the range of interactions taking place between the Attalids and non-Greek, nonpolis communities. Postcolonial Classics has taught us that the Greeks never monopolized power in the Hellenistic East.[13] Yet the most recent generation of scholarship on these kingdoms casts the polis as the privileged interlocutor of the king. It turns out that if a polis played its cards right, it could leverage its symbolic resources. The Anatolian interior, however, was filled with far fewer poleis than the Aegean coast. Since success depended on a rapid recognition of the tax base, the Attalids quickly shed their pretense. Each civic organism represented a unit of local support and a transit point for taxes. It mattered little whether the village was governed by an assembly modeled on Classical Athens or by a traditional council of elders. If the village wanted an assembly, with Athenian-style civic tribes to boot, the Attalids were happy to advise. In most cases, we in fact know absolutely nothing of how these communities functioned

---

[10] Strabo 12.4.3.
[11] Akman and Tosun 2012, 55 (Eski Doğu Garajı – Halk Pazarı Mevkii necropolis).
[12] Mileta 2008, 80–89.
[13] Scholars of Seleukid Babylonia provide several models of interpretation for the study of the fate of Anatolian elites and indigenous cultures after the Macedonian conquest. See Sherwin-White and Kuhrt 1993, 149–60; Kosmin 2014b, 173–75. Cf. on the Far East, from a nuanced postcolonial perspective, Mairs 2014, 185–87.

on the inside. Yet we can observe the process of their adhesion to Pergamon. Joining up with the Attalids did not mean relinquishing a fiscal territory and the prerogatives of a body politic. On the contrary, the very fact that these civic organisms held on to their own fiscal territories and maintained their own memberships is what keyed resource extraction and dialogue.

Still, certain towns and clusters of villages clamored for recognition as poleis, and the Attalids, hungry for honors and eager to set in place pliable institutions, then oversaw their transformation into "Greek cities." What difference did the change of status make? In other words, what did it mean to be born a polis with Pergamene midwifery? Was the new title the sign of a new sense of cultural identity, the outcome or rather the beginning of a process of acculturation? It is doubtful whether the so-called birth of a polis meant that populations nucleated and new settlements instantly gained orthogonal streets and public and commercial squares. Rather, it seems that with the name "polis" the Attalids handed their subjects two gifts: an ideological defense weapon and a new set of institutions. For excluding their walls, the name "polis" was their greatest defense. It was tantamount to a human right in Antiquity, which, in theory, guarded against arbitrary exactions and punishments or forced labor, demanding dignity and equal treatment in any higher-order political community. It was a small price to pay for the Attalids, who now oversaw the installation of recognizable institutions, tried-and-tested methods of tax collection, and a clean conduit for redistribution.

The Bottom

To begin our survey of inner Anatolia at the bottom, with the weakest, and then progressively work our way up the settlement hierarchy, we must begin with the communities of peasants known by the crude term *laoi* ("the people"). These dependent villages of indigenous farmers were usually located within the boundaries of great estates. The estates belonged to courtiers, generals, or private landowners, the local powerbrokers who had survived regime change. Villages of *laoi* were also found on royal estates and scattered about less neatly defined royal domains like forests. *Laoi* were neither serfs nor slaves.[14] Nor, however, were they fully free:

---

[14] For the state of the question on the status and condition of the *laoi*, see Papazoglou (1997, 113–40), emphasizing their freedom. Schuler (1998, 180–89) is more measured. Cf. the older

villagers' mobility was hindered, though they might also find themselves summarily uprooted. The shadowy existence of the Anatolian *laoi* tends to register on our radar when an estate changed hands, and the new owner claimed the tax liabilities of their villages.[15] The owner, so to speak, of their taxes might be the king, a polis, a larger-order town, a private individual, or the nearby temple. For example, in a dossier of Seleukid-era inscriptions chiseled on the wall of the great Temple of Artemis at Sardis, the taxes due from villages on the estate of a man called Mnesimachos are transferred to the goddess along with the rest of his estate. The Lydian villagers owe taxes in cash, their labor, certain "wine-jars," and still more levies on "the other products of the villages."[16] It is unlikely that any *laoi* ever had any say in these transactions. At best, the village headmen may have received timely notice and a new destination address for the taxes. In a very fragmentary inscription recovered in the theater at Pergamon, an Attalid military colony of the mid-third century receives a number of gifts and privileges. The king awards his cavalrymen revenues, land to cultivate and land for homes, and with that land, apparently, "its people."[17]

From the Attalid perspective, each group of *laoi* possessed a territorial definition, but not a territory. Unauthorized movements of population disrupted tax collection and the cruel demands of corvée labor. *Laoi* lacked secure property rights, and though they were meant to stay put, the *laoi*

---

view of Bikerman 1938, 178. The comparison of *laoi* to medieval European serfs is certainly imprecise and inappropriate, but scholars struggle to define their unfreedom precisely. One key issue is the extent to which the peasants were bound to the land. Some freedom of movement is implied by the terms of the sale of *laoi* along with their possessions to Laodike (*RC* 18 lines 1–13), but other texts (*RC* 11 lines 22–25) show limits. While villages of *laoi* paid taxes collectively, individuals owed corvée labor, and their possessions were taxed too, as a contractual formula states (*RC* 18 line 9; *I.Sardis* 1 Column I line 12). Landowners and the Hellenistic state had an interest in restricting and monitoring the movement of *laoi*. Of their legal condition, much of what we know comes from the Hefzibeh Dossier (*SEG* XXIX 1613), for which see the recent edition and commentary of Heinrichs 2018, with p. 305 on the vindication of the legal rights of *laoi* in the Jezreel Valley of the Galilee. Note also that Demetrios of Skepsis reports Attalos I's appointment of a judge for royal land in Aeolis (Ath. 15.697d).

[15] A notable exception – perhaps, since they do not identify themselves as *laoi* – is the case of two villages, one of the Kiddiokômitai and the other of the Neoteicheitai, both in the vicinity of the modern city of Denizli, the site in Phrygia on which Laodikeia-on-the-Lykos was to be founded (*I.Laodikeia* 1). Situated on a Seleukid royal estate belonging to Achaios the Elder, the two villages passed an honorific decree dated to 267 that demonstrates a precocious civic life, replete with an assembly, public festivals, and, therefore, revenues. Either this is a sensationally unique case, unlikely given the vagaries of survival, or the Attalids would have inherited other villages already fitted out with the requisite institutions for complex interaction.

[16] *I.Sardis* 1 lines 11–13.

[17] *RC* 16 C line 7. The *laoi* here are a plausible restoration of the text by Welles, supported by Virgilio (2008, 208).

held startlingly little control over the land under their feet. An intriguing and unique royal document from the hinterland of Aigai highlights the scope of their insecurity. The inscription is usually dated roughly to the third century, making Attalid authorship plausible. The curt tone of the memorandum signals orders for a group of *laoi*. It is a long list of taxes on everything from land to beehives – even the hunt is taxed at the rate of one leg per boar and one per deer. For certain work, the people are provided with tools at royal expense. Most importantly, they appear to have lost, no doubt by an unrecorded act of violence, the very means of subsistence. Mercifully, they now receive back lost land, vineyards, and houses, in sum, reads the text, "their property."[18] As it stands, we cannot determine the identity of those who drove these peasants off their land. We should not rule out the possibility that it was in fact an arm of a Hellenistic state. We know that in a shake-up of settlement structure, the Attalids themselves cleared out two tiny villages of the Lydian forest called Thileudos and Plazeira.[19]

The Ascendant Towns

Directly above the hapless *laoi* was a class of towns called in similarly unimpressive language the *katoikiai* ("the settlements"; singular *katoikia*).[20] The title sounds anodyne, but it conceals a partnership of fundamental importance for the Attalids. Historians have underestimated its significance because, like Polybius, they have tended to focus on Pergamon's relationship with the polis. However, by means of direct access to the king and his court, representatives of these towns exercised real power. Indeed, it was to satisfy the needs of one *katoikia*, probably Apolloniucharax, that those *laoi* of Thileudos and Plazeira in the Lydian forest lost their land. Now, of the many towns called *katoikiai* in our sources, it is often unclear which were Attalid foundations, rather than inheritances from earlier empires. That said, such settlements seem to proliferate – in our sources, at least – across the Lydian countryside after 188 (**Map 4.1**). A denser network of agrarian settlements inhabited by

---

[18] Malay 1983 (*SEG* XXXIII 1034), especially p. 351 n. 6. The property is returned at Side B 6–11. Malay dates the inscription by the letter-forms and suggests that the *laoi* are the addressee. Cf. the late fourth-century date of Descat 2003, 160–65.

[19] D2 Side B lines 20–24.

[20] Here, I group together all communities named in the sources as *katoikia* along with those representing themselves as "the inhabitants (*katoikountes/katoikoi*) in such and such a place." For terminology, see further Papazoglou (1997, 218–26); Schuler (1998, 33–40).

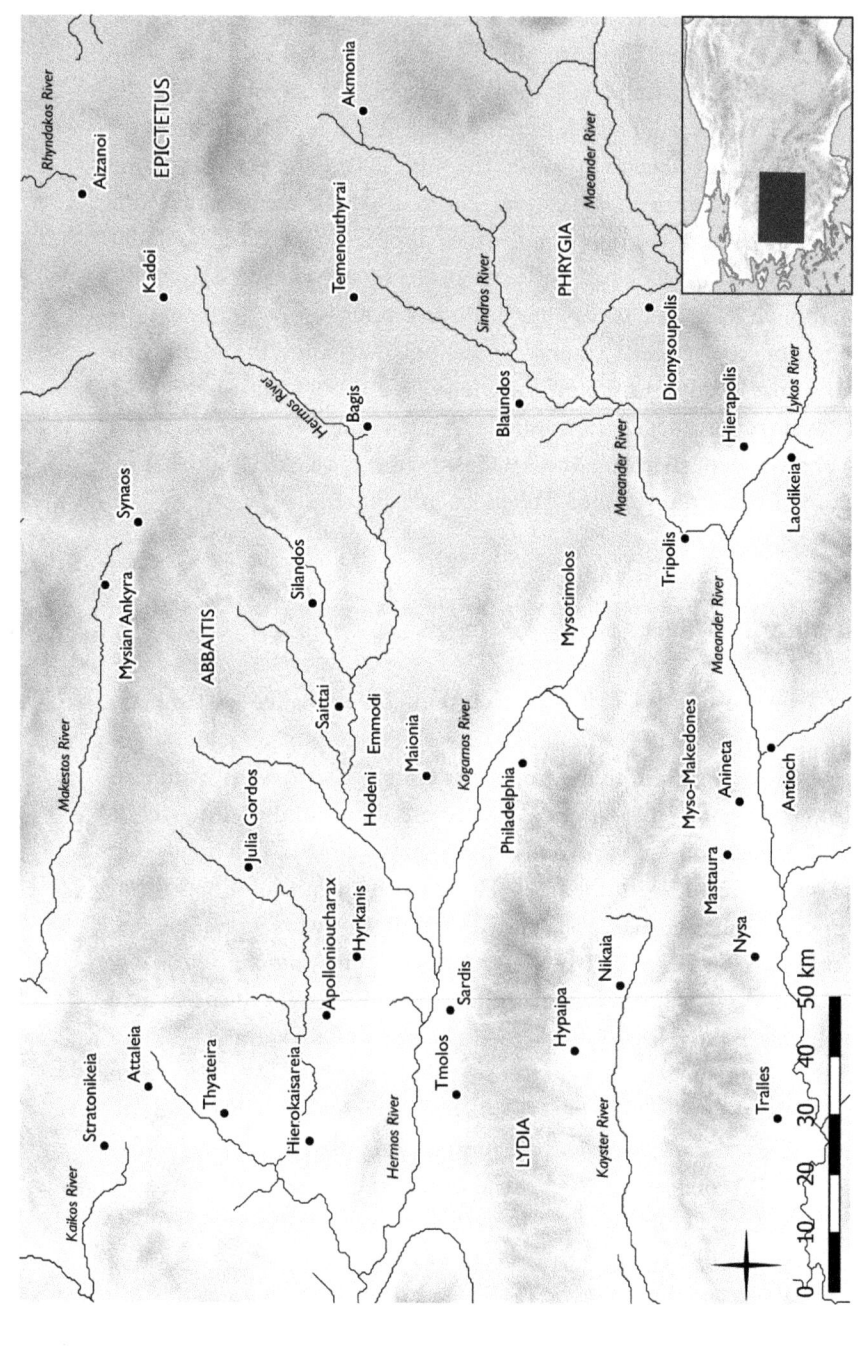

Map 4.1 Eastern Lydia and Mysia Abbaitis.

would-be conscript soldiers helped both to maintain Pergamene military manpower and to expand the tax base. Colonization is a potentially misleading description of the phenomenon, for the population of these towns was probably of local origin, or in the case of the Mysians, made up of recent migrants from an adjacent upland ecological zone. The timing of the Mysian migration, like the authenticity of the claim of certain settlers to Macedonian identity, is difficult to determine. The more interesting questions pertain to what the Attalids stood to gain by shoring up these towns and fostering civic consciousness among their inhabitants.[21]

The military character of the *katoikiai* has proven difficult to define. In part, this is because we can rarely pin down the location of towns known mostly from epigraphy, nor have we yet been able to conclusively match many toponyms to standing fortifications.[22] It also probable that the function of many settlements changed over time, as an early Hellenistic fortress and garrison developed into a full-fledged town by the second century. For the Attalids, the self-sufficiency of these agrarian communities was in fact crucial to their military value. Therefore, many towns occupied fertile plains. The inhabitants were registered for conscription; they were not a standing army maintained by the state.[23] Strategically, a dense belt of settlement formed across eastern Lydia, concentrating manpower where it was most needed: where the urbanized core of the empire met the stateless Anatolian hinterland, the approaches to the porous, ill-defined border with Galatia. It was a settlement policy of filling in blind spots.

The agricultural significance of the *katoikiai* was paramount. On the best land available, the Attalids nurtured client communities. We see this twin concern for keeping tabs on the soldiery and providing them with productive farms in one second-century Attalid's letter to an anonymous *katoikia* (RC 51). According to a framework detailed in the letter, each soldier received a lot that contained two kinds of land: a larger part for arable agriculture and a smaller part for the vine. Interestingly, the lots

---

[21] Daubner (2011, 54) views many of these settlements as late Attalid foundations, stocked with Macedonians fleeing the collapse of the Antigonid kingdom in 167. By contrast, the tentative proposal of Cohen (1991, 46) that the bulk of those in Lydia, at least, were Seleukid colonies, has long held sway. Recently, Mitchell (2018, 11–15) has argued persuasively that most are in fact pre-Seleukid, settled by Macedonians of the period of Alexander. Regardless of their origin, which in most cases was probably not Pergamene, the *katoikiai* played a uniquely significant role in the Attalid kingdom.

[22] Meriç 2009, 136–37. It is telling that even the largest Hellenistic sites among the fortifications of the Kayster Valley, with enceintes of ca. 430 × 230 m and acropolis-like overhangs, were not, in Meriç's view, urban settlements ("keine städtischen Ansiedlungen").

[23] **D2** Side A lines 19–22.

themselves are not uniformly equal, but the larger lots seem to go to those who are registered as living on the land. In other words, the Attalids wanted to tie soldier-settlers to the land. Trust was at stake. Indeed, the availability and the quality of the land were crucial to the compact between king and settler. For example, Polybius describes Attalos I in 218 leading a trusting band of Galatians, the Tolistoagii, with their wives, children, arms, and equipment in tow, on a circuitous journey in search of a "fertile place" to inhabit.[24] Attalos was personally playing the part of land-distributor (*geodôtês*), an office twice documented in Lydia of the troubled 160s, but nowhere to be found in Seleukid records.[25] The king successfully carved out settlements for the Tolistoagii near the Hellespont, but not without paying a price. To win the acquiescence of the nearby cities of Lampsakos, Ilion, and Alexandria Troas, Attalos must have paid dearly, but it was with such bargains struck on the fly that an empire was founded and later expanded.

It is often supposed that a strategic, not an agrarian logic drove earlier Achaemenid and Hellenistic colonization of western Anatolia. It is asserted that the Seleukid colonies in Lydia, for example, straddled important highways, while Attalid sites are ostensibly off the beaten path. It is an attractive argument, which rightfully credits Pergamon with bringing more territory than ever before under state control. However, the evidence for this claim is far less secure than its almost axiomatic use nowadays suggests. It was an argument originally developed almost a century ago by Robert in a discussion of the (still unverified) location of Attaleia in the upper Lykos Valley.[26] According to Robert, the Attalids were principally concerned with the agricultural productivity of settlement sites. Therefore, he suggested, site distribution under the Attalids should bear little relation to strategic routes and passes. Yet that corollary claim does not stand up to scrutiny. Frank Daubner has recently restated the argument, claiming that most new Hellenistic settlements in Lydia are Attalid, but unlike the Seleukids, or even the Persians before, Pergamene towns were founded in fertile plains, at a remove from major roads.[27] He points to the Hyrkanian Plain, but also names Stratonikeia in the upper Kaikos Valley as a probable Attalid foundation. Persian activity, though, is evident in the very name of the great plain, not to mention sites therein such as Dareioukome. In fact,

---

[24] Polyb. 5.77–78. Virgilio (2008, 210) suggests that the notion of a "fertile place" (*topos euphyês*) in which to settle (*pros katoikian*) may derive from Attalid propaganda.
[25] **D2** Side A lines 12–13, Side B lines 23–24; *SEG* XL 1062 line 5.   [26] Robert 1934, 89–92.
[27] Daubner 2011, 54; repeated by Bielfeldt 2019, 177.

according to an attractive model proposed by Nicholas Sekunda, Achaemenid colonization in Lydia was also oriented toward agriculture. Achaemenid nobles drew on the usufruct of scattered villages; and the colonists per se were ex-mercenaries, not reserves, who received land as a reward for past service. Their dispersed village communities and Iranian identities did not survive the Spartan incursions of the early fourth century.[28]

As for Lydian Stratonikeia, if it is in fact to be located at the village of Siledik, it actually occupied a strategic position astride two major routes into the plain of Kırkağaç: one south to Thyateira and another west to Pergamon. To be fair, we should not discount the quality of the surrounding land. Ephebes known as the Stratonikeians from an evidently well-known plain known as the Indeipedion were registered in the capital.[29] The site was both defensible and propitious for farming. Still, most damning to Robert's influential thesis is archaeologist Christopher Roosevelt's observations in his detailed study of long-term settlement patterns in Lydia. He points out that in the absence of more secure spatial data, the pattern which emerges right across the Persian and Hellenistic periods is consistent: settlements tend to be sited in defensible positions at the edge of fertile plains, near perennial routes of communication and mountain passes.[30]

Rather, what is distinctive about the Attalids is just how much they relied on these towns of modest size, mixed military-civilian and non-Greek character to sustain their rule. They multiplied in the second century in the same east Lydian/south Mysian zone that Aristonikos was to make his final redoubt after the fall of the dynasty. The region proved to be the rebel's greatest bulwark because earlier Attalids had cultivated it. That concern for the long-term agricultural prosperity of this kind of community is perceptible elsewhere, too, for example, from the Kardakon Kome near Telmessos in Lycia. A letter of Eumenes II to his official Artemidoros addressed the lamentable condition of the settlers.[31] When, in 181, Eumenes, in his own words, set about investigating the settlers' fitness to pay taxes, he found their orchards sparse and their land poor. In fact, some men had already fled the place and consequently evaded state control. Those who remained in the village had agreed to purchase much needed land from a local lord named Ptolemaios, but ultimately failed to pay up. Eumenes rescued the community by ordering the land transferred to the settlers' possession. Ultimately, he lowered the villagers' tax rate because

---

[28] Sekunda 1985, 27–29. [29] On the Stratonikeians in Indeipedion, see Rigsby 1988, 130–37. [30] Roosevelt 2019, 158–59. [31] **D3** lines 6–7.

they were "weak and weighed down by their private affairs (*ta idia*)." Through a pattern of interaction that would recur across Attalid Anatolia after 188, the villagers of Kardakon Kome gained lands and secured property rights. For the success of their private affairs was of great interest to the king, who hoped to tax it one day soon. Wherever needed, land was purchased, confiscated, or transferred to sustain the *katoikiai*. It seems too that the inhabitants of *katoikiai* held whatever land they acquired with royal aid on privileged terms, as a "sovereign possession," according to one document.[32] Fascinatingly, the Attalids alone seem to have extended to small farmers the private property rights that other rulers reserved for the henchmen whom they gifted with great estates; and Pergamon now conceded to the village what had been conceded, traditionally, to the polis.[33]

Just like the Seleukids and Achaemenids, who bequeathed an unknown number of these towns, the Attalids counted on a reserve of soldiers settled in the Anatolian countryside, such as those who commemorated their return from a campaign in the Chersonese and Thrace with a dedication at Sındırgı.[34] What changed now was that more of these soldiers were native farmers, rather than guards imported from the Near Eastern imperial center. Compare the vision of Seleukid colonization under Antiochos III, ca. 200 BCE, contained within Flavius Josephus' report of the settlement of Jews in *katoikiai* emplaced in restless parts of Lydia and Phrygia.[35] There, Jewish guards (*phylakes*) and their households are transplanted from faraway Mesopotamia. Certain elements do accord with the Attalid model, in particular, the distribution of two kinds of land and building materials, the civilian tinge to the place, and the emphasis on the bond of trust between colonists and king, reminiscent of Attalos and his Galatian clientele on the Hellespont. Yet the Seleukid colonies are explicitly described as garrisons (*phrouria*) established among populations in revolt, quite unlike the isolated Pergamene garrison found on the Yüntdağ.[36] Seleukid settlers could even come to dominate a nearby polis, as happened

---

[32] *RC* 51 lines 21–22 (κτήσεις κύ[ριαι]). This is one of many indications that private property existed well beyond the confines of the polis in Hellenistic Asia Minor.
[33] Schuler 1998, 191.   [34] *OGIS* 330.
[35] Joseph. *AJ* 12.147–52. The much-debated historicity of the events is immaterial to our purposes. This is how Josephus' Hellenistic source would have imagined the foundation of Seleukid *katoikiai* in Anatolia.
[36] Müller 2010.

when neighboring colonists inserted themselves into a treaty between the cities of Magnesia-under-Sipylos and Smyrna.[37] We have no evidence that the Attalids ever installed communities as overseers.[38]

The task now assigned to these towns, old and new, was different and more important. They were the eyes and ears of the king in the deeper countryside that had not yet known state power, and they were rewarded for this service handsomely. Just a hint of that promotion and those strengthened ties to the monarchy is contained in the name of one town near Satala in Lydia's upper Hermos valley, the "*katoikia* of the kings," presumably, the brothers Eumenes II and Attalos II.[39] It is difficult to imagine Seleukid settlers, whether in Lydia or in Jerusalem's Akra citadel, taking on such airs. In the decentralized Attalid state, the *katoikiai* became increasingly autonomous and increasingly capable of serving a fiscal function, as tax collectors in the remote countryside and as a fixed address for redistribution. To serve these functions, a town did not need coinage or walls, though many must have possessed a fortified enceinte or a sturdy tower. In fact, there was no urgent need for nucleation.[40] Likewise, the town did not need an assembly or a council, but any form of representation before the king would do. What they needed was a territory and a body politic. On a delimited, dependent territory, the *katoikia* raised taxes for the Attalids, a portion of which it kept for its own people, the body politic that also stood to gain from any royal kickbacks.

Subject to each Attalid *katoikia* was a dependent territory, often with *laoi* living on it, structurally, analogous to a Classical polis with its dependent territory (*chora*) and dependent villages (demes; *kômai*). In fact, across rural Anatolia of this period, we find articulated a newfound expression of territory, or one at least publicized for the first time in epigraphy. As Schuler explains in his exhaustive study of these communities, when we consider them from the perspective of their own self-representation – as opposed to the hegemonic perspective of the polis – much more about their

---

[37] *OGIS* 229 II.
[38] See *TAM* V 2 959, from Mernouphyta, which in the Roman period still saw itself as descended from *katoikountes* of Attalos I and Eumenes II. Cohen (1995, 218) asserts that the Attalids established a colony at Mernouphyta to oversee Seleukid Thyateira, but the claim is warrantless, as Mitchell (2018, 20 n. 57) correctly points out.
[39] *TAM* V 1 609.
[40] See, e.g., the recent proposal of Couvenhes (2020, 606–10) for the location of the *katoikia* of Attaleia, suggesting multiple foci of settlement, a military sector on Gördük Kale and a civilian one in the plain below at Selcikli.

senses of place and identity comes into focus.⁴¹ These Attalid towns joined a range of rural communities in asserting their territoriality.⁴² Under the shadow of Rhodes, for example, the upland *peripolia* of Lycia and Caria behaved similarly.⁴³ One could see here an aspect of a growing cottage industry in small-scale civic identities. This is a development from the bottom-up over which the Attalids had no control, but it represented an opportunity. Thonemann has drawn attention to the late Attalids' curious habit of detaching land from the royal domain and devolving it onto cities and towns.⁴⁴ They sacrificed aspects of sovereignty in these places for the sake of raising higher, more predictable revenues, or perhaps any taxes at all. However, of Thonemann's six cases, in only three was the Attalids' beneficiary a polis. As civic organisms, the *katoikiai* were evidently seen as fit to receive dependent territories, as well as grants of territorial inviolability.⁴⁵ One even wonders if the Attalids oversaw the occasional transfer of territory to a *katoikia* at the expense of a rival polis, as may have occurred around Lake Apolloniatis, in the territories of Apollonia-on-the-Rhyndakos and Miletoupolis.⁴⁶ Thus, even without further urbanization or an upgrade to the status of polis, the Attalids possessed ready-made vehicles for territorial integration.

One can also perceive here an increasing formalization of the body politic of these communities, which was not without consequence for the Attalids. Membership in the *katoikia* came to be defined more rigorously, meaning that the in-group could claim a larger share of the spoils of empire; the village could finally partake of the traditional leisure (*scholê*) of the city. Such is the implication of the plea of the settlers at

---

[41] Schuler 1998, 22–26.

[42] For earlier precedents, note a boundary stone marking the border between two unnamed villages (*MAMA* IV 75 of 211/10). Compare also the territorial definition of the Olympenoi, who clearly do not live in a polis, with that of the polis of Aigai, in the tax treaty that the two communities signed in the late fourth or early third century (*Staatsverträge* III 456). The logic of the agreement demands that the Olympenoi control a territory equally well defined to that of Aigai.

[43] Schuler 2010.   [44] Thonemann 2013b, 16–26.

[45] Herrmann and Malay 2007, 56 (**D2** Side B lines 4–6).

[46] *SEG* XLIII 879, an inscribed decree of the *katoikia* of Daphnous, a town located near a sanctuary of Apollo Daphnousios, which records honors for high-ranking, presumably, Attalid officials. The consensus is that this is an Attalid document (see, e.g., Ricl 2014, 143). As in the case of a similar dedication of the *katoikiai* of the Orneênoi and the Dandaênoi from the territory of nearby Miletoupolis (*I.Kyzikos* II 20), the benefaction itself is unstated. (The inscription is also increasingly accepted as a source for Attalid administration. See, e.g., Avram and Tsetskhladze 2014, 170.) Gifts of good land and the resources of the lake and other waterways are plausible in the crowded political ecology of Hellespontine Phrygia.

Apollonioucharax who petitioned Eumenes II for building materials to rebuild houses torched in the Galatian Revolt.[47] The translation of the passage has vexed commentators, but may be understood to highlight an unsuspectingly salient political identity in the Attalid kingdom. The text reads: "Regarding the houses in the suburb (*proastion*), which were burned and pulled down, (we request that) it be seen to that since we are co-citizens (*dêmotai*), some grant be provided for their reconstruction." Apparently, certain people who could claim membership in the *katoikia* dwelt outside its fortified core on exposed, vulnerable terrain before the walls or ramparts.[48] To Eumenes II or his official, it may not have been obvious why royal building crews should rebuild these particular homes, for so much stood in ruins. After all, they were located at some remove from the main settlement. So the emissaries of Apollonioucharax made their case, arguing in solidarity that "since we are the same people/citizens (*dêmotai*)" help was in order.[49] In other words: these are Attalid people and must be saved. Membership in the *katoikia* meant something.[50]

Naturally, we can begin to identify in this period a sharper profile for the rural body politic. In sleepy towns, dormant identities were awakened, amplified, or even invented. Take the example of a settlement called Kobedyle in the rural Kogamos Valley in eastern Lydia. In their decree, the settlers call themselves "the Macedonians from Kobedyle," though it is not clear whether they are colonists of a defunct regime, newly settled

---

[47] **D2** Side B lines 9–11.
[48] Interpretation of *proastion* here as suburb: Thonemann 2011a, 7. On its vulnerability, see the sources of Schuler 1998, 106 n. 20. Interestingly, the topographical term *proastion* (τὰ ἔξω τειχῶν, ἡ ἔξω πόλις) is a borrowing from the conceptual field of the polis.
[49] The translation of *dêmotai* as "same people/citizens" is that of Ricl (2011, 144), though she posits the speaker here as the city of Sardis.
[50] Thonemann (2011a, 7) is almost certainly right to see the settlers of Apollonioucharax (?) as the speaker here, but his translation of *dêmotai* as "poor" – i.e., "Since we are poor ..." – is not compelling, especially in a town with enough well-to-do residents to justify the *eisphora* wealth tax (**D2** Side A line 24). Herrmann and Malay (2007, 51) consider the translation "of the (same) people," but reject it as lacking sense. Admittedly, one cannot adduce the perfect parallel, but how many other documents of this length and detail from the region's sub-polis stratum do we possess? Nothing in the substantial corpus of Schuler 1998 comes close. Granted, Schuler (1998, 264 n. 313) records the term *dêmotai* as a hapax, which hitherto had only appeared in Phrygian Orkistos in 273 CE, but copious examples exist of villagers calling themselves *kômêtai* (Schuler 1998, 29–32). Recently, an inscribed funerary altar held at the museum of Eskişehir (Dorylaion) was published, terming the deceased a *dêmosios*. The suggestion of Karabulut (2020, 180) that the label means public slave/servant is debatable. In sum, the inhabitants of a *katoikia* call themselves οἱ κατοικοῦντες in order to distinguish themselves from others. To refer to their compatriots, so it seems, they could use the term *dêmotai*.

emigrants fleeing the Antigonid collapse, or simply Attalid soldiers trained to fight in the Macedonian manner.[51] In any case, the settlers date their decree by the regnal year of Eumenes II, declaring their allegiance and framing a context for their politics. Puzzlingly, the Macedonians award honors to a man whom they call their "citizen" (*politês*). Though not so named in the short, fragmentary text, Kobedyle is plainly a *katoikia* and not a polis.[52] In what sense, then, could it claim a citizenry? Getzel Cohen writes, "The use of the term πολίτης suggests that by the time of the inscription, namely 163/2 B.C., the inhabitants of Kobedyle had become citizens of a polis. However, the identity of this polis is unknown."[53] Yet the document more likely suggests that the term "citizen" was not the exclusive preserve of the polis. And who was to say that it should be? Kobedyle had not overstepped, at least not by the reckoning of the Attalids, for whom stronger civic identities were a boon. Cohen's interpretation ignores the logic of the grammar, which makes of the honoree a citizen of the body politic honoring him – a co-citizen.[54] It is not difficult to understand how a town like Kobedyle could manifest citizens if we keep in mind the fluidity of real-world politics. The ever-expanding civic consciousness of rural Anatolia gelled perfectly with the Attalid style of governance.

We can compare the similarly idiosyncratic language of the honorary decree for Nikanor son of Nikanor, found in modern Badınca, ca. 5 km from Alaşehir (Philadelphia).[55] An anonymous and atypical body politic awards the honors: τὸ κοινὸν τῶν πολιτῶν (association or council of citizens?). Georg Petzl conjectures that the honoring body was the *katoikia* of Adruta, which we know belonged to Philadelphia.[56] This may mean that the citizenry of the town, though subordinate to a royal foundation, maintained their own functioning civic institutions. On the other hand, Cohen writes, "From the mention of *politai* and ephebes we may conclude that even at this early stage in its development Philadelphia had the accessories of a polis."[57] However, there is no reason to assume that the

---

[51] *TAM* V 1 221 = *TAM* V 3 1423. Antigonid emigrants: Daubner 2011, 53. See also the earliest coins of Philadelphia, which bear a Macedonian shield on the obverse, a winged fulmen in wreath on the reverse (*SNG Copenhagen* 343).

[52] *Contra* Daubner 2011, 55. Mitchell (2018, 20 n. 61) notes incisively: "I would not infer from the use of the term *politês*, that Kobedyle was a *polis*."

[53] Cohen 1995, 214; cf. comments of Petzl, *TAM* V 3, p. 19. Commentators long assumed that the citizens of Kobedyle were citizens of a nearby polis, going so far as to promote the neighboring village of Kastolos, later a *kome* of Philadelphia, to that stand-in role. Mitchell (2018, 20) sees Kobedyle as a *katoikia* "around the city of Philadelphia" – with a citizenry of its own.

[54] Debord 1985, 349: "concitoyen"; Petzl (*TAM* V 3, p. 19): "Mitbürger."

[55] *SEG* XVII 524 = *TAM* V 3 1425. [56] *TAM* V 3, p. 20. [57] Cohen 1995, 214.

document belongs to Philadelphia, or even that it dates to a time after the accession of the city's namesake Attalos II (159). It is just as likely that Philadelphia did not yet exist, but that one of the towns later subsumed by that city had selectively adopted certain institutional indicia of a polis. Instead of seeing the anomalous "*koinon* of citizens" as a feature of a young polis, yet unformed, we should see it as another sign of the diversity of civic organisms and growing civic consciousness in the Anatolian countryside of the late Hellenistic period.

Temple People

In much of the countryside, signal communal activities continued to take place according to the rhythms of the agricultural calendar around indigenous or thinly Hellenized shrines and temples. Governors and garrison commanders vested local priests with power over large sectors of the rural population. Priests, then, demanded taxes and perquisites, but could also offer the farmers protection in return. The impact of Alexander's conquest on the power of these so-called Anatolian temple-states and their sacred villages is much debated. While some surely perished, others survived, either bound to a polis – often enough, uncomfortably and insecurely – or as independent entities. Of the independent variety, alongside a major, regional center such as Pessinous in eastern Phrygia, we must also consider small temple-towns, individual villages attached to a single cult and its priesthood. At both ends of that scale, the evidence suggests that the Attalids made use of the native cults as an interface with marginal populations. Moreover, where a rearrangement of the rural settlement structure seemed propitious, cult sites made for sturdy platforms on which to erect new cities.[58]

Across the Hellenistic East, the kings, who were often the newcomers, contended with the power of age-old temples and religious authorities. This is the form of interaction that gave us the Rosetta Stone, the Maccabean Revolt, and which resounds in cuneiform astronomical diaries from

---

[58] The enduring power of Anatolian temples in the Hellenistic period is now roundly acknowledged. At issue is the relationship of priestly to secular power in the form of kings and cities. Debord 1982 sees urban sanctuaries, at least, tightly controlled by polis elites. Dignas 2002, by contrast, highlights tensions that drew kings into the conflict. See Boffo 1985 on the *modus vivendi* of kings and temples, as well as distinctions between various communities designated sacred in the sources. For a preliminary list of temples in the Attalid orbit, see Rostovtzeff 1923, 370–71.

Babylonia. One of several ways in which the Attalids, who were not foreign to Anatolia, differed from their rivals was by their ability to penetrate deeper into out-of-the-way temples and beneath the hieratic elite. A remarkable dossier of Attalid correspondence illustrates a distinctive pattern. For example, in the Upper Kaikos Valley, the Attalids granted tax exemptions in 185 to a group of villagers attached to an obscure sanctuary of Apollo Tarsenos.[59] Keeping with traditional decorum, the villagers accessed the royal bureaucracy through their high priest. Afterward, however, village and priest passed a decree together in response to the benefaction, demonstrating the kind of burgeoning civic consciousness that we find in other small towns. Under Attalos III, villagers at Hiera Kome ("sacred village"), on the frontier with Caria, were more precocious: they contacted the king directly with their concerns.[60] Finally, Attalos III may also have confirmed the inviolability of a sanctuary of Anaitis-Artemis in the Hyrkanian Plain.[61] Again, it was the villagers, "those around the goddess," who sent ambassadors bearing documents and requests.[62] The Attalids, it seems, managed to diffuse the threat of so much social power concentrated in rural sanctuaries. Properly cultivated, the temples represented not an alternative, but rather a branch of the state.

Certain indigenous shrines seem to have formed the core of the new settlements that the Attalids constructed in the hinterland. The tantalizingly laconic sources for these foundations hint at an effort to anchor new cities in old cults. For example, a Pantheon shrine, a sanctuary of All Gods, may have formed the nucleus of the city of the Pantheôtai established in Lydia.[63] The ecumenical nature of the cult seems to have appealed to the Attalids, ever eager to attract the greatest number of adherents to their cause. In addition, the theophoric names of new cities of the interior, such as Phrygian Dionysoupolis and Hierapolis on the Upper Maeander, hearken back to earlier forms of political organization under the authority of god and priesthood. There are good reasons to believe that Hierapolis

---

[59] D14. Thonemann (2015b, 121) takes the *katoikoi* of Apollo Tarsenos to be a contingent of soldiers. The local priest's role as intermediary with the Attalids suggests an older community of temple dependents. See Debord 1982, 272.

[60] RC 69.

[61] RC 68; cf. Rigsby 1996, 440–41, with arguments for Roman authorship. On the Persian Goddess in Anatolia, see Debord 1982, 265–66.

[62] As noted by Debord (1982, 274), Welles' translation in *RC* of "city" in lines 1–2 does not fit the rural context, nor is it in the Greek. Cf. Rigsby 1996, 440: "The inviolability of the Persian [Goddess] among you I confirm."

[63] Habicht 1975, 79; Cohen 1995, 226–27. See further a dedication on behalf of Attalos III to All Gods (*pantes theoi*) from Zeytinli, *I.Adramyttion* 3.

was a Pergamene refoundation.⁶⁴ In the case of Dionysoupolis, Stephanus of Byzantium preserves in its bare bones the origin story for the city. Eumenes II and his brother Attalos founded Dionysoupolis after discovering an archaic cult statue (*xoanon*) of the god Dionysus on the spot. It is a self-serving legend, one which the Attalids themselves perhaps invented, but it is also a sophisticated fabrication. It is worth asking: Precisely *which* god Dionysus did Eumenes and Attalos find in the region of the Çal Dağ and Çal Ova? On the one hand, it is a curious coincidence that the Attalids discovered a pristine image of one of their dynasty's tutelary divinities in a region targeted for colonization. The cult of an Orphic and theatrical Dionysus Kathegemon ("the Guide"), as he was known on the citadel of Pergamon and, increasingly, in many parts of the kingdom, including urbanized Phrygia, was tied to king, court, and old Greek cities like Teos. On coins of Dionysoupolis' civic mint, this god appears. On the other hand, a very different, rural, Hittite-version of Dionysus, associated with Zeus, storms, and springs, remained current among the highlanders of Phrygia well into the Roman period. The logic of the story allows for either version of Dionysus to take center stage. On a bend in the great river, the Attalids had likely chosen a spot for their city with links to the cult of an Anatolian Dionysus. The foundation story reflects a bold attempt to introduce dynastic piety under cover of a local deity.⁶⁵

Among the cult centers of inner Anatolia, none grew more powerful in this period than the sanctuary of Cybele Agdistis at Pessinous on the

---

⁶⁴ Debord 1982, 273. Hierapolis possessed tribes of Eumenis and Attalis, for which see Kunnert 2012, 123. See further the *clipei* of Eumenes II and Attalos II among the reliefs of the city's Roman theater (Queyrel 2003, D9 nos. 1 and 2) with archaeological evidence of Pergamene influence gathered in Kelp 2016. However, a Seleukid foundation has also been proposed on the basis of the tribe Apollonias (Kolb 1974; Cohen 1995, 305).

⁶⁵ Steph. Byz. *Etymologicum Magnum* p. 233. The context here justifies the antiquarian definition of *xoanon*, though Byzantine texts employ the term erratically (Donohue 1988, 172–74). The rediscovery of the god's statue in this story is of a piece with the wider transportability of the image of the divine in Greek religion, what Didier Viviers and others have called its *mise-en-scène* (Viviers 2015). These are powerful epiphanies of the godhead. The act of rediscovery may indeed have been ritualized, as it was in the case of Hera's statue on Samos (Ath. 15.672a–673d). The rediscovery of the statue must be seen as the performance of myth. Compare in Classical Athens the procession of the statue of Dionysus from the small temple at the Academy to the sanctuary of the theater during the Great Dionysia. On Teos, Dionysus, and the Attalids: Hansen 1971, 451–52. The earliest bronze issues of Dionysoupolis, which float chronologically between the second and first centuries BCE, display standard Dionysian iconography: grapes, the mask of Silenus, and the young, ivy-crowned god himself (*BMC* 1–3). For the distinctively Anatolian Dionysus, see Tassignon 2002.

notional border between Phrygia and Galatia. Attracting Attalid interest from an early date, it was the source of the Magna Mater cult that the Attalids adroitly transferred to Rome during the crucible of the Hannibalic Wars.[66] The Settlement of Apameia placed the sanctuary under the direct control of Pergamon, though we cannot be sure it remained so. Certainly, the Attalids strove to make diplomatic partners of its priests and to construct its territory as a buffer zone fronting the land of the Tolistobogii.[67] Painstaking archaeological detective work has reconstructed the human landscape around Attalid Pessinous. The built sanctuary, in fact, seems to have been a contrivance of Eumenes II or Attalos II. Its predecessor, the pre-Hellenistic, Phrygian sanctuary of Matar, may have sat somewhere on the sacred rocks of the Sivrihisar Mountains. Historically, the most important settlements of the region were not in the Gallos Valley. The choice of the site at modern Ballıhisar seems to have been administrative. It lacks the Cybele cult's distinctively rocky geology, and archaeologists have found scant remains of Phrygian occupation; the first signs of settlement actually date to the second and first centuries BCE. The excavated remains do confirm Strabo's report of Attalid building in the sanctuary (*temenos*). Yet if urbanization should rank among this dynasty's preferred tools for integrating resource-rich stretches of inner Anatolia into a nascent empire, we would expect its effects to register here. Did the Attalids intervene decisively in the settlement history of Pessinous, urbanizing the sanctuary and its environs?[68]

A recent discovery presents the first unimpeachably direct evidence of Attalid activities in and around Pessinous after 188. It is an inscribed royal letter of the future Attalos II addressed to a local military commander named Aribazos, found at Ballıhisar in 2003 (**D15**). The fragment lacks a date, but the context seems to be the immediate aftermath of the Attalid takeover. Aribazos appears to be an ex-Seleukid officer, a traditional local powerbroker, as his Persian name implies. Over and above an undelivered

---

[66] Mileta 2010 reasserts Pessinous as the origin of Magna Mater. Cf., most recently, Orlin 2010, 77–80.
[67] The chief evidence is the dossier *I.Pessinous* 1–7.
[68] Strabo 12.5.3. Pottery of the early second century BCE was recovered from foundations for a stoa in the western agora. No remains of a Hellenistic temple have been found, *contra* commentary of Roller (2018, 724) on this passage. On the historical geography of the region and the transfer of the cult from its Phrygian to its Hellenistic-Roman site, see Strobel 2003–7. As Coşkun (2016, 59) points out, "We are in no position to tell for how long this sacred stone had been harbored in the Gallos Valley – quite possibly for a very short period of time."

gift promised to junior officers, Aribazos makes three demands of Attalos: confirmation of his estates, an enhanced position in the new Attalid bureaucracy, and directions for mercenaries under his command. It is in his description of his relationship to the rank-and-file soldiers in his district that the character of settlement at Pessinous emerges. For Aribazos identifies himself as the commander of two groups of soldiers, the *katoikoi* of Amorion and of certain Galatians, the former mercenaries, stationed in a "place" (*topos*) called Kleonnaeion.[69] Surprisingly, the toponym Pessinous is absent. This has led Thonemann to make the ingenious suggestion that Kleonnaeion *is* Pessinous or, rather, that alongside the temple community existed a second polity, this one with a Greek name and appearance. The arrangement may strikes us as strange, but the heterogeneous inhabitants of the Hellenistic East found it perfectly normal.[70] A series of coin-types also shows twin settlements at the site, a priestly polity and the place called Kleonnaeion, perhaps named after a Macedonian general. In short, the new royal letter shows that the Attalids inherited this complex tableau.

Nothing, however, indicates that the Attalids rearranged settlement around what was termed a *chorion* (rural stronghold) during the campaign of conquest in 207.[71] Perhaps, with Pergamene support, Kleonnaeion eventually grew into a small polis, but its coins alone and the preliminary results of excavation are inconclusive proof.[72] If indeed this was a far more sanguine case of twin-track, bicultural settlement than that which arose next to mighty Near Eastern temples in Jerusalem, Babylon, or Rough Cilicia, all under Seleukid rule, it was the result of the Attalids' much more cautious approach. Unlike in those cases, in which the Seleukids devised or were convinced to plant a polis under the priests' noses, in the case of Pessinous and Kleonnaeion, the Attalids were content to maintain the status quo during a limited, but still decades-long period of influence over the sanctuary. For the Attalids, all that distinguished Kleonnaeion from the nearby *katoikia* of Amorion was its proximity to Pessinous. It was just another rural soldier-town without a large urban core, but the shrine lent it administrative importance. It is probably not an accident that Aribazos declares himself registered among those at Kleonnaeion. He in fact tells us himself that

---

[69] Cf. Ricl 2014, 144–45: Galatians replace the mercenaries previously stationed in Kleonnaeion.
[70] Thonemann 2015b, 122–26.   [71] *I.Pessinous* 1 line 9.
[72] Again, coinage is not a straightforward indication of political status in this period. In 25 BCE, Augustus founded the new city of the *Sebastênoi Pessinountioi*. This project of urbanization dwarfed anything that preceded it. It is clear that the Attalids attempted nothing comparable.

Figure 4.1 Hellenistic grave stele of Doidalses from Mustafakemalpaşa (courtesy of Elmar Schwertheim).

Kleonnaeion was not a polis, but rather a *topos* ("place"), employing the standard military-administrative term for extra-urban sites.[73] This was a key administrative hub in a dispersed landscape, parasitically attached to the

---

[73] For the meaning of *topos*, consider, e.g., the *katoikountes en tô topô* of *I.Sardis* 1 lines 16–17; or those *ek tou topou* in the Kardakon Kome, Maier 1959–61, no. 76 lines 16–17. As a Pergamene administrative term, see also *OGIS* 339 line 12; *SEG* II 663; and the *topoi* of the ephebic lists of

central node of a regional network. Merely strengthening it meant bringing more of rural Anatolia into its first sustained contact with a Hellenistic state.

The Sons of Telephos

> The *katoikoi* [dedicate a monument to] Doidalses son of Apollonios.

So declares a gabled stele now in Bursa, Turkey, recovered in the late nineteenth century in the town of Kirmasti, today Mustafakemalpaşa, near the site of ancient Miletopoulis on the lower Rhyndakos. Beneath that text are two recessed panels. In one, a bull is led to sacrifice as a towering Zeus (?) looks on (**Fig. 4.1**).[74] In the other, two men huddle together, one clothed and leaning on a staff. The other figure is fully nude, in the guise of the hero, leaning on what appears to be a spear. A large drinking cup sits on the ground. Crammed below the images, the following epigram is scrawled in rude letters:

> If Doidalses, who often on account of his athletic victories donned mirthful crowns on his head, had a fatherland, which was distinguished for its strong young men, then his deeds would be recorded alongside the great feats of Herakles. Therefore, the sons of Telephos, having placed him on par with noble men, glorify him with an everlasting homage.

At first glance, this object and its poem, an awkward piece of pop-literature with a dissonantly Homeric vocabulary, look like artifacts of the almost absurdly fierce hometown pride that characterized Greco-Roman civilization. His fatherland? Doidalses lived in a hamlet outside the city of Miletoupolis. His fatherland was a *katoikia*. His deeds like Herakles? The comparison seems specious. What league did he even play in? Certainly not a Panhellenic one – was he even *Greek*? Local Greeks claimed kinship with Miletus, but there were also Bithynians and Mysians among the population of so-called Hellespontine Phrygia in the second century. As noted since discovery, the name Doidalses is Thracian or Bithynian. Finally, what sense did it make for this village, which evidently lacked a name worth mentioning, to honor its compatriot in the name of "the sons of Telephos"? Why would

---

the capital, *MDAI(A)* 32 (1907), 415–69; *MDAI(A)* 33 (1908), 384–400; *MDAI(A)* 35 (1910), 416–36. Capdetrey (2007, 262–64) treats *topos* and *topoi* as the incorporation into administrative language of pre-Seleukid spatial understandings. For Allen (1983, 91–98, esp. 93), while the *topoi* of the ephebic lists of Pergamon, in particular, form a distinct category of communities beyond the polis, in general, the term lacked specific connotations. By contrast, Chaniotis (2010, 456–60), makes the case anew for the definition of *topos* as non-polis territory.

[74] For the suggestion that the deity is in fact a Myso-Phrygian sky god, see Merkelbach 2001, 91.

these villagers highlight the heroic ancestor of the people of Pergamon, whose saga was illustrated on the inner frieze of the Great Altar?[75]

On closer inspection, the stele housed in Bursa no longer seems generic, but in fact illustrative of a specific moment in the history of Anatolia. Again, we find people outside the cities brandishing their own civic identity. The anonymous town here is a famous fatherland (*patra*), and its inhabitants gather to praise a victorious athlete in good, classical form. Doidalses' name sounds like a Thraco-Bithynian spin on Daedalus, but this was a time of shifting ethnic identities. Of the identity of Doidalses' community, Elmar Schwertheim has suggested that is a *katoikia* of Mysians.[76] Indeed, this was the time when a broad spectrum of indigenous people living under Attalid rule came to call themselves "Mysians." Many were soldiers organized on the *katoikia* model, but civilians also counted among their ranks. This was a vast population spread across a region stretching from the Cyzicene peninsula to eastern Lydia. Gradually drawn into the Attalids' web, by the end of the dynasty, Mysian youth had even gained access to the gymnasium at Pergamon.[77] The most important point of administrative contact we can trace was the federal entity (probably Koinon) of the Mysians of the Abbaitis, but other regions and tribes, such as the "Hellespontine Mysians," may have been similarly organized.[78] Their koinon consisted not of cities, but rather of a number of rural districts (*dêmoi*), which grouped settlements around a central place. As the epigram

---

[75] *I.Kyzikos* II 23.

> οἱ κάτοικοι Δοιδάλσην Ἀπολλωνίο[υ].
> {Reliefs}
> εἰ πάτραν ἐπίσαμον ὁ πολλάκις εἵνε-
> [κ]εν ἄθλων Δοιδάλσης ἱλαροῖς κρᾶ-
> [τ]α βαλ<ὼ>ν στεφάνοις
> [ἔ]σχε παρ' αἰζηοῖσιν ἐν Ἡρακλείοις ἂν ἔργοις
> ἐγράφεθ' ἁ ῥώμα τοῦδε καὶ ἁ δύναμις.
> τούνεκα Τηλεφίδαι νιν ἰσόθρονον ἀνδρά-
> σιν ἐσθλοῖς θέντες ἀειμνάστοις ἀγλά-
> ισαν χαρίσιν.

Schwertheim (*I.Kyzikos* II, 29): "Sie sind eben keine Telephiden, Abkömmlinge des Herakles, wie die Pergamener. Sie sind offenbar Thraker, wie der name Doidalses schon nahelegt.... Die Τηλεφίδαι sind die Pergamener." Merkelbach (2001, 91) suggests that the epigram is referring to a grant of Pergamene citizenship for Doidalses. Yet the plain reading of the text is that the "everlasting homage" is the monument itself.

[76] *I.Kyzikos* II, 28. However, Schwertheim's argument that we are dealing here with precisely one of the *katoikiai* of the Mysians visited by Attalos I in 218 (Polyb. 5.77–78) seems far-fetched.

[77] For some examples, see *MDAI(A)* 32 (1907) 428,275; 435,297; 443,319; 446,331 and 332; 447,334. See further Allen 1983, 92–93.

[78] Hellespontine Mysians as possible koinon: Debord 2001, 144.

indicates, the supremely flexible myth of Telephos, a figure at once the "barbarian-speaking Greek" and an archetypal Mysian, provided these populations with a heroic and Hellenic ancestry.[79] Just as importantly, it tied their identity to the Attalids'. The stele of Doidalses is an artifact of rural life under the Attalids, evidence that Pergamon achieved a far-reaching integration of its new territories, both ideological and institutional, without herding people into cities.

Pergamon's debt to Mysia is well known. In fact, the Attalids themselves publicized it soon after arriving on the Panhellenic stage. On Delos, Attalos I erected a very unusual statue group, the so-called Teuthrania Monument, which depicted two or perhaps all three generations of royalty, while also thematizing the landscape of the Kaikos Valley, which is to say, the part of Mysia best known from Greek literature.[80] The statue group included a number of eponymous heroes: Midios (Midapedion), son of Gyrnos (Gryneion) and Halisarna; Teuthras (Teuthrania) son of Midios and Arge; and Phaleros, son of Ib[...] and Rhaistyne, daughter of Selinus (the river god).[81] This seems to be a major departure from the conventions of the genre of royal ancestors (*progonoi*) monuments.[82] In place of queens and Olympian ancestors such as Herakles, all of which may have appeared on a contemporary Antigonid monument also on Delos, a network of Mysian toponyms was personified. The explanation for this strange choice is not that the Attalids were "bourgeois" rulers depicting a maximally elaborated family tree, nor that as "liberals" they were representing their kingdom like a polis with a hinterland (*chora*), though Gyrnos was associated with the founder-hero (*ktistês*) Pergamos. Rather, as Andreas Grüner has shown, the Teuthrania Monument alludes to a network of settlements, mostly, but not exclusively poleis, which the earlier lords of the valley, the Gongylids and the Demaratids, had first bound together into a unified political geography.[83] If the Arkadian Telephos had afforded these families of exiles a link back to Greece, the Mysian Teuthras had helped them to fashion a micro-empire in their adopted homeland. As has been noted, the dynastic myth of Telephos and his stepfather Teuthras had nothing to do with the site of Pergamon, but rather that of modern Eğrigöl Tepe. What

---

[79] Lycoph. *Alex.* 205–15, 1245–49; Stewart 1996a, 43–45.
[80] For reconstruction, see Schalles 1985, 127–35, esp. p. 135, "Das pergamenische Königreich wird nicht allein von seinen Herrschern repräsentiert, sondern auch von Ortsheroen und Flußgöttern, gewissermaßen als Substrate des mysischen Stammlandes."
[81] IG XI 4 1206–8 Robert 1973.
[82] For an overview of *progonoi* monuments, see Coppola, 2016, 26–31.
[83] Grüner 2016; cf. Scheer 2003, 221; Schalles 1985, 134.

was appropriated then from the previous dynasties was both a regional fiefdom and a Mysian pedigree. Before the international audience on Delos, the Attalids did not emphasize Heraklid/Telephid descent, for their Greekness was not at stake. Rather, in a manner that anticipates the inner frieze of the Great Altar, they showcased the landscape of Mysia. Given the early date of the monument, it is important to keep in mind that when the Attalids arrived on the international scene, they arrived as Mysians. As Pierre Debord underscores, the site of Pergamon was one of the mythohistorical centers of Mysia, a fact which does not in any way impugn Attalid Hellenicity.[84] Survival as a first-order Mediterranean power depended on solidarity with this population and therefore the promotion of a Mysian identity.[85]

Politically, the administrative unity of a region known as Mysia, indeed one centered on Pergamon, may already have existed under the satrap Orontes, ca. 360.[86] However, as a cultural geography, the boundaries of Mysia were always vague and shifted over time. On the one hand, the lowlying areas near the coast tend to show up earlier in the Greek sources, such as the Kaikos Valley in the southwest and the Hellespontine plains around Daskyleion and Cyzicus in the north. For example, in the Athenian tribute list of 454/3, the Μυσοί are a community on the Propontic coast of Asia Minor.[87] Yet much of historical Mysia lay at higher elevations and scarcely enters the record before the Attalids (**Map 4.1**). The upland regions contained the central plains around modern Balıkesir and the Savaştepe Valley, as well as the rougher country to the east, the upper valleys of the ancient Makestos and Hermos, up to Kadoi across Mount Dindymos from Phrygian Aizanoi. In addition, Mysians wandered into what epigraphers refer to as "northeast Lydia," though just when migration south of Mount Temnos began is anyone's guess. While Aeschylus describes Mysians by Mount Tmolos in the vicinity of Sardis in 472, the major wave of migration seems to have begun later, perhaps during the third century.[88] The result was ethnogenesis and the emergence of federalism among the Mysians of the Abbaitis, a region that encompassed both sides of Mount Temnos (Demirci Dağ), the Simav basin, the upper Makestos, the upper but now also the middle Hermos. For the Attalids, the economic importance of their

---

[84] Debord 2001, 145.   [85] Williamson 2016, 75–79, esp. 77.
[86] Osborne 1975. Cf. Weiskopf 1989, 70–75, with arguments against the notion of a satrapy of Mysia.
[87] *IG* I³ 259 Col. V line 15. On northern Mysia, see Avram 2004, 975–76.
[88] Aesch. *Pers.* 49–52. Migration during third century: Nollé 2010, 80; cf. Ma 2013a, 71.

regional hinterland must have been profound. The silver deposits of Balya lay in Mysian country between the upper Kaikos and the Balıkesir plain. Even at higher elevations, good land for growing grain was in abundance. The place name Kadoi seems to preserve an Anatolian root for grain.[89] Lower down in the Katakekaumenê of "northeast Lydia," wine was produced for export.[90]

Scholars have tended to see Mysia as a land of brigands and hill people but, first of all, a land of laborers.[91] One scholar goes so far as to call the "human resources of rural Mysia" one of the "two lungs of the Attalid monarchy," along with the old Greek cities of the coast.[92] For their part, the Mysians provided indispensable manpower for the entire enterprise. From early on, they fought the wars and defended the winnings. Teamed with a broader local milieu of Thraco-Bithynians, as well as natives of Pergamon and of Cyzicus, they garrisoned the capital as well as far-off possessions like Aegina.[93] When we find lists of Attalid soldiers' names, for instance, the 141 recorded in full at the sanctuary of Thermon in Aetolia or those attached to a citizenship grant for a garrison near Delphi, Mysians make up a near-majority.[94] Like all Hellenistic kings, the Attalids employed mercenaries, especially Galatians, but the contingents of Mysoi would seem to have been regular levies. In other words, with material and symbolic leverage, the Attalids managed to compel these warriors to join up. In fact, though their fame as fighters spread abroad, Mysians very infrequently emigrated into Hellenistic armies outside Asia Minor.[95]

By contrast, Mysia's debt to Pergamon is less often acknowledged. The Mysians stood to gain greatly from the growth of the Attalid empire, which perhaps explains why, returning from distant theaters of war, they remained at home. The Mysians' quiet fulfillment of their end of the bargain is revealed in the aforementioned dedication from Sındırgı, set

---

[89] Nollé 2010, 73–74.   [90] Strabo 13.4.11; Debord 1985, 354–55.
[91] In general, for historical geography and ethnography see Robert 1937, 185–98, and Robert 1962, 265–70, especially 268 for Mysian brigandage as social banditry, the War of Aristonikos as "révolte des paysans indigènes." For the expression "land of laborers," see Launey 1949–50, vol. 1, 43.
[92] Ma 2013a, 65b.
[93] Catling 2004–9, 432. The indirect evidence for a plurality of Cyzicenes and Pergamenes in the Attalid army is onomastic.
[94] Catling 2004–9. Thermon: *IG* IX 1² 1 60. Lilaia: *FD* III.3 1325 = *ISE* 81. However, for Mysian as a military pseudo-ethnicon, see Masson 1993; but *contra* Daubner 2011, 57 n. 60; Nollé 2010, 87, 105.
[95] Launey (1949–50, vol. 1, 436–49) discusses the evidence for Mysians in the army of Antiochos IV, concluding that Mysians tended not to emigrate.

up in 145 by demobilized "soldiers who had crossed to the Chersonese and places in Thrace."[96] They use the regnal year for a date, but explicit praise for the king is absent.[97] Signs of sycophancy are absent because the relationship was genuinely beneficial to both parties. The lightweight Attalid state was dependent on this source of manpower, but Mysia flourished under Pergamon, reaching its apogee.[98] The evidence for this claim is not an uptick in city-building, for the region remained rural. Rather, we can point to the assertion and embellishment of Mysian identity, the sudden appearance of civic institutions capable of producing decrees and coinage, and an increase in the number of people laying claim to the mantle of Mysia. An elevated status is nowhere more visible than in the domain of genealogy. The myth of Telephos, who helped the Greeks on their way to Troy, long linked to Mysia, gained a new salience within Attalid state religion.[99] It seems too that the Mysians now began to press on their connection to Troy itself. For example, like many in the Mediterranean, they could look to a brief mention of an ancestor in Homer's *Iliad*. Theirs was a certain Chromis, named as a leader of the Mysians at Troy.[100] The federal assembly of the Mysians of the Abbaitis went so far as to honor their Homeric ancestor as a forefather (*propatôr*).[101] Interestingly, they called him Chromios. Was it a slip of the chisel or a conscious play for a bigger name? Since the name Chromios belonged to a Trojan prince, a son of Priam and a companion of Hektor, the upgrade certainly suited the socially ascendant Mysians.[102]

Gravestones by nature bear out strong statements of identity, as a life is summed up in just a few words. It is telling, then, that a late Hellenistic or early Roman epitaph from rural Mysia reads, "So long! (Here lies) Menekrates son of Timarchos, a Mysian who fell in battle."[103]

---

[96] *OGIS* 330. No ethnic is given, but we can safely assume that Mysians made the dedication, given both the findspot in an area dense with Mysian settlements and our wider knowledge of the ethnic composition of the Attalid army.

[97] Ma 2013a, 69.   [98] Debord 1985, 349.

[99] For the myth in Pergamon, see Heres 1996. More generally, see Gantz 1993, 428–31, 576–80, 640–41.

[100] Hom. *Il.* 2.858.

[101] *OGIS* 446. On Roman-period coinage of Kadoi, the Mysian heroes Chromios and Ennomos are represented, for which see Nollé 2010, 106.

[102] Hom. *Il.* 5.160; 17.494, 534. Apollod. *Bibl.* 3.152.

[103] Herrmann 1962, 60 (no. 57) = *TAM* V 1 444.

Μενεκράτης Τιμάρχου
Μυσὸς χαῖρε ὁ πεσὼν
ἐν τῇ μάχῃ.

The form πεσών is redolent of epic, appearing 21 times in Homer's *Iliad*.

Menekrates or his survivors were not simply engaging in the conventional naming practice of adding what scholars call his "ethnic," his political affiliation to his father's name. He was asserting in death a heroic archetype, the "fallen Μύσος," which he expected to resonate with passersby. The choice of this mortuary pose implies an astounding development of Mysian identity. First, very simply, it implies that Mysian ethnogenesis had taken place. Second, the existence of the archetype implies that the martial exploits of these Mysians had been embedded in heroic narrative. The image evoked is a quotation from that narrative, which had become by Menekrates' time a genuine meme. Both are the result of interaction with the Attalids. An ethnographer of Hellenistic militaries is hard-pressed to fix the geographical origin of the Mysians, not only due to the usual gaps in our knowledge, but since so many different groups and individuals began to wear the name in this period.[104] The process of ethnogenesis had clearly begun much earlier, but now it accelerated to breakneck speed. New groups like the Masdyênoi appear in the record, already attached to the banner of Mysia, as if no other path to peoplehood existed.[105] In the northern region around modern Yalova, one group even claimed to be Pratomysioi – the "real Mysians," evidence of the newfound social currency of the ethnicon.[106] It is especially telling of the tempo of ethnogenesis at this moment that one community in Lydia named themselves the Myso-Makedones and another called itself the town of Mysotimolos. The one is a graft on top of an older identity tied to Mount Tmolos.[107] The other is an attempt to partake of the newfound Mysian glory without renouncing the older prestige identity of the Macedonians. These hybrid names may evidence migration and resettlement, but they certainly also echo a new and increasingly prestigious ethnic identity in the countryside.[108]

---

[104] Launey 1949–50, vol. 1, 437: "une masse indistincte, dont l'ethnique n'est jamais précisé par une indication de provenance." To the dossier we may add a Μύσος appearing in an unpublished inscription housed in the museum of Uşak (Ender Varinlioğlu, personal comm.).

[105] Masydênoi as Mysians: Launey 1949–50, vol. 1, 440–41; as possible Iranians: Ma 2013a, 72.

[106] Debord 2001, 142.

[107] The comment of Strabo (12.4.10) on a group of Mysians around Mount Olympos is instructive. Some call them Hellespontine Mysians, others call them Olympenian Mysians. Yet everyone, by Strabo's time, calls them Mysians. By way of contrast, consider the Olympenoi who appear in a late Classical or early Hellenistic treaty with the city of Aigai (*Staatsverträge* III 456). I would suggest that the Olympenoi of the treaty have not yet experienced the Mysian ethnogenesis. See further Eustathius, *Ad Dionysium Periegetam* 322: Ἡρόδοτος δὲ τοὺς ἐν τῇ Ἀσίᾳ Μυσοὺς Λυδῶν ἀποίκους λέγει, Ὀλυμπηνοὺς καλουμένους, ἀπὸ ὄρους Ὀλύμπου τοῦ Ἀσιανοῦ ("Herodotus says that the Mysians in Asia, those called Olympenoi after the Asian Mount Olympos, are colonists of the Lydians").

[108] On the settlements of the Mysomakedones and the town of Mysotimolos, see Cohen 1995, 220–22; Launey 1949–50, vol. 1, 444. For Cohen and Launey, the toponym is evidence of a

In particular, the startling appearance of the Myso-Makedones, a people positioning themselves as both the traditional and the emergent ethnic power in the countryside, forces us to consider what a remarkable rehabilitation of the image of Mysia the Attalids had effected. From the indelible image of Telephos in rags, an invention of Euripides that found its way into Aristophanes' play *Acharnians*, to the pithy comedian Menander's insulting expression "the last of the Mysians" (Μυσῶν ὁ ἔσχατος), we find a sustained line of contempt. The region of Mysia was considered a veritable wasteland. It was a defenseless land ripe for plunder, leaderless while Telephos was away on his hero's journey. For example, the Athenian politician Demosthenes contended that were it not for the Athenians' resistance, the Persians would have subjected Greece to "a proverbial 'looting of Mysia (Μυσῶν λεία).'" Here, worse than simply stuck outside "Greece," Mysia is stuck on the wrong side of history. In fact, these Anatolian highlands had long been vulnerable to the predation of Greeks and Persians. Marching his Spartans to the Hellespont, Agesilaus had raided the forests of Mysia for conscripts. Further, the region had long been a source for slaves. A manumission decree of 179 from Delphi for a Mysian named Apollonios recalls that past. Yet in the Attalid era, the Mysians were no longer the hunted. On the contrary, they were the hunters.[109]

The Çan Sarcophagus, a piece of Achaemenid military art, provides a useful point of comparison (**Fig. 4.2**). Discovered in an elite tomb in the Troad's Granikos Valley, it belonged to an early fourth-century Iranian or Iranized noble, who wished to be depicted in death as a hunter. Two painted reliefs are preserved on the sarcophagus, one a scene of hunting animals, stag and boar, the other a battle scene. In each, the main subject is shown stabbing a victim in the eye, in one panel, a boar, in another, a human, trapped beneath the rider on horseback. The lightly armed figure in the battle scene is a defeated Mysian. The juxtaposition of the images then implies a macabre analogy: as he hunted the stag, so too did the

---

colony founded by or containing both Mysian and Macedonian settlers. I am suggesting instead that it is evidence of the heady atmosphere of Mysian ethnogenesis, a more recent phenomenon than Macedonian colonization in Lydia.

[109] The expression "last of the Mysians" seems to mean "worst of the worst." For anti-Mysian prejudice of classical literature, see Cope 1877, vol. 1, 235–36; Stewart 1996b, 109. For "Mysian spoil," see Simon. Fr. 37 West (= Dem. 18.72); Arist. *Rh.* 1372b31. See also Soph. *Aj.* 721, Teukros' plunder of the hills of Mysia. Agesilaus: *Hell. Oxy.* 16.1. Manumission: *SGDI* II 2065 with Lewis 2011 on the highlands of western Asia Minor as an important source of slaves in the Classical period.

Figure 4.2 The Çan Sarcophagus from the Granikos Valley, early fourth century BCE (courtesy of C. Brian Rose and Troy Excavation Project).

occupant of the sarcophagus hunt Mysians.[110] To understand that cruel gesture, one must examine the relationship of the Achaemenid state to this population. Xenophon consistently portrays the Mysians, along with the Pisidians, as the most vexing inhabitants of Achaemenid Anatolia. He saw them as independent, but also menacing. Xenophon reports frequent Mysian raids on the king's land, not loose imperial control, but open enmity. The Oxyrhyncus Historian writes, "Many of the Mysians are autonomous and do not answer to the king."[111] Thus, for an Achaemenid baron like the one buried in the Çan Sarcophagus, interaction with the Mysians amounted to frequent, nearly ritualized violent clashes. As the Spartan officer Klearchos and the satrap Tissaphernes agreed, the point of any interaction with them was to mete out violent discipline.[112]

---

[110] Ma 2008b.   [111] *Hell. Oxy.* 21.1.
[112] The speech of Klearchos to Tissaphernes (Xen. *An.* 2.5.13): "I know that the Mysians are troublesome to you, and I believe that with the force I have I could make them your submissive servants; I know that the Pisidians also trouble you, and I hear that there are likewise many other tribes of the same sort; I could put a stop, I think, to their being a continual annoyance to your prosperity" (trans. Loeb).

While the Seleukids succeeded in drawing individual Mysians and bands of mercenaries into their service, they failed to fully integrate communities. The Persians' thorny "Mysian problem" becomes less visible after Alexander, but the essentially antagonistic structure of interaction persists. There can be no doubt that the Seleukids made use of the human resources of Mysia. We find Mysians next to Achaios at the siege of Selge and alongside Antiochos III at the Battle of Magnesia. Further afield in the Levant, we find entire contingents of Mysians in the armies of Antiochos IV. Yet the Seleukids' reach into rural Anatolia was limited. Large populations must have evaded state control. The Pamukçu stele of 209, which treats the appointment of Nikanor as high priest, indicates the presence of the Seleukid state in the very heart of Smooth Mysia. How far beyond the penumbra of an administrative outpost was this presence felt? What was the cost of control for the Seleukids? A model, at least, presents itself in the story of Josephus on the establishment of Mesopotamian Jewish colonists in "the most difficult places" of rural Phrygia and Lydia. The mechanisms of control appear to have been costly indeed and highly coercive, pitting colonists against natives. Josephus' story is all about trust: Antiochos III places his trust (*pistis*) in the Jews, the outsiders whom he imports and equips with arms, making them the watchmen for restless Anatolia.[113]

Taking a different tack, the Attalids placed their trust in the Galatians, Phrygians, Lydians, and, especially, in the Mysians themselves, who now changed from mercenaries into conscripts.[114] By devolving authority, the kings both economized on coercion and gained access to stores of resources hitherto untapped. Uniquely among the Hellenistic rulers of Anatolia, the Attalids granted villages – and not just cities – full property rights over the land.[115] Throughout rural Mysia, the Attalid experience produced increasingly formalized, recognizably Hellenistic-style polities. The Mysians, perhaps in tandem with the poorly understood but increasingly vocal Phrygians of the Epictetus – and all those who rallied to these identities – were the privileged partners of the Attalids, both at home and abroad. It is probably not an accident that we find a proudly self-identifying Mysian on Aegina in this period. A gravestone records the name of a certain Xenokles the Mysos, probably an agent of the Attalid occupation of the island.[116]

---

[113] Mysians in the Seleukid army: Polyb. 5.76.7; App. *Syr.* 32. Army of Antiochos IV: 2 Macc 5:24; Polyb. 30.25.3. Pamukçu stele: *SEG* XXXVII 1010. Antiochos III and Mesopotamian Jews: Joseph. *AJ* 12.147–52.

[114] Avram and Tsetskhladze 2014, 173.

[115] Schuler (1998, 191) notes the peculiarity of the Attalids in this regard.

[116] *AA* 22 (1907) 129.

A growing dossier of inscriptions documents nascent institutions, which would have provided Pergamon with an unprecedented reach into rural Anatolia. The Mysians of the Abbaitis now came to possess a council (*boulê*), an assembly (*dêmos*), and a mint. A decree in honor of Philomelos son of Ophelas, from the vicinity of Silandos, showcases an extensive civic armature.[117] Philomelos, who is described as a co-citizen (*politês*), served his fatherland (*patris*) on embassies and with liturgies. As a biographical encomium, the decree would not be out of place in many a late Hellenistic polis.

Equally conventional of civic life are the bronze coins, which are well represented in major collections and must have contributed significantly to the monetization of the region.[118] Coins associated with a federal mint issuing under the names "the Mysoi" (ΜΥΣΩΝ) and "the Mysoi Abbaeitai" (ΜΥΣΩΝ ΑΒΒΑ, ΜΥΣΩΝ ΑΒΒΑΙΤΩΝ) burst into circulation late in the Hellenistic period (**Fig. 4.3**).[119] The bronzes appear in three types, most commonly featuring a laureate Zeus on the obverse, a winged fulmen surrounded by an oak wreath and text on the reverse.[120] One does not need to search too far to find nearly identical coins, for example, those of the polis of Apollonia-on-the-Rhyndakos, with ΑΠΟΛΛΟΩΝΙΑΤΩΝ framing the winged fulmen in place of ΜΥΣΩΝ.[121] With an ecumenical Zeus as their primary icon, capable of serving double duty as an Anatolian sky god, along with the winged fulmen, perhaps copying a Macedonian shield emblem, these Mysians were fitting right in.[122] A second type seems to bear more idiosyncratic images: a female deity (?) crowned with *stephanê* and an enwreathed labrys, the woodsman's axe.[123] Finally, a third type, consisting of a young Herakles donning the lion's skin helmet on the obverse, and the demigod's club on the reverse, itself draped with the lion's skin, expresses strong affinities with Pergamene coinage and the Attalid house.[124] The draped club of Herakles, in particular, is precisely the image

---

[117] Malay and Petzl 2003. While the decree dates to the immediate aftermath of the War of Aristonikos, i.e., to the 120s, the institutions, logically, stretch back into the Attalid period.
[118] To size up the volume of this coinage, consider that Paris holds 15 examples of the Zeus/thunderbolt type, at least half of which are unique obverses.
[119] For coin legends, see Leschhorn 2009, 30. A second-century date is listed in both *BMC* Mysia and the catalogue of the ANS ("190–133 BC" for 1944.100.49830).
[120] *BMC* Mysia 1, nos. 1–5.   [121] Imhoof-Blumer and von Fritze 1913, 67–68.
[122] Winged fulmen as Macedonian shield emblem: Sekunda 2012, 19.   [123] *BMC* Mysia 1, no. 7.
[124] Note the rarity of the head of young Herakles in this region. *BMC* Mysia contains only one other mint that provides examples: Pergamon (nos. 111–13). See also the contemporary civic bronzes of Pergamon featuring Eurypolos, son of Telephos and grandson of Herakles (*SNG Paris* 1897).

Figure 4.3 Late Hellenistic bronze coin of the Mysoi Abbaeitai (6.31 g, ANS 1944.100.49830; courtesy of the American Numismatic Society).

that the Attalids had placed on their own coinage, the fractions of their new cistophori.[125]

All this minting represents, on the one hand, the newfound prestige of Mysian identity, an ethnogenesis that probably accelerated through the process of federalization.[126] On the other hand, minting of this sort presupposes the existence of sturdy institutions of public finance, a civic toolkit. These coins are not the occasional issues of a local warlord. This is the money of a Mysian polity, as both its text and the uniformity of the mintmarks declare. On this reckoning, coinage flows from the formalization of traditional modes of governance and cooperation. It is a common feature of the polis, but was at no point in the history of money its exclusive preserve. Support for this claim can be found elsewhere in the numismatic record for inner Anatolia under the Attalids and in the wake of their collapse. It is at this point in history that a number of rural communities appear for the first time in coinage. The Kaystrianoi, of the eponymous Kayster Valley in Lydia, like the Mysians of the Abbaitis, also minted second-century bronzes marked with the Attalids' signature draped club

---

[125] Marcellesi 2012 no. 46.
[126] Ethnogenesis was not necessarily a prerequisite for federalization: Hall 2015, 48.

of Herakles.[127] Two other groups, the Epikteteis (Phrygia) and the Poimanenoi ("shepherds") of the lower Aisepos on the conventional, arbitrary dating of their coins, began minting soon after the Attalid collapse.[128] The formalization of their institutions could very well have begun earlier. The Zeus/thunderbolt coinage of the Poimanenoi bears such a striking resemblance to the bronzes of the Abbaitis that it may originate in the same historical context.[129] This barrage of coinage echoes the politicization of the Anatolian countryside, a development from which the Attalids, first, and the Romans, later, stood to gain.

In the signal case of the Abbaitis, we know that politicization took the form of a federal koinon comprised of different sub-polities (*dêmoi*). While the constituent *dêmoi* passed decrees, they were in fact not poleis, but rather rural districts, networks of small settlements oriented around a central place. The koinon federalized the villages.[130] This is important to emphasize because the distinctly pro-Attalid communities of the Abbaitis never became a union of poleis. In certain places, such as Kadoi, (Mysian) Ankyra, and Synaos, an early Roman city eventually succeeded the central settlement of the former district, but this was only after the political concept of the Abbaitis had dissipated following the Mithridatic Wars.[131] Another such place was Gordos, south of Mount Temnos, between Thyateira and the river Hyllos, garrisoned first by a Seleukid commander (*hêgemon*) and later by a Pergamene "*hêgemon* of Mysians."[132] Something had changed. Under the new regime, the "[district of the] Mysians of the Abbaitis in Gordos (οἱ Μυσοὶ Ἀββαεῖται [?] ἐν Γόρδωι)" bestowed honors

---

[127] ANS 1944.100.48919; Paris B 702.

[128] As discussed in Chapter 3, the convention of dating civic bronzes in Asia Minor roundly "post-133" is problematic. Poimanenoi: *BMC* Mysia 175, nos. 1–3; www.mfa.org/collections/object/coin-of-poimanenon-with-head-of-zeus-3641. Epikteteis: *BMC* Phrygia 200–1, nos. 1–9; http://artgallery.yale.edu/collections/objects/117206.

[129] Cf. a coin of Peltai with obverse of Zeus and reverse of winged fulmen, ANS 1944.100.50544; Paris, Fonds général 1797. Cohen (1995, 318) conjectures Seleukid origins for Peltai. He notes too that Peltai was one of the few cities in Phrygia to mint in the second century BCE. The city, which possessed a *boulê*, also exhibits ties to Mysia in the form of a decree in honor of the city of Antandros (Michel, *Recueil* 542).

[130] Debord 2001, 144: "[L]e koinon est l'agent fédérateur des villages." Cf. Ma 2013a, 66–67: "*poleis*-like communities … In post-Attalid Asia Minor, Mysia Abbaitis appears organized as an extensive federal entity regrouping a number of *poleis*." For Mileta (2008, 74–75), *dêmoi* in the Attalid kingdom are indigenous cities without polis status, including those glimpsed in the Customs Law of Asia.

[131] Nollé 2010, 84. For the participation of both the Epikteteis and the Mysians of the Abbaitis on the Roman side in the Third Mithridatic War, see *OGIS* 445.

[132] *TAM* V 1 689, 690.

on a benefactor linked to the Attalids.[133] The inscription juxtaposes the Mysians in the district of Gordos, a member *dêmos* district, with the "entire people (σύμπας δῆμος)," that is, with the totality of the Mysians in the koinon of the Abbaitis.[134] Archaeology demonstrates the privileged position that rural Mysians achieved in the Attalid kingdom. In a 2012 salvage excavation in modern Gördes, a late Hellenistic chamber tomb built from rough-cut stone was uncovered 1 km from the later site of the Roman city of Julia Gordos. It contained three skeletons, and a child's remains were found in an adjacent cist grave. Among the contents of these tombs was a trove of second-century Pergamene dishes, demonstrating close economic ties and the metropolitan tastes of the rural Mysian elite.[135]

Another key document is a late Hellenistic funerary stele from Yiğitler in the Demirci district, attesting four different Mysian *dêmoi* of the Abbaitis, those of the Lakimeni, Hodeni, Mokadeni, and Ankyrani, all described in spatial terms as the people around (*peri*) a particular place.[136] These subpolities of the Mysian koinon would seem to have encompassed many villages and a polis-sized territory.[137] The process of federalization not only accelerated ethnogenesis; it seems to have given the Mysians a new sense of territoriality.[138] By helping put the Mysians on the map, the Attalids revealed and came to know these new territories for themselves. This was achieved without resorting to the laborious task of founding cities. Indeed, such confederations now proliferated on both sides of the Maeander in rural Anatolia. At times, smaller communities must have joined to achieve recognition or escape domination. Pergamon as well as Rhodes were surely also responsible for aggregating the rural population into more malleable units.[139] Whatever the impetus, the end result brought ever larger amounts of territory into administrative contact with the state. Yet if its ethnic and political landscape changed, the settlement pattern of Mysia remained starkly rural.

Already in 218, we find the desire of the Attalids to integrate the Abbaitis to their urbanized, coastal core in Aeolis. Attalos I had engaged

---

[133] SEG XXXIV 1198 lines 7–8. Nollé 2010, 81: "der abbaïtische Distrikt der Abbaïtischen Myser zu Gordos."
[134] Louis Robert *BE* (1984) no. 384. See, further, Debord 1985, 349; Nollé 2010, 80–81.
[135] Soyaker et al. 2013.
[136] Malay 1983. However, for a challenge to the suggestion of Malay that the Hodeni located themselves around a road (ὁδός), see Louis Robert *BE* (1984) no. 385.
[137] Schuler 1998, 193.
[138] Hall 2015, 48: "[E]thnicity was not simply a prerequisite for federalization, but rather one of the means by which it was accomplished."
[139] For Rhodes' consolidation of settlement in its Carian and Lycian territories, see Schuler 2010.

the Gallic Aigosages during the War with Achaios, and he first used them to secure the cities of Kyme, Myrina, Phokaia, Aigai, and Temnos. Next, he continued inland toward Thyateira. Polybius provides a description of the king's show of force in the countryside:

> Continuing his progress and crossing the river Lycus he advanced on the Mysian communities (κατοικίαι τῶν Μυσῶν), and after having dealt with them reached Carseae. Overawing the people of this city and also the garrison of Didymateiche he took possession of these places likewise, when Themistocles, the general left in charge of the district by Achaeus, surrendered them to him. Starting thence and laying waste the plain of Apia he crossed Mount Pelecas and encamped near the river Megistus (Makestos).[140]

Though the expedition of Attalos I may have proved successful only as a recruiting and plundering tour, Eumenes II was able to target and secure these same territories in the Peace of Apameia. As Robert first pointed out, the κατοικίαι τῶν Μυσῶν were hamlets and remained so for much of history.[141] The French epigrapher was convinced that Attalos had headed north from the Lykos near Thyateia to the upper Kaikos. From there, he would have entered the pass of Gelembe, continuing north toward the Balıkesir Plain, an area which was urbanized only in the second century CE under Hadrian. Passing the mining district of Balya, Attalos would have then entered Hellespontine Phrygia, effectively touring what Robert and early travelers considered the most accessible parts of rural Mysia. However, seeing no strategic or political value in these communities (even the minerals), Schwertheim preferred to locate them hard by the Hellespontine cities – the *katoikiai* of the athlete Doidalses.[142] Both interpretations seriously underestimate the Attalid ability to touch the most remote parts of the Abbaitis and bundle them together with hoary Teuthrania into a single Mysian kingdom. Now, Johannes Nollé has redrawn the route, which could have departed from the Gelembe pass and reached Sındırgı on the north side of Mount Temnos. On this reckoning, the army of 218 would have here entered the upper Makestos, marched the length of the Abbaitis, and finished by plundering the Phrygian Plain of Apia.[143] After 188, Eumenes II would return, but not as a city builder. We are thus forced to contemplate a full-scale ideological and administrative integration that reached deep into the countryside and preserved a traditional pattern of settlement.

---

[140] Polyb. 5.77 (Loeb trans.). [141] Robert 1937, esp. 188–98.
[142] Schwertheim 1988, 74 n. 33. [143] Nollé 2010, 85–89.

The Birth of a Polis

So far, our survey of the countryside of the Attalid kingdom has highlighted small communities with a large sense of self-importance. With their own territories, revenues, citizenries, and royal subsidies, towns and cities of the post-Apameian kingdom achieved an unprecedented degree of cohesion and recognition. In the countryside, Eumenes II and his brother Attalos interacted with a broad spectrum of civic organisms. The polis, the notionally autonomous city-state on an archaic Greek model, with its council and assembly, laws and norms, fictitious tribes of citizens, magistrates, coins, and walls, was just one type. Long the power brokers of Hellenistic monarchies, these cities now seem to have lost their monopoly on unmediated contact with the kings, as more and more of Anatolia's inhabitants were formally introduced to the state. Had the polis finally died? Quite the opposite: the ascendant towns and tribal polities now sent embassies to the Attalids, begging to be recognized as one, and recent epigraphical discoveries in Turkey even show us what the birth of a new polis looked like. Aristotle, if he had returned from the dead, would have been slightly puzzled by a Greek city of the second century BCE; certainly, though, he would have recognized it. The idea of the polis as a set of institutions and a cultural identity was still alive and well. Moreover, in practical politics, the name clearly carried weight. Yet to complete our survey of the settlement structure of Pergamene Anatolia, we need to know why, with political identities more fluid than ever, a semi-Hellenized community might still transform itself into a polis. What was at stake? And for the Attalids, what was gained and what was lost by acceding to these requests? What did it mean to be born a polis under Pergamon?

With a mounting body of evidence, we can now connect a number of Anatolian micro-histories to the high political history of the Mediterranean. The most colorful is that of Toriaion, an obscure Seleukid *katoikia* in Phrygia Paroreios, in the plain of Ilgın, not far from the road from Philomelium to Iconium, which ultimately led to the Cilician Gates and Syria.[144] In 1997, a long inscription was discovered at Mahmuthisar, containing a dossier of three royal letters, the correspondence of the new ruler Eumenes II and the community of Toriaion (**D8**).

---

[144] The fortress of Kale Tepesi is frequently identified with Toriaion (Thonemann 2008, 44–48; Mitchell 2018, 22–23). However, see now the careful archaeological dating of these fortifications to the Hittite Bronze Age by Johnson and Harmanşah 2015, 268–71.

The text makes the historical setting explicit. It is the immediate aftermath of the Attalid takeover, with the Treaty of Apameia still fresh in mind. Betraying a measure of insecurity, Eumenes boasts that his bundle of gifts is no empty or illusory touch of grace (*charis*), but a grant founded on Roman arms and diplomacy.[145] Belatedly, Toriaion, which soon again slipped back into obscurity, has now achieved minor fame, as the first site to document a process so often effaced across the Hellenistic world. From a soldier-settler town of a mixed milieu of Graeco-Macedonian colonists, Phrygians, and Galatians – a key ambassador bears the Celtic name Brennos – Toriaion was now promoted to a polis. In the first letter, Eumenes addresses himself to "the settlers," while in the second and third, his interlocutor is the council (*boulê*) and assembly (*dêmos*) of the Toriaitai. Yet the change here was more than titular and by no means just skin deep. The transformation of Toriaion did not take place in discourse alone, an exercise in "code-switching." Rather, the town-cum-polis received an itemized list of new institutions per their initial request: a constitution (*politeia*), their own laws (*idioi nomoi*), a council, an assembly, and magistracies, and of course also a gymnasium. Finally, to top it all off, the Toriaitai requested and received "as much as is consistent with these things."[146]

As much as is consistent with polis-style institutions – a curious periphrasis; or is it, as much as is consistent with *being* a polis? We must try to follow the king's train of thought. On the one hand, Eumenes defers explication to forthcoming letters, which, as we quickly learn, hammer out the details of Toriaion's fiscal liabilities and privileges. To become a polis was to be more deeply integrated into the fiscal system of the Attalid state, but also to strike a fiscal bargain. On the other hand, Eumenes is at a loss for words. The rhetoric here gestures at an implicit contract between king and city, a nod to notoriously slippery notions like "freedom" (*eleutheria*) and "autonomy" (*autonomia*). The king binds himself. He vows to respect the ill-defined sovereignty of the polis. In this way, the Attalids abjured the more coercive forms of leverage. However, they simultaneously produced a much more robust civic organism, now filled with added citizens. Presumably, the more nebulous territory of the *katoikia* was expanded and clarified. Collection of certain taxes was ceded to polis administrators. Even the lower tax rate worthy of a polis could still bring in more revenues, as the Toriaitai, for their own ends, eagerly

---

[145] On the insecurity of Eumenes' position, see Thonemann 2013b, 5–7.
[146] **D8** lines 10–11: ὅσα τούτοις ἐστι|ἀκόλουθα.

exploited a windfall of dominance over the neighboring Ilgın plain.[147] The Attalids had even more to gain by designing the new polis from the ground up. All of the new city's laws and thus the final shape of its new institutions were to be submitted to the king for review, lest any contradict the interests of Toriaion. In fact, the stone reads "lest any contradict *our* interests," as a felicitous and all-too-telling mason's error transmitted the royal "we."

Eumenes then makes a fascinating suggestion: if needed, he is prepared to mail Toriaion its laws – and with them, the blueprint for a new council, assembly, boards of magistrates, and civic tribes – each prepackaged and ready-made. The Attalids had them all in stock! This allowed the monarch to shape the new city to fit a radically decentralized fiscal system and to plant seeds for a new imperial culture. Unlike some earlier Hellenistic monarchs, the Attalids seem to have attended to this work "in-house," rather than farming it out.[148] In a similar fashion, Antiochos IV, whom the Attalids had helped establish on the Seleukid throne, dispatched a lawgiver to Jerusalem, the mysterious Geron the Athenian, a royal functionary charged with overhauling that community's institutions and stubborn sense of self, playing midwife for the birth of Antiocheia-in-Jerusalem.[149] Unfortunately, the Attalids' interventions are only alluded to in Eumenes' offer to Toriaion. Yet we may catch a further glimpse in a decree from Pergamon concerning Akrasos in rural Mysia. A group calling itself "the Macedonians around Akrasos" honored a very highly placed courtier of Eumenes II named Menogenes son of Menophanes for his goodwill toward them and toward the king. Like the Toriaitai, these Macedonians were probably former military reserves of the Seleukids, poised to take on the mantle of the polis in the new Attalid state. They had a special relationship with Menogenes, who is styled both the king's intimate and his bodyguard.[150] One could see in the Attalid courtier Menogenes, then, a parallel for Antiochos IV's Geron the Athenian: if not an authoritarian lawgiver, then the administrative tutor to a new polis.

---

[147] Schuler (1999, 130) surmises that the territory of Toriaion was not radically altered. However, the second letter (esp. lines 44–47) implies the possibility of future modifications. At the very least, Toriaion strengthened its hold on these lands.

[148] Cf. *RC* 3 lines 52–65. Antigonos Monophthalmos farmed out the work of drafting new laws for one polis to local agents, *nomographoi*, who were dispatched to the island of Kos to copy that city's laws.

[149] 2 Macc. 6:1; Savalli-Lestrade 1998, 117; Ma 2012, 79; Ma 2020, 87.

[150] *I.Pergamon* 176a. While the edition *OGIS* 290 line 4 reads [καὶ νομ]οφύλακα, Savalli-Lestrade (1998, 135–37) restores [σωματ]οφύλακα. Her restoration has won broad acceptance. Note, however, that the presence of a *tau* at the right end of the lacuna is difficult to reconcile with Fränkel's drawing, which shows only the oblique hasta.

Both personally and collectively, the advantages of inclusion in a polis were enormous. It could mean the difference between paying a harvest tax of 50%, as opposed to 10%.[151] This is why Eumenes, in responding to the request of the Toriaitai, carefully defined the shape of the new citizen body. "I permit you and the indigenous people living with you (*enchorioi synoikountes*) to organize yourselves into one citizen body."[152] With a single clause, the cultural politics of accommodation and consensus, so vital to the Attalids' success, were broadcast throughout a strategically vulnerable district of rural Anatolia. Two previously separate and distinct communities, living side by side, were now combined. The actual drafting of citizen rolls was left to the local elite. Again, the Toriaitai were of mixed ethnic origins, but they had long been organized on the Graeco-Macedonian model of the *katoikia*. All the while living alongside them, by contrast, was a group of people that the letter describes only as "the indigenous." The original editors of the inscription found it unbelievable that the non-Greek inhabitants of the town received the new citizenship.[153] Yet as Schuler points out, they were certainly non-Greeks whose ethnic identity, likely Phrygian, is deliberately effaced; their otherness is consciously played down.[154] His view is that the local Phrygian elite pushed for the merger, and others have pointed again to possible parallels in near-contemporary Jerusalem or Babylon.[155] We cannot know for sure where the push came from, but we can confirm that the Attalids capitalized on the desire of a local elite bent on self-promotion. Whether by design or in an accident of expediency, Eumenes now professed his brand of pluralism and held up Toriaion as a model for other aspirants. Now, to join a polis was not to decamp and resettle in a nucleated hub; nor was it necessarily a matter of shedding older, Anatolian cultural identities overnight. Why did Eumenes promote the polis to such an extent that Polybius could call him his generation's greatest benefactor of "Greek cities"? He did so to replace the chauvinism of what Pierre Briant has called the traditional *ethno-classe dominante* with a privileged model of sociopolitical organization.[156] He thereby created a constituency much bigger than "the Greeks," which stretched deeper than ever into Anatolia, exercising tools of dominance honed over centuries in the Aegean.

Hungering for legitimacy in the early, uncertain years of the Apameian order, Eumenes trumpeted his relationship with little Toriaion as the

---

[151] For rough estimates of tax rates, see Monson 2015, 189–96.   [152] **D8** lines 26–27.
[153] Jonnes and Ricl 1997, 19–20; see epigraphical appendix for textual problem here.
[154] Schuler 1999, 129.   [155] E.g., Ma 2012, 75–77.   [156] Briant 1988, 137.

paradigmatic example of his beneficence and trustworthiness. Underscoring the point, he writes, "Myself, I consider the granting of your requests of no small interest to me, but it is directly related to many larger issues."[157] Eumenes was making an example of Toriaion. That is to say, the promotion of Toriaion was designed to validate Attalid sovereignty, which, as Eumenes' invocation of Roman power proves, was still quite shaky. The specter of a Seleukid return lingered in the background. Ultimately, Attalid sovereignty in lands far removed from administrative centers hinged on the establishment of a network of loyal communities. The promotion of communities to the status of polis boosted loyalty and aided in tax collection. It is possible to reconstruct a pattern of behavior discernible from very early on. This is now particularly true in the region of the Milyas, a crucial zone of overland passage between the Aegean and the Mediterranean. The Milyas guarded the approach from the upper Maeander Valley and rocky and rebellious Pisidia, down to the Pamphylian plain and the Attalids' foundation at Antalya. The recent discovery of three fragmentary inscriptions from Olbasa allows us to piece together yet another creation narrative.

Intensive research in previously underexplored highland regions of southern Anatolia has uncovered many hints of a concerted Attalid effort to integrate parts of the region. One of the most interesting is a fragmentary letter from the citadel at Belenli, the site of Olbasa, overlooking the Lysis Valley. Even in its lacunose state of preservation, the document can be seen to be another grant of polis status in exchange for loyalty, taxes, and surveillance of strategic terrain. With Attalid support, the indigenous Milyadeis and Pisidians of the town of Olbasa gained their own version of the polis. The request granted involves the organization of a citizenry (*politeuesthai*) and the assignation of new territories and stable sources of revenue earmarked for the public life of the new city. Olbasa gained dominance over two nearby villages, Motoura, a Pisidian toponym, and a place called Kidoas (?) – an important reminder that the polis was always achieved at someone else's expense. Here again, the Attalids took a keen interest in deciding who was in and who was out. Certain populations were excluded from consideration for the new citizenship. However, the basis for this exclusion was not a cultural or ethnic litmus test. Rather, the Attalids seem to have been concerned to safeguard their own estates in the fertile valley of the Lysis, and therefore excluded a force of guards living on the land.[158]

---

[157] D8 lines 17–19.
[158] Letter: *SEG* XLVIII 1532. For Attalid authorship, see Schuler 1999, 124 n. 2. See also the ed. pr. of Milner 1998, 65–66.

When we next meet Olbasa in our sources, in a new (unpublished) inscription, which Thomas Corsten found built into a modern wall in Belenli, the Anatolian town is a full-fledged polis. The year must have been around 182/1, as the text announces the arrival of sacred ambassadors from the city of Pergamon, bringing word of the promotion of the Nikephoria to Panhellenic status.[159] Designed as a permanent celebration of Attalid victories over Antiochos III and Prousias I of Bithynia, Eumenes promoted the Nikephoria as a Panhellenic festival on par with the Olympic and Pythian games, to be rung in every five years with the pilgrimage of athletes and sacred delegations to the imperial capital, as well as a sacred truce (*asylia*), which protected a rebuilt extramural shrine and holy grove, the Nikephorion. In fact, the foundation of this festival crowned what amounted to the rebirth of the city of Pergamon.[160] The Pergamene ambassadors who arrived in Olbasa were making the rounds, coming, perhaps, from nearby Caria or the island of Kos. Other delegations were sent to the heart of mainland Greece, where the Aitolians duly validated the Attalids' signature festival. From now until the end of the dynasty, the polis of Pergamon, with the daughters of its elite citizens cast in a starring role as the priestesses of Athena Nikephoros, played host to an international event, a festival that celebrated the glory of the kings and showcased their city.[161]

So it was to this gathering of Greeks, a conclave of poleis, that Eumenes now invited Olbasa, the quintessential Hellenistic newcomer. Remarkably, just a few years removed from a momentous refoundation, the people of Olbasa possessed the civic armature required of participants. They received and honored the ambassadors with a decree duly passed by an assembly (*dêmos*). Moreover, they were even prepared to send their own citizens, to sacrifice in common (*synthuein*) with those gathered at the Nikephoria, to enter the competitions in Pergamon, to vie with Greeks, and to compete *as* Greeks. Indeed, victory seems assured, as the decree seems to anticipate honors.[162] Humble Olbasa acts as the peer of the capital city, the polis of Pergamon. Prayers for its people, for the people of Olbasa, and for the king and his family are uttered in the same breath. Similarly, in a Pergamene

---

[159] New Olbasa decree is announced by Corsten 2008, 116. On the Nikephoria, see Allen 1983, 123–29.

[160] Strabo 13.4.2.

[161] Notice Eumenes' express motivation to inaugurate and celebrate the festival with his brothers, his mother, *and* the people (*dêmos*) of Pergamon (e.g., IX 1^2 1 179 lines 12–13).

[162] This seems to be the expectation of the lacunose lines 14–16 of the unpublished decree (Thomas Corsten, personal comm.).

decree for Metris, priestess of Athena Nikephoros, blessings are at once counted for "our people and for all the other peoples (τῷ τε ἡμετέρῳ δήμῳ καὶ τοῖς ἄλλοις ἅπασιν)."[163] It then comes as no surprise that in the local skirmishes that later broke out between the Attalids and the ever-recalcitrant Pisidians, Olbasa never broke ranks with the kingdom. In fact, when the city had recovered from the damage of those conflicts, Olbasa passed a decree in honor of two Attalid officials, further revealing an institutional framework at once of the polis and of the kingdom.[164]

Paradoxically, what one might be tempted to call the Attalids' policy on settlement, in fact, largely ignores the issue of settlement itself. Their attitude toward these towns was a mixture of intense interest in the shape of institutions and total disinterest in engineering cultural homogeneity. A modification is in order of the standard view that the Attalids were liberal monarchs who left cities to themselves and rigorously promoted Hellenism. When a polis was born, the Attalids took pains to hand-select the new citizenry, but they do not seem to have minded where these people domiciled. Nor do they seem to have been much concerned with which gods the new citizens worshipped. On the contrary, while the Olbasa dossier shows a royal imprint on the political transformation of yet another Anatolian town, it also contains another precious glimpse of the ecumenicalism that helps explain Pergamon's success. Olbasa's invitation to the Nikephoria must be seen in the context of a series of letters that the Attalids wrote on the subject, published in cities and sanctuaries across the Greek world. Between those that survive, we can compare the language of official piety. The two from Delphi, one belonging to the Aitolians, vaunt the Attalids' piety "toward the gods," namely, Athena, the honoree of the hour, and, of course, Apollo.[165] The two from the eastern Aegean and Asia Minor speak of honoring Athena "especially (*malista*) among the other gods."[166] By contrast, the Olbasa text nods to Athena and, significantly, "all the other gods" (ἄλλοις θεοῖς πᾶσιν in line 2). Instead of coupling this distinctly Pergamene Athena with a Panhellenic Apollo or singling her out from the rest of the Olympic pantheon, the rhetoric of this letter aligns the new goddess with, literally, any god or goddess that the Anatolians held in reverence. The sleight of hand and the invention of tradition should be familiar from the story of the birth of Dionysoupolis. It demonstrates a sustained sensitivity to local

---

[163] *I.Pergamon* 167 = *OGIS* 299. [164] *SEG* XLIV 1108.
[165] *Syll.*³ 629 lines 8, 13; *Syll.*³ 630 lines 2, 15. [166] *RC* 49 line 16; *RC* 50 line 3.

identity, which was clearly lacking, for example, in the contemporary Seleukid transformation of Jerusalem into a polis.[167]

What the new evidence from Olbasa and Toriaion suggests is that following the Romans' departure, the Attalids initiated a flurry of surgical interventions in the countryside, promoting a certain number of towns by securing their territories and revenues and by granting them polis institutions. A long-lost and so forever enigmatic inscription copied in 1885 in the city of Uluborlu in Turkey's Lake District, the site of Apollonia ("in Pisidia"/in Phrygia Paroreios), records a boundary dispute between that city and the Pisidian community of Tymbriada.[168] It seems to be an honorific decree of this old, probably Seleukid colony of Apollonia, thanking an early Roman official (ca. 85–25 BCE?) for a brutally large transfer of territory away from the indigenous Tymbriada. These were prized lands on the eastern side of the lakes of Hoyran and Eğirdir, among them the so-called Snake's Head and the land of Ouramma, perhaps a former Hittite principality between the lakes and the Sultan Dağ mountain range. According to the decree's opening lines, a certain late Hellenistic king had awarded these lands to Tymbriada, a decision now being overturned. Whereas Hellenistic Tymbriada had triumphed, Roman Tymbriada seems to have been overpowered. Pinched between Apollonia and Antioch-near-Pisidia, it faded into insignificance in later Antiquity, parceled into imperial estates. Yet clearly it had avoided the predations of the neighboring colonies and even waxed in power with the aid of an earlier king. Perhaps, like Toriaion, Tymbriada had also briefly been a polis. Though the identity of the king has never been confirmed, an Attalid is most likely to have been the one meddling here. Indeed, Gustav Hirschfeld made the proposal in the nineteenth century, though William Ramsay argued, wrongly we now know, that Pergamene control never extended to this region.[169] Rostovtzeff even writes, "The victorious Eumenes would not give his own territory to an unimportant foreign [sic] city like [Tymbriada]."[170] As we have seen, such communities were in fact important partners of the Attalids, frequently receiving territory and even polis status. Following a suggestion of Ramsay, Hadrien Bru proposes Mithridates VI, though he can find no secure motive for the Pontic king's

---

[167] However, on the administrative history of Seleukid Jerusalem, see Ma 2020, esp. 88–89, tempering any view of ham-handedness.
[168] For new text and historical geography, see Bru 2017, 89–104.
[169] Hirschfeld 1888, 591–92; Ramsay 1918, 143.   [170] Rostovtzeff 1923, 364 n. 3.

support of the Pisidians of Tymbriada against the Hellenes of Apollonia.[171] With the Attalids, the motive is readily apparent.

That the populations of new poleis often remained fixed in place is the implication of two major projects of synoicism, notionally, the process of combining multiple settlements into a single conurbation. Apollonis, on the road between Sardis and the capital, was the product of one such synoicism. We hear of one of the brothers of Eumenes II carrying out the king's design, taking forethought (*pronoia*) to produce a city of happiness (*eudaimonia*).[172] That may have involved constructing a gymnasium on a hilltop near modern Mecidiye. It does not seem to have involved displacing the nearby settlers at Doidye and a place called "-espoura," whose own citizenries, nevertheless, probably fed the new body politic at Apollonis.[173] In short, a polis was born, but many of the people stayed put. This is just as apparent in the case of Philadelphia in southeastern Lydia, a foundation attributed to Attalos II. Numerous *katoikiai* already existed in the territory of the new polis. There were both Macedonian and indeed Mysian *katoikiai*, such as Kastollos.[174] The corpus of inscriptions from the territory of Philadelphia attests to the endurance of these towns – both as places of settlement and as civic organisms in their own right. Evidently, it was not at their expense that Philadelphia came into being. Philadelphia was a strange place; at least Strabo thought so, marveling at its layout.[175] What were its founders thinking? They had built the city on highly seismic land, and Strabo would have seen the devastation of the earthquake of 17 CE. The Augustan geographer thought that most of the population lived in the countryside in order to avoid the dangerous impact of an earthquake in the city. Yet, perhaps, many people had never known the alternative of dense urban living. In this scenario, the Attalids had left the choice of domicile to the people of Philadelphia, including the privileged

---

[171] Bru 2017, 104. [172] *TAM* V 2 1187.

[173] On Doidye, see Cohen 1995, 206. In particular, the dedication of its Makedones in 161/0 should alert us to its survival as a locus of identity and settlement after the foundation of Apollonis. However, its once presumed location on a hilltop 500 m from Apollonis appears to be a second-millennium BCE citadel. See Roosevelt 2019, 158 n. 71. On "-espoura," see Cohen 1995, 207; and on Apollonis in Lydia, 201–4. Politically, Apollonis seems also to have absorbed the citizens of a small community called Kamai. A political union (*sympoliteia*) preserved Kamai's identity well into the Roman period. Geographically, however, little changed for Kamai. As Robert argues (*BE* 1979 no. 426), Kamai endured as a distinct settlement.

[174] For the full range of settlements in the territory of Philadelphia, see remarks of Petzl in *TAM* V 3, ix–xi. For *katoikiai*, see Mitchell 2018, 20; *TAM* V 3 1423, 1429, 1669. Macedonian population already at Philadelphia, see further: Pleket 2011, 171; Mitchell 2018, 18 with n. 33. Mysian population at Kastollos, *IG* II^2 9977; **D2** Side A lines 3–4.

[175] Strabo 13.4.10.

Macedonian and Mysian settlers already on the land of the royal-name city in the lush if geologically precarious Kogamos Valley.

All this makes the Attalids stand out from their peers. Admittedly, we can discern certain shock-and-awe behaviors, typical of high Hellenistic royal urbanism. Closer to home, they did move the city of Gargara from the old Attalid haunt of Mount Ida down to the coast and perhaps also forcibly restocked it with refugees from Miletoupolis.[176] Some have suspected a refoundation of Aeolian Aigai, but only on the basis of its spectacular market building and terrace architecture.[177] On the Pamphylian coast, Attaleia appeared, though we know so little about its foundation, which may have simply added girth to the preexisting Korykos.[178] However, the impact of Attalid power on settlement was much more often precisely that sighted by Felix Pirson in an intensive study of the micro-region of Pergamon itself and its ports. If the kings had a free hand anywhere, it was here. Around the Gulf of Elaia, Pirson shows that settlement structure remains static, but a new hierarchy emerges.[179] In short, the Attalids' ideological preference was for integration by any means, not for urbanism at any cost. Alongside Polybius' claim that Eumenes II surpassed his rivals as benefactor of the polis, we must consider the evidence presented here. In many parts of rural Anatolia, the Attalids achieved integration without imposing cookie-cutter polis institutions or forcing nucleation. Rather, they forced interaction on the full spectrum of civic organisms emerging in the hinterland of the Aegean.

---

[176] Cohen 1995, 152; Strabo 13.1.58.   [177] Heinle 2015, 155–56.
[178] Cohen 1995, 337–38, on the vexed question of Attaleia and Korykos in Pamphylia (Strabo 14.4.1). Again, note continuity across the third and second centuries in the cemetery of the Halk Pazarı Mevkii necropolis (Akman and Tosun 2012, 55).
[179] Pirson 2012, 219–32.

5 | Hastening to the Gymnasium

> They hastened to have a share in the unlawful ceremony at the summons of the discus calling them to the palaistra.
>
> (2 Macc 4:41)

The Roman legate Gaius Sulpicius, Polybius tells us, was a man consumed, given over to madness, reveling in his quarrel with Eumenes II of Pergamon (31.6.5).[1] In 164, a perplexed Senate, facing a realignment of power in Asia Minor, dispatched Sulpicius to the region on a fact-finding mission.[2] On arrival, Sulpicius solicited allegations against the king by posting notices in the most important cities. Anyone who wished could come to Sardis at an appointed time and be heard. Sulpicius then retreated to the gymnasium of Sardis where he sat for 10 days, holding court and taking complaints. The Roman investigator appears to have been energetic, systematic, even primed for a fight, but mad? What to make of the characterization of Polybius? It no doubt reflects the depth of the Roman assault on the ideological underpinnings of Attalid power and indeed of the world in which the Achaean statesman had come of age. Wherein, then, lies that depth? It has long been noted that Sulpicius was appealing directly to Attalid subjects in Attalid territory.[3] The choice of Sardis as the venue must also have stung. The former satrapal capital had grown in significance under the Seleukids, and had acquired under the Attalids the distinction of a cistophoric mint, if not a royal residence.[4]

---

[1] ἅτε παρεστηκὼς ἄνθρωπος τῇ διανοίᾳ καὶ φιλοδοξῶν ἐν τῇ πρὸς Εὐμένην διαφορᾷ.
[2] For the wider historical context, see Hansen 1971, 125.
[3] See, e.g., Walbank 1957–79, vol. 3, 471.
[4] Tralles, with its secondary Attalid palace, seems to have supplanted Sardis in the administrative hierarchy. See Savalli-Lestrade 2001, 82–86. As for Sardis, the current state of archaeological knowledge of Hellenistic Sardis is presented by articles in Berlin and Kosmin 2019. (For earlier ideas, see Capdetrey 2007, 369–71; Ratté 2008.) Of note is the hypothesis that Antiochos I – not Attalos I, ca. 226/5 – was responsible for the poliadization of Sardis, making the second quarter of the third century decisive, in terms of both public, architectural change and private, material, cultural change at the domestic level. Frustratingly little is known of the Seleukid city plan, and Stinson (2019, 140) is rightly cautious, writing of "*at least* a gymnasium ... and a theater" by the late third century, while Berlin and Kosmin (2019, 238) add a stoa with shops in what they call the new, civic-oriented middle city. Cf. doubts of Kaye 2016, 553–56. The Attalid downgrade of

Yet Sulpicius was not the first hot-tempered invader to occupy the gymnasium of Sardis. Antiochos III had even brought an army into its confines during the siege of 215/14.[5] Seleukid forces remained quartered in the gymnasium when Sardis fell, one new imposition among many that would have served to chasten its people for their disloyalty. The next year, however, Antiochos eased the city's punitive fiscal burden, and simultaneously lightened the occupation. In both cases, the city's gymnasium was a focus of his beneficence. He restored the gymnasium to the Sardians in its "former condition" – no mean feat – and he set life in the place on firm ground for the future. Much as he later did for Herakleia-under-Latmos, the king earmarked royal revenues for an oil fund (*elaiochristion*), one which would provide 200 *metrêtai* of oil to the *neoi* each year (*SEG* XXXVII 859; *SEG* XXXIX 1283 and 1285). Scholarship has always recognized the affections of Hellenistic kings for the gymnasium and "those who frequent it."[6] The charged and politicized nature of this mode of interaction is on full display in the famous episode from Jerusalem (see the epigraph above), an incident roughly contemporaneous with the visit of Sulpicius to Sardis: a group of young Judean priests approached Antiochos IV as members of an incipient gymnasium under royal patronage; a cataclysm ensued.[7] Now, with the recent publication of the earmarking documents from Sardis and Herakleia, the subsequent discovery of more inscriptions relating to Attalid involvement with the gymnasium, it has become ever more clear that the institution of the gymnasium started to take on new significance ca. 200 BCE and, by mid-century, constituted a primary site of interaction between cities and kings. Though the evidence is sparse, this is very likely to have been the case in Sardis in 164. In the late

---

Sardis in favor of Tralles completes a shift, already under way, by which the Royal Road ceded prominence to the Common Road (Kosmin 2019, 88–89) and, I would add, to the Maeander Corridor. Ultimately, an Anatolian imperial geography replaced a Near Eastern one. The new stratigraphy of the theater of Sardis presents a caveat to the hypothesis of an Attalid turn away from Sardis. A first phase belongs to the second quarter of the third century; a second, the first theater in stone, ca. 175–150. Despite its scale and monumentality, on the same plan as the later Roman theater, seating ca. 10,000, it seems hazardous to assign the theater to Eumenes II, as Berlin (2019, 66–67). Indeed, Ladstätter argues (2016, 262–65; 2019, 204) that Ephesus received its first stone theater with its lavish stage building in the very same period, i.e., under Eumenes II. Yet why the Attalids – who are not known as theater builders – deserve the credit, is unclear.

[5] Gauthier 1989, 37–38.
[6] For a digest of earlier scholarship, see Schmidt-Dounas 2000, 52–61. For "those who frequent the gymnasium" and the various locutions of corporate identity, see Gauthier 2006, 481. Generally, on the Hellenistic gymnasium and ephebate, A. Chankowski 2010 (for the Greek cities of the Aegean and Asia Minor) and the catalogue of Kennell 2006 are fundamental.
[7] For the ephebes of Jerusalem, see Honigman 2014, 199–214.

160s, the Attalids were making gifts in support of gymnasium life in places as distant and different as Rhodes, once an enemy and always a rival, and the city of Delphi, not to mention in "free" Miletus and Kos, or in Andros, a garrisoned possession. Indeed, not more than a few years before his arrival, the gymnasium where Sulpicius set up shop would have hosted competitions during the inaugural celebration of the Panathenaia kai Eumeneia festival, which honored the goddess Athena and the Attalid king.[8] Sulpicius' presence in the gymnasium of Sardis was understood by all who observed as an affront – as it was meant to be, so much so, in fact, says Polybius, that the Greeks, as if for pity, rallied to the king (31.6.6).[9]

The Problem of the Attalids and the Gymnasium

If Hellenistic kings' interactions with the gymnasium, with the ephebate of the Greek city, and with the other institutions and groups that "had a share in the oil" form a pattern of behavior that extends across time and space, it is a pattern that is sharply pronounced among the Attalids, especially after 188.[10] Consider, by way of a contrast, how when the Seleukids came into control of Miletus, they set about rebuilding the city's sanctuary of Apollo at Didyma, a god who happened to be their tutelary divinity. The Attalids, on the other hand, also sent a message to the Panhellenic audience, but by paying for a gymnasium in the urban center of Miletus: a promise to promote the identity of each and every polis.[11] Klaus Bringmann counts 29 foundations for gymnasia in his corpus of royal gifts.[12] Of these, an impressive 13 are Attalid (**Graph 5.1**). And we can add considerably to that count. The practice certainly goes back to the dynasty's origins: Philetairos consecrated land in Thespiai to Hermes, god of the gymnasium par

---

[8] Panathenaia kai Eumeneia: *OGIS* 305; for recent comment on this festival, see Jones 2000, 5.
[9] Cf. the skepticism of Gruen 1984, 127, 181.
[10] See already Robert 1937, 84–85, for a list of Attalid gifts with special attention paid to the gymnasium. Stappmanns (2012, 247) casts the gymnasium of Pergamon as a gift from Eumenes II to the citizens of Pergamon.
[11] Cf. Marcellesi 2004, 173, on royal benefaction at Miletus: "Il n'y a guère de différence entre l'évergétisme séleucide et l'évergétisme lagide ou attalide dans la nature de dons." Of course the political imperatives had changed, but the focus of benefaction did too.
[12] The omission of Bringmann et al. 1995, no. 88 [E], from the list of gymnasium foundations in the synthesis of Schmidt-Dounas (2000, 55) seems to be a mistake, as does the omission of Bringmann et al. 1995, no. 83 [E], Demetrios Poliorcetes' dedication of "Rhodian spoils" as an oil fund in Thebes.

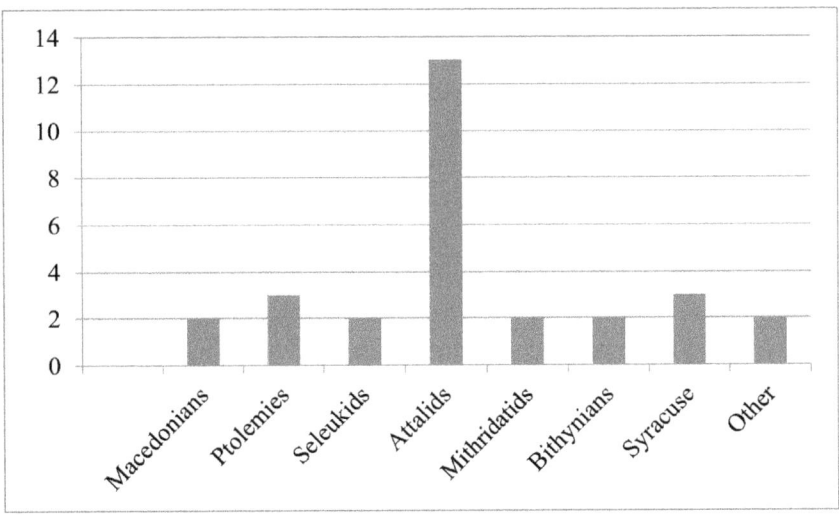

Graph 5.1 Royal gifts to gymnasia. (Data from Bringmann et al., 1995)

excellence, and earmarked its revenues for an oil fund.[13] Then, the practice intensified after Apameia: eight of the 13 foundations are securely dated post-188. In addition, the much-improved edition of the decree of Colophon for the Pergamene prince Athenaios now allows us to identify the royal gift of a *paidikê* (youth) palaistra in the background.[14] The decree for Korragos and the new documents from Metropolis and Toriaion show the integration of the polis gymnasium into the fiscal structures of the enlarged Attalid kingdom (**D1**, **D5**, and **D8**).[15] The Toriaion dossier may even illuminate *RC* 51, which Welles called a "letter of an Attalid king to military cleruchs, conferring various grants," and which he dated to the second century BCE. Its fragmentary line 24 reads, "From which [revenue source] I have given oil to the *neoi*" (ὧν ἔδωκα τοῖς νέοις εἰς τὸ ἔλαιον).[16]

---

[13] Bringmann et al. 1995, no. 88 [E], for which a date of ca. 270–263 is given. Cf. Philetairos' oil fund in Kyzikos (Bringmann et al. 1995, no. 241 [E]).

[14] Gauthier 2006 = **D10**.

[15] The Toriaion dossier was published after Bringmann et al. 1995, but it is discussed in a companion volume. See Bringmann 2000, 142.

[16] The partitive genitive must refer back to a revenue source, from the context, likely land, which is again earmarked for an oil fund. Potentially, *RC* 51 may support or vitiate the arguments laid out in what follows. The problem is that the community addressed is not identified in the surviving text. Thus we cannot determine if it is a *katoikia* or a polis. A polis is mentioned in line 14, but Welles takes it to be Pergamon itself, where some of the cleruchs will be quartered. In the case of Toriaion (**D8**), we can observe the transformation of the *katoikia* into a polis. There, it is a matter of debate whether the earlier *katoikia* possessed a gymnasium, which is then

Still, to gauge the full extent of the Attalid interest in the gymnasium, we must consider several other categories of evidence. The first is the paper trail left by courtiers, which points to the gymnasium as an interface between kings, represented by their most trusted officials, and the public. The prime example is a lamentably fragmentary decree found in southeastern Lydia, which honors a well-connected courtier named Asklepides, who at the end of a long career in the service of the Attalids served as overseer of an unnamed city, perhaps Apollonia-on-the-Maeander. The inscription describes the by-then-deceased Asklepides as having been both a citizen of Pergamon and an intimate (*syntethrammenos*) of the future Attalos II.[17] The package of posthumous honors awarded to this courtier is full of references to the multiple gymnasia of the city. What is clear from this difficult text is that one or more of the gymnasia was slated to host rituals in memory of the courtier.[18] At once an extension of the king's body and a representative of the citizenry of Pergamon, Asklepides found in the gymnasium of the unnamed polis an exquisitely convenient venue for local politics and the manufacture of collective memory.

Second, the archaeology of the gymnasium of the metropolis of Pergamon is a spectacular demonstration of the dynasty's attachment to the institution. First excavated at the turn of the century, a recent German research project has intensively reinvestigated the space (**Figs. 5.1** and **5.2**).[19] Its cascade of three terraces supported by huge retaining walls, the product of the original design and investment of Eumenes II, placed the monument at the center of the ancient spectator's visual encounter with the royal capital.[20] It evinces an unparalleled concern for the differentiation of space inside a gymnasium according to function, especially cultic. Room H seems to have housed the ruler cult, with statues of Eumenes and

---

officially recognized, or whether the creation of the gymnasium signals the creation of the polis. My view, argued infra, is that the gymnasium is a feature of the Hellenistic polis, but not a sine qua non. Moreover, evidence from Ptolemaic Thera shows that a garrison community might attract royal patronage for its gymnasium and interact with royal power on this score just as any polis would (*IG* XII 3 327 + p. 283). Fröhlich (2009, 62 n. 26) analyzes the Theran document alongside the corpus of Bringmann et al. 1995. See now a possible gymnasium at the Seleukid garrison town of Jebel Khalid on the Euphrates (Area C; Clarke 2016).

[17] Ed. pr. of the text: Malay 1999, no. 182; cf. text and commentary of *SEG* XLIX 1540, esp. for question of authorship; Aneziri and Damaskos 2004, 259 n. 89. For the identity of Asklepides and further speculation on authorship, see *SEG* LIII 1342 and Thonemann 2008, 50.

[18] See Kaye and Souza 2013. Apollonia-on-the-Maeander: Petzl 2001, 56; Thonemann 2003, 100–102. Cf. Patrice Hamon *BE* (2014) no. 426.

[19] For earlier research, see Radt 1999, 113–34.

[20] For gymnasium and urban plan of Pergamon, see Stappmanns 2012. On attribution to Eumenes II, see also Pirson 2012, 215.

The Problem of the Attalids and the Gymnasium 239

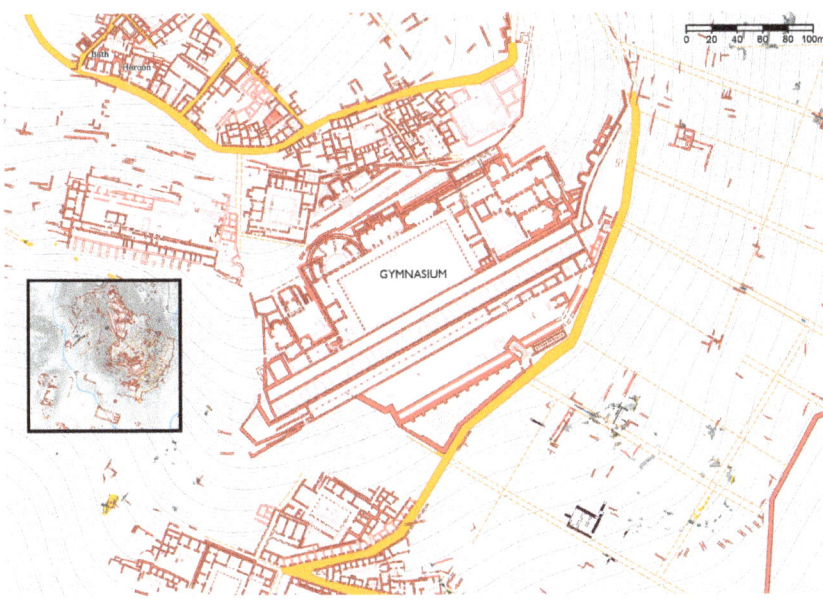

Figure 5.1 Plan of the gymnasium of Pergamon in relation to adjacent monuments and current reconstruction of street grid (courtesy of Pergamon Excavation of the German Archaeological Institute; https://geoserver.dainst.org/maps/5548/view).

Figure 5.2 Gymnasium of Pergamon, looking east across the palaistra of the upper terrace (courtesy of Pergamon Excavation of the German Archaeological Institute; photo: Ulrich Mania).

Philetairos next to one of Herakles.[21] Below, the sacred quarter of the Middle Terrace represents an unusual internal *temenos*. Crucially, it is the largest gymnasium on record in the Hellenistic world.[22] At ca. 20,000 m^2, it approaches double the size of a normal city's gymnasium.[23] With its three terraces and two temples, *xystos* and *paradromis* (running tracks), a precinct 212 m long at its greatest extent, and with an open-air palaistra measuring 35 × 75 m, it is in fact the largest integrated building complex in the entire city of Pergamon. Further, a recent revision of the city's street plan highlights the central importance of the gymnasium to the city of Eumenes II. A decade of soundings and geophysical prospection have ruled out a grid plan with streets oriented toward towers on Eumenes' wall. Instead, streets of various modules are oriented neatly toward the entrances and specific features of the gymnasium.[24] Set just below the old, so-called wall of Philetairos, which became, in effect, a lower boundary for the Upper/Old City with its palace district, religious monuments, and public spaces, the gigantism of the new gymnasium served to anchor the street plan and visual axes of the neighborhoods of the Lower/New City. The western entrance was fronted with a public fountain alongside the city's main arterial road. Indeed, for the New City of Eumenes II and his successors, this gymnasium complex appears to have been the sole public space of note, with the date of the Lower Agora now fixed in the early Roman period.[25] Wörrle has recently argued that one of the principal functions of the Pergamene gymnasium was to strengthen polis identity in Pergamon, which is often difficult to discern elsewhere in the city.[26] This building project may be simply the most resplendent evidence of negotiations that took place in many cities between elites and the Attalids. Poliad identity achieved stable footing, but the bonds of dependence were also strengthened. The *Großes Gymnasion* dates to the period of downhill urban expansion under Eumenes II, and evidence for a third-century gymnasium at Pergamon is extremely thin, limited to a single inscription, dated by the

---

[21] Hoff 2004, 384.   [22] Mathys et al. 2012, 271.
[23] Hoff 2009, 251–52. Ca. 10,000–15,000 m^2 seems to be the norm. Only the gymnasia of Messene and of the sanctuary of Olympia reach the same proportions. See also on these figures, Trümper 2015, 173 n. 24.
[24] Pirson 2012, 215–16. For the earlier street plan, see Wulf-Rheidt 1994.
[25] The results of recent test trenches and ceramic analysis have changed the chronology of the Lower Agora. It is now believed to be a post-Attalid monument of the first century BCE and first century CE. See Pirson 2014b, 129–31; Pirson 2015, 122–26.
[26] Wörrle 2007; Bielfeldt 2010.

notoriously unreliable criterion of letter forms (*I.Pergamon* 9).[27] On any reckoning, Eumenes II placed the gymnasium at the center of civic life in the polis of Pergamon. And yet only when the dynasty fell did responsibility for the oil fund pass from the royal treasury to the gymnasiarch.[28] The institution remained to the end a joint venture of king and citizenry.[29]

Finally, indirect and circumstantial evidence of Attalid involvement with the gymnasium abounds. The city of Tralles can stand as a case study. It has produced a Hellenistic victor list, mentioning *neoi*, which Wilhelm Dittenberger dated to the second century, and possessed a gymnasium by the time of Augustus.[30] While the proximity of ancient Tralles to a modern Turkish military installation puts 65% of the site off-limits to archaeology, an impressive Roman bath–gymnasium complex has been identified. Throughout Asia Minor, complexes of this sort stand over the remains of Hellenistic gymnasia, in many cases, over a gymnasium that the Attalids are known to have patronized.[31] At Apameia, the Attalids received Tralles as a "gift," stripping it of its Seleukid dynastic title, but adorning it with a cistophoric mint and a palace.[32] An ostotheke that was found 7 km east of Aydın/Tralles bears the names of several Attalid officials and their wives, attesting to the city's importance as an administrative center with an open-air military camp on its outskirts.[33] In many ways, Tralles resembles Ephesus, where a gymnasium foundation is known only by indirect means, namely, through an ephebic dedication to (Hermes), Herakles, and King

---

[27] Radt 1999, 115; Mathys et al. 2012, 271. Also of relevance here is the problem of the date of the main temple in the gymnasium of Pergamon, likely that of Asklepios. The orientation of the Ionic temple fits with the rest of the complex. However, the building contains pieces of an older Doric building. These have been tentatively attributed to the (yet-to-be-discovered) extra-mural Nikephorion, which was destroyed by Philip V in 201. See Radt 1999, 131.

[28] See Paul Jacobstahl in *MDAI(A)* 33 (1908), 381–83,3, with corrections of Hugo Hepding in *MDAI(A)* 35 (1910), 419.

[29] Wörrle 2007, 215: "eine Art joint venture von König und Demos."

[30] *Syll.*^{3} 671 = *I.Tralleis* 107; Strabo 12.8.18.

[31] For the Roman bath–gymnasium phenomenon in Asia Minor and its physical relationship to the Hellenistic gymnasium, see Yegül 2010, 154–80, esp. 155–57. On Roman administrative centers built on top of Hellenistic gymnasia, see further Burkhalter 1992. For the modern obstacles to excavation at Tralles, see Dinç 2003, 4. Dinç notes a first-century BCE predecessor to the bath–gymnasium complex, destroyed in the earthquake of 26 (p. 33). However, the claim is also made that Apatourios of Alabanda built a gymnasium in Tralles (p. 4). This figure, known only from Vitr. *De arch.* 7.5.5, is in fact believed to have been active in the second century BCE – see Howe et al. 1999, 268. But Vitruvius mentions only Apatourios' *ekklêsiastêrion* at Tralles, not, as Dinç writes, a theater and a gymnasium (p. 4). More recent excavations have focused on the western necropolis. For discussion, see Saraçoğlu 2011. Note the lack of Classical or Hellenistic remains in Ateşlier 2015.

[32] Polyb. 21.46.10; Plin. *HN* 35.72; Vitr. *De arch.* 2.8.9.   [33] *SEG* XLVI 1434.

Eumenes.³⁴ Ephesus too was a gift city, and has produced epigraphic evidence for the local presence of royal officials, the *hêgemônes* and *strategoi* who dedicate to Eumenes II and Queen Stratonike (SEG XXXIII 942). It was an Ephesian *neos* that Attalos II considered the right kind of young man to be educated alongside the future Attalos III.³⁵ One can easily imagine that the king was just as familiar with the *neoi* of Tralles as he was with their coevals in Ephesus.

This chapter offers a new explanation for the profound connection between Pergamon and the gymnasium, which casts the Attalids as participants and agents of change in the social history of ancient Greece. It argues that benefaction of the gymnasium was one more way in which the Attalids deftly synched local, civic culture with imperial fiscal structures. This is a mode of interaction that is not exclusively, but rather characteristically Attalid.³⁶ What is unexplained is its efflorescence during the Pergamene *floruit* – and what longer-term effects Pergamon may have had on this famous incubator of Hellenes. To date, scholarship has identified the pattern, but neither explained it adequately nor charted the ramifications. One has long struggled to divine the motivations behind individual royal gifts.³⁷ Nevertheless, the Attalid affinity for the gymnasium is usually understood, first, as a straightforward expression of Pergamene Panhellenism and, second, as part of a general tendency among Hellenistic kings to use the gymnasium to manufacture loyal, worshipping subjects. To take but two examples, Robert calls the gymnasium "this characteristic edifice of Greek culture" and "the place set aside for the royal cult and demonstrations of loyalty toward the Hellenistic kings."³⁸ For Dreyer, the kings wanted to use the gymnasium "to create bonds of loyalty by influencing children and the youth, and to recommend themselves to the adult citizens as benefactors and supporters of Greek culture."³⁹ Both statements collapse the evolution of the gymnasium into a synchronic

---

[34] Bringmann et al. 1995, no. 266 [E].
[35] Knibbe 1964–65, 1–6; for important emendations of this text, see also Jean and Louis Robert *BE* (1968) no. 464; see also Engelmann 1975; Herrmann 1976, 233–34.
[36] See Savalli-Lestrade 2005, 15 n. 18; Hoff 2009, 260.   [37] See Veyne 1976, 228–30.
[38] Robert 1960, 124–25: "cet édifice caractéristique de la culture grecque ... le lieu par élection où se manifestait le culte royal avec le loyalisme envers les souverains hellénistiques." For the manufacture of loyal subjects, see also Gauthier 1989, 93.
[39] Dreyer 2004, 218: "wollten durch den frühen Einfluß auf Kinder und Jugendliche neue Loyalitätsbindungen schaffen und sich den erwachsenen Bürgern als Wohltäter und Förderer hellenischer Kultur empfehlen." See also Schmidt-Dounas (2000, 60), for whom the gymnasium guarantees the continuity of Greek culture, and the Attalids, as the supreme patrons of Greek culture, are the natural benefactors of the gymnasium.

snapshot. It is a remarkable fact that for Aristotle in the fourth century BCE, the gymnasium was not an essential feature of the polis.[40] For the city's takeover of the gymnasium was a process transpiring over the course of the philosopher's life. By contrast, for Pausanias, writing in the second century CE about the modest settlement of Panopeas in Phokis, a proper polis needed a gymnasium.[41] Between the age of Aristotle and the time of Pausanias, a major change occurred. Did the Attalids spur or accelerate it?

There is no denying that the Attalids represented themselves as the avatars of the Greeks.[42] One aspect of their *Kulturpolitik* was to establish themselves in centers of international significance to Hellenes, such as Delphi, Delos, and later Athens, and to pose as the champions of the Hellene in the never-ending war against the Barbarian – in their day, figured as the Galatian. In these respects, their politics were Panhellenic, as Lynette Mitchell understands the term. In her study of the origin and development of concepts of Panhellenism in Archaic and Classical Greece, Mitchell stresses "the very complexity and flexibility of Panhellenism that makes it so difficult, on the one hand, to define, and, on the other, to control."[43] Key elements of an earlier Panhellenic ideology remained vital in the Hellenistic period, chief among them, the related themes of supra-poliad unity (*koinê homonoia*) and commitment to a war of liberation against the Barbarian, both spelled out in Chremonides' decree of 269/8 (*IG* II² 686 + 687).[44] These may be the wellsprings of the visual rhetoric of Attalid art, but they will not help explain Attalid involvement with the gymnasium.[45] Some might imagine a cultural Panhellenism behind this behavior, a concern to unify Hellenes around a shared *paideia* in the nascent Library of the capital as much as in the gymnasia of the cities. We should not confuse motivation with effect. In the most general terms, the gymnasium created and sustained a Panhellenic community of shared cultural practice. But by patronizing the gymnasia, the Attalids were sustaining polis identities, not suppressing them. Paradoxically, Pergamene ideology was by no means supra-poliad; it exalted particularism. For Polybius, Eumenes II was his generation's greatest royal benefactor of Greek cities (*poleis Hellênidas*) (32.8.5).[46]

---

[40] Arist. *Pol.* 1321b.   [41] Pausanias 10.4.1.   [42] Gruen 2000; Schalles 1985.
[43] L. Mitchell 2007, xviii.
[44] L. Mitchell 2007, 208. For the complicated question of the date of Chremonides' decree, see *SEG* LVI 190.
[45] For Attalid visual rhetoric, see Stewart 2004, 228–32; Seaman 2016.
[46] Cf. Bringmann et al. 1995, no. 313 [E], an honorific decree of Delphi for Eumenes II, which mentions both his tireless effort on behalf of "Hellenes" and his many gifts to "Greek cities"; and

There is also no denying that the gymnasium cemented the loyalties of Attalid subjects, but it tied people to Pergamon even as it enhanced their sense of belonging to a particular polis. Young men who enjoyed a youth spent in a palaistra equipped at royal expense – on the condition that they parade and sacrifice to the king on his birthday – were bound to fall into line as adults. Yet this drastically reduces the complexity of their experience. Young men may have been wrestling beneath portrait statues of the royal family, but they were also preparing for close combat under teachers picked by the city that they swore to defend.[47] By patronizing the gymnasium, the Attalids did not create an impassive and apolitical elite. In fact, they produced bands of *neaniskoi*, crack troops, the fighting force of the young men's association.[48] These *neaniskoi* might defend royal affairs (*basilika pragmata*), as they did in Ionian Metropolis during the War of Aristonikos, or, alternatively, they might pursue the specific military objectives of their home cities.[49] Sometimes, we cannot tell which it was, or whether it might have been both. For example, in the letter of Eumenes II to the polis of the Tabênoi (?), the mysteriously named *neaniskoi tôn oikeiôn* ("of the clan"), fought under a local big man/courtier named Koteies against the Galatians.[50] Patrice Hamon, however, has provided a new reading of the text, which also sees the group "going out against Apameia (προσελήλυθ' [ἐ]π' Ἀπάμειαν)," that is, attacking another city.[51] At any rate, the society of the gymnasium, while influential, represented a

cf. *RC* 52 where Eumenes represents himself, in accordance, it seems, with the Ionians' own claim, as (1) benefactor of "all Hellenes," (2) defender of these Hellenes against barbarians, and (3) benefactor for the welfare of "those inhabiting Greek cities" (lines 8–12); finally, cf. Bringmann et al. 1995, no. 49 [E], from Kalauria, documenting a benefaction of Eumenes II to Poseidon, the polis, and "the other Hellenes." I do not argue that a chauvinistic Pergamene Panhellenism did not exist, only that it does not adequately explain the dynasty's intensive involvement with the gymnasium.

[47] On portrait statues of the Attalids in gymnasia throughout the kingdom, see Hoff 2018, 264. Notably, these were not necessarily all cult statues.

[48] For *neaniskos* as essentially a technical term, referring to the "*neos* at arms," see Bremen 2013, 35.

[49] *I.Metropolis* 1 = **D5**. For a possible Attalid-trained ephebic artillery force at Metropolis, see Aybek and Dreyer 2011, 213. In general, Ionia in the 180s witnessed widespread inter-polis warfare without royal interference. See Ager 2007; Ma 2000, 350–51.

[50] The polis of the Tabênoi, addressed in a royal letter (*SEG* LVII 1109), has not been identified. The stone was found near Phrygian Hierapolis (Pamukkale), which fits with the mention of Apameia. Yet if the addressee were Carian Tabai, the stone would need to be considered a *pierre errante*. The ed. pr. is Guizzi 2006. Guizzi translates *neaniskoi tôn oikeiôn*, "giovani dei 'familiari,'" while Thonemann (2013b, 16) terms the group the "wider clan" of Koteies. See also Ritti et al. 2008, no. 3. Further on the episode, see Thonemann 2013b, 15–16; Ma 2013a, 60 n. 44 on the identity of the addressee.

[51] Patrice Hamon *BE* (2009) no. 440.

small share of the kingdom's population. If loyalty alone were at stake, the Attalids would have been much better off putting their money elsewhere. Surely, grain funds or important public buildings such as *bouleuteria* (council houses) were gifts better suited for the desired result.

Recent scholarship on the Hellenistic polis, with its insistence on the survival and vitality of polis institutions after the Battle of Chaironeia (338 BCE), proposes a different explanation. For Andrzej Chankowski, the cities of Asia Minor stood to gain the most from the interaction.[52] In his model, unlike the gymnasia of the cities of Antigonid Macedonia or of the Syracusan *epikrateia*, the gymnasia of Attalid cities produced citizen soldiers. In other words, the civic institution lay outside the recruitment structure of the royal army. And because the cities profited the most, so the argument goes, civic initiative and agency must lie behind this pattern of royal behavior. In short, the gymnasium survived because it helped the polis survive; Attalid patronage simply tracked alongside.[53] Yet the case of Toriaion (**D8**), on which the argument hinges, in fact points up the weakness of any explanation founded on assumptions of *cui bono*. Eumenes II offered to provide Toriaion with several ready-made institutions, among them, an oil fund that he supported with an earmark. While Chankowski recognizes the gift as evidence of the Attalids' active promotion of the gymnasium, he reduces Eumenes to an automaton.[54] The king may have had a model in mind, but not one invented in his own chancery. Rather, we must imagine, Eumenes adopted a model of interaction that took shape in cities such as Herakleia-under-Latmos in the third century.[55] For Chankowski, Toriaion demonstrates once again the inability of the kings to come up with their own ideas in the face of the "vitality of the institutions of the polis." The popularity of the gymnasium "in and of itself" justified the choice.[56] On this account, the Hellenistic kings affected neither the

---

[52] A. Chankowski 2009, 98–103.   [53] A. Chankowski 2010, 438–40.
[54] A. Chankowski 2009, 101: "Il s'agit donc d'une pratique administrative récurrente."
[55] *SEG* XXXIX 1283 and 1285. On the antiquity of the arrangement in Herakleia, I am agnostic. I am unwilling to take these cities at their word when they claim to have held a privilege "*ex archês.*"
[56] A. Chankowski 2009, 114: "l'incapacité des souverains à s'appuyer sur une autre modèle que celui de la cité, et la vitalité des institutions de la cité qui diffusent dans différentes régions du monde grec les mêmes modèles socio-culturels ... la popularité du modèle civique du gymnase *justifie à elle* seule son instauration" (emphasis added). Similarly, Daubner 2015, 40: "We should not assume that this connection reveals much about the relationship of the ruler to the gymnasium or any particular interest in this institution on his part, but it is important for his relation to the polis."

diffusion nor the shape of an institution born fully formed in fourth-century Athens.

The search for the prime mover in this interaction is futile. For new poleis, we can only guess at what preceded the formalization of the gymnasium in places such as Phrygia, Cappadocia, or Judaea.[57] For the old, coastal poleis of Asia Minor, our first glimpse of the institution is often no earlier than the second century BCE.[58] Instead, we ought to seek models for the Hellenistic polis that reflect more faithfully the staggered vision of polis actors: local concerns in the foreground, but the king, ever present, on the horizon.[59] Our challenge is to make plain the links between local and high politics that were once so obvious. Our difficulty in so doing is acute when it comes to the king and the gymnasium. For example, one has struggled to understand why third-century Halikarnassos asked "King Ptolemy" for "permission (*synchôrein*)" to renovate its gymnasium, "so that the *neoi* should have a gymnasium and the *paides* should reclaim the *paidikê palaistra* that the *neoi* are currently using."[60] The city had sent an embassy to the king before it announced a public subscription.[61] This is a curious detail. In what sense did Halikarnassos need royal permission to renovate its gymnasium? Léopold Migeotte, plausibly, suspects that the Halikarnassians were fishing for a contribution from the king, which they may well have obtained.[62] What we know for certain is that the king figured from the beginning in the city's planning. It is unclear in which sense, if any, they were required to contact Alexandria before undertaking a public works project that would marshal the city's resources and loyalties. The course of action, it seems, simply implied royal participation. In the panorama of their city that Halikarnassos presented to Ptolemy, the king could find himself.

To explain the Attalids' promotion of the gymnasium by recourse to its popularity is to risk a circular argument. Indeed, the institution reached the peak of its popularity in the second century, with an ephebate attested in

---

[57] See Bringmann 2004 for the process by which a new polis might adopt the institution of the gymnasium.
[58] On the chronological spread of the evidence and the resultant historiographical difficulties, see A. Chankowski 2010, 435.
[59] On the historiographical challenge, see Ma 1999, 1. [60] Migeotte 1984, no. 101 lines 10–13.
[61] Migeotte 1984, no. 102.
[62] Migeotte (1984, 318–19) also offers more nuanced translations of "*synchôrein*." Similarly, Hamon (2009, 357 n. 18) prefers the French "concession" for *synchôresis* in the decree for Eirenias (*SEG* XXXVI 1046 Block I lines 4–6). In any case, if Ptolemy did provide funds to Halikarnassos, and the subscription was only meant to cover a shortfall, as Migeotte speculates, this text would need to be added to the corpus of Bringmann et al. 1995.

65 cities. Yet surely royal – and especially Attalid – patronage and promotion helped swell the ranks. Consequently, the gymnasium as we know it is also an artifact of Hellenistic monarchy. An institution that we usually think of as quintessentially civic was transformed by the kings it eventually outlived. The second-century Attalids encountered this institution at a particular point in its development. This was not the *ephebeia* of late Classical Athens or Eretria, which molded large age classes into the core of the citizen-army, some 500–600 young men at a time in Lykourgan Athens, as the gymnasium found architectural expression in the urban enceinte for the first time.[63] For that institution, Nigel Kennell's formulation "citizen training system" is more apt.[64] Nor was this yet the gymnasium of the period that the French have named the *basse époque héllenistique* (late and sub-Hellenistic), a gymnasium in which cities buried their greatest benefactors and rendered them a founder-hero's cult, a space that Robert famously labeled the "second agora."[65] To understand the efflorescence of Attalid involvement with the gymnasium we need to marry high political history to a deeper understanding of the development of this institution. Perhaps an Attalid political culture that fostered ties with civic elites is part of the story.[66] But the other dynasties needed their civic elites too, and their kings too could strike a civic pose in a local gymnasium. After all, the Antigonids Philip V and Perseus had their names inscribed on a donor list in the gymnasium of Larisa, without formal distinction, just

---

[63] For Lykourgan Athens and the precipitous drop in ephebic participation in the following century and a half, see Oliver 2007, 175–76; Perrin-Saminadayar 2007, 63–86. For the dramatic change in the siting of the gymnasium, which took place during the Classical period, see Delorme 1960, 442–43. On the various locations for the gymnasium in the Hellenistic city, see Hoff 2009, 252–54.

[64] Kennell 2006 (*A Register of Greek Cities with Citizen Training Systems*), esp. xii for the chronological peak of 65 cities with an ephebate in the second century BCE.

[65] For periodization, see Thonemann 2016, 8: "[T]he modern historiography of the later Hellenistic period is, frankly, a bit of a mess." For Hamon (2009, 377–79), the historical rupture that marks the *basse époque héllenistique* eludes explanation on the present state of the evidence. On the "second agora": Robert, *OMS* II, 812–14, esp. 814 n. 3; VI, 422–23. On public burial in the late Hellenistic gymnasium, see Chiricat 2005; Bremen 2013, 39; cf. Kaye and Souza 2013, 99. Such burials are crucial evidence for the transformation of the gymnasium into a "second agora," with towering benefactors honored as founder-heroes in a newly politicized space. However, a reexamination of the posthumous honors for the Pergamene courtier Asklepides (*SEG* XLIX 1540) confirms the standard chronology: this is a development that seems to postdate the collapse of the Attalid kingdom.

[66] For a distinctive Attalid relationship to civic elites, see Kertész 1992; Dreyer 2009; but also Polyb. 32.8.5.

like ordinary citizens.[67] In what follows, I analyze the role and functioning of the gymnasium in cities both inside and outside the territory allotted to the Attalids at Apameia. Sulpicius, the Roman disrupter in Sardis, came to meet Attalid subjects where they were accustomed to meeting their king.[68] How that had come to be the normal state of affairs has not been adequately explained.

The Gymnasium as a Civic Institution

When the ambassadors of Eumenes II approached the assembly (*plêthos*) of the Achaeans in 185 to offer an endowment, which would in the future pay the wages of the league's Council (*boulê*), they were shouted down (Polyb. 22.7–8; Diod. Sic. 29.17).[69] The arguments of Apollonidas of Sikyon had won the day. Apollonidas had cast the gift as, in principle, worthy of the Achaeans but, in practice, given the identity of the donor and the purpose of the endowment, both utterly shameful and totally illegal (*paranomotatê*) (Polyb. 22.8.1–2). The Achaeans, he pointed out, had laws (*nomoi*) that prohibited archons and private individuals from accepting a king's gift (*dôra*). The Achaean Council, then, as a collection of private individuals acting in their capacity as archons, had no business accepting one. Now, we know that the Achaeans were far from allergic to royal beneficence – they had been accepting Ptolemaic gold for years.[70] For Apollonidas and his camp, however, the form of the Attalid gift was unacceptable. It threatened to undermine the autonomy of the *boulê*, as gift obligated countergift, and to invite more unwanted royal advances: this year it was Eumenes II, but next year, warned Apollonidas, it would be Prousias, and then Seleukos. An Achaean civic institution would become unmoored.

We can consider, by way of contrast, that in 161/0 the Rhodians accepted a gift of grain from this same Eumenes. Proceeds from the sale of the grain were earmarked for an education fund, the instruction, presumably, taking place at least in part in the gymnasium (Polyb. 31.31). The critic of this gift is no Rhodian but Polybius himself, who takes the

---

[67] Bringmann et al. 1995, no. 106 [E]; see Habicht 1983 for the identification of the other donors as "true" Lariseans, and not Philip's Macedonian settlers. This text tells against Macedonian exceptionalism.
[68] Cf. Hatzopoulos 2001: "Macedonian Palaces: Where King and City Meet."
[69] For discussion, see Bringmann et al. 1995, no. 68 [L]. Note that, for Diodorus, the ambassadors approach the *synodos*.
[70] Noeske 2000.

Rhodians to task for abandoning their usual sense of decency (*to prepon*). In his view, they had acted indecently in soliciting money (*eranizesthai*) for the education of their sons when none was lacking.[71] Were the arguments of Apollonidas of Sikyon about Attalid interference in the Achaean Council on the mind of the Achaeans historian, as Frank Walbank suggests?[72] Probably not. Polybius finds fault with the recipient, not the donor. Moreover, as has been pointed out, Polybius makes his critique from the standpoint of private morality.[73] It is a critique, however, that he applies to the body politic (*politeia*) – and not without reason. The Rhodians who secured the gift from Eumenes were acting more like private individuals than representatives of the state, hence the metaphor of Polybius: the *philos* (friend/kin/associate) who inappropriately seeks an *eranos*-loan from his fellow *eranistai*.[74] Whereas Apollonidas had *nomos* as law to buttress his claim, Polybius had merely *nomos* as custom, the inarticulate rules of *philia* (friendship). Apollonidas speaks only of high politics (*pragmata*), invoking the warring natures (*enantiai physeis*) of king and democracy (22.8.6). Polybius speaks of the conduct of fathers on behalf of sons (31.31.1). They were arguing about two entirely different species of civic institution.[75]

The moralizing of Polybius on the Rhodians and Eumenes II throws into high relief the distinctiveness of the gymnasium as a civic institution in the decades after Apameia. Despite what the wooden language of polis decrees would have us believe, neither the membership nor the interests of the gymnasium were identical with the body politic. The gymnasium had its own law; even when subjected to the law of the polis, it retained its own norms; and its ideology, in a world where most cities and koina called themselves democracies, was elitist.[76] Its collective psychology and heroic archetypes were antisocial.[77] Its doors were literally closed to certain citizens, but unlike those of the Achaean Council, never to kings. If it was for Pausanias, in the second century CE, the sine qua non of the polis, it had not been for Aristotle, in the fourth century BCE.[78] For the Hellenistic period, one cannot assume that each and every polis contained

---

[71] Ascertaining the economic condition of Rhodes after Pydna and the Roman punitive action regarding the tax status of Delos is a historical problem, as this passage from Polybius suggests.
[72] Walbank 1957–79, vol. 3, 515.   [73] Bringmann et al. 1995, 243.
[74] For the *eranos*-loan, see Millett 1991, 152–59.   [75] Cf. Eckstein 2009, 259.
[76] For the problem of defining *demokratia* in the epigraphy of the Hellenistic city and in royal chancery language, see Rhodes and Lewis 1997, 528–64, esp. 533–34; and the epigraphical register of Carlsson 2010, 334–43. For aristocratic *kalokagathia* and the Hellenistic gymnasium, see Gehrke 2004, 415.
[77] Bremen 2013.   [78] Gauthier 1995, 7.

a gymnasium.[79] Gauthier, more than any other scholar, has recognized the peculiar separateness of the gymnasium as a civic institution. He writes of gymnasia that function "outside the cadre of the polis," the activities of which are but partially or even "in no way civic."[80] His insight comes across in editions of various texts – honorific decrees of the city of Xanthos for Lyson and of Colophon for Athenaios, for example – and in his prolegomenon to the study of the institution.[81] In stark contrast, much recent scholarship emphasizes the civic character of the gymnasium without qualification.[82] For Hans Gehrke, the gymnasium is not quite the city in miniature, but close.[83] The catalog of Kennell is billed as a list of "state-run systems of citizen training."[84]

We must contend with the distinctiveness of the gymnasium as a civic institution if we are to understand how it became a privileged site of contact with the Attalids. This is precisely why the only systematic attempt to analyze gymnasium society in its ambiguous and even oppositional relationship to civic society at large, Riet van Bremen's analysis of the *neoi*, is also the only treatment to give court and king their due.[85] We often count the gymnasium as one of the central institutions of the Hellenistic polis. In the case of Lysimachus and the city of Nikaia in Bithynia, Strabo tells us, the panoptic, geographic center of the entire urban plan was a single stone at the center of the gymnasium.[86] Yet this very centrality remains difficult to understand. The Korragos decree (**D1**) shows that a city could plausibly argue to have had a gymnasium "from the beginning." We in fact know that Toriaion did have one from the beginning (**D8**).

---

[79] Gehrke (2004, 414) is agnostic.   [80] Gauthier 1995, 8; Gauthier 1980, 212.
[81] Xanthos and Lyson (*SEG* XLVI 1721): Gauthier 1996; Colophon: Gauthier 2006; prolegomenon: Gauthier 1995.
[82] Dreyer 2004, 234: "Der Verbindung zwischen den Neoi und den Demos war demnach unauflöslich; die Neoi waren in ihren verschiedenen, hier umrissenen Aggregat-zuständen ein Abbild der gesamten Bürgerschaft."
[83] Gehrke 2004, 416: "In der körperlich-geistigen Formierung sowie in Ritual und Ausstatung wurde mithin fassbar und sichtbar, wie eng das Gymnasion mit der Identität der Polis verbunden war."
[84] Kennell 2006, vii. Despite its title, that corpus seems to register the totality of gymnasium society, not just ephebes. See, further, Kennell 2015, on the ephebeia's function to produce citizen-warriors. See also Habicht 1983, 31–32 (on Larisa): "Bau und Unterhaltung einer solchen, der Erziehung der Jugend gewidmeten Anlage war natürlicherweise eine *Sache der Bürgerschaft* und wurde in Larisa, wie dies auch für viele andere Städte bezeugt ist, *selbstverständlich* so angesehen" (emphasis added).
[85] Bremen 2013, 47. Cf. Gehrke 2004, the essay entitled, "Eine Bilanz: Die Entwicklung des Gymnasions zur Institution der Sozalisierung in der Polis," which puzzlingly makes no mention of kings.
[86] Strabo 12.4.7.

It may not have been a sine qua non, but it was also far from superfluous. Because in hard times too it was important to have one, Philetairos gave the Cyzikenes 20 talents for oil and a gathering (*synagôgê*) during the Galatian crisis of the 270s.[87] And in calmer times, the resumption of gymnasium life was a sign that things had returned to normal: recall that after Antiochos III's siege of Sardis the restoration of the gymnasium took priority. The gymnasium was also central because interactions with royal power were central to the political economy of the Hellenistic polis. Paradoxically, these interactions tended to take place in the gymnasium because it remained on the periphery of social and political life as long as kings stalked its peristyle colonnades.

Financing the Gymnasium

If we are willing to hazard a few generalizations about the Hellenistic gymnasium, we can identify several regional and historical trends.[88] One such trend is the gradual elaboration of this institution, throughout the Hellenistic world, from the Classical transition to the second century BCE, manifest in the construction of ever more rooms and the appearance of the first gymnasia in stone. We can observe an increasing complexity in administrative practice and an increase in scale: more instruction, more festivals – more activity. All of this would seem to imply a commensurate increase in financing, if not financial sophistication. Yet the reality was much messier. For gymnasiarchs, there were new responsibilities mandated both by the terms of private foundations, which added events to the calendar, and by law, not just the law of the gymnasium but the law of the polis. For instance, each year, officials of the gymnasium of Tauromenion in Sicily were required to document with an inscription both the number of their competitions and the impact on the budget, all in compliance with an ordinance known as the *dogma neaniskôn*.[89] On Athenian Delos, admittedly a special case, the gymnasiarch was both the primary agonothete of the island and chief administrator of gymnasium life.[90] An honorary decree for the gymnasiarch of 157/6 praises him for having accomplished all of the sacrifices, "which the laws and decrees of the

---

[87] Bringmann et al. 1995, no. 241 [E].
[88] On generalization, see the reflections of Gauthier 1995, 9; Gehrke 2004, 414.
[89] *IG* XIV 422; see Schuler 2004a, 180–81 for problem of date (second or first century BCE) and discussion.
[90] Roussel 1916, 189.

demos had prescribed for him (ὅσας προσέταττον αὐτῶι οἵ τε νόμοι καὶ ψηφίσματα τοῦ δήμου)" (*SEG* XLVII 1218 lines 16–17).[91] Similarly, the gymnasiarch of Attalid Andros performed his sacrifices to the royal family "according to the laws (ἐ[κ] τῶν νόμων)" (**D9** line 10).

As the responsibilities grew, so too did the prospects for failure. In a thorough review of the finances of the gymnasium, Schuler identifies the appearance of new controls and greater centralization in the second century, a response to a demonstrable weakness in the institution's ability to sustain itself.[92] In particular, he adduces the cases of Beroia and Iasos, where the polis assumed tighter control of a gymnasium that had either lost or mismanaged funds.[93] Here, arguments about the strength and vitality of the institution fall flat. The *neoi* and *presbyteroi* of Iasos were quite explicit in their statement to their city's *boulê* and *demos*: they could not do it on their own; their best attempt at accounting for the money, a process of review called διόρθωμα, had been unsuccessful.[94] Neither association had been able to recover the public money (*koina chrêmata*) that it had lent out. Generally, new regulations were a response to the problem, as the administrative techniques and habits of accountability were transferred from the polis to the gymnasium. But we might also see new regulations as one of the causes of financial meltdown in the first place. In this new era, the gymnasiarch who administered public funds would be held to the standards of the polis.[95] Meanwhile, he oversaw a patrimony that was a patchwork of foundations, dues, and ad hoc gifts. For those who had to manage the money, the financial hodgepodge of the Hellenistic gymnasium was sometimes more of a liability than an asset.[96]

The financial shortcomings of the Hellenistic gymnasium are no secret. We have several examples of building projects paused, if finally completed. No doubt there were many that were abandoned, and so we lack an honorific decree or a donor's dedication. In the aforementioned case of Halikarnassos, a local benefactor provided stopgap funding when the

---

[91] For discussion, see Migeotte 2009.
[92] Schuler 2004a, 180. For shortfalls in late Hellenistic public finance, see, e.g., Hegelochos' bailout of Kyaneai: *SEG* LVI 1721. It is worth noting that political scientists can point to the surprising power of weak institutions to determine resource allocation in favor of interest groups, e.g., on Zimbabwe, Herbst 1990.
[93] *SEG* XLIII 381 (esp. Side A lines 13–16); *I.Iasos* 23.   [94] *I.Iasos* 23 lines 15–17.
[95] For these standards, see Fröhlich 2004a.
[96] On "Mischfinanzierung" and disorder ("Unregelmässigkeit"), see Schuler 2004a, 179, 185. Similarly, Moretti 1982, 56: "Ma in età ellenistica il carattere aleatorio, eventuale, del contributo pubblico impone il ricorso ad alter forme di finanziamento." Finally, Delorme 1960, 456: "les fonds proviennent constamment de ressources occasionnelles."

public subscription, and perhaps also the appeal to Ptolemy, failed. Indeed, royal benefactors were not entirely reliable, as Priene learned when several second-century monarchs reneged on their promises.[97] Yet the problem was not confined to large projects – to "people getting in over their heads." The month-to-month and year-to-year operation of the gymnasium was a relentless challenge. We can see the ensuing financial bind in the Thessalian city of Pherai, in its early second-century list of gymnasiarchs "since the time of Alexander the Great."[98] In several years, the list reads, μετέλιπε; the strange form is a *hapax*, but one easy to interpret: in those years, there was no gymnasiarch, perhaps no activity at all.[99] In effect, the city did not merely countenance a closure of the gymnasium; it preserved the memory. Another year, the list reads, ἁ πόλις. In this year, the city was prepared to play an unusually large role as the sole funder of the gymnasium.[100]

As Olivier Curty's study of the office demonstrates, it was only the most generous of gymnasiarchs, men such as Adaios of Amphipolis, who assumed the cost of a regular and continuous supply of oil from the beginning until the end of a term.[101] Accordingly, when faced with the inevitable shortfall, members of the gymnasium had several options. They could appeal to the city for help, which was the solution in Pherai, but also in Beroia and Iasos.[102] Or they could turn to "crowd sourcing," with participants paying more or even all of the costs.[103] Or, finally, they could turn to benefactors, either local or royal, who tended to set up foundations. If managed well, these foundations ensured smooth functioning. Yet, as Schuler points out, benefactors with broader horizons might have their own ideas about the management of the money.[104] He cites the micromanaged case of Pharsalos, where Leonidas of Halikarnassos, a man with mercantile connections, insisted that city magistrates called *tagoi* and

---

[97] Bringmann et al. 1995, no. 270 [E].
[98] Habicht 1976. On the text, see A. Chankowski 2010, 38 n. 85.
[99] Habicht (1976, 191) conjectures that the funding gap came in some phase of the First Macedonian War, in other words, the late third century.
[100] Column B line 7. See further the case of Priene in the early first century BCE. The benefactor Zosimos reinstituted the association of the *neoi* after a hiatus (*I.Priene* 114 lines 17–19).
[101] Curty 2015, 278. Adaios of Amphipolis: *SEG* XLIII 371.
[102] See Schuler 2004a, 187 n. 147. It was often the case that the gymnasium received an annual subvention from the polis, which normally made up only part of an operating budget, while the gymnasiarch added a personal contribution.
[103] Generally considered a late Hellenistic phenomenon, but see Schuler 2004a, 183, for earlier cases of the "Spartan reality" behind the luxury of the honorific decrees.
[104] Schuler 2004a, 185–86.

tamiai (treasurers), not the gymnasium crowd, manage his foundation.[105] In this way, the gymnasium could lean on the fiscal structures and competence of the city to solve its problems. We should not underestimate, however, the advantages accruing to the gymnasium from its incorporation into a system of royal finance. In fact, royal benefaction could qualitatively change the institution, rather than simply grow it. Once integrated into the Attalid fiscal system, some of the typical precariousness of bookkeeping disappeared. This is one lesson that can be drawn from the earmarking episode of Eumenes II in Toriaion (**D8**). When the king takes charge of organizing an oil fund, he has at his disposal not just resources, the revenue of the *agoranomia* or various tracts of *chora basilikê*, but the financial know-how of his officials (the *hemiolios*), and a flexibility that no city or individual could ever match.[106]

The creation of royal as much as civic bonds of dependence marked a departure from what seems to have been a merely notional state of autarky. If the patrimony of the mid-Hellenistic gymnasium consisted of a mixed bag of foundations and subsidies from various quarters, the money that the city might provide, termed *gymnasiarchikon*, vel sim., was always supplemented from elsewhere.[107] In other words, the city's contribution was not expected to cover the entire budget of the gymnasium. Kings, local benefactors, or the membership itself invariably picked up different costs. By the same token, the monarch's gifts alone were not sufficient. For example, Ptolemaic soldiers of the local garrison tacked on an impressive 4,656 drachmas to a foundation of Ptolemy VI for the gymnasium of Thera.[108] In another case, a sensational lease document from Attalid Teos, excavated in 2016, shows a valuable piece of real estate in the gymnasium's property portfolio. The *neoi* and other gymnasium members (*metechontes tou gymnasiou*) were mandated to offer the land with its built structures for at least 150 drachmas of annual rent, but raised 450 drachmas at auction.[109] Yet gauging financial independence is difficult since we lack even a single complete inventory of a given gymnasium's resources. Instead, it is more fruitful to investigate the issue of control or ownership of this complex patrimony. To do so, we must consider the case of Beroia in the

---

[105] For the family of merchants to which Leonidas belonged, see Miller 1974.
[106] For the *hemiolios*, see Müller 2005.
[107] For the *gymnasiarchikon*, see Migeotte 2000, 153, noting its obscurity; we hear of it only when gymnasiarchs substituted their own money in its place and were duly honored.
[108] *IG* XII 3 327. For discussion, see Migeotte 2013, 117–18. [109] Adak and Stauner 2018, 5–7.

decades before 168/7.[110] The Macedonian city has produced the very richest documentation, showing that the gymnasium's members – rather than the polis or the Antigonid king in Pella – controlled and effectively owned this wealth.

The basic purpose of the famous law of Beroia was to transform the gymnasiarch into a civic magistrate and thereby subject him to civic controls on the administration of patrimony. Of the old regime, we are not informed, but one assumes that the gymnasiarch's election had taken place in the cadre of the gymnasium.[111] The first words of the law (*nomos*) proper change all that: Ἡ πόλις αἱρείσθω γυμνασίαρχον ("The *polis* shall select the gymnasiarch") (Side A lines 22–23). From now on, the gymnasiarch will submit accounts three times per year to a board of city auditors (*exetastai*) (Side B lines 91–97).[112] In the event that he must pay a fine for maladministration, a city official, the *politikos praktôr*, will exact it (Side B lines 96–103). Yet these measures seem to be the extent of the city's new involvement. One of the law's stated aims is to prevent wasteful use of the "revenues (*prosodoi*) of the *neoi*" (Side A lines 13–14). Some of the means of regulating these *prosodoi* may now be civic, but the patrimony itself is never conceptualized as such. It remains, throughout the text, the possession of the *neoi* (Side A lines 13–14, 30–31; Side B lines 60, 86–97).[113] The key passage is Side B lines 86–97, which sets out guidelines for the administration of the *prosodoi* of the *neoi*. It begins, Κυριευ|έτω δὲ ὁ γυμνασίαρχος τῶν προσόδων ὑπαρχουσῶν τοῖς νέοις καὶ ἀπὸ τούτων| ἀναλισκέτω ("for the duration of his term, the gymnasiarch shall be *kyrios* [owner/executor] of the revenues, and he shall spend from them"). What money is left at the end of the year is combined with fines, and the next gymnasiarch becomes *kyrios* of the total (*plêthos*).[114] In other words, the money never passes through city coffers. Control of the patrimony of the gymnasium passes directly from one gymnasiarch to the next, even under the newly centralized regime. Moreover, if the gymnasiarch himself pays a fine, he pays it to the *neoi* (ἀποτινέτω τοῖς νέοις [Side B line 95]).[115]

---

[110] Gauthier and Hatzopoulos 1993 = *SEG* XLIII 381. For a date pre-168/7, see Hatzopoulos 1996, vol. 1, 137–38.
[111] Gauthier and Hatzopoulos 1993, 51.
[112] For *extestai* as civic magistrates, see Fröhlich 2004a, 117–68.
[113] This is demonstrated grammatically either by use of a genitive of possession or by a participle of the verb ὑπάρχειν with a dative of possession.
[114] For *kyrieia* as possession, see Chaniotis 2004, 186.
[115] Gauthier and Hatzopoulos 1993, 127–28: "En ce sens, 'les *neoi*,' groupe par définition mouvant et hétérogène (citoyens et étrangers), continuent à former, après l'adoption de la loi, une entité, que tout à la fois reconnaît et contrôle."

The law presents an ironclad distinction between the "revenues of the *neoi*" and the "revenues of the city."[116] Gauthier goes so far as to argue that the burden of financial surveillance remains with *les habitués du gymnase*. He draws attention to three men who are elected in an assembly in the gymnasium (*ekklêsia en tôi gymnasiôi*) and who, presumably, take their oaths of office before that same body. These men are charged with the stringently quotidian tasks of helping the gymnasiarch keep watch over the *neoi* and over their finances (Side A lines 35–62). Yet unlike the gymnasiarch, they are not civic magistrates.[117] Furthermore, *neoi* or affiliated alumni would seem to play an important role in the auditing process, since the law permits "whoever wishes to do so to inspect the accounts of the gymnasiarch along with the *exetastai* (the city's auditors) (ἐάν τινες βούλωνται, μετὰ τού|των συνεγλογίζεσθαι αὐτόν)" (Side B lines 92–93). The record of the final rendering of accounts is displayed on a notice board (*sanis*) in the gymnasium. Over the course of the next 24 months, anyone may contest in court (*euthunein*) the accuracy of these accounts (Side B lines 107–9). Consequently, whoever brings such a claim will have spent time in the gymnasium, if only to inspect the public record. Finally, Gauthier ascribes to the ὁ βουλόμενος ("he who so desires") in Side B line 92 sole responsibility for reporting to the civic *praktôr* malfeasance discovered during the quadrimestral audits.[118] This has the effect of greatly limiting the role of the civic *exetastai*, which is why Pierre Fröhlich believes that the responsibility of these officials is simply implied.[119] Clearly, the very law that transformed the gymnasiarch into a civic magistrate, ultimately, preserved and enshrined many self-regulating aspects of the institution.

Despite the fact that the case of Beroia is unique in terms of these rich details, it still allows us to generalize. In fact, the law's motivation clause is explicit on this point: ἐν αἷς πόλεσιν γυμνάσιά|ἐστιν καὶ ἄλειμμα συνέστηκεν οἱ γυμνασιαρχι ν|κοὶ νόμοι κεῖνται ἐν τοῖς δημοσίοις, καλῶς ἔχει καὶ πα|ρ' ἡμῖν τὸ αὐτὸ συντελεσθῆναι "(Since) ... in those cities in which there are gymnasia and an oil fund established, there are gymnasiarchal laws in the public archives, so it is fitting that for us too it should be accomplished" (Side A lines 6–9). The stated goal of the law was to bring the institutions of Beroia into alignment with those of other poleis. Moreover, we have no

---

[116] Moretti (1982, 56–57) underlines that the expression *koinai prosodoi* elsewhere refers to gymnasiaum patrimony; Gauthier and Hatzopoulos 1993, 124–28, 140 (insisting on the point); Fröhlich 2004a, 380.

[117] Similarly, the *aphêgoumenos* of Side B lines 2–5 is an appointee of the gymnasiarch, a kind of *hypogymnasiarchos* and not a civic magistrate. See Gauthier and Hatzopoulos 1993, 65.

[118] Gauthier and Hatzopoulos 1993, 140.   [119] Fröhlich 2004a, 266.

reason to believe that these other cities were exclusively Macedonian or Antigonid. On the contrary, because its teachers were itinerant and its benefactors elite and therefore cosmopolitan, the gymnasium developed in a very broad context.[120] It is true that Philip V (and Perseus?) took an unusually heavy-handed approach to the gymnasium, laboring to standardize certain aspects of ephebic and gymnasium life in Antigonid cities.[121] For this reason, Andrzej Chankowski argues that models elaborated on the basis of the Beroia law have limited applicability.[122] Yet the law itself (notoriously) never mentions the king. And while we should not rule out royal support for the Beroia gymnasium, the text is silent on this score. It depicts a city in the process of assuming a certain measure of control over a gymnasium in its midst. The law is both witness to the strength of polis identity under monarchic rule and to the jealousy with which the gymnasium guarded its financial independence.[123]

Adorning the Gymnasium

When the gymnasiarch on Attalid Andros received his honors, it was, as is so often the case, because he had performed exceptionally. He had exceeded his duties. As the decree describes his accomplishment, in the shorthand of insiders, he had "embellished the gymnasium (τὸ γυμνάσιον κεκόσμηκεν)" (**D9** line 6). He had added to it. In this instance, this meant building an entryway (*pylôn*) and dedicating an exedra and a statue of the king in a luminous variety of marble.[124] The language of *kosmêsis*, of

---

[120] On the cosmopolitanism and broad horizons of the gymnasium crowd, see Schuler 2004a, 186. Consider also the shared iconography, the "international" or stock themes of statuary in the mid-Hellenistic gymnasium, for which see Hoff 2004, 391–93.

[121] For the "règlementation minutieuse" of Philip V, see Gauthier and Hatzopoulos 1993, 145–46. The crucial text for Philip's program of standardization is his partially published letter to Amphipolis (Hatzopoulos 1996, no. 16), on which see SEG XLIII 369; XLVI 717. Further on the Antigonid reform of ephebic life, see Intzesiloglou 2006.

[122] A. Chankowski 2009; cf. Prag 2007, 99. Despite the efforts of activist kings, the gymnasia of Antigonid Macedonia were perhaps less standardized than one has supposed. In both Beroia and Amphipolis, royal law was adapted and harmonized with civic (Rousset 2017, 63–69).

[123] The lack of any mention of the king led early commentators (SEG XXVII 261) to date the law *after* the fall of the dynasty. See now Gauthier and Hatzopoulos 1993, 125–26. Dreyer (2004, 234) adduces it as an example of a city asserting control over a gymnasium by one of several means at its disposal; also, Moretti 1982, 59.

[124] For the meaning of *pylôn*, see Delorme 1960, 358; entryways more generally, Hoff 2009, 254. For the luminous royal portrait statue, see Robert 1960, 117–18; for the ancient meaning of *exedra*, as opposed to what epigraphers typically mean by it, see Hellmann 1992, 126–30. The *exedra* is a full room or hall, at times with a porch attached, in other words, a much more substantial gift than a semi-circular statue base at the edge of the palaistra; cf. the *exedra* of SEG

adornment and elaboration, is familiar to the epigraphy of the gymnasium, where one, it seems, can always add something.[125] The material basis of its life was of course oil; without oil, the gymnasium, in fact, ceased to exist.[126] Therefore, a great variety of arrangements grew up to ensure a consistent supply of quality oil, many of them involving kings.[127] It has even become a matter of dispute whether one can assume that any *other* royal gift to a gymnasium was, by default, supplementary to an earlier gift of oil. For example, the honorific decree of Colophon for Menippos mentions "royal banquets (*basilika deipna*)" in the gymnasium, evidence of a late Attalid endowment.[128] While Bringmann et al. see a gift of oil accompanying the banquet endowment, Filippo Canali de Rossi has criticized their interpretation.[129] Regardless, a king who had already seen to the provision of oil – or found a gymnasium well stocked – could choose another form of embellishment. That he had so many options at his disposal speaks to the distinctiveness of the gymnasium as an institution.

Scholarship on the Hellenistic gymnasium has accounted for the many costs associated with the gymnasium: those which were fixed, such as oil, wood for heating baths, and water, and those that were a boon, such as renovations, distributions of food and drink, and so on.[130] However, we have perhaps not yet appreciated the sheer size of the institution's appetite for benefaction, at least from the second century on. We know, for example, that the gymnasium could scarcely function without pay for teachers. So, cities very often took charge of this aspect of gymnasium finance.[131] In Delphi, the foundation of Attalos II provided wages for

XXVI 139 line 45, which Ma 2008a places in a shrine of the Nymphs, not in an Athenian gymnasium as previously conjectured.

[125] For *kosmêsis*, see first Robert 1937, 349 n. 1. However, that note belongs to the publication of an honorific decree for a gymnasiarch of Sebastopolis in Caria, from the second century CE. Only a portion of Robert's parallels are to do with the gymnasium, and many of them are from Roman times. Yet these later benefactors have clearly inherited a Hellenistic model, one which may have been forged in the context of the gymnasium. See, for example, the decree of 196 BCE of the Xanthian *neoi* for Lyson, SEG XLVI 1721 lines 15–16: καὶ πολλὰ τῶν ἰδίων εἰς ανηλώσας ἐκόσμη|σεν ("and he decorated by spending much of his own money"); further, e.g., see the honors for Diodoros Pasparos from the gymnasium of Pergamon, *MDAI(A)* 32 (1907) 257,8.

[126] Curty 2015, 278.   [127] Fröhlich 2009.   [128] Bringmann et al. 1995, no. 262a [E] line 47.

[129] Bringmann et al. 1995, 304; *ISE* 149. On a related problem, note Bringmann et al. 1995, no. 215 [L], the gift of 75 talents for oil that Hieron II gave Rhodes. To many, this has seemed like too much money for oil alone. In fact, as a result, the text of Polyb. 5.88.5–8 has been amended with Diod. Sic. 26.8.1.

[130] Gauthier 1995, 5; Dreyer 2004, 227.

[131] For the public appointment of specialist instructors as a defining feature of the Hellenistic gymnasium, see Kah 2004, 63, with sources collected in Roesch 1982, 307–54. Aybek and Dreyer (2011, 212–13) suspect an Attalid ballistics trainer for ephebes at Metropolis.

teachers (*Syll.*³ 233). But one could always hire more specialized teachers, from farther afield, who commanded higher salaries. The Boeotian Koinon even mandated, it seems, that its member cities do so, which implies that local, cheaper teachers sufficed in the absence of outside intervention.[132] As a rule, what was necessary could always stand for improvement. The provision of water is another case in point. Specific body care practices necessitated a secure supply of water.[133] So it is no surprise that royal benefactors took pains to keep the water flowing, as Philip III seems to have done in Mylasa. In a land grant of 318/17, the king stipulated that the grant-holder provide water from a fountain on his land to a gymnasium and palaistra down the line.[134] Yet where the prestige of the dynasty was at stake, as in the city of Pergamon, or on the incredible ship of Hieron II, the *Syrakousia*, with its floating gymnasium, a king could always add more lavish means of water conveyance.[135] Proximity to water had always affected topography, but the second century witnessed a major uptick in the construction of bathing facilities set within gymnasium complexes.[136] Effectively, one could fill up the ritual calendar of the gymnasium. Various kings, Attalids among them, seem to have succeeded in doing just that on Kos.[137] Space, by contrast, was more readily available, especially if one built vertically on the dramatic, terraced slopes of the Hellenistic gymnasium. Perhaps, the peristyle around a palaistra could accommodate only so many exedrae. But one could always build new rooms, rooms with specific functions and higher prestige, such as a library, an *ephêbikê exedra* (instruction room), or the *akroaterion* (audience room) that the Attalids are believed to have financed at Aigai.[138] Or instead of rooms, the

---

[132] *SEG* XXXII 496 (from Thespiai).

[133] Delorme 1960, 304: "Point n'est besoin de montrer la nécessité de l'eau dans les gymnases." The siting of gymnasia on hillsides also facilitated water conveyance (Hoff 2009, 252–53). On cold and hot baths (so-called Hellenistic *Schwitzbaden*) in this context, see Trümper 2014, 211–12.

[134] Bringmann et al. 1995, no. 298 [E]. However, an alternative interpretation exists: the benefactor might be one of the descendants of the original grant-holder, not Philip III. See Bringmann et al. 1995, 371–72.

[135] Pergamon: Radt 1999, 121; Hieron II: Ath. 5.207d.

[136] Hoff 2009, 255. See also Delorme 1960, 446–47, on water needs as a determinative factor for the topography of the early gymnasium.

[137] Bringmann et al. 1995, nos. 225–29 [E]; see also Savalli-Lestrade 2010, esp. 83. In her model, Hellenistic royalty came to monopolize the festival or sacred time of the cities. I am reluctant to go so far, but the royal dominance of the civic festival calendar certainly came at the expense of local observance. Moreover, as she demonstrates, once on the sacred books, it was actually very difficult to remove rites associated with even defunct dynasties.

[138] Bringmann et al. 1995, no. *357 [E]. On these rooms and the increase in their functional differentiation over the course of the Hellenistic period, see Hoff 2009, 256–59; Trümper (2015,

benefactor could provide entire buildings: a gymnasium for the *presbyteroi* to match that for the *neoi*; or a *paidikê palaistra* where one was lacking, as in Attalid Colophon, where the Homereion had to suffice until Athenaios' purpose-built structure was finished.[139] The gymnasium offered seemingly endless opportunities for *kosmêsis*, and so for the display of royal virtue.

Social Status and the Gymnasium

When the Attalid dynasty fell, the gymnasium of Pergamon became a meeting place for self-styled *aristoi andres* ("best men").[140] Yet if the membership had changed, it had in fact become more demotic with an influx of new citizens.[141] However, what remained the same was the current of aristocratic agonism that had long animated the civic gymnasium.[142] This was not so much the "citizen training system" as the nursery of the self-styled "beautiful and noble aristocratic youth" (*kalokagathikos neos*). From the mid-second century, it was a key context for the production of a new hereditary aristocracy, which successfully distinguished itself from an indistinct mass of citizens.[143] For example, the biography of Menippos of Colophon, who as a mere *neos* served on embassies to the Attalid capital, narrativizes how a youth's aristocratic virtue might redound to his city's credit.[144] Nevertheless, if for lack of status or simply money, a young citizen could not participate in its elitist culture, the gymnasium was happy to leave him untrained. In Beroia, the gymnasium excluded broad categories of people, some of whom must have included citizens: the freedman, the freedman's son, the physically unfit (*apalaistros*), the drunkard, the madman, anyone who had prostituted themselves, and, importantly, anyone who plied a manual or common trade (*agoraia technê*).[145] In other words, citizenship did not guarantee admission – not

---

169) sees such rooms as characteristic of *late* Hellenistic gymnasia. On libraries in gymnasia of this period, see Adak and Stauner 2018, 12 n. 37; Prag 2007, 94.

[139] Athenaios and Colophon: Gauthier 2006 = **D10**. [140] *SEG* L 1211 line 12.

[141] See Wörrle 2007, 513. Indeed, Kennell (2015, 176) notes class tensions in the late second century (post-Attalid) gymnasium of Pergamon.

[142] Gehrke 2004, 414–15.

[143] On the emergence of an aristocracy in the Hellenistic city from the mid-second century, see Hamon 2007, 84.

[144] *SEG* XXXIX 1244 = *Claros* I, 63–104 Column I lines 11–12.

[145] Side B lines 27–29. Regarding *apalaistroi*, we find them making a dedication to a gymnasiarch in Demetrias, along with *paides* and οἱ ἐκ τοῦ γυμνασίου: A. S. Arvanitopoulos, *Polemon* 1 (1929), 126–28. It seems that a group of physically unfit youths might be eligible for distributions of oil that took place in the gymnasium, even if they found themselves excluded from the palaistra itself. See Gauthier and Hatzopoulos 1993, 81–84.

even de jure.¹⁴⁶ The social stigma attached to banausic labor surely prevented many from entrance, as perhaps so too did a property qualification adumbrated in the Ephebic Law of Amphipolis.¹⁴⁷ On the other hand, one could grow up to be a citizen without passing through the gymnasium. Mid-third-century Athens minted just two dozen ephebes per year.¹⁴⁸ Surely, the body politic was replenished from elsewhere. Here, we can indeed generalize about the Hellenistic polis. Passing through the gymnasium or ephebate did not constitute an obligatory step toward citizenship or any other juridical status.¹⁴⁹

Scholarship has underestimated the extent to which the elite of the gymnasium disputed the egalitarian ethos of citizenship. One tends to recognize aristocratic origins, or emphasize a late turn toward elitism and exclusivity, while the sources themselves tell the story of an institution dominated in most periods and places by the few. Lykourgan Athens in this respect represents a notable exception. Consider that in Argos of the 420s, a select group of youths (*logades*) trained at public expense launched an oligarchic coup.¹⁵⁰ The Argos incident highlights the ever-present potential for conflict. These "disruptive *neoi*," in Van Bremen's apt formulation, stood in a different relationship to power from the rest of their community.¹⁵¹ They looked to their heroes, to aristocrats, princes, and kings, for support, even when it discomfited or even enraged polis society. They were at once a threat to social cohesion and a vital connection to royal and later Roman authority. For the other citizens – including other elites – the task was to constrain the would-be aristocrats of the gymnasium, while still profiting from their ties to imperial power.

---

[146] *Contra* Gehrke (2007, 418), who contends that all citizens had a de jure right to participate. For the ephebate, see full discussion of A. Chankowski 2010, 277–84. Note that the admission of noncitizens to the ephebate was rare before the influx of Romano-Italians. By contrast, Chankowski (p. 277) remarks on the regular participation of noncitizens in many other activities of the gymnasium.

[147] Hatzopoulos 1996, vol. 1, 209 n. 1; see now text of Lazaridou 2015, lines 14–19. However, Hatzopoulos (2016, 155–56) suggests that fathers or tutors with property valued above 30 minas may have been required by royal writ to register their sons for the ephebate, making it a matter of choice for the poor. Rousset (2017, 70–75) instead argues that lines 14–19 reflect conditions in the Augustan age, when the ephebate was obligatory for all citizens of Amphipolis.

[148] Kennell 2006, x, citing Pélékidis 1962, 164–65.

[149] Gauthier and Hatzopoulos 1993, 83: "Le passage par le gymnase ou par l'éphébie n'y constituait pas ou n'y constituait plus, pour autant que nous le sachions, l'étape obligée vers la citoyenneté ou vers quelque statut juridique privilégié."

[150] Thuc. 5.67.2; Diod. Sic. 12.75.7; Plut. *Alc.* 15.3.   [151] Bremen 2013, 36–44.

Ionian Metropolis, for example, honored Apollonios for his successful negotiation of fiscal and territorial disputes, but also for securing an oil fund from Attalos II "through his own persistence (διὰ τὴν ἰδίαν ἐκτένειαν)" (**D5** Side B line 24).[152] The effort is private, but the good, we are assured, is public. In the civic discourse of the decree, Apollonios wins high repute in other cities and obviously the affection of Attalos, but never presses his own advantage at the expense of Metropolis and "the common good of the city" (τὰ κοινὰ τῆς πόλεως πράγματα) (Side B lines 16–17). Each of his actions manifests civic virtue, none more so than his death, which a second decree relates came leading the *neaniskoi* (armed youth of the gymnasium) against the rebel Aristonikos, "for the sake of his own virtue (*arête*) and that of his fatherland (*patris*)" (Side A line 37). This is the official image of Apollonios that the people of Metropolis have left us: a man of the court and of the gymnasium, firmly embedded in civic society. It is an image, however, that we cannot take at face value.[153] The city granted the sons of Apollonios the right to build a hero shrine (*hêrôon*) for his bones "before the city gate on their own property (πρὸ τῆς πύλης ἐν τοῖς ἰδίοις)" (Side A line 42). Jones sees Apollonios "as receiving true heroic honors from his city, even if the tomb is on private property."[154] That the tomb is on private property does not make the honors any less heroic, only less civic. The tomb is outside the city's enceinte. The city's grant of approval is one last attempt to fix a larger-than-life benefactor in civic discourse.[155] Jones has also pointed out that Apollonios evinces a convergence of the public heroization of the Classical and Hellenistic periods with the private heroization of the period of the Roman Empire.[156] In death as in life, the Attalids' friends in the city gymnasia walked a very thin line.

If we accept the rhetoric of these cities wholesale, the disjuncture between the elites of the gymnasium and civic society at large disappears. Yet that rift is the background to Attalid patronage of the gymnasium. In the case of Eirenias and Miletus, it deserves more attention. Eirenias, as we recall, was one of the ambassadors of the Ionian Koinon to Eumenes II in 167/6.

---

[152] Translation here and below of Side A line 42 from Jones 2004.
[153] *Contra* Rowe 2002, 127–30.   [154] Jones 2004, 483.
[155] The rhetoric of the Metropolis decrees is in some ways rather banal. Formally, the Hellenistic honorific decree tends to reduce each individual biography to what Ma (2007, 218) calls a "cipher of civic virtue." Ma's essay, which characterizes the honorific decree as social constraint rather than sycophancy, has shaped my analysis here and in the following treatment of Eirenias of Miletus. The distinctiveness of the Metropolis case consists of repeated assimilation of the private (*to idion*) to the public (*to koinon*), particularly with regard to heroic cult.
[156] Jones 2010, 35.

They met on Delos, and Eumenes followed up with a letter to the Ionians the same year (*RC* 52). Sometime later, but before 164, Miletus honored its citizen Eirenias with a gilded statue on a very large, round base, which bears a decree (*SEG* XXXVI 1046).[157] The honorific decree for Eirenias informs us of the massive foundation of Eumenes II for the construction of a gymnasium: 160,000 medimnoi of wheat for sale, the proceeds of which were lent out at interest, and also sufficient wood for building. That wood was much needed. While Miletus had possessed at least two gymnasia since 206/5, it now began construction of a much larger complex with the new revenue and material. To give a sense of the scale, the palaistra of Eumenes' gymnasium is estimated at ca. 7,000 m², embarrassingly larger than the so-called Hellenistic Gymnasium endowed by Miletus' own citizen Eudemos (1,600 m²).[158] Consensus places the so-called gymnasium of Eumenes II under a Roman bath in the city's "Westmarkt Areal." The unexcavated building relates to a slate of other structures that form a self-contained neighborhood. The gymnasium's propylon aligns directly with the stadium to its east in an unusually axial orientation, implying an integrated plan.[159] A Milesian decree for Eumenes II was inscribed on one of the antae of the propylon (*I.Milet* 307), though whether the entire complex was completed in the king's lifetime can be doubted.[160] In addition, the aligned, so-called Westmarkt is now seen to have consisted of running tracks, including a *xystos*. Finally, adjoining the running tracks is a peristyle known as the "Hofhaus am Athena-Tempel," which is now interpreted as the possible *temenos* for the ruler cult of Eumenes II.

The decade-long involvement of Eirenias in the execution of such a monumental undertaking, which left its mark on an entire sector of the city of Miletus, produced a dossier of inscriptions. These have been ordered in relative sequence around fixed points like the letter of Eumenes II to the Ionians. Most of the documents illuminate the afterlife of the royal gift: the exceptional, full-blown ruler cult for a living Attalid that seems to have

---

[157] See also editions of Bringmann et al. 1995, no. 283 [E 1]; *I.Milet* 1039.
[158] The foundation of Eudemos provides the *terminus ante quem* for the other gymnasia (*Milet* I 3 145).
[159] Hoff 2009, 254: the Eumenes-Gymnasion in Miletus and the gymnasium of Messene are exceptions to the rule that Hellenistic gymnasia do *not* share axial alignment with other major monuments and urban plans.
[160] Bringmann et al. 1995, no. 284 [E 2]. Schaaf (1992, 62) concludes that the propylon undoubtedly belongs to the gymnasium complex. See also Kleine 1986 and esp. Emme 2013, 269, 347–48, with Taf. 76, p. 464. Emme suggests that the "Westmarkt"/*xystos* could also be a second-century monument. See further Trümper 2015, 196 n. 92.

sprung up in response, then promises of further benefactions, then further embassies of Eirenias as representative of the Milesians. However, what interests us most here is the prehistory of the gymnasium's foundation. While the honorific decree of the Milesians for Eirenias postdates the letter of Eumenes to the Ionians, the foundation mentioned in the decree for Eirenias predates the audience on Delos.[161] In other words, before he met Eumenes as an ambassador of the Ionians to deliver a koinon decree, or as a representative of Miletus bearing a civic decree, Eirenias approached the king in a private capacity, as an advocate of the gymnasium. According to Herrmann, this would represent the beginning of warm relations between Miletus and Pergamon.[162] The text reads: ἐντυχὼν δὲ καὶ βασιλεῖ Εὐμένει κατὰ τὴν δο|θεῖσαν ὑπὸ τοῦ πλήθους αὐτῶι συνχώρησιν καὶ διὰ τῆς ἰδίας συστάσεως|προτρεψάμενος αὐτὸν δοῦναι τῆι πόλει δωρεάν ("He met with King Eumenes, according to the permission granted to him by the people, and, by means of his own good relations with the king, prevailed upon him to give the city the gift") (*SEG* XXXVI 1046 Block I lines 4–6).

The point to stress is that the gift of the gymnasium of Eumenes II to Miletus came about through the initiative of one man, acting alone, but with the crucial permission of the Milesian assembly (*plêthos*).[163] In what sense did Eirenias need "permission"? For Herrmann, Eirenias sought a safeguard from the city.[164] To switch perspectives, might the city of Miletus not have wanted protection from Eirenias? The city, after all, later enshrined that detail of procedure in the decree, defining the gift in no uncertain terms as its own (*dôrea têi polei*). This is in contrast to a common formulation by which the recipient of royal patronage of the gymnasium is

---

[161] The Milesians voted cultic honors for Eumenes in recompense for the foundation. On this exceptional lifetime deification, see further Allen 1983, 114–19. These were announced to the king in a decree that Eirenias delivered. It is very likely that one of these honors was a *temenos*, the very precinct mentioned in *RC* 52 (line 60 of Welles' text) and possibly the peristyle "Hofhaus am Athena-Tempel." For the chronology, see the useful table of Herrmann 1965, 113–14.

[162] Herrmann 1965, 111.

[163] This is the unambiguous interpretation of Herrmann (1965, 78, 111), who translates *synchôrêsis* as "Erlaubnis" and "Zustimmung"; cf. *I.Milet* 1040: "Einverständnis," *pace* Kleine 1986, 131. For *synchôrêsis*, granted by the city to the gymnasium, cf. *I.Pergamon* 252 lines 39–40. For further evidence of the informal character of the first meeting of Eirenias and Eumenes, see the Milesian decree for Eumenes from the propylon of the gymnasium (*I.Milet* 307 lines 17–18). There, Eirenias' presentation to the king regarding the gymnasium is described as τά τε ὑπὸ Εἰρ[η]|νίου ἐμφανισθέντα αὐτῶι ("the things explained to Eumenes by Eirenias") – not as a decree of the Milesians.

[164] Herrmann 1965, 111: "sich sichern."

expressed as the members in the dative plural.¹⁶⁵ A great deal of money was at stake, and Eirenias would prove to have a hand in its administration until the end.¹⁶⁶ As we witnessed earlier, in the case of one King Ptolemy and the gymnasium of Halikarnassos, asking permission (*synchôrêsis*) was no pleasantry; it was a way of aligning interests. Yet one has typically seen the interests of Miletus and Eirenias aligned from the very beginning, the initial approach, and, therefore, explained the episode as simply the intervention of a leading citizen on behalf of his city.¹⁶⁷ There is no textual support for that reconstruction, only the familiar, banal, and suspicious statement that Eirenias always acted to the advantage of his polis and for the fame of his fatherland (Block I lines 2–4).

By the same token, one has wavered over the nature of another mission reported in the decree, which Eirenias made to the court of the Seleukid king Antiochos IV. Again, Eirenias traded on his rapport with a royal interlocutor, in this instance, the king's sister-wife Laodike IV. The result was a grant of tax immunity to the People (*demos*) for certain goods (*genêmata*) exported from the region of the Milesia into the Seleukid kingdom. In the view of H. W. Pleket, Eirenias acted on behalf of Miletus, "or at least not without its consent," though we are in fact given no indication either way.¹⁶⁸ Herrmann writes of diplomacy at Antioch, though Eirenias is not designated as *presbeutês* (ambassador), as he is elsewhere in the decree.¹⁶⁹ All we really know is that in retrospect, the city claimed the gift – for each and every citizen: πρὸς ἐπαύξησιν δὲ ἀνήκουσαν τῶν τε τῆς πόλεως καὶ τῶν ἑκάστου τῶν|ἰδιωτῶν προσόδων ("for the increase of the respective incomes of the city and of each individual")

---

¹⁶⁵ An interesting case is that of Rhodes, Hieron II, and Gelon II after the earthquake of 227/6 (Bringmann et al. 1995, no. 215 [L] = Polyb. 5.88.5–8; Diod. Sic. 26.8.1). Polybius records among other gifts, 10 talents πρὸς ... τὴν ἐπαύξησιν τῶν πολιτῶν, a phrase commonly rendered simply as, "for the welfare of the citizenry," whereas the oil is provided τοῖς ἐν τῷ γυμνασίῳ, "for those in the gymnasium."

¹⁶⁶ See Bringmann et al. 1995, no. 286 [E]. After the death of Eumenes II, the Milesians transferred some of the revenues of the gymnasium foundation to a different (new?) foundation for a ruler cult, which included a grain distribution to Milesian citizens. In his capacity as supervisor of the building of the gymnasium, curiously, Eirenias was responsible for the transfer of the money at the public bank.

¹⁶⁷ E.g., Dreyer 2004, 234; Gauthier 1985, 67 n. 220; Hamon 2009, 356–57.

¹⁶⁸ Pleket 1973, 256.

¹⁶⁹ Herrmann 1987, 175; *I.Milet* III, p. 23: "ein weiteres Mal in diplomatischer Mission am pergamenischen Hof"; Eirenias is designated as *presbeutês* in *SEG* XXXVI 1046 Block I line 9. The embassy in question delivered an honorific decree to Eumenes II voted in response to the gift of the gymnasium.

(Block II lines 5–6).¹⁷⁰ It was just one more demonstration that Eirenias was a virtuous, model citizen (*agathos politês*) (Block II line 7).¹⁷¹

In reality, Eirenias was not the model citizen. He was an extraordinary citizen and, therefore, worthy of extraordinary honors. Note that the round monument on which his decree was inscribed is suspiciously similar in form to the Ionian monument for Eumenes II – only bigger.¹⁷² Yet the city's treatment of Eirenias was not quite royal. Eumenes had been able to choose the site of his extraordinary monument: the *temenos* that Miletus had voted in his honor (*RC* 52 line 60).¹⁷³ By contrast, the siting of the monument for Eirenias was subject to a further decision (or vote?) of the *demos*, not left up to a board of magistrates or simply, as so often, designated loosely in the decree as "the most conspicuous spot" in the agora or gymnasium (*SEG* XXXVI 1046 Block II line 13). Unfortunately, we do not know where the monument stood, as its fragments were not found in situ.¹⁷⁴ But it is worth noticing that there was no role for the gymnasium crowd in the siting of the monument, while there had been one in the earlier case of Eudemos.¹⁷⁵ The *demos* had taken the decision out of their hands.

Again, for Miletus, Eirenias was a different kind of benefactor, which meant that he received unusual honors, but also unusual scrutiny. This is how we should understand the phrase "provided that the honor is confirmed in court (τῆς δὲ τιμῆς ἐπικυρωθείσης ἐν τῷ δικαστηρίῳ)" (Block II

---

¹⁷⁰ For this interpretation, see Bresson 2000, 131–49; cf. Hamon (2007, 357 n. 22), who sees tax immunity for goods exported from the city, not by the citizens.

¹⁷¹ Marcellesi (2004, 181 n. 93) best captures the subtlety of the situation beneath the rhetoric of the decree. Discarding an old idea about a thaw in Seleukid-Attalid relations, she envisions a skillful courtier playing the two dynasties against each other.

¹⁷² Compare the lengths of the bases: 2.65 m (Eirenias) and 1.64 m (Eumenes II). *I.Milet* III, p. 22: "ein wahrhaft 'königliches' Denkmal"; larger than the monument of Eumenes II: Kleine 1986, 130. Note also that both Eirenias and Eumenes received gilded statues, as an honor that may have once been reserved for royals is transferred to the domain of civic benefactors. See Gauthier 1985, 46 n. 116. At Miletus, no one else seems to have received such a statue until early Imperial times. See Herrmann 1965, 87 n. 49. On the technique and proliferation of Hellenistic gilding, cf. Ma 2013b, 253–54. Ma attributes the late Hellenistic increase in gilded statues to the introduction of gold leaf.

¹⁷³ The location of the *temenos* is controversial. One has suspected that it was near the future site of the gymnasium of Eumenes II, but the findspot of the remains of the king's round monument was the so-called Hofhaus am Athena-tempel. See Kleine 1986, 139.

¹⁷⁴ For the findspot, see Kleine 1986, 130. The blocks were discovered in a fountain house in a village southeast of the site.

¹⁷⁵ *Milet* I 3 145 = *Syll.*³ 577. The decision of the city is contained therein: to erect two stelai, one in the Delphinion, in an exedra dedicated by Eudemos himself, the other in the *paidikê palaistra*, in "which place seems appropriate (*epitêdeion*)" (lines 84–87).

line 14). While Herrmann points out that such provisory ratification clauses, usually in a genitive absolute, are a common feature of Greek decrees, those that refer specifically to the confirmation of honors by a process of judicial review are much fewer in number.[176] We hear nowhere else of this Milesian *dikastêrion*, but parallels illuminate the spirit of the institutional arrangement. If assemblies tended to vote up or down on honorific decrees, the precise nature or size of the honor (*timê*) or "gift (*dôrea*)" of recompense might fall to others to decide.[177] This was a means of checking corruption, of legitimating each honor individually. As third-century Achaian Dyme insisted, the polis itself had judged each metic singly before awarding citizenship (κρίνασα καθ' ἕνα ἕκαστον) (*Syll.*³ 529 lines 9–10). Herrmann also adduces as parallels grants of naturalization, which, along with the honor of *isoteleia* (tax equality for noncitizens), fourth-century Athens submitted to a process of review called *dokimasia*.[178] However, a more proximate phenomenon appears in Athens of the third century, which Gauthier has termed "*dokimasia* of rewards."[179] Athens awarded outsized honors (*megistai timai*) to men who had played a decisive role in the city's affairs on an international stage. One such man was the Athenian Phaidros of Sphettos, a major figure of influence in Ptolemaic Alexandria, who received a portfolio of honors just before 250 (*IG* II² 682).[180] A rider to the decree informs us that Phaidros had proposed his own honors in decree form, but that the gift (*dôrea*) was subject to the review (*dokimasia*) of a court (*dikastêrion*) (lines 92–101). Eirenias too may have had his own ideas about which honors he merited, but civic institutions existed to check him. This was the dynamic that structured relations between the gymnasium elite, their cities, and their

---

[176] Herrmann 1965, 88, where parallels are adduced.
[177] Rhodes and Lewis 1997, 514–15, with Hellenistic parallels. On anxiety over the size and nature of public rewards for public benefactions, which appears already in fourth-century Athens, see Domingo Gygax 2016, 240–43.
[178] Herrmann 1965, 88–89. Ma (2013b, 70–75) treats the mechanics and politics of the grants of public space (*topos*) for honorific portrait statues. When a city's own assembly voted to erect a statue, the grant of a *topos* was a tautologous display of communal power. Normal practice was to appoint a magistrate or board to carry out the work (e.g., the *archê* appointed in *I.Oropos* 294). Any further review of the honors in the form of *dokimasia* represents, then, an important check on status-seekers. The Cyzikene priestess Kleidike is another one of the few on record facing such scrutiny. However, an assembly (*demos*) ratified her honors rather than a special court as in Eirenias' Miletus (*CIG* 3657 = Michel, *Recueil* 537).
[179] Gauthier 1985, 78: "*dokimasia* de la recompense."
[180] For the latest discussions of this inscription, see *SEG* LVI 193.

Attalid patrons after 188. The gift itself was the end result of a negotiation on two levels: the city came to terms with the king, but also with its leading citizens.

The Gymnasium as an Association

Any insistence on friction and negotiation – on the gap or social distance between the gymnasium regulars and the rest – may still seem strained. We need to examine how the group organized and represented itself, how it took action. This was a voluntary association that straddled the divide between public and private. In fact, it was made up of several smaller groups called *paides*, *epheboi*, *neoi*, *presbyteroi*, and even *apalaistroi*, each with its own rules and habits.[181] Each group also possessed its own sense of corporate identity, but as institutions, their functions varied. In most cases, they all acted together, either passing a decree or partaking of the perquisites of belonging. Men and boys who frequented the gymnasium but did not belong to a subgroup, some probably noncitizens, seem to have been subsumed under the category of "those who belong to the gymnasium (οἱ μετέχοντες τοῦ γυμνασίου)" or "those who have use of the oil (οἱ ἀλειψάμενοι)," κτλ.[182] Moderns have struggled to define the umbrella grouping them all together.[183] In particular, the German tradition in legal history has taken up the problem, and German contains words like *Vereinswesen* and *Verein* that lack precise linguistic and cultural equivalents in the English language.[184] Scholars have also doubted whether the ancient names of the associations connoted juridical status.[185] For our purposes, it will suffice to think of the gymnasium as a kind of collective, but not one loosely organized by "weak ties" alone.[186] Members chose to participate, rather than find themselves automatically enrolled as citizens of a certain age class.[187] In fact, it must have been the strength of this

---

[181] *paides*: Gauthier and Hatzopoulos 1993, 65–69; *epheboi*: Chankowski 2010; *neoi*: Dreyer 2004 and Bremen 2013; *presbyteroi*: Fröhlich 2013; *apalaistroi*: see above n. 145.

[182] Kennell 2006, s.v. *gymnasiou*; Gauthier 2006, 485 n. 5; Adak and Stauner 2018, 11–12.

[183] Van Bremen (2013, 31–36) considers the definitional problem anew from the standpoint of the *neoi*.

[184] Ziebarth 1896; Poland 1909. See now also the regional corpora Kloppenborg and Ascough 2011; Kloppenborg et al. 2014, along with publications of the Copenhagen Associations Project, such as Gabrielsen and Thomsen 2015.

[185] Fröhlich 2013, 67.

[186] Since Granovetter 1973, sociology has reconsidered the paradoxical strength of "weak ties" in social networks.

[187] Never an age class nor even the *porte-parole* for one: Fröhlich 2013, 79–81.

collective as an institution that led many cities to impose a battery of officials on gymnasia – the civic gymnasiarch, his assistant the *paidonomos*, and the *grammateus* (secretary) – just when the power of the Attalids was peaking in mid-second-century Pergamon.[188] An institution this strong was liable to run its own line out to royal power, which is what happened in Termessos of 319, during the Wars of the Diadochoi, when the *neoi* picked a different dynast from their older peers.[189]

The boldest and indeed most common expressions of the institutional identity of the gymnasium are its decrees. There are scores of inscriptions that emanate from a decision of the collective to honor its patron and publicize the act. It is easy enough to characterize these as harmless exercises in citizenship. What gives pause is the curious use of the procedure of *prographê*, whereby a gymnasium decree became a draft that the polis later decided to incorporate into a civic decree. We have reason to believe that this was a contentious process and that intergenerational or intra-elite conflict lurks behind our documents.[190] A case in point is Attalid Colophon. Prince Athenaios, the youngest son of Attalos I, seems to have endowed that city with a youths' palaistra, perhaps already in the 180s when he was still a *neos* himself.[191] An inscription records honors for Athenaios (**D10**). The first editor of the text, Theodore Macridy, described it as an honorary decree for Athenaios, but as Gauthier made clear, the stone actually bears two decrees, the first providing for a statue of the prince in the sanctuary of Claros, the second for public sacrifice and games on his birthday.[192] The motivation clause for the second decree indicates that a certain collective of the gymnasium, perhaps "the regulars of the place" (οἱ μετέχοντες τοῦ τόπου), had already passed its own decree, or "pre-decree," the aforementioned *prographê*. In it, the group honored Prince Athenaios as a benefactor: ψήφισ|[μα προεγράψαντο περὶ τοῦ] τιμῆσαι Ἀθήναιον ὄντα|[εὐεργέτην (lines 6–8). It is worth noting that the

---

[188] From Attalid Teos, note also the oversight of the *timouchoi*, one of two leading boards of magistrates, in the administration of the property of the *neoi* (Adak and Stauner 2018, 20).

[189] Diod. Sic. 18.46–47; for Van Bremen (2013, 36–40), this episode is paradigmatic of her "disruptive *neoi*." See further on the episode, Köse 2017, 42–43.

[190] For this genre of decrees, see Robert 1926, 507–9; Robert 1937, 149–52. According to Hamon (2009, 360–62), the *prographê* of the Council (*boulê*) was a normative feature of probouleutic deliberation in the Hellenistic polis. For *neoi* decrees as such, see Gauthier 1996, 1–34, esp. 9–11. An honorific decree from Roman Smyrna refers to a vote by three bodies: the *gerousia*, the *neoi* of the Mimnermeion, and the *synodos* of the *paideutai* (I.Smyrna I 215).

[191] Gauthier 2006, 488.

[192] Macridy 1905, 161–63; Gauthier 2006, 465, where the honors of the second decree are also qualified as "gymnasiaux."

honors ratified in the second decree, the athletic events, are distinctly gymnasium-oriented, as is their administration, and even participation in the feast to follow: the gymnasiarch distributes the leftover meat to *hoi aleipsamenoi* (oil users), victors of past stephanephoric games, and various archons (lines 21–26). We catch a glimpse of the confrontational manner in which the *neoi* may have presented a gymnasium decree to the Council in an earlier civic decree of Colophon, which depicts a full 153 of them making one such submission.[193] Van Bremen adduces alongside these texts the vivid scene of the Pergamene *neoi* descending on the Council and Assembly of the royal capital en masse (κατὰ πλῆθος) in order to demand honors for the gymnasiarch Metrodoros (*I.Pergamon* 252 line 37).[194] As she points out, these are all cases of *neoi*, with all of youth's potential for disruption, demanding that honors performed in the context of the gymnasium be promoted to citywide acclamation. These young men were not asking for permission to practice their citizenship in the simulation room of the gymnasium.[195]

Intriguing evidence admits that the city did not dictate the circumstances under which the gymnasium passed its decrees, rendered its accounts, or appointed its magistrates. For example, the surviving fragment of the mid-second-century calendar of the gymnasium of Kos, attesting Ptolemaic, Cappadocian, but especially Attalid benefactions, speaks of a "council" (*boulê*), perhaps taking place in the sacred grove of Asklepios known as the Kypariss(i)on (**D11** line 22). Unfortunately, whatever qualifier preceded the word *boulê* is gone.[196] Bringmann et al. hypothesize a meeting of instructors (*Konferenz der Lehrer*).[197] Edward Hicks had proposed a regular meeting of the Council of the polis of Kos, which representatives of the gymnasium were required to attend.[198] Yet much more likely is an occasion akin to the annual conclave in the gymnasium, termed *synodos en tôi gymnasiôi*, which the civic benefactor and Attalid courtier Kephisodoros required of the ephebes and *paides* of Apameia (**D6** lines 15–16). Civic calendars do not seem to have had any bearing on the dates

---

[193] See the new edition of Gauthier 2005, 101–2.   [194] Bremen 2013, 48.
[195] See also the case of the *neoi* of Xanthos, *SEG* XLVI 1721, with text and analysis of Gauthier 1996. The *neoi* seek their city's permission to have the gymnasiarch Lyson honored in the city's main sanctuary, the Letôon.
[196] The term does not appear in the index of Kennell 2006. He indicates (personal comm.) that he knows of no comparanda.
[197] Bringmann et al. 1995, 252. However, *contra*, see *IG* XII 4 1 281: "concilium magistrorum."
[198] Paton and Hicks 1891, no. 43. Note also Maiuri 1925, no. 434, on the Attalid connection to a shadowy *politeuma* on Kos. I am at a loss over this text. I cannot determine whether it relates to the gymnasium per se.

of these meetings. We even hear of the civic calendar of Iasos falling out of touch with the calendar of the city's gymnasium. Herrmann has demonstrated that, at least in late Hellenistic or early Imperial times, the association used a different era than the city proper.[199]

The organizational homologies between the gymnasium and polis institutions are undeniable. The various associations of the gymnasium imitate civic habits of record-keeping, honoring their benefactors, and publicity.[200] The question is whether, from an emic perspective, the gymnasium was ever an antagonist of the polis, or just the city writ small, as it is usually understood from our etic perspective. Indeed, already for Aristotle, the nonpolitical association (*chrematistikê koinônia*) had looked to the polis as its model.[201] For the philosopher, both groups aimed at the advantage (*to sympheron*) of their members. Yet surely, interests could and did diverge. The association of maritime traders in Aristotle's treatment, for example, may have differed with their city's port officials over the most advantageous way to organize harbor dues. Regarding the gymnasium and the city, these rival tendencies peaked in the second century BCE.[202] Witness what happened on Athenian Delos in 141/0. Up until then, the Athenian practice had been to elect the island's gymnasiarch in the assembly in Athens. However, in that year, the electing body consisted of the Athenian governor (*epimelêtes*) and "those who frequent the gymnasium (οἱ ἀλειφόμενοι)" (*I.Delos* 2580 lines 31–32). In the following year, the old practice was reinstituted for good – and spelled out ([χ]ει[ροτονη]θεὶς ὑπὸ τοῦ δήμου) (line 34). According to Christian Habicht, the reasons for this "messiness" are unclear.[203] Of course, ad hoc circumstances in Athens or on Delos may have led to this power play by the gymnasium's regular membership. Yet as a lapse in a city's control over a gymnasium, albeit one separated by a stretch of sea, it can be regarded as paradigmatic, rather than anomalous. In the absence of vigilance and pressure from the city, those who controlled the gymnasium were the elite, even the noncitizen population – which is to say,

---

[199] Herrmann 1995.   [200] Fröhlich 2013, 66–79.
[201] *Eth. Nic.* 1160a; cf. *Eth. Eud.* 1241b. The fourth century saw an explosion in the number of these associations. For Arnaoutoglou 1998, they contributed to the ideological coherence of the polis. Gabrielsen 2009 expresses a less sanguine view.
[202] Was the power of gymnasia also as great as it would ever be? Note that ca. 130, Ptolemy Euergetes II issued an edict liquidating the assets of all sorts of associations, certainly including gymnasia (Lenger 1964–88, no. 50).
[203] Habicht 1995, 262: "Unregelmäßigkeit."

those who were present – and those who, like the king and his courtier, could with money make themselves present.[204]

Close study of its architectural ensemble and place in urban plans of the period confirms the impression that the gymnasium restricted access in ways that must have served to exclude elements of the citizenry. In fact, it was only in Hellenistic times that the building complex of the gymnasium acquired a specific architectural typology. Above all, this included a large peristyle court, with rooms and exedrae forming a perimeter around a large central court. Architectural historians emphasize the integrity of the design: the gymnasium complex formed a *closed* architectural unity. The peristyle helped produce this effect, as did strong walls and built entryways, which eventually gained inviting propylaea. The unity of these complexes, often sited on slopes, made them at once key landmarks, glimpsed by all who approached the city or summoned its vista to mind, and also simple to close off – even from local outsiders. For all their iconicity, gymnasia were never as accessible as civic spaces like the Hellenistic theater or agora. In short, they were not open spaces. Of late, Ralf von den Hoff goes so far as to call their closure "hermetic." In practice, it was much easier to see inside than to get inside, with propylaea serving as visual provocations: both barriers and windows. Moreover, pathways in and out of gymnasia do not communicate directly or even align along clean axes with public spaces like agorai. For example, from the agora of Sikyon, one can gaze directly up toward the terrace of a large Hellenistic gymnasium (**Fig. 5.3**). Yet one enters not from the east side facing the agora, but rather from a small, side gate on the north, which itself lacks direct communication with the theater it faces. Additionally, unlike most civic sanctuaries, gymnasia, which included shrines, tend to stand apart from processional routes.[205]

At Pergamon, as noted, the *Großes Gymnasion* anchored the street plan of the East Slope of Eumenes' city, marking a middle ground between the

---

[204] The gymnasium of Delos received a great deal of royal patronage in the second century, but none of it Attalid. See Bringmann et al. 1995, nos. 153, 189–91. As for the *presence* of royal figures in the gymnasium, while Roman emperors do appear in epigraphy as gymnasiarchs, Hellenistic kings do not – unless one follows Robert in taking one of the Attalids as the gymnasiarch of Bringmann et al. 1995, no. *357 [E], from Aigai. The job requirements were too strict, though in late Hellenistic cities endowments produced "posthumous gymnasiarchs." In Beroia, at least, the daily presence of the gymnasiarch was expected. Similarly, I know of no certain cases of princes enrolled as ephebes before the two Cappadocians in Athens in 79/8 (*IG* II² 1039 b^i + c^i + p). Thus, I am skeptical of the claim that a Nikomedes (the future III or IV; Bringmann et al. do not treat the issue) was an ephebe on Delos (Bringmann et al. 1995, no. 189 [E] = *I.Delos* 1580).

[205] Hoff 2009, 254–55.

Figure 5.3 Hellenistic Sikyon, view east/southeast from the terraces of the city's gymnasium toward the adjacent agora (Sklifas Steven/Alamy Stock Photo).

Old and New City. The terraced complex was highly visible, both from the plain below and beyond Eumenes' walls, and along the axes of major streets that terminated at the structure's two original gates. Indeed, the more impressive of the two gates, the western, contains a covered staircase, which is rotated toward alignment with the streets of the East Slope. Building on the work of Bielfeldt, Pirson singles out the Pergamene gymnasium as a rare and singularly monumental civic space in the royal capital.[206] Yet as these and other scholars have noted, the citizens of Pergamon remain invisible or anonymous in the epigraphy and archaeology of the gymnasium until the final years of the dynasty. Only under Attalos III did the *demos* begin to dedicate statues in the gymnasium and gymnasiarchs to receive honors.[207] The architecture itself conflicts with any straightforward characterization of Eumenes' gymnasium as open to every citizen of

---

[206] It is worth noting that the Ionic Temple R, which sits on a podium above the Upper Gymnasium, was produced in marble. According to Bielfeldt (2010, 185), the connotations of marble at Pergamon were exclusively royal, while Pirson (2012, 218) observes a conspicuous lack of marble in those spaces that both scholars deem civic, such as the Upper Agora, as compared with royal showpieces like the sanctuary of Athena or the Great Altar terrace. This may be further proof that Temple R, with its independent entrance, was not as well integrated with the ensemble of the gymnasium as the ephebic inscriptions on its wall might indicate. See Trümper 2015, 176–77.

[207] On these dedications, see Hoff 2004, 388–90.

Pergamon. On the contrary, access was tightly controlled (**Fig. 5.1**). One did not enter – as visitors do today – directly from the nearby sanctuaries of Demeter or Hera. Rather, the two original entryways, while set on the main thoroughfare of the city, were quite narrow and did not lead to the decorated Upper Gymnasium. Further, the entire complex of the gymnasium was enclosed, with walls on the east and west and a monumental retaining wall on the south. Late in the Hellenistic period, up-to-date bathing facilities were added to the complex. One entered these baths via the palaistra, which limited access to those already inside.[208] We may place this architectural closure in the context of a broader second-century pattern of creating self-contained ensembles in urban planning, segmenting the city according to function. However, the assumption that the Pergamene gymnasium restricted access because the institution it housed restricted access to citizens is unfounded.[209] Access was restricted, but neither limited nor guaranteed to the citizens. For those who belonged, this was a civic space, distinguished by the very absence of the kind of constraint that polis ideology typically placed on Hellenistic rulers. Visible but not transparent, the gymnasium belonged to the new collectivities on which the Attalid state was built.

New Collectivities

Among those who frequented the Delian gymnasium in the 140s were a sizable number of noncitizens.[210] Delos was especially cosmopolitan, but in this respect, it fits a pattern. As the Beroia law and a host of ephebic lists show, the Hellenistic gymnasium did not exclude noncitizens. In another illustrative case, from Eriza in Caria or from Phrygian Themisonion, a gymnasiarch named Chares was honored in 115/14 for providing oil to the "ephebes, *neoi*, and resident aliens."[211] On the other hand, under the Attalids, it was not the gymnasium's role to fully assimilate outsiders into

---

[208] Trümper 2015, 216.

[209] Many architectural studies (Trümper 2014, 211 n. 35; Pirson 2012, 217; Hoff 2009, 254) point to Kobes 2004, an epigraphical analysis of restrictions on access to the gymnasium, in order to justify the claim that access was restricted to citizens. Focusing on the law from Beroia, Kobes' article in fact shows that exclusion was based *not* on citizenship, but rather on gender and social criteria. He also cites decrees from Miletus (*Syll.*³ 577) and Teos (*Syll.*³ 578) that imply the regular presence of foreign teachers.

[210] Habicht 1995, 262.

[211] Michel, *Recueil* 544 lines 19–20: τοῖς τε ἐφήβοις καὶ νέοις καὶ τοῖς|ἐπιδημοῦσιν ξένοις. On this text, see also Wilhelm, *Neue Beiträge* VI, 45–48.

the civic corps. If a noncitizen could access the gymnasium, once inside, he still retained his political status. The Attalids' gymnasium did not so much produce new citizens as new collectivities, rooted in the realities of social life and Mediterranean mobility. The *non*citizens of Mylasa – a colorful example – in a late Hellenistic decree of their own, honored Leontiades adoptive son of Philiskos, the gymnasiarch who at his own expense had provided them with 80 months' worth of oil, which he made available all day and up until night. (Arbitrary closures, apparently, were common, at least for noncitizens.) In their short text, this group of subalterns twice emphasizes that as metics, *paroikoi*, and aliens, they lacked a share in the public oil distributed in the gymnasium. Yet with their dedication of a portrait statue of Leontiades, the group publicly memorialized their participation in a certain form of civic life.[212] Ultimately, the new collectivities of the gymnasium, these broader cross-sections of the Hellenistic polis, were the targets of the Attalids' gifts. Indeed, the creation and the performance of the new collectivities owed much to royal sponsorship. So much so, in fact, that the Attalids' constant care for the gymnasium cannot have been reflexive adherence to a static model of social organization in the polis. Rather, with imperial motives, the Attalids helped increase the formal participation of noncitizens in civic rituals, profiting from the enduring vitality of the polis as a source of identity, while also contributing to a radical overhaul of social relations.

We hear echoes of this process in documents that refer to limited distributions of consumable, which is to say, perishable goods to the typically broad-based gymnasium society: certainly oil, but also food, and perhaps sweet wine, too. These were events like the "royal banquets" of the gymnasium, the *basilika deipna* mentioned in the long decree of Colophon for Menippos (*SEG* XXXIX 1244 Column II line 47). We will return to them shortly, but it is enough to point out here that the Colophonians had hoped to reconstitute with civic monies a royal foundation for (annual?) banquets for *neoi* and *presbyteroi*. Publishing the inscription from Claros, the Roberts found a comparable institution in the endowment of Philetairos for the *synagôgê* (gathering) of the *neoi* in Kyzikos.[213] At such banquets, Attalid money convened a group in the gymnasium that almost certainly included noncitizens.

---

[212] *SEG* LIV 1101. On the apparent paradox of noncitizen participation in what scholarship has – from an etic perspective – categorized as civic life, see Ma 2008b, 376.
[213] Bringmann et al. 1995, no. 241 [E] lines 15–16; *Claros* I, 100.

The protocols of the gymnasium banquet carried over the old status distinctions of the polis, but reorganized them according to a different logic, creating new symbolic frontiers between a select group of citizens, claiming aristocratic status, and the indistinct mass of other citizens.[214] Inside the gymnasium, it was presence itself, which trumped political rights exercised on the outside. The charters for the gymnasium feasts of Critilaos from Aigiale (Amorgos) and of Elpinikos from Eretria mandate different eating arrangements for citizens, metics, Romans, and temporary residents (*parepidêmountes*) – a larger piece of meat for the table of the ephebes. They do not, however, bar one from eating for lack of citizenship.[215] These two texts date to ca. 100, but already in the gymnasium honors that a certain Lydian city granted to Asklepides, courtier of Attalos II, a group of participants decidedly larger than the citizenry alone is envisioned.[216] To have a share in the distribution of the gymnasium banquet, it was more important to be present than to be a citizen. The new collective was not a virtual community. Its bonds were forged in real life. Thus, in the case of Critilaos, a share in the banquet goes to "those citizens who are present (τοῖς τε πολίταις τοῖς ἐπιδημοῦσιν)," just as it does to "those foreigners who are temporarily resident (ξένοις τοῖς παρεπιδημοῦσιν)" (lines 72–73). Gauthier underscores the point: this was a religious, not a civic festival, and one which demanded physical participation.[217] The *basilika deipna* of the gymnasium of Attalid Colophon would have been no different. For nowhere in the entire corpus of royal gifts to gymnasia is there a single instance of a distribution made exclusively to citizens in the manner of the grain fund of a Hellenistic polis. Habicht has restored one for the Gymnasium of Ptolemy in Athens, a conjecture that is worth reconsidering (*IG* II² 836).[218]

---

[214] For the "new symbolic frontiers" of aristocracy in the late Hellenistic polis, see Hamon 2007, 94.

[215] Critilaos: *IG* XII 7 515. It should be noted, at Critilaos' banquet, the youth of the city are *required* to be present; Elpinikos: *IG* XII 9 324 = *Syll.*³ 714.

[216] See *SEG* XLIX 1540 line 22.

[217] Gauthier 1980, 212: "Le caractère religieux (exigent la participation physique) et nullement civique de la fête est ainsi fortement marqué."

[218] Bringmann et al. 1995, no. 17 [E]. Habicht 1982, 115–17, restores: [... σίτου]|τοῦ διαμε[τρουμένου τοῖς πολίταις εἰς τὴν σ]|τοὰν τὴν ἐν [τεῖ παλαίστρᾳ τοῦ γυμνασίου τοῦ]|βασιλέως Π[τολεμαίου κτλ.] (lines 1–4). My own autopsy of the stone in the Epigraphical Museum of Athens (EM 7473) revealed no further trace of the intended recipients of Ptolemy's largesse, as the stone is broken on both sides. The restoration πολίταις seems suspect. See already Robert and Robert 1948, 127–28. On the topographical relationships and pseudo-civic ideology of the Gymnasium of Ptolemy, see Cesare 2018, 219–29. Another possible exception is a distribution at a festival in Miletus with posthumous ruler cult for Eumenes II (Bringmann

On the contrary, the terms of at least one Attalid foundation, that of either Eumenes II or Attalos III for the gymnasium of Andros, imply a distribution in the manner of Critilaos and Aigiale: food for participation (**D9**). The honorific decree praises the gymnasiarch of Andros for having discharged his duties generously and lawfully, which in part meant organizing a procession and a feast on the king's birthday. The gymnasiarch seems to have been generous in leading his own cow in procession, but indeed lawful in then sacrificing the animal immediately (παραχρῆμα) (line 8). The mandate to sacrifice immediately prevented the gymnasiarch from slaughtering the animal later, among different company.[219] It ensured that those who ate the meat were those who showed up on the king's birthday, that the feast took place only in the gymnasium. At Aigiale, Critilaos showed the very same concerns for his feast: ἡ δὲ δημοθοινία γενέσθω ἐν τῷ γυμνασίῳ ἐπάναγκες ("the banquet absolutely must take place in the gymnasium") (lines 59–60). And the flowers, the sacrificial victims, along with their skins – they were all to be consumed "immediately," again, παραχρῆμα (line 62). Both rituals incorporate elements of civic ideology. For example, at Aigiale, the procession begins at the city's prytaneion, while on Andros, a sacrifice is made on behalf of the *demos*. Yet in each case, the focus of the ritual is squarely on the patron of the gymnasium and his family: Critilaos and his prematurely deceased, heroized son Aleximachos, or the king, his father, and their queens.

We may now return to the issues raised in the case of Colophon and Menippos. Not long after the War of Aristonikos, the Colophonians had voted to revive so-called royal banquets. The city assumed control and financial responsibility for an Attalid institution. However, sufficient public money did not materialize, and the city resorted to the appointment of magistrate-liturgists called *epimênioi* to make up the difference. Menippos then intervened to release both the city and any would-be elite peers of the entire financial burden. The city had suffered greatly in a war that ushered in a profound change of the social fabric of the region's poleis. After Aristonikos, we see fully, on the one hand, the emergence of peerless super-citizens and, on the other, the erosion of distinctions between ordinary citizens and noncitizen permanent residents. Leading citizens like

---

et al. 1995, no. 286 [E]). However, it is noteworthy that the Milesians had *modified* an earlier foundation of Eumenes II. All this points to the hazard of assuming citizen-only distributions in the gymnasium. Roussel (1916, 188) refers to one such distribution at the Hermaia of the Athenian cleruchy of Salamis in 131/0. Yet in that text, the gymnasiarch in fact invites *everyone* (*IG* II 594 line 5).

[219] Robert 1960, 122–23.

Menippos, but also Polemaios of Colophon, and Moschion of Priene, instituted public feasts that created the new collectivities that crisis seemed to demand.[220] As Fröhlich observes, these feasts were at once a gathering of the entire population and also a means of distinguishing elite groups, which is to say, of maintaining – if reorganizing – the status distinctions of the polis.[221] As heirs to the kings' legacy and ex-ephebes themselves, the outsized civic benefactors of the period knew the gymnasium as the civic institution in which presence counted the most, in which the role one played was the youth, the king, the hero, Alexander or Herakles, and not the middling citizen. The "royal banquets" of the gymnasium, then, were the perfect model for the new "inclusive" public feasts. Menippos, who as a mere *neos*, according to his epigraphical biography, proved his worth to Colophon on embassies to the Attalid kingdom (*Attalikê basileia*), was responsible for reconstituting the kings' feasts. Yet he was also credited with sponsoring a lavish public feast (*dêmothoina*) during the Epiphany of Dionysus that fed citizens on the first day, and metics and holders of *isoteleia* on the second.[222] These men literally towered above their co-citizens: life-size portrait statues of Polemaios and Menippos stood on columns over 9 m tall in the Sanctuary of Apollo at Claros. The monument of Menippos, on which his decree was inscribed, squeezed itself between a statue of Antiochos IV and the Temple of Apollo itself.[223] The social distance between Menippos and the other Colophonians recalled the gulf between the kings and the rest. And like the kings, they found in the gymnasium a civic space that conformed to the realities of power and demography.

As we read in the roughly contemporary Colophonian decree for Polemaios, the War of Aristonikos had sent refugees pouring into the city.[224] Polemaios helped provide for the outsiders, and seems to have promoted the idea of a public subscription (*epidosis*) for their welfare. At his wedding, he treated citizens to a sweet wine distribution called *glykismos*, while to noncitizens he gave a portion of meat. The wedding of Polemaios, just like the public feast of Menippos, was an occasion for the ritual performance of a new collectivity in Colophon. In this respect, these rituals mimicked long-standing practice in the gymnasium, an institution

---

[220] On the traditional chronology, Archippe of Kyme is also thought to have held sway in this period. For the low chronology, see Hamon 2005, 135–36; for the high, see Bremen 2008.
[221] Fröhlich 2005, 245.   [222] SEG XXXIX 1244 Block II lines 36–41.   [223] Étienne 2004, 104.
[224] SEG XXXIX 1243 = *Claros* I, 11–62.

with which both men were familiar.²²⁵ Indeed, in Pergamon itself and elsewhere in the region, post-Attalid elites soon began using the rituals of the gymnasium to integrate outsiders.²²⁶ The long decree of Sestos in honor of Menas, former Attalid *stratêgos* of the Chersonnese and the Thracian *topoi*, priest of King Attalos in his city, and twice gymnasiarch, provides a wealth of detail.²²⁷ During Menas' second stint as gymnasiarch, post-Attalid Sestos was in dire circumstances, with the raids of nearby Thracians preventing the cultivation of its territory. In this case, the integration of outsiders was vital for the survival of the city. Menas consecrated his inaugural Hermaia kai Herakleia festival "for the salvation of the *demos* and the *neoi*," and "he invited to the sacrifice not only those who have a share of the oil, but everyone else as well, even giving a share to foreigners (ἐκάλεσεν ἐπὶ τὰ ἱερὰ οὐ μόνον τοὺς μετέχοντας τοῦ ἀλείμματος| ἀλλὰ καὶ τοὺς λοιποὺς πάντας ποιούμενος τὴν μετάδοσιν τῶν ἱερῶν καὶ τοῖς ξέ|νοις)" (lines 60–67).

We have lingered over the historical context of the decree of Colophon for Menippos because the novelties of civic life in the sub-Hellenistic world refract earlier interventions by kings. It has long been recognized that a veritable cult of civic benefactors in the first century BCE was modeled on Hellenistic ruler cult. Yet it also pays bearing notice that the Attalid kings, in effect, piloted the expansion of participation in civic rituals that we tend to associate with the chaos and rapid social change that transpired after their demise. The choice of the gymnasium as the quintessential beneficiary of Pergamene redistribution meant that participation of noncitizens in a steeply hierarchical political community was normalized within its walls. Outside, civic intellectuals were just then debating the ethics of an unbridled philanthropy that reduced co-citizens to clients and blurred boundaries with outsiders.²²⁸ The logic of the "inclusive" public feasts of the sub-Hellenistic period and the earlier *basilika deipna* of the gymnasium was the same, namely, the creation of a new collectivity that transformed the status distinctions of the polis without breaking them. The polis remained a powerful source of identity, but the meaning of citizenship and participation in civic life had changed forever. From the Andros inscription, we can discern the logic of an Attalid-sponsored public banquet in the polis (**D9**). For the processions that led up the feasts, two texts

---

²²⁵ The *glykismos* in particular, which Robert and Robert (*Claros* I, p. 50) see as invariably including noncitizens, may have originated in the gymnasium. See, e.g., *I.Histriae* 59 line 14.
²²⁶ See the ephebic lists of post-Attalid Pergamon: *MDAI(A)* 32 (1907) 416–20.
²²⁷ *I.Sestos* 1 = *OGIS* 339.   ²²⁸ Gray 2020.

suggest similarly broad participation.[229] On Kos, ca. 180, Ariarathes IV celebrated military success with a procession that entailed the participation of the gymnasiarch, the *neoi*, and the ephebes, and he promised to crown three groups: citizens, *paroikoi*, and temporary residents of Kos (*SEG* XXXIII 675, lines 6–7). The Attalids were very active patrons of the gymnasium of Kos in this period and very close allies of Ariarathes IV.[230] We may imagine that Attalid festivals on Kos were similarly organized. Moreover, we know much of the procession that welcomed the victorious Attalos III home to Pergamon (*OGIS* 332 lines 33–38). It included the priesthood and the magistrates of the city of Pergamon, but also its ephebes and *neoi*, gymnasiarch, *paides* and *paidonomos*, and finally the citizens, their wives and daughters, as well as the other inhabitants (*enoikountes*).

The aim here was to provide a framework of explanation for the Attalids' habit of funding gymnasia in cities under their control or influence. Scholars have taken the benefits of the arrangement to be self-evident. On this reckoning, the Attalids gave to the gymnasium in order to produce loyal subjects or, in slightly less Machiavellian terms, out of an ill-defined Panhellenism.[231] As for the cities, the last wave of work on the Hellenistic polis argues that the vitality of civic institutions after Chaironeia left the Attalids with little choice; the cities imposed this model of giving on the kings, further strengthening polis identity in the face of royal power. Behind these explanations lies a pair of related assumptions about the true beneficiary of the arrangement, and so about who initiated it. Yet both sides had something to gain, and, usually, we cannot know who pushed first. Taking a fresh look at the exchange brings out the true nature of the sovereignty play. Attalid patronage of the gymnasium strengthened polis identity, but it weakened popular control of communal self-representation before royal power. An elite group, theoretically open to noncitizens, now negotiated directly with Pergamon over a city's fate. Those who had a share of the oil also had access to the king, who now had a bridgehead into civic life, precisely what Apollonidas of Sikyon was trying to prevent by blocking the gift of Eumenes II to the Council of the Achaean Koinon. Correspondingly, we can now better sense the full sting of the sovereignty

---

[229] On late Hellenistic civic processions, see A. Chankowski 2005.
[230] See Bringmann et al. 1995, nos. 226–28.
[231] These explanations stem ultimately from Robert; the more Machiavellian ones go back to Rostovtzeff.

violation of Sulpicius, the Roman who entertained complaints against the Attalids from a seat in the gymnasium of Sardis.

In the mid-second century, the gymnasium was not "the city writ small," but rather, the preferred site of interaction between cities and kings. Eumenes II, who made an architectural spectacle out of one, unparalleled in its size and spatial complexity, the singular visual reference point for his new capital city, helped focalize civic life into its confines. He helped further politicize the gymnasium, and eventually, after the Attalids were gone, it emerged as a "second agora," in which the city's heroized dead were buried and the collective voice of the free inhabitants routinely expressed. Under the Attalids, what facilitated the rise of the gymnasium, it has been argued, were the dynamics of the institution at this juncture in its historical development, such as its peculiar system of finance, or the seemingly endless opportunities for embellishment it offered its patrons. The gymnasium also offered members of this dynasty, ever the financial sophisticates capable of exploiting the anonymizing power of money, a way to launder money to their supporters. We must also be aware that the Attalids faced an institution in flux, and that the intensity of their benefactions must have affected or exploited the following processes. Curty has written of a mid-second-century transitional period in the evolution of the gymnasiarchy, which saw the gymnasiarch take over the oil supply, just as the city began to take charge of honoring the gymnasiarch. The mid-second century also witnessed a race to amass social capital in the gymnasium, in evidence with the formal appearance of the gymnasium's *presbyteroi* as an association. The Attalids participated in and stood to profit from any struggle over the definition of the gymnasium as a public space. They certainly contributed to increasing its profile, as the monumental, marble architecture of the gymnasium now begins to turn up in the archaeological record.[232]

---

[232] For the transitional "period charnière" in the evolution of the gymnasiarchy, see Curty 2015, 267–91. Appearance of *presbyteroi*: Fröhlich 2013, 91. Total absence of marble architecture from gymnasia before the second century: Hoff 2009, 260. Note the lack of any marble (or any other stone remains) from the earliest, ostensibly third-century phases of the "Gymnasium of Ptolemy" in Athens. I cannot assume, as Cesare (2018, 216–17) does, that the "Gymnasium of Ptolemy" and the Diogeneion were major architectural *erga* of the last quarter of the third century, which transformed and "modernized" the built environment of Athens' city center (yet failed to garner the attention of Herakleides Kritikos). Notably, Mavrojannis (2019, 1–10) argues that it was Ptolemy Lathyros who donated the "Gymnasium of Ptolemy" as a massive architectural complex in 116 BCE. In a similar vein, Prag 2007 credits Roman administrators with raising the profile of the civic gymnasium in Sicily.

This chapter was also an essay on the distinctive nature of the gymnasium as a civic institution. If this was the preferred site of interaction with royal power, what might that say about its relation to other civic institutions? The gymnasium enjoyed a measure of autonomy from those other civic institutions, it was argued, and occupied a unique position vis-à-vis king and court. Ironically, this fact has become obscure to us precisely because both parties – the kings *and* the cities – wanted it to be so. At every turn, cities sought to constrain the elites of their gymnasia and bind them ideologically to the polis. As for the Attalids, they certainly intended their patronage of the gymnasium to be perceived as gifts to "Greek cities (*poleis Hellēnidas*)" in the terms of Polybius (32.8.5). A final example comes from Chios, where an inscription records two gifts of "Attalos," one for the renovation of the city's walls, and a second for the heating of the gymnasium.[233] One struggles to relate these gifts chronologically to the voluntary subscription (*epidosis*) of Chios for wall construction, particularly because the Attalid text also lists the names and properties of locals.[234] Yet in epigraphic terms, the association of the two public goods, sturdy walls and a gymnasium, could not have been any tighter. We lack an explicit statement of the Chians on what the gymnasium meant to them, but the *epidosis* document provides stark testimony for the walls: the freedom (*eleutheria*) and autonomy (*autonomia*) of the homeland (*patris*) (lines 1–2). If the Attalids had convinced at least some of the Chians to think similarly of the gymnasium, they had achieved success.

---

[233] Maier 1959–61, no. 51 = Bringmann et al. 1995, no. 231 [E]. For Migeotte (1992, 180), Attalos II is certainly possible; for Schalles (1985, 105 n. 634), it must be Attalos II. While Bringmann et al. list Attalos I as the donor, neither historical nor epigraphical arguments favor either candidate decisively.

[234] See Migeotte 1992, no. 60. An Attalid gift close in time to the Chian public subscription: Maier 1959–61, vol. 1, 194.

6 | Pergamene Panhellenism

The aim of the preceding holistic account of the Attalid fiscal system has been to recast the so-called liberal or bourgeois monarchy as a line of administrative savants, who won an empire not by the spear but by making the cultural reproduction of local constituencies, the elite of the gymnasium, the polis community, and emergent civic organisms in rural Anatolia, all depend on efficient taxation. When we view the Attalid kingdom from this perspective, the kings themselves fade out of view – just as they do on their own coin types.[1] Yet, if we follow the taxes back to the metropole, the relationship between culture and power only increases in salience. For we find the Attalids taking a hyperactive role in collecting, curating, producing, and circulating cultural artifacts.[2] From the Library of Pergamon to the Academy of Athens, tax revenues funded the Attalids' spending spree on culture. Taxes allowed the Attalids to capture pride of place in the archaeological record of Panhellenic centers such as Delphi and Delos. In addition, the manner in which the citadel of Pergamon and its hinterland were developed with the proceeds of empire also represented a cultural statement to would-be subjects. No picture of Attalid political economy can be complete without a consideration of the role of culture in determining the outcome of the Settlement of Apameia. In other words, did the cultural pageantry and positioning of the Attalids contribute to the ideological integration of the new state?

According to a standard reference article on the dynasty, cultural ideology masked real weakness, while monuments and bibliophilic lore have obscured the fact that Pergamon controlled neither its destiny nor its notional territory.[3] Again, the scale, costliness, and prestige of Pergamene

---

[1] The inconspicuousness of the Attalids is in part an effect of our lack of confirmed portraits in any medium. In sculpture, a mix of charismatic and sober portraits – contrast, for example, the Terme Ruler with a head in Malibu – pervades the pages of Queyrel 2003 (see, here, esp. pp. 234–35). While many of Queyrel's identifications remain conjectural, note the persistent tendency among art historians to interpret even lost Attalid portraits as mixing divine, royal, and extraordinary elements with a noncharismatic or civic aspect, the so-called "bürgerliche Bild" (Schalles 1985, 148–49; Hoff 2018, 264).

[2] See, most recently, Kuttner 2015.   [3] Kosmetatou 2003, 173–74.

cultural output would seem to belie such pessimism about its material basis. Yet the subject of an Attalid *Kulturpolitik*, of a commitment to "culture as policy," has largely been approached as a matter of understanding the subtlety, even genius with which these unpedigreed latecomers to royalty constructed authentic Hellenic cultural credentials, not only by patronizing Athens and the Panhellenic sites of Old Greece but by cleverly building bridges of fictive kinship to Arkadia and coopting the Muses of Thespiai.[4] Meanwhile, in Anatolia itself, we risk losing track of the kind of local reception that postcolonial scholarship has recovered for the other multiethnic kingdoms such as Ptolemaic Egypt and the Seleukid Near East. And yet it is this internal, Graeco-Anatolian – in ancient terms – Asian audience that counts for assessing the impact of the cultural content of Attalid imperialism. However, unlike Hellenistic Egypt and the Near East, Anatolia was home to both indigenous Greeks and indigenous non-Greeks. Here, the encounter with the subaltern was strange and unique. In fact, mutual intelligibility was unparalleled, especially since a large population of Phrygians spoke the Indo-European language closest to Greek.[5] Therefore, neither inauthenticity nor cultural appropriation is a suitable lens through which to view the Attalids. In the Mysian context, Greek identity was also bound to take its own forms, distinct from those of the mainland and the islands of the Aegean. Helpfully, by providing a cultural profile of the Greeks of the kingdom's geographical core, recent studies of the Classical polis network of the Kaikos Valley and of collective memory and cult in Pergamon under the Gongylids shed light on specifically local resonances of the Telephos myth.[6] We must also consider what particular currents of Panhellenism issuing forth from the Library may have meant for an audience of East Greeks. For all their connections abroad, the Attalids could not afford to ignore cultural dialogue with the Greeks at home.

On the other side of the ledger, the extent to which the Attalids acted like Anatolian kings has been seriously underappreciated in accounts of their rise. In fact, the Anatolian substrate of Attalid cultural identity is rarely investigated beyond takedown references to the mixed parentage of Philetairos: his mother was a Paphlagonian of ill repute, and his father, on shaky onomastic grounds, is usually counted a Macedonian. In the Classical period, the lords of the Kaikos Valley had been Greeks and Persians, but the population was a mix of Greeks, who have left us a few

[4] Gruen 2000; Étienne 2003. On Thespiai, see Schalles 1985, 36–37. On Arkadia, see *I.Pergamon* 156.
[5] Obrador-Cursach 2019, 238–40.   [6] Dignas 2012; Grüner 2016.

Atticizing grave stelai, and, presumably, a silent majority of Anatolians.[7] In the Bronze Age, the region had lacked the Aegean connections of the Milesia or the Troad.[8] We must recall that for Herodotus Pergamon was not one of the eleven Aeolian poleis, and that for Xenophon, the citadel was still "Pergamon of Mysia."[9] Of course, the muted Hellenism of early Pergamon informs the idea that the Attalids "emerged from the sidelines of history to become one of the dazzling centres of antiquity."[10] Cruelly, the Anatolian cultural background of the Attalids is thereby rendered invisible when it should help us explain how Pergamon transformed itself from vassal to continental empire, adroitly governing both the coastal poleis and the inland *ethnê* and *demoi*. Measured against the coastal cities of the deltas of the great Anatolian rivers – Smyrna on the Hermos, Ephesus on the Kayster, and Miletus on the Maeander – early Pergamon is often rated a Hellenic backwater. Yet it was no accident that a city-state on the margins of two cultural spheres emerged with an empire. The Attalids represent a culturally "bilingual," distinctly Anatolian response to the diasporic Graeco-Macedonian model of empire. This was not a settler state, and the Attalids were not "chameleon kings," who manipulated local expectations.[11] In a groundbreaking study, Ann Kuttner has shown that the creative incongruity of Pergamene eclecticism in art and architecture is riven with Anatolian materials, motifs, and topophilia. As she points out, the Attalids continually proclaimed themselves something other than Hellenes.[12]

The goal of this chapter is to take stock of the Attalids' cultural diplomacy to their own people. This means taking seriously the dynasty's claim to rule a place called Asia, which is part of, but also apart from, Hellas. That claim is voiced already in an epigram of Philetairos, inscribed at Pergamon on an Olympic victory monument, which makes a distinction between Hellenes and Asians.[13] Yet we find the programmatic statement reflected in the 184/3 decree of Telmessos in Lycia, a document for the scramble that pitted the Attalids against Anatolian rivals from Bithynia and Galatia. The inscription recounts that Eumenes II, savior and benefactor, declared war and undertook danger "not only on behalf of those ruled by him, but also

---

[7] Grave stelai: Kelp 2014, 360–66. It has proven difficult to assess the cultural profile of Classical Pergamon from the relatively few imported Greek fine wares of the fifth and fourth centuries recovered in excavations, for which see Agelidis 2014, 76 n. 3.
[8] Horejs 2014. [9] Hdt. 1.149; Xen. *An.* 7.8.8. [10] Gehrke 2014, 124.
[11] For a critique of the concept of "chameleon kings" (coined by Ma 2003a, 179), see Strootman 2017, 179.
[12] Kuttner 2005, 140. [13] *I.Pergamon* 11 lines 5–8.

on behalf of the other inhabitants of Asia."[14] Asia was the theater of war. The population of Asia looked to Eumenes for salvation. We can understand the ease with which such Pan-Asianism coexisted with Hellenizing tendencies only if we recognize the Attalids as the heirs of Anatolian kings such as Mausolus of Caria and Croesus of Lydia, occupying the same geographical niche defined by East Greece and the Anatolian steppe. We must avoid reducing the cultural universalism of the Attalids to an antithesis of Greeks and barbarians. This is the temptation of the mythic allegory of the Gigantomachy on the Great Altar and of the historical analogies of the Little Barbarians on the Athenian acropolis.[15] In mainland Greece, the Attalids joined the Aetolians and others in portraying victory over the Gauls as a replay of the triumph of a united Hellas over the Persians. Unsurprisingly, at Athens, Attalos I catered to the Athenian version of the mythic cycle, which also juxtaposed Trojans and Greeks, as well as Amazons and Greeks. Meanwhile, in their own kingdom, the Attalids invested in the prestigious legacy of Troy and leaned heavily on the support of Aeolian cities allegedly founded by Amazons. Therefore, we begin by investigating the intellectual orientation of the official Panhellenism of the Library of Pergamon, in order to reconstruct a few of the lineaments of the cultural dialogue between the Attalids and the Greeks of Asia Minor. Next, we consider ancient perceptions of the capital as an Anatolian royal city rather than an inauthentic polis, first, from the perspective of its tumulus burials and, second, from the vantage of its mountaintop palace and urban plan. Pergamene Panhellenism, then, emerges as the particularistic expression of the civilization *of* cis-Tauric Asia. Finally, we reevaluate the relationship of culture to power in Attalid interactions with new or potential subjects in the highlands of central and southern Anatolia. In places like Galatia and Pisidia, we come to see Pergamene Panhellenism as a truly universalistic expression: civilization *in* cis-Tauric Asia.

The Library of Pergamon

The Attalids had always courted intellectuals, but Eumenes II was the first to attract an academic superstar to the capital, the Stoic philosopher and

---

[14] Allen 1983, no. 7 lines 6–10. On a possible Pergamene claim to an Asian kingdom by dint of affiliation with Dionysus-Sabazios, see Burkert 1993, 265 n. 34, on Cic. *Nat. D.* 3.58.
[15] Stewart 2004, 200–1; cf. Queyrel 2017, arguing strongly against the Galatian allegory; doubts also expressed by Ridgway 2018, 253.

literary critic Crates of Mallos. Crates arrived at an opportune moment: the physical setting of the Library, wherever it was, now took shape amid a flurry of book buying and book production on the city's famous parchment.[16] In addition, an entire cast of Pergamene intellectuals now found themselves working for much higher stakes. As a Stoic, Crates must have cherished the opportunity to steer an ascendant king and the population of his new empire toward virtue and harmony with nature. He is best known for his work on the text of Homer, especially allegorical and lexical exegesis in pursuit of knowledge of the cosmos. For the Stoics, such knowledge on the global scale directly informed ethics on the local.[17] However, we sorely lack any idea of the librarian's position on the ethical relationship of a wise man to his community of origin (*patris*). Yet the issue was a central concern of the Early Stoa, treated at length by Zeno of Citium in his *Politeia*. Building on Cynic critiques of norm and convention, Stoic cosmopolitanism reconsidered the act of political affiliation. Meanwhile, Pergamon's territorial monarchy was faced with the task of securing commitments from subjects whose primary affiliation remained the conventional one, the community of origin.

Symbolically, as a vast store of cultural prestige, the Library contributed to the power of the dynasty. As a self-proclaimed *kritikos*, Crates busied himself with the creation of a classical literary canon.[18] This put the Attalids in direct competition with the Ptolemies of Alexandria. Emulation of Athens aside, Pergamon became a center of cultural production in its own right. For example, one suspects that the Library produced a royally commissioned, specifically Pergamene edition of Homer.[19] Yet if the Library, under the stewardship of Crates, made a distinctive ideological contribution to the maintenance of an empire, which, as I have argued, promoted local, civic identities and institutions, it managed to do so by blunting the hardest edges of Stoic cosmopolitanism. Early Stoicism had inherited a critical stance on the *patris* from Diogenes the Cynic. The radical stance of an early Stoic named Aristo recalls the view of Diogenes. Aristo is cited for the claim that "the fatherland [*patris*] does

---

[16] For an overview of the question of the Library's location, see Coqueugniot 2013, expressing skepticism about the traditional identification of the rooms behind the North Stoa of the Sanctuary of Athena Polias. Cf. Seaman 2016, 415. For the related testimonia, see Platthy 1968, 159–65, esp. testimonium 151: some translators take Strabo 13.4.2 to say that Attalos II built libraries. See further on architecture Hoepfner 2002. As a physical space for the collection of books, the library (βιβλιοθήκη) begins to appear in inscriptions only in the second century BCE – see Hendrickson 2014.

[17] Brown 2009. [18] Nagy 2011. [19] Finkelberg 2006, 238.

not exist by nature."[20] And for a Stoic, what does not exist by nature is of no concern. Aristo, however, was a dissident, and Zeno and his immediate successors, principally Chrysippus, counseled politically active men. In principle, the true polis of wise men stretched beyond the boundaries of any particular city. In fact, the achievement of the ultimate goal (*telos*) of Stoicism entailed the dissolution of each individual city-state. That the true foreigner (*xenos*) was the morally bad was a belief held by Zeno, who placed virtue over institutions.[21] The realization of that *telos*, though, was safely set in the distant future. For the contemporary Stoic sage, to live a cosmopolitan life was to emigrate to the court of a king, even an enlightened barbarian, in order to promote virtue among the greatest number of people. Nevertheless, Chrysippean doctrine suggests the possibility of serving the fatherland and privileging its citizenship, if only as a worst-case scenario for a sage rendered immobile by circumstance. These ideas may have caused some embarrassment for later thinkers of the Middle Stoa, but they formed part of the intellectual background of Crates of Mallos. Later, too, arrived the more humanistic cosmopolitanism of universal community. The Stoicism of Crates would seem to have taken membership in the polis for granted, but harbored doubts about its citizens' common destiny.[22]

A more traditional attitude is in evidence in the writings of Arkesilaos of Pitane, an Academic and a client of Eumenes I, who began an epigram for a fallen friend from inland Anatolia, crying, "Far, far away are Phrygia and sacred Thyateira, your native land (*patris*), Menodoros, son of Kadanos."[23] Plainly, no Pergamene school of thought existed.[24] Moreover, Stoicism seems to have gravitated back toward practical ethics under Panaetius, said to have been a student of Crates.[25] Rather, it is noteworthy that the intellectual climate of the Library contained an element of ambivalence about the more exclusive claims of the community of origin on an individual, even if the identity of the average Attalid subject remained rooted in place. Yet a different strain of scholarship, alive and well in the same

---

[20] Brown 2009, 554–55; Plut. *De exil.* 600 E.   [21] Schofield 1999, 760.
[22] Stoic obligation to honor one's native land: Long 1986, 190. See here also Brown 2009, 555; Sellars 2007, 13. Stoic cosmopolitanism lived out in a *real* city: Sellars 2018, 161–64.
[23] Diog. Laert. 4.6.31.
[24] Pfeiffer 1968, 235. The Stoic Blossius of Cumae, a Gracchan exiled from Rome, ended his life at the court of Aristonikos (Plut. *Ti. Gracch.* 20; Cic. *Amic.* 11.37). This has led some to ascribe a radical and utopian social agenda to the regime of the last of the Attalids. For skepticism, see Africa 1961 and the careful work of Daubner (2006, 176–86, esp. 181) on the many strange bedfellows of the usurper's coalition.
[25] Pfeiffer 1968, 245. On Panaetius' innovations, see Long 1986, 211–16.

Library, responded directly to that silent majority's firm sense of place. This was what Rudolph Pfeiffer once termed "the new antiquarianism" of Pergamon, associated with periegetic art historians such as Antigonos of Karystos and Polemon of Ilion. Polemon deserves close attention, since we know enough about his oeuvre to try to reconstruct its target audience. Born a subject of the Attalids, he is widely believed to have been present at their court.[26] Like the Attalids, he was honored at Delphi, which he adorned with a history of its treasuries.[27] He too was deeply familiar with the tribes of Athens and the city's acropolis, as well as cities such as Sikyon, dear to Pergamon. Yet the Panhellenism of an author nicknamed *Helladikos* encompassed scores of cities with little or no direct connection to the kings.

The titles and fragments of the works of Polemon point to an abiding interest in the histories of individual cities.[28] For example, he wrote books on the cities of the regions of Phocis, Lakedaimon, and Pontos. For each city, the antiquarian recorded genealogies, laws, institutions, festivals, and local lore. He wrote in an old, popular tradition, which had survived for centuries, usually alongside, but occasionally mixed in with the historiography of political affairs and military events.[29] Polemon aimed to distinguish himself from certain rivals in Alexandria by using autopsy to claim more accurate knowledge. He traveled to these locations and studied their monuments and inscriptions. One can imagine that the realia of his traveler's accounts resonated with readers' lived experiences and ritualized memories, perhaps more so than the erudite poems of the library-bound Callimachus.[30] The Attalids were famous for collecting art, and research such as Polemon's will have lent their prize pieces robust object histories, a context that stuck to the statues accumulating in Pergamon through purchase and spoliation. In fact, in the presentation of art in the citadel's sanctuary of Athena Polias, the Attalids pointed proudly to objects' provenance, appropriating prestige without denying individual cities their own histories. The island polis of Aegina, under Attalid rule from 206, is a case in point. In the Pergamene sanctuary, two images from Aegina were

---

[26] Engels 2014, 86–89, though see p. 77, arguing that Polemon's *To Attalos* is addressed to Apollo, not a king. Cf. Kosmetatou 2001, 124–25.
[27] *Syll.*³ 585. Pfeiffer 1968, 247.
[28] Titles: *Suda* s.v. Πολέμων (Π1888); with summary and analysis of fragments by Karl Deichgraeber in *RE*, s.v. Polemon.
[29] Bravo 2007.
[30] On the "realism" of Pergamene antiquarianism, celebrated in the nineteenth century, see *RE*, s.v. Polemon, 1319; Pfeiffer 1968, 251.

juxtaposed side by side, one a classical work of the Aeginetan sculptor Onatas, in the Severe Style, the other, a Hellenistic sculpture by the Boeotian Theron, but inscribed, "(The image is) from Aegina" (*I.Pergamon* 48–49). The juxtaposition of old and new artifacts, in different styles, both from Aegina, gestured toward the particularity of that city's history, continually unfolding. The local histories of Polemon, like the statues of Aegina, belonged to a Panhellenic cultural patrimony, now under Attalid management. As Kuttner points out, from our perspective, the notion of a common patrimony of the Greeks sits in tension with the Attalids' admiration for historically located pedigree and respect for original place.[31]

Polemon's literary output can be considered a response to a crisis of Greek identity, even a reaction against the unmooring tendencies of conquest-driven migration and Stoic cosmopolitanism.[32] He wrote auto-ethnography for a Panhellenic public. The modern label "antiquarianism" misleadingly implies pedantry; these writings invoked the deep past to buttress contemporary attachments to communities of origin. The figure of Polemon is an important clue about the specific character of Pergamene Panhellenism, which reaffirmed local differences for imperialist aims. One can detect the ideology as early as the reign of Philetairos, who when dedicating in Thespiai and Aigai, employed each city's local dialect.[33] With the increase in their power, the Attalids were able not only to deploy local knowledge but to expropriate it, occasionally right along with the hard currency of cultural artifacts. The paradoxical, even jarring effects of this policy are evident in the signal case of Athens. Attalos I could not convince a certain Lakydes, head of the Academy, to join his court. In an extraordinary gesture for a royal patron, Attalos bowed to the primacy of the place: the king built a garden in Athens for the use of the philosophers, known as the Lakydeion.[34] From Athens, the Attalids were also not at liberty to remove colossal masterpieces such as the Athena Parthenos or Promachos. In a novel twist, they made copies for their own acropolis.[35] Close study of the cult and sanctuary of Athena Polias, as well as that of Demeter and Kore further down the slope, shows Athenian influence but not slavish imitation. Imperial Pergamon evoked, honored, and emulated,

---

[31] Kuttner 2015, 49, 51. For Massa-Pairault (2010, 19), Polemon's object histories simply reflect the unspecified "'politica culturale' del regno."
[32] Engels 2014, 88–92.   [33] *OGIS* 310, 311, and 312.   [34] Diog. Laert. 5.67.
[35] Schalles 1985, 53–54.

but, contrary to a scholarly cliché, never claimed to replace or supersede Athens.[36]

The Panhellenism of Polemon's work is also noteworthy for its geographical limits. The Greek world, for Polemon, was a much smaller place than the effectively limitless domain once envisioned by Isocrates. The fourth-century philosopher had argued that education and acculturation could produce Hellenes, and by the second century, that vision was a reality. When Antiochos IV invaded Egypt, he was able to pick out the Greek residents of the polis of Naukratis, in order to award them each a gold stater.[37] Polemon, however, did not go looking for Greeks in Egypt. Whereas Polybius, for example, took the entire inhabited world (*oikoumenê*) as the stage of his history, or the narratives of earlier periegetes such as Herodotus and Hecataeus of Miletus wandered off into barbarian lands, Polemon's setting was an anachronistic vision of the confines of Hellenism.[38] As is often remarked, he restricted himself to studies of the Greeks of the mainland, the Aegean islands, Sicily, Magna Graecia, and, indeed, East Greece. For a Hellenistic intellectual, these were noticeably parochial interests. The exceptions, Carthage and Caria, seem to prove the rule, since their earlier histories had been so intertwined with the Greeks.[39] Polemon's project highlighted the differences between cities, celebrating the peculiarities of sanctuaries. Yet it also drew a boundary around a comfortably antiquated version of the Hellenic world, one which the Attalids now targeted for support.

Another view of this Panhellenic audience, with its strong local loyalties, emerges from a Polybian vignette about a boxing match at Olympia. It took place on the eve of the Third Macedonian War, as Greece faced the prospect of the destruction of the old geopolitical order at the hands of Rome. The story also highlights popular antipathy for kings. The match pitted a reigning champion named Kleitomachos against a challenger, Aristomachos, whom Ptolemy VI had trained for the occasion. Hungry

---

[36] See here the cogent arguments of Agelidis 2014 (esp. 99, 106), regarding the development of the cult of Athena Polias at Pergamon. At home, the Attalids emphasized the Trojan, not the Athenian connection.

[37] Polyb. 28.20.11.

[38] On the evolution of the antiquarian tradition, see Momigliano 1990, esp. p. 67. He is the rare commentator who considers Polemon worldly, though see too Massa-Pairault 2010, 18, alleging encyclopedism.

[39] *RE*, s.v. Polemon, 1299. Interestingly, a fragment mentions Telmessos, the Attalid possession in Lycia. On Carthage, the subject of the work does not seem to have been the origins, institutions, or customs of the Carthaginians, but a Punic textile bound up with the history of the western Greeks.

for an upset, the Olympic crowd began by cheering on the underdog Aristomachos. Polybius describes Kleitomachos on his heels, nearly vanquished, pleading with the crowd, "Did they think he himself was not fighting fairly, or were they not aware that Kleitomachos was now fighting for the glory of the Greeks and Aristomachos for that of King Ptolemy? Would they prefer to see an Egyptian conquer the Greeks and win the Olympic crown, or to hear a Theban and Boeotian proclaimed by the herald as victor in the men's boxing match?"[40] In an instant, the two competitors, confirmed Hellenes insofar as they had managed to enter an Olympic boxing ring, assumed different, oppositional ethnic identities. The speech ignited the crowd, which carried the Boeotian champion to victory over his Egyptian challenger. The incident does more than simply demonstrate the celerity with which a mob can descend into the humiliation of a perceived outsider; it also captures a specific, popular notion of Hellenicity at a critical juncture in the political history of the ancient Mediterranean. After a century and a half of increased migration and the forging of polyglot monarchies on the eastern lands of Alexander's conquests, the claims of the community of origin were as strong as ever. The determinant criteria for belonging to the community of Hellenes, at least the one conjured up during the Olympic bout, were backward-looking: identification with an ancestral polis, an *ethnos*, and a particular place in Old Greece. Idle curiosity did not bring us the methodologically rigorous antiquarianism of Polemon, but rather popular prejudice about the distinctiveness of a homeland. Polemon's agenda is thus entirely Attalid in that these self-proclaimed stewards of the Greek cultural heritage evince an acute interest in topographic authenticity.

They shared that interest with another second-century intellectual, the historian Demetrios of Skepsis in the Troad. He has been imagined as an "independent country squire," for Diogenes Laertes calls him a wealthy and noble man, who also may have had access to a first-rate local library – Neleos of Skepsis was purported to have once been in possession of Aristotle's books.[41] Unsurprisingly, Demetrios seems to have taken pride in his native city and participated in its rivalry with nearby Ilion for pride of place in Homeric lore.[42] Yet his ancient reputation implies a broader stature both in the Attalid kingdom and in the world of letters. He practiced textual criticism of Homer and topographic exegesis. He

---

[40] Polyb. 27.9.12. Loeb trans. Paton, modified.
[41] Pfeiffer 1968, 250. On the question of library access, Biraschi (2011, n. 12) is agnostic.
[42] On this polemic, see Ellis-Evans 2019, 27–29.

delighted in distinguishing spatial homonyms and, like Polemon, could boast of autopsy, pointing to the very hill on which the Judgment of Paris took place. In fact, Strabo, delving into the hydronymy of Mount Ida, urges his reader to trust Demetrios, a local person with experience of the terrain.[43] The geographer made great use of the scholar, whom Diogenes Laertes also praises as an excellent *philologos*.[44] Just as Demetrios' fragments bear witness to an awareness of Attalid affairs and high politics, it can confidently be assumed that his ideas circulated in the emerging Library of the capital, even if he worked from home.[45] Moreover, his creation, the *Trojan Catalogue* (Τρωικὸς διάκοσμος), a mammoth commentary of 30 books on the 62-line description of Troy's federative army (*Iliad* 2.816–77), Anatolian history as much as local, provided the Attalids – true Trojans on his reckoning – with a model for their pan-Asian empire.

Demetrios' sprawling study was an attempt to organize the populations and lands of the Anatolian peninsula into a coherent whole. His description of his work as a *diakosmos* (ordering) implies as much.[46] On the one hand, his interests were restricted to the substance of the Homeric account, the subject of the exegesis. On the other hand, one senses that Homer's lines were felt to be an inadequate ethnography of contemporary Anatolia. Demetrios needed to account for entire peoples and regions, features of his world that seemed to be sorely missing from the poem. A further mystery was the origin of the toponym Asia itself, which Demetrios located squarely within Attalid territory, in Maeonia-Lydia.[47] To the bedeviling problem of where to draw the line between Trojans and non-Trojan allies, Demetrios offered an intriguing solution. Modern Homeric philology tends to posit a single Trojan contingent, made up of bands of warriors native to the various cities of the Troad, coupled with five allied contingents from distinct geographical zones. These were the likes of Hektor's Trojans and Aeneas' Dardanians, in other words, the true Trojans. Demetrios, by contrast, seems to have divided the Trojan core, at least, into nine so-called dynasties. Where did Pergamon fit in? Interestingly, whereas the

---

[43] Strabo 13.1.43.
[44] Diog. Laert. 5.83–84: πλούσιος καὶ εὐγενὴς ἄνθρωπος καὶ φιλόλογος ἄκρως ("A wealthy and well-born person, as well as an acute *philologos*").
[45] High politics: e.g., a comment on Antiochos III in *FGrHist* 2013 T 3. Attalid affairs: *FGrHist* 2013 F 6 and F 31a, both on the Καλὴ Πεύκη ("Beautiful Pine"), a lost work of Attalos I, which, according to Ellis-Evans (2019, 87–88), transmits boastful Pergamene claims to the wood and resin of the forests of Mount Ida.
[46] Trachsel 2017, 2–5. Technically, the work does not claim to be a catalogue at all.
[47] *FGrHist* 2013 F 41.

future site of the city and indeed the entire Homeric Mysia, on the basis of the primary text of Homer's epic alone, can be assigned to allied units, in Demetrios' exegesis, the Kaikos Valley and its Telephid rulers belong to the Trojan core. His Trojans ruled "up to the Kaikos."[48] Yet adding the Attalids' ancestors to Priam's kingdom was clearly a stretch. Strabo even seems to waver in his endorsement of Demetrios' schema, uncertain of the existence of the ninth dynasty, which belonged to Eurypylos son of Telephos, lord of the Kaikos. In an earlier part of the epic cycle, Achilles and company had mistaken Telephos' Teuthrania for Troy. Was it Troy after all? Pergamon was indeed an alternate name for Priam's citadel. Strabo's hesitation may also have stemmed from the fact that among the nine dynastic captains, only Eurypylos arrived at Troy *after* the events described in the *Iliad*. The *Odyssey* knows of the event, but a scholiast states that Priam was obliged to convince Eurypylos to enter the war as the allied king of Mysia.[49]

A centuries-old tradition had linked the houses of Telephos and Priam: the mother of Eurypylos was Astyoche, a Trojan princess, and Andromache bore Pergamos, the eponymous founder of the city. The Attalids have been justly accused of constructing mythological links to the winning side of the war as well. In a grotesque twist, Neoptolemos fathered Pergamos, and the position of the stoa of Attalos I at Delphi seems to have stressed the Aeacid connection.[50] Equally ancient must have been the tradition of Telephos' Arkadian origins, which provided the Attalids with a prestigious link to Herakles (and Alexander). What is new in the work of Demetrios of Skepsis is the identification of the Attalids' forefathers as primeval Trojans. This anchored the dynasty to the rest of Anatolia – not just the Kaikos Valley.[51] The Attalids now gained access to the deep, pan-Anatolian past to which Demetrios was determined to award cultural primacy. Many mountains were called Ida, but it was the one in the Troad, he argued, on which Zeus had been born. It was a daring argument, mounted against the authority of fifth-century Athenian tragedy. What was the proof? Demetrios took a characteristically empiricist tack, declaring that the rites of Rhea (Cybele) were indigenous to the Troad

---

[48] Strabo 13.1.2. [49] Schol. Hom. *Od.* 11.520.
[50] On the Aeacid connection, see Schalles 1985, 114–15.
[51] Cf. Bielfeldt 2019, 187: "Telephus is the expression of a Pergamene particularism."

and Phrygia alone. Any claim to the contrary was mythology, he declared, not history.[52]

So much had changed since Trojans in Phrygian dress had graced the tragic stages and red-figure pots of Athens. As is well known, Homer depicts a war between Achaeans and Trojans, not Greeks and barbarians. Those categories had yet to be developed. It took the events of the Persian Wars to initiate a change in self-perception that recast the Trojans in the role of eastern, in the case of Paris, specifically Phrygian barbarians.[53] Inevitably, the idealized civilization of Priam's kingdom militated against any such downgrade. It has even proven possible to regard the *Ilioupersis* (Sack of Troy) depicted on the northern metopes of the Parthenon as a cautionary tale in hubris for imperial Athens.[54] However, it is difficult to deny that the fifth-century Athenians inflated their participation in the mythological war of the epic cycle to match their leading role in recent history's clash with Persia. The conflation of Troy with Persia followed suit. In the agora, the iconographic program of the Painted Stoa was the first to juxtapose the Battle of Marathon with *Ilioupersis*. Later, on the Periklean acropolis, in addition to the Parthenon metopes, one can point to a colossal bronze "Trojan Horse" set up in the sanctuary of Artemis Brauronia, stocked with local, Athenian heroes. If in this montage, the acropolis of Athens came to stand in for the citadel of Troy, this was of a piece with Athenian attempts to claim their own primacy in the Troad by rescripting the Aeolian and Ionian migrations.[55] In other words, not only were the Trojans barbarians, by this account, but their occupation of Ilion was illegitimate.

As we have seen, the conception of Demetrios of Skepsis was entirely different. It served Hellenistic Pergamon's imperial needs, not those of classical Athens. In Demetrios' conception, Trojans claimed primacy in the Troad, and Pergamenes were counted among their ranks. Ties of kinship bound them to Phrygians, construed as a population of primordial Anatolians. Demetrios' work brings into focus the multifaceted character of the Trojan connection in Attalid cultural politics, which represented far more than a means of currying favor with the Romans.[56] Indeed, Ilion was the fulcrum by which the Attalids made themselves kinsmen of the

---

[52] *FGrHist* 2013 F 61. Cf. *CIG* II 3538, a late second-century oracle from Klaros, which makes the rocky peak of Pergamon the birthplace of Zeus.
[53] Hall 1988, 1991.   [54] Ferrari 2000.   [55] Rose 2014, 146–50.
[56] Indeed, Demetrios disagreed with the idea that Aeneas was progenitor of Rome (*FGrHist* 2013 T 3; Gruen 1992, 41–42).

descendants of Aeneas. In 205, we find Ilion and Pergamon set side by side as signatories to the Roman-brokered Treaty of Phoinike. The dynasty's benefactions at Ilion and other interests in the Troad are well documented.[57] Yet at the very same time, Attalos I effected the transfer of the cult of Idaean Cybele to Rome from a seat in Pessinous, the ancient Phrygian cult center. Gruen has written of the way in which the Trojan lineage allowed the Romans to acquire a character "distinct from that of the Greeks but solidly within the Greek construct."[58] In an analogous fashion, the same lineage gave the Attalids a purchase on a distinct, Anatolian identity, now firmly embedded in the Homeric matrix. Troy was a bridge to Rome, but also to Pessinous.

The Attalids' stake in the glory of Troy was then of critical importance to their imperial project and no mere window dressing. It may be that a hint of their Trojan affinity is admitted by the historical narrative presented on the Athenian acropolis in the form of the dedication known as the Little Barbarians. In the reconstruction of Andrew Stewart, the Attalid monument presented a universal history, unfolding from the beginning to the present, a series of challenges to the civilizational order: Giants, Amazons, Persians, and, finally, Galatians. The Attalids could rely on a local tradition of assimilating the enemy of the hour to the Persian barbarian, as well as a Panhellenic one that likened the Galatian bands to Xerxes' army.[59] For Stewart, the dedication "created a Pergamene-Periklean alliance across time and space to defeat the entire gamut of civilization's foes."[60] Yet the Trojans were conspicuously absent from the rogues' gallery. By contrast, the Periklean prototype, as represented by the Parthenon metopes and the Stoa Poikile, included an *Ilioupersis*. The sack of Troy was later represented on highly visible temples such as the Argive Heraion and the temple of Asklepios at Epidauros, and the iconography reemerged in the Troad itself at Ilion and Chrysa.[61] The Attalids seem to have taken part in the construction of the new Athenaion at Ilion, which, ironically or not, featured an *Ilioupersis* on its metopes with Trojans in eastern garb.[62] We have no

---

[57] Kosmetatou 2001. Note that a tribe of Ilion was named Attalis (*I.Ilion* 121).
[58] Gruen 2010, 247.
[59] The Macedonians were cast as the Persians in Chremonides' decree *IG* II² 687. On Galatians as Persians, see Stewart 2004, 200–1. Note especially the epic *Perseis* of Mousaios of Ephesus (*FGrHist* and *BNJ* 455), associated with the court of Attalos I. Fragments liken and compare the Galatians to the Persians.
[60] Stewart 2004, 200.   [61] On these monuments, see Ridgway 1997, 25–30, 34–40.
[62] On Pergamene participation in the construction of the temple, deduced principally from stylistic and technical affinities, see Rose 2014, 185. Tellingly, Webb (1996, 149) wavers between Persikomachy and *Ilioupersis*.

way of knowing what, if any, role Pergamene artisans or patrons had in the selection of the theme for the Athenaion. Its appearance, unusual in the Hellenistic period, must be related to the special relationship of the Troad to the Homeric past, especially at a time when Iliadic tourism was booming. On the other hand, we know that the Attalids did not evoke a Trojan theme among their dedications on the Athenian acropolis. This may have been because they saw themselves as the successors of Priam, as civilized a king as any who had ever lived.

The Attalid Way of Death

Faced as they were with the task of ruling a vast and diverse Anatolian territory, the Attalids' choice to play the part of Priam's heirs makes perfect sense. Like Priam's rule, they could argue, theirs too was just and rightful. Likening their empire to the Trojans' alliance, moreover, would have promoted an ideology of consent and cast a shadow over coercive measures. In the archaeological record, one can detect an allusion to the glory of the heroes of Troy in the form of a series of burial mounds (tumuli) scattered around the periphery of the city of Pergamon. Most of the tumuli of Pergamon are Hellenistic, built in the third and second centuries BCE.[63] In fact, adjacent to the city's gate, the early second-century fortification wall of Eumenes II sliced through a third-century tumulus encasing a chamber tomb, effectively incorporating it into the bulwark. Since Archaic times, the names – and cults – of Homeric heroes had been associated with particular hilltops, natural and man-made. On his way through the Troad, Alexander had visited a certain mound then known as the tomb of Achilles.[64] Under the Attalids, the citizens of Ilion undertook a major public works project at the site now known to archaeologists as the Neolithic settlement of Sivritepe. They artificially increased the height of the mound, from 5 to 13 m, an intervention that was sure to capture the imagination of would-be pilgrims. The site was soon roundly recognized as the Tumulus of Achilles.[65] Now, at just this moment, members of the ruling clique of Pergamon were burying themselves in tumuli. Surely, one impression conveyed by the choice of tomb type was the desire to assert Trojan filiation. Were the tombs, then, just one more baldly transparent effort to

---

[63] For the spatial distribution of the known tumuli at Pergamon, see Kelp 2014, 356. Maltepe, the second largest of 11, seems to be a construction of the Roman period.
[64] Arr. *Anab.* 1.11.12.   [65] Rose 2014, 190–93.

Figure 6.1 Yığma Tepe (courtesy of Pergamon Excavation of the German Archaeological Institute).

invent tradition? Quite the opposite: the tumuli fit into a well-documented Anatolian tradition, which informs us about the Attalids' cultural identity and helps explain their success.

With just a glance over the tumulus field at Pergamon, one notices both considerable diversity in mortuary practice, but also the unique grandeur of the Yığma Tepe tomb (**Fig. 6.1**) Given their number, differences in size and in the nature of the excavated grave goods, it must have been the case that kings and nonroyal elites alike shared this burial custom. The smaller tumuli, such as Tumuli 2 and 3, have a diameter of ca. 30 m and are braced by a low stone wall called a *krepis*. Both lack a burial chamber and contain only an andesite sarcophagus buried below ground level. Grave goods from Tumulus 3 are modest compared with those of Tumulus 2, which include a golden oak-leaf wreath. Another significant example is the tumulus on the saddle of the Ilyas Tepe, facing the east side of the acropolis. It is also just 37 m in diameter (5 m tall), but it contains a *dromos* (entry corridor) and an elaborate, Macedonian-style chamber tomb covered with a barrel vault. Yet the subterranean burial in a stone sarcophagus recalls the rite practiced by the builders of Tumuli 2 and 3.[66] The occupant of the tomb is thought to be an important general of the

---

[66] Kelp 2016, 603.

third-century reign of Attalos I. None, though, matches the grandeur of Yığma Tepe, which is 158 m across, 35 m tall, and surrounded by a deep ditch, the very source of its material, a cavity that enhances the visual impact of the mound. Despite several attempts to find it by digging and with geophysical prospection, a burial chamber has never been located, but a monumental *krepis*, without an entrance, has been exposed. New excavations have uncovered thin rows of stones above and perpendicular to it, which may be late additions to the monument. Ceramic finds from the excavations of the early twentieth century, taken together with the style of the masonry, offer a provisional date in the second BCE. An important clue for the identification of the occupant of the tomb is the orientation of the Yığma Tepe along an axis that joins both the west side of the Temple of Athena and the stairway of the Great Altar, over 3 km away. The city-builders Eumenes II or Attalos II are therefore the most likely candidates. Given its unique size and suggestive spatial context, the fact that we await the hard proof need not deter us from an analysis of the tumulus as a royal burial monument.[67]

Comparison of the Attalid tumulus tradition with the burial customs of the major Hellenistic dynasties is instructive. The Ptolemies, we know, were interred and displayed alongside the body of Alexander inside a mausoleum known as the Sema or Soma. That building lay within the segregated royal quarter of the city of Alexandria, attached to a complex that also included the Library and the Museum. The monument housed Alexander's cult as well as the dynasty's. With this novelty, the Ptolemies clearly broke with pharaonic precedents, but in good Egyptian fashion, they had themselves mummified.[68] While aided by archaeology, our picture of the Seleukid practice is in fact less complete. We know that Antiochos I built a sacred precinct for the remains of his father Seleukos I, known as the Nikatoreion, set within the palace district of Seleukeia Pieria. The precinct contained a large, non-standard Doric temple that covered a crypt, in which, it has been conjectured, Seleukos I's descendants joined him in death. This combination of precinct, temple, and, therefore, posthumous ruler cult, all housed within a palace district, was repeated in breakaway Bactria at Ai Khanoum. It seems to represent the Seleukid way of death.[69]

---

[67] No hard proof: Kelp 2014, 357. For recent archaeological work and preliminary dating, see Pirson 2016, 184–87; on latest geophysical results, Pirson 2019b, 110–13. Wilhelm Dörpfeld, who first excavated Yığma Tepe, believed it contained the heroon of Pergamos. *Contra*, see Kosmetatou 1995, 140–41. Other possibilities include the tumulus of Auge, observed by Pausanias (8.4.9). On Auge and the Kaikos Valley, see Williamson 2016, 74–75.

[68] Thompson 2003, 114; Erskine 1995, 41.   [69] Seleukid royal burial: Canepa 2010, 7–10.

In the case of the Antigonids of Macedon, direct testimony is lacking. However, it seems very likely that they were buried in tumuli. Certainly, several of their Temenid predecessors were buried in chamber tombs under the Great Tumulus of the royal necropolis, which was not attached to the palace, but lay on the outskirts of Vergina/Aigai. Though the necropolis of Pergamon has not (yet) produced the exposed architectural facades of the conventional Macedonian tomb, shared features include the barrel vault on Ilyas Tepe, the common *krepis*, and the wreath of Tumulus 2.[70] The fundamental point of similarity between Pergamon and Macedonia is a consistent if not continuous tradition of tumulus building, which the powerful, almost by default, make their own. In Macedonia, we can trace it from the Iron Age mounds at Vergina to the proliferation of large (50–100 m wide) tumuli at Hellenistic Pella.[71]

Tempting as it is to interpret the Pergamene tumuli as little more than a claim to Macedonian identity, shoring up the link to Alexander that was tenuous at best, we risk overstating the importance of a single point of reference among many. Moreover, by positing diffusion from Macedon, we mistake correlation for causation.[72] It is important to understand that in this respect, the Macedonians themselves were just one party to a heritage from prehistoric southeastern Europe. The neighboring Thracians were another, and as they moved from the central Balkans eastward, the practice spread into the region of modern Kırklareli in the Thracian Chersonnese.[73] With another Iron Age migration, that of the population that came to be known as the Phrygians, the tomb type appeared around Gordion.[74] To try to pick apart the issue of influence hundreds of years later is next to impossible, though Barbara Schmidt-Dounas has suggested that it was, in fact, Anatolia that influenced the growth in the size of the later tumuli of Macedonia.[75] In short, for an Attalid subject, a tumulus did not read as

---

[70] On underground, built chamber tombs in the Macedonian tradition, see Palagia 2016, 383. On the golden oak-leaf wreath in Macedonian burials, see Kyriakou 2014.

[71] On Macedonian tumuli, see Schmidt-Dounas 2016, esp. 102, 111.

[72] Link to Alexander: Kosmetatou 2003, 167–68. [73] Yıldırım 2016.

[74] For the combination of linguistic and material cultural evidence that seems to confirm Herodotus' report (7.73) that the origin of the Phrygians lay in southeastern Europe, see Roller 2011, 560–61. Cf. Obrador-Cursach 2019, 242–43, on this "linguistic minefield," noting some similarities, not necessarily genetic, between Phrygian and Thracian, as well as the considerable distance between Phrygian and the Greek dialect of Macedonian.

[75] Tumuli at Hellenistic Pella based on impressions of Macedonian soldiers in the "East," which in this context, could mean only Anatolia: Schmidt-Dounas 2016, 111. Cf. Boardman and Kurtz 1971, 277–83, esp. 279: "While the chamber tombs within tumuli, survivors of Bronze Age practice or derived from Anatolian tradition, may have contributed something to the

Macedonian. In Anatolia itself, an impressive number of models for the Yığma Tepe were available. The landscape was saturated with tumuli – from the fuzzy eastern border inland to the boundaries of the coastal city-states. They flanked the capitals of earlier Anatolian empires such as royal Phrygia and Lydia, and had more recently become a defining feature of the Granikos Valley in the Troad. Because these are highly durable monuments, an ancient viewer saw an accretion of tumuli from different periods. Their dates of construction, only a minority of which have been established by modern excavation, were hardly discernible in antiquity. Yet significantly, a chronological synopsis of the tumulus tradition in Anatolia demonstrates continuity of practice. It also provides a broader context for interpretation.

The earliest point of reference for the Yığma Tepe is indeed the tumulus field at Gordion, capital of Iron Age Phrygia, filled with some 240 examples.[76] The Phrygians began building them in the ninth century BCE and increased their size and the richness of their contents in the eighth. If the number of such tombs seems to diminish in the sixth century BCE, Hellenistic examples have also been recorded at Gordion.[77] Now dated ca. 740 BCE, the most monumental of all is Tumulus MM, a royal burial consisting of a wooden chamber covered by a tumulus 53 m high and 300 m in diameter. In the second century BCE, it lay in a part of Galatia that bordered Attalid territory, but one can also find Phrygian tumuli in areas directly under Pergamene control. For example, in the late eighth or early seventh century BCE, Phrygians had built a spectacular series of tumuli far from Gordion, on the piedmont above the plain of Elmalı (Bayındır), in the southern Milyas.[78] Similarly, in western Phrygia, a recent survey identified 65 tumuli, most of which cannot be dated without excavation. The painted Taşlık tumulus exhibits Phrygo-Lydian architecture, but may date to the Achaemenid period, as does the painted tomb at Tatarlı. On the other hand, the find-rich Kocakızlar Tumulus, 80 m in diameter and erected in open country 3 km from the site of Midaion, is

---

development of the Macedonian tomb, they had nothing to do with its final form, especially in its detailed resemblance to a house."

[76] A total of 44 have been investigated archaeologically.

[77] An early series ends in the sixth century: Roller 2011, 562. Hellenistic examples: Liebhart et al. 2016, 629.

[78] Others date the Bayındır tumuli to the sixth and early fifth century BCE, labeling them Phrygo-Lydian. See Bayburtluoğlu 2004, 158–59. See further on the state of the question, Tiryaki 2016, still allowing for an eighth- and seventh-century date for the Bayındır necropolis, but dating many of the Milyan tumuli to a period of local dynastic rule under the Achaemenids, 525–470 BCE.

Hellenistic.[79] After the collapse of the Phrygian state, Lydian royals and elites adapted the practice to their own architectural traditions in the second quarter of the sixth century BCE.[80] Certain Lydian tumuli possess a *krepis*. Ten kilometers from Sardis is a field known today as the Bin Tepe ("thousand hills"); around 100 tumuli have been identified at Bin Tepe, and 500 in greater Lydia. Of these 600, only 54 have been dated to within a century. While several of the largest and most prominent, such as Kocamutaf Tepe, associated with king Alyattes, date to the period of Mermnad rule, the tumulus tradition is best represented in Lydia during the first century of the Achaemenid period.[81] At the same time, tumuli of the Lydian style appeared at Delpınar in Persian-controlled Pisdia.[82] The Achaemenid period also witnessed the proliferation of tumuli in Troad's Granikos Valley, such as the one at Kızöldün, dated ca. 500–490 BCE, the source of the Polyxena sarcophagus. These seem to belong to a mixed milieu of Anatolian, Greek, and Persian estate-holders. Once they were dispossessed of their lands, these sites were largely abandoned.[83]

Clearly, dramatic shifts in the historical center of power affected the distribution of tumuli. A succession of empires left their mark on the landscape. The Attalids, it seems, as heirs to one of the petty fiefs of the Persian period, picked up where the likes of the Gongylids left off. Yet high political history hardly explains the ubiquity, durability, and historical continuity of the phenomenon. Salvage archaeology in contemporary Turkey, driven by the twin threats of economic development and looting, provides a reasonably random sample. The last 26 years of accidental discoveries has produced 43 excavated tumuli. Chronologically, they run the gamut from Iron Age to Late Roman. Significantly, 18, or 42%, have been dated to the Hellenistic period. Their spatial distribution is very broad, with a clustering in the upper Maeander and Lykos river valleys, which Ute Kelp has related to Attalid influence and even a possible refoundation of Hierapolis.[84] Another discernible pattern is that the tumuli seldom lie within a 5-km radius of recorded settlements (**Map 6.1**). Whether they belong to rural estate holders or to rulers residing in nearby towns and cities, the tumuli do seem to promote claims of land possession.[85] In political terms, they also present the face of power to wayfarers traversing a demarcated territory.

---

[79] Sivas and Sivas 2016. [80] Roosevelt 2009, 140; Luke and Roosevelt 2016, 408.
[81] Roosevelt 2019, 148–49. [82] Hürmüzlü 2016. [83] Rose and Körpe 2016.
[84] Kelp 2016, 605–8.
[85] Cf. an unusual Hellenistic tumulus at the center of the Carian city of Hyllarima: Henry 2013.

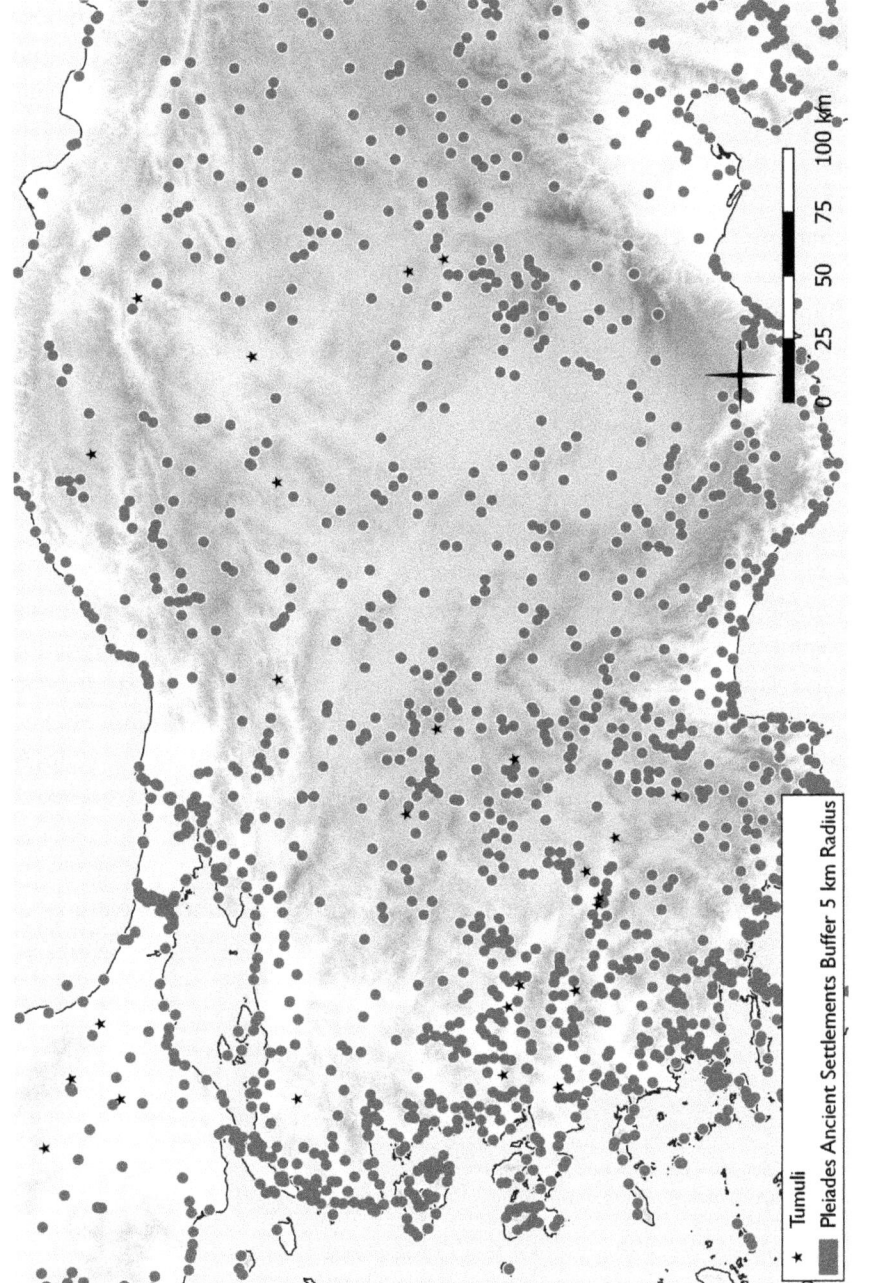

Map 6.1 Tumuli recorded in salvage excavations (*Müze Çalışmaları ve Kurtarma Kazıları Sempozyumu Yayınları*, 1990–2016) and ancient settlements in the Pleiades data set (pleiades.stoa.org).

From the Aegean to the Euphrates, a dense scatter of tumuli emerged over the course of the first millenium BCE. Ultimately, Pergamon's tumuli belong to what can be termed an Anatolian *koinê* of burial practices.[86] In burial, the Attalids behaved precisely as their regional rivals did. The salvage results proffer a more or less approximate idea of the likely appearance of royal or princely Bithynian, Galatian, and indeed Pontic tumuli. At Üçtepeler, for example, near Bithynian Izmit (Nicomedia), excavations have revealed a late Hellenistic tumulus 75 m across and 12 m high, containing a vaulted burial chamber and a *dromos* – a strong candidate for a Bithynian royal tomb.[87] Philetairos' native Paphlagonia recently produced a roughly contemporaneous tumulus with a painted burial chamber, at Selmanlar.[88] It is now well understood that the Galatians abandoned La Tène burial practice for the Anatolian tumulus.[89] At Karalar (Blucium), an inscription identifies the tomb's occupant as Deiotarus the Younger. Galatian tumuli have also been investigated outside Gordion and at Yalacık, near Ankara.[90] The Mithridatids are a fascinating case because they vacillated between Greek, Persian, and Anatolian traditions. Down to ca. 180 BCE, the kings of Pontos were laid to rest in the rock-cut tombs of the royal necropolis of Amaseia. With the transfer of the capital to Sinope under Pharnakes I, a change occurs, and it has been conjectured that later kings, including Mithridates VI, were buried in tumuli.[91] The results of the excavation of a Hellenistic tumulus at Arafat Tepesi, 50 km from Çorum, as well as data from an intensive survey of the hinterland of Sinope, render the idea quite plausible.[92] The spectacular monuments of Orontid Commagene also belong in our reckoning, but so too those of Cappadocia. While no Ariarathid royal burial is securely identified, the stone tumulus at Avanos in Nevşehir province is a candidate, while salvage excavations have dated two more Cappadocian mounds to the Hellenistic period.[93]

To be fair, this sample contains a great variety of technical features of construction, size, and placement in the landscape. The tumulus is also an

---

[86] Harl 2011, 757.   [87] Turgut and Aksoy 1996; Gabelko 2017, 328.   [88] Bal 2014.
[89] Coşkun 2014, 142–47.
[90] Karalar and overview of Galatian burial: Darbyshire et al. 2000, 85–87. Gordion's Galatian tumulus: Temizsoy and Kaya 2001. Yalacık: Mermerci and Yağcı 1991.
[91] Fleischer 2009, esp. 118. By contrast, Højte (2009, 128) suggests the possibility that the Amaseia complex remained in use down to the end of the dynasty and housed the remains of Mithridates VI.
[92] Arafat Tepesi: İpek and Çakar 2009; Sinop: Doonan 2009, 72.
[93] Avanos: Thierry 2016. Belkuyu and Devebağırtan tumuli: Başal 2000.

enormous expenditure of wealth, and ostentatious consumption always had a local history and a distinctive role in social structure.[94] Yet what seems to justify analysis on this scale is Pergamon's own Pan-Asian political claims – enunciated in the Telmessos decree of 184/3. In death, how did the powerful comport themselves within the political space delineated for "the inhabitants of Asia"? Further, the bird's-eye view makes plain the stark difference between, on the one hand, Asia (Minor), as construed as the coastal Aegean zone conjoined with inner Anatolia, and, on the other, mainland Greece and the islands. Archaic and Classical Greece witnessed a boom-and-bust cycle of ostentation in burial, the record of which includes tumuli among other forms such as *peribolos* monuments. Broadly speaking, the fifth century seems to have witnessed restraint in the form of burial. Restraint seems to end, at least in Athens, already during the Peloponnesian War. A new cycle of ostentation began that petered out toward the end of the fourth century. The disappearance of monumental tombs like tumuli from the landscape of Greece is often tenuously attributed to sumptuary laws, though it surely also must reflect the redirection of disposable income toward other ends, such as house-building and public works.[95] A sharp decline in the number of tumuli can be discerned already ca. 600 BCE.[96] They disappear from the Kerameikos at Athens and also from the great tumulus fields of Thessaly at Krannon and Pharsalos.[97] Of course, there are some outliers such as the Macedonian-style Tomb of the Erotes at Eretria, but by and large, the tumulus is not a feature of the landscape in Hellenistic Greece. This contrasts markedly with the situation in East Greece. So what? Here, the tumulus tradition appears to be unbroken. From the archaic period, for instance, comes the sixth-century tumulus at Belevi near Ephesus, as well as the archaic tumuli of Larisa-on-the-Hermos.[98] Scores have also been detected in surveys of the Ionian cities Klazomenai and Teos.[99] Classical tumuli are known from the territory of

---

[94] On the problem of comparison, regarding burial in democratic Athens and aristocratic Thessaly, see Morris 1992, 147–48.

[95] Athens: Whitley 2001, 364–75; Morris 1992, 128–44.

[96] Schnapp-Gourbeillon 2016, 212; Kurtz and Boardman 1971: "Chamber tombs went out of fashion in the Classical period." Among Hellenistic exceptions, Pergamon is singled out for special mention (p. 283).

[97] Thessaly's tumuli dated sixth to fourth centuries BCE: Stamatopoulou 2016, esp. 181–83.

[98] Larisa-on-the-Hermos: Kurtz and Boardman 1971, 176–77. Belevi tumulus: Kasper 1976–77.

[99] Ersoy and Koparal 2008. At Teos, Koparal and Tuna 2017 (pp. 213–15) record numerous tumuli, both in the *chora* and in the urban core (*asty*). The phenomenon seems to have begun in full force during the Archaic period, when the city was founded (seventh century, in their view), and stretched into the Classical period (tumulus at Kayalıca, e.g.).

Parion.¹⁰⁰ A recent salvage excavation investigated the Biçerova tumulus, a fifth-century tomb 2.5 km from Kyme.¹⁰¹ Hellenistic examples from Pergamon's immediate regional context are not lacking. In the second century, at the modern site of Maltepe near ancient Phokaia, a tumulus was founded on the archaic city wall in the second century.¹⁰² Near the port of Elaia, the Seç Tepe tumulus was also in use at this time.¹⁰³ In Anatolia, Greeks were not outsiders, socially distanced from the rest – though the modern discipline of Classics has often portrayed them this way. A possible royal tomb at Yığma Tepe, therefore, aligns the Attalids not only with Anatolian kings of an earlier age but with the Graeco-Anatolian aristocracy of many neighboring cities.

City as Acropolis

With the conquest and acquisition by award of new territories, as well as a westward push to seize Aegean islands and gain ever more influence at Rome, it is a curious fact that the Attalids never moved their capital, but retained and embellished a mountain redoubt. As the landscape archaeologist Christina Williamson has shown, that mountainous viewshed makes of the lower Kaikos Valley an inward-looking, landed microregion. Indeed, standing atop the peak of Pergamon (329 m asl), the best line of sight points east and inland, up the Kaikos Valley toward modern Kınık and Soma. By contrast, it is only on a very clear day that the sea and the port city of Elaia are visible (**Fig. 6.2**).¹⁰⁴ With respect to the urbanism of their capital, then, the Attalids made a distinctive, even suprising choice. In Macedonia of the early fifth century, Archelaus had moved the Argead capital down from Aigai to the coastal estuary at Pella. In time, the polis of Pella was refounded on the so-called Hippodameian grid and appended to a royal residence. While the Ptolemies and the Seleukids both inherited the seats of ancient empires, they chose to stake out new cities according to Greek conventions of space. Further, Alexandria and the Syrian Tetrapolis both hugged the Mediterranean. Even contemporary Anatolian rivals did things differently. Mithridates I shifted his capital from inland Amaseia to the polis of Sinope on the Black Sea; the Bithynian Prousias I refounded Kios as Prousa-on-the-sea.¹⁰⁵ Logistically, the Attalids certainly could have decamped to Ephesus and ruled from a city that had hosted Antigonids,

---

¹⁰⁰ Tombul 2015. ¹⁰¹ Korkmaz et al. 2016. ¹⁰² Özyiğit 2009–11. ¹⁰³ Kelp 2016, 603.
¹⁰⁴ Williamson 2016, 86. ¹⁰⁵ Kaye 2013, 44–45.

Figure 6.2 View to the southwest of the Kaikos Valley from the acropolis of Pergamon (author's photo).

Ptolemies, and Seleukids. In fact, in recent excavations conducted above the city's theater (Panayırdağ), a lavish peristyle house on the scale of the Attalids' Palast V (2,400 m²) has been revealed. The excavator has dated the building to the second century and noted many Pergamene architectural features, suggesting an Attalid governor's residence, perhaps even a secondary palace.[106] Yet their capital remained what had been an important sub-satrapal stronghold of the late Persian period, which, as the military history reminds us, retained its defensive value. Less obvious, perhaps, is the ideological value of presenting this vertiginous and asymmetrical urban facade to would-be subjects.

Standard accounts of the monumentalization of the Pergamene acropolis underscore the builders' reverence for Classical Athens.[107] It was not Philetairos, in fact, but one of his immediate predecessors, Barsine or Lysimachus, who seems to have replaced the cult of Apollo with that of

---

[106] Baier 2013, 53–56; Ladstätter 2016, 263: major remodeling or rebuilding of palatial residence on Panayırdağ in Attalid period.

[107] The Atheno-centric interpretation of Pergamene spatial aesthetics is noticeably muted in the account of Seaman (2016, 411): "They *appear* to have evoked and thus competed with fifth-century Athens" (emphasis added).

Figure 6.3 Model of ancient Athens (courtesy of American School of Classical Studies at Athens: Agora Excavations).

Athena Polias as the central cult of the city. Yet the late fourth-century construction of the sanctuary and temple of Athena Polias, along with the introduction of the Panathenaia festival by the time of Eumenes I, it has been argued, speak to a wider effort to liken Pergamon, supposedly lacking traditions of its own, to storied Athens.[108] For Schalles, the equation of the two cities in Attalid self-presentation is assured by the time of Attalos I, who reorganized Athena's terrace.[109] However, if we zoom out from the sanctuary and consider the cityscape as a whole, the equation breaks down. Athens is a democratic city with an acropolis (**Fig. 6.3**); Pergamon represents an altogether different, Anatolian, and oligarchic model of urbanism,

---

[108] Massa-Pairault 2010, 3–4; Gehrke 2014, 123.
[109] Schalles 1985, 54. Reorganization of sanctuary by Attalos I: Kästner 2014b, 439–42.

City as Acropolis 309

Figure 6.4 Model of Hellenistic Pergamon (bpk Bildagentur; Antikensammlung/ Staatliche Museen/Berlin/Germany; Art Resource, NY).

in which the city *is* an acropolis (**Fig. 6.4**).[110] Astoundingly, the excavated residential quarter (*Wohnstadt*) is laid out on a slope of about 20–25%, a fine point of comparison to the core of Lydian Sardis, which registers at 16–20%.[111] As once described by an excavator of Sardis, Pergamon is "a typical Anatolian acropolis town," built on the spur of a mountain, just like the Lydian royal capital.[112] Many Lycian cities also seem to cascade down steep hillsides, a type of urbanism that is widely recognized as pre-Greek and indigenous. For example, at Xanthos, major changes in elevation (in sum, over 50 m) separate the city's various districts. Some 25 m above the lower city stands the palace and dynastic monuments of the so-called Lycian acropolis; at about the same elevation is the public space of the presumed Lycian agora. Another 25 m up the hill, one reaches the citadel of Xanthos, conventionally known as the Roman acropolis, but exhibiting Classical-period remains.[113]

---

[110] Arist. *Pol.* 1330b: περὶ δὲ τόπων ἐρυμνῶν οὐ πάσαις ὁμοίως ἔχει τὸ συμφέρον ταῖς πολιτείαις· οἷον ἀκρόπολις ὀλιγαρχικὸν καὶ μοναρχικόν, δημοκρατικὸν δ' ὁμαλότης, ἀριστοκρατικὸν δὲ οὐδέτερον, ἀλλὰ μᾶλλον ἰσχυροὶ τόποι πλείους. "As to fortified positions, what is expedient is not the same for all forms of constitution alike; for example, a citadel-hill (*akropolis*) is suitable for oligarchy and monarchy, and a level site for democracy; neither is favorable to an aristocracy, but rather several strong positions" (Loeb trans. Rackham).
[111] Cahill 2008, 119.   [112] Hanfmann 1975, 6.
[113] Borchhardt and Bleibtreu 2013, 5, 10–11: Episcopal Basilica on the "Roman Acropolis," also known as the Upper Hill, contains spolia from two Classical temples. Cf. Cavalier and des

Moreover, it was not only the siting of the city that evoked Anatolian precedents, but planners' treatment of the mountainous terrain. To a far greater extent than the prototypical Greek polis, Pergamon was "sculpted" out of towering volcanic rock.[114] As has long been noted by archaeologists, the landscaping of Pergamon's peak into its several iconic, monumental terraces, a process accelerated if not completed by Eumenes II, finds a close parallel in Sardis.[115] In the center of the Lydian city ("Acropolis North"), the revetment of the natural spurs of the mountain also created a series of terraces linked together by handsome staircases. Excavation has exposed the Lydian revetment, which consists of the kind of fine ashlar masonry found in royal tombs.[116] These ashlar terrrace walls were, in a sense, the face of the Lydian royal capital. The best understood of the terraces lie in Sardis sectors Field 49 and ByzFort. The latter is estimated to have enclosed an area of 1.2 ha. While visible from afar, these sculpted bluffs also stand apart from the lower city and its more expansive residential quarters. Yet their connection to the highest point of the acropolis seems assured. A tunnel cut in the bedrock in the valley between ByzFort and Field 49 leads the way. In essence, this regional technique of boldly terracing the mountainside creates dramatic vistas by taking advantage of natural contours. It does not seek to regularize the terrain or organize it modularly. As Nicholas Cahill puts it, "The Lydians, however, treated their sloping ground very differently from the later Greeks."[117] Then, when, in the early Hellenistc period, the Sardians finally returned to this area, perhaps already or soon to become denizens of a polis, they recreated the spatial aesthetic of the Lydian period. Current excavations in Field 49 show a remarkable investment in stabilizing and raising the level of the hill with massive subterranean foundations that follow the Lydians' alignments (**Fig. 6.5**).[118] In Sardis as in Pergamon, the geometry of Priene's fourth-century grid is nowhere to be found, but alongside the grandeur of the untreated rock, it is the sculpted earth and the terrace wall that stand as monuments and showpieces in their own right. It has proven difficult to find a precedent for the urban plan of Lydian Sardis in Anatolia, prompting considerations

Courtils (2001, 155), reporting only Classical spolia from a large basilica at the foot of the Upper Hill.
[114] Seaman 2016, 408.
[115] Hanfmann 1975, 28–33; Greenewalt et al. 1986, 17; Cahill 2008, 119.
[116] See most recently, Ratté 2011.   [117] Cahill 2008, 119.
[118] Cahill 2019, 28–35. While no trace of a Hellenistic terrace wall survives in Field 49, the excavator expresses confidence in the existence of one along the line of the Lydian terrace.

Figure 6.5 Archaic terrace walls of Sardis, reconstruction drawing by Philip Stinson (©Archaeological Exploration of Sardis/President and Fellows of Harvard College).

of Near Eastern influence.[119] On the other hand, the local vassals of the intervening Achaemenid period offered the Attalids a blueprint for a high-elevation capital.

First, Lycian dynasts were well accustomed to residence in cities built on precipitous slopes that descended from a fortified peak, often containing a necropolis. Just as in Xanthos, we often find important monuments on a level terrace, which is usually not the highest point, but again, set on a spur lower down the mountain. In Xanthos, this is the Lycian acropolis, with its dynastic heroa, palaces, and public buildings. Elsewhere in the same river valley, one finds the same pattern at Tlos and also at Pinara. It is telling that at Pinara the large (ca. 1.7 ha) *basileia* terrace was once referred to as the "lower acropolis."[120] In the east of Lycia, the city of Arykanda controls a steep pass into the plain of Elmalı. The earliest remains show it to have been a minor dynastic center, but one which conforms neatly to the pattern of a lofty fortified acropolis, set high above a city that itself clings to the sides of a mountain. The city grew in importance in the Hellenistic period, and, in fact, it seems that Arykanda received its stunning terraces at about the same time that Pergamon's were completed (**Fig. 6.6**).[121] Second, the

---

[119] Cahill 2008, 120, pointing to Neo-Assyrian Dur-Sharrukin and Neo-Hittite Carchemish. On the terrace (8.41 ha and 12 m high) of the palace at Dur-Sharrukin as a point of comparison for Lycian royal residences, see Borchhardt and Bleibtreu 2013, 174.

[120] Borchhardt and Bleibtreu 2013, 123.   [121] Knoblauch and Witschel 1993, 258.

Figure 6.6 Late Hellenistic terraces at Arykanda (author's photo).

Hekatomnids of Caria had provided the Attalids with an obvious model in Halikarnassos, the capital of Mausolus, as well in other cities such as Amyzon. The Hekatomnid influence on Attalid urbanism is glimpsed through Pergamon's participation in the fourth-century BCE Ionian Renaissance, a cultural program that effectively restored parity between western Anatolia and mainland Greece.[122] Indeed, the Hekatomnid

---

[122] Pergamon and the fourth-century BCE Ionian Renaissance: Pedersen 2004; and on the significance of the Ionian Renaissance, see Pedersen 2013, esp. p. 44.

inheritance is also detectable in many other ways, for example, in the mythological gamesmanship that gave both royal houses an Arkadian pedigree and links to Herakles. Yet as a builder, specifically, Mausolus propagated the technique of using terrain and terrace to give a royal city an iconic facade. His two grand terraces dominated the cityscape of Halikarnassos, one belonging to the Temple of Mars, while the other, twice as large and visible from the island of Kos, supported the Mausolleion.[123] Another Hekatomnid terracing project has been identified at the sanctuary of Artemis in Amyzon, girding a spur of Mount Latmos. Two terraces joined at an angle form a line 168 m long, comparable to the 160 m of the upper terrace of Pergamon's theater. However, the visual effect of the rusticated terrace walls at Amyzon is to minimize the impact of the buildings themselves – the propylon, and even the temple.[124] In this architectural idiom, platform is as significant as superstructure. One can hardly say the same of Classical Athens, the Propylaia, the Parthenon, and the Acropolis.

Gallograeci

Around 281, a large, migratory movement of Celtic-speaking peoples arrived in the Balkans. Under their leader Brennos, they fought through Macedonian territory and threatened to sack Delphi, where Antigonos Gonatas and a coalition of Greeks featuring Aetolian and Athenian contingents stopped the Celtic advance. Reversing course, two offshoots of the original migration, one under Leonnorios and another under Luturios, set off for Anatolia. With their passage across the Hellespont, in 279/8, they came to be known as the Galatians – the Celts of Anatolia. Bands of Galatian warriors, sometimes serving as mercenaries in the armies of Bithynian, Attalid, and Pontic kings, at other times operating as unattached raiding parties, fought in the nude behind the long, oval shields distinctive of Europe's La Tène tradition. Torques around their necks, their hair dressed with lime, Asia's newest barbarians struck fear into the hearts of the city-dwellers of the coast. Down into the 260s, "Galatian war" (πολεμὸς Γαλατικός) was a common experience and a "Galatian fund" (τὰ Γαλατικά) a possible line item in city budgets. Ultimately, most – but not all – of the migrants settled in the central highlands, what had once been the upland

---

[123] Carstens 2002, 403. [124] Pedersen 2004, 429–32.

core of the Phrygian and Hittite empires.[125] By then, they had formed three separate tribes. Each group claimed its own loosely defined territory around a regional emporium: the Tolistobogii in the west, holding Gordion; the Trocmi in the east, around Tavium, in the bend of the Halys; and the Tectosages in between, occupying Ancyra. We know that the Celts did not find these lands empty, and archaeology continues to reveal a subtle process of accommodation to preexisting conditions and culture. Beyond convening a pantribal council to try homicide cases once per year, the Galatians seem rarely if ever to have acted as a unified bloc in politics or war. Nevertheless, a capable set of adversaries confronted the Attalids on their eastern flank. As many have pointed out, the Galatians also presented Pergamon with an opportunity to garner much-needed legitimacy. The Attalids needed the Galatians.

This was certainly the case for Attalos I. He was the first king of Pergamon, the first of the dynasty to take the title of *basileus* and wear the diadem, and indeed the Hellenistic ruler who squeezed the most out of his triumphs over Galatians. Polybius' eulogy for Attalos reads, "For having conquered the Gauls, the most formidable and warlike nation of Asia, he built upon this foundation, and then first showed he was really a king."[126] This account of the birth of the Attalid kingdom as such in the years after 241 is very partial, but also very telling. It occludes the broader context of a breakdown of Seleukid authority beyond the Taurus and perhaps also Pergamon's enduring vassalage, but it grounds the Attalid kingship in the memory of specific, historical victories over the Galatians girded with myth. This is most evident in several large dedications in the Sanctuary of Athena at Pergamon, which Attalos now remodeled, using free-standing sculpture to depict, it seems, multiple battle scenes featuring Seleukid and Galatian enemies, while the dismembered La Tène-style arms appeared as trophies on the surrounding architecture.[127] The connection between the

---

[125] Strobel 1996, 98. [126] Polyb. 18.41.7–8.
[127] Multiple battle scenes with Seleukids and Galatians on the so-called Great Dedication or Long Base (19.6 m long), erected not long after 223 BCE in Athena's sanctuary at Pergamon: *OGIS* 273–279; Marszal 2000, 208–9; for oft-cited alternatives cf. Mitchell 2003, 285; Kunze 2012, 316. The controversy around the reconstruction of the Long Base, as well as the earlier Round Monument, itself a thank-offering for the victory over Galatians at the Kaikos in the late 230s (*OGIS* 269; Kästner 2014b, 440–43), requires cautious conjecture about Pergamene messaging. Certain scholars maintain that the Long Base supported the "Large Gauls" (Ludovisi Gaul and "Dying Trumpeter"); others, such as Stewart (2004, 210–12), place those statues before the Greek audience at mainland Delphi; finally, Ridgway (2018, 252–54) reasserts the case that the Large Gauls are in fact Roman originals – not Roman copies of Pergamene originals. Thus, the visual rhetoric of Galatian victory at Pergamon itself – before the internal Attalid

Attalid claim to kingship and the Galatian triumphs recorded in Athena's sanctuary appears so tight that scholars have long dated an alteration to the portrait head known as the Berlin Attalos, an update which may have added its diadem, to a moment not long after the "battle near the source of the Kaikos River against the Tolistoagioi Galatians" (*OGIS* 276).[128] Not only was this piece of local history soon internationalized when a team of high-profile Greek sculptors arrived to commemorate them in Pergamon, but Attalos also trumpeted the importance of his victory in the centers of Old Greece, Delos, Athens, and probably also at Delphi. In so doing, he joined other Hellenistic kings in a Panhellenic discourse that cast the Galatians as a barbaric threat to cosmic order. The Battle of the Kaikos has come to be seen by scholars as a kind of "Pergamene Marathon," in a construct which allegorizes the Attalids as the Athenians and the Galatians as the Persians. On the mainland, that interpretation holds more weight, as Greeks do seem to have interpreted the defense of Delphi in 279 in those terms.[129] In Asia, by contrast, the nature of events meant that the Galatians' crossing simply could not fit into the same mythico-historical tradition. Moreover, at home, the goal, as we have seen, was different: not only or even necessarily to burnish Hellenic credentials, but rather to normalize Attalid rule in Asia. For this reason, and because real-life Galatians inhabited the borderlands and surely some of the territory they already claimed, the Attalids' rhetorical rendering and interactions with the Galatians were more complicated than is usually assumed.

Rhetorically, the fit between the Galatians and the Persians, as expressed, for example, in Hellenistic panegyric, was in fact rather awkward. What

---

audience – was perhaps less strident and othering than we have thought. Note also that an internal Anatolian audience may not have recognized contemporary Galatians by arms depicted – anachronistically – on the balustrade reliefs of Eumenes II's stoa and propylon: Coşkun (2014, 148–51) argues that such La Tène *realia* were not present in the battles commemorated.

[128] For Tolistoagioi as Tolistobogioi, see Strobel 1996, 238–39 n. 377. According to Livy 38.16, Attalos I was the first to stop paying the Galatians tribute. However, note that the evidentiary basis is shaky for the use of the so-called Berlin Attalos to tell a story of pristine kingship earned in battle against the Galatians. There were clearly two phases for the head of the marble portrait statue, which stood 3 m and seems to have been displayed in the cultic Room H of the Upper Terrace of the gymnasium of Pergamon. Yet the question of whether and when the diadem was added, along with, or opposed to, the fuller head of hair, remains debated. For Stewart (2014, 63), the diadem was recut in the second phase; while Smith (2019, 79–82) presents a strong case for the diadem as an addition. Cf. Hoff (2018, 265, with Grüßinger et al. 2012, Kat. 5.8), maintaining that the diadem was original – and dating the remodeling of the second phase to the post-Attalid early first century BCE.

[129] Paus. 10.20; Strobel 1996, 221–22.

kind of barbarian was the Celt? The contemporary answer shades toward tropes of reckless ferocity, mindlessness, and bodily austerity. Barbaric traits, certainly, but hardly an established antithesis of all things Greek. One third-century elegiac poet goes so far as to *contrast* the effeminate Persian of his purple cloth and tents with the impetuous Galatian who camps in the open air.[130] The Persians of yore remained an important touchstone in political invective. Opponents could paint a Seleukid, even an Antigonid or Lysimachus as a new Xerxes.[131] However, the effectiveness of the Persians in a historical analogy drawn to make sense of the Galatians in Anatolia was limited by the fact that one barbarian menace had crossed from Asia and left; whereas the other had crossed into Asia and remained, an event that cried out for explanation. In response, Hellenistic historiography seems to have generated a novel set piece, the unwelcome Crossing of the Gauls, while debating culpability. In multiple source traditions, narratives were built around this critical event. For instance, a chapter heading of Pompeius Trogus reads, "How the Gauls Entered Asia (*transierunt in Asiam*) and Waged War with Antiochos and the Bithynians."[132] In historical memory, the Gauls' crossing to Asia merited its own treatment, distinct from other episodes. The epithet of that very Antiochos I, namely, Soter (Savior), is elsewhere attributed to his expulsion of the "Galatians who had invaded (*esbalein*) Asia from Europe."[133] One of our earliest and best accounts, that of third-century Nymphis-Memnon of Herakleia Pontika, represents an apologetic perspective on the crossing. Amassed on the European side, the patriotic historian relates, the Gauls had long been harassing Byzantium, which his faithful Herakleia had supported with gold. Earlier, the Gauls had repeatedly attempted to cross, without success.[134] At last, on terms of an alliance with Herakleia and the

---

[130] Stewart 2004, 201. The text is *SH* 958, on which see Barbantani 2001, 118–35, who attributes this piece of encomiastic poetry to an Alexandrian poet, rather than Mousaios of Ephesus, writing for an Attalid, against commonplace in scholarship (e.g., Kosmetatou 2000, 51–52).

[131] Diod. Sic. 21.12, e.g., on Lysimachus.

[132] Pomp. Trog. *Prol.* 25. On this historiographical tradition, the ideas here are indebted to several forthcoming articles by Thomas J. Nelson, who in discussing Trogus' sources for the account of the Galatians' crossing, suggests either Hieronymos of Cardia or a third-century Seleukid courtly writer.

[133] App. *Syr.* 65.343. This is typically seen as a reference to the so-called Elephant Battle, ca. 270–268 BCE, which is widely believed to have resulted in the creation of the savior cult and the adoption of the title *Soter* by Antiochos I. Cf. Coşkun 2012, esp. p. 62 n. 17, which casts the Elephant Battle as a fantasy of a Seleukid court poet, but also nicely summarizes the historiographic set piece transmitted by Appian: juxtaposition of Europe and Asia means that (in the fantasy) Anatolia was emptied out of Galatians.

[134] *FGrHist* 434 F 1 11.2: πολλάκις μὲν ἐπιχειρήσαντας [εἰς] τὴν Ἀσίαν περαιωθῆναι.

other cities of the Northern League, it is stressed, Nicomedes I of Bithynia "transferred the Galatian population to Asia (τὸ Γαλατικὸν πλῆθος εἰς Ἀσίαν διαβιβάζει)." In a case of special pleading, Nymphis-Memnon contends that the inhabitants of Asia (*oiketorês Asias*) actually benefited from the arrival of the Galatians, who, he claims, supported democracies against kings. Clearly, the singular event of the migration of the Celts across the continental divide resisted assimilation to the Persian invasion. It also left a wound that stung so long as these newcomers menaced "the inhabitants of Asia."

In short, the new northern barbarians threatened civilization in Asia, not Greece. Geographically, the concept of a Graeco-Macedonian mainland that was distinct from the continental notion of Asia had emerged in Alexander's wake.[135] In the early third century, the painter of the Boscoreale Frescoes had personified the two as opposing female figures, inveterate enemies. Of course, in 279/8, many of those who incurred losses would have counted among them the assault on their dignity as Hellenes. This is precisely what the decree for Sotas from Ionian Priene reports: "It happened that many of the Greek inhabitants of Asia were ruined. They were not able to struggle with the Barbarians (πρὸς τοὺς βαρβάρους ἀνταγωνίζεσθαι)."[136] Yet the Attalids were not obliged to adopt the same stance – even in triumph. They could, for example, adopt the stance of the Lycians of Tlos. The epigram of Neoptolemos son of Kressos commemorates the defense of the city, perhaps during the initial wave of migration in the 270s and 260s: "I am Neoptolemos son of Kressos. In the Temple of the Three Brothers the citizens of Tlos set (me), glory of my spear. For them, so many Pisidians and [Paeonians] and Agrianians and Galatians I confronted and scattered away."[137] For a Greek-speaking Lycian of the Hellenistic period, the Galatians were no more barbarous an enemy than the neighboring Pisidians. Similarly, when Eumenes II addressed the inhabitants of the town of Apolloniucharax in Lydia, with its local milieu of Mysians, the king described the Galatians straightforwardly as "enemies (*polemioi*)."[138]

In Anatolia, there was nothing to gain by representing the Galatian as the non-Greek foil to the Hellene. Rather, advantage was to be had by entering the fight against the Galatians on the side of *all* of the inhabitants of Asia, irrespective of cultural identity. A decree from Lycian Telmessos, almost 100 years later than Sotas' from Ionian Priene, strikes a very

---

[135] Kosmin 2014a, 124–25. [136] *OGIS* 765. [137] Trans. Barbantani 2007, 75.
[138] **D2** Side A line 15.

different note, though the Galatians are still named as enemies. The Telmessians honor Eumenes II as the city's savior, who, invoking "the gods," undertook a war against Prousias I, Ortiagon, and the Galatians, "not only on behalf of those subject to him, but on behalf of all inhabitants of Asia ([ὑπὲρ ἄ]λλων τῶν κατοικούντων τὴν Ἀσίαν)." An Attalid king, just as a Seleukid, could claim to be "king of Asia," the title that the *Suda*, for example, applies to Attalos II.[139] That pseudo-Achaemenid rank required of its holder both a multifaceted cultural politics and a means of projecting power across the conceptual geography of Asia. In Asia, the ideological value of the victories over the Galatians was not Hellenic respectability, but a stronger claim to rule the nebulous territory allotted at Apameia.[140]

The historiography of the Galatians' crossing evokes the specter of Asia's salvation from the beginning. Polybius, as preserved by Livy, also depicts the Gauls mounting their campaign from the European side of the Propontis where their cupidity overtook them, as "a desire for crossing into Asia seized them."[141] The goal of what scholars take to have been a migration aimed at finding land for about 20,000 people is distorted into an expedition to plunder all of cis-Tauric Asia.[142] According to Livy, the Galatians divided up the revenues of the entire territory into three (*tres partes*), with the Trocmi drawing tribute from the Hellespont, the Tolistobogii living off Aeolis and Ionia, and the Tectosages assigned the interior. While it is clear from this account that everyone settled upland, in historical Galatia, the barbarians continued to threaten all of cis-Tauric Asia. Thus, when Polybius praises the Romans for suppressing the Galatians in 189, he explicitly commends them for removing that threat.[143] In a dramatic reversal, the local heroes of these narratives stand up to the Galatians, especially at places already imbued with meaning in myth, and ultimately eject them from Asia altogether, or at least from the more civilized reaches of its western seaboard. The Attalids vied with other Anatolian rivals for this role. During the War with Achaios, Polybius writes, Attalos I brought yet another band of Gauls over from Europe,

---

[139] *Suda* s.v. Ἄτταλος (A4316).

[140] Cf. Koehn 2007, 110–35, esp. 129, for the compelling view that the Galatians were a distinct ideological resource for the Attalids, by means of which they pursued territorial expansion in Asia Minor. However, a purported defense of *Greek* civilization in Asia is absent from the decree of Telmessos.

[141] Livy 38.16.4: *Cupido inde eos in Asiam transeundi, audientes ex proprinquo quanta ubertas eius terrae esset cepit.*

[142] For the size of the population on the move, see Strobel 2002, 3, 12, with ancient references and plausibility.

[143] Polyb. 3.3.5.

the Aigosages. They damaged the cities of the Hellespont and threatened to take Ilion, but were fought off by the citizens of Alexandria Troas. In the end, Prousias freed the cities of the Hellespont from the danger. In effect, by correcting the mistake of Attalos, he reversed that of his forebearer Nicomedes I, giving "a good lesson to the barbarians from Europe in the future not to be overready to cross to Asia."[144]

The assault of the Aigosages on Ilion in 218 would have recalled an earlier attack on the same city during the initial migration in 279/8. By 218, Ilion seems to have received its sturdy, 2.5–3 m thick fortification wall. On the other hand, Strabo tells us that in 278, the Galatians, fresh from Europe, had reconnoitered Ilion as a potential stronghold. Finding it unwalled, and so unsuitable, they moved on, and the city survived unscathed.[145] The appearance of two such incidents in our sources may not be a coincidence, but instead an indication of the significance to observers and memory makers of the heroic defense of Troy, perhaps seen as a symbol for the salvation of Asia. In other words, if Ilion could hold, the rest of Asia could also survive the onslaught. This is the implication of a complex of oracles that seems to have circulated in the third century as a series of *post eventum* interpretations of the Gauls' crossing. Addressed to the king of Bithynia, one oracle ominously forecast a wave of destruction, but in congratulating "the Hellespont" seems to hint at Ilion's survival. "O thrice blessed Hellespont, and the divinely built walls of men ... by divine commands which [city] the dreadful wolf will frighten under mighty compulsion."[146] This oracle may have issued from from the Temple of Apollo in Chalcedon, though it was at some point in Antiquity associated with the name of the

---

[144] Polyb. 5.111.7.
[145] Strabo 13.1.27, preserving Hegesianax of Alexandria Troas (*FGrHist* 45). However, Strabo 13.126 vexingly attributes the walls of Ilion to Lysimachus in the early third century, in time for the Galatian episode of 279/8. On the actual date of the walls, Rose (2014, 168–70) assigns them to Antiochos Hierax (230s); for other opinions, see Cohen 1995, 155; Strobel 1996, 244–45. There is a certain danger in using Strabo and his sources to help date the fortifications, since these authors clearly exaggerate the modesty of Hellenistic Ilion, in their words, just a village-city (*kômopolis*), on which see Ellis-Evans 2019, 28–31. However, what is important here is the enduring historical memory: even a brief Galatian occupation of perhaps an unwalled settlement was, nevertheless, evocative of a Trojan defense of Asia.
[146] See Parke 1982, esp. p. 443, for restoration of Ilion in the lacuna in line 11. Zos. 2.37.12–14 (trans. Parke):

> Τρὶς μάκαρ Ἑλλήσποντε, θεόκτιτα τείχεά τ' ἀνδρῶν,
> <...> θείαισιν ἐφετμαῖς
> ἣν λύκος αἰνόλυκος πτήξει κρατερῆς ὑπ' ἀνάγκης

Chaonian prophetess Phaennis. Pausanias records her prophecy that an Attalos, ruling in Pergamos, son of a bull and reared by Zeus, would rout the Gauls who had ravaged Asia and harmed those who inhabited its coast.[147] While we cannot be certain of the precise origin or authorship of these oracles, nor their relationship to each other, together they preserve a precious, near-contemporary perspective on events. The mythic archetype through which the inhabitants of Asia understood the Gallic crossing was the Trojan, not the Persian War, and they called on their kings to play the part of Priam, not Miltiades. In managing the migration, individual kings may have, in certain contexts, claimed to be champions of the Greeks, but they remained the helmsmen of Hellenistic states on Asian soil.

Despite their intercourse with the enemy, the Attalids managed to spread the idea that they were responsible for, as Pausanias puts it, driving the Galatians away from the sea and out of "lower Asia" (κάτω Ἀσίας).[148] Pausanias' testimony is what Karl Strobel has envisioned as the official Pergamene version of the settlement of the Galatians after the victory of Attalos I.[149] This version of events is demonstrably false: not only were individual Celts settled in the urban west of the peninsula, but Galatia as a constellation of tribal polities in central Anatolia in time became a protectorate of the enlarged kingdom of Pergamon.[150] Yet the important point to note here is that the Attalids' territorial claim is to parts of Asia that are emptied out of Galatians. That this territorial claim of an Asia without Galatians was foundational for Pergamon is glimpsed on the long, blue marble Base of Philetairos on the island of Delos. Its verse inscription, which seems to have been erected by Attalos I, celebrates the founder's achievements in war, principally, that "he drove the Galatians far beyond his frontiers (*oikeioi horoi*)." He did not merely defeat them; he expelled them, defining a border in the process.

This is an exaggeration, since while Philetairos may have skirmished with the Galatians, no major victory on the scale of Antiochos I's Elephant Battle was ever trumpeted. Further, the verse essentially backdates the birth of the Attalid kingdom by depicting the vassal Philetairos chasing the barbarians beyond borders that were scarcely notional. Yet the rhetoric worked. By Strabo's writing, it was impossible to conceive of a place as both Pergamene and permanently settled with Galatians.[151] The geographer describes a two-part process of settlement. First, the Galatians wandered about overrunning Attalid and Bithynian territory, and second, those two

---

[147] Pausanias 10.15.3. [148] Paus. 1.4.5–6, 1.8.1. [149] Strobel 1996, 252 n. 440. [150] Mitchell 1993, vol. 1, 25–26, 57. [151] Strabo 12.5.1.

monarchies granted them permission to settle in historical Galatia. This neat picture obscures the fact that these dynasties contested each other's borders and surely competed with Galatian leaders for influence in many places. It also exculpates those who bear the guilt of inviting the Galatians to Asia by crediting them with the creation of a homeland on the periphery of the Mediterranean system.

In the Pergamene version of the Galatian settlement story, elements of truth are combined with major distortions. Both help us understand what was at stake for the Attalids in conjuring up certain Galatians while also interacting with those of flesh and blood. The extent to which any Hellenistic monarch was directly responsible for the creation of historical Galatia is difficult to determine. Yet it was Mithridates I of Pontos, the lord of those parts, who seems to have played the greatest role.[152] Apart from the confusing notice in Strabo, the only evidence for Attalid involvement is the episode with the Aigosages, and they were settled in the west, deep inside Pergamene territory. Indeed, it is likely that many Galatians lived inside the Attalid kingdom. This is suggested, for example, by the appearance of Middle La Tène metalwork outside the Galatian core, or even by the Celtic name of one of Toriaion's ambassadors to Eumenes II. Galatian princes such as Ortiagon and Eposagnatus collaborated with the Attalids. After the dynasty's fall, a portrait statue of Adobogiona, the Galatian princess who married the powerful citizen Menodotos, was erected inside the Temple of Hera at Pergamon, where it stood next to images of Attalos II and Stratonike.[153] One has the impression that the Galatians never fully vacated the territory. Yet generally, this was a migration aimed at the acquisition of land, not the booty or mercenary pay of the ancient, even modern stereotypes.[154] Mithridates could offer large amounts of relatively fertile and resource-rich territory in the Anatolian highlands. Unsurprisingly, no Greek city on the Aegean seaboard offered to redistribute choice, alluvial land. In fact, the landless, non-Hellenes of Priene seem to have collaborated with the Galatians and avenged themselves on the landed classes.[155]

---

[152] *FGrHist* 740 F 14.
[153] Statue of Adobogiona: *MDAI(A)* 37 (1912), 294–96. For display context, see Agelidis 2012, 181. According to Strobel (2009, 137), the queen presented a decidedly non-Greek portrait. Further on this line of Galatian royalty, see Mitchell 1993, vol. 1, 28–29.
[154] Cf. Hansen 1971, 31: "[T]he Gauls regarded the districts assigned to them merely as a place in which the women and children could remain while the men went forth on their raids and to which the booty could be brought for safekeeping."
[155] *I.Priene* 17 lines 5–6.

The old picture of the Galatians as semi-nomadic or unsettled has been completely overturned by anthropological and paleoenvironmental studies, although it still haunts scholarship.[156] The region between the Sangarius and the Halys was much more heavily forested in Antiquity and, to the incoming Celts, may have resembled the Central European lands of their origin.[157] In any case, its diverse resources supported a mixed agricultural regime for a sedentary population. Evidence from the well-studied site of Gordion provides a picture of long-term demographic and economic stability at odds with the turbulence of Pergamene art and rhetoric. For example, landscape analysis shows that the arrival of the Galatians did not alter land-use patterns or rates of erosion. A decline in the intensity of land use that had begun in the late Iron Age simply continued. This is indirectly confirmed by recent work on the domestic architecture of the Hellenistic town. Some houses were abandoned, some were taken over; in the end, the Galatians may have changed the layout of Gordion's urban plan and even its typical house type, but they preserved the character of the settlement.[158] Moreover, soil studies show that the rate of sedimentation in nearby streams was unaffected, continuing its decline. The Galatians, unlike, say, the LBA Hittites, did not direct or centralize land use in such a way that erosion was significantly curbed. Nor, however, did they degrade hill slopes with intensive pastoralism like, say, the later nomadic Turks.[159] Defying their reputation for disruptiveness, the Galatians maintained the structure of the agropastoralist economy, even if the Anatolian, Phrygian-Luwian population now found itself attached to Celtic tribes and clans.[160]

Hellenistic Galatia would appear to have been more or less economically self-sufficient, lacking strong ties to Aegean and Pontic trade networks such

---

[156] Mitchell 1993, vol. 1, 15; but corrected by Darbyshire et al. 2000, 78. Still, see Coşkun 2016, 55: "for the most part nomadic." Similarly, Stewart writes (2004, 208) of the Ludovisi Gaul: "[S]ince the Gauls were nomads, the inclusion of women in the carnage is unproblematic."

[157] Strobel 1996, 81–107, esp. 81–87 on the poor fit of nomadism as a model for understanding Galatian settlement in Anatolia. See also, already, Allen 1983, 138: "The aims of the Galatians seem from the beginning to have been settlement and security."

[158] Wells 2012, 263: "house clusters." See also Voigt 2003, 16, on a complex of buildings marked off by a 2-m-thick wall.

[159] Note, though, the presence of sheep-shears, one pair of which has been termed Celtic, and a wide array of textile kit from the abandonment levels of Mid-Hellenistic Gordion. See Stewart 2010, 101, 113.

[160] Kealhofer 2005, 147; Marsh and Kealhofer 2014, 697–98; Kealhofer and Marsh 2019, 96–98. Their own data and excavation results from Gordion, however, seem at odds with the unsupported claim (p. 95) that "Galatians – Celts from central Europe who established hegemony in central Anatolia in the 3rd c. BCE – are known to have disrupted settlement across the region."

as had existed in the age of Alexander. Again, if we look to Gordion, the extended absence of imported Greek tablewares and amphoras during the second and third quarters of the third century was once attributed to hostilities, but perhaps it is the presence of these artifacts that needs to be explained. Mark Lawall has argued that caches of Rhodian amphoras at the site represent nontrade events, such as the expedition of Manlius Vulso. Goods from the Mediterranean or Black Sea arrived on an irregular basis through pulsatile trade.[161] The regular contacts remained the pre-Hellenistic ones – links with the other emporia of Ancyra and Tavium, and with sites such as Boğazköy. In what excavators call the Early Hellenistic B and Middle Hellenistic periods (ca. 275–235 and ca. 235–189, respectively), finewares were either local or regional, such as the so-called Galatian ware, a Central Anatolian form, well known from the eastern lands of the Trocmi.[162] Similar conclusions can be drawn from an analysis of coin hoards from this region. Over time, large-denomination silver and even gold coins filtered in, accumulating in what appear to be savings, not circulation hoards. Perhaps the contexts in which coinage was useful were limited, though the significant amounts of third-century bronze recovered at the site are suggestive. While these smaller denominations and possible countermarking at Gordion show some low-level monetization, it does not appear that Galatia was fully integrated into the monetary systems to which Pergamon belonged.[163] While we cannot take too seriously the claim of Diodorus that Eumenes II, though not being too rich, "subdued the entire *ethnos* of the Galatians" with liberal but judicious gift giving, the anecdote may point to the informal nature of Attalid power in many parts of Galatia.[164] Conditions were never ripe, then, for an expansion east of the Sangarius, since the normal preexisting infrastructure never materialized. The Attalid imperial geography of a lower Asia defined in opposition to an up-country Galatia gained traction and was later endorsed by Pausanias. The cultural politics of Pergamon excluded those who were already outside.

The topography, however, did not always align with the cultural identity of Anatolia's inhabitants, and a large part of western highland Phrygia, specifically, stretches of what later geographers called Phrygia Epictetus, fell squarely between Galatia of the Tolistobogii and the Attalid core (**Map 6.2**). Inside the Epictetus of Strabo, in this period, lay

---

[161] Lawall 2008.   [162] Özsait and Özsait 2003; Stewart 2010, 100.
[163] *IGCH* 1401, 1403, 1404, 1405, 1406. Kenneth Harl's forthcoming *Coins from the Excavations at Gordion, 1950–2008* will shed much light on these hoards and the monetary history of Hellenistic Galatia.
[164] Diod. Sic. 31.14.

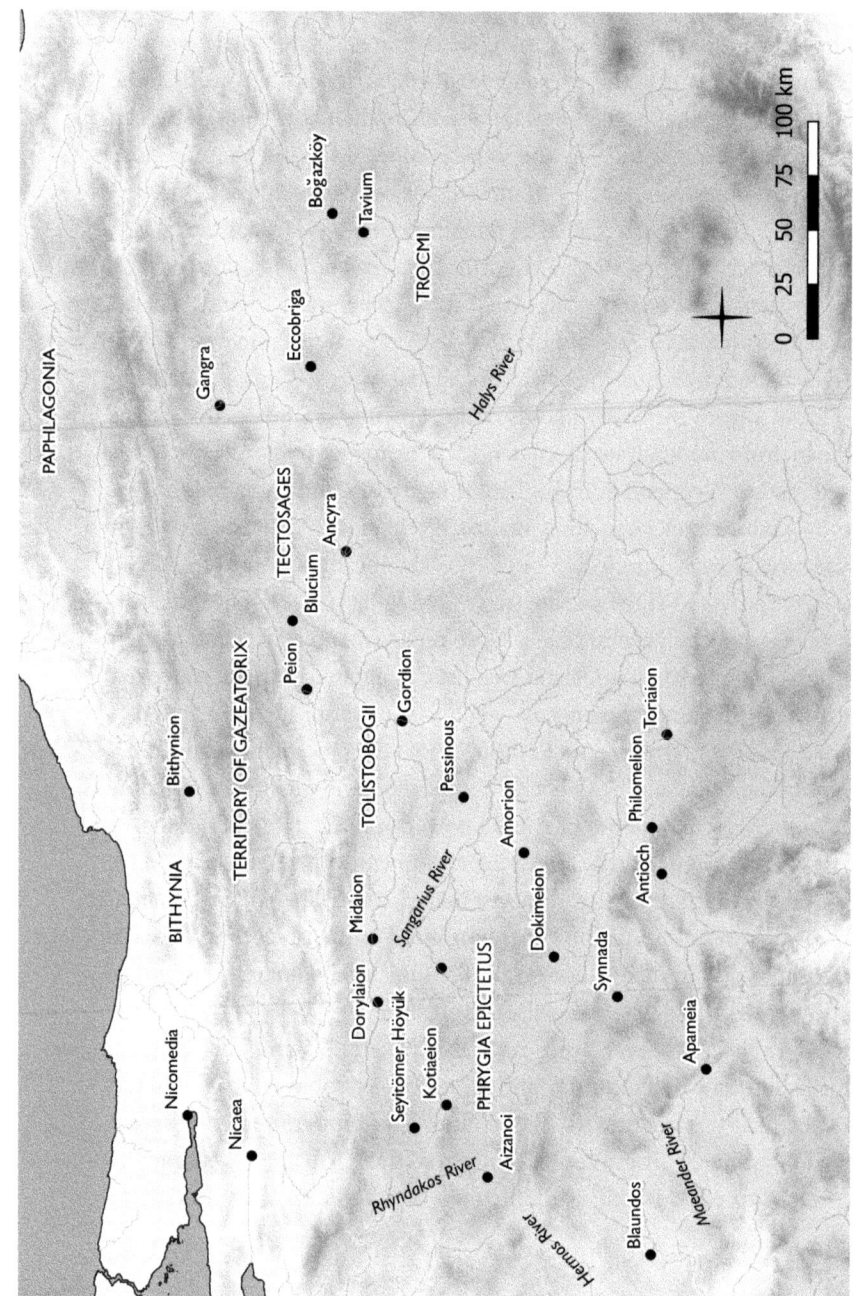

Map 6.2 Central Anatolia.

the shifting boundaries between Bithynia, Paphlagonia, the Attalid kingdom, and the territory of the Tolistobogii.[165] Naturally, Pergamene activity is detectable all along this contested frontier zone. In the west, Attalos I was a major benefactor of the sanctuary of Zeus at Aizanoi, and a Pergamene official may have been resident in the handsome house uncovered nearby.[166] In the east of this buffer zone, the Attalids were present, we now know, not just at Pessinous, but also in Amorion. An important and early Galatian ally, Eposognatus, would seem to have held sway near here.[167] Presumably, the Attalids controlled the fortified mound of Seyitömer, as well as other former Seleukid strongholds with Macedonian identities, such as Dorylaion (Şarhöyük) in the north.[168] In southwestern Phrygia, we know that the Attalid monetary system reached into places such as Synnada, Lysias, and Dionysoupolis.[169] This was a militarized frontier, but it was not a cultural no-man's land. Or, rather, it did not lack a coherent, even if hybrid, cultural identity. It was widely seen, from some point in the second century, as Gallograecia (Γαλλογραίκια) or *Hellēnogalatia*. The Latinate term, which appears in our earliest source, the younger Eratosthenes of Cyrene, and persists into Byzantine times, admits a Roman perspective. It recalls the speech of Manlius Vulso in Livy, the contemptuous comparison of the Galatians with the true *Galli* of Europe. Contrasted with the European Gauls, "These are a degenerate lot, mixed, and really, they are called Gallo-Greeks (*hi iam degeneres sunt, mixti, et Gallograeci vere, quod appellantur*)." Significantly, in the same speech, Vulso calls them Phrygians with Gallic arms.[170]

Ironically, the pejorative usage of the Roman outsider may preserve an insider's perspective.[171] The second-century inhabitants of the Epictetus may indeed have seen themselves as Gallo-Greeks, and aspects of their material culture were, in fact, Phrygian. Note that Livy's passive "they are called" lacks a subject. By whom were they called Gallograeci? We should

---

[165] On the fuzziness of the northern and western frontiers of the Tolistobogii, see Darbyshire et al. 2000, 79 n. 11. On the difficulty of defining the boundaries between Phrygia, Mysia, and Bithynia, see Strabo 12.4.4. On the border between the Tolistobogii and the Epictetus, see Strabo 12.5.2.

[166] Thonemann 2013c, 23.   [167] Livy 38.18.1.

[168] Seyitömer: Aydın 1991; Topbaş 1992; Topbaş 1993; İlaslı 1996.

[169] I am skeptical of the idea that the Attalids urbanized these valleys of the Maeander's tributaries. For example, excavations at Blaundos show exiguous Hellenistic remains (Filges 2003, 37–42). In fact, Willet (2020, 488) shows systematically how underurbanized this region was relative to the rest of Asia Minor.

[170] Livy 38.17.9. The same slur also entered Cicero's rhetoric (*Har. resp.* 28).

[171] Darbyshire et al. 2000, 83.

take seriously the possibility that the term was one of self-ascription. Pompeius Trogus, for one, believed that the migrants themselves had come up with the idea.[172] For Strabo, Gallograecia was distinct from and lay west of Galatia proper. The Galatians, he writes, "occupied that which is now called 'Galatia and Gallograecia.'"[173] These inhabitants of the Pergamene frontier may have been uniquely positioned to claim shares in both the Hellenistic *koinê* and the barbarian prestige promoted by warring Galatian tetrarchs. Indeed, scraps of evidence tell us that the sociopolitical structures of second-century Galatia were indeed becoming quite sophisticated without shedding Celtic institutions. The nobles Ortiagon and Chiomara, for example, gave their son the evocative Greek name Paidopolites ("son citizen"), but his career in public life culminated with an appointment as a tribal judge.[174] Ideologically, the notion of Gallograecia would have potentially been at odds with the Attalids' claim to an Asia without Galatians. In practice, however, the cultural makeup of the region boded well for its integration into the rest of the kingdom. Inscriptions show that Neo-Phrygian held a status here that it lacked farther east. Its everyday material culture also differed from that of the Galatian heartland. If we compare Gordion in its final, pre-189 phase to a site like Dorylaion/Şarhöyük, the contrast is striking. At Gordion, local potters had already dropped most Greek forms from their repertoire after ca. 275. In the town that Vulso conquered, just a few imported drinking cups existed. There appears to have been no real demand for drinking cups, as none of the imports were replicated in local fabrics.[175] On the other hand, at Şarhöyük (Dorylaion, now Eskişehir), which had been the western outpost of the Hittites, Hellenistic houses have revealed a broad assemblage of Greek vessels that were duly copied in the Phrygian gray ware tradition, such as unguentaria, echinus bowls, and fish plates. Aegean-style drinking was entrenched here, as demonstrated by a series of mold-made bowls that spawned local imitations.[176] These patterns are surely the result of a multiplicity of factors, many of which are not recoverable. It is difficult to know what direct effects, if any, the sovereignty of a handful of Galatian elites had on the culture of the many, particularly in light of the fast pace of the leaders' own assimilation. What we see among the Attalids' Gallogrecian subjects, then, is perhaps an even higher degree of cultural fluidity, almost entrepreneurial in nature, stimulated by the region's

---

[172] Just. *Epit.* 25.2.11. [173] Strabo 12.5.1.
[174] Mitchell 1993, vol. 1, 43, citing *Suda* s.v. Παιδοπολίτης (Π866). [175] Stewart 2010, 231–37.
[176] Sivas 2018, 105; and on mold-made bowls, see Yedidağ 2015.

enduring link to the Aegean. Pergamene cultural politics needed to be sophisticated and imaginative enough to keep pace. The result was the extraordinary investment in the sanctuary of the Mother of the Gods at Pessinous.

Pessinous and Aizanoi

The originality and creativity of Attalid cultural politics were on full display at the sanctuary of Cybele Agdistis in Pessinous. Rather than impose, imitate, or merely appropriate, the Attalids combined different elements of Greek, Phrygian, and Galatian culture in novel ways, in order to stretch and secure their influence along a restive eastern frontier. Several decades of excavation and a remarkable epigraphic dossier show that Pergamon transformed an open-air sanctuary in remote eastern Phrygia into a place of Pan-Asian and indeed international repute. It was once presumed that the Attalids intruded here on a native priesthood, its "temple state," and a cult with deep roots in Phrygian or even Hittite religion, but that view has become untenable. In the Iron Age, several modest Phrygian settlements dotted the slopes of the Sivrihisar Mountains and the Gallos Valley. Beneath the riverside platform of the large, Julio-Claudian temple in Pessinous itself, modest late Phrygian houses have been uncovered and a presumed, nonmonumental "cult annex."[177] However, nothing suggests that the site was a focal point of the valley before Hellenistic times, let alone a place of wider significance for Phrygian religion.[178] With no sign of a Phrygian sanctuary of Cybele in Pessinous, scholars have gone looking for a rock-cut shrine in the surrounding high places, on the order of the Midas Monument in Yazılıkaya. Several surveys of the environs, including the presumed Mount Dindymos, which gave the goddess her epithet Meter Dindymene, have turned up a handful of Phrygian cult sites, such as Tekören and Hamamtepe. None, however, is securely identified as a shrine of the Great Mother. Nor do any of these sites appear to have attracted long-distance pilgrimage or much attention at all. Following Altay Coşkun, it is even possible to doubt the authenticity of the earliest witness to the Pessinountine cult, the early fourth-century historian Theopompus,

---

[177] Verlinde 2015, 63.
[178] Coşkun 2016, 59, noting also the lack of any significant Iron Age settlements in the Gallos Valley.

as cited by Ammianus Marcellinus.[179] This would make Diodorus, in the first century BCE, our earliest literary source.[180]

As a result, it has become clear that the so-called temple state of Pessinous grew significantly – or was born as such – in the Hellenistic period. Whereas we once puzzled over how Attalos I, as early as 205/4, could have pilfered the aniconic cult stone for transfer to Rome, in the form of an Idaean Magna Mater, the archaeology now forces us to contend with the question of what was there for the alleged temple-robber to take.[181] The late Iron Age in Phrygia was characterized by dispersed settlement patterns and the absence of the state.[182] It took an outside power, then, to reconfigure the late Phrygian cult on such a grand scale. Therefore, Strobel has argued that one of the Successors, either Antigonos or Lysimachus, drew the cult down from the mountains and equipped its client-priests with a citadel and a sanctuary.[183] This reconstruction has been aided by insecure dates for both the earliest monumental architecture under the Roman temple, that is, the *emplekton* citadel, as well as the hilltop necropoleis of the bustling Hellenistic emporion. The theory also receives a measure of support from Thonemann, who argues that Pesssinous was the site of Kleonnaion, a Graeco-Macedonian settlement of the late fourth century. However, current readings of the pottery seem to point to the later Attalids and Galatian tetrarchs as the primary builders of the sanctuary, even if the citadel in Sector B receives an earlier date in the third century. Moreover, Strabo tells us, in no uncertain terms, that the "Attalic kings" equipped (κατεσκεύασται) the *temenos* with a temple and marble stoas.[184]

Strabo's description credits the Attalids with sponsoring the construction of the first monumental architecture in the sacred precinct. While Strabo takes for granted the prior existence of the sanctuary, he cannot be construed to point to a rebuild or an expansion of earlier buildings. Rather, the geographer's use of the same verb elsewhere suggests that, from a conceptual standpoint, *temenos* and emporion alike were empty spatial

---

[179] Coşkun 2018, 212–13.   [180] Diod. Sic. 3.59.8.
[181] Some, such as Gruen (1990, 5–33) and Bremmer (2004, 558), have cast doubt on the historicity of the tradition of an Attalid transfer of the cult from Pessinous to Rome, while others, such as Burton (1996) and Devreker (2018, 248), continue to uphold the idea.
[182] Thonemann 2013c.
[183] Strobel 2003–7, 208–9, noting, however, stratigraphy that indicates major new constructions in the early second century BCE.
[184] Strabo 12.5.3. Kleonnaion at Pessinous: Thonemann 2015b, 122–26. However, as Coşkun (2018, 218) points out, no compelling archaeological evidence has emerged for an early Hellenistic floruit for the site under the likes of Antigonos, Lysimachus, the early Seleukids, or indeed Philetairos, though one is often assumed (e.g., by Roller 2018, 725).

containers for humans to fill with their works.¹⁸⁵ The Attalids had encountered, then equipped the sacred place with architecture that was appropriate to its holiness, or so it may have seemed in the Augustan age. Perhaps, by Strabo's time, Pergamene and Roman building had obscured the oddity and contingency of the Attalids' original investment, which a recent redating of the opening letter of the epigraphic dossier puts in the late third century.¹⁸⁶ In other words, it appears that the Attalids grafted their marble design on to a modest, open-air Phrygian sanctuary. As the Pergamene Temple of Cybele has never been located, it has been suggested that it stood on the site of an earlier mountain-top shrine. Philetairos' Doric temple and sancuary of Meter on Mamurt Kale, 30 km southeast of Pergamon, may have provided a precedent.¹⁸⁷ The lost marble slabs of the epigraphic dossier, long thought to have formed part of the wall of an Attalid temple, as well as several column capitals discovered in upland Dinek, are intriguing hints.¹⁸⁸ Or the Attalid temple may lie unexcavated under the village of Ballıhisar. Either way, the new temple was part of a complex of buildings. Strabo's mention of the Attalids' marble stoas, along with the latest analysis of the pre-Roman architecture beneath the massive terrace in Sectors B and H, the core of the Hellenistic town's residential quarters, points to a break with the past. The material culture inside these buildings,

---

[185] We can approach the philological problem through the translation of Roller (2014, 543) of Strabo 12.5.3: "Pessinous is the greatest emporium in that region, having a sanctuary of the Mother of the Gods, which is greatly revered. They call her Angdistis. In antiquity the priests were essentially the masters and benefited from a great priesthood, yet today these honors have been greatly reduced, although the emporium remains. The precinct was developed by the Attalid kings in a manner befitting a sacred place, with a temple and stoas of white stone (Πεσσινοῦς δ' ἐστὶν ἐμπόριον τῶν ταύτῃ μέγιστον, ἱερὸν ἔχον τῆς μητρὸς τῶν θεῶν σεβασμοῦ μεγάλου τυγχάνον. καλοῦσι δ' αὐτὴν Ἄγδιστιν. οἱ δ' ἱερεῖς τὸ παλαιὸν μὲν δυνάσται τινὲς ἦσαν, ἱερωσύνην καρπούμενοι μεγάλην, νυνὶ δὲ τούτων μὲν αἱ τιμαὶ πολὺ μεμείωνται, τὸ δὲ ἐμπόριον συμμένει. κατεσκεύασται δ' ὑπὸ τῶν Ἀτταλικῶν βασιλέων ἱεροπρεπῶς τὸ τέμενος ναῷ τε καὶ στοαῖς λευκολίθοις)." Difficulties arise around translating the verb κατασκευάζειν. Verlinde (2015, 39–40) strongly objects to the translation "enlarged, reconstructed," for which see, still, Devreker (2018, 248). Yet the epigraphic study of Uzunoğlu (2018) rightly cautions against taking the verb to mean construct, unequivocally, "from scratch." The problem resolves itself if we accept that the Attalids did indeed "develop" the *temenos*, which they were the first to monumentalize. Note further Strabo's usage with regard to his own city of Amaseia (12.3.39), "marvelously equipped by foresight and nature (κατεσκεύασται δὲ θαυμαστῶς προνοίᾳ τε καὶ φύσει)." We also learn that the harbor of Assos was "created by means of a large mole (ὁ δὲ λιμὴν χώματι κατεσκεύασται μεγάλῳ)" (13.1.57).

[186] *I.Pessinous* 1; Mileta 2010; see also Coşkun 2016.

[187] Roller's comment (2018, 725) on Strabo 12.5.3, "Remains of a temple of Hellenistic date are visible," is therefore quite misleading. On Mamurt Kale, utterly transformed despite cultic continuity, see, most recently, Bielfeldt 2019, 178–86.

[188] Verlinde 2015, 68.

wall paintings, and pottery is said to be broadly second-century and Pergamene.[189]

If indeed an Attalid, posing as a new Midas, wrested Pessinous from obscurity, the question remains, to what end? Again, finding the answer requires us to take seriously the dynasty's claim to rule over all of the inhabitants of Asia and, not only that, to represent the cultural ambitions of those now invited, once again, to join civilization. The epigraphic dossier from Sivrihisar and the new Attalid letter, found in a house in Ballıhisar, reinforce the impression that Pergamon was deeply involved with the priesthood, the cult, and the sanctuary, from as early as 207. This cannot have been because Attalos I anticipated the Roman request for aid a few years later or guessed at the Sibyl's oracular pronouncement. The king had his own reasons, strategic and ideological, for investing considerable resources in the remote Gallos Valley. Most of the epigraphic dossier records correspondence between the Attalids and a priest named Attis, who is a Galatian, we learn, when his brother is identified as a hostile leader named Aioiorix.[190] By a process that remains obscure to us, Galatians had entered the Pessinountine priesthood, in which they formally retained their non-Phrygian identity.[191] The Attalids' cultivation of Attis was not aimed at instigating defection, since Galatian leaders had diverse interests and rarely engaged in collective action. He was their partner after 188, it seems, because Attalos I had conquered Pessinous around 207. Surely, its territory floated in and out of Pergamene control over the following decades, but this did not necessitate what has often been described as secret communication. On the contrary, the Attalids would have publicized their relationship with Pessinous' priests to the greatest extent possible. Here is an example of a context in which the Attalids encountered a flesh-and-blood Galatian subject, one ensconced in a (pseudo-?) Phrygian priesthood that occupied a militarily advantageous borderland position. The letters and the building project both attest to their zeal to win over such powerbrokers, who undoubtedly also received other offers, not only from their distant kin in Ancyra or Peion but also from the Bithynians, with whom the Attalids fought a series of border wars that stretched over many decades.

The war of Attalos I and Prousias I of Bithynia over the Epictetus (208–205) is now seen to form the backdrop of the first letter of the

---

[189] Verlinde 2015, 64–65.   [190] *RC* 56 line 5.
[191] The Phrygian-Galatian distinction within the priesthood was maintained under Roman rule. Note that the Galatians may not have provided the apparently punning name *Galloi* for the castrate priests; for a summary of the issue, with linguistic details, see Bøgh 2007, 323–24.

Pessinous dossier. Christian Mileta has argued persuasively that *I.Pessinous* 1 is not a royal letter to the priest Attis, traditionally dated to the late 160s, but an internal Attalid directive issued during this, much earlier war with Prousias.[192] Its brusque message, voiced not to an ally but to a subordinate officer, is to take Pessinous (rendered "Pessongoi") by hook or by crook. The motivation for such an action is made explicit in the final sentence of the communiqué, which, if the letter were addressed to a priest, would be absurd: "For as the place is holy, it must be taken by all means" (ἱεροῦ γὰρ τοῦ χωρίου ὄντος ληπτέον ἐστὶ πάντως).[193] The local priests surely took the holiness of the sanctuary for granted! Our copy of the document was a reinscription of the first century CE, when the sacred status of the land was at issue. Attalos' memorandum seems to have been dug out of an archive in order to be offered as evidence to secure the sanctuary's inviolability (*asylia*). Ironically, the original concern of Attalos, in the third century BCE, had been to take the place by force. Commentators have also noted the strategic connotation of the word *chorion*. It may be surmised that the king saw the immense value of a fortified indigenous sanctuary because he already anticipated its development as a platform for cultural pageantry. The Bithynians were a great threat to the Attalids in war and diplomacy – but nowhere near as adept at cultural politics.

The Attalids' distinctive ability to reorganize a Phrygian cultic landscape in the service of securing the borders is also discernible at the site of Aizanoi. It lies in the northwestern Epictetus, in a plain around the river Penkalas, one of the sources of the Rhyndakos. The sanctuary of Aizanoi, as it now stands, is a Roman creation. At its center is a Roman temple of Zeus with a subterranean chamber that seems to have housed the cult of Cybele. Although the tidy work of the Roman builders has again obscured earlier activity on the site, recent excavations have managed to shed light on the Bronze and Iron Age mound beneath the temple's terrace – and on Hellenistic remains. In Aizanoi, too, Attalos I faced off against Prousias I for control of strategic territory, which Macedonian cleruchs had perhaps already settled.[194] Yet the sacredness of the topography was also clearly a draw. A bilingual inscription of 128 CE from the wall of the Roman temple tells us that both Attalos I and Prousias I had once donated land to the city

---

[192] Mileta 2010, 116–17.   [193] *I.Pessinous* 1 lines 8–9.
[194] Habicht 2006, 3–4, on the chronology of the Bithynian conflict. Evidence for a Macedonian settlement is slim: Berges (2010, 42) notes Macedonian shield iconography in the archive of the large house. Note, though, the presence of a "High Hellenistic," i.e., third- or early second-century, Iron Age Phrygian-type oven housed in a mud brick structure (Hoff 2011, 130–31 with fig. 10).

and to the god.¹⁹⁵ By Hadrian's time, that land had fallen into private hands. An unpublished inscription is said to indicate that Attalos I distributed land to cleruchs, making it difficult to sort out the original relationship between king, sanctuary, settlers, and the Hellenistic political community that preceded the Roman *civitas Aezanitarum*.¹⁹⁶ Many scholars assume that a pre-Hellenistic sanctuary of some importance benefited from Attalid patronage or, alternatively, was dispossessed.¹⁹⁷ Control of a powerful Anatolian temple was the prize, on this view, and Attalos behaved much like other Hellenistic kings by assigning lands to a prominent indigenous sanctuary.¹⁹⁸ However, as in Pessinous, the antiquity of the temple institutions may be chimeric, or rather, the Attalids may have changed the cult so thoroughly that it bore only a distant relation to its Phrygian forerunner.

Archaeologically, the site of Aizanoi is complex, but excavation of a 7-m-deep trench on the settlement mound and the remains of a large Hellenistic house suggests wholesale transformation under the Attalids. The deep trench on the settlement mound did not turn up late Bronze or early Iron Age material. However, an early Bronze Age building was uncovered, which some suspect could be cultic.¹⁹⁹ In the later Iron Age (seventh to fourth centuries BCE), a Phrygian village existed at Aizanoi, but its gray ware pottery is idiosyncratic and out of sync with wares from major centers such as Gordion or Dorylaion.²⁰⁰ Clearly, the village was not the administrative seat of a robust, ancient Anatolian temple-state. No such temple has been found, but rather, the local, pre-Hellenistic cult of significance in the area seems to have been housed in the cave sanctuary of Steunos, typologically, a classic, rural shrine of Phrygian Matar, set above a streambed 2 km southwest of the settlement.²⁰¹ At Aizanoi itself, the laying of foundations for, first, a Roman pike wall and, then, the massive Roman temple has obliterated that building's predecessor. Nevertheless, excavator Klaus Rheidt all but assumes that an Attalid temple once existed, arguing that Pergamon transformed Aizanoi into one of the most important

---

¹⁹⁵ Bringmann et al. 1995, no. 253 [E].

¹⁹⁶ Daubner 2011, 54 n. 46. It is not clear to me if this unpublished inscription is among the series of boundary stones mentioned by Rheidt 2008, 109.

¹⁹⁷ Debord 1982, 273.   ¹⁹⁸ Allen 1983, 87; Laffi 1971, 21–25; Roller 1999, 336.

¹⁹⁹ Lochner 2010, 29; Berndt-Ersöz 2006, 163.   ²⁰⁰ Dikbaş 2010, 44.

²⁰¹ A Palaeo-Phrygian date is evidenced by the step-like structure and circular shafts on a ridge above the cave. Roller (1999, 337–38) contends that here, as in comparable installations at Midas City and Fındık, Iron Age shrines remained in use during the Hellenistic and Roman periods.

sanctuaries of Asia Minor.²⁰² The suggestion of the excavator that the original Pergamene cult statue can be glimpsed in a Roman bronze figurine of Zeus of Aizanoi, as well as in the iconography of a Roman coin type, encourages us to reckon with the transformation of the local god on the Attalids' watch. This is now Zeus with a bushy beard, glimpsed in depictions of Zeus Bronton, which are particularly common in this very area of northwest Phrygia – and indeed reminiscent of the indigenous King Teuthras on the Telephos frieze.²⁰³ The deity worshipped at Aizanoi in Attalid times was surely an older Anatolian weather god propitiated by farmers, but the Greek language and architectural idiom now became vehicles for the religious imagination of conservative Phrygia. Local worshipers now saw their aniconic, male weather god (Ata?) anthropomorphized, and they named him "Zeus," shorthand in these parts for "great god," surely adding an epithet such as Bronton or any other from the region's rich palette.²⁰⁴ In a powerful display of Pergamene creativity, the god showed the Anatolian face assigned to him by Greek artists in the cosmology of the Great Altar. It also seems probable that the occupant of the large Hellenistic house somehow oversaw this hypothetical Pergamene temple of Zeus-Ata and, considering the sturdy, bronze lock fixture from a chest in one of its rooms, perhaps also its finances. The 46 clay bullae found in the house, surely a fraction of the original archive's contents, suggests a spike of administrative activity. Further, a cache of 18 nearly complete ceramic vessels, largely of Pergamene origin and datable to the second quarter of the second century BCE, along with a female statue head of fine crystalline marble, give us a sense of the scale and intense pace of change at Aizanoi.²⁰⁵

Evidently, Attalos I took the same steps at Aizanoi that Strabo's unspecified "Attalic kings" took at Pessinous. Picking up on a local mythographic

---

[202] Rheidt 2008, 108–11.
[203] For the iconography of Zeus Bronton along the border between Phrygia and Bithynia, see Şahin 2001, 174–75.
[204] On Phrygian gods represented in Greek, see Parker 2017, 79; further on the meaning of "Zeus" as "great god" in rural western Anatolia, as well as the unusually rich palette of Zeus epithets and Greek as a vehicle for religious imagination in conservative Phrygia, pp. 94, 107–10, noting too the agricultural Zeus Ἀναδότης "sender up" in Aizanoi (*SEG* XLV 1719). On the persistence of Phrygian deities worshipped under the name Zeus in northwest Phrygia, see Şahin 2006, a large dossier of dedications from a rural sanctuary in the territory of Nakoleia (second and third centuries CE).
[205] For the archive, see Berges 2010; the statuette, Lochner 2010, 34–35. For dates for the pottery from the destruction layer, closed just after the midpoint of the second century, see Ateş 2017, esp. 94.

tradition, he erected monuments to match the sacredness of the place, fixing the focus of the surrounding countryside on a new temple and its annexes. Similarly, if there were powerful priests in Hellenistic Aizanoi, it would seem that they were Pergamene creations, not just clients. Centuries later, Pausanias, in his description of the Meter sanctuary at the cave of Steunos, calls it one of the most famous such caves in Greek or barbarian lands. Yet this fame was anchored in the relatively recent past, though the periegete credited primeval Arcadian colonists with the foundation of the Phrygian cult.[206] The cave has been thoroughly explored, and small finds indicate heavy traffic between the first century BCE and the end of the first century CE, when the cult seems to have been transferred to the Roman temple's subterranean chamber.[207] In the recent discovery of a votive dump for the same cult of Meter at the village of Ilicikören, 5 km south of the settlement mound, we can see that the increase in longer-distance traffic to shrines of the Aizanitis had started already in the second century BCE.[208] Significant numbers of Phrygian worshippers began to patronize a cult annex at Ilicikören, and this may have been a secondary effect of the Attalid elaboration of the sanctuary at Aizanoi. Nearly all of the pottery from Ilicikören is local and indigenous, and many of the figurines are, like those from Steunos, distinctly Anatolian in form. The goddess stands and wears a *polos* on her head, whereas she already appears seated in Greek iconography after the sixth century BCE.[209] That a high volume of these decidedly un-Greek figurines appears in the sanctuary site's preserved cult annexes from the second century BCE suggests that the Attalids had elaborated religious life at Aizanoi in such a way as to make contact with a population of the Phrygian countryside that had remained largely hidden from the state during the later Iron Age.

The large house and Greek cult statue of the lost temple notwithstanding, one has the impression that the cultural identity of the local population remained Phrygian under Attalid rule, and yet the cave of Steunos is notable precisely for its mixture of Greek and Phrygian cult fixtures.[210] While the Phrygian and Greek conceptions of Meter/Matar had been influencing each other since the sixth century BCE, differences endured, and we should try to capture, to the extent possible, the Phyrgian perspective at Aizanoi.[211] It is often said that the combination of the cults of Meter and Zeus was facilitated by the early assimilation of Phrygian Matar and Greek Rhea, but we should not overlook the way in which the Attalids also

---

[206] Pausanias 8.4.3; 10.32.3.　[207] Roller 1999, 336–41.　[208] Ateş 2010; Ateş 2015.
[209] Standing: Bøgh 2007, 332.　[210] Roller 1999, 337.　[211] Bøgh 2007, 316.

drew on much older traditions of paired deities, Mother and Father (Ata). The so-called Male Superior God of the early Phrygian pantheon, shown with Matar in double idols, survived into the Hellenistic period as Zeus Papas/Papias. In fact, the popular rural cult of Papias even appears outside Phrygia, in a dedication from Lasnedda in Lydia, dated to the late Attalid period.[212]

It has also been suggested that the Male Superior God was worshipped on step structures like the one above the cave at Steunos.[213] In the Phrygian cultural context of this Hellenizing building program, the Attalids' new subjects probably understood Zeus as a strange new Ata, seductively endowed with human form and granted a Greek-style temple. The Attalids had long shown abundant creativity when it came to recasting Phrygian religion in monumental form. Philetairos had encased the Phrygian stone-cut base for an earlier cult-statue and a stone-cut altar inside his building complex on the sacred mountain of Asporden (Mamurt Kale). The impulse to combine creatively emerged from the Attalids' deep familiarity with both cultural traditions and the pressing need to integrate rural Anatolia. The luxury of appropriation was not available; they need to manufacture temple power. At the imperial center, the votives tend to be, as expected, rather more Greek in appearance, but the apparent clash of styles is repeated. The sacred geography of the countryside of the Kaikos Valley contained multiple rock-cut Meter/Matar shrines.[214] Matar seems to have had royal associations in Phrygian religion since ca. 700 BCE, and indeed we find the cult of Meter Basileia at Pergamon. Yet it is a civic priesthood, held by priestesses, not male eunuchs. The cult statue has been identified, and it is a magnificent Atticized and seated Cybele, holding her tympanum. Her sanctuary has not been conclusively identified, and may have been, in good Anatolian fashion, attached to the craggy rock of the highest peak of the Pergamene acropolis.[215] In other words, the cultural background of the Attalids matched their cultural politics, which is why at Pessinous and Aizanoi, they correctly identified places charged with local meaning but bereft of a

---

[212] *TAM* V 2 1321; Cohen 1995, 215.   [213] Bøgh 2007, 320–22; Berndt-Ersöz 2006, 170–71.
[214] I am referring here to Kapıkaya and also the newly discovered sanctuary at Mulla Mustafa Tepesi. On its rescue excavation, see Pirson 2013, 131–33, with illustration of Greek-style figurine of Meter-Cybele, fig. 54.
[215] On Meter-Cybele at Pergamon and its hinterland, see Agelidis 2012, 177–79; and now also Pirson et al. 2015, on a shrine built into the rock formations of Pergamon's rugged eastern slope, possibly dedicated to Meter-Cybele.

built environment. Iconoclastically, they developed them into showpieces that were no less important to their ambitions than the royal capital.

Pergamon in Pisidia

In the highlands above coastal Lycia and the plain of Pamphylia, the Attalids encountered a far less pliant set of indigenous populations. Geographically, Greater Pisidia includes the mountainous Pisidian heartland, with its deep river valleys and flat alluvial plains, as well as, in the west, the Milyas, the Lysis Valley, and the Kibyratis, and, in the north, Phrygia Paroreios.[216] Already present in rapidly urbanizing Pisidia were precisely the robust forms of social and military organization that were missing in far more rural parts of Attalid Phrygia. Surely, the process had begun earlier, but our first tangible proof of these far-reaching changes dates to around 200 BCE. Ethnic Pisidians, members of the dominant group of Luwian-speakers living in the mixed milieu of the territory of a former Hittite vassal state, began to nucleate in ever greater numbers. Over 50 Hellenistic cities have been recorded. To compare, a Turkish census of 1950 lists only 12 towns across the same region with at least 2,500 inhabitants, or roughly the same size of small Greek and Roman cities.[217] The urban form and governing institutions of these new cities were, in part, modeled on the Greek polis. Indigenous urban antecedents were few and far between, limited, it seems, to Panemoteichos I and the site of Düzen Tepe. In addition to new Greek-style magistracies, a bicameral system appeared in many cities, consisting of a popular assembly (*ekklesia*) and a council of elders (*gerousia*), with Termessos and Adada, at least, representing themselves as democracies. Before long, a competitive peer-polity system emerged, a veritable city-state culture, rife with rivalry, war, a creative discourse about kinship and descent, and even colonizing migrations, a place that Mitchell has likened to a microcosm of Archaic Greece.[218] Recent research has shown that Pisidian ethnogenesis, perhaps directed by mercenaries of the Persian period and buoyed by a rising population, was followed by a period of acculturation to Hellenistic habits in the century or so after Alexander. When the Attalids arrived in 188 BCE,

---

[216] On definition of the region and its annexes, see Talloen 2013, 13–18. See further Mitchell 1998a, for the scope of the Pisidian Survey of the British Institute of Archaeology at Ankara. On the definition of Milyas, see Syme 1995, 177–92; and on Phrygia Paroreios, see Bru 2017, 15–30.
[217] Mitchell 1998a, 238.   [218] Mitchell 1992, esp. 25.

the urban transformation was in full swing, so much so that we soon find Pisidians migrating westward and founding new cities in the Milyas and Kibyratis.

The famously martial Pisidians were indeed capable of mounting stiff resistance on the battlefield, which is why we find Attalos II campaigning in person against them for a considerable number of years. They were also conspicuously active agents in their own acculturation, fashioning a Hellenistic cultural bricolage that contains many indigenous elements in novel combinations with Greek ones. A fine example is the phenomenon of partly rock-cut temples, which are faced with a Greek *naos*, often in the Doric order.[219] The extent of the Attalids' involvement in Pisidia and the depth of their interference in local society has become increasingly clear.[220] Again, however, the imperial project's success remains unexplained as long as the cultural politics are simply termed Hellenization. While the Attalids fought a high-profile war against the proud city of Selge, coercion may have been the exception rather than the rule. Selge, then, comes to look like a lone and isolated holdout, grasping for Bithynian or Roman support. Archaeological remains and a growing epigraphic record point to a broader projection of soft power that had the effect of reducing rebellion and keeping open this vital link to the eastern Mediterranean via Attaleia. Further, Pergamon's tactful support of the cultural aspirations of Pisidian cities allowed for their rapid and precocious integration within the kingdom of Asia.

While historians once doubted that the Attalids' presence in Pisidia was ever more than episodic, several decades of intensive archaeological work have served to highlight Pergamon's impact on the region.[221] By contrast, Seleukid activity appears to have been limited, both in its geographic scope (to the north) and in terms of its effect: colonies were planted along major arteries connecting Apameia to Lykaonia, such as Pisidian Antioch, Seleukeia Sidera, Laodikeia Katakekaumene, and, most likely, Apollonia; vestiges of the previous regime may be detected in Macedonian shield reliefs spread around the region and in Sagalassos' use of the elephant as a civic badge.[222] In two key cities, Termessos and Selge, the third century

---

[219] Talloen 2013, 107–8.
[220] Kosmetatou 1997; Waelkens 2004; Köse 2004; Köse 2017, 66–68; Talloen 2013, 86–87.
[221] See, e.g., Allen 1983, 102. Pisidia figures scarcely in Allen's account, as his book was researched before a wave of archaeological surveys and excavations in the region. For Pisidia as a "frontier," see *RC*, 239. Cf. Bresson 2019, 292: "routes of circulation of men and goods ... from Pergamon to Pamphylia and Pisidia."
[222] Daubner 2011, 46. Macedonian identity of Seleukid Sagalassos: Kosmetatou 1997, 22.

witnessed a prelude of budding civic consciousness and Greek-style urbanism. However, as Veli Köse has shown in a detailed analysis of the datable evidence, the new civic identity in Pisidia did not begin to take monumental form before ca. 200 BCE.[223] The advent of the Attalids in Pisidia came amid a boom in fortification and, in many places, for the first time, the laying out of an agora and the construction of public buildings in stone ashlar. Much of the impetus for these changes was demonstrably ground-up.[224] Yet the more we know about the timing of these developments, the more Pergamene influence is apparent. In Pisidia, Attalid influence was deep and unprecedented.[225]

For example, the well-studied site of Sagalassos now helps date Pisidia's cultural revolution quite precisely. From the Persian into the early Hellenistic period (fifth to third centuries), the site was occupied, though the character of the settlement has been difficult to tease out from Classical and Hellenistic pottery recovered in the vicinity of the later Upper Agora. Flanking Sagalassos, however, was a primitively fortified sister settlement, Düzen Tepe, which maintained an Anatolian, seemingly anachronistic form of urbanism and material culture until its abandonment, just as the more outward-looking Sagalassos took shape around its first agora.[226] Düzen Tepe has been thoroughly explored and, along with Panemoteichos I, attests to the admittedly attenuated existence of a form of urbanism in Iron Age Pisidia. However, the emergence of some 50 cities in the Hellenistic period represents a sharp break with the past. The timing of that break and the character of one of the most important new cities were revealed in controlled excavations of the Upper Agora of Sagalassos in 2014 and 2015. Those digs put to rest old theories of rapid Hellenization immediately subsequent to Alexander's siege. In fact, the layout of the first, beaten-earth agora took place ca. 200 BCE, with the first ashlar buildings, such as the city's market building, arriving about half a century later.[227] This new date for the onset of the acceleration phase of urban change at

---

[223] Köse 2017, 44–59. This represents a major down-dating of key evidence adduced by Waelkens 2004. On different evidence, Waelkens and Vandeput (2007, 101) argue, "In fact, in general Attalid rule may have had less impact on the urban developments in Pisidia than was previously assumed." However, the strength of Waelkens' thesis that chronological fine-tuning of the archaeology reveals a more modest Pergamene impact on the region has now been considerably weakened.

[224] Mitchell 1992; Vanhaverbeke and Waelkens 2005.   [225] Kosmetatou 1997, 32.

[226] Sequential rather than contemporaneous settlement at Sagalassos and Düzen Tepe: Talloen 2013, 26.

[227] Cf. Waelkens 2004, 464–66, on the market building of Sagalassos, which he dated to the third century.

Sagalassos accords well with evidence from across Pisidia and coincides neatly with the appearance of the Attalids.[228] Admittedly, the kings stimulated and contributed to a process already underway. Yet two cities, Apollonia and Ariassos, even chose to publicize a break with the past by inaugurating new city-eras in 188.[229]

Perhaps the strongest indication of the Attalids' presence is the distinctive form of urbanism that ultimately took root in Pisidia. It has become evident that the Pisidians took over or adapted specifically Pergamene urban features from the start. Some scholars have seen Attalid influence in the choice of a trapezoidal agora at Selge, Sagalassos, and Termessos.[230] Interestingly, the centerpiece of the newly constituted community was not, for example, a gymnasium. Exceptionally, it seems, Termessos and Sagalassos acquired one in the second century.[231] The absence of that venue for royal munificence may help explain the oft-noted lack of honorific decrees for kings from Pisidia. In fact, civic life and the interaction with royal power were happening elsewhere. Across the region, the focal point of early civic life was the so-called Pergamene market building. In most places, this "market building," as the earliest monumental architecture, will have fulfilled a variety of administrative functions on the new city's agora.[232] The Pisidians tended to have added a *bouleuterion* soon thereafter, with the full complex taking shape ca. 150–100 BCE, though a firm early Imperial date for the *bouleuterion* at Sagalassos now reinforces the idea that in the initial layout of the agora, the market building stood alone.[233] In smaller cities, such as Sia and Adada, the *gerousia* may have gathered on the agora in assembly places flanked by steps, the Pisidian version of a council house or *ekklesiasterion*. Dating these structures is difficult, but they are associated with paved, well-demarcated agoras, which themselves begin to appear only in the second century BCE. Ultimately, we have to contend with the fact that Pergamene market buildings anchored early civic life in Pisidia.[234]

---

[228] Vanhaverbeke et al. 2010; Talloen and Poblome 2016, 120.
[229] Kosmetatou 1997, 30 n. 91 with references.
[230] The idea seems to go back to Martin 1974, 154–61. See Kosmetatou 1997, 33; cf. Waelkens 2004, 454; Waelkens and Vandeput 2007, 101.
[231] Termessos: Köse 2017, 67. In Sagalassos, geophysical prospection has detected gymnasium, for which see Degryse and Waelkens, 2008, 4.
[232] Köse 2005, 143–48.   [233] Köse 2017, 61–64; Talloen and Poblome 2016, 118–19.
[234] Termessos contains the only securely Hellenistic theater in Pisidia. For a date in the early second century BCE, see Waelkens 2004, 450.

What this visual quotation means is that the Attalids provided nascent urban communities in Pisidia with a specific vocabulary with which to express their civic identity, one drawn directly from a model built up in the metropole. New civic functions and big-ticket transactions were now conducted in surroundings that recalled Pergamon. Just decades before, the Attalids had developed their own spectacular multistoried stoa, with its substructure and rooms both behind and below the colonnades, bordering and in fact buttressing – as part of a giant terrace wall – the Upper Agora. The Pergamene market building had been a key feature of the Graeco-Anatolian synthesis in urban planning: inspired by East Greek antecedents, but innovatively designed to take advantage of the slope and enhance the prominence of the kind of terrace façade proper to Anatolian royalty. In hilly Pisidia, the idea caught on quickly. Market buildings of this type or a local variation are ubiquitous in a region in which many suspect Attalid builders were active.[235] This does not mean that in every case we should suspect a royal architect, let alone Pergamene sovereignty. Several examples have been found in Pamphylia, but also in Caria at Herakleia-under-Latmos and Alinda. On the contrary, the local variations, built on flatter ground, without stoas on the top floor or storage galleries in the central story, show that smaller cities, such as the unidentified cities at Melli and Kapılıtaş, freely adapted the Pergamene blueprint to meet their own needs (**Fig. 6.7**). Does divergence in design tell us that a city remained outside the Attalids' direct control? It is foolhardy to use these buildings as a proxy for the kingdom's borders. Large cities such as Termessos, Pednelissos, and Selge all contain buildings that hew closely to type, but can hardly have shared the same political status. The density and variety of these earliest of all of the region's public buildings in stone are stark reminders of the power of Pergamene cultural affinity to mold new civic identities in a strategic province.

The appearance of the first temples in Pisidian sanctuaries also seems to coincide with the arrival of the Attalids and the departure of the Seleukids.[236] At the turn from the third to the second century, a slew of large Ionic peripteral temples were built in the cities of Termessos, Selge, and Pisidian Antioch. In each case, it seems to be the most important local indigenous deity, now Hellenized and placed at the helm of a new civic

---

[235] Technical features of the construction of the Stoa of Attalos II in Termessos provide evidence for the activity of Attalid builders in the region. See Kosmetatou 1997, 32–33, citing Korres 1984.
[236] For two recent discussions, see Talloen 2013, 103–7; Köse 2017, 52–55.

Figure 6.7 Late Hellenistic Pergamene market building of the unidentified city at Melli in Pisidia (courtesy of Veli Köse and © Pisidia Survey Project).

pantheon, which acquired a new home. At Termessos, Temple N5 housed, most likely, Zeus Solymeus. On the acropolis of Selge, Zeus Kesbelios gained one such temple, and so too did Pisidian Antioch's main god, Mên, at the site of Karakuyu. Several factors point to an impetus from the outside. First, the similarity in architectural form is striking. Further, save for a possible temple at Panemoteichos I, there are no local precedents. Rather, the model is drawn from coastal Asia Minor. Finally, the scale of building would seem to have outstripped the revenues of these cities. This is especially true at Termessos, where two new temples, N5 and N7 (for Artemis), appeared in rapid succession. It is possible that competition between the two Hellenistic dynasties set off a cascade of construction across Pisidia, but the bulk of the activity appears to have been Attalid. While this is partly due to chronology, the behavior also fits a pattern discernible at Phrygian Aizanoi and at Pessinous, whereby the Attalids brought Greek temple architecture to indigenous sanctuaries.[237] At Selge,

---

[237] Compare also the Attalids' promotion of Mên Askaênos at Antioch and elsewhere. The sanctuary of Mên at Karakuyu, 3.5 km southeast of Antioch, seems to have origins in the second century BCE. While its Ionic peripteral temple dates, in its present form, to the Antonine period, close comparison with the temple of Dionysus at Teos and the temple of

at least, a Seleukid-era temple may have preceded the Ionic peripteral one that most scholars date to the period of Attalid rule. Polybius gives us a tantalizing hint of the existence of that temple (*hieron*) of Zeus during the siege of Achaios in 218.[238] Yet the appearance of the city's Kesbedion sanctuary, like much of the cultic landscape of Pisidia, changed indelibly over the course of the second century.

Architectural sculpture on some of the earliest public buildings in the region also provides a window onto the transformative impact of Pergamon in Pisidia. A traditional theme of military valor, a mainstay of third-century Pisidian ossuaries and even the earlier sepulchral monument of Alketas at Termessos, now found its way onto fortification walls, gates, public buildings, and monuments in the form of the weapons frieze. This was a distinctively regional, militaristic expression of civic identity, a Pisidian way of representing the new community.[239] However, alongside the traditional repertoire of arms, we also find an imported iconography in an up-to-date style, indeed, direct quotations from the Great Altar of Pergamon. For example, a fragmentary frieze from Termessos depicts Iphigeneia as priestess in the service of Artemis in Tauris.[240] Both stylistically and with its engaging continuous narrative, the monument recalls the Telephos Frieze. Current interpretations place the two fragments on the base of a pseudo-monopteros shrine to Artemis Tauropolos. Local lore may even have claimed that the cult-statue within was the original, which Iphigeneia herself whisked away from Tauris. If so, the people of Termessos used the Iphigeneia myth and the new medium to make an Attalid-style argument for authenticity, grounded in the primacy of place. Two other examples both feature the Gigantomachy, which admittedly also appears in a variety of non-Attalid contexts in Hellenistic Asia Minor. Yet at Termessos, the two badly damaged frieze slabs, unfortunately missing a secure architectural context, display a Gigantomachy that echoes the Great Altar in particular.[241]

Athena Polias at Priene suggests a predecessor built by the Attalids between 175 and 125 BCE. See Mitchell and Waelkens 1998, 68; Raff 2011, 139–40; cf. Khatchadourian 2011, 159–60. Mên appears to have been a pan-Anatolian deity, who took on an entirely new form and prominence in the second century BCE. See Hübner 2003, esp. 189–90.

[238] Polyb. 5.76.2.
[239] Baldıran 2016, esp. fig. 17, a Hellenistic architectural relief trophy from Amblada.
[240] Stähler 1968; Ridgway 2000, 85–86.
[241] Talloen (2013, 103) attributes the frieze to the temple of Zeus Solymeus. For echoes here of the Great Altar, see Ridgway 2000, 87.

Pergamon in Pisidia 343

Figure 6.8 Late Hellenistic frieze of Gigantomachy in the agora of the unidentified city at Melli in Pisidia (courtesy of Veli Köse and © Pisidia Survey Project).

A second example is from the unidentified site of Melli, the sensational recent discovery of a Gigantomachy frieze on three sides of a rectangular block of local limestone, perhaps the base of a lost monument from the city's nascent agora (**Fig. 6.8**).[242] It has been dated to the second half of the second century or the beginning of the first century BCE. Most legibly, it features Artemis and Apollo with his bow drawn, taking on one serpentine Giant, while Herakles confronts another. The sculptor appears to have been influenced by images of the Temple of Artemis in Magnesia, but much of the iconography, especially the violent hair-pulling and limb-treading, the form of the Giants' bodies, as well as the distinctive baroque style, point to Pergamene influence. Art historians taking a bird's-eye view would rightly caution us from mistaking the appearance of the baroque style as surefire proof of an Attalid presence. Further, we cannot hope to reconstruct the path by which these motifs and techniques arrived in second-century Pisidia. Traveling Rhodian craftsmen are just as likely as royal work gangs to have brought them here. The reception of the Great Altar in Rome, by

[242] Köse 2004.

contrast, will probably always remain much better understood. Yet why should these memes have landed at all, and so quickly, in a place like Melli? It seems they provided the Pisidians with the means to vindicate their own cultural claims in a changing world. In the case of Iphigeneia and Termessos, we can discern a typical Mediterranean play for mythological inclusion. The Gigantomachy of Melli takes the armed struggle for civic identity, perhaps here too in allegorical form, the memory of specific battles, and elevates it all to the cosmic plain. The Pisidian townsmen join the gods' defense of civilization, not Hellenism as such. What does the reception of the Great Altar in Pisidia tell us about how subjects from the semi-Greek periphery may have interpreted the Great Altar's own Gigantomachy? It seems to call into question a common conception of the message of the Altar, voiced most recently by Filippo Coarelli, as a statement of the defense of the ostensibly timeless values of Panhellenism.[243] Rather, it reveals a message of cultural universalism suited to the needs of communities still on the fringes of the poliad system.

Pergamon's armed interference in Pisidia certainly provoked resistance. Some scholars have even seen the symmachy struck between Adada and Termessos as a military alliance against the Attalids.[244] Still, the dynasty's lasting prestige in a region it ruled for just half a century underscores the effectiveness of its cultural diplomacy. Naming practice among an indigenous population, which continued to speak Luwian and Phrygian, is revealing in this regard. In northern Pisidia and the Paroreios, for example, the name Attalos is ubiquitous and persists for generations, with many occurrences at Neapolis, which, Hadrien Bru has argued, was in fact an Attalid colony.[245] An example from the early Roman village of Tynada in the territory of Pisidian Antioch emblematizes the multifaceted cultural identity of the elite families that will have been the power brokers in Attalid times. The *demos* of the village of Tynada had honored a certain Attalos son of Philetairos with a statue.[246] Two brothers named Attalos and Orokendeas, sons of Kralos, erected the statue. The two dynastic names are flanked by two local names, one certainly Anatolian, Orokendeas, which itself combines the Greek "of the mountain" (Oro-) with the common Pisidian name Kendeas. The same mixedness is evident in a

---

[243] Coarelli 2017, 200. Cf. Queyrel 2017, arguing too against a Galatian allegory in the Gigantomachy of the Great Altar.
[244] *TAM* III 1 2. For this interpretation, see Kosmetatou 1997, 28; Waelkens and Vandeput 2007, 102; cf. Hopp 1977, 73 n. 81; Brandt 2002, 395.
[245] Bru 2017, 49–61.   [246] Labarre and Özsait 2015, 96 (no. 4).

family from Antioch itself. A man named Attalos and his wife Tateis erected a monument for a certain Manes son of Opnadeios. In a single family, three onomastic layers are visible: the Greek dynastic name, Anatolian names common in Phrygia (Tateis and Manes), as well as a Pisidian name (Opnadeios).[247] To the ruling classes of mountain towns in the process of becoming city-states, the Attalids offered an entrée to a shared Mediterranean, in which it was possible to become Greek and still remain Pisidian.

On the island of Delos in 113 BCE, less than a generation after the Bequest of Attalos, we find the arrival of the Pisidians on the trans-Mediterranean stage advertised in a display context redolent of dynastic memory. Six envoys of the "*demos* of the Pisidians of Prostanna," perhaps returning from an embassy to the Roman Senate, honored Marcus Antonius, the quaestor of the province of Asia, with a statue.[248] The Pisidian ethnic identity shines through in the new community's nomenclature. Here too, the persistence of indigenous names is also striking: five out of six are Anatolian, an impressive ratio after almost a century of urban living, half of that spent under a regime whose cultural politics have often been described as a Hellenizing mission. These ambassadors represented the Pisidians of Prostanna on Delos before Roman power and were already accustomed to the normal Hellenistic exchange of honors. One can only imagine that most nonelite Pisidians retained much more than their old names. Yet the findspot of the statue base points to a genuine affinity with the Attalids. It was a monument for one of Asia's new Roman rulers, but placed near the stoa known as the Portique du Sud, it inevitably garnered some of the prestige of the province's former kings.[249] The stoa on the east side of the southern end of the processional way may very well have been a gift of Attalos I. Multifigure statue groups stood at each end, one starring the Pergamene general Epigenes. The other seems to have commemorated a victory of a mounted Attalos I over Galatians, which, perhaps, even depicted the fearsome barbarians.[250] In such a context, men like Motoxis and Mistanisthos of Prostanna were perfectly at home. The Attalids had offered their fathers a version of civilization that was not the exclusive possession of Greeks.

---

[247] *SEG* VI 576; Bru 2017, 211.   [248] *I.Delos* 1603; Robert 1965, 83 (no. 1).
[249] Bru 2017, 22.
[250] *IG* XI 4 1109. For the monument, see Bruneau and Ducat 2005, 168. See Schalles 1985, 60–68, esp. 61, on the possibility of Galatian figures. Cf. Stewart 2004, 223, proposing a chariot monument instead.

In practice, that invitation could have looked much like the unpublished decree from Olbasa, a strange and unexpected recent addition to the dossier of the Nikephoria festival. What is so surprising about this discovery is the off-the-beaten-path location of the find. By contrast, the previously known invitations were addressed to political and cultural elites, powerful city-states such as Kos and likely Iasos, as well as to the Aetolians and the Delphic Amphictiony.[251] The new inscription shows a small, just-hatched city in the Milyas region of western Pisidia following the same standard conventions as the "Greek cities": receiving a Pergamene sacred embassy, recognizing the refounded festival as crowned games and the sanctuary of Athena Nikephoros as inviolable, and arranging to participate themselves. This is remarkable given the way historians have understood the motivation and the message behind Eumenes II's 182/1 upgrade of the Nikephoria to penteteric games, in which the musical section was promoted to isopythian status, the athletic and equine to isolympic. In the treatment of Allen, for example, the games became Panhellenic in an "outward sign to the Greek world of [Eumenes'] authority and influence after the Treaty of Apameia."[252] For Domenico Musti, the festival instantiated a tripartite vision of Classical Greece: Olympia, Delphi, and Athens – but in second-century Asia.[253] To be sure, grandiose Hellenocentric rhetoric was not missing from the fanfare. Famously, the Amphictionic decree is full of it. That text even describes the Pergamene ambassadors talking up the role of the Attalids as solicitous benefactors of "all the Greeks, both singly and according to city."[254] However, as Kent Rigsby points out, these arguments appear to have been tailored for Delphi.[255] They would have made little sense in Pisidia, retailed to a population not yet, or even just now, identifying as Hellenes. After all, the trigger for the reorganization of the festival had been the triumph over Prousias I, Ortiagon, and the Galatians, which the people of Telmessos moved in 184/3 to commemorate with sacrifices to Athena Nikephoros.[256] That text, again, had celebrated a victory on behalf of *all* of the inhabitants

---

[251] New Olbasa Decree: Corsten 2008. Nikephoria dossier with earlier bibliography: Rigsby 1996, 363–77 (nos. 176–179).

[252] Allen 1983, 129.

[253] Musti 1998. See also Musti 2000. His arguments against the consensus on periodicity have failed to convince. See Allen 1983 121–29; Jones 1974; Jones 2000.

[254] Lines 13–14: ἀ]πελογίσαντο δὲ καὶ οἱ θεωροὶ τὴν τοῦ βασιλέως [εὔ]νοιαν ἣν ἔχων|δ[ια]τελεῖ κ[οινῆι τ]ε πρὸς ἅπαντας τοὺς Ἕλληνας καὶ καθ' ἰδίαν π[ρὸ]ς τὰς πόλεις.

[255] Rigsby 1996, 376–77. Cf. Koehn 2007, 71, 134, taking the Amphictionic decree as a rather too complete statement of Attalid ideology.

[256] Bithynian war as trigger: Hopp 1977, 42; cf. Allen 1983, 128.

of Asia. Civilization in Asia, the Lycians of Telmessos claimed, was worth saving. Taken together, this evidence suggests that the ambassadors fanning out from Pergamon to announce the Nikephoria carried a culturally differentiated message. For Olbasa, then, participation in the festival was a means not of becoming Greek, but rather of claiming a share in civilization.

We find the Anatolian content of that message emblazoned on an intriguing coin type minted in the name of Athena Nikephoros, a rare silver tetradrachm (Attic standard) known from just three examples (**Fig. 3.9**).[257] A date for the coin floats between the relaunch of the festival in 182/1 and ca. 165, making the coin broadly contemporaneous with the epigraphic dossier and a complementary instrument of ideology.[258] The image on the coin's reverse seems to be a cult statue, though an epiphany has also been considered.[259] In any case, this is not the expected Greek iconography – neither the helmeted profile of Athena of two other series minted in the name of Nikephoros nor the seated goddess of the Philetairoi. Yet another Classical model may have presented itself in the form of the Pheidian knock-off from the presumed Library's eastern hall: the Parthenos type carried a Nike.[260] Instead, what this coin depicts is an Anatolian goddess with a number of Greek accoutrements: an aegis, a long *peplos*, the shield resting on her left leg, and the Nike in her right hand. Instead of the familiar Corinthian or Athenian helmet, the goddess wears a high *polos* and a long veil. Her pectoral and the manner in which she extends her arms are reminiscent of Artemis of Ephesus. The coin depicts an Anatolian mother goddess, perhaps Meter Basileia, who, on one theory, had been worshipped in Pergamon under the name Athena Polias since the late fourth century.[261] Another parallel worth considering is an image of a syncretized Athena Magarsia on a coin image from Mallos in Smooth Cilicia (**Fig. 6.9**). It is interesting to compare the two, since the posture

---

[257] Le Rider 1973; Mørkholm 1984; Faita 2001; Marcellesi 2012, 125–27 (no. 44). The three coins were struck from two dies, but as Marcellesi (2012, 127) points out, nothing proves this was a one-off issue. Cf. Thonemann 2015a, 85.

[258] The date of the Sitochoro hoard (*IGCH* 237; ca. 168–165) provides the lower limit of the chronology.

[259] Epiphany: Meadows 2018, 303; see also Hölscher 2017, 238, for a similar interpretation of epiphany at Myra. However, for the cult statue glimpsed on the coin, see Rigsby 1996, 363; Agelidis 2014, 109.

[260] Marcellesi 2012, 57–58. For the reconstruction of the Pheidian imitation in the Library as a Nikephoros, see Coqueugniot 2013, 120. Demargne (1984, 1041) does not outline a distinct iconography for Nikephoros, but points to the frequency with which a Pheidian Parthenos is represented as such in the Hellenistic period.

[261] Agelidis 2014, 95–99.

Figure 6.9 Left: reverse of silver tetradrachm of Demetrios II depicting Athena Magarsia, ca. 145–142 BCE (14.26 g, ANS 1984.116.1; courtesy of the American Numismatic Society); right [from Figure 3.9]: reverse of silver tetradrachm in the name of Athena Nikephoros, reign of Eumenes II, ca. 180–165 BCE (16.06 g, BM 1975,0208.1 © The Trustees of the British Museum).

of the goddess of Magarsos is so much more upright that scholars have been tempted to see there a *chiton* and *chlamys* as Greek textiles draped on an older, wooden Anatolian statue – a cultural intrusion. On our coin, by contrast, it is much harder to pick apart the two traditions. In a more subtle blending of cultures, arms flailing out stiffly in the North Syrian–Anatolian manner, Pergamene Athena Nikephoros strikes the unmistakable pose of the Greek contrapposto. Tellingly, it is not obvious whether we should see in the peculiarly hybrid figure an archaic original or a second-century sculptor's idea of a traditional Anatolian *xoanon*.[262] She confounds our categories.

Yet if the coin represents, as has been supposed, the cult-statue from the extramural Nikephorion, the image ought to have been new under Eumenes II.[263] Though an earlier mintmark of Lysimachus provided

---

[262] Fleischer 1978, 349. Further, on the comparison with Athena Magarsia, see Marcellesi 2012, 125 n. 45. The earliest of those coins date to the reign of Demetrios II (146–138). See, further, Fleischer 1973, 260–63; Houghton 1984, esp. 110.

[263] Many scholars attribute the Nikephorion to Attalos I, who, having granted Athena the epithet some time in the late 220s, laid out the extramural sanctuary ca. 200 BCE – which Philip V promptly destroyed (Polyb. 16.1.5–6). Others prefer a date in the early 190s under Eumenes II, e.g., Allen 1983, 128.

cutters with an in-house model for an Anatolian goddess as an iconic badge for the city of Pergamon, the new image does not entirely reflect the prototype.[264] This was not quite the archaic Trojan *palladion* nor the "original" cult statue, which Auge had brought from Arkadia. Such an image may well have existed since the fourth century in the form of an archaizing cult statue housed in the Temple of Athena Polias on the Pergamene acropolis.[265] Indeed, the visual language for such a statement was available to engravers, as can be seen from a silver tetradrachm of Knidos of the 160s. There, an up-to-date, anthropomorphic Artemis leans on what is clearly her own archaic idol.[266] Yet in this case, Eumenes made no such distinction between the present and the past. This was the goddess that the king wanted subjects such as the Pisidians of Olbasa to picture presiding over the Nikephoria. The numismatists have queried her origins. Le Rider sees an old Asian deity, coming to the surface in this form; Mørkholm suspects an import, the Cappadocian goddess Ma, riding into town in the 180s with Queen Stratonike.[267] But perhaps such speculation is misplaced. We have good reason to suppose that the cult of Athena in Attalid Pergamon had always belonged to a multicultural system. The city's very first temple for her, now credited to the acropolis-building activity of Herakles and Barsine (330–325), bore an unusually late, bilingual Lydian-Greek inscription. In a very prominent position, then, 4 m up on a column of the pronaos of the city's central temple, a donor named Partaras had explicitly equated the Lydian goddess Malia with Athena.[268] It seems that Greek and Anatolian elements were present from the beginning in the worship of Athena Polias at Pergamon, just as they had been, for example, in Classical Lycia – the local goddess in Eumenes' time remained

---

[264] Schalles 1985, 13 n. 67; Agelidis 2014, 110.

[265] The key evidence here is a pre-Hellenistic gold stater of Pergamon with a martial Athena on the reverse, Fritze 1906, 49–50 (nos. 8–10); Marcellesi 2012, 44 (no. 5). For the image as a *palladion*, the cult statue of Athena Ilias, see Schalles 1985, 13–19, attributing the coin to Herakles and Barsine. Cf. Agelidis 2014, 78–88, associating the coin with Alexander and strengthening the case for Trojan overtones. For Auge's mythical foundation of the Athena cult, see *I.Pergamon* 156, lines 23–24, though her cult is represented with the self-same *palladion* on the Telephos Frieze (Panel 20).

[266] Meadows 2018, 301–3.

[267] Le Rider 1973, 72; Mørkholm 1984, 192. According to Agelidis (2014, 110), the Cappadocian princess could only strengthen the indigenous elements of Athena's cult already present at Pergamon. Later too, another Cappadocian god became Zeus-Sabazios – rather than the typical Dionysus-Sabazios – thereby facilitating his incorporation into the cult of Athena Nikephoros in the time of Attalos III (*OGIS* 332).

[268] *I.Pergamon* 1. Payne and Sasseville 2016; Parker 2017, 40. Date of the temple: Schalles 1985, 20.

"an Athena who had been denatured."[269] Yet by emphasizing Anatolian features in the creation of an imperial Nikephoros, Eumenes code-switched in order to convince elites in places like Olbasa that they belonged. What effects if any this had on popular religion can be doubted. As Robert Parker has argued, Anatolia contained a large "zone of indifference to Athena," in which, under her name, native goddesses were worshipped with native rites.[270] But in Pisidian Apollonia, for example, Nikephoros did enter the official civic pantheon, presumably, due to Pergamene influence.[271] Similarly, at Blaundos, a late Hellenistic priest with the telling name of Philetairos Diogenous served a cult of Athena Nikephoros and Homonoia.[272] The ecumenical quality of this odd tetradrachm is further evidenced by the absence of a legend that tags the cult as the possession of any particular city. That is to say, Athena Nikephoros is not "of the Pergamenes," the way Apollo Aktaios is "of the Parians" or Apollo Smitheus is "of the Alexandrians." This is a glaring omission given that the design otherwise matches the almost 40 civic coinages minted ca. 175–140 with portraits of poliad deities – but suitably labeled.[273] The collective behind the coin of Eumenes was both Pan-Asian and politically idiosyncratic. It was, in short, the Attalid coalition.

Intervention in Greater Pisidia was costly and fraught with risk. It resulted in military and – in the case of Selge – even diplomatic defeat at Rome. What justified all the effort? On the one hand, there was the need for passage. Important army tracks already ran through the region, the basis of the future Via Sebaste, connecting both Pamphylia and Lykaonia to southern Phrygia. It is significant that in the crucial zones of transition, such as the country of the Orondeis and the Milyas, there is a case to be made for the existence of Attalid settlements. A colony at Neapolis among the Orondeis will have secured passage to Lykaonia and indeed the Kalykadnos Valley of Rough Cilicia. The Milyas was, in Ronald Syme's description, "A land of long plains and easy transit."[274] To control it was to keep the new foundation of Attaleia on the Mediterranean coast connected to the Aegean core of the kingdom. What this meant in practice may become clear as we learn more about the Attalids' southern port from

---

[269] Parker 2016, 74, 79, 81.   [270] Parker 2016, 78.
[271] First suggested by Sterrett 1888, 367 no. 532; see also Talloen 2013, 90.
[272] SEG XLVI 149 = Filges 2006, 321 no. 1.
[273] Meadows 2018, 304. As a sign of how far the coin of Eumenes departs from the same civic conventions it invokes, consider that Le Rider (1973, 75–79) argues for a minting authority on the model of the Confederacy of Athena Ilias – neither polis nor kingdom, but cultic koinon.
[274] Syme 1995, 186.

salvage excavations, such as those recently conducted in a necropolis full of Hellenistic chamber tombs at the site of Antalya's Doğu Garajı. On the other hand, the goal – or perhaps simply the achievement – was to integrate the region to the kingdom, if not always administratively, by ties of culture. Once again, colonies were not the preferred tool of this empire. Yet the Pergamene imprint here was profound, though these effects must be understood in the broader context of epochal changes in Pisidian society, largely driven from below. The long-term cultural complexity of particular pockets of the region is stunning. The Iron Age artifacts from the Bayındır tumuli in the plain of Elmalı exhibit Phrygian, Lydian, and also East Greek influence. Centuries later, Strabo tells us that four languages were still spoken in the Kibyratis.[275] Ranged against such diversity and cultural fluidity, an attitude of Hellenic chauvinism would have spelled disaster.

In summary, the shrewd cultural ideology that contributed so much to the Attalids' success was not simply an antipodal Panhellenism that pitted the Greeks of the polis against everyone else. In short, the Polybian perspective, Eumenes' special pitch at Delphi or Attalos' at Athens, is not the full story. The Attalids were capable of playing several games at once. Their own cultural background prepared them for it. They had indeed arrived from the Aegean's semi-Greek periphery, but they returned to that same Anatolian hinterland in order to build an empire. A scholarly trope labels them parvenus. This invariably means that they lacked Hellenic credentials and, therefore, always stressed their links to Greece. "For Pergamon had no Greek mother-city and no proper past," writes Stewart.[276] Yet the sting of parvenu status was just as much a result of their lack of illustrious ancestors in non-Greek or pre-Greek Asia. An anecdote from Strabo describes the Attalids' crucifixion of the grammarian Daphitas on a mountain near Magnesia-on-the-Maeander. His crime? Poking fun in this distich: "Purpled with stripes, mere filings of the treasure of Lysimachus, ye rule the Lydians and Phrygia."[277] The joke turns on the idea that their (modest) pecuniary inheritance did not make them the rightful successors of Alexander, Croesus, and Midas. The reproach

---

[275] Strabo 13.4.17. See, further, Corsten and Hülden 2013, on the recent survey of the archaic site near the Gölhisar Gölü known as "Old Kibyra," which has turned up both Lydian and Lycian tombs.
[276] Stewart 1996a, 43.
[277] Strabo 14.1.39. For the crucifixion of Daphitas of Telmessos, see Fontenrose 1960, proposing a historical context of the initial stages of the rebellion of Aristonikos in the last days of Attalos III.

responds to the Attalid claim to cis-Tauric Asia, a place full of Greeks, non-Greeks, and many people with multiple, fluctuating identities. These were "the inhabitants of Asia," by no means a corporate identity, but still an imagined collectivity, personified in the Telmessos decree of 184/3 that praised Eumenes as its savior. Moreover, it may also have been present in the background at Magnesia in 208, in that city's claim to be "the first of those dwelling (*katoikountes*) in Asia" to vote for stephanitic games.[278] The task for Pergamene ideologues was to construct a Pan-Asian collective identity, while deploying the relevant symbols of power across a culturally heterogeneous territory.

To try to tell the more complete story of Pergamon's cultural politics, it was necessary for the purposes of the analysis to make a dangerously arbitrary distinction between essentialized Greek and Anatolian subjects on the receiving end of the message. Many communities had since Alexander's arrival sensed the economic and political benefits of presenting themselves as Greek to the outside. Further, in the second century, intensifying Hellenizing tendencies among elites in Galatia and Pisidia further contributed to a shared Greco-Anatolian culture. Yet by picking out the non-Greek elements in the Attalids' self-presentation, we recover another audience for these theatrics and restore to history those who in many places were the silent majority underneath the Hellenic veneer. People who would never see Athens in their lives saw in Pergamon an Anatolian royal capital; in the Yığma Tepe tumulus, an answer to the taunt of Daphitas.

The risk of essentialism may also have been justified by the need to specify the ideological value of the Library of Pergamon. It was suggested that scholars such as Polemon of Ilion and Demetrios of Skepsis did not simply validate the dynasty's weak association with Old Greece, but strengthened its claim to rule the Greeks of Asia, in part, by seeking to redress an imbalance of prestige between Hellenic East and West. So-called antiquarian research gave heft to the pretense that the king treasured the traditions of each city under his rule. It also placed Pergamon conveniently within the core of Priam's ancient kingdom. Finally, we examined the tenets of cultural diplomacy and ideological outreach to two peoples of highland central Anatolia. Indeed, Pergamon was obsessed with imaginary Galatians, but not simply as a barbaric antithesis. Internally, the expulsion of the Galatians from the western lowlands – κάτω Ἀσίας – was the

---

[278] *I.Magnesia* 16 lines 16–18; Thonemann 2007, esp. 158, citing the roughly contemporary claim of Cyzicus to have been the first city in Asia to found a cult of Athena (*Anth. Pal.* 6.342).

territorial kingdom's founding creation myth. In truth, along the contested frontier of the Epictetus and nearby at Pessinous, the Attalids transformed local shrines in order to precipitate interactions with real-life Galatians. These flesh-and-blood Galatians were scarcely distinguishable from their Phrygian neighbors. Certain elites among them no doubt asserted Greek identity. The Attalids jockeyed with the Bithynians and the Galatian tetrarchs for their loyalties. The overarching goal was not to pacify a population. In Pisidia, where coercive power was least likely to work against a burgeoning city-state system, a lasting cultural affinity was established. Panhellenism cannot explain the integration of aspirant Pisidians, but as the ritual and symbolism of the refounded Nikephoria imply, a much broader notion of civilization in Asia can.

Conclusion

Why Pergamon? Our story began with ten Roman commissioners, who in 188 BCE drew up a new map for cis-Tauric Asia after the defeat of Antiochos III at Magnesia-under-Sipylos. That map was an artifact of the Settlement of Apameia. A century-old Mediterranean interstate system had broken down at the end of the third century, and the Romans' map proposed just two pieces of a new geopolitical order, the partition of the Anatolian peninsula between two allies, Rhodes and Pergamon. The failure of Rhodes to integrate or even retain control over its share along the south coast in Lycia and Caria is emblematic of the fact that enforcement of the settlement fell to the actors on the ground. The Romans withdrew and did not soon return, even as Pan-Anatolian wars between Pontos, Pergamon, Bithynia, and their respective allies embroiled the entire region for a decade. While a cunning and opportunistic diplomacy had helped put the Attalids in a position to win an empire, sovereignty over these vast new territories and peoples was never guaranteed. This was the basic assumption of an inquiry into the mechanics of imperial rule, rapid state formation, and the ideological tendencies of the Pergamene kings. My central argument was that the Attalids creatively employed noncoercive means to capture control of Greek cities and Anatolian rural communities, ultimately, making local civic culture depend on their tax revenues.

Other scholars have pointed up the historical contingencies of Pergamon's meteoric rise. Most recently, Thonemann has argued that the atypicality of the Attalid state was a direct result of just such an "exogenous process of state-formation."[1] In the last monographic treatment of the subject, Allen queried Attalid divergence by noting the similarity of the careers of Philetairos and the Phrygian Philomelid dynasts: both were semi-independent Seleukid vassals who sought to broaden their influence with gifts to cities and sanctuaries. He writes, "If we knew more about such dynasties in Asia Minor, we would probably find other features reminiscent of the policies of the early Attalids."[2] In other words, any number of other local candidates might have emerged to dominate cis-Tauric Asia after

---

[1] Thonemann 2013b, 45–47. [2] Allen 1983, 19–20.

systemic collapse. If not the Phrygian Philomelids, then why not the Pylaimenid dynasty of Gangra in Paphlagonia? Mitchell has gone so far as to describe the Attalids and the Pontic Mithridatids as peers living "parallel lives."[3] So, why Pergamon? Bracketing the personalities – the daring of Eumenes II or the loyalty of his brother Attalos II – I have tried to illuminate the structures that propelled this particular dynasty toward an overnight empire. Three themes emerge.

The first is timing. This study has aimed to contribute to our understanding of the nature of a historical conjuncture, in which the Attalids were primed to become agents of structural change. Much has been made of the vitality of the polis under Hellenistic monarchy and indeed Roman rule, the strength of its institutions, and its endurance as a locus of identity. As was most apparent in Chapter 5's discussion of the gymnasium, the diachronic development of the institutions of the Greek city-state must also be kept in mind. The polis not only survived the Battle of Chaironeia (338 BCE); it thenceforth developed in iterative ways *with* monarchy. In 188, when regime change took place at the top, these cities had accumulated half a millennium's worth of experience in public finance. The combination of an intense buildup of social power over their citizenry and knowledge sharing about public administration made cities like this extremely effective tax collectors for a higher-order polity such as a federative koinon or a "composite" kingdom. To integrate subject cities into a state apparatus and appropriate their social power and administrative efficiencies, the task for royal bureaucrats was to access civic institutions without provoking resistance. No other Hellenistic state ever combined so much interleaving of royal and civic symbols – so many interlocking institutions. Apollonidas of Sikyon argued contemptuously in the presence of Eumenes II that monarchy and democracy were two forces of nature at war. The king proved him wrong.

What have been described as consensual ideologies were important, but the Attalids were not modern liberals; theirs was not a constitutional monarchy. On the contrary, as the Korragos Decree (**D1**) shows, Pergamene officials had already accessed city budgets by 188. They constantly interfered in the day-to-day operation of the polis, not as was once thought, by packing boards of *stratêgoi*, super-legislators with probouleutic powers yet beholden to kings. The appointment of a city governor (*epi tês poleôs*) seems to have been rare, and the role of such officials may have

---

[3] Mitchell 2005.

been mostly supervisory. True interference took the form of earmarking arrangements (Chapter 1). Mastery of the technique of earmarking was an essential tool for maximizing revenue while minimizing coercion, but it relied on civic institutions, public banks, budgeting, and accountability measures, all of which were centuries in the making. Cities had also become habituated to negotiating the terms of taxation with Hellenistic kings and even had experience in cooperating with royal authorities in the process of tax collection. One of the main conclusions of the overview of the Attalid fiscal system (Chapter 2) is that the established rules of the game did not change. On the other hand, Pergamon massively expanded the scale of cooperation in rolling out the cistophoric monetary system that helped integrate cis-Tauric Asia without closing it off to the outside (Chapter 3). The Attalids also took advantage of autonomous change taking place inside cities, for example, the concentration of elite youth in gymnasia that were surprisingly independent and financially complicated institutions (Chapter 5). I argued that the Attalids had an overlooked role in the transformation of the gymnasium into the so-called second agora. Finally, we saw that a coercion-light approach to settlement took advantage of an upsurge in civic consciousness in rural Lydia, Phrygia, and Mysia in order to render these populations legible.

A second theme is money. Countering a modern view that sees the Attalids as exceptionally rich, I began from the premise that this was in every measurable way a middling power by the standards of Hellenistic royalty. In quantitative terms, the imprecision of our numbers aside, this is plain to see. The 9,000 talents that Lysimachus entrusted to Philetairos was what a mid-sized kingdom collected in a year – a nest egg, but hardly enough money to purchase the prestige that Antiquity would eventually accord Pergamon. Further, the Attalids were frenetic gift-givers, but their donations were small. For example, their gifts of money make up just 9% of the total amount recorded for all dynasties combined. Nevertheless, even ancient observers associated money and wealth with Pergamene kings, the *attalicae divitiae* (Attalid riches) of the early Christian morality play. Modern observers have also marveled at the Attalids' wealth. For the nineteenth century with its suspicion of new money, these princes were Mommsen's "Medici of Antiquity," and in line with an economistic turn in ancient history, a 2013 conference volume on Attalid Asia Minor made money a central line of investigation. Many scholars of Hellenistic art and literary culture produced under the dynasty's auspices have puzzled: Where did the all the money come from? The truth is that the amount of money was not as important as the manner in which it was acquired and spent. This is a truth that the cognoscenti of the Hellenistic public seem to have known, people like Polybius, who noted the modest size of gifts made in expectation of great honors after the Rhodian earthquake. That Eumenes II was not "exceedingly rich" (οὐ λίαν εὐπορούμενος) is also the very irony of his success in capturing an Anatolian empire, according to the following story of Diodorus (31.14), from the context of the Third Macedonian War:

> Ὅτι ὁ Εὐμένης ξενολογήσας τά τε ὀψώνια ἅπασιν ἀπέδωκε καὶ δωρεαῖς ἐτίμησε καὶ ἐπαγγελίαις ἐψυχαγώγει πάντας, ἐκκαλούμενος τὴν εὔνοιαν, οὐχ ὁμοίως τῷ Περσεῖ. ἐκεῖνος γὰρ δισμυρίων Γαλατῶν παραγενομένων εἰς τὸν πρὸς Ῥωμαίους πόλεμον ἀπετρίψατο τὴν τηλικαύτην συμμαχίαν, ἵνα φείσηται τῶν χρημάτων· ὁ δὲ Εὐμένης οὐ λίαν εὐπορούμενος ξενολογῶν δωρεαῖς ἐτίμα τοὺς δυναμένους μάλιστα χρείας παρέχεσθαι. τοιγαροῦν ἐκεῖνος μὲν οὐ βασιλικὴν μεγαλοφροσύνην ἀλλ' ἰδιωτικὴν τοῦ τυχόντος ἀναλαβὼν μικροψυχίαν, ἅμα τῇ βασιλείᾳ πάσῃ καὶ τὸν τηρηθέντα πλοῦτον ἐπεῖδεν αἰχμάλωτον· οὗτος δὲ τῆς νίκης πάντα δεύτερα τιθέμενος οὐ μόνον ἐκ μεγάλων κινδύνων ἐρρύσατο τὴν βασιλείαν, ἀλλὰ καὶ πᾶν τὸ τῶν Γαλατῶν ἔθνος ὑποχείριον ἐποιήσατο.

> Eumenes, having recruited a force of mercenary troops, not only gave all of them their pay, but honored some with gifts and beguiled them all with promises, evoking their goodwill. In this he did not at all resemble Perseus. For Perseus, when twenty thousand Gauls arrived to join him in the war against Rome, alienated this great body of allies in order to husband his wealth. Eumenes, however, though not exceedingly rich, when enlisting foreign troops honored with gifts all who were best able to render him service. Accordingly, the former, by adopting a policy, not of royal generosity, but of ignoble and plebeian meanness, saw the wealth he had guarded taken captive together with his whole kingdom, while the latter, by counting all things else second to victory, not only rescued his kingdom from great dangers but also subjugated the whole nation of the Gauls. (trans. after Loeb)

The juxtaposition of the two kings in a single war, the one who lost everything, the other whose greatest ambitions were now realized, is a rhetorical set piece. In Chapter 6, we examined evidence for the presence of the Attalid state in Galatia. The alleged subjugation of an entire *ethnos* is an imperial fantasy of cis-Tauric Asian supremacy. What matters is the moral of the story: Eumenes is the more royal of the two kings because he cleverly stretches less money into more kingship. This is evidently not Hellenistic kingship as raw luxury and opulence (*tryphê*), but rather a different paradigm.[4] Crucially, money and the redistribution of royal wealth allow

---

[4] On *tryphê*, see Stewart 2014, 206–26.

Eumenes to succeed by a practicing a form of trickery, by actually leading the Galatian mercenaries astray (*psychagôgeô*). In effect, Diodorus presents a model for the method of this book. Overall, I have tried to see behind the financial trickery in order to recover the substantive goals and effects of what has always been seen as a distinctive Attalid relationship with money and an uncannily creative approach to public finance. This starts in Chapter 1 with the habit of earmarking, which was not the inevitable result of the expropriation of all civic revenues, nor the manipulation of honor-seeking kings by city elites. Rather, the Attalids negotiated the shape of earmarks, meaning that civic fiscal priorities were embedded in the royal tax code. Earmarking saved on the costs of redistribution if the revenues stayed put in the local economy. Even as it buffered risk and signaled providence, the technique involved an element of false transparency. Staring at an inscription on stone, a taxpayer was able to "follow the money," from tax collection to spending on public goods. Meanwhile, the community became ever more dependent on royal largesse to meet its basic cultural needs. Chapter 3 examined the quintessential case of Attalid dissembling around money, the cistophoric coinage. These strange coins lack the typical image of the king's face, instead displaying traditional badges of civic identity. This was a proxy coinage, a monetary system in disguise. Naturally, scholars have always disagreed on whether the coins belonged to the king or to a monetary union of cities.

As demonstrated, cities were partners in a radical monetary experiment, but the cistophoric coinage required Attalid coordination. As a lightweight coinage, it economized on silver. Profits skimmed off the top were shared, and therefore the coins contributed to both the ideological and economic integration of the kingdom. In Chapter 5, the logic of Pergamon's obsession with the gymnasium was unraveled. The Attalids clearly outstripped their rivals in giving to civic gymnasia. This behavior either has been credited to the dynasty's supposedly reflexive Panhellenism, or we have given the Attalids an unearned benefit of the doubt: they wanted to help the polis manufacture its own citizens and ensure the survival of civic culture. Why was money on the gymnasium well spent? I argued that the gymnasium was an easy mark for kings bent on posing as champions of the cities, but actually out to dominate them. The financial vulnerability of the gymnasium and its ambiguous position in the civic landscape made it the perfect target.

Money also made a difference in the overlooked history of the arrival of the Attalid state in the Anatolian countryside. Chapter 4 detected a certain parsimony around settlement, a reluctance to undertake large urbanization projects that involved coercing populations into cities. On the other hand, the Attalids gave lavishly to monumentalize what had been modest indigenous sanctuaries at Phrygian Aizanoi and Pessinous in Galatia. Archaeology suggests that the kings transformed these sanctuaries beyond recognition, in a sense, inventing Anatolian temple-states that became a focus of interaction with imperial power in the countryside. Especially noteworthy in this regard is the Pergamene officer's peristyle house and archive adjacent to the Temple of Zeus at Aizanoi, as well as the Pessinous dossier of royal correspondence. The Attalids' ability to triumph by displaying wealth in cunningly confusing ways is also on display in the anecdote from Polybius about the destructive sea battle off Chios (201), in which the Rhodian and Pergamene navies clashed with Philip V. Ultimately, Attalos abandoned his ship and fled by land to Erythrai. Polybius tells us that the exigencies of war forced the king to employ an artifice (*technikon*; 16.6.6): he ordered his sailors to leave all of his royal tableware and robes on deck of the abandoned ship. In hot pursuit, the Macedonians were mesmerized by the display of wealth, and the king escaped without his shirt.

A third theme sounded was that Pergamon combined into a single polity what historically have been two distinct halves of cis-Tauric Asia: the urbanized, Greek Aegean littoral and the rural, highland Anatolian interior. No ancient historian is ever sure where Asia Minor ends and Anatolia begins. As an eminent historian of the Greek East puts it so hesitantly, the second concept encompasses the first, doesn't it?[5] For someone working within the scholarly framework of Classics, using Greek and Latin sources, and approaching the peninsula from the west, this book suggests, Anatolia is a lot closer than we think. Stand in one of the "bourgeois" Attalid palaces atop the vertiginous capital, and, on very clear day, you may just be able to glimpse the Aegean. The best sightlines are all inland and up the Kaikos river valley toward the Mysian heartland. I am wary of reifying a geographical trope by insisting on this divide. However, distinct differences in language, culture, and settlement pattern have often separated the two zones, and the tension continues to permeate modern Turkish society and politics. Consider these closing remarks of Bernard Lewis in his classic *The Emergence of Modern Turkey* (1961):

> Anatolia, the Turkish heartland, had always taken second place to Rumelia, the home of most of the cosmopolitan ruling class of the

[5] Sartre 2009, 9.

Empire – even the Young Turk Revolution, in its successive phases, had rested on Macedonia and Thrace, and Kemal himself was born in Salonika. But the shift in the centre of gravity and the cult of Anatolianism made Anatolia the real as well as the sentimental centre of the nation, and gave to the Anatolians an opportunity that they had not had before. The great Rumelian bureaucratic, religious, and military families are dwindling and losing their importance. The Anatolian country boys – *Memleket çocukları* – and still more the Anatolian country lords and gentry are inheriting their places, and making Turkey a Turkish state in fact as well as in name.[6]

I have tried to make the case that Pergamon, like a second Troy, a resurrection of the Mysian satrapy of Orontes, or the flash empire of Achaios, spanned this divide. The Attalids brought the Anatolian gentry into a coalition with Greek coastal elites, which even the succession struggle of the War of Aristonikos failed to break asunder.[7] From this perspective, there is nothing strange about the story that Attalos I, playing the role of dragoman, led the Romans to the Magna Mater at Pessinous. The westerners' Greek-speaking kin from the polis of Ilion simply lacked that access. We knew that the Attalids haunted the centers of Old Greece, but I have also emphasized and explained why they were at home in Anatolia. We saw again and again that Pergamon was not a bulwark of the Greek cities against steppe invaders. In fact, the Attalids themselves reached back up those river valleys. They mobilized the Mysians of the Abbaeitis. They connected the Mediterranean to the Aegean by investing heavily in Pisidia and the Milyas. The cistophoric coinage tied the two zones together, as did the reorganization of the Nikephoria festival in "Panhellenic" form, now bringing obscure Anatolian conurbations into the imagined community. We can compare Eumenes II to Midas, king of Phrygia in the Iron Age, whose name was known in Delphi. Eumenes went much farther in inhabiting both worlds: he was as comfortable on the Halys as he was in Delphi. The Attalids were cut in the mold of the fourth-century Hekatomnids of Caria, perfectly positioned to harness the social power of the Greek poleis with the manpower and natural resources of rural Anatolia. They were able to project authority by using both cultural idioms, Greek and Anatolian. And the result was actually quite similar to the impact of Mausolus, who also collected a dream team of Greek artists to work on his grandest project. The ripple effect on what we call the Classical or Hellenistic world was extremely durable. Yet unlike the theme of money, neither the literary

---

[6] Lewis 1968, 486.   [7] Daubner 2006, 187–90.

nor epigraphic sources revealed the story here. Archaeology and the analysis of material culture became much more important, and disciplinary boundaries were broached to reveal the true shape of the object of study.

In conclusion, two further reflections on the historiographical contribution may be offered. First, while I think that it was the Attalids themselves who were so fixated on taxation, I willingly chose the fiscal perspective, whereas previous monographs took foreign relations and constitutional history as their focus.[8] My goal was to meet the challenge sounded by Purcell, who reflects in a programmatic essay on Mediterranean customs tax, "These matters may be studied from an administrative, institutional, fiscal perspective, or from the social and economic angle. Some scholars have chosen one route, usually the former. There is much to be gained from attempting to combine the two, difficult though the exercise may be."[9] In the administrative and institutional details offered in this book, the description of the facts of taxation, a certain measure of the skeleton of an ancient state has been exposed. However, the skeleton is simply a guide to the living organism, a skeleton key that unlocks the state's interior and allows us to see an ancient imperialism from the inside. The goal of the presentation was to provide a dynamic account of the Attalid state's functioning, of the "workings of empire, practical and, especially, ideological."[10] What was once called the "machinery of monarchical government"[11] was put back in motion; the Attalids were seen staking their claim to rule. Insofar as the distinctiveness of Attalid imperialism was emphasized, the specter of comparison with historically and geographically proximate empires was raised. Yet the results will not fit neatly into the typologies of historical sociology. For the claim of distinctiveness was also advanced for this historical moment, for the power scramble set off by the Settlement of Apameia, for the conjuncture of monarchy (*basileia*) and other forms of sociopolitical organization in the second century BCE.

As ancient historians, we have struggled mightily to disabuse ourselves of the notion that Rome's extension of power in the eastern Mediterranean was inevitable before it was. On a comparatively miniature scale, we must be willing to do the same for the Attalids. This involves resisting the entire design of the dynasty's self-representation, from its Great Altar to its posturing as savior of "all who inhabit Asia," all of which is an attempt to render inevitable what was in fact a highly contingent outcome. The old question of whether the Attalids were "constitutional monarchs" or

---

[8] McShane 1964; Allen 1983.   [9] Purcell 2005, 205.   [10] Ma 1999, 24.
[11] Walbank 1984, 68–74.

"financier tyrants" is really a question of whether we approve of their success. Shall we cry when we turn the page at Chaironeia or, like Apollo's statue in Cumae, at the defeat of Aristonikos, the last of the Attalids?[12] The interesting question to ask is, How was success achieved? For over a century, at least since Giuseppe Cardinali's essay, "L'amministrazione finanziaria del comune di Pergamo,"[13] scholarship has recognized the peculiarity of the Attalid approach to public finance. With the more recent turn toward the study of euergetism, the dynasty's unusual pattern of giving has been noted. Yet perhaps because no study has taken the logic of Attalid fiscality as its singular focus, the crucial role played by this aspect of governance in the successful enforcement of the Settlement has escaped notice.

The earmarking arrangements, a monetary system dominated by the cistophori, and much of the fiscal apparatus of the Attalid state relied on civic institutions and promoted civic identities, preserving and elaborating the collective of polis or *katoikia*. The acme of the Attalids coincides with what coins and inscriptions show to have been a time of peak complexity in the social organization of these communities, a period in which civic bonds were renewed after the dislocation and even cosmopolitanism of the early Hellenistic period. Yet as we saw in the case of the gymnasium, as Attalid power spread across the new map, new collectivities were also produced. Indeed, a number of other important collectivities, such as the associations of the *technitai* (actors) of Dionysus and the associations of the Attalistai, fell outside the scope of this study. Attalid monarchy after Apameia – perhaps even simply late Hellenistic monarchy, taking Macedonia under Philip V and Perseus also into account – distinguishes itself by its capacity to both create and successfully incorporate these collectivities into a multiscalar state. One may protest that the presence of Rome on the horizon aided the process along, but we have reason to believe that the kings actively subscribed to a model of *basileia* different from the one our textbooks so often reproduce.

An entry from the *Suda* is often adduced in those textbooks. The foundation of *basileia*, we are told, rests on the king's virtue in war and administrative competence. Thus in favor of the so-called personal monarchy founded on "spear-won land (*doryktêtos chôra*)," one quotes *Suda* s. v. βασιλεία (B147): οὔτε φύσις οὔτε τὸ δίκαιον ἀποδιδοῦσι τοῖς ἀνθρώποις τὰς βασιλείας, ἀλλὰ τοῖς δυναμένοις ἡγεῖσθαι στρατοπέδου καὶ χειρίζειν

---

[12] August. *De civ. D.* 3.11.   [13] Cardinali 1915–16.

πράγματα νουνεχῶς. In Arthur Eckstein's translation, "Kingship does not derive either from royal descent or from formal legitimacy, but rather from the ability to command armies and to govern effectively. (We see this with the Successors of Alexander.)"[14] Thus in fact the connection to *early* Hellenistic monarchy is explicit. In stark contrast, the legitimacy of monarchy in the Attalid kingdom, 188–133, depended on the king living up to the ideal of the lexicon's next *lemma*, *Suda* s.v. βασιλεία (B148):

> ὅτι ἡ βασιλεία κτῆμα τῶν κοινῶν, ἀλλ' οὐ τὰ δημόσια τῆς βασιλείας κτήματα. διὸ τὰς ἐξ ἀνάγκης καὶ μεθ' ὕβρεως εἰσπράξεις ὥσπερ τυραννικὰς ἀκολασίας μισεῖν δεῖ, τὰς δὲ σὺν λόγῳ καὶ φιλανθρωπίᾳ τῶν εἰσφορῶν ἀπαιτήσεις ὥσπερ κηδεμονίαν τιμᾶν.

> Since kingship entails the possession of *ta koina* ["the commons" or common funds], but the public's property does not belong to the monarchy, it follows that one must detest as the excesses of a tyrant royal interventions made with force and arrogance, but one must honor like a solemn duty requests for contributions made persuasively and humanely. (my trans.)

The first and frequently cited definition of *basileia* is indeed appropriate to the Age of the Successors, for it explains the acquisition of monarchy. The second more fully defines its essence in the late Attalid context: as a specific set of possessions (*ktêmata*), rights, and obligations; as a relationship with rules, negotiable though they are. Common and public property coexist, and they appear distinct, if still contiguous. Resolving this paradox or, rather, understanding how the ancients themselves dealt with it, must be the goal of future research. Only in this way can we make sense of the distinction between early and late Hellenistic monarchy brought out by the contrasting definitions in the *Suda*. This will also involve a form of seeing double, as we have argued was the ancient way, and thus trading the traditional twin foci of Hellenistic history, city and king, for a unified vision.

---

[14] Eckstein 2009, 249.

Appendix of Epigraphical Documents

The following inscriptions have been discussed in detail and are referred to throughout by these numbers. Each lemma has two parts: a genetic summary of editions, with key restorations described in parentheses; and a date, with discussion where controversy exists.

D1: Honorific Decree of an Anonymous City for Korragos

Ed. pr. Holleaux 1924. De Sanctis 1925, 68–78. *I.Prusa* 1001, with excellent photo. Virgilio 2003, no. 31.

Date: 188–171. If Korragos is identical to Corragus Macedo (Livy 38.13.3; 42.67.4), this text likely dates to just after 188. In any case, the context is "postwar," so 186–183, 168–166, as well as 156–154 (A. Chankowski 2010, no. 406) have been proposed. Much turns on what event is meant by παράληψιν in l. 8.

D2: Royal Documents of Eumenes II from Taşkuyucak

Ed. pr. Herrmann and Malay 2007, no. 32 = *SEG* LVII 1150. Thonemann 2011a (a very different text, most importantly with respect to the addressee of the document represented by Side A: a new reading of ll. 5-6, the toponym Ἀπ[ολ]-|λωνιουχάρακος replaces the name and patronymic of the ed. pr.: Ἀπ[ολ]-|λωνίου Χάρακος. Consequently, Thonemann understands Side B as the petition of Apollonioucharax, restoring in ll. 16-17 ὑ-|μῶν for ed. pr.'s <ἡ>-|μῶν. Also significant is the restoration of και[νὴ γῆ (?) in the lacuna of Side A l. 4. Side B l. 24 contains unjustified punctuation before συντετάχαμεν). Cf. Bencivenni 2015, reattributing Side B to Eumenes II, but *contra*, see Patrice Hamon *BE* (2016) no. 433.
Date: 165/4.

D3: Letter of Eumenes II to Artemidoros Concerning the Kardakon Kome

Ed. pr. Segre 1938, with photo missing the left part of the inscription. Maier 1959–1961, v. 1, no. 76. Virgilio 2003, no. 28. For commentary, see Ashton 1994; Tietz 2003, 346–52.
Date: 181.

D4: Letter of Eumenes II to Temnos

I.Pergamon 157. *RC* 48 (with two major changes: Welles eliminated much of the publication clause as restored by Fränkel in Fragment D ll. 25–27, and Welles excluded Fränkel's Fragment E, arguing that it belongs to an honorific decree). Bold restorations are offered by Piejko 1987, 724 (for Fragment D l. 3: καὶ δύο (?) μ]έρη τῆς δεκ[άτης ἀφίημι ὑμῖν]; and for Fragment D *passim* Piejko 1989 restores ἵ|να δὲ καὶ ἱκανῶς ἔχητε εἰς τὴν διο]ίκησιν τῆ[ς π]όλεως καὶ [εἰς τὰ] ἱερὰ καλῶς ἔχων εἶναι ἐδόκει μοι ὑπο]υργ[ήσασθα]ι κατὰ πόλιν σ[τοάν, | ἀφ' ἧς ἡ ἀεὶ γενησομένη πρόσοδος προστιθεῖ]το ταῖς ἄλλ[αις ταῖς τῇ | πόλει ὑπαρχούσαις προσόδοις καὶ τελ] έσματ[α — —]; cf. Herrmann in *SEG* XXXIX 1332).
Date: Reign of Eumenes II (197–158/7).

D5: Honorific Decree of Metropolis for Apollonios

Ed. pr. *I.Metropolis* 1, with poor quality photo = *SEG* LIII 1312. Jones 2004, (offering different restorations for Side B ll. 28–36, the final fragmentary ll. of the lateral face; as does Philippe Gauthier *BE* (2004) no. 281; as does Virgilio 2006).

Date: 145/4 or 144/3. This is the date of the decree on Side B; Side A bears a posthumous decree for Apollonios of 130. Thus, the decree of Side B seems to have been republished after Apollonios' death in the Revolt of Aristonikos. See further, *SEG* LXIV 1093.

D6: Honorific Decree of Apameia for Kephisodoros

Ed pr. *MAMA* VI 173, with good photo. Bringmann et al. 1995 no. 254 [E], (incorporating restorations of Louis Robert *BE* (1939) no. 400 for ll. 11–15, most importantly [τοῦ βασιλέως ἀργ] for [καὶ τοῦ δήμου, ἀργ] in l. 12). See also A. Chankowski 2010, no. 395 (with new restoration in l. 16 for [γυμνασίωι τῶν τε ἐφήβ]ων, either [τῶι γυμνασίωι τῶν τε νέων καὶ τῶν ἐφήβ]ων or [τῶι γυμνασίωι τῶν τε νέ]ων).

Date: 188–159, or perhaps more precisely 168–166 (Robert).

D7: Decree of Teos Awarding Land to the *Technitai* of Dionysus

Ed. pr. Demangel and Laumonier 1922, with poor photo of squeeze = *SEG* II 580. Pickard-Cambridge 1953, no. 7 (incorporating new restoration of heading of Robert 1937, 39–44). Bringmann et al. 1995 no. 262 [E]. Csapo and Slater 1995, with English translation. Le Guen 2001, no. 39. Aneziri 2003, no. D2. Meier 2012, no. 51.

Date: 229–223, 218–206, or the decades following 188. Most discussion of the text concerns the date. While the most recent treatments of Le Guen and Aneziri opt for pre-188 dates, criteria such as the measurable "friendlinesss" of relations between the *technitai* and Teos are not to be relied upon. Things did turn sour, but several commentators have still suggested a post-188 date (summarized by Meier 2012, 360 n. 692).

D8: Letters of Eumenes II to Toriaion

Ed. pr. Jonnes and Ricl 1997, with rather poor photo = *SEG* XLVII 1745. Gauthier *BE* (1999) no. 509 raises several contextual issues that are dealt with variously in the following editions, which otherwise reproduce the ed. pr. (the transliteration and meaning of ed. pr.'s ἐγ χωρίοις in l. 27 – ἐγγχωρίοις after Schuler 1999 – and a possible restoration of ‹ἡ›μῖν for edd. pr.'s ὑμῖν in l. 30; Virgilio 2003, no. 30, which prints ε[ὐ]

(?)|δοκιμάζῃ in ll. 45–46, following Gauthier; *ISE* 196). *I.Sultan Dağı* 393 (after autopsy prints ἡμῖν in l. 30). Similarly, Bencivenni 2003, 333–56, with long commentary. See also restoration of Müller 2005, 357 with n. 8 (ἑτέραν – scil., πρόσοδον for ed. pr.'s ἑτέρων – in l. 44). A new restoration in Savalli-Lestrade 2018 (proposing in ll. 23–24 the word δωρ[ε]|ά for δολ[ί]|α, the noun "gift" for the adjective "deceitful").

Date: The document is typically dated shortly after 188 and related to the Settlement of Apameia. However, Savalli-Lestrade 2018 places it in the context of the war with Prousias I of Bithynia, ca. 184 BCE.

D9: Honorific Decree of Andros for an Anonymous Gymnasiarch

Ed. pr. Sauciuc 1914, no. 4. Paschalis 1925, no. 26. *IG* XII Suppl. 250. Allen 1983, no. 21. Bringmann et al. 1995, no. 230 [E] (incorporating all the restorations of Robert 1960, 116–25, which were made from a squeeze of Klaffenbach, most importantly l. 8: ὑπὲρ τοῦ βασιλέως συνεπόμπευσεν ἀγῶν ἴδιον βοῦν καὶ [ἔθυ]σεν παραχ[ρ]ῆμα τὰ πο[μπευθέντα ἱερεῖα]). Petrocheilos 2010, no. 9.

Date: Middle of the second century. Petrocheilos argues for 175–159 in order to take account of the two royals in l. 10: ταῖς βασιλίσσαις.

D10: Honorific Decree(s) of Notion/Colophon-on-the-Sea for (Prince) Philetairos

Ed. pr. Macridy 1905. Holleaux 1906 (with major improvements of first 18 ll.). Holleaux 1938–57, v. 2, 51–60 (incorporating the restorations of Robert 1937, 153–54 and passim, most notably, ll. 6–7: ψήφισ[μα προεγράψαντο περὶ τοῦ] τιμῆσαι). Kotsidu 2000, 358–60. Allen 1983, no. 20. Gauthier 2006, with Robert's photographs (contains a number of new restorations, including οἱ με-||[τέχοντες τοῦ τόπου (?), τῶν νέων] in ll. 5–6). A. Chankowski 2010, no. 208 endorses Gauthier's restoration in l. 33: παλαίστρα.

D11: Festival Calendar of Gymnasium of Kos

Ed. pr. Paton and Hicks 1891, no. 43. *Syll.*³ 1028. Herzog 1928, no. 9. *LSCG* 165. *Iscr.Cos.* ED 45. Bringmann et al. 1995, no. 225 [E] (from a squeeze). Kotsidu 2000, 244–49. *IG* XII 4 1 281.

Date: 158–138, for which see *IG* XII 4 1 281, using regnal dates of Attalos II from titulature in ll. 40–41.

D12: Letter of the Future Attalos II to Amlada

Ed. pr. Jüthner et al. 1903, no. 22 = *OGIS* 751. Schroeter 1932, 49. *RC* 54 (taking account of restoration of Holleaux 1918, 17–19 in ll. 6–7: ἐπισκευ[ῆς ἕνε]-||[κ]ε). Swoboda, *Denkmäler* 74. Allen 1983, no. 23.

Date: Late 160s, if the revolt of the Galatians is the war referred to in l. 5 (ἐν τῷ Γαλατικῷ πολέμῳ), but no later.

D13: Letter of an Attalid King to Cleruchs

Ed. pr. *I.Pergamon* 158. RC 51, (crucially, exchanging Fränkel's restoration for Robert's – no citation, but see Virgilio 2003: "Robert apud Welles" – in l. 17: εἰ[κοστήν, ἐκ δὲ το]ῦ for ed. pr.'s ἐ[κ μὲν τοῦ οἴνο]υ). Segre 1935. Virgilio 2003, no. 29, with excellent photos of all three fragments.

Date: Reign of Eumenes II (197–158/7)?

D14: Letter of the Future Attalos II Concerning the *Katoikoi* of Apollo Tarsenos

Ed. pr. Conze and Schuchhardt 1899, 212–14. Schroeter 1932, Fragment 17. RC 47. Piejko 1989, 395–409 (proposes lengthy new restorations, though the stone is lost and neither a photo nor a squeeze exists. Of particular interest are two restorations *contra* Welles, but following Wilhelm 1943, 35–40 and 61, as well as Feyel 1940, 137–41: πανηγύρεως in l. 4 and πανήγυριν in l. 12; cf. criticism of Piejko's text in *SEG* XXXIX 1337). Chandezon 2003, no. 50, which calls itself a conservative retreat while including the aforementioned restorations in ll. 4 and 12.

Date: 185.

D15: Letter of the Future Attalos II to Two Royal Officials from Pessinous

Ed. pr. Avram and Tsetskhladze 2014 = *SEG* LXIV 1296, earlier references *SEG* LV 1401. Ricl 2014 and Thonemann 2015a suggest important corrections, reviewed by Patrice Hamon *BE* (2015) no. 658 and *SEG* (notably, editors diverge over punctuation of the long prepositional phrase that begins [κ]αὶ διὰ in l. 7, which captures the *status quo ante*. Hamon's suggestion of particle and punctuation incorporated into *SEG* text in ll. 8–9: γεγράφεναι ἡμᾶ[ς|δ᾽ ἅ[etc.; φιλάνθρωπον. Also, in l. 10, ἔχ⟨ει⟩ν replaces edd. pr.'s {EXON}; and in l. 13 ἐσθῆναι ἔχειν replaces edd. pr.'s ἔχου̣[τ]⟨α⟩ς̣ ἔχειν, clarifying the nature of the petitioner's request).

Date: Edd. pr.'s low date of ca. 160 increasingly seen as implausible, first, on the prosopography: Could the official Herodes, presumably the one active at Toriaion (**D8**) in the 180s, have remained so at Pessinous in the 160s? A context in the 180s is now generally also favored on historical grounds. For high date in 180s, see Thonemann (ca. 183, in context of the war with Prousias I of Bithynia and Ortiagon, *pace* Savalli-Lestrade 2018, 175; even a few years earlier, Coşkun 2016, 54 n. 18).

Bibliography

Adak, Mustafa, and Konrad Stauner. 2018. "Die Neoi und das Temenos des Dionysas. Eine hellenistische Pachturkunde aus Teos." *Philia* 4: 1–25.

Africa, Thomas W. 1961. "Aristonicus, Blossius, and the City of the Sun." *International Review of Social History* 6: 110–24.

Agelidis, Soi. 2012. "Kulte und Heiligtümer in Pergamon." In *Pergamon: Panorama der antiken Metropole*, 2nd ed., edited by Ralf Grüßinger, Volker Kästner, and Andreas Scholl, 175–83. Petersberg: Michael Imhof Verlag.

2014a. "Cults and Sanctuaries in Pergamon." In *Pergamon: A Hellenistic Capital in Anatolia*, edited by Felix Pirson and Andreas Scholl, 380–401. Istanbul: Yapı Kredi Yayınları.

2014b. "Vom Palladion zur Nikephoros: Der Kult der Athena im Kontext der Herrschaftslegitimation im spätklassischen und hellenistischen Pergamon." *Istanbuler Mitteilungen* 64: 75–128.

Ager, Sheila L. 1996. *Interstate Arbitrations in the Greek World, 337–90 B.C.* Berkeley: University of California Press.

2007. "Keeping the Peace in Ionia: Kings and Poleis." In *Regionalism in Hellenistic and Roman Asia Minor*, edited by Hugh Elton and Gary Reger, 45–52. Pessac: Ausonius.

Akman, Ayşe, and Aynur Tosun. 2012. "Attaleia Nekropolü (Eski Doğu Garajı – Halk Pazarı Mevkii) Kurtarma Kazısı 2010 Yılı Çalışmaları." *Müze Çalışmaları ve Kurtarma Kazıları Sempozyumu Yayınları* 20: 47–68.

Akyürek Şahin, N. E., and Hüseyin Uzunoğlu. 2019. "New Inscriptions from the Museum of Bursa." *Gephyra* 17: 239–85.

Allen, Richard E. 1983. *The Attalid Kingdom: A Constitutional History*. Oxford: Clarendon Press.

Andreades, Andreas M. 1933. *History of Greek Public Finance*. Translated by Carroll N. Brown. Cambridge, MA: Harvard University Press.

Aneziri, Sophia. 2003. *Die Vereine der dionysischen Techniten im Kontext der hellenistischen Gesellschaft: Untersuchungen zur Geschichte, Organisation und Wirkung der hellenistischen Technitenvereine*. Stuttgart: Steiner.

2012. "Vereine und Kollegien: Kulte in den griechischen Vereinen." In *Thesaurus Cultus et Rituum Antiquorum, ThesCRA. VIII: Private Space and Public Space, Polarities in Religious Life, Religious Interrelations between the Classical World and Neighbouring Civilizations*, edited by Antoine

Hermary and Bertrand Jaeger, 69–75. Los Angeles, CA: J. Paul Getty Museum.

Aneziri, Sophia, and Dimitris Damaskos. 2004. "Städtische Kulte im hellenistischen Gymnasion." In *Das hellenistische Gymnasion*, edited by Daniel Kah and Peter Scholz, 246–72. Berlin: Akademie Verlag.

Aperghis, Gerassimos G. 2004. *The Seleukid Royal Economy: The Finances and Financial Administration of the Seleukid Empire*. Cambridge: Cambridge University Press.

Apostolou, Eva. 1995. "Les drachmes rhodiennes et pseudo-rhodiennes de la fin du IIIe siècle et du IIe siècle av. J.-C." *Revue Numismatique* 150: 7–19.

Arnaoutoglou, Ilias. 1998. "Between *koinon* and *idion*: Legal and Social Dimensions of Religious Associations in Ancient Athens." In *Kosmos: Essays in Order, Conflict, and Community in Classical Athens*, edited by Paul Cartledge, Paul Millett, and Sitta von Reden, 68–83. Cambridge: Cambridge University Press.

Arslan, Melih, and Ülkü Devecioğlu. 2011. "Der hellenistische Münzschatz von Apameia: Ein Vorbericht." In *Kelainai, Apameia Kibotos: Stadtentwicklung im anatolischen Kontext; Akten des internationalen Kolloquiums, München, 2.-4. April 2009 = Développement urbain dans le contexte anatolien*, edited by Latife Summerer, Askold I. Ivantchik, and Alexander von Kienlin, 309–18. Pessac: Ausonius.

Ashton, Richard. 1994. "The Attalid Poll-Tax." *Zeitschrift für Papyrologie und Epigraphik* 104: 57–60.

———. 2001. "The Coinage of Rhodes 408–c. 190 BC." In *Money and Its Uses in the Ancient World*, edited by Andrew Meadows and Kirsty Shipton, 79–115. Oxford: Oxford University Press.

———. 2005a. "The Coinage of Oinoanda." *Numismatic Chronicle* 165: 65–84.

———. 2005b. "Recent Epigraphic Evidence for the Start of the Rhodian and Lykian League Plinthophoroi." *Numismatic Chronicle* 165: 85–89.

———. 2016. "The Late Hellenistic Brass and Bronze Coinage of Apameia: A Sketch." In *Kelainai-Apameia Kibotos: Une métropole achéménide, hellénistique et romaine*, edited by Askold I. Ivantchik, Latife Summerer, and Alexander von Kienlin, 379–433. Bordeaux: Ausonius.

Ashton, Richard, and Philip Kinns. 2003. "Opuscula Anatolica II." *Numismatic Chronicle* 163: 4–40.

Ashton, Richard, and Andrew Meadows. 2008. "The Letoon Deposit: Lycian Coinage, Rhodian Plinthophori, and Pseudo-Rhodian Drachms from Haliartos (yet again) and Asia Minor." *Numismatic Chronicle* 168: 111–34.

Ateş, Güler. 2010. "Bilder aus gebranntem Ton: Neues über den Kult der Kybele in der Aizanitis." In *Aizanoi und Anatolien: Neue Entdeckungen zur Geschichte und Archäologie im Hochland des westlichen Kleinasien*, edited by Klaus Rheidt, 48–57. Mainz on Rhine: Philipp von Zabern.

2015. "Aizanoi und Pergamon, Türkei: Ländliche Heiligtümer der Meter-Kybele im Umland von Aizanoi und Pergamon." *E-Forschungsberichte des Deutschen Archäologischen Instituts* 3: 135–38.

———. 2017. "Aizanoi Helenistik Ev Seramik Buluntuları." *Süleyman Demirel Üniversitesi Fen-Edebiyat Fakültesi Sosyal Bilimler Dergisi*, no. 41: 91–112.

Ateşlier, Suat. 2015. "Aydın and the Nearby Ancient Cities." In *Cultural Heritage of Aydın*, edited by Filiz Özdem, 71–142. Istanbul: Yapı Kredi.

Atkinson, Anthony Barnes. 1977. "Optimal Taxation and the Direct versus Indirect Tax Controversy." *Canadian Journal of Economics* 10: 590–606.

Austin, Michel M. 1986. "Hellenistic Kings, War, and the Economy." *Classical Quarterly* 36: 450–66.

———. 2006. *The Hellenistic World from Alexander to the Roman Conquest: A Selection of Ancient Sources in Translation*, 2nd ed. Cambridge: Cambridge University Press.

Avram, Alexandru. 2004. "The Propontic Coast of Asia Minor." In *An Inventory of Archaic and Classical Poleis*, edited by Mogens Herman Hansen and Thomas Heine Nielsen, 974–99. Oxford: Oxford University Press.

Avram, Alexandru, and Gocha R. Tsetskhladze. 2014. "A New Attalid Letter from Pessinus." *Zeitschrift für Papyrologie und Epigraphik* 191: 151–81.

Aybek, Serdar, and Boris Dreyer. 2011. "Eine wehrhafte Stadt in späthellenistisch-römischer Zeit: Die Katapult-Arsenale der Stadt Metropolis (Ionien)." *Istanbuler Mitteilungen* 61: 205–17.

———. 2012. "Gewichte und Agoranomoi aus Metropolis." *Zeitschrift für Papyrologie und Epigraphik* 182: 205–14.

———. 2016. *Der Archäologische Survey von Apollonia am Rhyndakos beim Uluabat-See und der Umgebung Mysiens in der Nordwest-Türkei 2006-2010*. Berlin: Lit Verlag.

Aydal, Sabri, Stephen Mitchell, Thurstan Robinson, and Lutgarde Vandeput. 1997. "The Pisidian Survey 1995: Panemoteichos and Ören Tepe." *Anatolian Studies* 47: 141–72.

Aydın, Nurullah. 1991. "Seyitömer Höyük Kurtarma Kazısı 1989." *Müze Çalışmaları ve Kurtarma Kazıları Sempozyumu Yayınları* 1: 191–203.

Bagnall, Roger S. 1976. *The Administration of the Ptolemaic Possessions outside Egypt*. Leiden: Brill.

Baier, Christof. 2013. "Attolitur monte Pione: Neue Untersuchungen im Stadtviertel oberhalb des Theaters von Ephesos." *Jahreshefte des Österreichischen Archäologischen Institutes in Wien* 82: 23–68.

Bal, Nimet. 2014. "Selmanlı Tümülüslü Kurtarma Kazısı." *Müze Çalışmaları ve Kurtarma Kazıları Sempozyumu Yayınları* 22: 337–48.

Baldıran, Asuman. 2016. "Amblada Antik Kenti ve Civar Köylerdeki Helenistik Roma Dönemi Arkeolojik Materyaller." In *Amblada'nın (Yeniceköy) Deşifresi*, edited by Sedat Şimşek, 104–49. Konya: Selçuk Üniversitesi Matbaası.

Barbantani, Silvia. 2007. "The Glory of the Spear: A Powerful Symbol in Hellenistic Poetry and Art. The Case of Neoptolemus 'of Tlos' (and Other Ptolemaic Epigrams)." *Studi Classici e Orientali* 53: 67–138.

———. 2001. *Phatis nikephoros: Frammenti di elegia encomiastica nell'età delle Guerre Galatiche: Supplementum Hellenisticum 958 e 969*. Milan: Vita e Pensiero.

Bartusis, Mark C. 2012. *Land and Privilege in Byzantium: The Institution of Pronoia*. Cambridge: Cambridge University Press.

Başal, Şinasi. 2000. "1998 Yılı Tümülüs Kazıları." *Müze Çalışmaları ve Kurtarma Kazıları Sempozyumu Yayınları* 10: 179–88.

Bauchhenss-Thüriedl, Christa. 1971. *Der Mythos von Telephos in der antiken Bildkunst*. Würzburg: K. Triltsch.

Bauslaugh, Robert. 1990 "Cistophoric Countermarks and the Monetary System of Eumenes II." *Numismatic Chronicle* 150: 39–66.

Bayburtluoğlu, Cevdet. 2004. *Lykia*. Antalya: Suna & İnan Kıraç Research Institute on Mediterranean Civilizations.

Bayburtoğlu, Bülent, and Selahattin Yıldırım. 2008. "Gold and Silver in Anatolia." In *Anatolian Metal IV*, edited by Ünsal Yalçin, 43–53. Bochum: Deutsches Bergbau-Museum.

Bean, George E. 1968. *Turkey's Southern Shore: An Archaeological Guide*. New York: Praeger.

Bellinger, Alfred Raymond. 1949. "The Chronology of the Attic New Style Tetradrachms." *Hesperia Supplements* 8: 6–30.

Bencivenni, Alice. 2003. *Progetti di riforme costituzionali nelle epigrafi greche dei secoli IV–II a.C.* Bologna: Lo scarabeo editrice.

———. 2015. "Alcune questioni aperte sull'iscrizione attalide di Apolloniou Charax (*SEG* 57, 1150)." *Studi Ellenistici* 29: 207–14.

Berges, Dietrich. 2010. "Ein königlich-pergamenischer Beamter in Aizanoi." In *Aizanoi und Anatolien: Neue Entdeckungen zur Geschichte und Archäologie im Hochland des westlichen Kleinasien*, edited by Klaus Rheidt, 38–43. Mainz on Rhine: Philipp von Zabern.

Berlin, Andrea M. 2019. "The Archaeology of a Changing City." In *Spear-Won Land: Sardis from the King's Peace to the Peace of Apamea*, edited by Andrea M. Berlin and Paul J. Kosmin, 50–67. Madison: University of Wisconsin Press.

Berlin, Andrea M., and Paul J. Kosmin. 2019a. "Conclusion." In *Spear-Won Land: Sardis from the King's Peace to the Peace of Apamea*, edited by Andrea M. Berlin and Paul J. Kosmin, 235–40. Madison: University of Wisconsin Press.

Berlin, Andrea M., and Paul J. Kosmin. eds. 2019b. *Spear-Won Land: Sardis from the King's Peace to the Peace of Apamea*. Madison: University of Wisconsin Press.

Berndt-Ersöz, Susanne. 2006. *Phrygian Rock-Cut Shrines: Structure, Function, and Cult Practice*. Leiden: Brill.

Bielfeldt, Ruth. 2010. "Wo nur sind die Bürger von Pergamon? Eine Phänomenologie bürgerlicher Unscheinbarkeit im städtischen Raum der Königsresidenz." *Istanbuler Mitteilungen* 60: 117–201.

———. 2019. "Pergamum and Sardis: Models of Neighborliness." In *Spear-Won Land: Sardis from the King's Peace to the Peace of Apamea*, edited by Andrea M. Berlin and Paul J. Kosmin, 165–90. Madison: University of Wisconsin Press.

Bikerman, Elias J. 1938. *Institutions des Séleucides*. Paris: P. Geuthner.

Biraschi, Anna M. 2011. "Demetrios von Skepsis (2013)." In *Die Fragmente der Griechischen Historiker Part V. Brill Online Reference Works*. Leiden: Brill.

Black, John, Nigar Hashimzade, and Gareth Myles. 2012. *A Dictionary of Economics*. Oxford: Oxford University Press.

Boardman, John, and Donna C. Kurtz. 1971. *Greek Burial Customs*. London: Thames & Hudson.

Boehm, Ryan. 2018. *City and Empire in the Age of the Successors: Urbanization and Social Response in the Making of the Hellenistic Kingdoms*. Berkeley: University of California Press.

Boehringer, Christof. 1972. *Zur Chronologie mittelhellenistischer Münzserien 220–160 v. Chr.* Berlin: De Gruyter.

Boffo, Laura. 1985. *I Re ellenistici e i centri religiosi dell'Asia Minore*. Florence: La Nuova Italia.

———. 2013. "La 'presenza' dei re negli archivi delle poleis ellenistiche." In *Archives and Archival Documents in Ancient Societies: Legal Documents in Ancient Societies IV, Trieste 30 September–1 October 2011*, edited by Michele Faraguna, 201–44. Trieste: EUT Edizioni Università di Trieste.

Bogaert, Raymond. 1968. *Banques et banquiers dans les cités grecques*. Leiden: A. W. Sijthoff.

———. 1984. "Les banques affermées ptolémaïques." *Historia* 33: 181–98.

———. 1998. "Liste géographique des banques et des banquiers de l'Égypte ptolémaïque." *Zeitschrift für Papyrologie und Epigraphik* 120: 165–202.

Bøgh, Birgitte. 2007. "The Phrygian Background of Kybele." *Numen* 54: 304–39.

Bohne, Anke. 2012. "Vom Museumsexponat zur Karikatur – Die Rezeption des Pergamonaltars im Deutschen Kaiserreich." In *Pergamon: Panorama der Antiken Metropole*, 2nd ed., edited by Ralf Grüßinger, Volker Kästner, and Andreas Scholl, 398–401. Petersberg: Imhof.

Boldizzoni, Francesco. 2011. *The Poverty of Clio: Resurrecting Economic History*. Princeton, NJ: Princeton University Press.

Bonney, Richard, ed. 1995. *Economic Systems and State Finance*. Oxford: Clarendon Press.

———. 1999. *The Rise of the Fiscal State in Europe, c. 1200–1815*. New York: Oxford University Press.

Borchhardt, Jürgen, and Erika Bleibtreu. 2013. *Strukturen Lykischer Residenzstädte: Im Vergleich zu Älteren Städten des Vorderen Orients*. Antalya: Suna-Inan Kirac Research Institute on Mediterranean Civilizations.

Brandt, Hartwin. 2002. "Adada: Eine pisidische Kleinstadt in hellenistischer und römischer Zeit." *Historia* 51: 385–413.

Bravo, Benedetto. 2007. "Antiquarianism and History." In *A Companion to Greek and Roman Historiography*, edited by John Marincola, 491–502. Malden, MA: Blackwell.

Brélaz, Cédric. 2005. *La securité publique en Asie mineure sous le Principat (Ier–IIIème s. ap. J.-C.): Institutions municipales et institutions impériales dans l'Orient romain*. Basel: Schwabe Verlag.

Bremen, Riet van. 2008. "The Date and Context of the Kymaian Decrees for Archippe (*SEG* 33, 1035–1041)." *Revue des Études Anciennes* 110: 357–82.

―――. 2013. "Neoi in Hellenistic Cities: Age Class, Institution, Association?" In *Groupes et associations dans les cités grecques, IIIe siècle av. J.-C.–IIe siècle apr. J.-C.: Actes de la table ronde de Paris, INHA, 19–20 juin 2009*, edited by Pierre Fröhlich and Patrice Hamon, 31–58. Geneva: Droz.

Bremmer, Jan N. 2004. "Attis: A Greek God in Anatolian Pessinous and Catullan Rome." *Mnemosyne* 57: 534–73.

Bresson, Alain. 1993. "La circulation monétaire rhodienne jusqu'en 166." *Dialogues d'histoire ancienne* 19: 119–69.

―――. 1996. "Drachmes rhodiennes et drachmes d'imitation: Une politique économique de Rhodes." *Revue des Études Anciennes* 98: 65–77.

―――. 2000. *La cité marchande*. Bordeaux: Ausonius.

―――. 2001. "Timôn de Syracuse et les drachmes rhodiennes à Délos." *Revue des Études Anciennes* 103: 131–56.

―――. 2005. "Coinage and Money Supply in the Hellenistic Age." In *Making, Moving and Managing: The New World of Ancient Economies, 323–31 BC*, edited by Zosia H. Archibald, John K. Davies, and Vincent Gabrielsen, 44–72. Oxford: Oxbow Books.

―――. 2006. "Marché et prix à Délos: Charbon, bois, porcs, huile et grains." In *Approches de l'économie hellénistique*, edited by Raymond Descat, 311–39. Saint-Bertrand-de-Comminges: Musée archéologique de Saint-Bertrand-de-Comminges.

―――. 2007. "L'entrée dans les ports en Grèce ancienne: Le cadre juridique." In *Gens de passage en Méditerranée de l'Antiquité à l'époque moderne: Procédures de contrôle et d'identification*, edited by Claudia Moatti and Wolfgang Kaiser, 37–78. Paris: Maisonneuve & Larose.

―――. 2007–8. *L'économie de la Grèce des cités*, 2 vols. Paris: A. Colin.

―――. 2014. "Le change à Délos et la question du *kollybos*." *Bulletin de Correspondance Hellénique* 138: 515–33.

―――. 2016. *The Making of the Ancient Greek Economy: Institutions, Markets, and Growth in the City-States*. Princeton, NJ: Princeton University Press.

―――. 2018. "Coins and Trade in Hellenistic Asia Minor: The Pamphylian Hub." In *Infrastructure and Distribution in Ancient Economies: Proceedings of a Conference Held at the Austrian Academy of Sciences, 28–31 October 2014*, edited by Bernhard Woytek, 67–143. Vienna: Austrian Academy of Sciences.

———. 2019. "From Xerxes to Mithridates: Kings, Coins and Economic Life at Kelainai-Apameia." In *The Power of Individual and Community in Ancient Athens and Beyond: Essays in Honour of John K. Davies*, edited by Zosia H. Archibald and Jan Haywood, 285–310. Swansea: Classical Press of Wales.

Briant, Pierre. 1988. "Ethno-classe dominante et populations soumises dans l'empire achéménide: Le cas de l'Égypte." In *Method and Theory: Proceedings of the London 1985 Achaemenid History Workshop*, edited by Amélie Kuhrt and Heleen Sancisi-Weerdenburg, 137–73. Achaemenid History 3. Leiden: Brill.

———. 1989. "Table du roi, tribut et redistribution chez les Achéménides." In *Le tribut dans l'empire perse*, edited by Pierre Briant and Clarisse Herrenschmidt, 35–44. Paris: Peeters.

Bringmann, Klaus. 2000. *Geben und Nehmen. Monarchische Wohltätigkeit und Selbstdarstellung im Zeitalter des Hellenismus. Mit einem numismatischen Beitrag von Hans-Christoph Noeske*. Berlin: Akademie Verlag.

———. 2004. "Gymnasion und Griechische Bildung im Nahen Osten." In *Das hellenistische Gymnasion*, edited by Daniel Kah and Peter Scholz, 323–33. Berlin: Akademie Verlag.

Bringmann, Klaus, Hans von Steuben, Walter Ameling, and Barbara Schmidt-Dounas. 1995. *Schenkungen hellenistischer Herrscher an griechische Städte und Heiligtümer*, 2 vols. Berlin: Akademie Verlag.

Brown, Eric. 2009. "Hellenistic Cosmopolitanism." In *A Companion to Ancient Philosophy*, edited by Marie Louise Gill and Pierre Pellegrin, 549–60. Oxford: Blackwell.

Bru, Hadrien. 2017. *La Phrygie Parorée et la Pisidie septentrionale aux époques hellénistique et romaine*. Leiden: Brill.

Bruneau, Philippe, and Jean Ducat. 2005. *Guide de Délos*, 4th ed. Athens: École française d'Athènes.

Buck, Carl Darling. 1955. *The Greek Dialects: Grammar, Selected Inscriptions, Glossary*. Chicago: University of Chicago Press.

Burkert, Walter. 1993. "Bacchic *Teletai* in the Hellenistic Age." In *Masks of Dionysus*, edited by Thomas H. Carpenter and Christopher A. Faraone, 259–75. Ithaca, NY: Cornell University Press.

Burkhalter, Fabienne. 1992. "Le Gymnase d'Alexandrie: Centre administratif de la province romaine d'Égypte." *Bulletin de Correspondance Hellénique* 116: 345–73.

Burton, Paul J. 1996. "The Summoning of the Magna Mater to Rome (205 B.C.)." *Historia* 45: 36–63.

Cadell, Hélène, and Georges Le Rider. 1997. *Prix du blé et numéraire dans l'Égypte lagide de 305 à 173*. Brussels: Fondation égyptologique reine Elisabeth.

Cahill, Nicholas. 2008. "Mapping Sardis." In *Love for Lydia: A Sardis Anniversary Volume Presented to Crawford H. Greenewalt, Jr.*, edited by Nicholas Cahill, 111–24. Cambridge, MA: Harvard University Press.

———. 2019. "Inside/Out: Sardis in the Achaemenid and Lysimachean Periods." In *Spear-Won Land: Sardis from the King's Peace to the Peace of Apamea*, edited by Andrea M. Berlin and Paul J. Kosmin, 11–36. Madison: University of Wisconsin Press.

Callataÿ, François de. 2006. "Réflexions quantitatives sur l'or et l'argent non monnayés à l'époque hellénistique." In *Approches de l'économie hellénistique*, edited by Raymond Descat, 37–84. Saint-Bertrand-de-Comminges: Musée archéologique de Saint-Bertrand-de-Comminges.

———. 2007. "Les monnaies en argent d'Oinoanda: Après Apamée (188 av. J.-C.) ou après Mithridate (85–82 av. J.-C.)?" In *Liber Amicorum Tony Hackens*, edited by Ghislaine Moucharte, Maria Beatriz Borba Florenzano, François de Callataÿ, Patrick Marchetti, Luc Smolderen, and Panayotis Yannopoulos, 203–11. Louvain-la-Neuve: Association de numismatique professeur Marcel Hoc.

———. 2011a. "Productions et circulations monétaires dans le Pont, la Paphlagonie et la Bithynie: Deux horizons différents (Ve–Ier s. av. J.-C.)." In *Nomisma: La circulation monétaire dans le monde grec antique: Actes du colloque international, Athènes, 14–17 avril 2010*, edited by Thomas Faucher, Marie-Christine Marcellesi, and Olivier Picard, 455–82. Athens: Ecole française d'Athènes.

———. 2011b. "Quantifying Monetary Production in Greco-Roman Times: A General Frame." In *Quantifying Monetary Supplies in Greco-Roman Times*, edited by François de Callataÿ, 7–29. Bari: Edipuglia.

———. 2013. "The Coinages of the Attalids and Their Neighbours: A Quantified Overview." In *Attalid Asia Minor: Money, International Relations, and the State*, edited by Peter Thonemann, 207–44. Oxford: Oxford University Press.

Callataÿ, François de, Georges Depeyrot, and Leandre Villaronga. 1993. *L'argent monnayé d'Alexandre le Grand à Auguste*. Brussels: Cercle d'études numismatiques.

Canepa, Matthew P. 2010. "Achaemenid and Seleucid Royal Funerary Practices and Middle Iranian Kingship." In *Commutatio et Contentio: Studies in the Late Roman, Sasanian, and Early Islamic Near East*, edited by Henning Börm and Josef Wiesehöfer, 1–21. Düsseldorf: Wellem.

Capdetrey, Laurent. 2004. "Le 'basilikon' et les cités grecques dans le royaume séleucide: Modalités de redistribution de la richesse royale et formes de dépendance des cités." In *Le roi et l'économie: Autonomies locales et structures royales dans l'économie de l'empire séleucide*, edited by Véronique Chankowski and Frédérique Duyrat, 105–29. Topoi Supplément 6. Lyon: De Boccard.

2007. *Le pouvoir séleucide: Territoire, administration, finances d'un royaume hellénistique (312–129 avant J.-C.)*. Rennes: Presses universitaires de Rennes.

Carbone, Lucia Francesca. 2014. "Money and Power: The Disappearance of Autonomous Silver Issues in the Roman Province of Asia." *Revista Numismática OMNI* 8: 10–34.

——— 2020. *Hidden Power: Late Cistophoric Production and the Creation of Provincia Asia (128–89 BC)*. New York: American Numismatic Society.

Cardinali, Giuseppe. 1915–16. "L'amministrazione finanziaria del comune di Pergamo." *Atti della Accademia delle scienze dell'Istituto di Bologna: Memorie* 10: 181–93.

Carlsson, Susanne. 2010. *Hellenistic Democracies: Freedom, Independence and Political Procedure in Some East Greek City-States*. Stuttgart: Steiner.

Carruthers, Bruce G. 2005. "The Sociology of Money and Credit." In *The Handbook of Economic Sociology*, 2nd ed., edited by Neil J. Smelser and Richard Swedberg, 355–78. Princeton, NJ: Princeton University Press.

Carstens, Anne Marie. 2002. "Tomb Cult on the Halikarnassos Peninsula." *American Journal of Archaeology* 106: 391–409.

Carter, Giles F. 1983. "A Simplified Method for Calculating the Original Number of Dies from Die-Link Statistics." *American Numismatic Society Museum Notes* 28: 195–206.

Carusi, Cristina. 2008. *Il sale nel mondo greco (VI aC–III dC): Luoghi di produzione, circolazione commerciale, regimi di sfruttamento nel contesto del Mediterraneo antico*. Bari: Edipuglia.

Cary, Max. 1932. "Sources of Silver for the Greek World." *Mélanges Glotz* 1: 133–42.

Catling, Richard W. V. 2004–9. "Attalid Troops at Thermon: A Reappraisal of *IG* IX 1(2) 60." *Horos* 17–21: 397–439.

Cavalier, Laurence, and Jacques des Courtils. 2001. "The City of Xanthos: From Archaic to Byzantine Times." In *Urbanism in Western Asia Minor*, edited by David Parrish, 148–71. Journal of Roman Archaeology Supplementary Series 45. Portsmouth, RI: Journal of Roman Archaeology.

Cesare, Riccardo Di. 2019. "Hellenistic Gymnasia in the Heart of Athens." In *Development of Gymnasia and Graeco-Roman Cityscapes*, edited by Ulrich Mania and Monika Trümper, 215–36. Berlin: Edition Topoi.

Çevik, Nevzat, and Isabelle Pimouguet-Pédarros. 2004. "The Fortified Site of Kelbessos." *Anatolia Antiqua* 12: 283–91.

Chameroy, Jérémie. 2012. "Chronologie und Verbreitung der hellenistischen Bronzeprägungen aus Pergamon: Der Beitrag der Fundmünzen." *Chiron* 42: 129–79.

Chameroy, Jérémie, and Ivana Savalli-Lestrade. 2016. "Pergame: Cité et capitale dynastique au miroir de la prosopographie interne et des trouvailles monétaires." In *L'eolide dans l'ombre de Pergame*, edited by Ivana Savalli-Lestrade, 229–84. Topoi Supplément 14. Paris: De Boccard.

Chandezon, Christophe. 2003. *L'élevage en Grèce, fin Ve-fin Ier S. aC: L'apport des sources épigraphiques*. Bordeaux: Ausonius.

———. 2004. "Prélèvements royaux et fiscalité civique dans le royaume séleucide." In *Le roi et l'économie: Autonomies locales et structures royales dans l'économie de l'empire séleucide*, edited by Véronique Chankowski and Frédérique Duyrat, 131–48. Topoi Supplément 6. Paris: De Boccard.

Chaniotis, Angelis. 2004. "Justifying Territorial Claims in Classical and Hellenistic Greece: The Beginnings of International Law." In *The Law and the Courts in Ancient Greece*, edited by Edward M. Harris and Lene Rubinstein, 185–229. London: Duckworth.

Chaniotis, Angelos. 1999. "Milking the Mountains: Economic Activities on the Cretan Uplands in the Classical and Hellenistic Period." In *From Minoan Farmers to Roman Traders: Sidelights on the Economy of Ancient Crete*, edited by Angelos Chaniotis, 181–220. Stuttgart: Franz Steiner Verlag.

———. 2008. "Policing the Hellenistic Countryside: Realities and Ideologies." In *Sécurité collective et ordre public dans les sociétés anciennes*, edited by Cédric Brélaz and Pierre Ducrey, 103–54. Geneva: Fondation Hardt.

———. 2010a. "Epigraphic Bulletin for Greek Religion 2007." *Kernos*, no. 23: 271–327.

———. 2010b. "New Evidence from Aphrodisias Concerning the Rhodian Occupation of Karia and the Early History of Aphrodisias." In *Hellenistic Karia. Proceedings of the First International Conference on Hellenistic Karia, 29 June–2 July 2006*, edited by Riet van Bremen and Jan Mathieu Carbon, 455–66. Bordeaux: Ausonius.

Chankowski, Andrzej. 2005. "Processions et cérémonies d'accueil: Une image de la cité de la basse époque hellénistique." In *Citoyenneté et participation à la basse époque hellénistique*, edited by Pierre Fröhlich and Christel Müller, 185–206. Geneva: Droz.

———. 2009. "Les souverains héllenistiques et l'institution du gymnase: Politiques royales et modèles culturels." In *L'huile et l'argent: Gymnasiarchie et évergétisme dans la Grèce hellénistique*, edited by Olivier Curty, 95–114. Paris: De Boccard.

———. 2010. *L'éphébie hellénistique: Étude d'une institution civique dans les cités grecques des îles de la Mer Égée et de l'Asie Mineure*. Paris: De Boccard.

Chankowski, Véronique. 2007. "Les catégories du vocabulaire de la fiscalité dans les cités grecques." In *Les catégories du vocabulaire de la fiscalité dans les cités grecques*, edited by Jean Andreau and Véronique Chankowski, 299–331. Pessac: Ausonius.

———. 2011. "Cults as Consumers and Generators of Value." In *The Economies of Hellenistic Societies, Third to First Centuries BC*, edited by Zosia H. Archibald, John K. Davies, and Vincent Gabrielsen, 142–65. Oxford: Oxford University Press.

Chiricat, Edouard. 2005. "Funérailles publiques et enterrement au gymnase à l'époque hellénistique." In *Citoyenneté et participation à la basse époque hellénistique*, edited by Pierre Fröhlich and Christel Müller, 207–23. Geneva: Droz.

Chrubasik, Boris. 2013. "The Attalids and the Seleukid Kings, 281–175 BC." In *Attalid Asia Minor: Money, International Relations, and the State*, edited by Peter Thonemann, 83–120. Oxford: Oxford University Press.

Clarke, Graeme. 2016. "Area C: The Palaestra." In *Jebel Khalid on the Euphrates, vol. 5: Report on Excavations 2000–2010*, edited by Graeme Clarke, Heather Jackson, C. E. V. Nixon, John Tidmarsh, Karyn Wesselingh, and Lisa Cougle-Jose, 37–48. Sydney: Meditarch.

Coarelli, Filippo. 2017. "Il 'Grande Altare' di Pergamo: Cronologia e contesto." In *Géants et Gigantomachies entre Orient et Occident: Actes du colloque organisé par Centre Jean Bérard (CNRS/EFR) AOROC – ArScAN – LABEX Les passés dans le présent, Naples, 14–15 novembre 2013*, edited by Françoise-Hélène Massa-Pairault and Claude Pouzadoux, 193–201. Naples: Centre Jean Bérard.

Cohen, Getzel M. 1991. "*Katoikiai, katoikoi* and Macedonians in Asia Minor." *Ancient Society* 22: 41–50.

———. 1995. *The Hellenistic Settlements in Europe, the Islands, and Asia Minor*. Berkeley: University of California Press.

Conze, Alexander, and Carl Schuchhardt. 1899. "Die Arbeiten zu Pergamon 1886–1898." *Mitteilungen des Deutschen Archäologischen Instituts, Athenische Abteilung* 24: 97–240.

Cook, John M. 1973. *The Troad: An Archeological and Topographical Study*. Oxford: Clarendon Press.

Cope, Edward Meredith, and John Edwin Sandys. 1877. *The Rhetoric of Aristotle with a Commentary*, 3 vols. Cambridge: Cambridge University Press.

Coppola, Alessandra. 2016. "Kings, Gods and Heroes in a Dynastic Perspective: A Comparative Approach." *Erga-Logoi. Rivista di storia, letteratura, diritto e culture dell'antichità* 4: 17–37.

Coqueugniot, Gaëlle. 2013. "Where Was the Royal Library of Pergamum? An Institution Found and Lost Again." In *Ancient Libraries*, edited by Jason König, Aikaterini Oikonomopoulou, and Greg Woolf, 109–23. Cambridge: Cambridge University Press.

Corsten, Thomas. 2008. "Research in the Kibyratis in 2006 and 2007." *ANMED. News of Archaeology from Anatolia's Mediterranean Areas* 6: 112–16.

Corsten, Thomas, and Oliver Hülden. 2013. "Forschungen in der Kibyratis im Jahre 2011." *Araştırma Sonuçları Toplantısı* 30: 353–60.

Coşkun, Altay. 2012. "Deconstructing a Myth of Seleucid History: The So-Called 'Elephant Victory' Revisited." *Phoenix* 66: 57–73.

———. 2014. "Latène-Artefakte im hellenistischen Kleinasien: Ein problematisches Kriterium für die Bestimmung der ethnischen Identität(en) der Galater." *Istanbuler Mitteilungen* 64: 129–62.

———. 2016. "Attalos I and the Conquest of Pessinus. *I.Pessinus* 1 Reconsidered." *Philia* 2: 53–62.

———. 2018. "The Temple State of Kybele in Phrygian and Early Hellenistic Pessinus: A Phantom?" In *Pessinus and Its Regional Setting*, vol. 1, edited by Gocha R. Tsetskhladze, 205–43. Colloquia Antiqua 21. Leuven: Peeters.

Cottier, Michel, Michael, H. Crawford, Charles V. Crowther, Jean-Louis Ferrary, Barbara M. Levick, Olli Salomies, and Michael Wörrle. 2008. *The Customs Law of Asia*. Oxford: Oxford University Press.

Couvenhes, Jean-Christophe. 2020. "Attaleia de Lydie et Philétaireia-sous-l'Ida dans l'accord entre Eumène Ier et les soldats mutinés (*OGIS* 266): Des colonies militaires." In *New Perspectives in Seleucid History, Archaeology and Numismatics: Studies in Honor of Getzel M. Cohen*, edited by Roland Oetjen, 603–22. Berlin: De Gruyter.

Crawford, Michael H. 1985. *Coinage and Money under the Roman Republic: Italy and the Mediterranean Economy*. Berkeley: University of California Press.

Csapo, Eric, and William J. Slater. 1995. *The Context of Ancient Drama*. Ann Arbor: University of Michigan Press.

Curty, Olivier. 2015. *Gymnasiarchika: Recueil et analyse des inscriptions de l'époque hellénistique en l'honneur des gymnasiarques*. Paris: De Boccard.

Dahmen, Karsten. 2010. "The Numismatic Evidence." In *A Companion to Ancient Macedonia*, edited by Joseph Roisman and Ian Worthington, 41–62. Malden, MA: Wiley-Blackwell.

Darbyshire, Gareth, Stephen Mitchell, and Levent Vardar. 2000. "The Galatian Settlement in Asia Minor." *Anatolian Studies* 50: 75–97.

Daubner, Frank. 2006. *Bellum Asiaticum: Der Krieg der Römer gegen Aristonikos von Pergamon und die Einrichtung der Provinz Asia*. Munich: H. Utz.

———. 2008. "Der pergamenische Monatsname Eumeneios." *Epigraphica Anatolica* 41: 174–80.

———. 2011. "Seleukidische und attalidische Gründungen in Westkleinasien: Datierung, Funktion und Status." In *Militärsiedlungen und Territorialherrschaft in der Antike*, edited by Frank Daubner, 41–64. Berlin: De Gruyter.

———. 2015. "Gymnasia: Aspects of a Greek Institution in the Hellenistic and Roman Near East." In *Religious Identities in the Levant from Alexander to Muhammed: Continuity and Change*, edited by Michael Blömer, Achim Lichtenberger, and Rubina Raja, 33–46. Turnhout: Brepols.

Davies, John K. 2011. "The Well-Balanced Polis: Ephesos." In *The Economies of Hellenistic Societies, Third to First Centuries BC*, edited by Zosia Archibald, John K. Davies, and Vincent Gabrielsen, 177–206. Oxford: Oxford University Press.

Debord, Pierre. 1982. *Aspects sociaux et économiques de la vie religieuse dans l'Anatolie gréco-romaine*. Leiden: Brill.

———. 1985. "La Lydie du Nord-est." *Revue des Études Anciennes* 87: 345–58.

———. 2001. "Les Mysiens: Du mythe à l'histoire." In *Origines Gentium*, edited by Valérie Fromentin and Sophie Gotteland, 135–46. Bordeaux: Ausonius.

Degryse, Patrick, and Marc Waelkens, eds. 2008. *Sagalassos VI: Geo- and Bio-Archaeology at Sagalassos and in Its Territory*. Leuven: Leuven University Press.

Delorme, Jean. 1960. *Gymnasion: Étude sur les monuments consacrés a l'education en Grèce (des origines à l'Empire Romain)*. Paris: De Boccard.

Delrieux, Fabrice. 2007. "Frappes monétaires et cités grecques d'Asie Mineure occidentale de la mort d'Alexandre le Grand à la paix d'Apamée." In *Economies et sociétés en Grèce classique et hellénistique: Actes du colloque de la SOPHAU, Bordeaux, 30–31 mars 2007*, edited by Patrice Brun, 129–59. Toulouse: Presses Universitaires du Mirail.

Demargne, Pierre. 1984. "Athena." In *Lexicon Iconographicum Mythologiae Classicae*, II.1:955–1044. Zurich: Artemis & Winkler Verlag.

Descat, Raymond. 1985. "Mnésimachos, Hérodote et le système tributaire achéménide." *Revue des Études Anciennes* 87: 97–112.

———. 2003. "Qu'est-ce que l'économie royale?" *Pallas* 62: 149–68.

Devreker, John. 2018. "Pessinus and Its Sacred Places." In *Pessinus and Its Regional Setting*, vol. 1, edited by Gocha R. Tsetskhladze, 245–61. Colloquia Antiqua 21. Leuven: Peeters.

Dignas, Beate. 2002. *Economy of the Sacred in Hellenistic and Roman Asia Minor*. Oxford: Oxford University Press.

———. 2012. "Rituals and the Construction of Identity in Attalid Pergamon." In *Historical and Religious Memory in the Ancient World*, edited by Beate Dignas and R. R. R. Smith, 119–44. Oxford: Oxford University Press.

Dikbaş, Gülşen. 2010. "Aizanois anatolisches Erbe: Zum Verhältnis der Grauen Keramik zur roten Glanztonkeramik." In *Aizanoi und Anatolien: Neue Entdeckungen zur Geschichte und Archäologie im Hochland des westlichen Kleinasien*, edited by Klaus Rheidt, 44–47. Mainz on Rhine: Philipp von Zabern.

Dinç, Rafet. 2003. *Tralleis: Rehberi*. Istanbul: Arkeoloji ve Sanat.

Djurslev, Christian, and Daniel Ogden. 2018. "Alexander, Agathoi Daimones, Argives and Armenians." *Karanos. Bulletin of Ancient Macedonian Studies* 1: 11–21.

Dmitriev, Sviatoslav. 2005. *City Government in Hellenistic and Roman Asia Minor*. Oxford: Oxford University Press.

———. 2007. "Memnon on the Siege of Heraclea Pontica by Prusias I and the War between the Kingdoms of Bithynia and Pergamum." *Journal of Hellenic Studies* 127: 133–38.

———. 2010. "Attalus' Request for the Cities of Aenus and Maronea in 167 B.C." *Historia* 59: 106–14.

Domingo Gygax, Marc. 2009. "Proleptic Honours in Greek Euergetism." *Chiron* 39: 163–91.

2016. *Benefaction and Rewards in the Ancient Greek City: The Origins of Euergetism*. Cambridge: Cambridge University Press.

Donohue, Alice A. 1988. *Xoana and the Origins of Greek Sculpture*. Atlanta, GA: Scholars Press.

Doonan, Owen P. 2009. "Sacred Landscapes and the Colonization of the Sinop Promontory." In *Sacred Landscapes in Anatolia and Neighboring Regions*, edited by Charles Gates, Jacques Morin, and Martin Zimmermann, 69–78. Oxford: ArchaeoPress.

Douglas, Mary. 1967. "Primitive Rationing: A Study in Controlled Exchange." In *Themes in Economic Anthropology*, edited by Raymond Firth, 119–47. London: Tavistock Publications.

Doyle, Michael W. 1986. *Empires*. Ithaca, NY: Cornell University Press.

Drew-Bear, Thomas. 1975. "Studies in Greco-Roman Phrygia." *Harvard Studies in Classical Philology* 79: 356–57.

Drew-Bear, Thomas, and Georges Le Rider. 1991. "Monnayage cistophorique des Apaméens, des Praipénisseis et des Corpéni sous les Attalides. Questions de géographie historique." *Bulletin de Correspondance Hellénique* 115: 361–76.

Dreyer, Boris. 2004. "Die Neoi im hellenistischen Gymnasion." In *Das hellenistische Gymnasion*, edited by Daniel Kah and Peter Scholz, 211–36. Berlin: Akademie Verlag.

———. 2009. "City Elite and the Administration of the Attalid Kingdom after the Peace of Apameia: Evidence, Research, and Methodological Thoughts." In *Greek History and Epigraphy: Essays in Honour of P. J. Rhodes*, edited by Lynette G. Mitchell and Lene Rubinstein, 33–45. Swansea: Classical Press of Wales.

Dreyer, Boris, and Gregor Weber. 2011. "Lokale Eliten griechischer Städte und königliche Herrschaft." In *Lokale Eliten und hellenistische Könige: Zwischen Kooperation und Konfrontation*, 14–54. Berlin: Verlag Antike.

Duyrat, Frédérique. 2014. "Greek Monetary Standards: An Introduction." *Dialogues d'Histoire Ancienne* 12: 103–23.

Ecker, Avner, Gérald Finkielsztejn, Gilles Gorre, Sylvie Honigman, and Danny Syon. 2017. "The Southern Levant in Antiochos III's Time: Between Continuity and Immediate or Delayed Changes." In *Antiochos III et l'Orient: Journées d'études franco-allemandes, Nancy 6-8 juin 2016*, edited by Christophe Feyel and Laetitia Graslin-Thomé, 161–207. Paris: De Boccard.

Eckstein, Arthur M. 2009. "Hellenistic Monarchy in Theory and Practice." In *A Companion to Greek and Roman Political Thought*, edited by Ryan K. Balot, 247–65. Malden, MA: Wiley-Blackwell.

———. 2012. *Rome Enters the Greek East: From Anarchy to Hierarchy in the Hellenistic Mediterranean*. Malden, MA: Wiley-Blackwell.

Einhorn, Robin L. 2006. *American Taxation, American Slavery*. Chicago: University of Chicago Press.

Emme, Burkhard. 2013. *Peristyl und Polis: Entwicklung und Funktionen öffentlicher griechischer Hofanlagen*. Berlin: De Gruyter.

Engelmann, Helmut. 1975. "Zu einem Brief von Attalos II." *Zeitschrift für Papyrologie und Epigraphik* 19: 224.

Engelmann, Helmut, and Dieter Knibbe. 1989. "Das Zollgesetz der Provinz Asia. Eine neue Inschrift aus Ephesos." *Epigraphica Anatolica* 14: 1–206.

Engels, David. 2014. "Polemon von Ilion: Antiquarische Periegese und hellenistische Identitätssuche." In *Athen und/oder Alexandreia?: Aspekte von Identität und Ethnizität im hellenistischen Griechenland*, edited by Klaus Freitag and Christoph Michels, 65–98. Cologne: Böhlau.

Errington, R. Malcolm. 2010. "Alabanda und Rom im 2. Jh. v. Chr." *Epigraphica Anatolica* 43: 125–30.

Erskine, Andrew. 1995. "Culture and Power in Ptolemaic Egypt: The Museum and Library of Alexandria." *Greece & Rome* 42: 38–48.

Étienne, Roland. 2003. "La politique culturelle des Attalides." *Pallas* 62: 357–77.

——— 2004. *Sanctuaire de Claros, l'architecture: Les propylées et les monuments de la voie sacrée: Fouilles de Louis et Jeanne Robert et Roland Martin, 1950–1961*. Paris: Éditions Recherche sur les Civilisations.

Evans, Jane DeRose. 2018. *Coins from the Excavations at Sardis: Their Archaeological and Economic Contexts: Coins from the 1973 to 2013 Excavations*. Archaeological Exploration of Sardis Monographs 13. Cambridge, MA: Harvard University Press.

——— 2019. "The Mint at Sardis." In *Spear-Won Land: Sardis from the King's Peace to the Peace of Apamea*, edited by Andrea M. Berlin and Paul J. Kosmin, 97–113. Madison: University of Wisconsin Press.

Evans, Richard. 2012. *A History of Pergamum: Beyond Hellenistic Kingship*. London: Bloomsbury.

Faita, Antonia S. 2001. "The Medusa-Athena Nikephoros Coin from Pergamon." In *Athena in the Classical World*, edited by Susan Deacy and Alexandra Villing, 163–79. Leiden: Brill.

Faraguna, Michele. 2006. "L'Economia della Macedonia Ellenistica: Un Bilancio." In *Approches de l'économie hellénistique*, edited by Olivier Picard, 85–119. Saint-Bertrand-de-Comminges: De Boccard.

Ferrari, Gloria. 2000. "The Ilioupersis in Athens." *Harvard Studies in Classical Philology* 100: 119–50.

Feyel, Michel. 1940. "La fête d'Apollon Tarsenos." *Revue des Études Anciennes* 42: 137–41.

Filges, Axel. 2003. "Stadtentwicklung im Gebiet des Oberen Mäander. Die Lydisch-Phrygische Grenzregion am Beispiel von Blaundos." In *Stadt und Stadtentwicklung in Kleinasien*, edited by Elmar Schwertheim and Engelbert Winter, 35–50. Asia Minor Studien 50. Bonn: Habelt.

——— 2006. *Blaundos: Berichte zur Erforschung einer Kleinstadt im lydisch-phrygischen Grenzgebiet*. Istanbuler Forschungen 48. Tübingen: E. Wasmuth.

Finkelberg, Margalit. 2006. "Regional Texts and the Circulation of Books: The Case of Homer." *Greek, Roman and Byzantine Studies* 46: 231–48.

Finkielsztejn, Gérald. 2010. "The *Sekoma*: A Volume Standard for Liquids." In *Maresha Excavations: Final Report III*, edited by Amos Kloner, Hava B. Korzakova, and Gérald Finkielsztejn, 193–203. IAA Reports 45. Jerusalem: Israel Antiquities Authority.

Flament, Christophe. 2010. *Contribution à l'étude des ateliers monétaires grecs: Étude comparée des conditions de fabrication de la monnaie à Athènes, dans le Péloponnèse et dans le royaume de Macédoine à l'époque classique*. Louvain-la-Neuve: Association de numismatique professeur Marcel Hoc.

Fleischer, Robert. 1973. *Artemis von Ephesos und verwandte Kultstatuen aus Anatolien und Syrien. Études préliminaires aux religions orientales dans l'Empire Romain* 35. Leiden: Brill.

——— 1978. "Artemis von Ephesos und Verwandte Kultstatuen aus Anatolien und Syrien." In *Studien zur Religion und Kultur Kleinasiens*, edited by Sencer Şahin, Elmar Schwertheim, Jörg Wagner, and Karl Dörner, 324–58. Leiden: Brill.

——— 2009. "The Rock-Tombs of the Pontic Kings in Amaseia (Amasya)." In *Mithridates VI and the Pontic Kingdom*, edited by Jakob Munk Højte, 109–19. Aarhus: Aarhus University Press.

Fontenrose, Joseph. 1960. "The Crucified Daphidas." *Transactions and Proceedings of the American Philological Association* 91: 83–99.

Francotte, Henri. 1909. *Les finances des cités grecques*. Liège: H. Champion.

French, David. 2012. *Roman Roads and Milestones of Asia Minor, vol. 3: Milestones, Fasc. 3.1: Republican*. BIAA Electronic Mongraph 1. London: British Institute at Ankara.

——— 2016a. *Roman Roads and Milestones of Asia Minor, vol. 3: Milestones, Fasc. 3.9: An Album of Maps*. BIAA Electronic Mongraph 9. London: British Institute at Ankara.

——— 2016b. *Roman Roads and Milestones of Asia Minor, vol. 4: The Roads, Fasc. 4.1: Notes on the Itineraria*. BIAA Electronic Monograph 10. London: British Institute at Ankara.

Fritze, Hans von. 1906. "Zur Chronologie der autonomen Prägung von Pergamon." In *Corolla Numismatica: Numismatic Essays in Honour of Barclay V. Head*, edited by George Francis Hill, 47–62. London: H. Frowde.

Fröhlich, Pierre. 2004a. *Les cités grecques et le contrôle des magistrats (IVe-Ier siècle avant J.-C.)*. Geneva: Droz.

——— 2004b. "'Logistèrion,' à propos d'une inscription de Kymè récemment publiée." *Revue des Études Grecques* 117: 59–81.

——— 2005. "Dépenses publiques et évergétisme des citoyens dans l'exercice des charges publiques à Priène à la basse époque hellénistique." In *Citoyenneté et participation à la basse époque hellénistique*, edited by Pierre Fröhlich and Christel Müller, 225–56. Geneva: Droz.

2009. "Les activités évergétiques des gymnasiarques à l'epoque hellénistique tardive: La fourniture de l'huile." In *L'huile et l'argent: Gymnasiarchie et évergétisme dans la Grèce hellénistique*, edited by Olivier Curty, 57–94. Paris: De Boccard.

2013. "Les groupes du gymnase d'Iasos et les presbytéroi dans les cités à l'époque hellénistique." In *Groupes et associations dans les cités grecques, IIIe siècle av. J.-C.–IIe siècle apr. J.-C.: Actes de la table ronde de Paris, INHA, 19–20 juin 2009*, edited by Pierre Fröhlich and Patrice Hamon, 59–111. Geneva: Droz.

Gabelko, Oleg. 2017. "Bithynia and Cappadocia: Royal Courts and Ruling Society in the Minor Hellenistic Monarchies." In *The Hellenistic Court: Monarchic Power and Elite Society from Alexander to Cleopatra*, edited by Andrew Erskine, Lloyd Llewellyn-Jones, and Shane Wallace, 319–42. Swansea: Classical Press of Wales.

Gabrielsen, Vincent. 2009. "Brotherhoods of Faith and Provident Planning: The Non-Public Associations of the Greek World." In *Greek and Roman Networks in the Mediterranean*, edited by Irad Malkin, Christy Constantakopoulou, and Katerina Panagopoulou, 230–48. London: Routledge.

2011. "Profitable Partnerships: Monopolies, Traders, Kings, and Cities." In *The Economies of Hellenistic Societies, Third to First Centuries BC*, edited by Zosia Archibald, John K. Davies, and Vincent Gabrielsen, 216–50. Oxford: Oxford University Press.

Gabrielsen, Vincent, and Christian Ammitzbøll Thomsen, eds. 2015. *Private Associations and the Public Sphere: Proceedings of a Symposium Held at the Royal Danish Academy of Sciences and Letters, 9–11 September 2010*. Scientia Danica 9. Copenhagen: Det Kongelige Danske Videnskabernes Selskab.

Gantz, Timothy. 1993. *Early Greek Myth: A Guide to Literary and Artistic Sources*, 2 vols. Baltimore, MD: Johns Hopkins University Press.

Gauthier, Philippe. 1976. *Un commentaire historique des Poroi de Xénophon*. Geneva: Droz.

1980. "Études sur des inscriptions d'Amorgos." *Bulletin de Correspondance Hellénique* 104: 197–220.

1989. *Nouvelles inscriptions de Sardes II*. Geneva: Droz.

1991. "Ateleia tou somatos." *Chiron* 21: 49–68.

1993. "Epigraphica II.4: Prostagmata attalides à Egine (OGI 329)." *Revue de Philologie* 67: 41–48.

1995. "Notes sur le rôle du gymnase dans les cités hellénistiques." In *Stadtbild und Bürgerbild im Hellenismus*, edited by Michael Wörrle and Paul Zanker, 1–12. Munich: C. H. Beck.

1996. "Bienfaiteurs du gymnase au Létôon de Xanthos." *Revue des Études Grecques* 109: 1–34.

2005. "Un gymnasiarque honoré à Colophon." *Chiron* 35: 101–12.

2006. "Les décrets de Colophon-sur-Mer en l'honneur des Attalides Athènaios et Philétairos." *Revue des Études Grecques* 119: 473–503.

Gauthier, Philippe, and Miltiades B. Hatzopoulos. 1993. *La loi gymnasiarque de Beroia*. Paris: De Boccard.

Gawlinski, Laura. 2015. "Securing the Sacred: The Accessibility and Control of Attic Sanctuaries." In *Cities Called Athens: Studies Honoring John McK. Camp II*, edited by Kevin F. Daly and Lee Ann Riccardi, 61–87,

Gehrke, Hans-Joachim. 2004. "Eine Bilanz: Die Entwicklung des Gymnasions zur Institution der Sozialisierung in der Polis." In *Das hellenistische Gymnasion*, edited by Daniel Kah and Peter Scholz, 413–19. Berlin: Akademie Verlag.

2014. "A Brief History of Pergamon." In *Pergamon: A Hellenistic Capital in Anatolia*, edited by Felix Pirson and Andreas Scholl, 122–41. Istanbul: Yapı Kredi Yayınları.

Gentner, Wolfgang, Hildegund Gropengiesser, and Günther A. Wagner. 1980. *Blei und Silber im ägäischen Raum: Eine archäometrische Untersuchung und ihr archäologisch-historischer Rahmen*. Heidelberg: Max-Planck-Institut für Kernphysik und Archäologisches Institut der Universität.

Giovannini, Adalberto. 1982. "La clause territoriale de la paix d'Apamée." *Athenaeum* 60: 224–36.

Goitein, Shlomo D. 1967–93. *A Mediterranean Society: The Jewish Communities of the Arab World as Portrayed in the Documents of the Cairo Geniza*, 6 vols. Berkeley: University of California Press.

Gökyıldırım, Turan. 2016. *İstanbul Arkeoloji Müzeleri Lydia Sikkeleri Kataloğu*. Istanbul: Istanbul Arkeoloji Müzeleri.

Goldstone, Jack A., and John F. Haldon. 2009. "Ancient States, Empires, and Exploitation: Problems and Perspectives." In *The Dynamics of Ancient Empires: State Power from Assyria to Byzantium*, edited by Ian Morris and Walter Scheidel, 3–29. Oxford: Oxford University Press.

Gossman, Lionel. 2006. "Imperial Icon: The Pergamon Altar in Wilhelminian Germany." *Journal of Modern History* 78: 551–87.

Grandinetti, Paola. 2010. "Le élites cittadine di Mileto, Priene e Kyme all'età ellenistica." In *La cité et ses élites: Pratiques et représentation des formes de domination et de contrôle social dans les cités grecques*, edited by Laurent Capdetrey and Yves Lafond, 81–103. Pessac: Ausonius.

Grandjean, Catharine. 2007. "De la drachme au denier." *Revue Européenne des Sciences Sociales* 45: 19–30.

Graninger, Denver. 2011. *Cult and Koinon in Hellenistic Thessaly*. Leiden: Brill.

Granovetter, Mark S. 1973. "The Strength of Weak Ties." *American Journal of Sociology* 78: 1360–80.

Greenewalt, Crawford H., Marcus L. Rautman, and Recep Meriç. 1986. "The Sardis Campaign of 1983." *Bulletin of the American Schools of Oriental Research Supplementary Studies* 24: 1–30.

Gruen, Erich S. 1984. *The Hellenistic World and the Coming of Rome*, 2 vols. Berkeley: University of California Press.

1990. *Studies in Greek Culture and Roman Policy*. Leiden: Brill.

1992. *Culture and National Identity in Republican Rome*. Ithaca, NY: Cornell University Press.

2000. "Culture as Policy: The Attalids of Pergamon." In *From Pergamon to Sperlonga: Sculpture and Context*, edited by Nancy Thomson de Grummond and Brunilde Sismondo Ridgway, 17–31. Berkeley: University of California Press.

2002. *Diaspora: Jews amidst Greeks and Romans*. Cambridge: Cambridge University Press.

2010. *Rethinking the Other in Antiquity*. Princeton, NJ: Princeton University Press.

Grüner, Andreas. 2016. "Teuthrania: Eine kleinasiatische Polis der klassischen Zeit und ihre Bedeutung für die Herrschaftsideologie des attalidischen Pergamon." In *L'éolide dans l'ombre de Pergame*, edited by Ivana Savalli-Lestrade, 65–86. Topoi Supplément 14. Lyon: Maison de l'Orient Mediterranéen.

Grüßinger, Ralf, Volker Kästner, and Andreas Scholl, eds. 2012. *Pergamon: Panorama der antiken Metropole*, 2nd ed. Petersberg: Michael Imhof Verlag.

Guizzi, Francesco. 2006. "Il re, l'amico, i Galati. Epistola inedita di Eumene II alla città di Tabai." *Mediterraneo antico* 9: 181–203.

Güney, Hale. 2015. "Unpublished Coins of the Bithynian Kingdom." *Numismatic Chronicle* 175: 357–63.

Habicht, Christian. 1956. "Über die Kriege zwischen Pergamon und Bithynien." *Hermes* 84: 90–110.

1970. *Gottmenschentum und Griechische Städte*, 2nd ed. Munich: Beck.

1975. "New Evidence on the Province of Asia." *Journal of Roman Studies* 65: 64–91.

1976. "Hellenistische Gymnasiarchenliste aus Pherai." In *Demetrias I*, edited by Vladimir Milojčić and Dimitrios Riga Theocharis, 181–97. Bonn: Habelt.

1983. "Makedonen in Larisa." *Chiron* 13: 21–32.

1989. "The Seleucids and Their Rivals." In *Rome and the Mediterranean to 133 BC*, edited by A. E. Astin, F. W. Walbank, M. W. Frederiksen, and R. V. Ogilvie, 324–87. CAH^2 8. Cambridge: Cambridge University Press.

1990. "Athens and the Attalids in the Second Century B.C." *Hesperia* 59: 561–77.

1995. "Ist ein 'Honoratiorenregime' das Kennzeichen der Stadt im späteren Hellenismus?" In *Stadtbild und Bürgerbild im Hellenismus*, edited by Michael Wörrle and Paul Zanker, 87–92. Vestigia 47. Munich: C. H. Beck.

2006. *The Hellenistic Monarchies: Selected Papers*. Ann Arbor: University of Michigan Press.

Hall, Alan S. 1986. "R.E.C.A.M. Notes and Studies No. 9: The Milyadeis and Their Territory." *Anatolian Studies* 36: 137–57.

Hall, Edith. 1988. "When Did the Trojans Turn into Phrygians? Alcaeus 42.15." *Zeitschrift für Papyrologie und Epigraphik* 73: 15–18.

——— 1991. *Inventing the Barbarian: Greek Self-Definition through Tragedy*. Oxford: Clarendon Press.

Hall, Jonathan M. 2015. "Federalism and Ethnicity." In *Federalism in Greek Antiquity*, edited by Peter Funke and Hans Beck, 30–48. Cambridge: Cambridge University Press.

Hamon, Patrice. 2005. "Le conseil et la participation des citoyens: Les mutations de la basse époque hellénistique." In *Citoyenneté et participation à la basse époque hellénistique*, edited by Pierre Fröhlich and Christel Müller, 121–44. Geneva: Droz.

——— 2007. "Élites dirigeantes et processus d'aristocratisation à l'époque hellénistique." In *Aristocratie antique: Modèles et exemplarité sociale. Actes de la Journée d'étude de Dijon, 25 novembre 2005*, edited by Henri-Louis Fernoux and Christian Stein, 79–100. Dijon: Éditions universitaires de Dijon.

——— 2008. "Kymè d'Éolide, cité libre et démocratique, et le pouvoir des stratèges." *Chiron* 38: 63–106.

——— 2009. "Démocraties grecques après Alexandre. À propos de trois ouvrages récents." *Topoi* 16: 347–82.

Hanfmann, George M. A. 1975. *From Croesus to Constantine: The Cities of Western Asia Minor and Their Arts in Greek and Roman Times*. Ann Arbor: University of Michigan Press.

Hansen, Esther V. 1971. *The Attalids of Pergamon*, 2nd ed. Ithaca, NY: Cornell University Press.

Harl, Karl. 1991. "Livy and the Date of the Introduction of the Cistophoric Tetradrachma." *Classical Antiquity* 10: 268–97.

Harl, Kenneth W. 2011. "The Greeks in Anatolia: From the Migrations to Alexander the Great." In *The Oxford Handbook of Ancient Anatolia, 10,000–323 B.C.E.*, edited by Sharon R. Steadman and John Gregory McMahon, 752–74. Oxford: Oxford University Press.

Harris, Edward M., David M. Lewis, and Mark Woolmer. 2016. *The Ancient Greek Economy: Markets, Households and City-States*. Cambridge: Cambridge University Press.

Hatzopoulos, Miltiades B. 1996. *Macedonian Institutions under the Kings*, 2 vols. Paris: De Boccard.

——— 2001. "Macedonian Palaces: Where King and City Meet." In *The Royal Palace Institution in the First Millennium: Regional Development and Cultural Interchange between East and West*, edited by Inge Nielsen, 189–200. Aarhus: Aarhus University Press.

——— 2016. "Comprendre la loi éphébarchique d'Amphipolis." *Tekmeria* 13.

Hedrick, Charles W. 1999. "Democracy and the Athenian Epigraphical Habit." *Hesperia* 68: 387–439.

Heinle, Melanie. 2015. *Eine historische Landeskunde der Aiolis*. Istanbul: Ege Yayınları.

Heinrichs, Johannes. 2018. "Antiochos III and Ptolemy, Son of Thraseas, on Private Villages in Syria Koile around 200 BC: The Hefzibah Dossier." *Zeitschrift für Papyrologie und Epigraphik* 206: 272–311.

Hellmann, Marie-Christine. 1992. *Recherches sur le vocabulaire de l'architecture grecque, d'après les inscriptions de Délos*. Paris: De Boccard.

Hendrickson, Thomas. 2014. "The Invention of the Greek Library." *Transactions of the American Philological Association* 144: 371–413.

Henry, Olivier. 2013. "Un tumulus en ville." In *Le mort dans la ville: Pratiques, contextes et impacts des inhumations "intra-muros" en Anatolie, du début de l'Age du Bronze à l'époque romaine*, edited by Olivier Henry, 123–34. Istanbul: Institut Français d'Études Anatoliennes.

Herbst, Jeffrey. 1990. *State Politics in Zimbabwe*. Berkeley: University of California Press.

Heres, Huberta. 1996. "The Myth of the Telephos Frieze in Pergamon." In *Pergamon: The Telephos Frieze from the Great Altar*, edited by Renée Dreyfus and Ellen Schraudolf, 2:83–108. San Francisco: Fine Arts Museums of San Francisco.

Herrmann, Peter. 1962. *Ergebnisse einer Reise in Nordostlydien*. Vienna: Böhlau.

——— 1965. "Neue Urkunden zur Geschichte von Milet im 2. Jahrhundert v. Chr." *Istanbuler Mitteilungen* 15: 71–117.

——— 1976. "Nochmals zu dem Brief Attalos' II. an die Ephesier." *Zeitschrift für Papyrologie und Epigraphik* 22: 233–34.

——— 1987. "Milesier am Seleukidenhof. Prosopographische Beiträge zur Geschichte Milets im 2. Jhdt. v. Chr." *Chiron* 17: 171–92.

——— 1995. "Eine 'pierre errante': Ephebenkatalog aus Iasos in Milet." *Arkeoloji Dergisi* 3: 93–99.

Herrmann, Peter, and Hasan Malay. 2007. *New Documents from Lydia*. Vienna: Verlag der Österreichischen Akademie der Wissenschaften.

Herzog, Rudolf. 1928. *Heilige Gesetze von Kos*. Berlin: Verlag der Akademie der Wissenschaften, in Kommission bei de Gruyter.

Hirschfeld, Gustav. 1888. "Review of J. Sterrett 'The Wolfe Expedition to Asia Minor' Boston 1888." *Göttingische gelehrte Anzeigen* 15: 577–92.

Hocquet, Jean-Claude. 1999. "Venice." In *The Rise of the Fiscal State in Europe, c. 1200–1815*, edited by Richard Bonney, 381–416. Oxford: Oxford University Press.

Hoepfner, Wolfram. 2002. "Bibliotheken in Wohnhäusern und Palästen." In *Antike Bibliotheken*, edited by Wolfram Hoepfner, 86–96. Mainz: Philipp von Zabern.

Hoff, Ralf von den. 2004. "*Ornamenta γυμνασιώδη? Delos und Pergamon als Beispielfälle der Skulpturenausstattung hellenistischer Gymnasien.*" In *Das hellenistische Gymnasion*, edited by Daniel Kah and Peter Scholz, 373–405. Berlin: Akademie Verlag.

2009. "Hellenistische Gymnasia: Raumgestaltung und Raumfunktionen." In *Stadtbilder im Hellenismus: Die hellenistische Polis als Lebensform 1*, edited by Albrecht Matthaei and Martin Zimmermann, 245–75. Berlin: Verlag Antike.

2011. "New Research in Aizanoi 2007–2009." In *Archaeological Research in Western Central Anatolia*, edited by A. Nijet Bilgen, 122–39. Kütahya: Üçmart Press.

2018. "Ruler Portraits and Ruler Cult in the Pergamon Gymnasion." In *Development of Gymnasia and Graeco-Roman Cityscapes*, edited by Ulrich Mania and Monika Trümper, 253–71. Berlin: Edition Topoi.

Højte, Jabob Munk. 2009. "The Administrative Organisation of the Pontic Kingdom." In *Mithridates VI and the Pontic Kingdom*, edited by Jakob Munk Højte, 95–108. Aarhus: Aarhus University Press.

Holleaux, Maurice. 1906. "Note sur une inscription de Colophon Nova." *Bulletin de Correspondance Hellénique* 30: 349–58.

1918. "Études d'histoire hellénistique." *Revue des Études Anciennes* 20: 9–19.

1923. "Polybe et le tremblement de terre de Rhodes." *Revue des Études Grecques* 36, no. 168: 480–98.

1924. "Inscription trouvée à Brousse." *Bulletin de Correspondance Hellénique* 48: 1–57.

1957. *Études d'épigraphie et d'histoire grecques. T.5 Rome, la Macédonie et l'Orient grec Pt. 2 Rome et le conquête de l'Orient*. Paris: Librairie d'Amérique et d'Orient Adrien-Maisonneuve.

Hölscher, Fernande. 2017. *Die Macht der Gottheit im Bild: Archäologische Studien zur griechischen Götterstatue*. Heidelberg: Verlag Antike.

Honigman, Sylvie. 2014. *Tales of High Priests and Taxes: The Books of the Maccabees and the Judean Rebellion against Antiochos IV*. Berkeley: University of California Press.

Hopp, Joachim. 1977. *Untersuchungen zur Geschichte der letzten Attaliden*. Munich: Beck.

Horejs, Barbara. 2014. "Pergamon and the Kaikos Valley in Prehistoric Times." In *Pergamon: A Hellenistic Capital in Anatolia*, edited by Felix Pirson and Andreas Scholl, 106–19. Istanbul: Yapı Kredi Yayınları.

Houghton, Arthur. 1984. "The Seleucid Mint of Mallus and the Cult Figure of Athena Magarsia." In *Festschrift für Leo Mildenberg: Numismatik, Kunstgeschichte, Archäologie*, edited by Arthur Houghton, Sylvia Hurter, Patricia Erhart Mottahedeh, and Jane Ayer Scott, 181–92,

Howe, Thomas Noble, Ingrid Rowland, and Michael Dewar, eds. 1999. *Vitruvius' Ten Books on Architecture*. Cambridge: Cambridge University Press.

Howgego, Christopher J. 1995. *Ancient History from Coins*. London: Routledge.

Hübner, Sabine. 2003. "Spiegel und soziale Gestaltungskraft alltäglicher Lebenswelt: Der Kult des Men in Lydien und Phrygien." In *Religion und Region: Götter und Kulte aus dem östlichen Mittelmeerraum*, edited by Elmar Schwertheim and Engelbert Winter, 179–200. Bonn: Habelt.

Huret, R. D. 2014. *American Tax Resisters*. Cambridge, MA: Harvard University Press.

Hürmüzlü, Bilge. 2016. "Display of Power: The Mortuary Landscape of Pisidian Tumuli." In *Tumulus as Sema: Space, Politics, Culture and Religion in the First Millennium BC*, edited by Olivier Henry and Ute Kelp, 491–500. Berlin: De Gruyter.

Hutchins, Zachary McLeod, ed. 2016. *Community without Consent: New Perspectives on the Stamp Act*. Hanover, NH: Dartmouth College Press.

İlaslı, Ahmet. 1996. "Seyitömer Höyüğü 1993 Yılı Kurtarma Kazısı." *Müze Çalışmaları ve Kurtarma Kazıları Sempozyumu Yayınları* 6: 1–20.

Imhoof-Blumer, Friedrich, and Hans von Fritze. 1913. *Die antiken Münzen Mysiens 1: Adramytion-Kisthene*. Berlin: G. Reimer.

Ingvaldsen, Håkon. 2010. "The Hellenistic Coinage of Metropolis." In *Metropolis Ionia. II, Yollarin kesistigi yer: Recep Meriç İçin yazilar = The Land of the Crossroads: Essays in Honour of Recep Meriç*, edited by Serdar Aybek and Ali Kazım Öz, 177–84. Istanbul: Homer Kitabevi.

Intzesiloglou, Babis G. 2006. "The Inscription from the Kynegoi of Herakles from the Ancient Theatre of Demetrias." In *Inscriptions and History of Thessaly: New Evidence*, edited by G. A. Pikoulas. Volos: Πανεπιστήμιο Θεσσάλιας Τμήμα ΙΑΚΑ.

İpek, Önder, and Metin Çakar. 2009. "Çorum İli, Osmancık İlçesi, Koyunbaba Mahallesi, Arafat Tepesi Kurtarma Kazısı." *Müze Çalışmaları ve Kurtarma Kazıları Sempozyumu Yayınları* 17: 161–70.

İslamoğlu, Huri. 2004. "Politics of Administering Property: Law and Statistics in the Nineteenth-Century Ottoman Empire." In *Constituting Modernity: Private Property in the East and West*, edited by Huri İslamoğlu, 276–319. London: I. B. Tauris.

Jacquemin, Anne, Dominique Mulliez, and Georges Rougemont. 2012. *Choix d'inscriptions de Delphes, traduites et commentées*. Athens: Ecole française d'Athènes.

Jenkins, Gilbert K. 1978–80. "Hellenistic Gold Coins of Ephesos." In *Festschrift Akurgal*, edited by Cevdet Bayburtluoğlu, 183–88. Anadolu 21. Ankara: Üniversitesi Dil ve Tarih-Coğrafya Fakültesi.

Jesus, Prentiss S. de. 1978. "Metal Resources in Ancient Anatolia." *Anatolian Studies* 28: 97–102.

Johnson, Peri and Ömür Harmanşah. "Landscape, Politics, and Water in the Hittite Borderlands: Yalburt Yaylası Archaeological Landscape Research Project 2010-2014." In *The Archaeology of Anatolia: Recent Discoveries (2011-2014) I*, edited by Sharon Steadman and Gregory McMahon, 255–277. Newcastle upon Tyne: Cambridge Scholars Press.

Jones, Arnold H. M. 1971. *The Cities of the Eastern Roman Provinces*, 2nd ed. Oxford: Clarendon Press.

Jones, Christopher P. 1974. "Diodoros Pasparos and the Nikephoria of Pergamon." *Chiron* 4: 183–205.

———. 2000. "Diodoros Pasparos Revisited." *Chiron* 30: 1–14.

———. 2004. "Events Surrounding the Bequest of Pergamon to Rome and the Revolt of Aristonicos: New Inscriptions from Metropolis." *Journal of Roman Archaeology* 17: 469–86.

———. 2010. *New Heroes in Antiquity: From Achilles to Antinoos.* Cambridge, MA: Harvard University Press.

Jones, Nicholas F. 1979. "The Autonomous Wreathed Tetradrachms of Magnesia-on-Maeander." *American Numismatic Society Museum Notes* 24: 73–80.

Jonnes, Lloyd, and Marijana Ricl. 1997. "A New Royal Inscription from Phrygia Paroreios: Eumenes II Grants Tyriaion the Status of a Polis." *Epigraphica Anatolica* 28: 1–30.

Jüthner, Julius, Fritz Knoll, Karl Patsch, and Heinrich Swoboda. 1903. *Vorläufiger Bericht über eine archäologische Expedition nach Kleinasien, unternommen im Auftrage der Gesellschaft zur Förderung deutscher Wissenschaft, Kunst und Literatur in Böhmen.* Prague: J. G. Calve.

Kah, Daniel. 2004. "Militärische Ausbildung im hellenistischen Gymnasion." In *Das hellenistische Gymnasion*, edited by Daniel Kah and Peter Scholz, 47–90. Berlin: Akademie Verlag.

Kallet-Marx, Robert. 1995. *Hegemony to Empire: The Development of the Roman Imperium in the East from 148 to 62 B.C.* Berkeley: University of California Press.

Karabulut, Büşra. 2020. "New Inscriptions from the Museum of Eskişehir." *Gephyra* 19: 173–88.

Kasper, Sander. 1976–77. "Der Tumulus von Belevi (Grabungsbericht)." *Jahreshefte des Österreichischen Archäologischen Institutes in Wien* 51: 127–80.

Kästner, Volker. 2012. "Das Heiligtum der Athena." In *Pergamon: Panorama der antiken Metropole*, 2nd ed., edited by Rolf Grüßinger, Volker Kästner, and Andreas Scholl, 184–93. Petersberg: Michael Imhof Verlag.

———. 2014a. "The Altar Terrace." In *A Hellenistic Capital in Anatolia*, edited by Felix Pirson and Andreas Scholl, 456–77. Istanbul: Yapı Kredi Yayınları.

———. 2014b. "The Sanctuary of Athena." In *Pergamon: A Hellenistic Capital in Anatolia*, edited by Felix Pirson and Andreas Scholl, 438–53. Istanbul: Yapı Kredi Yayınları.

Kaye, Noah. 2013. "The Silver Tetradrachms of Prousias II of Bithynia." *American Journal of Numismatics* 25: 21–48.

———. 2015. "Defining the Role of Hellenistic Monarchy in the Taxation of Sale." In *Sale and Community: Documents from the Ancient World*, edited by Eva Jakab, 81–98. Trieste: Edizioni Università di Trieste.

2016. "The Dedicatory Inscription of the Stoa of Attalos in the Athenian Agora: Public Property, Commercial Space, and Hellenistic Kings." *Hesperia* 85: 537–58.

Kaye, Noah, and Randall Souza. 2013. "New Readings of the Decree for Asklepides Son of Theophilos Pergamenós from Kadiköy (SE Lydia)." *Epigraphica Anatolica*, no. 46: 91–100.

Kazhdan, Alexander. 1995. "Pronoia: The History of a Scholarly Discussion." *Mediterranean Historical Review* 10: 133–63.

Kealhofer, Lisa. 2005. "Settlement and Land Use: The Gordion Regional Survey." In *The Archaeology of Midas and the Phrygians: Recent Work at Gordion*, edited by Lisa Kealhofer, 137–48. Philadelphia: University of Pennsylvania Museum of Archaeology and Anthropology.

Kealhofer, Lisa, and Ben Marsh. 2019. "Agricultural Impact and Political Economy: Niche Construction in the Gordion Region, Central Anatolia." *Quaternary International* 529: 91–99.

Kearsley, R. A. 1994. "The Milyas and the Attalids: A Decree of the City of Olbasa and a New Royal Letter of the Second Century B.C." *Anatolian Studies* 44: 47–57.

Kelp, Ute. 2014. "The Necropoleis of Pergamon." In *Pergamon: A Hellenistic Capital in Anatolia*, edited by Felix Pirson and Andreas Scholl, 354–75. Istanbul: Yapı Kredi Yayınları.

2016. "Some Remarks on Tumuli of Late Hellenistic and Early Roman Times in Phrygia and the Development of Provincial Art." In *Tumulus as Sema: Space, Politics, Culture and Religion in the First Millennium BC*, edited by Olivier Henry and Ute Kelp, 601–12. Berlin: De Gruyter.

Kennell, Nigel. 2005. "New Light on 2 Maccabees 4:7–15." *Journal of Jewish Studies* 56: 10–24.

2015. "The Ephebeia in the Hellenistic Period." In *A Companion to Ancient Education*, edited by W. Martin Bloomer, 172–83. New York: Wiley.

Kennell, Nigel M. 2006. *Ephebeia: A Register of Greek Cities with Citizen Training Systems in the Hellenistic and Roman Periods*. Hildesheim: Weidmann.

Kertész, István. 1992. "Zur Sozialpolitik der Attaliden." *Tyche* 7: 133–41.

Khatchadourian, Lori. 2011. "The Cult of Mên at Pisidian Antioch." In *Building a New Rome: The Imperial Colony of Pisidian Antioch (25 BC–AD 700)*, edited by Elaine K. Gazda and Diana Y. Ng, 153–72. Ann Arbor, MI: Kelsey Museum of Archaeology.

Kinns, Philip. 1986. "Asia Minor." In *A Survey of Numismatic Research, 1978–1984, vol. 1: Ancient, Medieval and Modern Numismatics*, edited by Martin Price, 150–79. London: International Numismatic Commission.

1999. "The Attic Weight Drachms of Ephesus: A Preliminary Study in the Light of Recent Hoards." *Numismatic Chronicle* 159: 47–97.

Kleine, Jürgen. 1986. "Pergamenische Stiftungen in Milet." In *Milet 1899–1980. Ergebnisse, Probleme und Perspektiven einer Ausgrabung. Kolloquium, Frankfurt a.M. 1980*, edited by Wolfgang Müller-Wiener, 129–40. Tübingen: E. Wasmuth.

Kleiner, Fred S. 1972. "The Dated Cistophori of Ephesus." *American Numismatic Society Museum Notes* 18: 17–32.

——— 1978. "Hoard Evidence and the Late Cistophori of Pergamum." *American Numismatic Society Museum Notes* 23: 77–105.

——— 1980. "Further Reflections on the Early Cistophoric Coinage." *American Numismatic Society Museum Notes* 25: 45–52.

Kleiner, Fred S., and Sydney P. Noe. 1977. *The Early Cistophoric Coinage*. New York: American Numismatic Society.

Kloppenborg, John S., and Richard S. Ascough, eds. 2011. *Greco-Roman Associations, vol. 1: Texts, Translations, and Commentary: Attica, Central Greece, Macedonia, Thrace*. Beihefte zur Zeitschrift für die neutestamentliche Wissenschaft 181. Berlin: De Gruyter.

Kloppenborg, John S., Richard S. Ascough, and Philip A. Harland. 2014. *Greco-Roman Associations, vol. 2: Texts, Translations, and Commentary: North Coast of the Black Sea, Asia Minor*. Beihefte zur Zeitschrift für die neutestamentliche Wissenschaft 204. Berlin: De Gruyter.

Knibbe, Dieter. 1964–65. "Epigraphische Nachlese im Bereich der ephesischen Agora." *Jahreshefte des Österreichischen Archäologischen Institutes in Wien* 47: 1–44.

Knoblauch, Paul, and Christian Witschel. 1993. "Arykanda in Lykien. Eine topographische Aufnahme." *Archäologischer Anzeiger* 1993: 229–62.

Knoepfler, Denis. 1997. "Alexandreion nomisma: L'apparition et la disparition de l'argent d'Alexandre dans les inscriptions grecques: Quelques reflexions complementaires." *Topoi* 7: 33–50.

Kobes, Jörn. 2004. "Teilnahmeklauseln beim Zugang zum Gymnasion." In *Das hellenistische Gymnasion*, edited by Daniel Kah and Peter Scholz, 237–46. Berlin: Akademie Verlag.

Koehn, Clemens. 2007. *Krieg – Diplomatie – Ideologie zur Außenpolitik hellenistischer Mittelstaaten*. Stuttgart: Franz Steiner Verlag.

Koenigsberger, H. G. 1989. "Composite States, Representative Institutions and the American Revolution." *Historical Research* 62: 135–53.

Kohl, Markus. 2002. "Das Nikephorion von Pergamon." *Revue archéologique* 34: 227–53.

Kolb, Frank. 1974. "Zur Geschichte der Stadt Hierapolis in Phrygien: Die Phyleninschriften im Theater." *Zeitschrift für Papyrologie und Epigraphik* 15: 255–70.

Koparal, Elif, and Numan Tuna. 2017. "Results of the Field Surveys at Teos and Environs (2007–2009): Revealing the Archaic Landscape." *Journal of Greek Archaeology* 2: 199–220.

Korkmaz, Erdal, Zuhal Küçükgüney, and Dilara Doğu. 2016. "İzmir İli, Aliağa İlçesi, Bozköy Kyme Antik Kenti Doğusu Biçerova Tümülüsü Kurtarma Kazısı." *Müze Çalışmaları ve Kurtarma Kazıları Sempozyumu Yayınları* 24: 329–46.

Korres, Manolis. 1984. "Vorfertigung und Ferntransport eines athenischen Grossbaus und zur Proportionierung von Säulen in der hellenistischen Architektur." In *Bauplanung und Bautheorie der Antike*, edited by Wolfram Hoepfner, 201–7. Berlin: E. Wasmuth.

———. 2000. "Anathematika kai timetika tethrippa sten Athena kai stous Delphous." *Bulletin de Correspondance Hellénique Supplement* 36: 292–329.

Köse, Veli. 2004. "Ein neuer Gigantenfries aus Melli in Pisidien." *Istanbuler Mitteilungen* 54: 393–408.

———. 2005. "The Origin and Development of Market-Buildings in Hellenistic and Roman Asia Minor." In *Patterns in the Economy of Roman Asia Minor*, edited by Stephen Mitchell and Constantina Katsari, 139–66. Swansea: Classical Press of Wales.

———. 2017. *Akkulturation in Pisidien*. Ankara: Bilgin Kültür Sanat Yayınları.

Kosmetatou, Elizabeth. 1995. "The Legend of the Hero Pergamus." *Ancient Society* 26: 133–44.

———. 1997. "Pisidia and the Hellenistic Kings from 323 to 133 BC." *Ancient Society* 28: 5–38.

———. 1998. "Cistophori and Cista Mystica: A New Intepretation of the Early Cistophoric Types." *Revue Belge de Numismatique et de Sigillographie* 144: 11–19.

———. 2000. "Lycophron's 'Alexandra' Reconsidered: The Attalid Connection." *Hermes* 128: 32–53.

———. 2001. "Ilion, the Troad, and the Attalids." *Ancient Society* 31: 107–32.

———. 2003. "The Attalids of Pergamon." In *A Companion to the Hellenistic World*, edited by Andrew Erskine, 159–74. Malden, MA: Blackwell.

Kosmin, Paul J. 2014a. *The Land of the Elephant Kings: Space, Territory, and Ideology in the Seleucid Empire*. Cambridge, MA: Harvard University Press.

———. 2014b. "Seeing Double in Seleucid Babylonia: Rereading the Borsippa Cylinder of Antiochus I." In *Patterns of the Past: Epitēdeumata in the Greek Tradition*, edited by Alfonso Moreno and Rosalind Thomas, 173–98. Oxford: Oxford University Press.

———. 2019. "Remaking a City: Sardis in the Long Third Century." In *Spear-Won Land: Sardis from the King's Peace to the Peace of Apamea*, edited by Andrea M. Berlin and Paul J. Kosmin, 75–90. Madison: University of Wisconsin Press.

Kotsidu, Haritini. 2000. *ΤΙΜΗ ΚΑΙ ΔΟΞΑ: Ehrungen für hellenistische Herrscher im griechischen Mutterland und in Kleinasien unter besonderer Berücksichtigung der archäologischen Denkmäler*. Berlin: Akademie Verlag.

Kovenko, V. 1940. "Balya Lead Mines (Turkey)." *Bulletin of Mineral Research and Exploration* 21: 587–93.

Kraay, Colin M. 1976. *Archaic and Classical Greek Coins*. London: Methuen.

Kraft, John C., Helmut Brückner, Ilhan Kayan, and Helmut Engelmann. 2007. "The Geographies of Ancient Ephesus and the Artemision in Anatolia." *Geoarchaeology* 22: 121–49.

Kremydi-Sicilianou, Sophia. 2007. "ΜΑΚΕΔΟΝΩΝ ΠΡΩΤΗΣ ΜΕΡΙΔΟΣ: Evidence for a Coinage under the Antigonids." *Revue Numismatique* 163: 91–100.

Krengel, Elke. 2016. "Orphik in Pergamon: Die Bedeutung des Schlangenpaares auf den Cistophoren und römischen Prägungen." *Jahrbuch für Numismatik und Geldgeschichte* 66: 15–55.

Kunnert, Ursula. 2012. *Bürger unter sich: Phylen in den Städten des kaiserzeitlichen Ostens*. Basel: Schwabe.

Kunze, Christian. 2012. "Hellenistische Skulpturen aus Pergamon." In *Pergamon: Panorama der antiken Metropole*, 2nd ed., edited by Ralf Grüßinger, Volker Kästner, and Andreas Scholl, 313–19. Petersberg: Michael Imhof Verlag.

Kuttner, Ann. 1995. "Republican Rome Looks at Pergamon." *Harvard Studies in Classical Philology* 97: 157–78.

——— 2005. "'Do You Look like You Belong Here?' Asianism at Pergamon and the Makedonian Diaspora." In *Cultural Borrowings and Ethnic Appropriations in Antiquity*, edited by Erich S. Gruen, 137–206. Stuttgart: F. Steiner.

——— 2015. "Hellenistic Court Collecting from Alexandros to the Attalids." In *Museum Archetypes and Collecting in the Ancient World*, edited by Maia W. Gahtan and Donatella Pegazzano, 45–53. Leiden: Brill.

Kwass, Michael. 1999. "A Welfare State for the Privileged? Direct Taxation and the Changing Face of Absolutism from Louis XIV to the French Revolution." In *Crises, Revolutions and Self-Sustained Growth: Essays in European Fiscal History, 1130–1830*, edited by W. M. Ormrod, Margaret Bonney, and Richard Bonney, 344–76. Stamford, Lincolnshire: Shaun Tyas.

Kyriakou, Athanasia. 2014. "Exceptional Burials at the Sanctuary of Eukleia at Aegae (Vergina): The Gold Oak Wreath." *Annual of the British School at Athens* 109: 251–85.

Labarre, Guy, and Mehmet Özsait. 2015. "Colonisation et interculturalité en Pisidie et Phrygie Parorée." *Epigraphica Anatolica* 48: 87–114.

Ladstätter, Sabine. 2016. "Hafen und Stadt von Ephesos in hellenistischer Zeit." *Jahreshefte des Österreichischen Archäologischen Institutes in Wien* 83: 233–62.

——— 2019. "Ephesus: Sardis's Port to the Mediterranean in the Hellenistic Period." In *Spear-Won Land: Sardis from the King's Peace to the Peace of Apamea*, edited by Andrea M. Berlin and Paul J. Kosmin, 191–204. Madison: University of Wisconsin Press.

Laffi, Umberto. 1971. "I terreni del tempio di Zeus ad Aizanoi." *Athenaeum* 49: 3–53.

Laum, Bernhard. 1933. *Die geschlossene Wirtschaft: Soziologische Grundlegung des Autarkieproblems.* Tübingen: Mohr.

———. 1964. *Stiftungen in der griechischen und römischen Antike: Ein Beitrag zur antiken Kulturgeschichte.* Leipzig: Teubner.

Launey, Marcel. 1949–50. *Recherches sur les armées hellénistiques*, 2 vols. Paris: De Boccard.

Lawall, Mark L. 2008. "Rhodian Amphora Stamps from Gordion 189 BC." In *Philias Charin: Mélanges à la mémoire de Niculae Conovici*, edited by Alexandru Avram, Vasilica Lungu, and Marian Neagu, 111–20. Bucharest: Editura Daim.

Lazaridou, Kalliopi D. 2015. "Ἐφηβαρχικὸς νόμος ἀπὸ τὴν Ἀμφίπολη." *Ἀρχαιολογική Ἐφημερίς* 154: 1–45.

Le Guen, Brigitte. 2001. *Les associations de technites dionysiaques à l'époque hellénistique*, 2 vols. Paris: De Boccard.

Le Rider, Georges. 1973. "Un tétradrachme d'Athéna Niképhoros." *Revue Numismatique* 15: 66–79.

———. 1975. "Contremarques et surfrappes dans l'Antiquité grecque." In *Numismatique antique: Problèmes et méthodes, actes du colloque organisé à Nancy du 27 septembre au 2 octobre 1971 par l'Université de Nancy II et l'Université Catholique de Louvain*, edited by Jean-Marie Dentzer, Philippe Gauthier, and Tony Hackens, 27–56. Louvain: Éditions Peeters.

———. 1989. "La politique monétaire du royaume de Pergame après 188." *Journal des Savants*, 163–90.

———. 1993. "Les ressources financières de Séleucos IV (187–175) et le paiement de l'indemnité aux Romains." *Cahiers du Centre Gustave Glotz* 4: 23–24.

———. 1999. *Antioche de Syrie sous les Séleucides: Corpus des monnaies d'or et d'argent I: De Séleucos I à Antiochos V c. 300–161.* Mémoires de l'Académie des Inscriptions et Belles-Lettres. Nouvelle série 19. Paris: Académie des Inscriptions et Belles-Lettres.

———. 2001. "Sur un aspect du comportement monétaire des villes libres d'Asie Mineure occidentale au IIe siècle." In *Les cités d'Asie mineure occidentale au IIe siècle aC*, edited by Alain Bresson and Raymond Descat, 37–60. Pessac: Ausonius.

Le Rider, Georges, and François de Callataÿ. 2006. *Les Séleucides et les Ptolémées: L'héritage monétaire et financier d'Alexandre le grand.* Monaco: Rocher.

Lemaire, André. 2002. "Nouvelle inscription araméenne d'époque achéménide provenant de Kenger." *Epigraphica Anatolica* 34: 179–84.

Lenger, Marie-Thérèse. 1964–88. *Corpus des ordonnances des Ptolémées.* Brussels: Fondation égyptologique Reine Elisabeth.

Leschhorn, Wolfgang. 2009. *Lexikon der Aufschriften auf Griechischen Münzen II: Ethnika und "Beamtennamen."* Vienna: Verlag der Österreichischen Akademie der Wissenschaften.

Levi, Margaret. 1988. *Of Rule and Revenue.* Berkeley: University of California Press.

Levick, Barbara. 2007. "Girdled by Hills: Culture and Religion in Phrygia Outside the Polis." In *Regionalism in Hellenistic and Roman Asia Minor*, edited by Hugh Elton and Gary Reger, 107–16. Pessac: Ausonius.

Lewis, David L. 2011. "Near Eastern Slaves in Classical Attica and the Slave Trade with Persian Territories." *Classical Quarterly* 61: 91–111.

Lewis, David M. 1962. "The Chronology of the Athenian New Style Coinage." *Numismatic Chronicle* 2: 275–300.

Liebhart, Richard F., Gareth Darbyshire, Evin Erder, and Ben Marsh. 2016. "A Fresh Look at the Tumuli of Gordion." In *Tumulus as Sema: Space, Politics, Culture and Religion in the First Millennium BC*, edited by Olivier Henry and Ute Kelp, 627–36. Berlin: De Gruyter.

Lochner, Ina. 2010. "Der Siedlungshügel von Aizanoi in vorrömischer Zeit." In *Aizanoi und Anatolien: Neue Entdeckungen zur Geschichte und Archäologie im Hochland des westlichen Kleinasien*, edited by Klaus Rheidt, 22–37. Mainz on Rhine: Philipp von Zabern.

Long, Anthony A. 1986. *Hellenistic Philosophy: Stoics, Epicureans, Sceptics*. Berkeley: University of California Press.

Lorentzen, Janet. 2014. "Die Stadtmauer des hellenistischen Pergamon. Neue Erkenntnisse zur Datierung von Bau und Niederlegung sowie der städtebaulichen und fortifikatorischen Bedeutung." In *Bericht über die 47. Tagung für Ausgrabungswissenschaft und Bauforschung vom 16. bis 20. Mai 2012 in Trier*, edited by Martin Bachmann, Ulrike Wulf-Rheidt, Hansgeorg Bankel, and Andreas Schwarting, 101–8. Stuttgart: Koldewey-Gesellschaft.

Loukopoulou, Louisa D. 1987. "Provinciae Macedoniae Finis Orientalis: The Establishment of the Eastern Frontier." In *Two Studies in Ancient Macedonian Topography*, edited by Miltiades B. Hatzopoulos and Louisa D. Loukopoulou, 61–100. Athens: Kentron Hellenikes kai Romaïkes Archaiotetos, Ethnikon Hidryma Ereunon.

Lozanov, Ivaylo. 2015. "Roman Thrace." In *A Companion to Ancient Thrace*, edited by Julia Valeva, Emil Nankov, and Denver Graninger, 75–90. Malden, MA: Wiley-Blackwell.

Luke, Christina, and Christopher H. Roosevelt. 2016. "Memory and Meaning in Bin Tepe, the Lydian Cemetery of a 'Thousand Mounds.'" In *Tumulus as Sema: Space, Politics, Culture and Religion in the First Millennium BC*, edited by Olivier Henry and Ute Kelp, 407–28. Berlin: De Gruyter.

Lytle, Ephraim. 2012. "A Customs House of Our Own: Infrastructure, Duties and a Joint Association of Fishermen and Fishmongers (*IK*, 11.1a-Ephesos, 20)." In *Tout vendre, tout acheter. Structures et équipements des marchés antiques. Actes du colloque international d'Athènes (GDRI, EfA, Société Archéologique d'Athènes), 16–19 juin 2009*, edited by Véronique Chankowski and Pavlos Karvonis, 213–24. Bordeaux: Ausonius.

Ma, John. 1999. *Antiochos III and the Cities of Western Asia Minor*. Oxford: Oxford University Press.

2000. "Fighting Poleis of the Hellenistic World." In *War and Violence in Ancient Greece*, edited by Hans Van Wees, 337–76. London: Duckworth.

2003a. "Kings." In *A Companion to the Hellenistic World*, edited by Andrew Erskine, 175–95. Malden, MA: Blackwell.

2003b. "Peer Polity Interaction in the Hellenistic Age." *Past and Present* 180: 9–39.

2007a. "Hellenistic Honorific Statues and Their Inscriptions." In *Art and Inscriptions in the Ancient World*, edited by Zahra Newby and Ruth E. Leader-Newby, 203–20. Cambridge: Cambridge University Press.

2007b. "Review of G. Aperghis 'The Seleukid Royal Economy' Cambridge 2004." *Hermathena* 182: 182–88.

2008a. "The Inventory *SEG* XXXVI 139, and the Athenian Asklepieion." *Tekmeria* 9: 7–16.

2008b. "Mysians on the Çan Sarcophagus? Ethnicity and Domination in Achaimenid Military Art." *Historia* 57: 243–54.

2008c. "Paradigms and Paradoxes in the Hellenistic World." *Studi Ellenistici* 20: 371–86.

2013a. "The Attalids: A Military History." In *Attalid Asia Minor: Money, International Relations, and the State*, edited by Peter Thonemann, 49–82. Oxford: Oxford University Press.

2013b. *Statues and Cities: Honorific Portraits and Civic Identity in the Hellenistic World*. Oxford: Oxford University Press.

2020. "The Restoration of the Temple in Jerusalem by the Seleukid State: II Macc. 11.16–38." In *New Perspectives in Seleucid History, Archaeology and Numismatics: Studies in Honor of Getzel M. Cohen*, edited by Roland Oetjen, 80–93. Berlin: De Gruyter.

MacDonald, David. 1992. *The Coinage of Aphrodisias*. London: Royal Numismatic Society.

Mackil, Emily. 2016. *Creating a Common Polity: Religion, Economy, and Politics in the Making of the Greek Koinon*. Berkeley: University of California Press.

Mackil, Emily, and Peter van Alfen. 2006. "Cooperative Coinage." In *Agoranomia: Studies in Money and Exchange Presented to John H. Kroll*, edited by Peter van Alfen, 201–46. New York: American Numismatic Society.

Macridy, Theodore. 1905. "Altertümer von Notion." *Jahreshefte des Österreichischen Archäologischen Institutes in Wien* 8: 155–73.

Magie, David. 1950. *Roman Rule in Asia Minor to the End of the Third Century after Christ*, 2 vols. Princeton, NJ: Princeton University Press.

Maier, Franz Georg. 1959–61. *Griechische Mauerbauinschriften*, 2 vols. Heidelberg: Quelle und Meyer.

Mairs, Rachel. 2014. *The Hellenistic Far East: Archaeology, Language, and Identity in Greek Central Asia*. Berkeley: University of California Press.

Maischatz, Thomas. 2003. *Neandreia: Untersuchungen zur Bebauung und Stadtentwicklung*. Bonn: Habelt.

Maiuri, Amedeo. 1925. *Nuova Silloge Epigrafica di Rodi e Cos*. Florence: Le Monnier.

Malay, Hasan. 1983. "A New Inscription Concerning the Lakimeni, Hodeni, Mokadeni, and Ankyrani." *Epigraphica Anatolica* 1: 25–28.

Malay, Hasan, and Georg Petzl. 2003. "Posthumous Decree for Philomelos, Son of Ophelas, Issued by the Council and the People of the Mysoi Abaitai." *Epigraphica Anatolica* 36: 19–23.

Manganaro, Giacomo. 2000. "Kyme e il dinasta Philetairos." *Chiron* 30: 403–14.

Mann, Michael. 2012. *The Sources of Social Power, vol. 1: A History of Power from the Beginning to AD 1760*, 2nd ed. Cambridge: Cambridge University Press.

Manning, Joseph G. 2007. "Hellenistic Egypt." In *The Cambridge Economic History of the Greco-Roman World*, edited by Walter Scheidel, Richard P. Saller, and Ian Morris, 434–59. Cambridge: Cambridge University Press.

2009. *The Last Pharaohs: Egypt under the Ptolemies, 305–30 BC*. Princeton, NJ: Princeton University Press.

Mannzmann, Anneliese. 1962. *Griechische Stiftungsurkunden: Studie zu Inhalt und Rechtsform*. Münster: Aschendorff.

Marcellesi, Marie-Christine. 2000. "Commerce, monnaies locales et monnaies communes dans les états hellénistiques." *Revue des Études Grecques* 113: 326–58.

2004. "Milet et les séleucides: Aspects économiques de l'évergétisme royal." In *Le roi et l'économie: Autonomies locales et structures royales dans l'économie de l'empire séleucide*, edited by Véronique Chankowski and Frédérique Duyrat, 165–88. Topoi Supplément 6. Paris: De Boccard.

2008. "Une cité devenue capitale royale: L'histoire monétaire de Pergame dans son contexte micrasiatique." In *Pergame: Histoire et archéologie d'un centre urbain depuis ses origines jusqu'à la fin de l'antiquité*, edited by Markus Kohl, 245–56. Villeneuve d'Ascq: Presses Université Charles de Gaulle.

2010. "Le monnayage royal et ses interactions avec les monnayages civiques: L'exemple du royaume attalide." In *Des rois au prince: Pratiques du pouvoir monarchique dans l'Orient hellénistique et romain (IVe siècle avant J.-C.–IIe siècle après J.-C.)*, edited by Ivana Savalli-Lestrade and Isabella Cogitore, 193–206. Grenoble: ELLUG, Université Stendhal.

2012. *Pergame de la fin du Ve au début du Ier siècle avant J.C.: Pratiques monétaries et histoire*. Pisa: F. Serra.

Marek, Christian. 1989. "Amastris: Geschichte, Topographie, archäologische Reste." *Istanbuler Mitteilungen* 39: 373–89.

2016. *In the Land of a Thousand Gods: A History of Asia Minor in the Ancient World*. Princeton, NJ: Princeton University Press.

Marinescu, Constantin A. 2000. "The Posthumous Lysimachi Coinage and the Dual Monetary System at Byzantium and Chalcedon in the Third Century BC." In *XII. Internationaler Numismatischer Kongress, Berlin 1997: Akten*, edited by Bernd Kluge and Bernhard Weisser, 333–37. Berlin: Staatliche Museen zu Berlin.

Marsh, Ben, and Lisa Kealhofer. 2014. "Scales of Impact: Settlement History and Landscape Change in the Gordion Region, Central Anatolia." *The Holocene* 24: 689–701.

Marszal, John. 2000. "Ubiquitous Barbarians: Representations of the Gauls at Pergamon and Elsewhere," in *From Pergamon to Sperlonga: Sculpture and Context*, edited by Nancy Thomson de Grummond and Brunilde Sismondo Ridgway, 191–234. Berkeley: University of California Press.

Martin, Roland. 1974. *L'urbanisme dans la Grèce antique*, 2nd ed. Paris: Picard.

Martin, Thomas R. 1985. *Sovereignty and Coinage in Classical Greece*. Princeton, NJ: Princeton University Press.

Martinez-Sève, Laurianne. 2004. "La fiscalité séleucide: Bilan et perspectives de recherche." In *Le roi et l'économie: Autonomies locales et structures royales dans l'économie de l'empire séleucide*, edited by Véronique Chankowski and Frédérique Duyrat, 81–104. Topoi Supplément 6. Paris: De Boccard.

Marzano, Annalisa. 2013. *Harvesting the Sea: The Exploitation of Marine Resources in the Roman Mediterranean*. Oxford: Oxford University Press.

Massa-Pairault, Françoise-Hélène. 2010. *Pergamo e la filosofia*. Rome: Giorgio Bretschneider.

Masson, Olivier. 1993. "Une question delphique: Qui étaient les 'Mysiens' de Lilaia?" *Revue des Études Grecques* 106: 163–67.

Mathys, Marianne, Verena Stappmanns, and Ralf von den Hoff. 2012. "Das Gymnasion: Architektur, Nutzung, und Bildwerke." In *Pergamon: Panorama der antiken Metropole*, 2nd ed., edited by Ralf Grüßinger, Volker Kästner, and Andreas Scholl, 270–77. Petersberg: Michael Imhof Verlag.

Mattingly, Harold B. 1971. "Some Problems in Second Century Attic Prosopography." *Historia* 20: 26–46.

——— 1990. "The Beginning of Athenian New Style Silver Coinage." *Numismatic Chronicle* 150: 67–78.

——— 1993. "The Ma'Aret En Nu'man Hoard of 1980." In *Essays in Honour of Robert Carson and Kenneth Jenkins*, edited by Martin Price, Andrew Burnett, and Roger Bland, 69–86. London: Spink.

Mavrojannis, Theodoros V. 2019. "The Royal Donations of Ptolemy IX Soter II Lathyros in Athens: The Gymnasium of Ptolemy and the Horologium of Andronicus Cyrrhestes." *Ostraka* 28: 117–59.

McDonald, A. H. 1967. "The Treaty of Apamea (188 B.C.)." *Journal of Roman Studies* 57: 1–8.

McNicoll, Anthony, and N. P. Milner. 1997. *Hellenistic Fortifications from the Aegean to the Euphrates*. Oxford: Clarendon Press.

McShane, Roger B. 1964. *The Foreign Policy of the Attalids of Pergamum*. Urbana: University of Illinois Press.

Meadows, Andrew. 2001. "Money, Freedom, and Empire in the Hellenistic World." In *Money and Its Uses in the Ancient Greek World*, edited by Andrew Meadows and Kirsty Shipton, 53–63. Oxford: Oxford University Press.
  2002. "Stratonikeia in Caria: The Hellenistic City and Its Coinage." *Numismatic Chronicle* 162: 79–133.
  2008. "Alabanda in Caria: The Hellenistic City and Its Coinage." D.Phil. thesis, Oxford University,
  2009. "The Eras of Pamphylia and the Seleucid Invasions of Asia Minor." *American Journal of Numismatics*, 51–88.
  2013. "The Closed Currency System of the Attalid Kingdom." In *Attalid Asia Minor: Money, International Relations, and the State*, edited by Peter Thonemann, 149–206. Oxford: Oxford University Press.
  2018. "The Great Transformation: Civic Coin Design in the Second Century BC." In *TYPOI: Greek and Roman Coins Seen through Their Images: "Noble" Issuers, "Humble" Users?*, edited by Panagiotis P. Iossif, François de Callataÿ, and Richard Veymiers, 297–318. Liège: Presses Universitaires de Liège.
Meadows, Andrew, and Arthur Houghton. 2010. "The Gaziantep Hoard, 1994 (CH 9.527; 10.308)." In *Coin Hoards X: Greek Hoards*, edited by Oliver D. Hoover, Andrew Meadows, and Ute Wartenberg, 173–224. New York: American Numismatic Society.
Meier, Ludwig. 2012. *Die Finanzierung öffentlicher Bauten in der hellenistischen Polis*. Mainz: Verlag der Antike.
  2013. "Priests and Funding of Public Buildings on Cos and Elsewhere." In *Cities and Priests: Cult Personnel in Asia Minor and the Aegean Islands from the Hellenistic to the Imperial Period*, edited by Marietta Horster and Anja Klöckner, 41–48. Berlin: De Gruyter.
Meissner, Burkhard. 2008. "Reparationen in der klassischen griechischen Welt und in hellenistischer Zeit." In *Kriegskosten und Kriegsfinanzierung in der Antike*, edited by Friedrich Burrer and Holger Müller, 246–59. Darmstadt: Wissenschaftliche Buchgesellschaft.
Melloni, Maria Francesca. 2018. "Decreto di Pergamo per il sacerdote Athenaios." *Axon* 2: 185–210.
Meriç, Recep. 2004. *Metropolis: City of the Mother Goddess*. Izmir: Metropolis Sevenler Derneği.
  2009. *Das Hinterland von Ephesos: Archäologisch-Topographische Forschungen im Kaystros-Tal. Ergänzungshefte zu den Jahresheften des Österreichischen Archäologischen Institutes in Wien 12*. Vienna: Österreichisches Archäologisches Institut.
Meritt, Benjamin D. 1935. "Inscriptions of Colophon." *American Journal of Philology* 56: 358–97.
Merkelbach, Reinhold. 2001. *Die Nordküste Kleinasiens (Marmarameer und Pontos). Steinepigramme aus dem griechischen Osten 2*. Munich: Saur.

Mermerci, Doğu, and Remzi Yağcı. 1991. "Yukarı Bağdere, Yalacık Tümülüsü 1989 Kurtarma Kazısı." *Müze Çalışmaları ve Kurtarma Kazıları Sempozyumu Yayınları* 1: 163–76.

Meshorer, Yaakov. 1981. "The 'Cista Mystica' and Worship of Kore-Persephone at Samaria." *Eretz-Israel: Archaeological, Historical and Geographical Studies* 15: 356–57 (Hebrew).

Migeotte, Léopold. 1984. *L'emprunt public dans les cités grecques: Recueil des documents et analyse critique*. Québec: Les Éditions du Sphinx.

———. 1992. *Les souscriptions publiques dans les cités grecques*. Quebec City: Éditions du Sphinx.

———. 2000. "Les dépenses militaires des cités grecques: Essai de typologie." In *Economie antique: La guerre dans les économies antiques*, edited by Jean Andreau, 145–76. Saint-Bertrand-de-Comminges: Musée archéologique départemental de Saint-Bertrand-de-Comminges.

———. 2003. "Taxation directe en Grèce ancienne." In *Symposion 1999: Vorträge zur griechischen und hellenistischen Rechtsgeschichte*, edited by Gerhard Thür and Francisco Javier Fernández Nieto, 297–313. Cologne: Böhlau.

———. 2006. "La planification des dépenses publiques dans les cités hellénistiques." *Studi Ellenistici* 19: 77–97.

———. 2009. "À propos de gymnasiarque de Délos." In *L'huile et l'argent: Gymnasiarchie et évergétisme dans la Grèce hellénistique*, edited by Olivier Curty, 159–67. Paris: De Boccard.

———. 2013. "Les souscriptions dans les associations privées." In *Groupes et associations dans les cités grecques (IIIe siècle av. J.-C.–IIe siècle apr. J.-C.): Actes de la table ronde de Paris, INHA, 19–20 juin 2009*, edited by Pierre Fröhlich and Patrice Hamon, 113–28. Geneva: Droz.

———. 2014. *Les finances des cités grecques aux périodes classique et hellénistique*. Paris: Les Belles Lettres.

Migeotte, Léopold, and Vassa Kontorini. 1995. "ΛΟΓΕΙΑ ΤΗΣ ΔΙΔΡΑΧΜΙΑΣ à Rhodes." *Bulletin de Correspondance Hellénique* 119: 621–28.

Mileta, Christian. 2008. *Der König und sein Land: Untersuchungen zur Herrschaft der hellenistischen Monarchen über das königliche Gebiet Kleinasiens und seine Bevölkerung*. Berlin: Akademie Verlag.

———. 2009. "Überlegungen zum Charakter und zur Entwicklung der Neuen Poleis im hellenistischen Kleinasien." In *Stadtbilder im Hellenismus*, edited by Albrecht Matthaei and Martin Zimmermann, 70–89. Berlin: Verlag Antike.

———. 2010. "Überlegungen zur Datierung der Inschriften des Inschriftendossiers I. Pessinous 1–7." In *Studia Hellenistica et Historiographica: Festschrift für Andreas Mehl*, edited by Thomas Brüggemann, 107–20,

Miller, Stephen G. 1974. "A Family of Halikarnassians in North-Central Greece." *American Journal of Archaeology* 78: 151–52.

Millett, Paul. 1991. *Lending and Borrowing in Ancient Athens*. Cambridge: Cambridge University Press.

Milner, Nicholas P. 1998. *An Epigraphical Survey in the Kibyra-Olbasa Region Conducted by A. S. Hall*. London: British Institute of Archaeology at Ankara.

Mitchell, Lynette G. 2007. *Panhellenism and the Barbarian in Archaic and Classical Greece*. Swansea: Classical Press of Wales.

Mitchell, Stephen. 1992. "Hellenismus in Pisidien." In *Forschungen in Pisidien*, edited by Elmar Schwertheim, 1–28. Asia Minor Studien 6. Bonn: Habelt.

———. 1993. *Anatolia: Land, Men, and Gods in Asia Minor*, 2 vols. Oxford: Clarendon Press.

———. 1994. "Three Cities in Pisidia." *Anatolian Studies* 44: 129–48.

———. 1998a. "The Pisidian Survey." In *Ancient Anatolia: Fifty Years' Work by the British Institute of Archaeology at Ankara*, edited by Roger Matthews, 237–53. Ankara: British Institute at Ankara.

———. 1998b. "Archaeology in Asia Minor 1990–98." *Archaeological Reports* 45: 125–99.

———. 1999. "The Administration of Roman Asia from 133 BC to AD 250." In *Lokale Autonomie und römische Ordnungsmacht in den kaiserzeitlichen Provinzen vom 1. bis 3. Jahrhundert*, edited by Werner Eck and Elisabeth Müller-Luckner, 17–46. Munich: R. Oldenbourg Verlag.

———. 2003. "The Galatians: Representation and Reality." In *A Companion to the Hellenistic World*, edited by Andrew Erskine, 280–93. Malden, MA: Blackwell.

———. 2005. "Anatolia between East and West: The Parallel Lives of the Attalid and Mithridatid Kingdom in the Hellenistic Age." In *Studi ellenistici 16*, edited by Biagio Virgilio, 521–30. Pisa: Giardini.

———. 2008. "Geography, Politics, and Imperialism in the Asia Customs Law." In *The Customs Law of Asia*, edited by M. Cottier, M. H. Crawford, C. V. Crowther, J.-L. Ferrary, B. M. Levick, O. Salomies, and M. Wörrle, 165–201. Oxford: Oxford University Press.

———. 2018. "Dispelling Seleukid Phantoms: Macedonians in Western Asia Minor from Alexander to the Attalids." In *The Seleukid Empire, 281–222 BC: War within the Family*, edited by Kyle Erickson, 11–35. Swansea: Classical Press of Wales.

Mitchell, Stephen, and Marc Waelkens. 1998. *Pisidian Antioch: The Site and Its Monuments*. London: Classical Press of Wales.

Momigliano, Arnaldo. 1970. "J. G. Droysen between Greeks and Jews." *History and Theory* 9: 139–53.

———. 1990. *The Classical Foundations of Modern Historiography*. Berkeley: University of California Press.

Mommsen, Theodor. 1879. *Römische Forschungen*, vol. 2. Berlin: Weidmann.

———. 1881. *Römische Geschichte. Zweiter Band, Von der Schlacht von Pydna bis auf Sullas Tod*. Berlin: Weidmannsche Buchhandlung.

Monson, Andrew. 2015. "Hellenistic Empires." In *Fiscal Regimes and the Political Economy of Premodern States*, edited by Walter Scheidel and Andrew Monson, 169–207. Cambridge: Cambridge University Press.

Monson, Andrew, and Walter Scheidel. 2015. "Studying Fiscal Regimes." In *Fiscal Regimes and the Political Economy of Premodern States*, edited by Andrew Monson and Walter Scheidel, 3–28. Cambridge: Cambridge University Press.

Moretti, Luigi. 1982. "Sulla legge ginnasiarca di Berea." *Rivista di Filologia* 110: 45–63.

Mørkholm, Otto. 1965. "The Municipal Coinages with Portrait of Antiochus IV of Syria." In *Congresso Internazionale di Numismática: Roma, 11–16 settembre 1961. II, Atti*, 63–67. Rome: Istituto Italiano di Numismatica.

——— 1978. "The Era of the Pamphylian Alexanders." *American Numismatic Society Museum Notes* 23: 69–75.

——— 1979. "Some Reflections on the Early Cistophoric Coinage." *American Numismatic Society Museum Notes* 24: 47–61.

——— 1982. "Some Reflections on the Production and Use of Coinage in Ancient Greece." *Historia* 31: 290–305.

——— 1984. "Some Pergamene Coins in Copenhagen." In *Festschrift für Leo Mildenberg: Numismatik, Kunstgeschichte, Archäologie*, edited by Arthur Houghton, Sylvia Hurter, Patricia Erhart Mottahedeh, and Jane Ayer Scott, 181–92. Wetteren: Editions NR.

Morris, Ian. 1992. *Death-Ritual and Social Structure in Classical Antiquity*. Cambridge: Cambridge University Press.

——— 2010. *Why the West Rules – For Now: The Patterns of History, and What They Reveal about the Future*. New York: Farrar, Straus and Giroux.

Mourgues, Jean-Louis. 1995. "Le préambule de l'édit de Tiberius Julius Alexander: Témoin des étapes de son élaboration." *Bulletin de Correspondance Hellénique* 119: 415–35.

Müller, Helmut. 2005. "Hemiolios, Eumenes II, Toriaion und die Finanzorganisation des Alexanderreiches." *Chiron* 35: 355–84.

——— 2010. "Ein Kultverein von Asklepiasten bei einem attalidischen Phrourion im Yüntdag." *Chiron* 40: 427–57.

——— 2012. "Pergamon als Polis – Institutionen, Ämter und Bevölkerung." In *Pergamon: Panorama der antiken Metropole*, 2nd ed., edited by Ralf Grüßinger, Volker Kästner, and Andreas Scholl, 254–59. Petersberg: Michael Imhof Verlag.

Müller, Helmut, and Michael Wörrle. 2002. "Ein Verein im Hinterland Pergamons zur Zeit Eumenes' II." *Chiron* 32: 191–236.

Mulliez, Dominique. 1998. "La chronologie de la prêtise IV (170/69–158/7) et la date de la mort d'Eumène II." *Topoi* 8: 231–41.

Musti, Domenico. 1998. "I Nikephoria e il ruolo panellenico di Pergamo." *Rivista di filologia e di istruzione classica* 126: 5–40.

——— 2000. "Un bilancio sulla questione dei Nikephoria di Pergamo." *Rivista di filologia e di istruzione classica* 128: 257–98.

Nagy, Gregory. 2011. "The Library of Pergamon as a Classical Model." https://chs.harvard.edu/curated-article/gregory-nagy-the-library-of-pergamon-as-a-classical-model/.

Nicolet-Pierre, Hélène. 1989. "Monnaies de Pergame." In *Kraay-Mørkholm Essays: Numismatic Studies in Memory of C. M. Kraay and O. Mørkholm*, edited by Georges Le Rider, 203–16. Louvain-La-Neuve: Institut supérieur d'archéologie et d'histoire de l'art, Séminaire de numismatique Marcel Hoc.

Noe, Sydney P. 1954. "Countermarked and Overstruck Greek Coins at the American Numismatic Society." *American Numismatic Society Museum Notes* 6: 85–93.

Noeske, Hans-Christoph. 2000. "Zum numismatischen Nachweis hellenistischer Stiftungen am Beispiel ptolemäischer Geldgeschenke." In *Schenkungen hellenistischer Herrscher an griechische Städte und Heiligtümer*, edited by Klaus Bringmann, Hans von Steuben, Walter Ameling, and Barbara Schmidt-Dounas, T.2. Bd.1:221–48,

Nollé, Johannes. 1992. "Zur Geschichte der Stadt Etenna in Pisidien. Mit einem Exkurs zur Interpretation von Götterdarstellungen auf den kaiserzeitlichen Stadtmünzen Kleinasiens." In *Forschungen in Pisidien*, edited by Elmar Schwertheim, 61–141. Bonn: Habelt.

——— 2010. "Beiträge zur kleinasiatischen Münzkunde und Geschichte 10." *Gephyra* 7: 71–124.

Ober, Josiah. 2015. *The Rise and Fall of Classical Greece*. Princeton, NJ: Princeton University Press.

Obrador-Cursach, Bartomeu. 2019. "On the Place of Phrygian among the Indo-European Languages." *Journal of Language Relationship* 17: 233–45.

Ogden, Daniel. 2013. *Drakōn: Dragon Myth and Serpent Cult in the Greek and Roman Worlds*. Oxford: Oxford University Press.

Ohlemutz, Erwin. 1968. *Die Kulte und Heiligtümer der Götter in Pergamon*. Darmstadt: Wissenschaftliche Buchgesellschaft.

Oliver, Graham J. 2007. *War, Food, and Politics in Early Hellenistic Athens*. Oxford: Oxford University Press.

Onat, Saadet. 1959. "Aydın İlinin Dalama Bucağına Bağlı Şahnalı Köyü Civarında Bulunmuş Olan Kistoforlar." *Ankara Üniversitesi Dil ve Tarih-Coğrafya Fakültesi Dergisi* 17: 139–46.

Orlin, Eric. 2010. *Foreign Cults in Rome: Creating a Roman Empire*. Oxford: Oxford University Press.

Ormrod, William M., Margaret Bonney, and Richard Bonney, eds. 1999. *Crises, Revolutions and Self-Sustained Growth: Essays in European Fiscal History, 1130–1830*. Stamford, Lincolnshire: Shaun Tyas.

Orth, Wolfgang. 2008. "Der Dynast Philetairos von Pergamon als Wohltäter." In *Vom Euphrat bis zum Bosporus: Kleinasien in der Antike: Festschrift für Elmar Schwertheim zum 65. Geburtstag*, edited by Engelbert Winter and Frank Biller, 1:485–95. Bonn: Habelt.

Osborne, Michael J. 1975. "The Satrapy of Mysia." *Grazer Beiträge. Zeitschrift für die klassische Altertumswissenschaft* 3: 291–309.

Oy, Harun. 2017. "West Anatolian Mining in Early Bronze Age (3000–2000 BC)." *Journal of Ancient History and Archaeology* 4: 12–24.

Özsait, Mehmet, and Nesrin Özsait. 2003. "La céramique dite 'galate' du bassin du Kızılırmak." *Anatolia Antiqua* 11: 323–42.

Özyiğit, Ömer. 2009–11. "Recent Discoveries at Phocaea." *Empuries* 56: 25–40.

Pafford, Isabelle. 2013. "Priestly Portion vs. Cult Fees – The Finances of Greek Sanctuaries." In *Cities and Priests: Cult Personnel in Asia Minor and the Aegean Islands from the Hellenistic to the Imperial Period*, edited by Marietta Horster and Anja Klöckner, 49–64. Berlin: De Gruyter.

Palagia, Olga. 2016. "Commemorating the Dead: Grave Markers, Tombs, and Tomb Paintings, 400–30 BCE." In *A Companion to Greek Architecture*, edited by Margaret M. Miles, 374–89. Chichester: Wiley Blackwell.

Panagopoulou, Katerina. 2007. "Between Necessity and Extravagance: Silver as a Commodity in the Hellenistic Period." *Annual of the British School at Athens* 102: 315–43.

Papazarkadas, Nikolaos. 2004–9. "Ἀττικὰ ἐπιγραφικὰ σημειώματα." *Horos* 17–21: 91–108.

Papazoglu, Fanoula. 1997. *Laoi et Paroikoi: Recherches sur la structure de la société hellénistique*. Belgrade: University of Belgrade.

Papini, Massimiliano. 2016. "Commemorations of Victory: Attalid Monuments to the Defeat of the Galatians." In *Pergamon and the Hellenistic Kingdoms of the Ancient World*, edited by Carlos A. Picón and Seán A. Hemingway, 40–43. New York: Metropolitan Museum of Art.

Parke, Herbert W. 1982. "The Attribution of the Oracle in Zosimus, *New History* 2.37." *Classical Quarterly* 32: 441–44.

Parker, Robert. 2016. "Athena in Anatolia." *Pallas* 100: 73–90.

———. 2017. *Greek Gods Abroad: Names, Natures, and Transformations*. Berkeley: University of California Press.

Paschalis, Dimitrios. 1925. Ἡ Ἄνδρος, ἤτοι ἱστορία τῆς νήσου ἀπὸ τῶν ἀρχαιοτάτων χρόνων μέχρι τῶν καθ' ἡμᾶς. Athens: Hestia.

Paton, William R., and Edward Lee Hicks. 1891. *The Inscriptions of Cos*. Oxford: Clarendon Press.

Payne, Annick, and David Sasseville. 2016. "Die lydische Athene: Eine neue Edition von *LW* 40." *Historische Sprachforschung* 129: 66–82.

Pedersen, Poul. 2004. "Pergamon and the Ionian Renaissance." *Istanbuler Mitteilungen* 54: 409–34.

———. 2013. "The 4th Century BC 'Ionian Renaissance' and Karian Identity." In *4th Century Karia: Defining a Karian Identity under the Hekatomnids*, edited by Olivier Henry, 33–64. Istanbul: Institut Français d'Études Anatoliennes-Georges Dumézil.

Pélékidis, Chrysis. 1962. *Histoire de l'éphébie attique des origines à 31 avant Jésus-Christ*. Paris: De Boccard.

Pelling, Christopher. 1996. "The Triumviral Period." In *The Augustan Empire, 43 BC–AD 69*, edited by Alan K. Bowman, Edward Champlain, and Andrew Lintott, 1–69. *CAH*² 10. Cambridge: Cambridge University Press.

Pernicka, Ernst. 2014. "Possibilities and Limitations of Provenance Studies of Ancient Silver and Gold." In *Metalle der Macht – Frühes Gold und Silber*, 153–64. Halle (Saale): Landesamt für Denkmalpflege und Archäologie in Sachsen-Anhalt, Landesmuseum für Vorgeschichte.

Pernicka, Ernst, Thomas C. Seeliger, Günther A. Wagner, Friedrich Begemann, Sigrid Schmitt-Strecker, Clemens Eibner, Önder Oztunali, and István Baranyi. 1984. "Archaeometallurgische Untersuchungen in Nordwestanatolien." *Jahrbuch des Römisch-Germanischen Zentralmuseums Mainz* 31: 517–99.

Perrin-Saminadayar, Éric. 2007. *Éducation, culture et société à Athènes: Les acteurs de la vie culturelle athénienne, 229–88: Un tout petit monde*. Paris: De Boccard.

Petrocheilos, Nikolaos. 2010. Συμβολὲς στὴν ἱστορία καὶ προσοπωγραφία τῆς ἀρχαίας Ἄνδρου: Ἐπιγραφικὲς καὶ φιλολογικὲς μαρτυρίες. Andros: Kaïreios Bibliotheke.

Petzl, Georg. 1978. "Inschriften aus der Umgebung von Saittai I." *Zeitschrift für Papyrologie und Epigraphik* 30: 249–76.

———. 2001. "Varia Epigraphica." *Epigraphica Anatolica* 33: 51–56.

Pfeiffer, Rudolf. 1968. *History of Classical Scholarship: From the Beginnings to the End of the Hellenistic Age*. Oxford: Clarendon Press.

Picard, Olivier. 2006. "Monétarisation et économie des cités grecques à la basse période hellénistique: La fortune d'Archippè de Kymè." In *Approches de l'économie hellénistique*, edited by Raymond Descat, 85–119. Saint-Bertrand-de-Comminges: De Boccard.

———. 2009. "Le décret amphictionique sur le tétradrachme stéphanéphore et les Technites." In *Kermatia philias: Timetikos tomos gia ton Ioanne Touratsoglou*, 33–43. Athens: Hypourgeio Politismou.

———. 2010. "Rome et la Grèce à la basse période hellénistique: Monnaies et impérialisme." *Journal des Savants*, 161–92.

Piejko, Francis. 1987. "The Settlement of Sardis after the Fall of Achaeus." *American Journal of Philology* 108: 707–28.

———. 1989. "Two Attalid Letters on the 'Asylia' and 'Ateleia' of Apollo Tarsenus, 185 B.C." *Historia* 38: 395–409.

Pirajno, Franco, Taner Ünlü, Cahit Dönmez, and M. Bahadır Şahin. 2019. *Mineral Resources of Turkey*. Cham: Springer.

Pirson, Felix. 2012. "Hierarchisierung des Raumes? Überlegungen zur räumlichen Organisation und deren Wahrnehmung im hellenistischen Pergamon und seinem Umland." In *Manifestationen von Macht und Hierarchien in*

Stadtraum und Landschaft: Wissenschaftliches Netzwerk der Abteilung Istanbul im Rahmen des Forschungsclusters 3 "Politische Räume" des Deutschen Archäologischen Instituts, edited by Felix Pirson, 187–232. Istanbul: Ege Yayınları.

2013. "Pergamon: Bericht über die Arbeiten in der Kampagne 2012." *Archäologischer Anzeiger*, 79–164.

2014a. "Elaia, der (maritime) Satellit Pergamons." In *Häfen und Hafenstädte im östlichen Mittelmeerraum von der Antike bis in byzantinische Zeit: Neue Entdeckungen und aktuelle Forschungsansätze*, edited by Sabine Ladstätter, Felix Pirson, and Thomas Schmidts, 339–56. Istanbul: Zero Prod.

2014b. "Pergamon: Bericht über die Arbeiten in der Kampagne 2013." *Archäologischer Anzeiger*, 101–56.

2014c. "Urban Space and Urban Planning in Hellenistic Pergamon." In *A Hellenistic Capital in Anatolia*, edited by Felix Pirson and Andreas Scholl, 208–25. Istanbul: Yapı Kredi Yayınları.

2015. "Pergamon: Bericht über die Arbeiten in der Kampagne 2014." *Archäologischer Anzeiger*: 89–163.

2016. "Pergamon: Die Arbeiten des Jahres 2015." *E-Forschungsberichte des Deutschen Archäologischen Instituts* 3: 179–200.

2019a. "Pergamon." In *Hellenistic and Roman Anatolia: Kings, Emperors, City States*, edited by Oğuz Tekin, 70–87. Istanbul: Yapı Kredi Yayınları.

2019b. "Pergamon: Bericht über die Arbeiten in der Kampagne 2018." *Archäologischer Anzeiger*: 1–157.

Pirson, Felix, Güler Ateş, Melanie Bartz, Helmut Brückner, Stefan Feuser, Ulrich Mania, Ludwig Meier, and Martin Seeliger. 2015. "Elaia: Eine aiolische Polis im Dienste der hellenistischen Residenzstadt Pergamon?" In *Urbane Strukturen und bürgerliche Identität im Hellenismus*, edited by Albrecht Matthaei and Martin Zimmermann, 22–55. Mainz: Verlag Antike.

Pirson, Felix, Güler Ateş, and Benjamin Engels. 2015. "Die neu entdeckten Felsheiligtümer am Osthang von Pergamon – Ein innerstädtisches Kultzentrum für Meter-Kybele?" In *Natur – Kult – Raum: Akten des internationalen Kolloquiums Paris-Lodron-Universität Salzburg, 20.–22. Jänner 2012*, edited by Katja Sporn, Sabine Ladstätter, and Michael Kerschner, 281–301. Vienna: Österreichisches Archäologisches Institut.

Platthy, Jenö. 1968. *Sources on the Earliest Greek Libraries: With the Testimonia*. Amsterdam: Hakkert.

Pleket, Henry W. 1973. "Economic History of the Ancient World and Epigraphy: Some Introductory Remarks." In *Akten des VI. Internationalen Kongresses für Griechische und Lateinische Epigraphik*, 243–57. Vestigia 17. Munich: C. H. Beck.

2011. "Review of G. Petzl 'Tituli Asiae Minoris, vol. V: Tituli Lydiae, fasc. 3: Philadelpheia et Ager Philadelphenus' Vienna 2007." *Mnemosyne* 64: 171–74.

Poland, Franz. 1909. *Geschichte des griechischen Vereinswesens*. Leipzig: B. G. Teubner.
Polanyi, Karl. 1957. "The Economy as an Instituted Process." In *Trade and Market in the Early Empires: Economies in History and Theory*, edited by Karl Polanyi, Conrad A. Arensberg, and Harry W. Pearson, 243–70. Glencoe, IL: Free Press.
Pollitt, Jerome J. 1986. *Art in the Hellenistic Age*. Cambridge: Cambridge University Press.
Prag, Jonathan R. W. 2007. "Auxilia and Gymnasia: A Sicilian Model of Roman Imperialism." *Journal of Roman Studies* 97: 68–100.
Price, Martin. 1989. "The Larissa 1968 Hoard (IGCH 237)." In *Kraay-Mørkholm Essays: Numismatic Studies in Memory of C. M. Kraay and O. Mørkholm*, edited by Georges Le Rider, 233–43. Louvain-la-Neuve: Institut supérieur d'archéologie et d'histoire de l'art, Séminaire de numismatique Marcel Hoc.
Pritchard, David M. 2015. *Public Spending and Democracy in Classical Athens*. Austin: University of Texas Press.
Prokopov, Ilya. 2012. *The Silver Coinage of the Macedonian Regions: 2nd–1st Century BC*. Wetteren: Moneta.
Psoma, Selene. 2013. "War or Trade? Attic Weight Tetradrachms from Second Century BC Attalid Asia Minor in Seleukid Syria after the Peace of Apameia and Their Historical Context." In *Attalid Asia Minor: Money, International Relations, and the State*, edited by Peter Thonemann, 265–300. Oxford: Oxford University Press.
Purcell, Nicholas. 2005. "The Ancient Mediterranean: The View from the Customs House." In *Rethinking the Mediterranean*, edited by William V. Harris, 200–228. Oxford: Oxford University Press.
Queyrel, François. 2003. *Les portraits des Attalides: Fonction et représentation*. Athens: École française d'Athènes.
———. 2017. "Les Galates comme nouveaux géants: De la métaphore au glissement interprétatif." In *Géants et Gigantomachies entre Orient et Occident: Actes du colloque organisé par Centre Jean Bérard (CNRS/EFR) AOROC – ArScaN – LABEX Les passés dans le présent, Naples, 14–15 novembre 2013*, edited by Françoise-Hélène Massa-Pairault and Claude Pouzadoux, 203–15. Naples: Centre Jean Bérard.
Radt, Stefan L., ed. 2002–11. *Strabons Geographika: Mit Übersetzung und Kommentar*, 10 vols. Göttingen: Vandenhoeck & Ruprecht.
Radt, Wolfgang. 1994. "Die archaische Befestigungsmauer von Pergamon und zugehörige Aspekte." *Revue des Études Anciennes* 96: 63–75.
———. 1999. *Pergamon: Geschichte und Bauten einer antiken Metropole*. Darmstadt: Primus Verlag.
———. 2014. "Location and Development of Ancient Pergamon." In *Pergamon: A Hellenistic Capital in Anatolia*, edited by Felix Pirson and Andreas Scholl, 188–205. Istanbul: Yapı Kredi Yayınları.

Raff, Katherine A. 2011. "The Architecture of the Sanctuary of Mên Askaênos: Exploration, Reconstruction, and Use." In *Building a New Rome: The Imperial Colony of Pisidian Antioch (25 BC–AD 700)*, edited by Elaine K. Gazda and Diana Y. Ng, 131–52. Ann Arbor, MI: Kelsey Museum of Archaeology.

Ramsay, William Mitchell. 1918. "The Utilisation of Old Epigraphic Copies." *Journal of Hellenic Studies* 38: 124–92.

Ratté, Christopher J. 2008. "Reflections on the Urban Development of Hellenistic Sardis." In *Love for Lydia: A Sardis Anniversary Volume Presented to Crawford H. Greenewalt, Jr.*, edited by Nicholas Cahill, 125–33. Cambridge, MA: Harvard University Press.

——— 2011. *Lydian Architecture: Ashlar Masonry Structures at Sardis*. Cambridge, MA: Harvard University Press.

Reger, Gary. 2007. "Hellenistic Greece and Western Asia Minor." In *Cambridge Economic History of the Graeco-Roman World*, edited by Walter Scheidel, Ian Morris, and Richard P. Saller, 460–83. Cambridge: Cambridge University Press.

Reynolds, Joyce Maire. 1982. *Aphrodisias and Rome*. London: Society for the Promotion of Roman Studies.

Rheidt, Klaus. 2008. "Aizanoi in hellenistischer Zeit." In *Neue Funde und Forschungen in Phrygien*, edited by Elmar Schwertheim and Engelbert Winter, 107–22. Bonn: Habelt.

Rhodes, Peter J. 1993. *A Commentary on the Aristotelian Athenaion Politeia*. Oxford: Clarendon Press.

——— 2007. "διοίκησις." *Chiron* 37: 349–62.

——— 2013. "The Organization of Athenian Public Finance." *Greece and Rome* 60: 203–31.

Rhodes, P. J., and David M. Lewis. 1997. *The Decrees of the Greek States*. Oxford: Oxford University Press.

Ricl, Marijana. 2011. "Observations on a New Corpus of Inscriptions from Lydia." *Epigraphica Anatolica* 44: 143–52.

——— 2014. "A New Royal Letter from Pessinus: Some Corrections and Suggestions." *Epigraphica Anatolica* 47: 141–46.

Ridgway, Brunilde Sismondo. 1997. *Fourth-Century Styles in Greek Sculpture*. Madison: University of Wisconsin Press.

——— 2000. *Hellenistic Sculpture II: The Styles of ca. 200–100 B.C.* Madison: University of Wisconsin Press.

——— 2018. "The Ludovisi 'Suicidal Gaul' and His Wife: Bronze or Marble Original, Hellenistic or Roman?" *Journal of Roman Archaeology* 31: 248–58.

Rigsby, Kent J. 1979. "The Era of the Province of Asia." *Phoenix* 33: 39–47.

——— 1988. "Provincia Asia." *Transactions of the American Philological Association* 118: 123–53.

———. 1996. *Asylia: Territorial Inviolability in the Hellenistic World*. Berkeley: University of California Press.

Ritti, Tullia, H. Hüseyin Baysal, E. Miranda, Francesco Guizzi, and Nalan Fırat, eds. 2008. *Denizli-Hierapolis Arkeoloji Müzesi Yunanca ve Latince Yazılı Eserlerin Kataloğu: Denizli Yöresinden Gelen Yazıtlar = Museo Archeologico di Denizli-Hierapolis Catalogo delle iscrizioni greche e latine: Distretto di Denizli*. Pubblicazioni del Dipartimento di discipline storiche 25. Naples: Liguori.

Robert, Louis. 1926. "Notes d'épigaphie hellénistique." *Bulletin de Correspondance Hellénique* 50: 469–522.

———. 1934. "Voyages dans l'Anatolie septentrionale." *Revue Archéologique* 104: 88–94.

———. 1937. *Études anatoliennes: Recherches sur les inscriptions grecques de l'Asie Mineure*. Paris: De Boccard.

———. 1960. *Hellenica, Recueil d'Epigraphie, de Numismatique et d'Antiquités Grecques, XI–XII*. Paris: Adrien Maisonneuve.

———. 1962. *Villes d'Asie Mineure: Études de géographie ancienne*, 2nd ed. Paris: De Boccard.

———. 1965. *Hellenica, Recueil d'Epigraphie, de Numismatique et d'Antiquités Grecques, XIII*. Paris: Adrien Maisonneuve.

———. 1967. *Monnaies grecques: Types, légendes, magistrats monétaires et géographie*. Geneva: Droz,

———. 1973. "Statues de héros mysiens à Délos." In *Études déliennes: Publiées à l'occasion du centième anniversaire du début des fouilles de l'École française d'Athènes à Délos*, 1:478–85. Bulletin de Correspondance Hellénique Supplément. Athens: École française d'Athènes.

———. 1984. "Documents d'Asie Mineure." *Bulletin de Correspondance Hellénique* 106: 309–78.

Robert, Louis, and Jean Robert. 1954. *La Carie: Histoire et géographie historique, avec le recueil des inscriptions antiques. Tome II, Le plateau de Tabai et ses environs*. Paris: Adrien Maisonneuve.

———. 1976. "Une inscription grecque de Téos en Ionie: L'union de Téos et de Kyrbissos." *Journal des Savants*, 153–235.

Robert, Louis, and Jeanne Robert. 1948. *Hellenica, Recueil d'Epigraphie, de Numismatique et d'Antiquités Grecques, VI*. Paris: Adrien Maisonneuve.

Robinson, Edward Stanley Gotch. 1954. "Cistophori in the Name of King Eumenes." *Numismatic Chronicle* 14: 1–8.

Roelens-Flouneau, Hélène. 2019. *Dans les pas des voyageurs antiques: Circuler en Asie Mineure à l'époque hellénistique (IVe s.av.n.è – Principat)*. Bonn: Habelt.

Roesch, Paul. 1982. *Études béotiennes*. Paris: De Boccard.

Rojas, Felipe. 2019. *The Pasts of Roman Anatolia: Interpreters, Traces, Horizons*. Cambridge: Cambridge University Press.

Roller, Duane W. 2014. *The Geography of Strabo: An English Translation with Introduction and Notes.* Cambridge: Cambridge University Press.

⸺ 2018. *A Historical and Topographical Guide to the Geography of Strabo.* Cambridge: Cambridge University Press.

Roller, Lynn E. 1999. *In Search of God the Mother: The Cult of Anatolian Cybele.* Berkeley: University of California Press.

⸺ 2011. "Phrygian and the Phrygians." In *The Oxford Handbook of Ancient Anatolia, 10,000–323 B.C.E.*, edited by Sharon R. Steadman and John Gregory McMahon, 560–78. Oxford: Oxford University Press.

Rookhuijzen, Jan Zacharias van. 2018. *Herodotus and the Topography of Xerxes' Invasion: Place and Memory in Greece and Anatolia.* Berlin: De Gruyter.

Roosevelt, Christopher H. 2009. *The Archaeology of Lydia: From Gyges to Alexander.* Cambridge: Cambridge University Press.

⸺ 2019. "The Inhabited Landscapes of Lydia." In *Spear-Won Land: Sardis from the King's Peace to the Peace of Apamea*, edited by Andrea M. Berlin and Paul J. Kosmin, 145–64. Madison: University of Wisconsin Press.

Rose, C. Brian, and Reyhan Körpe. 2016. "The Tumuli of Troy and the Troad." In *Tumulus as Sema: Space, Politics, Culture and Religion in the First Millennium BC*, edited by Olivier Henry and Ute Kelp, 373–86. Berlin: De Gruyter.

Rose, Charles Brian. 2014. *The Archaeology of Greek and Roman Troy.* Cambridge: Cambridge University Press.

Rostovtzeff, Mikhail Ivanovitch. 1923. "Notes on the Economic Policy of the Pergamene Kings." In *Anatolian Studies Presented to Sir William Mitchell Ramsay*, edited by W. H. Buckler and W. M. Calder, 359–90. Manchester: Manchester University Press.

⸺ 1930. "Pergamum." In *Rome and the Mediterranean 218–133 B.C.*, edited by S. A. Cook, F. A. Adcock, and M. P. Charlesworth, 590–618. CAH^1 8. Cambridge: Cambridge University Press.

⸺ 1941. *Social and Economic History of the Hellenistic World*, 3 vols. Oxford: Clarendon Press.

Roussel, Pierre. 1916. *Délos: Colonie Athénienne.* Paris: De Boccard.

Rousset, Denis. 2017. "Considérations sur la loi éphébarchique d'Amphipolis." *Revue des Études Anciennes* 119: 49–84.

Rowe, Greg. 2002. *Princes and Political Cultures: The New Tiberian Senatorial Decrees.* Ann Arbor: University of Michigan Press.

Russell, Thomas James. 2017. *Byzantium and the Bosporus: A Historical Study, from the Seventh Century BC until the Foundation of Constantinople.* Oxford: Oxford University Press.

Saba, Sara. 2020. *Isopoliteia in Hellenistic Times.* Leiden: Brill.

Şahin, N. Eda Akyürek. 2001. "Büyük Çiftçi Tanrısı Zeus Bronton Arkeolojik ve Epigrafik Belgelerle Phrygia'da bir Zeus Kültü." *Olba* 4: 163–82.

2006. *Yazıdere (Seyitgazi) Zeus Kutsal Alanı ve Adak Yazıtları*. Istanbul: Ege Yayınları.
Sanctis, Gaetano de. 1925. "Epigraphica." *Rivista di Filologia e di Istruzione Classica* 53: 63–90.
Saraçoğlu, Aslı. 2011. "Hellenistic and Roman Unguentaria from the Necropolis of Tralleis." *Anadolu* 37: 1–42.
Sargent, Thomas J., and François R. Velde. 2002. *The Big Problem of Small Change*. Princeton, NJ: Princeton University Press.
Sartre, Maurice. 2009. "Préface." In *L'Asie Mineure dans l'Antiquité: Échanges, Populations et Territoires: Regards actuels sur une péninsule: Actes du colloque international de Tours, 21-22 octobre 2005*, edited by Hadrien Bru, François Kirbihler, and Stéphane Lebreton, 9–12. Rennes: Presses Universitaires de Rennes.
Sauciuc, Theophil. 1914. *Andros: Untersuchungen zur Geschichte und Topographie der Insel*. Vienna: Hölder.
Savalli-Lestrade, Ivana. 1992. "Eumène (Ier) et l'expansion de Pergame. À propos de *IG* XII Suppl., no. 142." *Revue des Études Grecques* 105: 221–30.
1996. "Courtisans et citoyens: Le cas des philoi attalides." *Chiron* 26: 149–82.
1998. *Les philoi royaux dans l'Asie hellénistique*. Geneva: Droz.
2001. "Les Attalides et les cités grecques d'Asie Mineure au IIe s. a.C." In *Les cités d'Asie Mineure occidentale au IIe siècle a.C*, edited by Alain Bresson and Raymond Descat, 77–91. Bordeaux: Ausonius.
2003. "L'élaboration de la décision royale dans l'Orient hellénistique." *Pallas* 62: 17–39.
2005. "Devenir une cité: Poleis nouvelles et aspirations civiques en Asie Mineure à la basse époque hellénistique." In *Citoyenneté et participation à la basse époque hellénistique*, edited by Pierre Fröhlich and Christel Müller, 9–37. Geneva: Droz.
2010. "Les rois hellénistiques, maîtres du temps." In *Des rois au prince: Pratiques du pouvoir monarchique dans l'Orient hellénistique et romain (IVe siècle avant J.-C.-IIe siècle après J.-C.)*, edited by Ivana Savalli-Lestrade and Isabella Cogitore, 55–83. Grenoble: ELLUG, Université Stendhal.
2018. "Nouvelles considérations sur le dossier épigraphique de Toriaion (*SEG* 47. 1745; *I. Sultan Dağı* I, 393)." *Zeitschrift für Papyrologie und Epigraphik* 205: 165–77.
Sawyer, Stephen W. 2016. "A Fiscal Revolution: Statecraft in France's Early Third Republic." *American Historical Review* 121: 1141–66.
Sayar, Mustafa H. 1999. "Pergamon und Thrakien. Ein Beitrag zur Geschichte Thrakiens in der hellenistischen Zeit." In *Steine und Wege: Festschrift für Dieter Knibbe zum 65. Geburtstag*, edited by Peter Scherrer, Hilke Thür, and Hans Taeuber, 245–51. Vienna: Österreichisches Archäologisches Institut.
Schaaf, Hildegard. 1992. *Untersuchungen zu Gebäudestiftungen in hellenistischer Zeit*. Cologne: Böhlau.

Schalles, H.-J. 1985. *Untersuchungen zur Kulturpolitik der pergamenischen Herrscher im dritten Jahrhundert vor Christus.* Tübingen: E. Wasmuth.

Scheer, Tanja S. 1993. *Mythische Vorväter: Zur Bedeutung griechischer Heroenmythen im Selbstverständnis kleinasiatischer Städte.* Munich: Editio Maris.

——— 2003. "The Past in a Hellenistic Present: Myth and Local Tradition." In *A Companion to the Hellenistic World*, edited by Andrew Erskine, 216–31. Malden, MA: Blackwell.

Schmidt-Dounas, Barbara. 2000. *Geschenke erhalten die Freundschaft. Politik und Selbstdarstellung im Spiegel der Monumente.* Berlin: Akademie Verlag.

——— 2016. "Macedonian Grave Tumuli." In *Tumulus as Sema: Space, Politics, Culture and Religion in the First Millennium BC*, edited by Olivier Henry and Ute Kelp, 101–42. Berlin: De Gruyter.

Schnapp-Gourbeillon, Annie. 2016. "Tumuli, Sema and Greek Oral Tradition." In *Tumulus as Sema: Space, Politics, Culture and Religion in the First Millennium BC*, edited by Olivier Henry and Ute Kelp, 205–17. Berlin: De Gruyter.

Schofield, Malcolm. 1999. "Social and Political Thought." In *The Cambridge History of Hellenistic Philosophy*, edited by Keimpe Algra, Jonathan Barnes, Jaap Mansfeld, and Malcolm Schofield, 739–70. Cambridge: Cambridge University Press.

Schroeter, Friedrich. 1932. *De regum Hellenisticorum epistulis in lapidibus servatis quaestiones stilisticae.* Leipzig: Teubner.

Schuler, Christof. 1998. *Ländliche Siedlungen und Gemeinden im hellenistischen und römischen Kleinasien.* Munich: Beck.

——— 1999. "Kolonisten und Einheimische in einer attalidischen Polisgründung." *Zeitschrift für Papyrologie und Epigraphik* 128: 124–32.

——— 2004a. "Die Gymnasiarchie in hellenistischer Zeit." In *Das hellenistische Gymnasion*, edited by Daniel Kah and Peter Scholz, 163–92. Berlin: Akademie Verlag.

——— 2004b. "Landwirtschaft und königliche Verwaltung im hellenistischen Kleinasien." In *Le Roi et l'Économie: Autonomies locales et structures royales dans l'économie de l'empire séleucide*, edited by Véronique Chankowski and Frédérique Duyrat, 509–43. Topoi Supplément 6. Paris: De Boccard.

——— 2005. "Die διοίκησις τῆς πόλεως im öffentlichen Finanzwesen der hellenistischen Poleis." *Chiron* 35: 385–403.

——— 2007. "Tribute und Steuern im hellenistischen Kleinasien." In *Geschenke und Steuern, Zölle und Tribute: Antike Abgabenformen in Anspruch und Wirklichkeit*, edited by Hilmar Klinkott, Sabine Kubisch, and Renate Müller-Wollermann, 371–406. Leiden: Brill.

——— 2010. "Sympolitien in Lykien und Karien." In *Hellenistic Karia: Proceedings of the First International Conference on Hellenistic Karia, Oxford, 29 June–2*

July 2006, edited by Riet van Bremen and Jan-Mathieu Carbon, 393–414. Pessac: Ausonius.

Schulz, Armin. 2000. *Die Stadtmauern von Neandreia in der Troas.* Bonn: Habelt.

Schumpeter, Joseph. 1991. *The Economics and Sociology of Capitalism.* Princeton, NJ: Princeton University Press.

Schwertheim, Elmar. 1988. "Studien zur historischen Geographie Mysiens." *Epigraphica Anatolica* 11: 65–77.

Seaman, Kristen. 2016. "Pergamon and Pergamene Influence." In *A Companion to Greek Architecture*, edited by Margaret M. Miles, 406–23. Chichester: Wiley Blackwell,

Segre, Mario. 1932. "Duo novi testi storici." *Rivista di filologia e d'istruzione classica* 60: 446–52.

———. 1935. "Epigraphica. II. Ἐστεγνοποιημένοι." *Rivista di filologia e d'istruzione classica* 63: 222–25.

———. 1938. "Iscrizioni di Licia I: Tolomeo di Telmesso." *Clara Rhodos* 9: 181–208.

Sekunda, Nicholas Victor. 1985. "Achaemenid colonization in Lydia." *Revue des Études Anciennes* 87: 7–30.

———. 2012. *Macedonian Armies after Alexander, 323–168 BC.* Oxford: Osprey.

Sellars, John. 2007. "Stoic Cosmopolitanism and Zeno's *Republic*." *History of Political Thought* 28: 1–29.

———. 2018. *Hellenistic Philosophy.* Oxford: Oxford University Press.

Seyrig, Henri. 1968. "Monnaies héllenistiques de Byzance et de Calcédoine." In *Essays in Greek Coinage Presented to Stanley Robinson*, edited by Colin M. Kraay and G. K. Jenkins, 183–200. Oxford: Clarendon Press.

———. 1973. *Trésors monétaires séleucides: Trésors du Levant anciens et nouveaux.* Paris: Librairie orientaliste P. Geuthner.

Sherwin-White, Susan, and Amélie Kuhrt. 1993. *From Samarkhand to Sardis: A New Approach to the Seleucid Empire.* London: Duckworth.

Shipley, Graham. 2000. *The Greek World after Alexander, 323–30 B.C.* London: Routledge.

Sivas, Tacîser Tüfekçi. 2018. "Excavations at Dorylaion/Sarhöyük in Phrygia Epiktetos." In *Pessinus and Its Regional Setting*, vol. 1, edited by Gocha R. Tsetskhladze, 99–127. Colloquia Antiqua 21. Leuven: Peeters.

Sivas, Tacîser Tüfekçi, and Hakan Sivas. 2016. "Tumulus Tombs in Western Phrygia." In *Tumulus as Sema: Space, Politics, Culture and Religion in the First Millennium BC*, edited by Olivier Henry and Ute Kelp, 613–26. Berlin: De Gruyter.

Smith, Roland R. R. 2019. "Diadems, Royal Hairstyles, and the Berlin Attalos." In *Art of the Hellenistic Kingdoms: From Pergamon to Rome*, edited by Séan A. Hemingway and Kyriaki Karoglu, 75–82. New York: Metropolitan Museum of Art.

Sommerey, Kai Michael. 2008. "Die Chora von Pergamon: Studien zur Grenzen, Siedlungsstruktur, und Wirtschaft." *Istanbuler Mitteilungen* 58: 139–70.

Sosin, Joshua D. 2002. "Two Attic Endowments." *Zeitschrift für Papyrologie und Epigraphik* 138: 123–28.

———. 2004. "Alexanders and Stephanephoroi at Delphi." *Classical Philology* 99: 191–208.

Soyaker, Sevgi, Eren Sülek, and Tülay Kocaman. 2013. "2012 Yılı Gördes Oda Mezar Kurtarma Kazısı." *Müze Çalışmaları ve Kurtarma Kazıları Sempozyumu Yayınları* 22: 441–50.

Stähler, Klaus. 1968. "Zu den Iphigeniereliefs in Termessos." *Archäologischer Anzeiger*, 280–89.

Stamatopoulou, Maria. 2016. "Forging a Link with the Past: The Evidence from Thessalian Cemeteries in the Archaic and Classical Periods." In *Tumulus as Sema: Space, Politics, Culture and Religion in the First Millennium BC*, edited by Olivier Henry and Ute Kelp, 181–204. Berlin: De Gruyter.

Stanier, Robert S. 1953. "The Cost of the Parthenon." *Journal of Hellenic Studies* 73: 68–76.

Stappmanns, Verena. 2012. "... das Mögliche wirklich werden lassen ... Zu Standort, Entwurf und Konstruktion des hellenistischen Gymnasions von Pergamon." In *Manifestationen von Macht und Hierarchien in Stadtraum und Landschaft: Wissenschaftliches Netzwerk der Abteilung Istanbul im Rahmen des Forschungsclusters 3 "Politische Räume" des Deutschen Archäologischen Instituts*, edited by Felix Pirson, 233–50. Istanbul: Ege Yayınları.

Sterrett, John Robert Sitlington. 1888. *The Wolfe Expedition to Asia Minor: 1884–1885*. Boston: Damrell and Upham.

Stewart, Andrew. 1996a. "A Hero's Quest: Narrative and the Telephos Frieze." In *Pergamon: The Telephos Frieze from the Great Altar*, edited by Renée Dreyfus and Ellen Schraudolf, 1:39–52. San Francisco: Fine Arts Museum of San Francisco.

———. 1996b. "Telephos/Telepinu and Dionysos: A Distant Light on an Ancient Myth." In *Pergamon: The Telephos Frieze from the Great Altar*, edited by Renée Dreyfus and Ellen Schraudolf, 2:109–19. San Francisco: Fine Arts Museum of San Francisco.

———. 2004. *Attalos, Athens, and the Akropolis: The Pergamene "Little Barbarians" and Their Roman and Renaissance Legacy*. Cambridge: Cambridge University Press.

———. 2014. *Art in the Hellenistic World: An Introduction*. Cambridge: Cambridge University Press.

Stewart, Shannan Marie. 2010. "Gordion after the Knot: Hellenistic Pottery and Culture." PhD dissertation, University of Cincinnati.

Stinson, Philip. 2019. "The Hellenistic City Plan: Looking Forward, Looking Back." In *Spear-Won Land: Sardis from the King's Peace to the Peace of Apamea*, edited by Andrea M. Berlin and Paul J. Kosmin, 139–44. Madison: University of Wisconsin Press.

Strobel, Karl. 1996. *Die Galater: Geschichte und Eigenart der keltischen Staatenbildung auf dem Boden des hellenistischen Kleinasien.* Berlin: Akademie Verlag.

——— 2002. "State Formation by the Galatians of Asia Minor: Politico-Historical and Cultural Processes in Hellenistic Central Anatolia." *Anatolica* 28: 1–45.

——— 2003–7. "Ist das phrygische Kultzentrum der Matar mit dem hellenistischen und römischen Pessinus identisch?" *Orbis Terrarum* 9: 207–28.

Strootman, Rolf. 2017. "Imperial Persianism: Seleukids, Arsakids and Fratarakā." In *Imperial Persianism: Seleukids, Arsacids, Frataraka*, edited by Rolf Strootman and Miguel John Versluys, 177–200. Stuttgart: Franz Steiner.

Stroud, Ronald S. 1998. *The Athenian Grain-Tax Law of 374/3 B.C.* Princeton, NJ: American School of Classical Studies at Athens.

Stumpf, Gerd. 1991. *Numismatische Studien zur Chronologie der römischen Statthalter in Kleinasien (122 v. Chr.–163 n. Chr.).* Saarbrücken: Saarbrücker Druckerei und Verlag.

Syme, Ronald. 1995. *Anatolica: Studies in Strabo.* Oxford: Clarendon Press.

Szaivert, Wolfgang. 1983. "Stephanephoren und Kistophoren: Die mittelhellenistische Großsilberprägung und die römische Ostpolitik in der Ägäis." *Litterae Numismaticae Vindobonenses* 2: 29–55.

——— 2005. "Der Beitrag der literarischen Quellen zur Datierung des Beginns der Kistophorenprägung." In *Vindobona docet: 40 Jahre Institut für Numismatik und Geldgeschichte der Universität Wien 1965–2005*, edited by Hubert Emmerig, 51–64. Vienna: Österreichische Forschungsgesellschaft für Numismatik.

——— 2008. "Kistophoren und die Münzbilder in Pergamon." *Numismatische Zeitschrift* 116–17: 29–43.

Takmer, Burak. 2007. "Lex Portorii Provinciae Lyciae: Ein Vorbericht über die Zollinschrift aus Andriake aus neronischer Zeit." *Gephyra* 4: 165–88.

Talloen, Peter. 2013. *Cult in Pisidia: Religious Practice in Southwestern Asia Minor from the Hellenistic to the Early Byzantine Period; A Study Based on the Archaeological Research at Sagalassos.* Turnhout: Brepols.

Talloen, Peter, and Jeroen Poblome. 2016. "The 2014 and 2015 Control Excavations on and around the Upper Agora of Sagalassos: The Structural Remains and General Phasing." *Anatolica* 42: 111–50.

Tanrıver, Cumhur, and Salih Kütük. 1993. "The Katoikia of Daphnous and the Sanctuary of Apollon Daphnousios in the Territory of Apollonia ad Rhyndacum." *Epigraphica Anatolica* 21: 99–102.

Tassignon, Isabelle. 2002. "Foyers dionysiaques de Phrygie et de Lydie." *Hethitica* 15: 233–44.

Tekin, Oğuz, and Aliye Erol-Özdizbay, eds. 2015. *Sylloge Nummorum Graecorum. Turkey 9: The Özkan Arıkantürk Collection.* Istanbul: Türk Eskiçağ Bilimleri Enstitüsü Yayınları.

Temizsoy, İlhan, and Vahap Kaya. 2001. "Kıranharman 'O' tümülüsü nakil çalışmaları." *Müze Çalışmaları ve Kurtarma Kazıları Sempozyumu Yayınları* 11: 149–56.

Thierry, Nicole. 2016. "Le tumulus d'Avanos et la ville sainte du grand Zeus Ouranos." In *Tumulus as Sema: Space, Politics, Culture and Religion in the First Millennium BC*, edited by Olivier Henry and Ute Kelp, 649–56. Berlin: De Gruyter.

Thompson, Dorothy J. 2003. "The Ptolemies and Egypt." In *A Companion to the Hellenistic World*, edited by Andrew Erskine, 105–20. Malden, MA: Blackwell.

Thompson, Margaret. 1961. *The New Style Silver Coinage of Athens*. New York: American Numismatic Society.

Thonemann, Peter, ed. 2003. "Hellenistic Inscriptions from Lydia." *Epigraphica Anatolica*, 95–114.

———. 2007. "Magnesia and the Greeks of Asia (*I.Magnesia* 16.16)." *Greek, Roman and Byzantine Studies* 47: 151–60.

———. 2008. "Cistophoric Geography: Toriaion and Kormasa." *Numismatic Chronicle* 168: 43–60.

———. 2009. "Estates and the Land in Early Hellenistic Asia Minor: The Estate of Krateuas." *Chiron* 39: 363–93.

———. 2011a. "Eumenes II and Apollonioucharax." *Gephyra* 8: 1–12.

———. 2011b. *The Maeander Valley: A Historical Geography from Antiquity to Byzantium*. Cambridge: Cambridge University Press.

———. 2013a. *Attalid Asia Minor: Money, International Relations, and the State*. Oxford: Oxford University Press.

———. 2013b. "The Attalid State: 188–133 BC." In *Attalid Asia Minor: Money, International Relations, and the State*, edited by Peter Thonemann, 1–48. Oxford: Oxford University Press.

———. 2013c. "Phrygia: An Anarchist History, 950 BC–AD 100." In *Roman Phrygia: Culture and Society*, edited by Peter Thonemann, 1–40. Cambridge: Cambridge University Press.

———. 2015a. *The Hellenistic World: Using Coins as Sources*. Cambridge: Cambridge University Press.

———. 2015b. "Pessinous and the Attalids: A New Royal Letter." *Zeitschrift für Papyrologie und Epigraphik* 194: 117–28.

———. 2016. *The Hellenistic Age*. Oxford: Oxford University Press.

Tietz, Werner. 2003. *Der Golf von Fethiye: Politische, ethnische und kulturelle Strukturen einer Grenzregion vom Beginn der nachweisbaren Besiedlung bis in die römische Kaiserzeit*. Bonn: Habelt.

Tiryaki, S. Gökhan. 2016. "*The Milyan Tumuli: An Overview of the Current State of Research.*" In *Havva İşkan'a Armağan LYKIARKHISSA: Festschrift für Havva İşkan*, edited by Şevket Aktaş, Erkan Dündar, Mustafa Koçak, and Serap Erkoç, 841–54. Istanbul: Ege Yayınları.

Tombul, Musa. 2015. "Parion, Adresteia Antik Yolu Üzerindeki Tümülüsler." In *Parion Kazıları 10. Yıl Armağanı*, edited by Cevat Başaran and Vedat Keleş, 167–78. Ankara: Atatürk Üniversitesi-Ondokuz Mayıs Üniversitesi.

Topbaş, Ahmet. 1992. "Kütahya Seyitömer Höyüğü 1990 Yılı Kurtarma Kazısı." *Müze Çalışmaları ve Kurtarma Kazıları Sempozyumu Yayınları* 2: 11–34.

———. 1993. "Seyitömer Höyüğü 1991 Yili Kurtarma Kazısı." *Müze Çalışmaları ve Kurtarma Kazıları Sempozyumu Yayınları* 3: 1–30.

Travaglini, Adriana. 1997. *Museo di Izmir I: Ripostigli di Monete Greche*. Milan: Ennerre.

Troxell, Hyla A. 1971. "The Peloponnesian Alexanders." *American Numismatic Society Museum Notes* 17: 41–94.

———. 1982. *The Coinage of the Lycian League*. New York: American Numismatic Society.

Trümper, Monika. 2014. "'Privat' versus 'öffentlich' in hellenistischen Bädern." In *Stadtkultur im Hellenismus*, edited by Albrecht Matthaei and Martin Zimmermann, 206–49. Mainz: Verlag Antike.

———. 2015. "Modernization and Change of Function of Hellenistic Gymnasia in the Imperial Period: Case-Studies Pergamon, Miletus, and Priene." In *Das kaiserzeitliche Gymnasion*, edited by Peter Scholz and Dirk Wiegandt, 167–222. Berlin: De Gruyter.

Turgut, Mehmet, and Taner Aksoy. 1996. "Kocaeli Ili, Üçtepeler Köyü, Büyük Tümülüs Kurtarma Kazısı." *Müze Çalışmaları ve Kurtarma Kazıları Sempozyumu Yayınları* 6: 399–413.

Ungern-Sternberg, Jürgen von. 2009. "Kriegsentschädigungen – Eine vertraglich geregelte Form der Beute?" In *Praeda: Butin de guerre et société dans la Rome républicaine/Kriegsbeute und Gesellschaft im republikanischen Rom*, edited by Marianne Coudry and Michel Humm, 247–64. Stuttgart: Franz Steiner Verlag.

Ure, Percy N. 1922. *The Origin of Tyranny*. Cambridge: Cambridge University Press.

Uzunoğlu, Hüseyin. 2018. "On the Use of κατασκευάζειν in Building Inscriptions." *Olba* 26: 387–404.

Vacante, Salvatore. 2011. "Alexander the Great and the Polis of Iasus: Salt and Democracy? Notes on the 'Little Sea' Inscription (*I.Iasos* 24 + 30) and the *Ekklesiastikon* Decree (*I.Iasos* 20)." *Klio* 93: 322–36.

Valverde, Luis Amela. 2007. "Cistóforos proconsulares de Apamea, Laodicea, Pergamum y Tralles." *Iberia* 10: 17–36.

Vanhaverbeke, Hannelore, and Marc Waelkens. 2005. "If You Can't Beat Them, Join Them? The Hellenization of Pisidia." *Mediterranean Archaeology* 18: 49–65.

Vanhaverbeke, Hannelore, Marc Waelkens, Kim Vyncke, Véronique de Laet, Sabri Aydal, Branko Mušič, Bea de Cupere, et al. 2010. "'Pisidian' Culture? The

Classical-Hellenistic Site at Düzen Tepe near Sagalassus (Southwest Turkey)." *Anatolian Studies* 60: 105–28.

Vélissaropoulos, Julie. 1980. *Les nauclères grecs: Recherches sur les institutions maritimes en Grèce et dans l'Orient hellénisé.* Geneva: Droz.

Verlinde, Angelo. 2015. "The Pessinuntine Sanctuary of the Mother of the Gods in Light of the Excavated Roman Temple: Fact, Fiction and Feasibility." *Latomus* 74: 30–72.

Veyne, Paul. 1976. *Le pain et le cirque: Sociologie historique d'un pluralisme politique.* Paris: Seuil.

Vial, Claude. 1984. *Délos Indépendante. Bulletin de Correspondance Hellénique Supplément 10.* Paris: De Boccard.

Virgilio, Biagio. 2003. *Lancia, diadema e porpora: Il re e la regalità ellenistica,* 2nd ed. Pisa: Giardini.

2004. "À propos des cités d'Asie Mineure occidentale au IIe siècle AC." *Revue des Études Anciennes* 106: 263–87.

2008. "Sur quelques concessions Attalides à des communautés sujettes." In *Pergame: Histoire et archéologie d'un centre urbain depuis ses origines jusqu'à la fin de l'antiquité,* edited by Markus Kohl, 205–22. Villeneuve d'Ascq: Presses Université Charles de Gaulle.

Viviers, Didier. 2015. "Quand le divin se meut: Mobilité des statues et construction du divin." In *Figures de dieux: Construire le divin en images,* edited by Sylvia Estienne, Valérie Huet, François Lissarrague, and Francis Prost, 27–38. Rennes: Presses universitaires de Rennes.

Voigt, Mary M. 2003. "Celts at Gordion." *Expedition Magazine* 45: 14–19.

Von Reden, Sitta. 2007. *Money in Ptolemaic Egypt: From the Macedonian Conquest to the End of the Third Century BC.* Cambridge: Cambridge University Press.

2010. *Money in Classical Antiquity.* Cambridge: Cambridge University Press.

Waelkens, Marc. 2004. "Ein Blick von der Ferne: Seleukiden und Attaliden in Pisidien." *Istanbuler Mitteilungen* 54: 435–71.

Waelkens, Marc, and Lutgarde Vandeput. 2007. "Regionalism in Hellenistic and Roman Pisidia." In *Regionalism in Hellenistic and Roman Asia Minor,* edited by Hugh Elton and Gary Reger, 97–105. Pessac: Ausonius.

Waggoner, Nancy M. 1979. "The Propontis Hoard (*IGCH* 888)." *Revue Numismatique* 21: 7–29.

Walbank, Frank W. 1957–79. *A Historical Commentary on Polybius,* 3 vols. Oxford: Oxford University Press.

1983. "Via Illa Nostra Militaris: Some Thoughts on the Via Egnatia." In *Althistorische Studien: Hermann Bengtson zum 70. Geburtstag dargebracht,* edited by Heinz Heinen, Karl Stroheker, and Gerold Walser, 131–47. Wiesbaden: Steiner.

1984. "Monarchies and Monarchic Ideas." In *The Hellenistic World,* edited by F. W. Walbank, A. E. Astin, M. W. Frederiksen, and R. V. Ogilvie, 62–100. CAH^2, 7.1. Cambridge: Cambridge University Press.

Walker, Stephen P., and Gary D. Carnegie. 2007. "Budgetary Earmarking and the Control of the Extravagant Woman in Australia, 1850–1920." *Critical Perspectives on Accounting* 18: 233–61.

Walser, Andreas Victor. 2015. "The Finances of the Cities of Asia Minor." *Topoi* 20: 411–33.

Webb, Pamela A. 1996. *Hellenistic Architectural Sculpture: Figural Motifs in Western Anatolia and the Aegean Islands*. Madison: University of Wisconsin Press.

Weiskopf, Michael. 1989. *The So-Called "Great Satraps' Revolt," 366–360 B.C.: Concerning Local Instability in the Achaemenid Far West*. Stuttgart: Franz Steiner.

Wells, Martin Gregory. 2012. "A Cosmopolitan Village: The Hellenistic Settlement at Gordion." PhD Dissertation, University of Minnesota.

West, David. 1976. "Review of A. Setaioli 'Il Proemio dei carmina Oraziani' Florence 1973." *Latomus* 35: 618.

Westermark, Ulla. 1960. *Das Bildnis des Philetairos von Pergamon: Corpus der Münzprägung*. Stockholm: Almqvist & Wiksell.

Whitley, James. 2001. *The Archaeology of Ancient Greece*. Cambridge: Cambridge University Press.

Wiegand, Theodor. 1904. "Reisen in Mysien." *Mitteilungen des Deutschen Archäologischen Instituts, Athenische Abteilung* 39: 254–339.

———. 1911. *Siebenter vorläufiger Bericht über Ausgrabungen in Milet und Didyma*. Berlin: Akademie der Wissenschaften.

Wilhelm, Adolf. 1943. *Griechische Königsbriege*. Leipzig: Scientia Verlag.

Will, Édouard. 1962. "Les premières années du règne d'Antiochos III (223–219 av. J.-C.)." *Revue des Études Grecques* 75: 72–129.

Willet, Rinse. 2020. *The Geography of Urbanism in Roman Asia Minor*. Sheffield: Equinox Publishing.

Williamson, Christina. 2016. "Mountain, Myth, and Territory: Teuthrania as Focal Point in the Landscape of Pergamon." In *Valuing Landscape in Classical Antiquity: Natural Environment and Cultural Imagination*, edited by Jeremy McInerney and Ineke Sluiter, 70–99. Leiden: Brill.

Winter, F. E. 1966. "Notes on Military Architecture in the Termessos Region." *American Journal of Archaeology* 70: 127–37.

———. 1971. "Addendum to AJA 70 (1966) 127–37: Notes on Military Architecture in the Termessos Region." *American Journal of Archaeology* 75: 190–91.

———. 1985. "Notes on Neandria." *American Journal of Archaeology* 89: 680–83.

Wörrle, Michael. 1979. "Epigraphische Forschungen zur Geschichte Lykiens III: Ein hellenistischer Königsbrief aus Telmessos." *Chiron* 9: 83–111.

———. 1988. "Inschriften von Herakleia am Latmos I: Antiochos III, Zeuxis und Herakleia." *Chiron* 18: 421–76.

———. 2007. "Zum Rang und Bedeutung von Gymnasion und Gymnasiarchie im hellenistischen Pergamon." *Chiron* 37: 501–16.

———. 2009. "Neue Inschriftenfunde aus Aizanoi V: Aizanoi and Rom I." *Chiron* 39: 409–44.

Wroth, Warwick. 1882. "Asklepios and the Coins of Pergamon." *Numismatic Chronicle* 2: 1–51.

Wulf-Rheidt, Ulrike. 1994. "Der Stadtplan von Pergamon: Zu Entwicklung und Stadtstruktur von der Neugründung unter Philetairos bis in spätantike Zeit." *Istanbuler Mitteilungen* 44: 135–75.

Yarrow, Liv. 2006. "Lucius Mummius and the Spoils of Corinth." *Scripta Classica Israelica* 25: 57–70.

Yaşar, Ersoy, and Elif Koparal. 2008. "Klazomenai Khorası ve Teos Suriçi Yerleşim Yüzey Araştırması 2006 Yılı Çalışmaları." *Araştırma Sonuçları Toplantısı* 25: 47–70.

Yedidağ, Turgut Yaşar. 2015. "Dorylaion Kalıp Yapımı Kaseleri." *Olba* 23: 235–72.

Yegül, Fikret K. 2010. *Bathing in the Roman World*. Cambridge: Cambridge University Press.

Yıldırım, Sahin. 2016. "The Emergence and the Development of Tumuli in Eastern Thrace." In *Tumulus as Sema: Space, Politics, Culture and Religion in the First Millennium BC*, edited by Olivier Henry and Ute Kelp, 359–70. Berlin: De Gruyter.

Zelizer, Viviana A. 1997. *The Social Meaning of Money: Pin Money, Paychecks, Poor Relief, and Other Currencies*. Princeton, NJ: Princeton University Press.

1989. "The Social Meaning of Money: 'Special Monies.'" *American Journal of Sociology* 95: 342–77.

Ziebarth, Erich. 1896. *Das griechische Vereinswesen*. Leipzig: S. Hirzel.

Ziesmann, Sonja. 2005. *Autonomie und Münzprägung in Griechenland und Kleinasien in der Zeit Philipps II. und Alexanders des Grossen*. Trier: Wissenschaftlicher Verlag Trier.

Index Locorum

Literary Texts

Aeneas Tacticus
  29.5: 116n143
Aeschylus
  Pers.
  49–52: 212
Anth. Pal.
  6.342: 352n278
Apollodorus
  Bibl.
  3.152: 214n102
Appian
  B Civ.
  4.1.4: 74
  Syr.
  32: 218n113, 316n133
Aristotle
  [*Ath. Pol.*]
  51.3–4: 86n41
  Eth. Eud.
  1241b: 271n201
  Eth. Nic.
  1160a: 271n201
  [*Oec.*]
  2.1.5: 98–100n84
  2.4: 77–8n10, 84n29, 116
  Pol.
  1.3.1257a31–42: 40
  1321b: 243n40
  1330b: 309n110
  Rh.
  1372b31: 216–17n109
Arrian
  Anab.
  1.11.12: 297n64
  7.9.6: 10–11n25
Athenaios
  5.207d: 259n135
  15.672a–673d: 205–6n65
  15.697d: 190–2n14

Augustine
  De civ. D.
  3.11: 362n12
BNJ
  124 F 54: 182n204
  455: 296n59
Caesar
  BCiv.
  2.32.2: 95–6n76
Cato the Elder
  fr. 95 b: 183
Cicero
  Amic.
  11.37: 288n24
  Deiot.
  19: 30n103
  Har. resp.
  28: 325n170
  Leg. Agr.
  2.50: 126n183
  Nat. D.
  3.58: 286n14
  Q.Fr.
  1.1.17: 152
  1.1.33: 159n111
De exil.
  600 E: 288n20
Demosthenes
  18.72 = Sim. Fr.37 West: 216–17n109
  On the Chersonese
  25: 11n28
Diodorus Siculus
  3.59.8: 328n180
  5.88.5–8: 258n129, 265n165
  12.75.7: 261
  18.46–47: 269n189
  21.12: 316n131
  26.8.1: 258n129, 265n165
  29.17: 248
  31.14: 26n79, 323–5n164, 357
  32.15: 28–9n94
  34.3: 29–30n99

Diogenes Laertes
   4.6.31: 288n23
   5.67: 290n34
   5.83–84: 293n44
Etymologicum Magnum
   p. 233: 205–6n65
Eustathius
   Ad Dionysium Periegetam
      322: 215n107
FGrHist
   45: 319n145
   244 F 77: 125
   434 F 1 11.2: 316–17n134
   434 F 9: 15–17n45
   740 F 14: 321n152
   2013 F 6: 293n45
   2013 F 31a: 293n45
   2013 F 41: 293–4n47
   2013 F 61: 295n52
   2013 T 3: 293n45
Galen
   De Simp. Med.
      XII 229 line 16 – 230 line 5: 183
Hell. Oxy.
   16.1: 216–17n109
   21.1: 217n111
Heraklides Lembos
   37: 184n212
Herodotus
   1.149: 285n9
   1.151.1: 188n3
   3.89–95: 9n17
   7.73: 300n74
Homer
   Il.
      2.816–77: 293
      2.858: 214n100
      5.160: 214n102
      17.494: 214n102
      17.534: 214n102
Scholia on Homer
   Od.
      11.520: 294n49
Horace
   Carm.
      1.1: 32–3
Josephus
   AJ
      12.4.1–11: 96–7n79
      12.138–44: 116n143
      12.142: 117n151
      12.147–152: 198n35, 218n113
      12.151: 62n81
      12.181: 79n13
      13.49: 86n38
Justin
   Epit.
      12.5.1: 326n172
      36.4.1–5: 29–30n99
Livy
   31.14.2: 186–7n223
   31.26.9–13: 21n68
   37.46.3–4: 140n36
   37.56.2: 159n113
   37.58.3–5: 140n36
   37.59.3–6: 140n36
   38.12.6: 22
   38.13.3: 35n2, 364
   38.16: 315n128
   38.16.4: 318n141
   38.16.14: 19
   38.17.9: 325n170
   38.38.14: 179n192
   38.39.15–16: 189n7
   38.84.4–5: 22–4n72
   39.7.1–2, 5: 140n36
   42.67.4: 35n2, 364
   44.14.3–4: 89n56
   45.18: 186–7n223
   45.20: 126–7n186
Lycophron
   Alex.
      205–15: 211n79
      1245–49: 211n79
1 Macc.
   10:34: 117n151
2 Macc.
   4:41: 234
   5:24: 218n113
   6:1: 226n149
Pausanias
   1.4.5–6: 320n148
   1.8.1: 320n148
   1.25.2: 19n58
   7.16.8: 28–9
   8.4.3: 334n206
   10.4.1: 243n41
   10.15.3: 320n147
   10.20: 315–16n129
   10.32.3: 334n206
Pliny the Elder
   HN
      13.70: 26
      33.15.51: 181
      35.72: 241n32
Plutarch
   Alc.
      15.3: 261n150

Sol.
  15.2: 78n11
Ti. Gracch.
  20: 288n24
Polyaenus
  Strat.
  4.8.1: 187n225
Polybius
  2.37.8–11: 127
  3.3.5: 318–19n143
  4.37.8–10: 178
  4.45.1–53.1: 178
  4.47.1: 98–100n84
  4.49.3: 21n57
  4.52.5: 98–100n84
  5.76.2: 342n238
  5.76.7: 218n113
  5.77–78: 20n62, 196n24, 210n76, 223n140
  5.88.5–8: 265n165
  5.111.7: 319n144
  16.1.5–6: 21, 348–9n263
  16.6.6: 359
  18.16.1–2: 47n34
  18.41.7: 314n126
  18.41.7–8: 19
  21.43.5–6: 22–4n72
  21.43.19: 180
  21.43.20–21: 179n192
  21.45.1: 64–5
  21.45.6: 65
  21.45.10: 189n7
  21.46.2–3: 78
  21.46.10: 144–5, 241n32
  22.7–8: 248
  22.8.1–2: 248
  22.8.6: 248–9
  22.20.1–8: 25n76
  25.4.4: 103–5n101
  27.9.12: 292n40
  28.20.11: 291n37
  30.1–3: 126–7n186
  30.5.11–16: 159n111
  30.6.6: 183
  30.21: 159n111
  30.24: 159n111
  30.31.7: 103
  31.5.5: 159n111
  31.6.6: 236
  31.31: 248
  31.31.1: 249
  32.8.3: 21
  32.8.5: 12–13n36, 25, 189–90n9, 243, 247–8n66, 282
  33.6: 28n90
  33.6.6: 28
Pompeius Trogus
  Prol.
  25: 316n132
SH
  958: 316n130
Sophocles
  Aj.
  721: 216
Steph. Byz.
  ε 63 Billerbeck: 125
Strabo
  4.3.2: 98–100n84
  12.3.39: 329n185
  12.4.3: 190n10
  12.4.7: 250–1n86
  12.4.10: 215n107
  12.5.1: 320–1n151, 326n173
  12.5.3: 123, 206–7n68, 328–9n184, 329n184, 329n185, 329n187
  12.7.3: 106
  12.8.5: 122–3
  12.8.18: 241n30
  13.1.2: 294n49
  13.1.4: 65
  13.1.14: 53n55, 138–9n30
  13.1.27: 319n145
  13.1.43: 293n43
  13.1.45: 182
  13.1.54: 113–14
  13.1.57: 329n185
  13.1.58: 233n176
  13.3.2: 101n90
  13.3.5: 124
  13.4.1: 188n5
  13.4.1–2: 14–15n43
  13.4.2: 26n82, 189n6, 229n160, 287n16
  13.4.10: 232–3n175
  13.4.11: 213n90
  13.4.17: 351n275
  13.56.1: 182n205
  13.126: 319n145
  14.1.24: 94–5n71, 124
  14.1.26: 94
  14.1.39: 94–5n71, 351–2n277
  14.2.3: 159n111
  14.2.29: 157
  14.3.9: 119
  14.4.1: 9n16, 233n178
  14.5.28: 182
Suda
  s.v. ἀργόλαι (A3781): 138n28
  s.v. Ἀριστοφάνης (A3933): 26n81

Suda (cont.)
   s.v. Ἀριστώνυμος (A3936) 26n81
   s.v. Ἄτταλος (A4316): 318n139
   s.v. βασιλεία (B147): 362–3
   s.v. βασιλεία (B148): 363
   s.v. Κράτης (K2342): 26n81
   s.v. Παιδοπολίτης (Π866): 326n174
   s.v. Πολέμων (Π1888): 289n28
Tertullian
  De ieiunio adversus psychicos
   294: 9
Thucydides
   2.13.3: 10–11n25
   5.67.2: 261
   7.28.4: 115n138
Vitruvius
  De arch.
   2.8.9: 241n32
   7.5.5: 157n103, 241n31
Xenophon
  An.
   2.5.13: 217n112
   7.8.8: 285n9
   7.8–24: 188n2
Zosimus
   2.37.12–14: 319n146

Papyri and Inscriptions

AA 22 (1907)
   129: 218–19n116
Austin 2006
   no. 84: 8–9n13
   no. 123 = *Syll.*³ 525: 166–7n145
   no. 125: 172n163
   no. 235: 34n1
   no. 236: 79–80n16
   no. 244 = *RC* 61: 28n91
   no. 405: 19–20n60
BCH 13 (1889)
   334: 98–100n84
Bringmann et al. 1995
   no. 17 [E]: 276–7n218
   no. 88 [E]: 236–7n12, 237n12, 237n13
   no. 106 [E]: 248n67
   no. 189 [E] = *I.Delos* 1580: 272n204
   nos. 225–29 [E]: 259n137
   no. 230 [E]: 367
   no. 231 [E] = Maier 1959–61, no. 51: 282n233
   no. 241 [E]: 237n13, 251n87, 275–6n213
   no. 253 [E]: 332n195
   no. 262 [E]: 366
   no. 262a [E] line 47: 258n128
   no. 266 [E]: 242n34
   no. 270 [E]: 253n97
   no. 283 [E 1]: 263n157
   no. 284 [E 2]: 263–4n160
   no. 286 [E]: 265n167, 276–7n218
   no. 298 [E]: 259n134
   no. 313 [E]: 243–4n46
   no. *357 [E]: 272n204
CID
   4 104: 36n4
CIG
   3538: 295n52
   3657 = Michel, *Recueil* 537: 267n178
CIIP
   IV 2 no. 3511: 72
CLA, 89–91, 116, 165–6n142
D1
   34n1, 35n2, 35–6n3, 35–6n3, 36n5, 43–4n28, 56, 364
D2
   Side A: 81, 84, 193–6n23, 196n23, 196n25, 201–2n50, 232n174, 317–18n138
   Side B: 56, 63n83, 72, 100n87, 103, 106n106, 193n19, 196n25, 200n45, 201n47
D3
   49, 84, 79n14, 141, 86n39
D4
   145n50
   Fragment D: 103
D5
   52, 82–108, 100n86, 112, 244n49
   Side A: 262
   Side B: 52–3, 262
D6
   10: 54, 56, 270
D7
   57, 366
D8
   28n92, 64, 79, 86, 109, 225–6n146, 226n147, 226n146, 227n152, 228n157
D9
   252, 257, 277
D10
   258n128, 269–70
D12
   79, 105–6
D13
   lines 16–17: 81–2
   lines 25–26: 86n39
   lines 25–27: 82
D14
   83

Text A: 87
Text B: 87
FD
   III.3 1325 = *ISE* 81: 213n94
Filges 2006
   321 no. 1 = *SEG* XLVI 149: 350n272
I.Adramytteion
   3: 204–5n63
I.Delos
   399: 70
   1443: 134n15
   1580 = Bringmann et al. 1995 no. 189 [E]: 272n204
   1603: 345n248
   2580: 271
I.Didyma
   488: 67–8
I.Ephesos
   1: 94
   201 = SEG XXVI 1238: 97
   3407: 52
   3408: 52
   3601: 115n141
I.Erythrai
   112: 66n91
   503, 27–28: 87n44
IG
   II 594: 276–7n218
   II^2
      682: 267
      686 + 687: 243
      687: 296n59
      835: 100n85
      836: 276
      1035: 100n85
      1039: 272n204
      1289: 42–3n25
      9977: 232n174
   IX 1^2 1
      60: 213n94
      179: 229n161
   XI 4
      1109: 345–6n250
      1206–8: 211n81
   XII 3 327: 237–8n16, 254n108
   XII 4 1 281: 270n197, 367
   XII 5 817: 173–4n171
   XII 7 515: 276–7, 276n215
   XII 9 324 = *Syll.*^{3} 714: 276n215
   XII Suppl. 250: 367
   XIV 422: 251n89
IGR
   4.915, a: 158n107

I.Histriae
   59: 279n225
I.Iasos
   3: 110
   23: 252n94, 252n93
I.Iznik
   1260: 86n40
I.Kyme
   12: 60n74
   27: 112
I.Kyzikos II
   20: 200–1n46
   23: 210n75
   28: 210n76
   29: 210n75
I.Laodikeia
   1: 187n15
I.Magnesia
   8: 103n99
   16: 352n278
   91: 98–100n84
   269: 86n40
I.Metropolis
   1 (**D5**): 52, 97, 100n86, 112, 244n49, 365
I.Milet
   54: 98–100n84
   307: 263, 264n163
   1039: 263n157
   1040: 264n163
I.Mysia (und Troas)
   1137–38: 87n44
I.Oropos
   294: 267n178
I.Pergamon
   1: 349–50n268
   9: 241
   11: 285–6n13
   15: 18n52
   20 = *OGIS* 269: 19n59
   24 = *OGIS* 276: 19n58
   48–49: 290
   138: 86n40
   152: 101
   152–55: 101
   156: 284n4, 349n265
   157: 50–1n49, 365
   158: 368
   167: 72n105
   167 = *OGIS* 299: 230n163
   176a: 226–7n150
   183: 86n40
   224: 106, 108, 108–9n115
   230: 82–3n23
   245: 188n5

I.Pergamon (cont.)
  246: 70, 111n125
  247: 162–3n129
  249: 114–15n137, 118
  251: 162–3n129
  252: 264n163
  613: 188n1
I.Pessinous
  1: 207n71, 329n186, 331n193
  1–7: 206n67
I.Priene
  17: 321–2n155
  111: 95n74
  111 = ISE 182: 93, 95n74
  114: 253n100
I.Prusa 1001 (**D1**)
  34n1, 35–6n3, 35n2, 35–6n3, 36n5, 43–4n28, 56, 364
I.Sardis
  1: 80–1n18, 81, 86n39, 190–2n14, 192n14, 192n16
  2: 103, 110–11, 145n50
Iscr.Cos.
  ED 45: 367
ISE
  81 = FD III.3 1325: 213n94
  149: 258n129
  182 = I.Priene 111: 93, 95n74
  196: 366
I.Sestos
  1 = OGIS 339: 101, 126, 148, 169n155, 176, 279n227, 279
I.Smyrna
  I 215: 269n190
I.Sultan Daği
  393: 366
I.Thespiai
  58–61: 47n33
I.Tralleis
  32: 86–7
  107 = Syll.^{3} 671: 241n30
Keil and Premerstein, *Bericht über eine Reise*
  nos. 204 and 205: 112–13n132
LSCG
  165: 367
Maier 1959–61
  no. 51 = Bringmann et al. 1995 no. 231 [E]: 282n233
  no. 76: 197–8n31, 365
MAMA
  IV 75: 200n42
  VI 173: 365

MDAI(A)
  9 (1884) 56–60: 87n44
  16 (1891) 292–93: 119n160
  32 (1907)
    257, 8: 258n125
    415–69: 208–9n73
    416–20: 279n226
    428: 210n77
    435: 210n77
    443: 210n77
    446: 210n77
    447: 210n77
  33 (1908)
    381–83, no. 3: 241n28
    384–400: 208–9n73
  35 (1908) 375, 1: 72n105
  35 (1910)
    416–36: 208–9n73
    419: 241n28
    425, 12: 101n90
  37 (1912), 294–96: 321n153
Michel, *Recueil*
  537 = CIG 3657: 267n178
  542: 221n129
  544: 274–5n211
Milet I 3
  145 = Syll.^{3} 577: 70, 263n158, 266–7n175, 274n209
  149: 71
ML
  45: 168
  69: 114
OGIS
  55 = TAM II 1: 96–7n79
  227: 199n37
  265: 50n45
  266: 18–19n56
  267: 18n51, 108–9n115
  269: 19n60, 19–20n60, 19n59, 314–15n127
  269 = I.Pergamon 20: 19n60, 19–20n60, 19n59, 314–15n127
  270: 27n86
  273–79: 19–20n60
  276: 19n58, 315
  276 = I.Pergamon 24: 19n58, 315
  276–79: 314–15n127
  299 = I.Pergamon 167: 230n163
  301: 124
  305: 25n77, 236n8
  308: 25n76
  310: 290n33
  311: 290n33

312: 290n33
323: 107
329: 62–3n82
330: 27–8n89, 101, 126n183, 214n96
332: 30n101, 280, 349n267
335: 18n54
339 = *I.Sestos* 1: 279
351: 28n90
445: 221n131
446: 214n101
484: 172, 174n176
515: 174n176
748: 88
751: 367
765: 317n136

OMS
  I
    120–23: 126n185
  II
    287–91: 163n131
    812–14: 247n65
  III
    290–91: 162n127

P.Cair.Zen.
  590036: 36n6
  I 59021: 165, 165n141

P.Rev
  73–78: 166n143

PSI
  4 406: 117n151

P.Tebt.
  3.2 894 Fr 5, r, 2: 66n91
  8: 96–7n79

RC
  3: 43n26, 66, 77n11, 226n148
  11: 190–2n14
  15: 85–6n37
  16 C: 192–3n17
  18: 190–2n14
  18 1–13: 190–2n14
  34: 188n5
  47: 83, 368
  48 (**D4**): 50, 145n50
  49: 230–1n166
  50: 230–1n166
  51: 195, 237, 368
    16–17: 81
  52: 25–6n78, 67, 69, 243–4n46, 263, 264n161, 266
  53: 57n63
  Fragment II A: 71n101
  54: 27n87, 367
  56: 330n190
  61 = Austin 2006 no. 244: 28n91
  67: 30n100
  68: 204n61
  69: 83–4n26, 204n60
  195–96: 50n47
  197: 50–1n48

Ritti et al. 2008
  no. 3: 115n140

RO
  22: 78n11
  81: 70

Robert, *Carie* II
  167: 65
  307: 66n88

SEG
  II 580: 57, 366
  II 663: 208–9n73
  IV 632: 71n101, 84n27, 102n96
  VI 576: 345n247
  IX 7: 30n102
  XII 511: 71n103, 71
  XIII 327: 100n85
  XVII 524 = *TAM* V 3 1425: 202n55
  XIX 867: 49
  XXIV 154 + XL 135: 119n161
  XXVI 139: 257–8n124
  XXVI 1238 = *I.Ephesos* 201: 52–3n54, 97, 101, 101n90
  XXVII 261: 257n123
  XXIX 1516: 79n14, 85, 116
  XXIX 1613: 190–2n14
  XXXI 1201: 117
  XXXII 1109: 108n114
  XXXII 1237: 84
  XXXIII 675: 280
  XXXIII 942: 242
  XXXIII 1034: 83n25, 193n18
  XXXIII 1039: 108n114
  XXXIV 1198: 222n133
  XXXVI 982A: 11–12n30
  XXXVI 1046: 246–7n62, 263–5, 265–6n169, 266–7
  XXXVII 849: 36n6
  XXXVII 859: 100–1n88, 103n99, 235
  XXXVII 923: 85–6n37
  XXXVII 1006: 106
  XXXVII 1010: 21–2n70, 218n113
  XXXVII 1186: 158–9n110
  XXXVIII 1476: 108
  XXXIX 1243: 43–4n28, 278–9n224
  XXXIX 1243 = *Claros* I, 11–62: 278–9n224

SEG (cont.)
  XXXIX 1244 = *Claros* I, 63–104: 260n144, 275, 278n222
  XXXIX 1283: 109–10n120, 235, 245n55
  XXXIX 1285: 36n6, 66–7n92, 235, 245n55
  XXXIX 1332: 365
  XL 1062: 103, 196n25
  XLI 649: 162
  XLI 1003: 78, 79n14
  XLIII 369: 257n121
  XLIII 371: 253n101
  XLIII 381: 66, 252n93, 255, 255n110
  XLIII 879: 200–1n46
  XLIV 949: 174n174
  XLIV 1108: 27n87, 62–3n82, 106n108, 118, 230n164
  XLV 447: 169–70n157
  XLV 1719: 333n204
  XLVI 149 = Filges 2006, 321 no. 1: 350n272
  XLVI 717: 257n121
  XLVI 1434: 102, 163–4n133, 241–2n33
  XLVI 1519: 83
  XLVI 1721: 250n81, 258n125, 270n195
  XLVII 1218: 252–71
  XLVII 1601: 118
  XLVII 1745: 62, 80n17, 366
  XLVIII 1404: 101n91
  XLVIII 1532: 114–15n137, 118, 228–9n158
  XLIX 875: 124–5n178
  XLIX 1540: 238n17, 247n65, 276n216
  L 1195: 59–61, 98, 188n5
  L 1211: 260n140
  LII 132: 42–3n25
  LII 1197: 102
  LIII 1312: 365
  LIII 1342: 238n17
  LIII 1706: 105
  LIV 1101: 275n212
  LIV 1229: 60n74
  LIV 1230: 60n74, 60n71
  LIV 1473: 71n103
  LV 1300: 84n27
  LV 1401: 368
  LVI 190: 243n44
  LVI 193: 267–8n180
  LVI 1721: 252n92
  LVII 1109: 159n113, 244n50
  LVII 1150: 364
  LXII 1489: 71n103
  LXIV 1296: 368

SGDI
  II 2086: 55

Staatsverträge
  III 456: 200n42, 215n107

Syll.[3]
  57: 71
  218: 165n141, 168
  233: 259
  270: 72n105
  524: 72–3
  525 = Austin 2006 no. 123: 166–7n145, 174n175
  529: 267
  577 = *Milet* I 3 145: 70, 263n158, 266–7n175, 274n209
  578: 274n209
  585: 289n27
  629: 230n165
  630: 230n165
  633: 95, 113–14n134, 116–17
  670: 27n86
  671 = *I.Tralleis* 107: 26–7n84, 37–9n10, 58, 241n30
  672: 26–7n84, 37–9n10, 58–9, 70
  714 = *IG* XII 9 324: 276n215
  1028: 367

TAM
  II 1 = *OGIS* 55: 96–7n79
  III 1 2: 113n133, 344n244
  III 1 14: 118
  V 1 211 = *TAM* V 3 1423: 202n51
  V 1 444 = Herrmann 1962, 60 (no. 57): 214n103
  V 1 609: 199n39
  V 1 689: 221–2n132
  V 1 690: 221–2n132
  V 2 959: 199n38
  V 2 1187: 232n172
  V 2 1321: 335n212
  V 3 1423 = *TAM* V 1 211: 202n51, 232n174
  V 3 1425 = *SEG* XVII 524: 202n55
  V 3 1429: 232n174
  V 3 1669: 232n174

Tebtunis Papyri
  3.2 894 Fr5, r, 2: 66n90

Subject Index

Page numbers in *italics* indicate figures; "n" indicates notes; "g" indicates graphs.

Achaeans, 248-9
Achaios, 19, 192n15, 222-3
Achilles, tomb of, 297-8
acropolis, 306-13, *307*, *309*
actors' guilds (*technitai*), 57, 171, 366
Adada, 113-14, 336, 339, 344
Adaios of Amphipolis, 253
Adobogiona, 321
Adramyttion, 106
Aegina, 289-90
Aelius Herodianus, 125
Aemilius Lepidus Paullus, L., 154
Aeschylus, on Mysians, 212
Afyonkarahisar hoard, 167-8
Agesilaus, 216
agio. See exchange
agoras
    Athens, 295, *308-9*
    Pergamon, 240, 247, 273n206, 281
    Pisidian, 27, 338-40
    Sikyon, *272-3*
    Xanthos, 309
agriculture, and the *katoikiai*, 195-8
Ahmetbeyli hoard, 167, 186
Aigai, 112-13, 233
Aigiale, and Critilaos, 276-7
Aigosages, 223, 319, 321
Aioiorix, 330
Aizanoi, sanctuary of Zeus, 325, 331-6, 341, 359
Alabanda, coinage, 141, 159-60
Alassos, 118
Alexander
    burial, 299
    and the Pisidians, 119
    and snakes, 138
    and the tomb of Achilles, 297
Alexander Balas, 28
Alexanders (coins), 131-3, 145, 184-5n213
    earmarked for Delphi's teachers, 58
Allen, R. E., 22, 346, 354

Amlada
    letter (**D12**), 79, 103, 105-6, 367-8
    taxation of, 104-6
Ammianus Marcellinus, 327-8
Amphipolis, 257n121, 257n122, 261
Amyzon, sanctuary of Artemis, 313
Anaitis-Artemis, sanctuary, 204
anarchy, monetary, 163
Anatolia, *3-4*, 359-60
Andros, decree (**D9**), 252, 257, 277, 279, 367
Antalya (Attaleia), 123, 190, 233
Antigonos Gonatas, 313
Antigonos Monophthalmos, 42-3, 77n9, 115n141, 226n148, 328
Antikythera hoard, 168
Antioch, 340-1, 344-5
Antiochis, 19
Antiochos Hierax, 19, 319n145
Antiochos I (Soter), 18, 234-5n4, 299, 316
Antiochos II, 18
Antiochos III Megas, 19-22, 62n81
    decree of Teos, 78
    and Jewish settlers, 218
    letter to Telmessos, 85
    and Sardis, 235, 251
Antiochos IV, 25, 218, 265
    and Naukratis, 291
    and Sardis gymnasium, 235
    sends Geron to Jerusalem, 226-7
Antony, Mark, 74-6, 104
Apameia
    coinage, 147, 151
    as *emporion*, 122-3
    and Kephisodoros, 54-6
    and the sanctuary of Cybele Agdistis, 206
    Treaty of, 78
Apatourios of Alabanda, 157n103
Aperghis, G. G., 97, 102-3
Apollo, sanctuary at Didyma, 68-9
Apollo Chresterios, 113, 188n4

Apollo Tarsenos, letter from Attalos II (**D14**), 83, 87–8, 204, 368
Apollodoros of Athens, 125
Apollonia ("in Pisidia"/in Phrygia Paroreios), 231–2
Apollonia-on-the-Rhyndakos, 35n2, 150–1n79, 200, 219
Apollonia Salbake, and Pamphilos, 65–7
Apollonidas of Sikyon, 248–9, 280
Apollonios, 97–101
    earmark for Metropolis (**D5**), 52–3, 262, 365
Apollonioucharax, 193
    D2, 44–51, 81, 84, 201, 317
    tax collection, 103
Appian, speech of Mark Antony, 74
Arafat Tepesi, 304
Argos, coup, 261
Ariarathes IV of Cappadocia, 24, 280
Ariarathes V, 27–8
Aribazos, letter from Attalos II (**D15**), 206–7, 368–9
Aristo, 287–8
Aristokles of Tralles, *154–5*, 154–5
Aristomachos (boxer), 291–2
Aristonikos, 4, 30, 197
Aristophanes, *Acharnians*, 216
Aristophanes of Byzantium, 26
Aristotle
    on the acropolis, 309n110
    on associations, 271
    on coinage, 40
    on the gymnasium, 243
Arkesilaos of Pitane, 288
army, and the gymnasia, 245, 247
Arsinoe II, 184
Artemidoros, 105
    letter from Eumenes II, 141–2, 365
Artemidoros of Ephesus, 157
Artemis
    Brauronia (Athens), 295
    coinage, 147
    Ephesia, 94–5
    sanctuary in Amyzon, 313
    sanctuary of Anaitis-, 204
    in Tauris, 342
    temple at Sardis, 192
    temples at Termessos, 341
Arykanda, 311, *312–13*
Ashton, Richard, 141–2
Asia, 285–6, 293
"Asia Minor" hoards, 167
Asklepides, 238, 247n65, 276

Asklepios, 70–1, 138, 241n27
associations, 362
    the Artists of Dionysus, 57, 142, 171, 366
    gymnasia as, 268–74
    maritime traders, 271
    presbyteroi, 281
Astyoche, 294
Ata (god), 333, 335
Athena, sanctuary at Pergamon, 314
Athena Magarsia, coin, 347–8, *348*
Athena Nikephoros, 29, 346, 350
    tetradrachms, 142, *143–4*, 347, *348*
Athena Parthenos, coin, 347
Athena Polias, 308, 349
Athenaios (Attalid prince), 28, 237, 250, 260
    decree of Colophon **D10**, 269–70
Athens, Acropolis, 308, *308–9*
    Gymnasium of Ptolemy, 276, 281–2n232
    harbor tax, 115
    Little Barbarians sculptures, 21, 286, 296
    Parthenon, 295–7
    sanctuary of Artemis Brauronia, 295
Attaleia (Antalya), 123, 190, 233
Attaleia (festival), 58
Attalos I, 19–21
    and Aizanoi, 333–4
    appointment of judge in Aeolis, 190–2n14
    and cult of Idaean Cybele, 296
    and Epictetus, 330–1
    and the Galatians, 314–15
    on his kingdom, 188
    Lakydeion, 290
    as land-distributor, 196
    and Magna Mater, 360
    and the Nikephorion, 348–9n263
    and Pessinous, 330–2
    and the Pisidians, 337
    purchase of land in Sikyon, 47
    and sanctuary of Zeus at Aizanoi, 325
    and the stoa in Delos, 345
    Teuthrania Monument, 211–12
    War with Achaios, 222–3
Attalos II Philadelphos, 25–9
    altar, 52
    and Attaleia, 123
    dossier **D14**, 83, 87–8, 204, 368
    education of Attalos III, 242
    and funds for Delphi, 70
    letter to Aribazos (**D15**), 206–7, 368–9
    letter to Amlada (**D12**), 367–8

Attalos III Philometer Euergetes, 5, 29–30, 204, 242
  letter to Hiera Kome, 83–4n26
  procession for, 280
  ruler cult, 70–1
  taxation, 91
  and temple villages, 204
Attic-weight silver coinage, 131, 142–7, *143–4*,
  143–5, *143*, *144–5*
Attis (priest of Cybele), 28, 330–1
Auge, 1, *138–9*
Augustus, 119, 207–8n72

Ballıhisar, 206–7
banquets, 275–80
Barsine, 15–17, 307, 349
basileia (monarchy), 355, 361–3
Bauslaugh, Robert, 111–12, 139n32, 177n184,
  179–80
Beroia Law, gymnasium, 252, 254–7, 260–1,
  274, 274n209
Biçerova tumulus, 306
Bisanthe, 124–5
Bithynia, 125
  coins, 161
Blaundos, 150, 325n169, 350
Blossius of Cumae, 288n24
Boscoreale Frescoes, 317
boundaries
  boundary guards (*orophylakes*), 116–17
  and civic fiscality, 112
Brélaz, Cédric, 116–18
Bremen, Riet van, 250, 261, 270
Brennos of Toriaion, 64, 67, 225, 313
Bringmann, Klaus, 236–7
bronze coinage, 172–3
bulls, and Tralles, 147, 162, 171
burials, 297–306, *298–9*, *303–4*. *See also*
      gravestones
    Gördes chamber tomb, 222
    Seleukos I Nikator, 299–300
    tomb of Achilles, 297–8
    Tomb of the Erotes, 305
    Yığma Tepe tomb, 298–9, *298–9*, 301, 306
Büyükçekmece hoard, 178n190
Byzantium, 125, 169–70n157, 170, 177–8

Cahill, Nicholas, 310–11
calendars, Kos festival (**D11**), 270, 367
Callataÿ, François de, 153, 185
Çan Sarcophagus, 216–17, *217–18*
Cato the Elder, 183
Cavafy, C. P., "In a Large Greek Colony"
      (poem), 4–6

Celts. *See* Galatians
centralization, 122–7
  of coinage, *134–5*, 149–52, *152*
Chalcedon, 170, 177–8
chamber tomb, Gördes, 222
"chameleon kings," 285
Chandezon, Christophe, 87–8
Chankowski, Andrzej, 116, 245–6, 257
Chankowski, Véronique, 76–7, 111
Chersonese, 126
Chiliomodi hoard, 184–5n213
Chios, gymnasium, 282
Chremonides, decree, 243, 296n59
Chromis/Chromios, 214
Chrysippus, 288
cista mystica, *134–5*, 134
cistophori, 129–31, 134–40, *134–5*, *135–6*, *135*,
  147–9
  Attic-weight, 142–7, *143–4*, *143–5*, *143*,
    144–5
  dating, 140–2
  Tralles, 152–63, *154–5*
cistophoric system, 40–1n17, 130–1, 169–77,
  356, 358
  and centralization, *134–5*, 149–52, *152*
  as closed, 163–9
  coins, 188–133, 131–40
  coordinated coinage, 173–7
citizenship
  granting, 267
  and the gymnasium, 249–50, 260–1, 274–9
  and the polis, 227–8, 230
  and taxation, 11, 127
  and towns, 193–203
civic fiscality, 111–13
Claros, inscription, 275
Classics, 7–8
Claudius Pulcher, C., 154, *154–5*
cleruchs, letter to (**D13**), 81–2, 86n39, 368
closure/closed currency systems, Ptolemaic, 163–9
Cohen, Getzel, 202
Coinage Decree, 168, 172
Colophon
  honorific decree D10, 237, 258, 260,
    269–70, 367
  and Menippos, 277–9
cooperative coinage, 175–7
Corcyra, 184–5
countermarks, 132–3, *133–4*, 171–2, 177–80
  and Toriaion, 62n80
coup, Argos, 261
Crates of Mallos, 26, 287–8
Critilaos, 276–7

Curty, Olivier, 253, 281–2
customs (taxes), 87–92
customs houses, 2, 92, 115–16
    Kyme, 60
    of Philetairos, 88
Customs Law of Asia (CLA), 88, 127
Cybele
    Agdistis (sanctuary) at Pessinous, 20, 205–9, 327, 359
    cult at Aizanoi, 331
Cyzicus, 88, 177–8, 352n278

Daphitas, 351
Daubner, Frank, 196
decentralization, 12, 131, 163
decrees
    Andros (**D9**), 252, 257, 277, 279, 367
    of Apameia for Kephisodoros (**D6**), 54–6, 270–1, 365–6
    Chremonides, 243, 296n59
    Colophon (**D10**), 237, 258, 260, 269–70, 367
    for Eirenias, 263
    Korragos (**D1**), 34–5, 38–40, 43, 56, 101, 112, 250, 355, 364
    sanctuary of Apollo at Didyma, 67–9
    of Sestos, 279
    of Telmessos, 24, 305
Deiotarus the Younger, 304
Delos
    Base of Philetairos, 320
    embassy from Pisidia, 345
    gymnasium, 251, 271
    Teuthrania Monument, 211–12
Delphi
    and Attalos I, 20
    endowments, 57–9
    sacred earmarking, 70
    wages for teachers, 258–9
Demeter, 142–4, 290
Demetrios I, 28
Demetrios Poliorketes, 184
Demetrios of Skepsis, 190–2n14, 292–5
    Trojan Catalogue, 293–4
Demosthenes, on Mysia, 216
denarii, 136
Didyma, sanctuary of Apollo, 236
Dignas, Beate, 70
Diodorus Siculus
    on Attalos III, 29
    on Eumenes II and the Galatians, 323
    on the Galatians, 25–6
    on Pessinous, 327–8
    on the wealth of Eumenes II, 357

Diogenes the Cynic, 287
Diogenes Laertes, 292–3
Dionysoupolis, 150, 204–5, 325
Dionysus, 205
    Kathegemon, 136–7, 205
Doidalses, son of Apollonios, 208–9, 209–11
dokimasia, 267–8
Dreyer, Boris, 98, 112, 242
Droysen, Johann, 7
Duyrat, Frédérique, 111
Düzen Tepe, 336, 338
Dyme, 267

earmarking, 36–40, 37–8g, 179–80, 356, 358. See also Toriaion, Dossier (**D8**)
    brokering, 51–9
    and institutions, 59–69
    meanings, 69–73
    Philetairos and Thespiai, 236–7
    private property sale, 44–51
    Sardis oil fund, 235
    as social process, 40–3
earthquakes, 265n165
    Strabo on, 232
Eirenias of Miletus, 67, 69, 262–8
Elaia, 18–19, 88, 306
Elephant Battle, 316n133
Elpinikos, 276
embassies
    and brokering earmarks, 51–3
    Pisidian to Delos, 345
    and Toriaion, 64
embezzlement, 9
empires, 5–6
    Neo-Assyrian Empire, 6
    Roman, 6
endowments, Delphi, 57–9
Engelmann, Helmut, 98, 112
Ephebic Law, 261
epheboi, 202, 246–7
D6, 55
Ephesus, 124, 306–7
    coinage, 133–4, *144–5*, 144–5, 151, *152*, 170, 184
    coinage imagery, 147
    Customs Law of Asia (CLA), 88
    gymnasium, 241–2
Epictetus, 20, 323–7, *324–5*, 330–1
    Aizanoi, 331–6
Epigenes, 345
Eposognatus, 325
Eratosthenes of Cyrene, 323–5
Eretria, Tomb of the Erote, 305

Eriza, 274
Erythrai, 184
ethnogenesis, Mysian, 123, 212, 220, 222
Eudemos of Miletus, 70
Eumeneia (festival), 58
Eumenes (brother of Philetairos), 15
Eumenes I, 14, 17–19
Eumenes II, 21–7, 187, 189, 223, 360–1
   and the Apameia earmark, 55–6
   coinage, *132*, 142, *143*, 165n134
   and Crates of Mallos, 286–7
   decree of Telmessos, 285–6
   Eirenias and Miletus, 262–8
   endowment for Eumeneia, 58
   and the Galatians, 323
   gift of grain to Rhodians, 248–9
   gymnasium, 237, 245, 250–1
   and Kardakon Kome (**D3**), 49, 84–5, 103, 105, 197–8, 365
   and the Korragos decree (**D1**), 35–6, 43
   letter to Artemidoros, 141–2, 365
   letter to the Tabênoi (?), 244
   letter to Telmessos, 85
   letter to Temnos (**D4**), 50, 103, 365
   letter to Toriaion (**D8**), 28n92, 62–4, 79–80, 109, 224–8, 254, 366
   and the Milesians, 67–9
   and the Nikephoria, 229–30, 348–50
   and the Peace of Apameia, 223
   and the Pergamon gymnasium, 236n10, 238–41, 281
   Polybius on, 21, 25, 189
   and Sulpicius, 234
   Taşkuyucak letter (**D2**), 44–51, 56, 201, 317, 364
   wealth of, 357–8
Euripides, and Telephos, 216
Eurypylos, 294
exchange, currency, 165–6, 168–70, 174
exedrae, 257

Fannius, C., 154
feasts. *See* banquets
festivals
   Attaleia, 58
   coins used at, 170–1
   Eumeneia, 58
   Hermaia kai Herakleia, 279
   Kos calendar (**D11**), 270, 367
   Little Panathenaia, 70
   Nikephoria, 24–5, 229–31, 346–7
   Panathenaia, 17, 308
   Panionia, 67–8
   Philetaireia, 47

First Macedonian War, 20
fiscal constitutions, 76–7
Flavius Josephus, 79n13, 198
fortifications, 117–22, 195
France, taxation, 109

Galatians, 33, 313–27, 352–3, 357–8
   burial practice, 304
   Diodorus Siculus on, 25–6
   incursion by, 105
Galen, on silver, 183
Gallograecia, 325–7
Gargara, 233
Gauthier, Philippe, 85, 250, 256, 276
Geron the Athenian, 226
gift exchange, 58, 68
Gigantomachy
   Great Altar (Pergamon), 24, 286, 342
   Melli, *343–4*, 343
   Termessos, 342
Gongylids, 15
Gordion (Phrygia), 301–2, 314, 322–3
Gordos, 221–2
gravestones. *See also* burials
   Menekrates, 214–15
   Xenokles, 218
Great Altar of Pergamon, 1–2, 26, 342
   Gigantomachy, 24
   and Telephos, 137
Great Dedication/Long Base, 314–15n127
Great Mother. *See* Cybele
Gresham's law, 164–5n137, 165
gymnasia, 236–48, *237–8g*, *239*, *239–41*, 356, 358
   adornment (*kosmêsis*), of 257–60
   architecture, *272–3*, 272–3
   as an association, 268–74
   as civic institution, 248–51
   financing, 251–7
   and new collectivities,, 274–82
   Sardis 234–6
   and social status, 260–8
gymnasiarchs, 252–7, 269
   Kephisodoros, 54–6
   Leontiades, 275
   Menas, 279
   Metrodoros, 270
Gymnasium of Ptolemy (Athens), 276, 281–2n232

Halikarnassos, 246, 252–3, 265, 312
Hannibal, 24
harbor tax, 115

head tax, 84–6, 104–5, 127
Hegesianax of Alexandria, 319n145
Hekatomnids, 312
Heliodoros Stele, 72
Hellenopolis, 125
Hera, 205–6n65, 321
Herakleia-under-Latmos, 109–10, 116, 235
Herakles, on coinage, 219–21
Herakles (son of Alexander), 15
Heraklides Lembos, 184n212
Hermaia, Salamis, 276–7n218
Herodes, 79–81, 102
Herodotus, 188, 285
Herrmann, Peter, 264–5, 267
Hiera Kome, 204
Hierapolis, 204–5, 302
Hieron II, 259
history, political, 14–30
hoards, 158, 161, 167, 323
    Afyonkarahisar, 167–8
    Ahmetbeyli, 167, 186
    Antikythera, 168
    "Asia Minor," **167**
    Büyükçekmece, 178n190
    Chiliomodi, 184–5n213
    Larissa (Sitochoro), 141n39, 166, 186–7n223
    Maaret-en-Nouman, 140
    Polatlı, 167
    Priene, 176n181
    Propontis, 177–8
    Şahnalı, 158–9
    Tell Kotchek, 178n188
Hofhaus am Athena-Tempel (Miletus), 263
Homer, 292–7
    Iliad, 214, 294
    Odyssey, 294
Horace, "Attalid offers," **32–3**

Iasos, 110, 252
iconography, coinage, 136–8, *138–9*
identity, and taxation, 11–12
Ilion, 292, 295–8, 319
Ilioupersis, Parthenon (Athens), 295–7
Ilyas Tepe tumulus, 298–9
indirect taxation, 76–7, 86–92, 115–16, 127–8
Ionian League, 25
I.Pessinous, 331
Iphigeneia, 342, 344

Jews, settlement, 198, 218
Jones, A. H. M., 111–12
Jones, C. P., 98–100

Jonnes, Lloyd, 80–1n18, 87n44, 112
Josephus, on Jewish colonists, 218
Julius Caesar, 74, 96
Justin, 29

Kabeiroi, 142–4
Kadoi, 189, 212–13
Kaikos River, battle, 315
Kaikos Valley, 15, *16–17*
Kale Tepesi, 224n144
Kardakon Kome, 104–6, 141, 197, 208–9n73, 365
    D3, 49, 84–5, 103, 197–8, 365
katoikiai, 193–9. *See also* Toriaion
Kayster region, 94, *99–100*
    mints, 220–1
    tax dispute, 97–101
Kennell, Nigel, 247
Kephisodoros, decree (**D6**), 54–6, 270–1, 365–6
Klearchos, 217
Kleiner, Fred, 111–12, 129, 148, 150–1, 153–4
    Early Cistophoric Coinage (*ECC*), 149–50, 152–3
Kleitomachos (boxer), 291–2
Kleonnaeion, 207–9
Kobedyle, 201–2
Korragos the Macedonian
    decree for (**D1**), 34–5, 38–40, 43, 56, 101, 112, 355, 364
    gymnasium, 237, 250
Korykos, 123
Kos, gymnasium, 270, 280, 367
Kosmetatou, Elizabeth, 136
Koteies, 244
Krateuas of Gambreion, 82
Kuttner, Ann, 285, 290
Kyme, 59–61, 184n212, 306
Kytenion, 108

Labraunda, 70
lagoons, 93–5
lakes, 94–5
Lakydeion, 290
Laodike III, decree of Teos, 78
Laodike IV, 265
laoi (the people), 191–3
Larissa (Sitochoro) hoard, 141n39, 166, 186–7n223
Le Rider, Georges, 129–30, 147–50, 184, 349
Lebedos, 42–3, 66, 77n9
Leonidas of Halikarnassos, 253
Leonnorios, 313
Leontiades, 275

Lewis, Bernard, *The Emergence of Modern Turkey*, 359–60
Library of Pergamon, 7–8, 286–97, 352
Little Barbarians (Athens), 21, 286, 296
Little Panathenaia (festival), 70
livestock
    coins used for, 170–1
    tax on, 87–8
Livy
    on Attalos I, 19
    on cistophori, 140
    on coinages, 186
    on the Galatians, 318, 325
    on Manlius Vulso, 22
Long Base/Great Dedication, 314–15n127
Loukopoulou, Louisa, 125–7
Luturios, 313
Lydia, 193–5, *194–5*, 302
Lysias (general), 19
Lysimachi, 15, 178
Lysimachus (king), 188, 319n145, 328, 356

Ma (goddess), 349
Maaret-en-Nouman hoard, 140
Macedonians
    burial practice, 300–1
    coinage, 186
Mackil, Emily, 175
Maeander Valley, 154–7, *156–7*
Magna Mater (Great Mother), 20, 206, 327, 360
Male Superior God, 335
Manius Aquilius, 89, 119–21n163
Manlius Vulso, 22–3, 64–5, 323, 325
Mann, Michael, *The Sources of Social Power*, 6–7
Marcellesi, Marie-Christine, 136, 140, 142n42, 162n127, 169n156
Marinescu, Constantin A., 177–8n186
maritime traders associations, 271
market buildings, 339–41
    Aigai, 233
    Melli, *340–1*
    Sagalassos, 337
Mater, 17, 20. *See also* Magna Mater
Mausolus, 312–13
Meadows, Andrew, 148
Meleager, and Sibloe, 47–50
Melli, market building, *340–1*
Menander, on the Mysians, 216
Menas, 148, 176, 279
Menekrates, gravestone of, 214–15

Menippos of Colophon, 258, 260, 275, 277–9
Menogenes (son of Menophanes), 226–7
Meris coinage, 130, 185, 186–7n223
Metellus, 28
Meter/Matar, 206, 327, 329, 332, 334–6, 347. *See also* Cybele; Demeter; Great Mother; Magna Mater; Mater
Metris (priestess of Athena Nikephoros), 230
Metrodoros, 270
Metropolis decree **D5**, 262, 365
    earmark for, 52–3
    decree for Metropolis, 108, 112
    gymnasium, 237
    tax dispute, 97–101
Miletus
    border guards, 116
    earmarking, 67–9
    gymnasium, 236, 262–8, 274n209, 276–7n218
Milyas, 119–20, *120–1*
mining, silver, 182–3
mints, 138–40
    centralization, 149–52, *152*
    Corcyra, 184–5
    Erythrai, 184
    Kyme, 184n212
    Mysia, 219–21, *220*
    Smyrna, 184
Mitchell, Lynette, 243
Mitchell, Stephen, 89, 121, 355
Mithridates I, 306, 321
Mithridates VI, 231, 304
Mithridatids, burial practice, 304
Mnesimachos, 80–1n18, 81–2
Mommsen, Theodor, 8–9, 356
monarchy (*basileia*), 355, 361–3
money, 40–2, 356–7. *See also* cistophoric system; taxation
    retariffing, 179
money-changers, 161
Mørkholm, Otto, 147–8n63, 149
Morzius of Paphlagonia, 24
Moschion of Priene, 278
Mount Ida, 294
Mousaios of Ephesus, *Perseis*, 296n59
Müller, Helmut, 102
Mummius, 29
municipal bronzes, 186
Mylasa, 70
Myrina, 170
Mysia/Mysians, 189n7, *194–5*, 195, 209–24
    coinage, 219–21, *220*
    in document of Eumenes II (**D2**), 44–6

Mysia/Mysians (cont.)
　mining, 182–3
　settlement, 232–3, 356
Myso-Makedones, 215–16

Nagy, Gregory, 7–8
naming practice
　Mysian, 215–16
　Pisidian, 344–5
Naukratis, and Antiochos IV, 291
negotiation, for taxation, 104–8, 128
Neleos of Skepsis, 292
Neo-Assyrian Empire, 6
neoi, and gymnasia, 270
Neoptolemos, son of Kressos, 317
New Fiscal History, 76, 127
New Institutional Economics (NIE), 13
New Style tetradrachms, 130, 145, 171–2, 185
Nicomedes I of Bithynia, 317
Nikanor, 202, 218
Nikatoreion, 299
Nikephoria (festival), 24–5, 229–31, 346–7
Nikephorion, 21, 229, 241n27, 348, 348–9n263
noncitizens, 274–9
　and the gymnasium, 268
Nymphis-Memnon, 316–17

oil
　earmarked in Toriaion, 63–4
　and gymnasia, 258
Olbasa, 114–15n137, 119, 228–31, 347
　decree, 62–3n82, 106, 118, 346
Olbia, 168, 173
Olympenoi, 200n42, 215n107
Oprasates, 106
oracles, 295n52, 319–20
Orophernes II, 27–8
orophylakes (boundary guards), 116–17
Ortiagon, 24, 105, 318, 326
Oxyrhyncus Historian, 217

paides, 55, 246, 261–70n145, 268, 270, 280
painting, used as dice board, 29
Pamphilos of Adramyttion, 106
Pamphilos of Apollonia Salbake, 65–7
Pamphylia, 176n181
Pamukçu stele, 218
Panaetius, 288
Panathenaia (festival), 17, 308
Panathenaia kai Eumeneia (festival), 236
Panemoteichos I, 336, 338
Panhellenism, 283–6
Panion, 124

Panionia (festival), 67–8
paraphylakitai (guards), 117–22
pastoralism, tax on, 87–8, 118–19
Pausanias, 19
　on the Galatians, 320
　on the gymnasium, 243
　on looted art works, 28–9
　on the Meter sanctuary, 334
　on prophecy of Phaennis, 320
Pella, 300–1n75, 306
Pergamon, *16–17*, 188–9
　acropolis, 306–13
　gymnasium, 238–41, *239*, *239–41*, 272–4
　Sanctuary of Athena, 314
Pergamon Museum, 1–2
Pergamos, 211, 294
Perseus (son of Philip V), 25, 186, 357
Persians, and Galatians, 296n59, 315–16
Pessinous, 296, 327–31
　as *emporion*, 123
　sanctuary of Cybele Agdistis,
　　205–9, 359
Pfeiffer, Rudolph, 289
Phaennis, 320
Phaidros of Sphettos, 267–8
Pharnakes I of Pontos, 24, 304
Pharsalos, 253–4
Pherai, gymnasium, 253
Philadelphia, 202–3, 202n53, 202n51, 232–3
philanthropic foundations, 37g
Philetairan Wall, 17
Philetaireia (festival), 47
Philetairoi, 131–2, *132*, 147
　dating, 140–1
　Eumenes II, 142, *143*
Philetairos, 8–9, 15–18, 188, 284
　and Asians, 285
　Base of, 320
　building complex on the mountain of
　　Aspordenon, 335
　coins minted under, 18
　and Cyzicus, 88, 251
　earmarking revenues in Thespiai, 236–7
　and the Galatians, 320–1
　and Kyme, 59–61
　and Panhellenism, 290
　property acquired by, 46
Philip III, 259
Philip V, 20–1, 186
　and the gymnasium, 257
Philomelos (son of Ophelas), decree, 219
Phoenician standard silver, 178
phoros, 78–9

Phrygians
    Epictetus, 20, 33, 323–7, *324–5*
    Gordion, 301–2
Picard, Oliver, 130, 149, 171
Piejko, Francis, 50–1
Pirson, Felix, 233, 273
Pisidia, 27, 119, *120–1*, 336–51, *340–1*, *343–4*
plinthophoros, Rhodian, 136, 157, 182n203
Pliny the Elder, on Eumenes II, 26
    on silver, 181
Poimanenoi, coinage of the, 221
Polatlı hoard, 167
poleis, 190–1, 224–33
    compared with gymnasia, 271–2
    harbors, 100n85
    money and financial systems, 80–1n18, 86n38, 90–2, 126–7, 162–3
    and subject cities, 112
Polemaios of Colophon, 278
Polemon of Ilion, 289–91
poll tax, 84–6, 104–5, 127
Polyaenus, on Eumenes II, 187
Polybius, 14, 291
    on Ariarathes, 28
    on Attalos I, 19, 47, 196, 223, 314, 359
    boxing match, 291–2
    on coinage, 127
    on empires, 4–5
    on Eumenes II, 21, 25, 189, 227, 233, 236, 243
    on financial disputes, 64–5
    on the Galatians, 318–19
    on gymnasia, 282
    on miserly kings, 37
    on Philip V, 21, 359
    on the Rhodians, 248–9
    on silver, 180
    tax collection, 103
    on the temple of Zeus at Selge, 342
    Third Macedonian War, 183
    Treaty of Apameia, 78
Polythrous, 71
Pompeius Trogus, 316, 326
Pompey, 154
"pork-barrel spending," **56**
Praisos (Crete), 72–3
presbyteroi, 281
Priene, 176n181, 253
proconsular cistophori, 130–55, *154–5*
prographê, 269–70
property, private, 44–51
Propontis hoard, 177–8
Prousias I, 20, 24, 306, 319
    war over Epictetus, 330–2
Prousias II, 24–5, 27, 106, 126, 161
providence (*pronoia*), 71–2
proxy coinage, 146, 160n115, 179n192, 184–6, 185n217, 358
Pseudo-Aristotle
    Oikonomika, 10
    on satrapal revenue, 77–8n10
    on taxes, 84–5, 116
Pseudo-Philip (Andriskos), 28
Psoma, Selene, 170–1
Ptolemaic monetary system, 163–9, 172–3
Ptolemaios (Lycian dynast), 49, 197
Ptolemies, burial practice, 299
Ptolemy Euergetes II, 271n202
Ptolemy I, 165
Ptolemy II, 165
Ptolemy Keraunos, 15
Ptolemy (king), and gymnasium of Halikarnassos, 265
Ptolemy V, 26
punishment, taxation as, 109
Purcell, Nicholas 115, 361

remonetization, 171–2, 179
religion
    cult of Idaean Cybele, 296
    and earmarking, 69–73
Rhea, 294–5
Rhode Island, 96n78
Rhodian Caria, *23–4*, 155, *156–7*
Rhodian coinage, 141–2, 157–8, 181, 182n203
Rhodians, gift of grain from Eumenes II, 248–9
Ricl, Marijana, 80–1n18, 87n44, 112
risk, 71, 75
Robert, Louis, 196, 223, 242
Rome, 6
    and Attalos I, 20
    and Attalos II, 28–9
    silver, 180–1
    taxation, 74–5
Roosevelt, Christopher, 197
Rostovtzeff, Mikhail, 12, 75, 87–8, 111, 231
royal banquets, 258, 275–80
royal gifts, 58, 237, 356
    of grain, 38g, 248–9
    to gymnasia, 237–8g
    of money, 38g
ruler cult, 30
    Attalos III, 70–1
    Eumenes II, 238–40, 263–4, 276–7n218
    Philetairos, 238–40
    Seleukos I, 299

sacrifices
  at banquets, 277
  earmarking for, 35, 42-4, 69-70
  in **D2**, 45, 47, 49-50
Sagalassos, 121-2, 338-9
Şahnalı hoard, 158-9
Salamis, Hermaia, 276-7n218
sales tax, 87-8
saltpans, 92-5
Samos, statue of Hera, 205-6n65
sanctuaries. *See* temples and sanctuaries
Sardis, 309
  acropolis, 310-11, *311*
  coin production, 133-4
  gymnasium, 234-6
  taxation as punishment, 109
Şarhöyük (Dorylaion), 326
Schuler, Christof, 80, 227, 252
Schumpeter, Joseph, 10
sculpture. *See also* stoas
  architectural, Pisidia, 342-3
Sekunda, Nicholas, 197
Seleukids
  mortuary practice, 299
  and the Mysians, 217-18
  and Pisidia, 337
  and the sanctuary of Apollo at Didyma, 236
  tax system, 103
Seleukos I Nikator, 15, 299-300
Seleukos II, 19
Seleukos III, 19
Seleukos IV, 25, 72
Selge, 27, 106, 337-42
  temples, 340-2
serpents, and coins, 137-8, *138-9*
settlements, 356, 358-9
  towns, 193-203
  villages, 191-3
Seyrig, Henri, 177-8n186, 178
Sibloe, 47-9
Sikyon
  gymnasium, *272-3*, 272
  purchase of land by Attalos I from, 47
silver. *See also* Attic-weight silver coinage
  sources, 180-3
slaves
  coinage used for purchase, 170-1
  manumission decree for Apollonios, 216
smuggling, 90, 116
Smyrna, mint, 184
snakes, and coins, 136-8, *138-9*
social status, and gymnasia, 260-8
Sosin, J. D., 57-9

Stalai, 72-3
states, defined, 5-6
stelai, 285
  dedicated to Doidalses, *208-9*, 209-11
  Pamukçu stele, 218
  Yiğitler, 222
Stephanos of Byzantion, 125, 205
Steunos, cave sanctuary, 332, 334-5
Stewart, Andrew, 296, 351
stoas
  Attalos I (Delphi), 294
  Attalos II (Athens), 2-3
  Attalos II (Termessos), 340n235
  Portique du Sud (Delos), 345-6
Stoicism, 286-8
Strabo, 14
  on Apameia, 122-3
  on Artemidoros of Ephesus, 157
  on Attaleia (Antalya), 123
  crucifixion of Daphitas, 351
  on Demetrios of Skepsis, 293-4
  on earthquake of 17 CE, 232
  on Elaia, 124
  on Ephesus, 124
  on Epictetus, 323-5, *324-5*
  on financial disputes, 65
  on the Galatians, 319-21, 325
  on the gymnasium, 250
  on Korykos, 123
  on languages, 351
  on Mysia, 212-13
  on Pergamon, 189
  on Pessinous, 328-30
  on settlement, 206
  on silver mining, 182
  on snake-men, 138
  on tax dispute in Ephesus, 94
  on Theophrastus, 113-14
  on the walls of Ilion, 319n145
strategos, 101-3
Stratonike, Queen, 24-5, 106, 242, 321, 349
Stratonikeia, 115, 159, 161, 168n152, 196-7
Strobel, Karl, 320, 328
subject cities, 112
  Metropolis as, 98n83, 112
Suda, on *basileia*, 362-3
Sulpicius, Gaius, 234-6, 281
surveillance, taxation, 113-22
Syrakousia (ship), 259

Tabênoi (?), letter from Eumenes II to the, 244
Taşkuyucak, Eumenes II inscription (**D2**),
  44-51, 56, 63n83, 317, 364

Tauromenion (Sicily), gymnasium, 251
tax farming, 96–104
taxation, 4, 8–14, 356, 361
    civic fiscality, 111–13
    direct, 76–86, 127
    indirect, 76–7, 86–92, 115–16, 127–8
    inventing new, 108–11
    and the *laoi*, 192
    negotiation for, 104–8, 128
    and Panhellenism, 283
    personnel, 95–104
    privileges of the, 227
    Roman, 74–5
    royal fiscality, 108–11
    surveillance, 113–22
teachers, wages for, 258–9
Tectosages, 314, 318
Telephos, 294
    and the Doidalses stele, 209–11
    Frieze, 137–8, *138–9*, 333
    and the Mysians, 214, 216
Tell Kotchek hoard, 178n188
Telmessos
    decree of, 24, 285–6, 305, 352
    letter from Eumenes II or Antiochos III, 85, 116, 317–18
    and the Nikephoria, 346–7
Temnos
    coinage, 145
    Eumenes II letter to (**D4**), 50, 103, 365
    tax holiday, 110–11
temples and sanctuaries. *See also under* Artemis; Cybele; Zeus
    Apollo at Didyma, 68–9, 236
    Athena at Pergamon, 314
    Meter, 334
    and their villages, 203–9
Teos, 66
    decree (**D7**), 57, 366
    first decree for Antiochos III and Laodike III, 78
    gymnasium, 274n209
    pastoralism tax, 119
    public grain fund, 42–3
    tribute, 77n9
Termessos, 113–14, 336–8, 344
    agora, 27
    and the gymnasium, 269, 339
    and Iphigeneia, 342, 344
    paraphylakeion, 118
    Stoa of Attalos II, 340n235
    temples, 340–1
    theater, 339–40n234

Tertullian, 9
Teuthrania Monument, 211–12
Teuthras, King, 1, 211, 333
theaters
    Sardis, 234–5n4
    Termessos, 339–40n234
Themisonion, 274
Theophrastus, 113–14
Theopompus, 327
Thera, gymnasium, 254
Third Macedonian War, 25, 183
Thonemann, Peter, 6–7, 47–8, 81–2, 93–4, 153–4, 177–8, 200, 207, 328, 354
Thrace, 125–6
Tieion, 15, 24, 188
Tissaphernes, 217
Tolistoagii/Tolistobogii, 196, *307*, 314, 318, 323–5
tolls/toll stations, 98–100, 112, 115
Toriaion, *62–3*, 112, 224–8
    Dossier (**D8**), 28n92, 62–4, 79–80, 102, 109, 224–8, 254, 366
    gymnasium, 64, 237, 245–6, 250–1
    indirect taxation, 86–7
towns, 193–203
trade, 322–3
Tralles, 149–52, 163–4, 234–5n4
    agoranomos, 86–7
    coinage, 144–5, 147, 171
    gymnasium, 241–2
    mint, 152–63, *154–5*
tribute (*phoros*), 77
Trocmi, 314, 318
"Trojan Horse," sanctuary of Artemis Brauronia (Athens), 295
Trojans, 293–7
Troy, and the Mysian, 214
Tynada, 344

United States, and taxation, 10

Van Alfen, Peter, 175
Via Sebaste, 119–21n163, 121, *122*, 350
villages, 191–3
    and temple, 203–9
Vitruvius, 157n103
Von Reden, S., 164n137, 165n140

wall, Kapıkaya, 121
water supply, 259
Weber, Max, 6
weights, coins, 136
Welles, Bradford, 50–1, 68–9, 237
Westmarkt Areal (Miletus), 263

Williamson, Christina, 306
Winter, F. E., 121
Wörrle, Michael, 85, 102, 240
Wreathed Coinages, *143–5*, 145–7, 183–6

Xanthos, 108, 309, 311
Xenokles, gravestone of, 218
Xenophon, 9
   Anabasis, 188
   on Mysians, 217
   on Pergamon, 285

Yiğitler, stele, 222
Yığma Tepe tomb, 298–9, *298–9*, 301, 306

Zelizer, Viviana, 41–2
Zeno of Citium, 288
   Politeia, 287
Zeus, 295n52
   Ata, 335
   Kesbelios, 341
   Papas/Papias, 335
   sanctuary of Zeus at Aizanoi, 325, 331–6, 341, 359
   Solymeus, 341
   Stratios, 45, 47–8
Zeuxis, letter to Herakleia-under-Latmos, 109–10
Zosimos, 253n100

For EU product safety concerns, contact us at Calle de José Abascal, 56–1°, 28003 Madrid, Spain or eugpsr@cambridge.org.

www.ingramcontent.com/pod-product-compliance
Ingram Content Group UK Ltd.
Pitfield, Milton Keynes, MK11 3LW, UK
UKHW050108230326
469255UK00017B/243